D0379757

# The Political Economy of Policy Reform

JOHN WILLIAMSON, EDITOR

# The Political Economy of Policy Reform

Institute for International Economics
Washington, DC
January 1994

John Williamson, Senior Fellow, was
economics professor at Pontifícia
Universidade Católica do Rio de Janeiro
(1978–81), University of Warwick (1970–
77), Massachusetts Institute of Technology
(1980, 1967), University of York (1963–68),
and Princeton University (1962–63);
Adviser to the International Monetary
Fund (1972–74); and Economic Consultant
to the UK Treasury (1968–70). He has
published numerous studies on
international monetary and Third World
debt issues, including *Economics of Soviet
Disintegration,*(1993), *Trade and Payments
After Soviet Disintegration,* (1992), *From
Soviet disUnion to Eastern Economic
Community?* with Oleh Havrylyshyn (1991),
*Currency Convertibility in Eastern Europe*
(1991), *Latin American Adjustment: How
Much Has Happened?* (1990), and *Targets and
Indicators: A Blueprint for the International
Coordination of Economic Policy* with Marcus
Miller (1987).

INSTITUTE FOR INTERNATIONAL
ECONOMICS
11 Dupont Circle, NW
Washington, DC 20036–1207
(202) 328–9000 FAX: (202) 328–5432

C. Fred Bergsten, *Director*
Christine F. Lowry, *Director of Publications*

*Cover design by Michelle M. Fleitz*

Copyright © 1994 by the Institute for
International Economics. All rights
reserved. No part of this book may be
reproduced or utilized in any form or by
any means, electronic or mechanical,
including photocopying, recording, or by
information storage or retrieval system,
without permission from the Institute.

For reprints/permission to photocopy
please contact the APS customer service
department at CCC Academic Permissions
Service, 27 Congress Street, Salem, MA
01970

Printed in the United States of America
96 95    8 7 6 5 4

**Library of Congress Cataloging-in-
Publication Data**

The political economy of policy reform /
John Williamson, editor.
      p.   cm.
   Includes bibliographical references
      1. Economic policy—Political aspects—
Case studies. I. Williamson, John,
1937–
HD87.P645    1993
338.9—dc20                          93-5038
                                         CIP

ISBN 0-88132-195-8

**Marketed and Distributed outside the USA and Canada by Longman Group UK
Limited, London**

The views expressed in this publication are those of the authors. This publication is
part of the overall program of the Institute, as endorsed by its Board of Directors, but
does not necessarily reflect the views of individual members of the Board or the
Advisory Committee.

This volume is dedicated to the memory of

**Bela Balassa**

Dr. Balassa was a Visiting Fellow at the Institute from 1985 to 1990 and coauthored major studies for us on Latin America, as well as a comprehensive study of *Japan in the World Economy*. He was one of the pioneers of the movement for the policy reforms discussed in this volume.

# Contents

# Preface

The Institute has conducted a number of studies of economic reform programs around the world, addressing most geographic regions: Latin America, most recently in *Latin American Adjustment: How Much Has Happened?* (1990); Eastern Europe, especially in *Currency Convertibility in Eastern Europe* (1991); the former Soviet Union, primarily in *Economic Consequences of Soviet Disintegration* (1992); Africa, in *African Economic Reform: The External Dimension* (1991); and East Asia, notably in *Pacific Basin Developing Countries: Prospects for the Future* (1991).

These studies had three common themes. First, all of them focused primarily on the economics of policy reform, albeit with the Institute's usual attention to the pragmatic implications of the various proposals and their impact on the real world. Second, most of our analyses derived at least partly from conferences sponsored by the Institute that considered papers presented by experts from individual countries on the experiences of those countries; we would then try to draw general lessons from the different experiences, with the ultimate aim of providing guidelines for future efforts in the region and perhaps elsewhere as well. Third, several of the projects—particularly concerning Latin America, Eastern Europe, and the former Soviet Union—were organized, led, and summarized by John Williamson, a Senior Fellow at the Institute who has developed the technique of synthesizing national case studies in search of such general conclusions.

This volume represents an effort to apply the conference technique, and the expertise that Dr. Williamson has developed on both the substance of policy reform and this methodology for appraising its success, to an even more difficult issue: the *politics* of the reform process. As explained in the introductory chapter, we selected a dozen countries that had achieved successful economic reform—across a wide spectrum, both geographically and in terms of per capita income—for analysis of the political process through which that reform had occurred. We added two countries where reform had been attempted but not yet concluded, a panel on the relevance of the debate for the emerging market economies of Eastern Europe and the former Soviet Union, and a final panel that helped pave the way for the concluding chapter—co-authored by Dr. Williamson and, because of the nature of the topic, political scientist Stephan Haggard of the University of California at San Diego. We hope that the resulting product will provide useful advice to would-be economic reformers in the future, as well as a better understanding of the political economy of the reform process for all those who are interested in it.

The Institute for International Economics is a private nonprofit institution for the study and discussion of international economic policy. Its purpose is to analyze important issues in that area, and to develop and communicate practical new approaches for dealing with them. The Institute is completely nonpartisan.

The Institute is funded largely by philanthropic foundations. Major institutional grants are now being received from the German Marshall Fund of the United States, which created the Institute with a generous commitment of funds in 1981, and from the Ford Foundation, the William and Flora Hewlett Foundation, the William M. Keck, Jr. Foundation, the C. V. Starr Foundation, and the United States–Japan Foundation. A number of other foundations and private corporations also contribute to the highly diversified financial resources of the Institute. About 16 percent of the Institute's resources in the latest fiscal year were provided by contributors outside the United States, including about 7 percent from Japan. The Pew Charitable Trusts provided substantial financial support for this project, as it has for much of the Institute's previous research on economic reform in Eastern Europe and the former Soviet Union.

The Board of Directors bears overall responsibility for the Institute and gives general guidance and approval to its research program—including identification of topics that are likely to become important to international economic policymakers over the medium run (generally, one to three years), and which thus should be addressed by the Institute. The Director, working closely with the staff and outside Advisory Committee, is responsible for the development of particular projects and makes the final decision to publish an individual study.

The Institute hopes that its studies and other activities will contribute to building a stronger foundation for international economic policy around the world. We invite readers of these publications to let us know how they think we can best accomplish this objective.

C. FRED BERGSTEN
Director
October 1993

## INSTITUTE FOR INTERNATIONAL ECONOMICS
11 Dupont Circle, NW, Washington, DC   20036-1207
(202) 328-9000   Fax: (202) 328-0900

C. Fred Bergsten, *Director*

**BOARD OF DIRECTORS**

*Peter G. Peterson, *Chairman*
*Anthony M. Solomon, *Chairman,
Executive Committee*

Leszek Balcerowicz
Raymond Barre
W. Michael Blumenthal
Miguel de la Madrid
Jessica Einhorn
George M. C. Fisher
Maurice R. Greenberg
*Carla A. Hills
W. M. Keck II
Nigel Lawson
Lee Kuan Yew
*Frank E. Loy
Donald F. McHenry
Ruben F. Mettler
Akio Morita
Kaneo Nakamura
Suliman S. Olayan
Paul H. O'Neill
I. G. Patel
Karl Otto Pöhl
Edzard Reuter
David Rockefeller
P. Roy Vagelos
Paul A. Volcker
*Dennis Weatherstone
Marina v.N. Whitman
Lynn R. Williams
Andrew Young

*Ex officio*
*C. Fred Bergsten
Richard N. Cooper

*Honorary Directors*
Alan Greenspan
Reginald H. Jones
George P. Shultz

**ADVISORY COMMITTEE**

Richard N. Cooper, *Chairman*

Robert Baldwin
Barry P. Bosworth
Susan M. Collins
Rimmer de Vries
Juergen B. Donges
Rudiger Dornbusch
Gerhard Fels
Robert J. Flanagan
Isaiah Frank
Jacob A. Frenkel
Gottfried Haberler
David D. Hale
Mahbub ul Haq
Dale E. Hathaway
Nurul Islam
Peter B. Kenen
Lawrence R. Klein
Lawrence B. Krause
Anne O. Krueger
Paul R. Krugman
Roger M. Kubarych
Robert Z. Lawrence
Jessica T. Mathews
Rachel McCulloch
Isamu Miyazaki
Michael Mussa
Richard R. Nelson
Sylvia Ostry
Rudolph A. Oswald
Tommaso Padoa-Schioppa
Jacques J. Polak
Jeffrey D. Sachs
Ernest Stern
Lawrence H. Summers
Alan Wm. Wolff
Robert Zoellick

*Member of the Executive Committee*

# The Political Economy of Policy Reform

# 1

# INTRODUCTION

# Introduction

C. FRED BERGSTEN AND JOHN WILLIAMSON

Economic reform has become a global stampede in the last quarter of the 20th century. Countries of every geographic region, income level, and ideology have joined the rush: Asians, Europeans, Latin Americans, and Africans; countries once among the richest in the world (such as Argentina, Australia, and New Zealand) and countries near the bottom; capitalists, socialists, and those in between. Competing theories of "how to do it"—the relationship between and the sequencing of structural transformation and macroeconomic stabilization, gradualism or shock therapy, and sundry other themes—abound in both the practical policy debate and analytical publications.

From the experience of the past decade or so, a growing consensus is emerging on the economics of reform. To be sure, application of general principles must be tailored to the circumstances of each individual country if it is to have the desired impact in the real world. But substantial agreement is now fairly widespread on the principles and policy actions upon which reform must be based.[1]

There is much less understanding, let alone consensus, on the political process through which economic reform can be achieved. Perhaps such a gap is inevitable, due to the greater complexity of politics and the even greater cross-country differences in this dimension.

---

1. The Institute has attempted to contribute to this evolving consensus, particularly through its work on reform in Latin America, Eastern Europe, and the former Soviet Union. Following the pioneering analysis of Balassa et al. (1986), John Williamson (1990, 1991, 1993) edited a series of studies. World Bank (1991) offers an authoritative summary of what it calls the "market-friendly view."

Nevertheless, it is critical to learn as much as possible about the politics of economic reform. Despite the breadth of the recent and current wave of reform, such reforms will continue to be on the agenda in many places for as far ahead as the eye can see. We cannot hope to discover a set of "golden rules" that will provide a blueprint for all reformers in all circumstances. But any guidelines, even if they apply only to limited degrees and with extensive caveats, could prove helpful to both officials and economists in the future.

The richness of the reform experience over the past decade or so, incomplete as that experience is in many countries, persuaded us that the time was ripe to make an effort of this type. We concluded that the only practical methodology was case studies: a careful examination of the specific reform processes in individual countries where, at least for now, success seems to have been achieved. To conduct such studies with the focus on the politics of reform, however, we needed a unique set of authors: economists who thoroughly understood the circumstances of the reform programs but were also close enough to the actual process in their countries to be able to analyze how the reforms came to be adopted initially and implemented subsequently.

Hence we invited a dozen or so economists, most of whom had held positions of political responsibility during periods when their countries had been trying to make the transition to a market economy, to write a paper about what they saw as the political factors that had made success possible. The decision to focus on the transition period was intended both to provide a degree of intellectual coherence to the enquiry and to illuminate a question that we thought had high contemporary policy relevance.

We quite deliberately chose a mix of countries from what would not long ago have been called the First, Second, and Third Worlds. We did this because of a conviction that the process of policy reform involved much the same things—stabilization where needed, liberalization and opening up everywhere—irrespective of whether a country might in the past have been classified as an industrial country,[2] whether it had been part of the socialist bloc, or whether it had been poor in the mid-1950s when the world was declared divided into three. (To recognize this broad similarity in the transition process is not to challenge Balcerowicz's insistence that the needed changes are more extensive and dramatic in the former Second World than elsewhere: see chapter 4.) If the economics of transition was broadly similar, then it seemed possible that the political lessons from a country in one class might be applicable elsewhere.

---

2. Spain and Portugal were classified that way because of geographical accident, while Australia and New Zealand were there because their resource endowments had given them high per capita incomes.

Our search for countries with a post-1960 transition that is now reasonably consolidated eventually led us to commission 11 papers: on Australia, Chile, Colombia, Indonesia, Korea, Mexico, New Zealand, Poland, Portugal, Spain, and Turkey. We also sought a paper on Bolivia, but our prospective author, Gonzalo Sanchez de Lozada, decided to run for the presidency instead (and won). Two of the papers that we commissioned did not materialize. Our prospective Chilean author, José Piñera, also decided to make a bid for the presidency of his country and hence did not write a paper or participate in the conference. However, since he had written an article for *International Economic Insights* in 1991 based on a seminar that he gave at the Institute, we circulated his paper to conference participants and have reprinted it in this volume. Second, our prospective Korean author, Il SaKong, did participate in the conference and talked about the Korean experience, but in the end he was unable both to get his new Institute off the ground and to write a paper for us, and somehow it was us that got crowded out. We decided, however, to retain both Chile and Korea in the sample of countries used to draw generalizations in the summary and synthesis paper by Williamson and Haggard that concludes the volume.

Although our initial plan was to limit papers to countries that had consolidated economic reform, someone (we cannot recall who we should thank) suggested that it would be illuminating to cover also some cases of attempted but nonconsolidated reform. To that end, we invited Luiz Carlos Bresser Pereira (Brazil) and Richard Webb (Peru) to discuss why the reform episodes with which they had been involved during their period in high office had not had the results they would have hoped for. Two of the political scientists commented afterward that they thought these papers had been more illuminating than those on the cases of successful reform. They too are covered in the summary and synthesis (chapter 12).

That still left out a number of countries that we would have liked to cover, and a lot more that we were criticized during the conference for not including, even though we thought our criterion provided us with a good reason for excluding them. Some examples will have to suffice. Argentina: is reform now consolidated? Venezuela: ditto, but we invited Miguel Rodríguez to comment in one of the sessions on Latin America, and he took advantage of the opportunity to say a little about the fascinating Venezuelan case (see chapter 6). Israel had an impressive stabilization program in 1985, but it was not accompanied by the sort of comprehensive liberalization and opening up that we were seeking to analyze. Czechoslovakia and Hungary: it is still a bit early to be sure that reform is consolidated. (Admittedly, we had something of the same qualm about including Poland and decided the other way.) Malaysia, Singapore, and Thailand: they are very strong performers, but they have reformed piecemeal over the years rather than having the sort of concentrated reform program that we sought. Mauritius and Sri Lanka: we didn't locate a potential author in time, and it is in any event impossible to cover every case that one would like to.

That leaves what many argued to be the most serious omission: sub-Saharan Africa. It is certainly true that a number of African countries have launched programs of policy reform in recent years, but we were not sure that the reforms had been consolidated even in the countries that started first, such as Ghana. What in retrospect we should have done is what we actually did in chapter 8 with respect to the other part of the world where this problem arose, Eastern Europe, and convened a panel with a more open format invited to discuss the implications of the thrust of the conference for the countries of the region.

As just implied, the case studies presented in chapters 3 through 7 do to some extent follow a common format, or at least the authors were asked to address a common set of questions. Those questions are laid out in the background paper, chapter 2, that Williamson wrote and circulated well before the conference. The authors of the country papers, most of whom were "technopols"—economists in key policymaking positions—during the reform programs that they describe and analyze, are a rather distinguished group: they include Leszek Balcerowicz, the architect of Poland's Big Bang that initiated the Second World's attempted transition to the market, and José Córdoba, President Carlos Salinas de Gortari's chief of staff. They were asked to focus on the political economy questions of how they managed to get their programs accepted (something that the crude versions of public-choice theory tend to suggest is impossible, see chapter 2), but the authors are all economists and hence they inevitably, and rightly, talk about the economics of the programs as well.

Chapter 8, with participants from Ukraine (Oleh Havrylyshyn), Russia (Vladimir Mau), and Bulgaria (Ambassador Ognian Pishev), contains the discussion of the panel that sought to assess the relevance of this debate for the economies in transition. Chapter 9 contains the account of the panel discussion that concluded the conference, introduced by one former technopol (Nicolás Ardito-Barletta, former president of Panama), two political scientists (Stephan Haggard and Joan Nelson), and the editor of the volume, John Williamson. As in most of the preceding chapters, the introductory presentations are followed by a concise but reasonably complete account of the ensuing conference discussion.

Chapter 10 contains an after-lunch speech to the conference by Enrique Iglesias, currently president of the Inter-American Development Bank and formerly foreign minister of Uruguay and executive secretary of the Economic Commission for Latin America and the Caribbean. He discusses the movement for policy reform in Latin America from the standpoint of one who has been at the center of the debate for many years.

Chapter 11 comprises an after-dinner speech by Jeffrey Sachs, concerning his experiences in urging and helping design policy reforms as adviser to the governments of a number of countries (at least Argentina, Bolivia, Poland, Russia, Slovenia, and Yugoslavia, and now several of the smaller former Soviet republics as well). It was a typically vigorous virtuoso performance, which, again not untypically, managed to stir up controversy. For example, a number of speakers in the remaining day and a half of the conference were moved to criticize or defend his attack on the claim that policy reform should be grounded in a social consensus. As another example, the International Monetary Fund felt that its role in Russia had been maligned, and accordingly Sachs' speech is followed by a reply by the director of the Fund's External Relations Department, Mr. Shailendra J. Anjaria, which is in turn followed by a rejoinder by Jeffrey Sachs.

The final chapter of the volume contains a summary and synthesis paper, similar to those that the Institute has often used to convey the flavor of the character and conclusions of its conferences to those who do not have the time to read the whole of the conference volume. Stephan Haggard, a political scientist who has devoted a large part of his professional career to analyzing the politics of economic reform in developing countries, agreed to coauthor that concluding chapter with Williamson. We hope this has helped to temper any tendency to reinvent wheels already familiar to political scientists that may be manifest in chapter 2. It certainly also brought a much-needed perspective to bear.

## References

Balassa, Bela, Gerardo M. Bueno, Pedro-Pablo Kuczynski, and Mario Henrique Simonsen. 1986. *Toward Renewed Economic Growth in Latin America*. Mexico City: El Colégio de Mexico; Rio de Janeiro: Fundação Getúlio Vargas; and Washington: Institute for International Economics.

Williamson, John. 1990. *Latin American Adjustment: How Much Has Happened?* Washington: Institute for International Economics.

Williamson, John. 1991. *Currency Convertibility in Eastern Europe*. Washington: Institute for International Economics.

Williamson, John. 1993. *Economic Consequences of Soviet Disintegration*. Washington: Institute for International Economics.

World Bank. 1991. *World Development Report: The Challenge of Development*. New York: Oxford University Press.

# 2

## IN SEARCH OF A MANUAL FOR TECHNOPOLS

# In Search of a Manual for Technopols

JOHN WILLIAMSON

Jorge Dominguez and Richard Feinberg have recently coined the useful term "technopols" to describe the burgeoning breed of economic technocrats who assume positions of political responsibility (quoted in Feinberg 1992). Outstanding examples currently holding office are President Carlos Salinas de Gortari and Finance Minister Pedro Aspe in Mexico, Prime Minister Aníbal Cavaco Silva and Finance Minister Jorge Braga de Macedo in Portugal, Economic Minister Domingo Cavallo in Argentina, Finance Minister Alejandro Foxley in Chile, President Lee Teng-hui in Taiwan, Prime Minister Yegor Gaidar in Russia, and Finance Minister Manmohan Singh in India.[1] (Examples in the Group of Seven countries do not spring readily to mind, which may help explain the lackluster performance of the world economy.)

To understand this definition of a technopol, one needs to know what a "technocrat" is. The *Concise Oxford Dictionary* defines a technocrat as one who advocates technocracy, which the dictionary defines as the "organization and management of a country's industrial resources by technical experts for the good of the whole community." This definition, however, does not fully capture the flavor of recent usage, which seems to have been confined to economists, and among economists those who are practitioners rather than merely advocates of the use of technical

---

1. This paper is presented here essentially as it was delivered at the January 1993 conference, where it served not only as an introduction to the issues of the conference but as a set of guidelines for the papers to be presented. By the time of the conference Prime Minister Gaidar had already been removed from office, but he reentered the government as first deputy prime minister shortly before this volume went to press.

(economic) skills.[2] In addition, "technocrats" as that term is currently understood are involved in managing all of a country's economic resources rather than just its industrial resources. What the Oxford definition correctly draws attention to, however, is that technocrats deploy technical (in particular, economic) skills to manage resources, and that those skills are deployed to further the general good rather than some private benefit.[3] Hence my own definition of a technocrat would be an economist who uses his or her professional and technical skills in government with a view to creating and managing an economic system that will further the general good.

Until recently technocrats were mostly senior civil servants. The technopols are those technocrats who have taken the risk of accepting political appointments, with the responsibility that entails. One would like to think that their proliferation reflects increasing acceptance that economists have skills whose exercise at the political level can help improve economic performance.

A successful technopol needs to combine two very different types of skill. One is that of a successful applied economist, able to judge what institutions and policies are needed in specific circumstances in order to further economic objectives. The other is the skill of a successful politician, able to persuade others to adopt the policies that he or she has judged to be called for. The aim of this conference will be to explore the political dimension of success: to seek to understand the circumstances under which reforms are possible and the rules of action that may help technopols to win the political support that will permit them to implement their agenda.

We will focus in particular on achieving the initial breakthrough, from a dirigiste, statist, "mercantilist,"[4] closed economy rendered unstable by populist macroeconomic policies, to an open, relatively stable economy using competitive markets to allocate resources. This focus reflects the particular point in history at which the conference is being held. For much of the postwar period most development economists and most developing countries assumed that catching up with the developed countries required a markedly different set of policies from the market-oriented and relatively open approach that the latter had cultivated. Experience—particularly in East Asia—has suggested that this is wrong, and that the key to successful development is to emulate the policies

---

2. *Webster's* offers an alternative definition of "a technical expert, especially one exercising managerial authority", which is closer to the sense in which the term has been used in recent years.

3. Despite the continuing rash of cases of corruption in the sort of high places often occupied by technocrats, I am not aware of anyone with claims to being among their number who has yet been implicated in ripping off the public for personal gain.

4. In the sense of Hernando de Soto (1989).

preached (if not always practiced) by the developed countries. Hence one has recently seen an unprecedented degree of consensus worldwide about the direction in which it is desirable to transform the economic policy regime (it is not only in the former communist countries that one can speak of a "transition").

The emphasis on technopols is not intended to imply that they are indispensable to policy reform. There are surely examples of political leaders who have themselves had little understanding of technical economic issues but who have selected a team of competent technocrats and delegated them enough authority to permit radical economic reforms. The results of this conference, it is hoped, will be of interest to such politicians as well as to technopols. One interesting question that we should pursue is whether there is a great advantage in having technopols hold key positions, or whether technocrats enjoying firm political backing can hope to accomplish as much.

As a background for this inquiry, this paper seeks to do three things. First, it discusses the relation of the quest for policy reform to the "new political economy" (alias "public choice theory"), which has sometimes been interpreted as precluding the very possibility of such reform. Second, it comments on the nature of the policy reforms that are typically sought during the initial reform phase. Third, it presents some hypotheses about the circumstances and rules of action that will help technopols to get their agenda implemented. Each of the country papers should assess whether those hypotheses appear to be borne out by the experiences of the country in question.


## The New Political Economy

A technocrat, and thus by extension a technopol, is defined above as a policymaker who is motivated to pursue the objectives postulated by traditional normative economic analysis. Public choice theory, and the new political economy of which it provides one strand, have dismissed this assumption as a hopelessly naive characterization of political motivation. In place of the Platonic assumption that policymakers selflessly dedicate themselves to disinterested pursuit of the public good, public choice theory posits that they behave as standard economic theory assumes *Homo economicus* to behave: they maximize their personal economic well-being. Bureaucrats fight for turf, politicians decide whether or not to hand out pork by calculating whether it will enhance their prospects of reelection, pressure groups seek rents (e.g., from the imposition of import restrictions) by offering political funding or support, and politicians give in to these pressures until they fear that the voters will perceive that they are being taken for a ride, and/or a predatory state seeks to maximize its own spending rather than the welfare of its citizens.[5]

This body of theory has yielded lots of policy prescriptions, all of them aimed at minimizing the role of government so as to curtail the damage done by policymakers seeking to maximize what has sometimes been termed a "social illfare function." But it has been argued that public choice theory yields no implications at all about how such recommendations can be implemented, because policymakers who are motivated as the theory hypothesizes will never choose to introduce policy reforms that will deprive them of the source of their patronage. For example, Gerald Meier (1991, 9) has written:

> How can policy reform be instituted? For these changes to occur, professional economic advice must have some influence. . . . But the dilemma is that in showing why governments do what they do, the new political economy at the same time shows why economists are not listened to.

Similarly, Jagdish Bhagwati (1989) has written of a "determinacy paradox": if all policymakers—politicians and bureaucrats—determine their actions with a view to maximizing their personal well-being, then normative analysis has no scope to influence policy. There will exist a determinate equilibrium outcome independent of any knowledge that may or may not exist of what policies would best promote the general social good, for no one is interested in maximizing the general good as opposed to his or her individual good.

Yet we have in recent years observed in various countries extensive policy reforms designed to curb the role of the state and increase that of markets, sometimes introduced by persons who appear to satisfy the definition of a technopol. This obviously does not imply that we should jettison the whole of public choice theory and the new political economy, for the occasions when policies are better explained by these approaches than by the precepts of traditional normative economics are altogether too frequent and flagrant to deny that the sort of political mafia hypothesized by those approaches does exist. What it does suggest is that pretensions to provide a universal characterization of political motivation must be rejected.[6] Just as we know that most individuals

---

5. See Meier (1991) for a general review of the new political economy. I find persuasive the criticisms of some of the strands of the new political economy by the political scientists Robert Bates, Stephan Haggard, and Joan Nelson in chapter 10 of that volume. Specifically, anthropomorphic theories of the state as maximizer would seem to violate the basic precept of the new approach, which stresses individual rationality in the pursuit of self-interest. Similarly, the concept of a political marketplace that balances narrow sectional interests against the general interest of consumers rests on no more solid a base than analogy.

6. The pioneers of public choice theory were much more circumspect than some who later jumped aboard the bandwagon of the new political economy as it rolled through (or over)

have other motives besides the striving for personal gain embodied in the term *Homo economicus* (for how else could we explain phenomena ranging from charitable donations to voluntary actions to reduce environmental threats?), so we should recognize that many, indeed perhaps most, politicians are moved by mixed motives. Most policymakers are driven by some mix (which varies from political *mafiosi* at one end of the spectrum to technopols somewhere near the other) of a desire to pursue the public good and a desire to advance their personal interests.

It is not necessary to believe that technopols—or economists who dispense advice intended to influence the course of public policy along the lines suggested by normative economics—have purely altruistic motives. Perhaps they are driven by a desire for a place in history or heaven, or an ambition to win prizes and public accolades, and judge that the best way of achieving those objectives is to fight special interests in order to promote a wider social good. What is preposterous is to deny that anyone finds either such motivations or altruism more powerful than a lust for more money or a longer period in office. Can one really believe that James Buchanan or Milton Friedman (to pick two examples not quite at random) could not have made themselves vastly richer had they devoted their talents to moneymaking rather than trying to change the world? And if they were capable of rising above the narrow objectives posited by public choice theory, how can any reasonable person claim that no politician is capable of doing likewise?

The objective of this conference is primarily to ask how one can strengthen the political muscle of those politicians who are most driven by concern for the general rather than a particular good. (One might equally reasonably want to inquire how one could increase the weight that the typical politician places on social rather than private objectives, which may or may not have much the same answer.) The new political economy is right to point to the importance of seeking institutional changes that will diminish the ability of policymakers to respond to rent seeking, and therefore the incentive of actors to seek rent, but it is unconvincing when pushed to the point of arguing that there can be no technopols anxious to make such changes.

## The Technocrats' Agenda

Normative economics is based on the assumption that the objective of economic policy is promotion of the general good. This can be formal-

---

the economics profession. Buchanan and Tullock (1962, 30) wrote:

> The model which incorporates this [maximizing] behavioral assumption . . . can, at best, explain only one aspect of collective choice. . . . it does not imply that all individuals act in accordance with the behavioral assumption made or that any one individual acts in this way at all times. Just as the theory of markets can explain only some fraction of all economic action, the theory of collective [public] choice can explain only some undetermined fraction of collective action.

ized as maximization of a social welfare function, a mathematical expression that ideally expresses the relative desirability of all alternative social states. It is well known that no such complete social welfare ordering can be established solely on the basis of the economics profession's favorite value judgment, namely, the Pareto criterion. The conclusion is that comparing alternative social states so as to give content to the concept of the general good requires the introduction, either explicitly or implicitly, of distributional weights that enable one to trade off the gain to one individual against the loss to another. The most common—highly conservative—procedure (rationalized, unconvincingly to my mind, by the compensation principle) is to treat an extra dollar as of equal significance no matter to whom it accrues. The alternative procedure that I prefer is to weight a dollar more highly the lower the income of the recipient. The parameter that expresses how rapidly the social value of income declines as the income of the recipient rises reflects, of course, a value judgment, and one that will vary between individuals, with a more rapid decline being associated with a more egalitarian set of values.

An elegant body of microeconomic theory shows that under certain circumstances the general good as characterized above will be promoted by a set of competitive markets and integration into the world economy. There is also a lot of empirical evidence—although not all of it is rigorous enough to satisfy the profession's econometric purists—that competitive markets and an open trade policy are in fact good for welfare.[7]

On the macroeconomic side, the social desirability of something close to price stability is universally agreed,[8] but there are significant differences about the two other traditional macroeconomic objectives of high employment and external balance. These are, however, disagreements about means rather than ends: presumably everyone would like output to be stable at the highest level consistent with the control of inflation and to avoid external imbalances so large as to threaten a debt crisis, but views differ over whether policy can expect to improve on the outcome

---

7. The most compelling evidence of the virtues of competitive markets over central planning is the superior long-term performance of market over planned systems that started off at similar levels: compare Austria with Czechoslovakia, East with West Germany, Estonia with Finland, mainland China with Taiwan, North with South Korea. The evidence for the superiority of open over closed trading policies accumulated gradually from the 1960s to the 1980s, primarily in the work of Bela Balassa and his associates at the World Bank. A massive study of the process of trade liberalization has recently been published in the seven volumes edited by Michaely, Papageorgiou, and Choksi (1991).

8. There remain those who argue that a moderate rate of inflation may be an efficient form of generating government revenue when the tax system is inadequate, those who see some merit in an upward drift of the price level so as to lubricate relative price changes or permit a moderately negative real rate of interest during recessions, and those who counsel caution in paying a high (even though temporary) price in terms of lost output to reduce inflation to very low levels.

given by following simple rules of prudence in government finance and fixed rates of growth in the money supply.

Two very important consequences follow from a decision to embrace what mainstream economists assume should be the objectives of government policy, as laid out above. First, it makes the state into an umpire rather than a favor-granting mechanism. In the extreme version, the state provides defense, law and order, and a legal system, and allows private agents to get on with their economic lives subject to the rule of law thus established. Less extreme models allow the government to supply a wider range of public goods and to compensate for market failures. Some would argue that this could go as far as establishing an industrial policy that would give special privileges to some enterprises over others, provided that the granting of privileges is based on a cost-benefit analysis employing known criteria and is thus both transparent and accountable. What are utterly unacceptable are arrangements that allow public office to be used to seek private gain, and thus nurture rent seeking.

The second important consequence is that public policy should be designed with a long time horizon in mind. The future matters; the pure rate of time preference is low; almost all worthwhile progress involves making short-run sacrifices for the sake of greater long-run benefits. Winning the next election matters to a technopol, but it matters so that the technopol can continue to implement his or her agenda, not for the sake of merely staying in office. An election won by abandoning principles is a Pyrrhic victory.

Once upon a time, when the movement toward policy reform in Latin America was first taking off, I made a list of the policy initiatives that were being urged on Latin America by the powers-that-be in Washington (Williamson 1990, chapter 2). The "Washington consensus"[9] offers a description of what is agreed about the set of measures that are typically called for in the first stage of policy reform on which this conference will focus, so that list is summarized in an appendix to the paper.

What I did not stress in my original presentation—or, for that matter, in subsequent elaborations—is the vast scope that this consensus leaves for disagreement. Apart from the issue of the speed of trade liberalization, to which I did draw attention, it also leaves room for different views on such questions as:

■ the desirability of maintaining capital controls

■ the need to target the current account

---

9. I have long ago taken the point of my discussant, Richard Feinberg, that I should have christened this list the "universal convergence" rather than the "Washington consensus", on the grounds that there is no complete consensus, while the very real convergence extends far beyond Washington, but my original term has nonetheless stuck.

- how rapidly and how far inflation should be reduced
- the advisability of attempting to stabilize the business cycle
- the usefulness of incomes policy and wage and price freezes (sometimes called "heterodox shocks")
- the need to eliminate indexation
- the propriety of attempting to correct market failures through such techniques as compensatory taxation
- the proportion of GDP to be taken in taxation and spent by the public sector
- whether and to what extent income should be deliberately redistributed in the interest of equity
- whether there is a role for industrial policy
- the model of the market economy to be sought (Anglo-Saxon laissez-faire, the European social market economy, or Japanese-style responsibility of the corporation to multiple stakeholders)
- the priority to be given to population control and environmental preservation.

These topics were not included under the Washington consensus because, chronic consensus-seeker that I am, I did not perceive that any particular view could come close to commanding a consensus in Washington. In some cases (e.g., as regards population control) I thought this state of disagreement was scandalous, while in other cases it struck me as quite natural. In most cases my personal views on these controversial issues are far removed from those of neoconservatives, so I find it ironic that some critics have condemned the Washington consensus as a neoconservative tract. I regard it rather as embodying the common core of wisdom embraced by all serious economists,[10] whose implementation provides the minimum conditions that will give a developing country the chance to start down the road to the sort of prosperity enjoyed by the industrialized countries. It therefore also provides a natural reference point for what one might expect technopols to aim at during the first stage of reform. Hence it is hoped that the country papers will analyze the extent to which policy reform covered this agenda, identify topics that were omitted or policies that were at variance with the consensus, and make mention of policy initiatives on subjects not covered by the standard list.

Since consensus does not extend to all important issues (for example, there is currently no consensus on how to get growth started again after

10. I paraphrase a comment of Luiz Carlos Bresser Pereira.

stabilization has succeeded, which is ironic given that in the Keynesian heyday this was the preeminent issue on which we thought we knew the answer), one would expect that there will normally be some topics in the last category. Sometimes one must expect that even technocrats will resort in such circumstances to an idiosyncratic ideology (of which a blind faith in markets and a belief in purchasing power parity are the two to which economists seem most professionally prone), which makes it relatively likely that policy will fail. But the fact that consensus is neither pervasive nor universal should not blind one to the reality that the stock of economic wisdom—of empirically reliable generalizations about the nature of the economic policies that can be expected to yield good results in due course—is substantial, and larger than it used to be. It is worth trying to be systematic about examining the political factors conducive to success in implanting those policies.

## Some Rules of Thumb for Technopols

The leading hypothesis about when policy reform may be possible is attributable to Mancur Olson (1982). He argues that societies have a natural tendency to become sclerotic. A society that faces no major crises experiences a buildup in the power of pressure groups and a consequent decline in flexibility. Policymakers become the prisoners of special interest groups, as posited by the new political economy.

Olson argues that what may change this situation and open the door to policy reform is a major crisis that undermines the previous system. Hyperinflation, military defeat, or some similar catastrophe can destroy existing coalitions and create opportunities for actors who were previously prevented from taking the initiative. Some of us might also argue that a sufficiently acute crisis may also create a consensus that the old order has failed and needs to be replaced, leading individuals and groups to accept that their special interests need to be sacrificed (along with those of other special interest groups) on the altar of the general good. But there may well be ambiguity about what constitutes a national crisis able to spark such a consensus: countries (e.g., Argentina, Ghana, and Zambia, or, in relative terms, Britain) have sometimes endured a long period of decline before it was recognized as constituting any sort of crisis.

Hence a crucial question that should be addressed by the authors of the country studies is, did policy reform emerge from the ashes of a national crisis? If so, what was the nature of the crisis that permitted a political initiative directed to achieving major reforms?[11]

---

11. This "crisis hypothesis" is endorsed by Grindle and Thomas (1991, 105) when it comes to the stimulus for major changes, such as those needed to make the transition to a

If it indeed proves difficult to identify cases of the sort of extensive policy reform needed to make the transition to an open, competitive, market economy that were not a response to a fundamental crisis, then one will have to ask whether it could conceivably make sense to think of deliberately provoking a crisis so as to remove the political logjam to reform. For example, it has sometimes been suggested in Brazil that it would be worthwhile stoking up a hyperinflation so as to scare everyone into accepting those changes that would finally make price stabilization attainable.

The following are not questions addressed to the authors of the country studies, but at a later stage of the conference we should ask whether the net effects of a crisis might be positive, or whether the direct costs always—or usually—outweigh the indirect benefits of permitting policy reform after the crisis has passed. Presumably no one with historical foresight would have advocated in the mid-1930s that Germany or Japan go to war in order to get the benefits of the supergrowth that followed their defeat. But could a lesser crisis have served the same function? Is it possible to conceive of a pseudo-crisis that could serve the same positive function without the costs of a real crisis? What is the least unpleasant type of crisis that seems able to do the trick? Or do we have to rely on technopols being able to make a more persuasive case to the public that mediocre performance is a calamity?

Even if a reforming government does not win legitimacy from an inherited crisis, and certainly if it does, the political scientists are unanimous in proclaiming that the time to introduce reforms is immediately after the government takes power. An incoming government enjoys a honeymoon during which the public will give it the benefit of the doubt and blame any sacrifices and difficulties on its predecessor. Presumably this honeymoon will be longer, and the scope for profound change greater, the deeper was the preceding crisis (compare the changes in US administration in 1933 and 1981 with those in 1961 and 1977). The country papers should describe whether the major reforms were introduced during such a honeymoon period and, if so, discuss how long the honeymoon lasted.

It is because of the honeymoon hypothesis that some political scientists argue that, from a political standpoint, the most difficult part of a reform program is not introducing the reforms but sustaining them until they have a chance to bear fruit and thus generate political support from the potential beneficiaries. How difficult this will be depends upon the

---

competitive, open, market economy, but they also argue that small changes will occur under conditions of politics as usual when there is no perception of a crisis. They envisage these small changes as falling in the pattern hypothesized by the new political economy. Thus their vision seems to be that the occasion creates the statesman rather than that the politician's values determine whether he operates as a normative economist would assume or as a member of the mafia postulated by public choice theory.

lag between the initial reforms and the emergence of politically significant beneficiaries—a topic on which most economists would probably be far more cautious now than a decade ago. It has even been suggested that programs should be designed to try and ensure the early emergence of some such group of beneficiaries, but the question arises as to whether such manipulation is compatible with the basic philosophy of economic reform, which is to provide a level playing field rather than favor particular groups. The country papers should certainly comment on how long it took for politically significant groups to recognize that they were benefiting from the program, what those first groups were, and whether their benefits were planned or accidental.

A complement to the crisis hypothesis has been suggested by Joan Nelson (1990, 335). She argues that reform will be easier where the opposition is discredited and disorganized (or repressed). The country papers should comment on the nature of the political and institutional opposition, and what role was played by opposition weakness in facilitating the implementation and subsequent maintenance of policy reform.

The preceding hypotheses relate to circumstances largely exogenous to government that may permit or facilitate policy reform. But the most interesting issues relate to those that can be controlled by technopols. One hypothesis might be thought of as a rival to the crisis hypothesis: it is plausible to suppose that the scope for reforms is greater where an incoming government has won a mandate for change by the substance of its preceding election campaign, rather than where it surprised its supporters after winning power. It would be helpful if the authors of country papers could describe the extent to which the government that introduced policy reforms had won a mandate for them by virtue of its campaign during the preceding election.

José Piñera (1991) has identified four features of Chile's experience with policy reform that he argues were crucial to its success.[12] Although Chile is in many ways atypical, his list provides an interesting supplement to the hypotheses that have been developed by political scientists, and it is presented here as providing a basis for discussion in the conference papers.

Piñera's first candidate is the presence in government of a team of economists with a common, coherent view of what needed to be done. The Chilean team was often referred to derogatorily as the "Chicago boys," but Piñera argues that what distinguished the team was not their indoctrination by tenets particularly associated with the University of Chicago, such as monetarism, but the fact that they all shared those

---

12. His presentation of this material at a meeting at the Institute for International Economics inspired the idea of convening a conference devoted to exploring the political dimensions of successful policy reform.

basic ideas in Paul Samuelson's *Economics* that were common to every university "where the great tradition of Anglo-Saxon economics was taught." They agreed that economic policy should be aimed at promotion of the general social good rather than fall prey to factionalism and special interest politics. "We simply applied the basic laws of supply and demand, of an open economy, of the efficiency of competition and free enterprise." Or, one might say, they implemented the Washington consensus long before the concept was conceived or (mis)named.

Piñera is not alone in drawing attention to the vital importance of an economic team with coherent views. The first of two broad generalizations that Joan Nelson (1990, 347) offers in drawing conclusions from a comparative study of 17 countries as to the political factors that permitted effective stabilization is that "the cases of clear failure all traced collapse in large part to deeply divided economic teams." But she argues that the need is broader than simply that the economic team should be intellectually united: the team must also command the instruments of concentrated executive authority.

This is presumably more likely to be true if another of Piñera's conditions is satisfied: the presence at the top of a leader with a vision of history, rather than a politician unable to lift his sights beyond the next election or a dictator preoccupied with defeating the next coup attempt. This condition may be described more prosaically as having a political leadership with an adequately long time horizon. This matters because policy reform is a long-term investment that may or may not have an electoral payoff before the next election (or coup), and hence it is only going to be pursued with the requisite degree of determination by those who think there are more important things in life than remaining in office.

Country papers should describe the characteristics and cohesiveness of the economic team that was responsible for designing and implementing the program of policy reform, including whether the team was headed by one or more technopols and whether that seems to have been an important factor in determining the successes and failures of the program. They should also try to characterize the attitude of the political leadership at the time that policy reforms were instituted as to the priority to be attached to the success of the reforms versus retaining the reins of power.

Another element that Piñera argued was crucial to the success of Chilean reform was a comprehensive program involving radical transformation of the economy, to be implemented rapidly. Liberalization was intended to cover all markets, not just trade or the capital market but also the labor market. Second-best theory provides a rationalization for this recommendation. He did not, however, demand that reform be instantaneous (he suggested five years to liberalize trade, for example). Indeed, it is hard to see how all reforms could be undertaken instantaneously: while most stabilization measures can be introduced rapidly, many liberalization measures and tax reforms require detailed preparation and legislative approval, which inevitably makes for a fairly lengthy period of implementation.

Presumably a recommendation for rapid and comprehensive reform is more appropriate in some situations than others. If a reform-minded government takes office when the economy is in a state of crisis, it may have no sensible alternative to a bold and comprehensive program such as that Piñera recommends. But if the economy is continuing to function, it may be more sensible to tackle issues one at a time. This will both avoid the danger of provoking a collapse and make it easier to retain political support, since only one or two interest groups will see their interests threatened at any particular time. The countries selected for study at the conference are mostly ones where relatively bold measures were taken, which may well reflect the fact that they started the reform process from a situation that called for such measures; but other countries such as China, Hungary, Malaysia, Singapore, and Thailand have made piecemeal reforms that have (arguably) got as far as those in some of the countries under study.

The country studies should certainly assess whether the reform program was comprehensive and implemented rapidly. The appendix may be used as a minimum checklist of what might be meant by a comprehensive program.

The final practice commended by Piñera is the will and ability to appeal to the general public through the media, bypassing vested interests. He argues that mobilization of public support was critical even in Chile at the time when it was ruled by Pinochet, and one would expect it to be vastly more important in a democracy. Piñera stresses that theoretical merit and internal consistency in a reform program are not enough to generate political support: the program also needs an upwelling of popular enthusiasm if it is to overcome the resistance of entrenched interests. Once again, each of the country papers should describe what efforts were made to mobilize public support for policy reforms, and with what degree of success.

The above list is based on the factors that one observer felt were important in sustaining reform in one particular country. Clearly one hopes that the authors of the country studies will add to it any factors that are not included but that seem to them to have been important in their own countries.

There are two traditional hypotheses that are sometimes used to explain when governments embark on a program of policy reform but that I personally do not find compelling. One of these is the association of reform with regime type: the notion that only military governments can institute reforms (as used to be asserted in Latin America), or conversely that only a democratic government can make the transformation to a market economy (as is widely asserted in Eastern Europe today). The wide range of regime types in the country studies to be discussed by the conference is enough to conclude that there is no necessary relationship of either type, for there are examples of both authoritarian and democratic governments among the reformers. Democratic governments enjoy both advantages (notably greater legitimacy in appealing for sacrifice) and disadvantages (notably the difficulty of getting democratic politicians to take measures whose payoff is expected only after the next election). It is hoped that the conference will shed light on just how much of a difficulty this is. Empirical evidence examined by John Helliwell (1992) suggests that authoritarian regimes enjoy a slight (though statistically insignificant) advantage in achieving economic growth.

There also seems little basis for postulating any general pattern of optimal sequencing of political versus economic liberalization. It does seem that the combination of a democratic political system and a competitive market economy is pretty stable; it is difficult to think of historical cases (with the notable exception of the Weimar Republic) where a society enjoying that combination has been destroyed from within. It also begins to seem that once a society has made substantial economic progress there is a natural emergence of pressures for democratization (the casual evidence on this is strongly confirmed by Helliwell's econometric analysis). Finally, it may be true that in Eastern Europe today it would be difficult for an undemocratic regime to make a successful transition to the market, because external support would be withdrawn. But it seems to me impossible to make a convincing general case for arguing that political must precede economic liberalization, or vice versa.

Second, the sample of successfully reforming countries to be examined at the conference (at a minimum this would include Australia, Chile, Korea, Mexico, New Zealand, Poland, Portugal, Spain, and Turkey) gives little reason to associate policy reform with the ideological coloration of the government. In particular, Australia, New Zealand, and Spain all pursued major reforms under left-of-center governments; in contrast, it is not difficult to think of avowedly right-wing governments that have eschewed policy reform and allowed their country to slide further into the morass of rent-seeking special interest groups.

A final subject that it is hoped the conference papers will illuminate is the role of external influences. External pressures come both from bilateral contacts with the governments of the major industrial countries and from multilateral agencies, notably international financial institutions such as the International Monetary Fund and the multilateral development banks. These external influences are presumably normally exercised with a view to strengthening the reform program. The most convincing theory of the way that the conditionality of the international institutions works is a highly political one: it says that the offer of financial assistance by an external agency gives reform-minded policymakers within the government extra leverage in winning internal arguments.[13] Is this the way that conditionality has worked? Was it an important factor in debate within the government? Are there improvements in the way the international organizations operate that might increase their effectiveness in promoting policy reform? Which was more important, pressures from international organizations or those from the governments of (which?) major industrial countries?

## Concluding Remarks

In summary, the country papers should focus primarily on the *politics* rather than the economics of achieving stabilization, liberalization, and opening of the economy. Nevertheless, it would be helpful to start each paper with a presentation of the major measures that were introduced and the chronology of their adoption. Use of the taxonomy incorporated in the "Washington consensus" (see the appendix) would facilitate comparison across countries. Each paper should also include a summary of the results of the introduction of the program, in terms both of changes in the main macroeconomic magnitudes (inflation, output, employment, the exchange rate, the balance of payments, reserves, etc.) and of the political standing of the government as measured by public opinion polls and election results. In particular, one wants to get a sense of how long it took before economic benefits became observable to the average elector, so that we can understand how great a problem arose in sustaining support for the reform program.

The main part of the paper should discuss how it proved possible to mobilize and maintain the political support that made policy reform possible. It is hoped that each paper will consider the set of hypotheses advanced above:

- the "crisis hypothesis" (that public perception of a crisis is needed to create the conditions under which it is politically possible to undertake extensive policy reforms) versus the "mandate hypothesis" (that a government may be able to introduce reforms if it campaigned on a program of reform in the preceding election)

- the "honeymoon hypothesis" (that extensive reforms have to be implemented immediately after a government takes office) and its

---

13. There are two competing theories. One is that the employees of international organizations are cleverer or better informed than those of national governments. The other is that international agencies compel national governments to do things that the latter do not perceive to be in their national interest. Neither seems very believable.

relation to the length of time before economic benefits began to materialize

■ the presence of a fragmented and demoralized opposition

■ the existence in government of a team of economists (headed by a technopol? did it matter?) with a common, coherent view of what needed to be done and commanding the instruments of concentrated executive authority

■ the presence at the top of a political leader with a vision of history, who is not unduly concerned about being reelected

■ the existence of a comprehensive program for transformation of the economy and a rapid timetable for implementation

■ the will and ability to appeal directly to the public and bypass vested interests.

In addition, the paper should classify the type of regime that undertook the reform program and describe the political coloration of the government (i.e., whether left or right of center). Furthermore, it should comment on the role of industrial-country governments and external financial agencies in strengthening or undermining the reform program.

## Appendix: The "Washington Consensus"

### Fiscal Discipline

Budget deficits, properly measured to include those of provincial governments, state enterprises, and the central bank, should be small enough to be financed without recourse to the inflation tax. This typically implies a primary surplus (i.e., before adding debt service to expenditure) of several percent of GDP, and an operational deficit (i.e., disregarding that part of the interest bill that simply compensates for inflation) of no more than about 2 percent of GDP.

### Public Expenditure Priorities

Policy reform consists in redirecting expenditure from politically sensitive areas, which typically receive more resources than their economic return can justify, such as administration, defense, indiscriminate subsidies, and white elephants, toward neglected fields with high economic returns and the potential to improve income distribution, such as primary health and education, and infrastructure.

### Tax Reform

Tax reform involves broadening the tax base and cutting marginal tax rates. The aim is to sharpen incentives and improve horizontal equity without lowering realized progressivity. Improved tax administration (including subjecting interest income on assets held abroad—flight capital—to taxation) is an important aspect of broadening the base in the Latin context.

## Financial Liberalization

The ultimate objective of financial liberalization is market-determined interest rates, but experience has shown that, under conditions of a chronic lack of confidence, market-determined rates can be so high as to threaten the financial solvency of productive enterprises and government. Under that circumstance a sensible interim objective is the abolition of preferential interest rates for privileged borrowers and achievement of a moderately positive real interest rate.

## Exchange Rates

Countries need a unified (at least for trade transactions) exchange rate set at a level sufficiently competitive to induce a rapid growth in nontraditional exports, and managed so as to assure exporters that this competitiveness will be maintained in the future.

## Trade Liberalization

Quantitative trade restrictions should be rapidly replaced by tariffs, and these should be progressively reduced until a uniform low tariff in the range of 10 percent (or at most around 20 percent) is achieved. There is, however, some disagreement about the speed with which tariffs should be reduced (with recommendations falling in a band between 3 and 10 years), and about whether it is advisable to slow down the process of liberalization when macroeconomic conditions are adverse (recession and payments deficit).

## Foreign Direct Investment

Barriers impeding the entry of foreign firms should be abolished; foreign and domestic firms should be allowed to compete on equal terms.

## Privatization

State enterprises should be privatized.

## Deregulation

Governments should abolish regulations that impede the entry of new firms or restrict competition, and ensure that all regulations are justified by such criteria as safety, environmental protection, or prudential supervision of financial institutions.

## Property Rights

The legal system should provide secure property rights without excessive costs, and make these available to the informal sector.

## Acknowledgments

The author is indebted to William R. Cline, I. M. Destler, Stephan Haggard, C. Randall Henning, Joan Nelson, and Marcus Noland for comments on a previous draft but absolves them of any responsibility for the views expressed.

## References

Bhagwati, Jagdish. 1989. "Is Free Trade Passé After All?" *Weltwirtschaftliches Archiv* Band 125, Heft 1: 17–44.

Buchanan, James M., and Gordon Tullock. 1962. *The Calculus of Consent.* Ann Arbor: University of Michigan Press

De Soto, Hernando. 1989. *The Other Path: The Invisible Revolution in the Third World.* New York: Harper and Row.

Feinberg, Richard. 1992. "Latin America: Back on the Screen." *International Economic Insights* 3, 4 (July-August): 52–56.

Grindle, Merilee S., and John W. Thomas. 1991. *Public Choices and Policy Change.* Baltimore: Johns Hopkins University Press.

Helliwell, John. 1992. "Empirical Linkages Between Democracy and Economic Growth." *NBER Working Paper* 4066. Cambridge, MA: National Bureau of Economic Research.

Meier, Gerald M. 1991. *Politics and Policy Making in Developing Countries.* San Francisco: International Center for Economic Growth.

Michaely, Michael, Demetris Papageorgiou, and Armeane Choksi. 1991. *Liberalizing Foreign Trade.* London: Blackwell.

Nelson, Joan M., ed. 1990. *Economic Crisis and Policy Choice.* Princeton, NJ: Princeton University Press.

Olson, Mancur. 1982. *The Rise and Decline of Nations.* New Haven, CT: Yale University Press.

Piñera, José. 1991. "Political Economy of Chilean Reform." *International Economic Insights* 2, 4 (July-August): 6–9, reprinted in chapter 5 of this volume.

Williamson, John. 1990. *Latin American Adjustment: How Much Has Happened?* Washington: Institute for International Economics.

# Comment

ROBERT H. BATES

Two claims lie close to the heart of John Williamson's paper. The first is that a precondition for good economic policy is that technocrats be in charge of making it. The second is that when economic policy *is* made by politicians, its chances of being good policy are enhanced if the politicians are socially regarding, public-spirited, and possess a sense of history. Both claims, Williamson argues, run counter to those of the new political economy, which, being based on the assumptions of self-interested behavior on the part of politicians, is therefore of limited utility in explaining successful cases of economic policy reform.

I agree with Williamson that "good" economic policymaking and the political preeminence of technocrats go together. Where Williamson sees causation, however, I see correlation—a point I will elaborate below. In addition, I disagree with his critique of the new political economy (but not the critique that he makes in the footnotes to his paper). I will explain here the reasons for my dissent, drawing on work recently published with Anne O. Krueger (Bates and Krueger 1993).

## Two Roads to Reform

Williamson, in my judgment, is right: good economic policymaking requires that economic decisions be made by technocrats. But what are technocrats? Generally, they are academics. They lack the normal prerequisites of political influence: wealth and power. Rather, they possess

*Robert H. Bates is a Professor at Duke University.*

expertise. If technocrats possess political power, it is generally because it is given to them by politicians. An understanding of the behavior of politicians is therefore central to any explanation of the role of the technocrat. Technocratic power and good policy may well go together, as Williamson claims, but the former does not cause the latter. Rather, the relationship is the result of the decision of politicians to delegate political power to otherwise powerless experts so as to secure economically superior public policy. To explain why technocrats possess power over economic policy, we must first, then, explain why politicians trust them and are willing to delegate to them control over economic decisions.

Politics is a competitive business: politicians compete to gain and to retain public office. The necessity of competing shapes the selection of public policies, either by causing individual politicians to "trim" or by enabling only those who sincerely believe in a particular policy position to win out in the competition for power. The assumption of competitive office seeking (Downs 1957; Mayhew 1974) does not negate the possibility that politicians also possess political convictions. Rather, it highlights the competitive nature of the political arena and the way in which those who prevail in the competition for office must respond to the pressures and incentives that originate within it, for example by endorsing certain economic policies in a search for political support. Building on these assumptions, we can identify two paths toward economic policy reform.

## The Politicians' Dilemma

The first path we can label "the politicians' dilemma" (Geddes forthcoming). Incumbents seek to retain power; challengers seek to unseat them. To remain in power, incumbent politicians turn their control over public spending into a source of political benefits: they adopt distributive strategies, financing programs and allocating "pork" so as to reward constituents and build organized followings. The dilemma arises from the fact that, while such strategies are rational for individual incumbents, they are collectively irrational for incumbents as a group. When each incumbent champions spending projects so as to retain office, deficits mount, and economic conditions worsen. The political popularity of incumbents as a group then declines, placing them at greater political risk from challengers.

Sophisticated politicians respond to this dilemma by creating institutions that possess the power to commit them to collectively rational strategies. In particular, they may create institutions that impose fiscal discipline, reducing the opportunities for distributive politics and enforcing limits on public spending. The form of the response is delegation: the creation of new agencies to which politicians delegate the responsibility for a particular policy domain.[1] These institutions act as agencies of restraint. Politicians staff them with technocrats and confer upon them special powers, thereby tying their own hands. Being vested with the defense of the collective interest, these agencies acquire special status; they come to be regarded as public institutions, whose mission is to defend the collective welfare rather than the private political interests of particular politicians.

This approach thus treats the creation of financial institutions and the empowerment of technocrats as a collectively rational response to the threat posed to incumbent elites by the pursuit of economically unsustainable policies. It helps to explain how self-interested politicians might reverse the decline of their economies, and thus of their political fortunes, by delegating power to financial institutions and to the technocrats who run them.

## The Partisan Model

The ''politicians' dilemma'' emphasizes the benefits of economic policy reform to all incumbent politicians. A second approach, called the ''partisan model,'' emphasizes the benefits of economic policy reform to a specific subset of incumbents: those whose constituents would directly benefit from the new set of policies (Kiewiet and McCubbins 1991). It views the benefits of economic policy reform as (at least in the short run) distributive. By this approach, the empowerment of the technocrats and financial institutions represents an attempt to institutionalize policies that serve particular interests—to stabilize the fortunes and protect the political triumph of particular industries, sectors, and regions of the economy that benefit from the new economic policies. For several reasons, I favor this approach.

Economic reform, while in the long run good for everyone, in the short run harms particular interests. These include those who derive their incomes from the untraded sector; the employees and owners of firms that will become unprofitable when faced with market prices; the beneficiaries of government subsidies for food or housing; and so on. In the short run, then, economic policy reform provokes distributive struggles, with partisan forces arrayed for and against. The technocrats implementing the reforms must be empowered to resist partisan challenges.

Reform-oriented governments possess a different political base than do those resistant to reforms. Within Africa, for example, governments based on constituencies in the highlands or forests adopt liberal economic policies that favor export agriculture; those based on constituencies in the semiarid zones adopt socialist policies, designed to tax export

---

1. The relevant central work is that of Krehbiel (1991).

agriculture and to promote the fortunes of "backward" regions (Bates 1991). Governments that have switched their economic policies, such as those in Asia (e.g., Korea), Latin America (e.g., Chile), or the former socialist countries (e.g., Hungary), first changed their political base.

Economic policy reform tends to correlate with discontinuous changes in the composition of governments, a result that would be expected were economic reforms to generate policies that favor some interests (and their political representatives) more than others.

There are logical as well as empirical reasons for favoring the partisan model. A full account of the power of technocrats must explain why politicians trust them at the outset. It must explain why private agents regard the reforms as credible. And it must explain how the reforms are sustained politically. An advantage of the partisan theory is that it does all three, and therefore provides a fuller account of successful reform.

To explain why politicians delegate power to technocrats, we must first explain how they come to trust them. Technocrats possess expertise—private information. Most politicians cannot directly evaluate that expertise; they can only evaluate its results. For a politician caught in a competitive political struggle, meaningful results take the form not just of aggregate economic growth but, more immediately, of positive economic rewards for influential political constituents. In checking out whether a technocrat is "sound," a politician is likely to listen to major economic interests in his constituency. Politicians are likely to come to trust those technocrats whose policies enhance the economic fortunes of key constituents and thus their own political fortunes as well.

An economic policy becomes credible when private agents understand that politicians possess no incentive to rescind it. In a competitive political world, should a politician violate the economic interests of those upon whose political support he depends, he would increase his chances of losing power. The clearest signal that a politician can send, then, is that arising from the public's perception of his political base. The partisan model highlights the mechanism—the politician's tie with his constituency—that can render policy commitments self-enforcing and therefore credible.

Economic technocrats become powerful, and thus reform becomes politically sustainable, when they serve the interests of powerful groups: industries, sectors, or regions of the economy. Over time, the fortunes of powerful groups become dependent upon the maintenance in place of a policy regime; they develop a vested interest in keeping the reforms in place. Politicians can costlessly dispose of unprotected academic advisers; they cannot do so, however, if those academics have become associated with a policy that is highly prized by powerful interests.

The partisan theory focuses on the distributive benefits of economic policies—the benefits that flow to interests that comprise political constituencies for office-seeking politicians. It therefore helps to explain how powerless academics gain the trust of powerful political elites, how their reforms gain credibility, and how they become politically self-sustaining.

## Conclusion

I thus agree with Williamson: the prominence of technocrats and the success of economic reforms go together. Where he sees causation, however, I see correlation. The relationship between economic success and technocratic prominence is, I feel, generated by an underlying political process: the competitive search for power by politicians. Politicians, seeking to retain or to gain power, themselves empower technocrats, and this comment has outlined two "causal processes" by which they may do so.[2]

## A Brief Addendum

As a political scientist, I would urge those studying the politics of economic policy reform to focus on the results of earlier research on the politics of economic policymaking in the advanced industrial countries (see Bates et al. 1991 and the references therein). Those results include the following:

- Countries whose governments rest upon strong trade union movements are better able to implement economic adjustment programs than countries in which trade unions are weak (or strong but in opposition to the government).

- Governments that pursue open trade policies tend to maintain large programs of job retraining, unemployment benefits, and social insurance.

- As the share of national product originating from foreign trade rises, so too does the public share of the national product. That is, countries that practice liberal trade policies tend to possess large, not small, public sectors.

Some participants at this conference expressed surprise about the role of labor in the politics of countries that mounted successful economic

2. I found the accounts of the politics of the "failed" cases of reform more illuminating than the successes. Ironically, the technocrats who have been politically more successful often appeared to be politically less insightful. The argument above may unravel this irony. The reason might be that, in the successful cases, the politicians took care of the politics, creating a political space for policy innovation by the technocrats, leaving them free to focus on the economics, and rendering their choices politically unchangeable.

reforms. Others highlighted the importance of "social safety nets," if only for reducing political opposition to reform packages. Still others debated whether economic adjustment in fact implied less activist governments. The discussion of all of these points could usefully have been informed by a fuller knowledge of these previous studies.

## References

Bates, Robert H. 1991. *Beyond the Miracle of the Market*. Cambridge: Cambridge University Press.

Bates, Robert H., and Anne O. Krueger. 1993. *Political and Economic Interactions in Economic Policy Reform*. Oxford: Blackwell.

Bates, Robert H., Philip Brock, and Jill Tiefenthaler. 1991. "Risk and Trade Regimes." *International Organization* 45, no. 1 (Winter): 1–18.

Downs, Anthony. 1957. *An Economic Theory of Democracy*. New York: Harper and Row.

Geddes, Barbara. 1993. *The Politicians' Dilemma: Reforming the State in Latin America*. Berkeley and Los Angeles: University of California Press (forthcoming).

Kiewiet, D. Roderick, and Mathew D. McCubbins. 1991. *The Logic of Delegation*. Chicago: University of Chicago Press.

Krehbiel, Keith. 1991. *Information and Legislative Organization*. Ann Arbor: University of Michigan Press.

Mayhew, David. 1974. *Congress: The Electoral Connection*. New Haven and London: Yale University Press.

# Comment

## JOHN TOYE

John Williamson, in a most stimulating paper, has presented a set of bold challenges to analysts of the politics of policy reform. These challenges are both theoretical, concerning the validity of public choice theory, and practical, proposing at least the section headings for a modern economic politician's manual. This comment follows the sequence of the Williamson paper, dealing first with the concept of the "technopol," then reflecting in turn on the new political economy, the "Washington consensus," and the appropriate rules of thumb in the politics of policy reform.

## The Concept of a "Technopol"

With all due respect to its originators Jorge Dominguez and Richard Feinberg, the term "technopol" should be quietly dropped from the professional vocabulary before it becomes entrenched through repeated use. The reason for this severe judgment is that the word has misleading overtones, and also that it fails to specify precisely what the concept is intended to mean. The misleading overtones come from its derivation from the term "technocrat." As the definitions quoted by Williamson suggest, the technocrat is a 19th-century ideal figure of industrial governance, much lauded by Saint-Simon, Comte, and others (Markham 1952, xxvi–xxvii). He stands as an antithesis to laissez-faire and free competition; he is a proponent of a planned industrial economy—at

*John Toye is Director of the Institute of Development Studies in Brighton. He is also a Professorial Fellow at the University of Sussex.*

considerable odds, therefore, with the policy objectives that a modern "technopol" is supposed to pursue.

Recent usage of the term "technocrat" to describe senior civil servants (see Williamson's introductory paper) is in line with this 19th-century origin rather than the aims of modern economic reform. The professional skills of such people are in administration and political management, not economics. It is not surprising that administered or planned economies, rather than efficient economies with minimalist governments, are what emerge when administrative "technocrats" form the ruling elite. Their struggle to keep economists in merely advisory positions in government, as minor technicians who can be consulted but, as necessary, overruled, is well-documented in economists' memoirs of their time in government.

The phenomenon that Williamson is describing is the economist-as-politician, who explicitly does battle with technocrats of industry or administration. If a new coinage is needed to dramatize the idea, "econopol," not "technopol," should be given currency.[1]

Having said that, however, one could argue that the second half of the neologism is as problematic as the first. The technopol is described by Williamson as having a political appointment and bearing political responsibility. There are as many ways to do these things as there are political systems. We need to distinguish between (at least) authoritarian regimes, democracies, and systems in transit from the one to the other. The implication in most of the paper is that technopols operate within political systems that are already democratic—that is, that their appointments are elective and the support that they need is public support. They are thus a product of a process of democratization that has already occurred.

If this is a correct reading, the definition sits uneasily with the later discussion of the optimal sequencing of political and economic liberalization, which cannot be an issue for this kind of technopol. The technopol is characteristic of a particular set of countries—illustrated by Spain, Portugal, Australia, New Zealand, Poland, Colombia, and India—where a democratic system is working, but where economic liberalization needs to be initiated and sustained. Technopols in authoritarian governments, like Indonesia under Suharto and Korea under Park Chung Hee, operate under quite different political constraints. In a third group,

---

1. Peter Self (1975, 4) made the point years ago that "economists are natural critics of technocracy." He also coined the term "econocrat," defined as a person who believes "that there exist fundamental economic tests or yardsticks according to which policy decisions can and should be made." Incidentally, Self regarded econocracy, so defined, as "much more ambitious, and consequently more dangerous to the public, than *any* kind of technocracy" (1975, 5, emphasis in original). Whether he would have maintained that judgment if econocrats operated as politicians (i.e., as "econopols") rather than as unelected officials is not clear, because he does not really consider this possibility.

exemplified by quite a few countries in sub-Saharan Africa, the initial breakthrough in economic liberalization has been made, and what is now being attempted is the construction of a properly democratic politics without destabilizing the economic reform process.

The concept of a technopol may well be a red herring. As Williamson suggests, it is far from clear that holding political office makes an economist any more effective in promoting reforms than operating under delegated authority from people who do hold political office. If there is a pragmatic justification for economists seeking political office, it must presumably derive from their comparative advantage, vis-à-vis other potential or actual politicians, in political skills. Otherwise, a division of labor would seem likely to be the more efficient solution.[2]

In studying modern economists-as-politicians, it will be important to establish how far they do exercise the politician's skills. One can hold political office while refusing to exercise political skills, but that choice makes one the prisoner of other politicians. One has a temporary platform, but little more than that. This seems to be the situation of Manmohan Singh, a distinguished economist and now India's finance minister. His political base, such as it is, is a nominated seat in the Upper House (Rajya Sabha) of the Indian Parliament. His announcement of a structural adjustment program in June 1992 followed within days of this nomination. It involved minimal politicking and minimal democratic consent. So he and his program remain highly vulnerable to adverse twists in the Indian political situation, which he can do very little to control, centered as it is on ethnic politics and the electoral calendar.

It is perhaps when the normal supply of political skills is failing for some reason that brief opportunities are created for economists to pursue "the objectives postulated by traditional normative economic analysis" from public positions. If some economists succeed in transforming this opportunity into a political career, they will have to do so through exercising the skills validated by traditional political practice. In that

---

2. Historically, British economists seem to have appreciated this argument of efficiency deriving from specialization and division of labor, and to have been increasingly reluctant to involve themselves in national politics. David Ricardo purchased the pocket borough of Portarlington, which he represented for four years (1819–23). As Lord Brougham put it, "finding but a very small body of his fellow members to agree with his leading positions," he had "generally to speak against the sense of his audience" (Hartwell 1971, 397). John Stuart Mill refused to spend any money, or to advance the interests of his constituents, when he became the member for Westminster briefly in the late 1860s. Both Mill and Ricardo sat as respected "independents" and never sought or found office. John Maynard Keynes actually refused three offers to represent Henry Asquith's Liberals in Parliament in 1920, believing that his voice and appearance were unsuitable for a politician and that he would find loyalty to the party line on economic policy too constraining (Skidelsky 1992, 21). By Keynes's time the respected independent member of Parliament was a dying breed, and (apart from providing the Lloyd George Liberals with a policy program in 1926–29) Keynes shied away from partisan politics.

case, actively realizing the agenda of normative economics is likely to have to take second place to a host of specifically political concerns—building a personal constituency, appealing for electoral support, negotiating with rival political groups. The economist-turned-politician may retain the vision and the rhetoric of normative economics, but is unlikely to practice his or her economic policymaking skills.

## The New Political Economy

I have explained my own understanding of the "new political economy" (NPE) elsewhere (Toye 1991, 321–37). It is in agreement at many important points with Williamson's as presented in his paper, and especially with his major proposition that "pretensions to provide a universal characterization of political motivation must be rejected." Within this overall agreement, I would differ in some points of emphasis.

The fundamental problems of the NPE arise from the axiom of methodological individualism. This simply prohibits any explanation of behavior that cannot be deduced from the rational calculations of the abstract individual. Social structure is acknowledged only to the extent to which it can be logically reduced to the rational self-interest of individuals. As a critique of organic sociological theories, this method is sharp and illuminating. But as a positive theory of society and polity, it is obviously partial. A reciprocal interdependence between actors and social structure provides a richer account of society than either organicism or individualism taken separately.

The extensive adoption in the 1980s of economic reform programs that curtail the role of the state is not quite the refutation of the NPE that it first seems, nor is it merely a result of the mixed motives of politicians in developing countries. The role of exogenous international agencies has been crucial to this process, and a residual reference at the end of Williamson's paper to their role is far less than sufficient recognition of this. The international financial institutions did not impose their policies of reform on unwilling countries, as is sometimes alleged. They were, however, vital catalysts in the process of developing countries' deciding to adopt the path of economic reform. This is not reflected in most NPE analyses, which effectively treat the political economy as closed.

Perhaps rather more stress should be laid on the rhetorical than on the scientific aspects of the NPE. It took a leaf from the book of neo-Marxism, exaggerating the pervasiveness of corruption and the obstacles to improvement as a persuasive tactic, in order to mobilize opinion in favor of new international initiatives that are much less respectful of the claims of national sovereignty than had been hitherto customary in relations with developing countries. Policy discourse does not just operate on the scientific level. Sometimes it is more like soothsaying than science. Prophecies of doom are used to change behavior; for them to be fulfilled would indicate their failure, not their success.

## The Washington Consensus

All over the world today, the Washington consensus is flying high. But meanwhile, down in the street below, people are still asking, "Is it a bird? Is it a plane? Is it a man?" Is the Washington consensus a statement of what economists actually believe about economic policy (i.e., the outcome of an opinion survey)? Is it instead a statement of what economists ought to believe, at least if they are "serious" economists (i.e., a synthesis of normative economics)? Or is it a statement of "wisdom" (going beyond what can be strictly proved in economics), which liberal economists must believe (i.e., a core vision, a professional creed, or a neoliberal ideology)? Like Superman, the Washington consensus is none of the things that it appears to resemble and yet is something of all of them. No one feels the need to test it empirically because the facts are too obvious; no one really wants to delve into welfare economics because its results are vulnerable to a whole raft of academic quibbles; and no one is really going to call in the Spanish Inquisition if the occasional economist harbors sincere doubts about, say, the privatization proposition. We are, as with Superman, in the realm of the Empowering Myth.[3]

The list approach to consensus (see the appendix to Williamson's paper) poses two different problems, one intellectual and the other practical. The intellectual problem is that it appears to freeze or concretize ideas, and thereby loses sight of the fact that they are always in flux, always embedded in a critical debate. The learning process disappears. Yet it is very clear that the new ideas of the 1980s that the consensus embodies did not simply materialize fully formed but underwent a whole series of modifications and qualifications. Different issues and fragments of analysis were added, while some of the strong policy stances that were taken in the first half of the 1980s have had to be modified when they turned out, in the light of serious criticism, to be intellectually unsustainable. At the moment "we are still . . . far from a consensual model of structural adjustment" (Ferreira 1992, 67). Unless we expect the learning process to stop, this will continue to be the case.

The problem at the practical level is that the "Washington consensus" or "universal convergence" looks remarkably like a body of settled conclusions immediately applicable to policy. It seems to be precisely what Keynes in his 1922 preface to the *Cambridge Economic Handbooks* denied

---

3. At this point unserious economists probably expect a really funny footnote comparing neoliberal economists to the designers of the telephone booth in which Clark Kent becomes the Caped Crusader. Perish the thought!

that the discipline of economics could provide. Even today there are some who believe that economics provides an analytical method rather than a doctrine. To them the art of policy remains the application of the logic of economic thinking to a set of specific circumstances, rather than the crafting of an agreed package, ready to go, with or without side orders of equity or population control.

To say this is emphatically not to deny the existence of an emerging consensus on policy questions in developing countries. Consensus is not the problem, rather consensus-mongering. The World Bank's *World Development Report 1991*, for example, although entirely well-intentioned, degenerates sometimes into the silliness of matching every inflexion of the consensus doctrine with one solid-looking academic research result.[4] Every attempt to define the consensus has the unintended effect of stimulating dissent as the learning process advances. Williamson suggests that the problem of disagreement can be handled by recognizing disagreement on a wide range of noncore issues, while insisting that all the core propositions have to be embraced by those who wish to be regarded as in possession of the wisdom of all serious economists. One can only repeat that there seems to be a conflation here of what economists believe with what is economic truth. We ought to question what other people believe, not believe it because they believe it. That, at least, is how we got to where we are now. Truth is always provisional, and it is the product of criticism just as much as the attempt to promote "economic correctness."[5]

Although, as Williamson suggests, the Washington consensus is the agenda of the economist-as-politician, it is not necessarily the case that the econopols went into politics to promote that agenda. Some of them went into politics as unserious economists and only became serious thereafter. Kwesi Botchwey, Ghana's long-serving finance minister and high priest of that country's economic recovery and structural adjust-

---

4. Some of the results relied on are much less solid-looking than they appear. For example, one of the Bank's own large and expensive studies of trade liberalization, quoted in the 1991 report, has been rightly criticized for its inadequate methodology and the extravagance of the authors' claims for the generality of their results (Greenaway 1993, 208–22, reviewing Papageorgiou et al. 1991). Williamson also refers to this study but in a noncommittal way (footnote 7 on page 10). It is not clear from this reference whether the study is being put forward as part of the evidence supporting the Washington consensus. After reading Greenaway's critique, one hopes not.

5. I owe the term "economic correctness" to Alice Amsden, who compared that notion with that of "political correctness" in an article in the *New York Times* (12 January 1993). The device of separating policy issues into core issues (in which certain beliefs are required by "economic correctness") and noncore issues (in which they are not) strongly reminds me of the judicious Richard Hooker's attempt to heal the divisive impact of Elizabethan Puritanism's ecclesiastical correctness by recognizing a category of beliefs about church government ("things indifferent") that could be legitimately based, not on Scripture, but on reason and tradition (Morris 1963, v–xiii).

ment programs, wrote his doctoral dissertation on the undesirable consequences of the trade and investment practices of multinational enterprises, and began his period of office with a set of policies very different from those adopted after 1983. One should examine those cases where the political process has imposed the Washington consensus on an econopol, as well as the reverse case that the Williamson paper emphasises.

## Rules of Thumb

One of the sets of questions that I and my colleagues Paul Mosley and Jane Harrigan investigated in our joint study *Aid and Power* (Mosley et al. 1991) concerned the conditions under which structural adjustment programs were most successfully implemented. Several of the hypotheses we formulated were very similar to those discussed by Williamson—namely, that an economic crisis provides a trigger for a reform episode, that a newly incoming government will do better than a long-established one at implementing reforms (because of the "honeymoon effect"), and that authoritarian regimes do better than democratic ones. We examined these hypotheses for nine countries in Latin America and the Caribbean (Ecuador, Jamaica, and Guyana), Africa (Kenya, Ghana, and Malawi), and Asia (Turkey, Thailand, and the Philippines).

The hypothesis of a "crisis" that triggers a reform episode proved difficult to substantiate because the depth of a crisis is so difficult to measure. Indeed, the objective identification of a crisis is no easier in the heady days of the Washington consensus than it was in the bad old days of those endless neo-Marxist debates about "the crisis." Which indicator should we measure? Loss of GDP, the balance of payments deficit, the rate of inflation, or the rate of acceleration of inflation? Is a crisis caused by one of these, or by a combination of some or all? How bad do things have to get? Economically, there is no situation so bad that it cannot get worse. Is it a matter of perception then? Does the crisis arrive when enough people perceive a crisis? If the crisis is defined subjectively, how do we measure the subjective perceptions independently of the reforming behavior that they are hypothesized to cause? Looking at country cases, it seemed that some reforming countries, such as Ghana, had experienced what on most objective measurements was a crisis. But other countries began reforms when their economic maladies were very much less severe. Given this vagueness and variability, Williamson's suggestion that it might be a good move to provoke an artificial crisis in order to trigger reform should best be read as an idea designed to provoke and tease.

The "honeymoon hypothesis," again despite its plausibility, did not come out particularly well either. Taking some African cases, one might ask whether authoritarian regimes either enjoy or need honeymoons.

New authoritarian regimes can quickly dispel any legitimacy that they may possess, as did the regime of Jerry John Rawlings in Ghana in 1982–83. Old authoritarian regimes, like that of Hastings Kamuzu Banda in Malawi, may prove just as effective in implementing reforms as the new Rawlings government, despite the former's many previous years in power (Toye 1992, 183–97). The "honeymoon hypothesis" is one whose relevance seems to depend critically on the nature of the regime. It seems to be more relevant where new governments are brought in on a wave of popular support, not by a coup or a putsch, and where the waning of popular support cannot be ignored by the judicious application of political repression.

However, to stress the analytic importance of the distinction between regime types is not to say that one type of regime can be relied on to achieve a better performance in the implementation of reform. *Aid and Power* is in agreement with Williamson's paper about this. The reason is, in part at least, that authoritarian regimes need some form of political patronage to secure the loyalty of selected parts of their national elite. Their leaders are anxious to retain certain sources of rent that can be used in this way. They often turn out to be half-hearted reformers, despite their ability to recruit technically powerful economic teams.

Since *Aid and Power* was completed, the reform process has widened not merely to encompass thoroughgoing economic reform, but also to include radical constitutional changes of various kinds usually described as improved transparency and accountability, good governance, multi-partyism, and electoral politics. As already indicated, the problem of optimal sequencing of economic and political liberalization does not appear to be the central issue. We seem to have either politically liberalized countries whose problem is to make progress on economic reform (typically in Eastern Europe and the former Soviet Union) or economically reformed countries struggling toward a semblance of democratic politics (typically in sub-Saharan Africa and China).

Since the African perspective is missing from the Williamson paper, it might be useful to end this comment by emphasizing how difficult the promotion of democratic politics in key African countries is proving in practice. In Ghana, Flight-Lieutenant Rawlings after 10 years of economic reform has now piloted his regime through three sets of elections at the district, the presidential, and the national parliamentary level. Against a divided opposition and four weak candidates, he won 58 percent of the presidential votes in what observers declared was a fair election. Unfortunately, the opposition groups decided not to contest the parliamentary election, and Rawlings's candidates took almost all the seats. There will thus be an electorally legitimated president but no effective parliamentary opposition within Ghana.

In Kenya, the situation is even worse. Again facing a multiply-divided opposition, Daniel arap Moi won the presidential election with 36 percent of the popular vote in what was a much less fair and open contest. The opposition still cannot find a basis for united action but has withdrawn cooperation with the government in a way that will make it difficult for Moi to construct a cabinet representing all main areas and groups in Kenya. Whereas the introduction of democratic politics may not have helped matters very much in Ghana, in Kenya it may actually have made them worse. In both countries the imperatives that the new system imposes for success have not been internalized. In sub-Saharan Africa, at least, it is not yet possible to sit back and contemplate the easy advance of self-reinforcing progress—now a little more economic progress, now a little political liberalization. At the same time, we must acknowledge that Africa has made more real progress in institution building in the last decade than many people ever expected.

## References

Ferreira, Francisco. 1992. "The World Bank and the Study of Stabilisation and Structural Adjustment." *DEP* 41. London: London School of Economics Development Economics Research Programme.

Greenaway, David. 1993. "Liberalising Foreign Trade Through Rose-Tinted Glasses." *Economic Journal* 103, no. 416.

Hartwell, R. Max, ed. 1971. *Ricardo's Principles of Political Economy and Taxation*. Harmondsworth, England: Penguin.

Markham, F. M. H., ed. and transl. 1952. *Selected Writings of Henri Comte de St-Simon (1760–1825)*. Oxford: Basil Blackwell.

Mill, John Stuart. 1924. *Autobiography*. Oxford: Oxford University Press.

Morris, Christopher, ed. 1963. *Richard Hooker's Of the Laws of Ecclesiastical Polity, Vol. 1*. London: Dent.

Mosley, Paul, Jane Harrigan, and John Toye. 1991. *Aid and Power: The World Bank and Policy-Based Lending in the 1980s* (2 vols.). London: Routledge.

Papageorgiou, Demetris, Michael Michaely, and Armeane Choksi. 1991. *Liberalizing Foreign Trade* (7 vols.). Washington: World Bank.

Self, Peter. 1975. *Econocrats and the Policy Process: The Politics and Philosophy of Cost-Benefit Analysis*. London: Macmillan.

Skidelsky, Robert. 1992. *John Maynard Keynes: The Economist as Saviour, 1920–1937*. London: Macmillan.

Toye, John. 1991. "Is There a New Political Economy of Development?" In C. Colcough and J. Manor, eds., *States or Markets? Neo-liberalism and the Development Policy Debate*, 321–338. Oxford: Clarendon Press.

Toye, John. 1992. "Interest Group Politics and the Implementation of Adjustment Policies in Sub-Saharan Africa." *Journal of International Development* 4, no. 2: 183–97.

World Bank. 1991. *World Development Report 1991*. Washington: World Bank.

# Discussion

*Max Corden* remarked that the first person to have thought about how to use political tricks to make the world a better place was Niccolo Machiavelli. The conference was really about "Machiavellian economics"! *Guy Pfeffermann* contrasted the effective way in which the Chilean government had used the media with the way in which the Venezuelan government had failed to argue the case for reform.[1]

*Anne Krueger* suggested that "ideas" were a critical conditioning circumstance that Williamson's paper had overlooked. The professional consensus at the time as to what was good economic policy had not differed much from what was practiced in the 1950s and 1960s. From a present perspective these policies are judged to have been inefficient, but the prevailing climate of ideas did not recognize that. Some well-intentioned teams had made a critical mistake early on in their policy reform efforts, which had undermined the adjustment programs before they really got off the ground. In some cases this may have been due to wishful thinking, but in others it was a matter of not having people on the team that were either sufficiently committed or sufficiently informed. One needed to pay attention not just to the team that was assembled but to the ideas it sought to implement.

*Fred Bergsten* questioned Krueger on the need to make a distinction between ideas and ideology. Specifically, he argued that the rise of "market economics" in the 1980s was distinct from the Reagan-Thatcher ideology and might well have made the same headway even in the

---

1. See Naim (1993, 134–37 and 150–52) for a discussion of the failure of the Carlos Andrés Pérez government to make its case for liberalization with the public (ed.).

latter's absence. Krueger replied that a proposition such as the likelihood of market forces subverting price controls was certainly not ideology but a matter of fact, and a fact that would be far more widely recognized today than formerly: the relation between changes in ideas and ideology was much less clear to her.

*Susan Collins* claimed that one feature of well-conceived adjustment programs had been their flexibility, with policymakers altering their particulars as short-term problems arose and mistakes were recognized.

*Nicolás Ardito-Barletta* argued for a distinction between external conditions (such as the presence of a crisis) that create the possibility for reform, and the internal decision factors (such as the existence of an effective team and its relationship with the political powers-that-be) that determine the viability of reform. The interaction of external and internal factors might create a domestic alliance with constituencies strong enough to build the credibility essential to successful reform. There was a critical learning process during which society realizes that current rules of conduct and organization have to be changed, and that realization might reconcile the satisfaction of the selfish purposes of politicians with the wider interests of the community at large. Statesmen, who are recognizable only ex post, are those who provide that essential but indefinable element called leadership that nurtures this process.

*Joan Nelson* endorsed the conclusion that the contrast between authoritarian and democratic governments had not proved a useful variable in explaining economic reform, but she suggested the need to distinguish between, on the one hand, economic reforms undertaken when basic political and systemic structures were stable and, on the other, the sweeping economic reforms associated with dramatic political change such as the collapse of an authoritarian regime. Under the latter circumstances the process of working out the new political rules of the game would rank at least as important as economic reform to most political players. This case was of particular relevance to many of the countries that had embarked on reform programs in the 1990s, but few of the cases being discussed at the conference fell in that category.

*Francisco Torres* followed up on Williamson's critique of the "new political economy," arguing that it was no longer very new. The truly new literature, represented (for example) by Alberto Alesina, focused attention on the political constraints faced by politicians and policymakers, not the nature of their objectives. It thus permitted analysis of the case treated by Williamson, where a technopol aims to advance the broad public interest but is constrained by the electoral and institutional features of the system. These politicians did not correspond to the rigid public choice model, but neither need they be completely altruistic.

Torres noted that the current Prime Minister of Portugal, Aníbal Cavaco Silva, was a distinguished economist who had authored the country's standard macroeconomics textbook and had been a research economist in the central bank before entering politics. He had assembled an impressive team of technocrats and managed to implement sustainable economic reform in parallel with political modernization. Torres argued, however, that the key to his success was not the coherent team of economists working for him, but his ability to inspire the technocrats (among others) with his vision of history while taking political constraints into account.

*Il SaKong* discussed what was meant by the term "technopol". He interpreted it as referring to political appointees rather than elected politicians; their status varied depending on the political system within which they were operating, whether it was a presidential system as in the United States or Korea or a parliamentary system as in Japan. An elected politician with an academic or economic background was in his view still a politician, not a technopol.

*Barbara Stallings* criticized the absence of reference to international factors in Williamson's paper and Robert Bates's comment on it. The simultaneous application across countries of similar reform models suggested a common international transmission mechanism of ideas. Where did the ideas come from? In part, they came presumably from international financial institutions and foreign governments. These were important not just in laying down conditionality but also in providing the external finance needed to support an adjustment program. So far as Bates's partisan model was concerned, we needed to know why politicians suddenly begin to change their agenda. Could that be because of outside pressures leading (*pace* Krueger) to changes in ideas?

*Gustav Ranis* queried whether the impact of the rest of the world, in terms of either ideas or money, was always beneficial. One should remember that easy access to external money during the 1970s had let countries off the hook and aborted reforms.

*Vladimir Mau* recalled that each of the leaders of the Soviet Union had considered himself both a political and an economic expert and had therefore concentrated decision-making power in both areas in his own hands. Mau emphasized that professional economists had assumed senior positions in public administration in Russia only during the past two or three years, after democratization had started and political and economic functions had been separated. Before that economists used to regard the economic process as an engine that operated according to definite economic laws and could be transformed with the appropriate set of tools. Mau also argued that it was possible to combine authoritarian (but not totalitarian!) and democratic systems, as in the case of France under General Charles de Gaulle.

In replying to the discussion, *John Williamson* differed with Il SaKong by stating that the term "technopol" was *not* intended to exclude elected officials. Unlike John Toye, he thought that current usage of the word "technocrat" did not preclude sympathy for the objective of extending the role of the market. Nor did Williamson deny the role of ideas in shaping reforms as Krueger (and Toye) had suggested. On the contrary, the difficulty of reaching agreement on appropriate policies in developing countries (as indeed in developed economies) was strong evidence of the significance of ideas. Finally, Williamson questioned whether either of Bates's hypotheses as to why self-interested politicians might shift power to economic reformers could explain the major cases where this had happened. Perhaps in Zambia power had shifted to a group that stood to benefit from the application of what economists regard as rational economic policies, so that the partisan model could provide an explanation. But that did not seem to have happened in Venezuela, Bolivia, nor even in Chile, where the generals initially had no concept of how they wanted economic policy to be run. According to José Piñera (chapter 5), their reform program was launched only after the economists had proposed a program addressed to national rather than (like the businessmen and lawyers) sectoral interests—a perspective that appealed to the patriotism of the military leaders governing Chile.

## Reference

Naim, Moises. 1993. *Paper Tigers and Minotaurs*. Washington: Carnegie Endowment for International Peace.

# 3

## AUSTRALASIA

# Australia

ROSS GARNAUT

Australia is almost one decade into a historic transformation, from an inward-looking, inflexible economy heavily specialized in exports of primary products to an open, market-responsive economy with a much more diverse pattern of exports. Australia has moved from having the most protected manufacturing sector of any OECD country to a set of policies that, if implemented as announced, will give it the most open trade policies among the advanced economies. It has been a slow and gradual transition, within an old and conservative democracy. But it has been consistent and inexorable, although since 1992 political cross-currents have become more important in the aftermath of recession.

If the end point of this transition is free trade, open and competitive financial markets, and a competitive, flexible, and highly productive real domestic economy, Australia is perhaps halfway through. It is also about halfway through the economic structural changes that are associated with policy reform. The reform having been gradual and slow, the benefits too have come slowly, and the reform process remains vulnerable to new political fashion pending its full reflection in economic activity and incomes.

For Australia, the internationalization of economic life has been closely associated with a reorientation in economic and political relations, from a historic focus on the North Atlantic to the Asia-Pacific region. This is an older transition that has been proceeding for a quarter of a century, but which has accelerated over the past decade, in the context of domestic economic reform and Asia-Pacific dynamism. The

*Ross Garnaut heads the Department of Economics in The Australian National University's Research School of Pacific Studies. He was personal economic adviser to Bob Hawke.*

success of outward-looking policies in East Asia has exercised subtle and indirect influences over Australian policy discussion.

The Australian transition has its origins in a domestic political debate that precedes "the Washington consensus" and predates the Thatcher and Reagan periods of "conservative" policy activism. These wider international political and ideological influences through the 1980s were important mainly for their effects on the policy orientation of the Australian conservative opposition parties, who through this period shifted from opportunistic defense of the status quo to economically rational versions of the Thatcher-Reagan positions (Kelly 1992; Walters 1992). The Australian government saw itself as reacting to Australian problems with policies that had some elements in common with the Atlantic Anglo-Saxon orthodoxies of the 1980s, but which were social democratic and in some respects very different from those pursued in America and Britain.

The story so far of policy decisions to achieve structural reform in Australia is principally the story of the Australian Labor Party government under the leadership of Prime Minister Bob Hawke, which was first elected in March 1983 and won successive national elections in December 1984, July 1987, and March 1990. In December 1991, Hawke was replaced by Paul Keating, who as treasurer had been a leading member in the Hawke cabinet. The transition followed a period of personal political rivalry. However, there has been no reversal of the Hawke government's decisions on reform since the change in leadership, although, with Australia in recession in the early 1990s, there has been some adjustment of the government's rhetoric away from internationalization and the strengthening of competitiveness, and toward demand expansion and assistance to particular industries as means of increasing employment and raising incomes.

The first section of this paper compares the economic reforms in Australia over the past decade with the so-called Washington consensus. The next section examines economic conditions in and the economic structure of Australia as causes and effects of reform. Then follow two case studies of the central "internationalizing" reforms of the Hawke government, namely, financial deregulation and trade liberalization. This is followed by a discussion of the political style and culture of Australian economic reform, focusing particularly on the hypotheses presented by John Williamson in chapter 2 of this volume. A concluding section sums up the Australian experience with the political economy of reform and assesses the prospective longevity of recent changes in economic strategy and policy.

## The Washington Consensus in Australia

The gradualist economic reforms that began in Australia in 1983 covered the whole range of issues encompassed in Williamson's definition of the

Washington consensus (chapter 2). Several elements of the reform program have been implemented in distinctive ways, and the program includes important elements that the Washington consensus does not explicitly cover.

With regard to fiscal discipline, the first element of the Washington consensus, there was a radical transformation of Australia's budgetary position between 1983 and 1990. A prospective federal government deficit of about 5 percent of GDP was converted into a substantial surplus over this period. This was achieved through the combination of considerable expenditure restraint, sustained efforts at raising revenues, and sustained economic growth. Federal expenditures as a proportion of GDP fell from about 30 percent in 1983 to about 23 percent in 1989. Recession corroded this position somewhat from 1990 on, however, and expansions in expenditure under the influence of recession politics have raised the structural component of the new federal budget deficit through 1992 and 1993. Taken together with the state government budgets, Australia's fiscal position moved from large primary and operational deficits in 1983 to a small primary surplus in 1989, and then back into modest operational deficit in 1992.

Fiscal discipline was maintained alongside the rigorous implementation of social democratic public expenditure priorities from 1983 on. One example of the rigor was a substantial redirection of social security expenditure toward low-income and low-wealth individuals and households, significantly affecting the distribution of after-tax and after-social security incomes (Harding 1992). Middle-class entitlements to social security were systematically removed or reduced through income and assets tests. A new, universal public medical insurance scheme was introduced, financed by a levy on incomes. More rigorous economic tests were applied to expenditure commitments of the previous government. A further example was the increase in federal government expenditure on education to finance places to support a doubling (from about one-third to about two-thirds) in the proportion of high school graduates continuing to tertiary education. A large expansion of university places was financed in part by the introduction of tuition fees. Students were provided with automatic access to loans to cover the fees, to be repaid through a tax surcharge on incomes above a specified level.[1]

There was a significant broadening of the income and indirect taxation base, supporting reductions in the marginal income tax rate from 60 percent to 47 percent and substantial reductions in rates on lower incomes. The federal revenue share of GDP was roughly maintained. A

---

1. In Australia, virtually all university education and the overwhelming majority of all forms of tertiary education are provided through public institutions. Places in universities were free of tuition charges until the late 1980s.

capital gains tax was introduced for the first time, and employee fringe benefits were taxed as income.

There was far-reaching liberalization of the financial sector, for both international and domestic transactions. The system of exchange controls that had been imposed during World War II was removed in December 1983, and all economically relevant controls on quantities of and interest rates for bank credit were removed in 1984 and 1985. Fifteen new banks with foreign equity were granted licenses to operate in Australia in 1985—the first significant new entrants into Australian banking in this century. The exchange rate was floated in December 1983, after a number of years of an adjustable peg against a basket of currencies.

There was far-reaching trade liberalization. Quantitative restrictions on imports, which had been about as important in Australia as in North America and Europe, were removed completely in a series of decisions stretched between 1983 and 1991. Tariffs and subsidies for agriculture, already low by OECD standards, were reduced further in the early years of the Labor government. Tariffs on manufactured goods, which had been higher than in any other OECD country except perhaps New Zealand, were set on a path toward normally low OECD levels. The average level of effective protection for manufacturing industry fell from 23 percent in 1982–83 to 19 percent in 1987–88 and is to be reduced to 5 percent by late in the 1990s under a program of liberalization announced in March 1991. (The corresponding average nominal rate by that time will be 3 percent.) Taking agricultural and manufacturing industry together, Australia is partway through a transition from (with New Zealand) the highest levels of protection in the OECD to the lowest, at least for trade in goods.

Australian policies on foreign direct investment have always been relatively liberal. Through the 1980s, most established restrictions were removed.

Australia has for a century relied relatively heavily on state-owned business enterprises—for example in railways, telecommunications, banking, civil aviation, and port services. In the first half of the 1980s the emphasis was on productivity-raising reform of these enterprises without changes in ownership. Beginning in the late 1980s, partial privatization and the introduction of or increase in competition from private businesses became an important part of the reform agenda.

Systematic attempts to remove business regulation that served no clear social purpose were made starting in 1984, and steps were taken to simplify the administration of other regulations. At the same time, the government's agenda in relation to equal opportunity, advancement of aboriginal Australians, the environment, and labor relations extended regulations in important ways. Major original research would be required to form a reliable judgment about whether the totality of changes in business regulation after 1983 assisted or retarded new entry, competition, and productivity.

The Australian reform experience differs from that of most countries in the role of and approach to labor unions. The Labor government consulted closely with the trade union movement on each aspect of reform and on most issues had the support of the movement's principal body, the Australian Council of Trade Unions. The legal position of trade unions was strengthened—in contrast to what occurred in Britain under the Thatcher government. Productivity-raising reforms of labor practices were implemented beginning in the late 1980s within the framework of, and limited by, a centralized industrial relations system.

## Economic Conditions and Structural Change

In Australia in early 1983, a deep recession was superimposed on long-term structural problems. The reforms of the 1980s were directed at these structural problems but interacted with cyclical fluctuations in important ways. The long economic boom from the second quarter of 1983 to the second quarter of 1990 strengthened the government's political position and increased government supporters' confidence in reform. However, the similarly deep recession that began in the second quarter of 1990 and the slow pace of recovery from late 1991 on encouraged political doubts about internationally oriented reform. The short-term macroeconomic objective of the government was always described as "fighting inflation and unemployment at the same time." In fact, employment growth had priority, and two decades of high inflation came to an end only with macroeconomic misjudgment and recession in 1990–91.

Australia (with, but more so than, New Zealand) has always been an unusual industrial economy. Australia's natural resource endowment relative to its labor and capital endowments is much greater than in other industrial economies, and its comparative advantage is therefore strong in unprocessed rural and mineral production. From the mid-19th century until the early postwar period, Australia enjoyed exceptionally high incomes through strong specialization in primary exports. Australian per capita income was the highest in the world by a wide margin through the late 19th century, and still fourth in the world (after the United States, Canada, and New Zealand) in the early postwar period (Anderson and Garnaut 1987).

Until the past two decades, the natural resource base was large enough for the country's primary industries alone to be able to generate almost all the internationally tradeable goods and services that were required to support relatively high Australian incomes. The internationally oriented primary industries were technologically advanced and highly productive by world standards. These industries carried many relatively unproductive, protected manufacturing and service industries. Inefficiency in the service industries was often supported by the protection of end users in the manufacturing sector or by state sponsorship of monopolistic positions. This pattern of Australian industry had broad support across the political spectrum until the late 1960s. It seemed to deliver the country's enviable standard of living.

The Australian economic model's capacity to deliver employment at high incomes for a rapidly growing population (in the country with the highest rate of immigration, proportionate to its size, in the world) was eventually undermined by three influences: the corrosion of the per capita natural resource endowment by population growth; the huge, unfavorable shift in world demand growth for primary products, with the corruption of world trade rules for agriculture and changes in demand patterns for metallic minerals, temporarily offset on a couple of occasions by increased energy prices; and the incapacity of an inflexible, inward-looking economy to take full advantage of technological changes in the manufacturing and service industries that were raising incomes in other advanced economies.

The 20th-century Australian model of economic policy, supported by high levels of protection for manufacturing industry, made Australia even more strongly specialized in exports of primary products than its relative resource endowments alone would have suggested. It caused Australia to stand aside from the great postwar multilateral reductions in manufacturing protection among the advanced industrial economies. Australia was the only OECD country (except for new Zealand) not to experience a large increase in the trade share of output and expenditure between the early postwar years and the mid-1980s.

The cyclical recession that brought the Hawke government to power in March 1983 was associated with what at that time was the largest fall in employment (see figures 1 and 2) and increase in unemployment since the Great Depression. Recession was precipitated by the interaction of increases in wage costs (won by the strong trade union movement in boom conditions following the late-1980s increase in world oil prices), a decline in Australia's terms of trade, and sharp monetary contraction.

The macroeconomic program of the Labor government embodied wage restraint (in cooperation with the trade union movement, in the context of the government's social democratic program) and early fiscal stimulus (although less than had been committed in the leadup to the 1983 election by the defeated conservative government), which was then withdrawn during the economic recovery between 1984 and 1988. One outcome of these policies was the strongest employment growth over a seven-year period that Australia had experienced in the 20th century (figures 1 and 2).

During the strong expansion of the 1980s, there was periodic concern about the large current account deficit. This concern was one motive for the severe tightening of monetary policy from 1988, during a virulent

millions employed

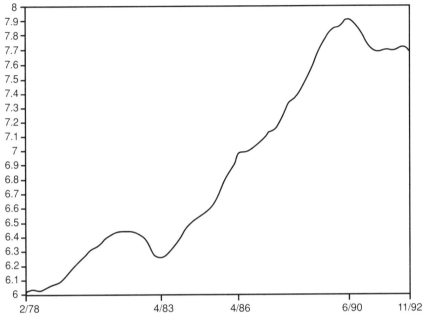

**Figure 1** Australia: trend estimate of employment

domestic boom, that in 1990 precipitated a recession as severe as that of the early 1980s.

By the 1980s, there was widespread recognition that the old pattern of economic policy and structure could no longer generate sustained high employment with living standards that were abreast of those in the world's most successful economies. There was widespread (although far from universal) recognition of a structural imperative for Australia to raise productivity growth by increasing international orientation, flexibility in resource use, and competition in domestic markets. Success would be reflected in a (much belated) rise in the export share of production, diversification of overseas markets, and—reflecting the direction in which opportunities lay for an internationally oriented Australian economy—rapidly expanding trade with the East Asian economies.

Structural transformation was facilitated by a large reduction in Australian costs relative to those of other industrial economies from 1985 on, although much of this gain was ceded in the period of tight monetary policy. (The mid-1980s levels of competitiveness were restored between late 1991 and mid-1993 with depreciation of the currency and low inflation).

The structure of the real economy responded powerfully to policy reform and the improvement in competitiveness. The export share of

percent

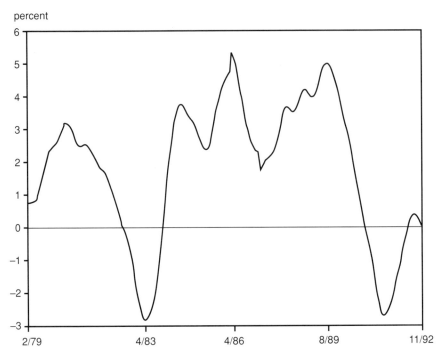

**Figure 2** Australia: annual percentage change in employment

output began to rise (figure 3). The 1979–80 peak reflects temporarily high export prices for primary (especially energy) prices. The 1980s increase was contributed entirely by nontraditional exports (manufactures and services). Figure 4 reveals the extent of the deterioration in world markets for Australian rural products: while improvements in competitiveness assisted rural as well as other exports, by the late 1980s the value of rural exports represented only about 4 percent of GDP, compared with 6 percent to 7 percent through the 1970s.

The increase in the export share of output was contributed entirely by East Asian markets, mostly those other than Japan. The share of Australian production absorbed by the European Community and the United States fell beginning in the mid-1980s, to a significant extent because of increased protection of their agricultural industries.

During the decade from 1983 the economic base of old Australia was continuing to corrode while the new structures were being established. This greatly increased the difficulty of economic policy. Although wage and fiscal restraint and reforms aimed at raising productivity proceeded to a depth and at a pace far beyond Australian experience in this century, both the extent and the pace fell short of what was required if the structural problems were to be solved without recession.

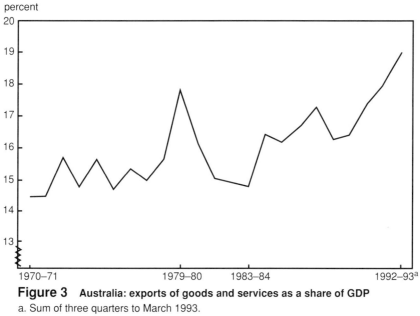

percent

**Figure 3** Australia: exports of goods and services as a share of GDP
a. Sum of three quarters to March 1993.
Source: ABS Catalogue 5302.0.

## Financial Deregulation

Australia's financial deregulation in the 1980s was, at that time, largely the sphere of economists, the financial press, and financial market operators and was of limited interest to the general public. Within the government, it was led by the prime minister and the treasurer, working on the advice of the central bank, a number of Treasury staff members, and their own personal advisory staffs.

The reforms had two aspects, which were implemented at different times and under different pressures. The main steps toward the first, the internationalization of the financial sector, were taken in December 1983. The second was reform of domestic finance and banking, including the entry of new banks financed with foreign equity. This aspect of reform had been commenced tentatively in 1982–83, during the last year of the conservative government of Malcolm Fraser, and mainly implemented between late 1983 and late 1985.

Australian banking and finance had been subject to far-reaching regulation in political response to the perceived failure of the financial system in the Great Depression, and to wartime and postwar pressures on the availability of foreign exchange. The need for reform had been discussed by specialists from the early 1960s on, as it became clear that Australia was not sharing in the opportunities for economic gains from increased international financial integration. The strains and inefficien-

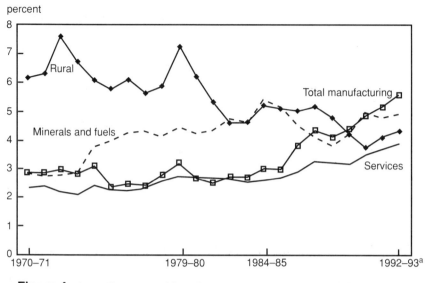

percent

**Figure 4** Australia: composition of exports as a percentage of GDP

a. Sum of three quarters to March 1993.

*Source:* ABS Catalogue 5302.0.

cies of the regulated system became more widely recognized and discussed through the 1970s and early 1980s, but the governments of those years failed to take action beyond the minimum necessary for the system to hold together month by month.

The collapse of the Bretton Woods arrangements between 1971 and 1973 provided an opportunity for systemic reform, but in Australia it led only to the patching up of the old system. Australia experienced a tendency toward payments surplus and currency appreciation during the pivotal years of international monetary crisis and change, 1971 and 1972. The conservative government resisted effective appreciation of the Australian dollar in order to protect traded goods, especially farm interests. The government shifted from a sterling peg to a US dollar peg, but the currency was not allowed to depreciate to the same extent that the US dollar did. This caused Australia to import much of the US inflation of those years.

The Labor government of Gough Whitlam (December 1972 to November 1975) was less inhibited about currency appreciation but combined it with excessive monetary and fiscal expansion, ending ultimately in the first deep recession of the postwar period in 1974–75. The Whitlam government implemented no systemic financial reform and extended international financial regulation by strengthening controls on capital inflows in late 1972 and 1973. By the time of the election of the Hawke government, authorities were operating an adjustable peg, with officials varying the exchange rate daily against a basket of currencies. The consequences included highly unstable domestic monetary conditions, which by 1983 clearly made it impossible to keep domestic demand growth on a steady path.

The inefficiency of domestic financial regulation was widely understood among financial market specialists by the 1970s. The political economy was, however, resistant to reform. Technocratic suggestions for reform during the period of the Fraser government (November 1975 to March 1983) were rejected, apparently because they would remove access by some groups of borrowers (farmers and homeowners in particular) to funds at regulated low rates.

By the beginning of the 1980s, the small corner of the economics profession that was interested in the financial sector, the many new operators in the financial markets at the fringes of banking, and the central bank had come firmly to the view that domestic financial deregulation was valuable and necessary. However, there was no uniformity of support for the abolition of exchange controls and the floating of the currency even in these circles. Some economists argued (correctly) that policy objectives could be achieved with a (strong) fixed rate, so long as domestic demand policies were appropriate and wages were responsive to changes in demand for labor. The senior leadership of the Treasury, the permanent official advisers to the government, was ambivalent in support of deregulation of the external financial sector.

In these circumstances, the treasurer in the Fraser government, encouraged by economists on his own and the prime minister's personal staffs, in 1981 commissioned a report on the financial system. The committee was led by a senior businessman, Keith Campbell, who was known to support financial deregulation. The publicity given to the work commissioned by the Campbell committee, and its final report (Campbell et al. 1981), raised the level of public discussion considerably and created widespread expectation that reforms along the lines eventually implemented by the Labor government were probably inevitable. The Labor Party, at that time still in opposition, criticized the report on populist grounds, although Bob Hawke and Paul Keating, who eventually became prime minister and treasurer, respectively, supported the Campbell recommendations on key issues in closed discussion within the party.

The Fraser government postponed consideration of the report's central recommendations, for fear of reaction from affected vested interests in what had become a highly competitive preelection political environment. Significantly, from this point on the established banks took steps to prepare themselves against competition from new foreign banks in Australia, including through mergers—in a market in which the number of players was already small. This anticipatory action increased the costs of rejection of or delay in deregulation.

The two main leaders of the Labor government had by mid-1983 come to the view that the Australian dollar's adjustable peg was inconsistent with national demand management in the circumstances of that time. This view was supported consistently by strong advice from the central bank and from economists on the leaders' personal staffs, but not by the leadership of the Treasury. The Treasurer was reluctant to act against Treasury advice, but the prime minister's clear commitment to reform on financial deregulation, and the logic of the case for floating the Australian dollar, overcame this reluctance between October and December 1983, as monetary instability arising out of variable capital inflows reached large proportions. The two leaders' commitment to internationalization of the Australian economy more generally predisposed them to accept advice from the central bank and their personal economic advisers to remove all exchange controls at the time of the float.

Domestic financial deregulation touched more sensitive nerves. With the encouragement of the prime minister, the treasurer sought to revive the Campbell report recommendations. In 1983, he commissioned a retired banker, Vic Martin, to review the Campbell conclusions from the perspective of a government that was concerned with improving distributional equity.

The Martin report's (Martin et al. 1984) conclusion that financial regulation was an inefficient means of achieving distributional objectives opened the way for far-reaching domestic deregulation. The domestic banks had been reconciled to increased competition from the time of discussion of the Campbell report. The prime minister and the treasurer—the latter with great energy and political skill, as he made this a central focus of his efforts—used detailed argument and forceful leadership to disarm Labor Party doubts about the entry of new banks and the competitive determination of interest rates. When deregulation was implemented, each step was accompanied by little political opposition.

Financial sector reform in Australia thus emerged as a result of several influences: near consensus among economic and financial experts and practitioners on the need for deregulation, a relative absence of general public interest in all but a few specific aspects of reform, and effective preparatory work commissioned by the government to lay a base for reform. The decisive factors in 1983 and 1984 were the acceptance by key political leaders that financial deregulation was necessary for wider policy reform, which they judged to be essential to restoration of sustained economic growth in Australia, and their preparedness to use their considerable political strength decisively at a time when developments in financial markets had created an opportunity for major change.

## Trade Liberalization

From the second and third decades of this century onward, Australia's high and increasing levels of protection for manufacturing industry had the support of all major political parties, most of the economics profession, and, overwhelmingly, the public at large. Business groups representing interests that were damaged by protection—that is, those in the primary export industries—judged it prudent to skirmish around the edges of policy rather than to fight protectionist interests head to head.

The background to the trade liberalization of the 1980s extends back to the 1960s, which witnessed a change in elite (but not popular) opinion about whether protection was in the national interest. In this context, the Whitlam Labor government implemented a 25 percent reduction of all tariffs under inflationary boom conditions in July 1973 but retreated into protectionist quantitative restrictions in the recession of 1974–75. The conservative government that succeeded Whitlam's reduced some protection for some industries between 1975 and 1983 but greatly increased protection for the most highly protected industries, with little effect on the average level of manufacturing protection.

The change in the climate of elite opinion on protection can be traced to work by academic economists through the 1960s. Economists began to examine closely and to publish studies on the costs of the highly differentiated Australian tariff. At first, the main reform advocated was movement toward a uniform tariff. By the late 1960s, the economics profession was advocating import liberalization with near unanimity and with increasing technical sophistication (Corden 1967, 1968; Lloyd 1988; Anderson and Garnaut 1987).

The new views of the Australian economics profession gradually influenced opinion in the bureaucracy, commencing with the Tariff Board. The Tariff Board was an advisory body established in the 1920s to place a buffer between protection policymaking and vested interest groups, in recognition of the corruption of the political process associated with unconstrained pressure by private interests. The Tariff Board was established to implement the established national policy of protection, and its views in its first four decades differed little from the general community's. The first breach in the protectionist line was Sir Leslie Melville's resignation as chairman of the board in 1962. The importance of individual views and the character of statutory officeholders for the direction of policy was underlined following the appointment of G. A. Rattigan as chairman in 1963. Rattigan was converted by the evidence to a freer trade position and made the public hearings and reports of the board important vehicles of public education. By the end of 1960s, the financial press, led by the *Australian Financial Review*, was giving extensive coverage to the Tariff Board's heresy and was itself playing a major role in publicizing the case against protection. The Tariff Board perspective gradually became more influential in other areas of government.

The near consensus of elite opinion in support of reduced protection in the early 1970s was not reflected in general public opinion. The polls showed (and continue to show) substantial majorities in favor of protection. Interestingly, despite persistent support for protection in the polls, the Whitlam Labor government's decision to reduce all tariffs by 25 percent in 1973 received large majority support at the time, most strongly among Labor Party voters, who otherwise tended to be somewhat stronger supporters of protection. This illustrates the autonomy of political leadership on protection policy issues, at least at times of consensus across the leadership of the major parties and of buoyant economic conditions.

Through the late 1960s and 1970s, lobbying by groups with vested interests in protection became more overt and strident. Protectionist interests had not needed to be strident in earlier times, when the climate of opinion had been strongly supportive. Their more open participation in the debate was partly a reaction to the emergence in public trade policy discussion of groups with an interest in trade liberalization. The changes in parliamentary leaders' attitudes, the information made available to the public by the Industries Assistance Commission (successor to the Tariff Board from 1974), and the improved understanding within the economics profession on the effects of manufacturing protection on farm incomes encouraged a number of farm industry groups into the public debate, especially the National Farmers' Federation, founded in 1977. The mining sector, perhaps mindful of its political weakness and vulnerability, and comprising large corporations with deep interests in government mineral leasing and taxation policies, entered the public political fray in early 1982, when five mining companies without large manufacturing assets argued for movement toward a low, uniform tariff.

Two highly protected sets of industries—the textiles, clothing, and footwear industry and the automobile industry—received large increases in assistance between 1974 and 1983, despite the change in the climate of elite opinion. These industries' established protection was so great that enterprises in them were able to invest heavily in political activity to preserve it; the establishment of strong industry organizations in defense of protection lowered the costs of new political mobilization; and developments in the wider economy were introducing pressures for these manufacturing industries to decline more rapidly than others in the recessions of the mid-1970s and early 1980s.

In addition, fortuitous political circumstances helped the cause of high protection for textiles, clothing, and footwear (Anderson and Garnaut 1987, chapter 6). International practice in these industries (especially textiles, clothing, and footwear, but also automobiles) was less liberal than in other areas of manufacturing, reflecting the rise of new centers of competitiveness in East Asia outside the North Atlantic economies that were most influential in setting the international rules. International practice eased the introduction of quantitative restrictions on imports of these commodities, the protective effect of which could then rise with changes in economic conditions without new government decisions. Through all these influences, it was the powerful incentive of the highly protected industries to invest heavily in political influence that was decisive in raising protection for textiles, clothing, footwear, and automobiles against the general trend.

Writing before the election of the Labor government in early 1983, Kym Anderson and I drew five main lessons from Australia's experience with protection policy. First, both the public and private interest theories of protection policymaking are relevant: neither on its own can explain Australian policy. Second, political leadership can exercise decisive influence over policy outcomes at certain moments in history. Third, protection is extremely difficult to remove once it has been granted. Fourth, sudden increases in import penetration tend to trigger protectionist responses, even in a climate of opinion generally unfavorable to protection. Fifth, while export interest groups have not been major actors in protection policymaking for most of Australia's history, they have been influential when they have been active (Anderson and Garnaut 1987). We thought in 1983 that there would be little change in the average level of manufacturing protection "in the immediate future." Working for lower protection were the change in political and intellectual leadership opinion in favor of a more open economy, the rise in countervailing power from export interests, and the desire to build closer and more cooperative relations with Australia's East Asian neighbors. The increasing understanding of the effects of protection on export performance had brought farm and mining industry groups into the policy debate, and the increasing understanding of the effects of protection on the interstate distribution of income had brought in the principal exporting states of Western Australia and Queensland.

Two factors were working against freer trade at that time. Long-term industry plans introduced by the Fraser government greatly increased the political costs of reducing protection before 1988 (for textiles, clothing and footwear) or 1992 (automobiles). And the deep recession of the early 1980s was unfavorable to early import liberalization.

We concluded that the prospects of future trade liberalization would be enhanced by further dissemination of information about the economic effects of protection; by compensating the states that benefited from protection for the effects of liberalization through Commonwealth-state financial arrangements; by public funding for political parties; and by Australian participation in discussion of trade liberalization within the Asia-Pacific region.

The Australian move toward free trade in the 1980s and 1990s is comprehensible in the context of the lessons that we drew in 1983 from earlier Australian experience. Bob Hawke as Labor prime minister held the personal belief that closer integration into the international economy, through trade liberalization and other means, was a necessary element of economic reform to build a modern economy in Australia. Trade liberalization did not feature in the program upon which the government was elected, but Hawke's consistent public position from the early days of his government was that sustaining economic growth in Australia required reductions in protection, and that these reductions would be implemented as employment strengthened during the economic recovery. Trade liberalization was discussed in these terms in the first week of the government, when the prime minister invited the author, known for his views on protection, to join his office as senior economic adviser. Hawke's perspective on trade policy was reflected in decisions on each of a series of industry policy issues that arose in the early years of the government, prior to the major trade liberalization decisions of 1988 and 1991.

Hawke's political style involved consultation among a wide array of interest groups, extended public discussion, and dissemination of information well in advance of decisions for change. The National Economic Summit Conference, discussion in the new Economic Planning Advisory Council and the Australian Manufacturing Council, speeches and exhortations by the prime minister himself, and the publication of reports to the government explaining the need for change (including the author's *Australia and the Northeast Asian Ascendancy* in 1989) were all instruments of public education, helping to prepare a climate of public opinion that expected and favored trade liberalization.

During the Hawke years, there was considerable discussion of and some movement toward reduction of the earlier bias in the allocation of Commonwealth revenues toward the less densely populated "export states." The governments of these states, especially Western Australia, moved more strongly than in earlier years to argue the case for compensatory reductions in protection.

Public funding of political parties was introduced at the Commonwealth level, although its effect on interest group pressures was diminished considerably by escalation in the costs of election campaigns. Requirements of public disclosure of large donations to political parties, and the expression of public displeasure at attempts to buy political influence, publicized by royal commissions into corruption in the states of Western Australia and Queensland, were probably more effective in constraining traditional forms of interest group behavior in relation to protection policy.

It was a theme of the Hawke government that close relations with East Asia and integration into Australia's Asia-Pacific environment were important elements of the reform program. It was part of the case for reducing protection that significant opportunities for expanding exports were emerging from economic growth in East Asia, including exports of nontraditional services and manufactured goods. Reductions in protection would make Australia's most productive industries more competitive and better able to take advantage of the East Asian opportunity. This was the position argued in *Australia and the Northeast Asian Ascendancy* (Garnaut 1989), the first contribution to mainstream public debate in Australia since the first decade of the Federation to argue the case for free trade rather than simply for lower protection. Australia's active sponsorship of and participation in multilateral trade negotiations in the 1980s was undertaken in close consultation with trading partners in East Asia.

The most important change in interest group behavior, toward the emergence of economywide trade union and business groups, was encouraged by the Hawke leadership style. The Australian Council of Trade Unions became more influential, relative to the individual unions that were its constituents, in public policy discussion and in consultation with government. The economywide Business Council, which included representatives of mining and service industries, became the most influential of the business groups. Economywide perspectives gave greater weight to the national interest in liberal trade, significantly constraining the political effectiveness of the advocacy by union and business groups of continued or increased protection for textiles, clothing, footwear, and automobiles. In the new climate of opinion, more favorable to liberal trade, the National Farmers' Federation and the Australian Mining Industry Council became more active in advocacy of trade liberalization.

## Political Style and Culture of Economic Reform

The reforms of the 1980s were conceived and implemented by a government that was unusually strong politically by the Australian standards of the past quarter century. By the time of his replacement as leader of the Australian Labor Party, Hawke had become the longest-serving Labor prime minister and the second-longest-serving prime minister in Australian history. Until the final months of his incumbency, and then only under leadership challenge from his deputy prime minister, he enjoyed unprecedently high personal standing in the electorate and wide margins of preference over opposition leaders, as measured by opinion polls.

The political strength of the government and its leader gave both of them unusual autonomy with regard to policy. Hawke's popularity does not seem to have been based on a particular set of policies, and this gave him and the government the capacity to lead policy in new directions.

From the beginning, Hawke expected to lead the Australian government for a long time. The government had a long time horizon, not because it judged policy outcomes during its term to be more important than reelection, but because it expected to be reelected. The leading figures in the government, Hawke and Treasurer Keating, also held the view that good long-term economic policy would earn community respect that, on balance, would be rewarded electorally.

Hawke's reform style was gradualist, emphasizing intensive public discussion of economic problems and policy alternatives and close consultation with interested parties. Public discussion and consultation were usually led by government, and vested interests were often coopted to support reform in the process.

The government's relationship with the trade union movement was closer and more influential than with other interest groups. The trade union movement generally offered either active or passive support for the reform program, and in turn it expected and received government support for its own preferred policies on labor market regulation and centrally determined employment conditions. The relationship with the trade union movement was a source of strength for the reform program, in a country in which the market power of unions was unusually strong. The relationship delivered a substantial reduction in real wages and real unit labor costs that was probably unique in Australian 20th-century history. It supported the beginnings of efficiency-raising reform of work practices in the context of enterprise-level bargaining, in what had been a highly centralized system for determining labor market conditions.

But the relationship with the trade union movement also placed limits on the reduction in real wages and the pace of reform of work practices. Given the severe and deteriorating nature of Australia's long-term economic weaknesses, these limits slowed structural change and the realization of the employment and other benefits of reform to a damaging extent.

Australian economic reform responded to the long-term deterioration of relative economic performance that had first become apparent to close observers in the 1960s. There was a sense in which the government was responding to a crisis, which became more severe with the collapse of the world system of agricultural trade in the 1980s. The crisis, however, was spread over time, and there was no inevitability that the problems would be addressed when they were, in the mid-1980s, rather than, say, the 1970s or the 1990s.

The economic problems that were felt politically as crises were short-term macroeconomic problems—the recessions of 1982–83 and 1990–91 and the current account deficit that followed the collapse in primary export prices in 1985–86. The instinctive Australian response to macroeconomic crisis, based on historical precedents since the 1930s, was not to pursue internationally oriented or market-oriented reform, but rather to stimulate domestic demand (for recession) and to increase protection and exchange controls (for balance of payments weakness). Government used the crisis atmosphere of 1983 and 1986 to advance the reform effort, but there is no sense in which the shape of the reform program itself was determined by crisis.

The rapid growth in employment from 1983 to 1990 validated the reform program in the eyes of the electorate, and especially within the government's own (social democratic) constituency. The growth in employment was not mainly a benefit of reform—the main benefits would come later. There were, however, some links between employment growth and reform. Wage restraint through the 1983–85 recovery contributed to employment growth, and the depreciation that occurred under floating exchange rates, together with deterioration in the terms of trade in 1985–86, eased adjustment. Financial deregulation contributed in an unfortunate way to employment growth by helping monetary expansion to get out of hand in 1987 and 1988, fueling unsustainable boom conditions and setting the scene for the 1990–91 recession. Recession, when it came, was moderated somewhat in its effects on employment by the growing importance of the manufactured and service exports that were emerging from economic reform: domestic demand contracted proportionately more in 1990–91 than 1982–83, but manufacturing employment rather less.

The conservative opposition parties' response to reform was initially populist and negative, opposing such measures as the broadening of the income tax base (through a capital gains tax and the treatment of employee fringe benefits as income) and the removal of middle-class social security entitlements. This might have been fatal to market-oriented reform had it not been for the exceptional personal popularity of the prime minister and his and the treasurer's political skills. The government's continued political success helped to destabilize the opposition parties after 1984. The attractions of market-oriented reform to parts of the traditional business support base of the conservative parties, and to some of their leading parliamentary representatives, together with the conservative appeal of the Reagan and Thatcher programs, led to deep division in the opposition parties and ultimately to their transformation into radical, economically liberal parties. From early 1990 on, the opposition parties' program was distinguished from the government's mainly in its embrace of far-reaching labor market deregulation, its commitment to go further in reducing public expenditure, and its advocacy of a value-added tax to finance reductions in personal income and business taxation. The opposition's failure to win office in recession conditions in the 1993 elections shook its own confidence in rapid and radical market-oriented reform and generated a new episode in policy and organizational introspection.

Hawke and Keating, the reform leaders, were political leaders, not technocrats. Hawke had a law degree and some exposure to economics from his time as a Rhodes scholar at Oxford. But his working life had been spent around and in politics. He had been an industrial advocate and then President of the Australian Council of Trade Unions, and for a period simultaneously president of the Australian Labor Party, until his election to Parliament as a member of the Labor opposition in 1980. While a trade union leader he had been a member of the board of the Reserve Bank and of a major committee of inquiry into the structural problems of the economy. He came to office with the view that Australia had long-term structural problems that required correction, and that community discussion and consensus would loosen the traditional political constraints on necessary reform. Hawke offered no detailed blueprint for reform, but he was predisposed to internationally oriented and market-oriented solutions. His personal advisers were appointed with this in mind. His speeches in his first year as prime minister established the directions and parameters but not the timetable for reform.

Keating had lived a life of politics from the time he quit high school. He recognized the tendencies in elite opinion in the 1980s and welded them to traditional labor and social democratic rhetoric. He accepted much of the technocratic program of the Treasury—which was largely unchanged from earlier years, when it had been ineffective—and harnessed the standing and professional strength of the Treasury to the government's policies.

Thus the Hawke government's reforms emerged from its leaders' views about the need for internationally oriented and market-oriented policies and from its electoral strength. There was never a blueprint or timetable for reform. Hawke and Keating's preferment of technocratic advisers with interests in market-oriented reform assisted in the gradual articulation of a wide-ranging program of reform in the early years of the government. As the government matured and the exercise of power became more deeply institutionalized, custody of the reform agenda passed to technocrats who were permanent public servants in the coordinating ministries, making strong use of the mandate that they had been given by the prime minister and, especially, the treasurer. The program was moved forward in step with the promotion of public discussion of the issues, and faster when there was political opportunity to do so.

## Assessment and Prospects

There is not yet widespread acceptance in Australia that the reforms of the 1980s have been successful. The recession is commonly attributed to the structural change emerging from reform, or more narrowly to financial deregulation. Recession has given strong voice to calls to slow trade liberalization and to reregulate parts of the economy. There is still little recognition of the extent of the favorable structural changes in the economy since the mid-1980s.

The inflationary boom of 1987–90 requires explanation, and if it could be shown to be an inevitable consequence of financial deregulation, it would be a mark against reform. There has been some suggestion that the boom emerged because financial reforms were implemented too far in advance of reforms in the real economy. Certainly it would have been better to move more quickly on reform of the real economy. But the government's style and Australian political culture placed speed limits on these changes. Financial reform helped to give impetus to other reforms and removed important allocative distortions. If the alternative to the actual sequence of reform had been delayed financial reform, it is not obvious that welfare would have been greater or the risk of recession less.

My own assessment is that financial deregulation complicated monetary management, by obscuring the continuing importance of old measures of money growth. There was also too little prior recognition of the professional weakness in the established banks, and therefore of the desirable role of prudential supervision by the central bank in the process and early years of deregulation.

For a time beginning in the early 1980s, the consensus of the major political parties on the directions of reform seemed to protect reform from the political dangers of recession, until the policy changes could be manifested clearly in new patterns of export specialization and higher employment and incomes.

The new prime minister from December 1991, Paul Keating, in a much more competitive electoral environment, tailored his rhetoric to the recession-induced doubts about market-oriented reform. There was no major retreat on structural reform, only a small retreat related to the scope of developing-country trade preferences. There was, however, significant recourse to fiscal expansion as an antirecessionary measure, which promised economic difficulties for later governments. The surprising outcome of the March 1993 election left the Keating government having to reconcile a less reformist and more expansionary rhetoric with structural and macroeconomic imperatives that had not changed fundamentally from the 1980s. Thus, Australians in mid-1993 are watching a painful political adjustment toward maintenance of a more cautious version of the 1980s programs.

An unusual era in Australian political economy has ended, and probably with it Australia's long entanglement in inward-looking, dirigiste approaches to economic management. Reform seems to have held its ground, even if it is now advancing at a much more measured pace.

# References

Anderson, K., and R. Garnaut. 1987. *Australian Protectionism*. Sydney: Allen and Unwin.

Campbell, K., et al. 1981. *Australian Financial System, Final Report of the Committee of Inquiry* (the Campbell Report). Canberra: Australian Government Publishing Service (September).

Corden, W. M. 1967. "Australian Tariff Policy." *Australian Economic Papers* 6, no. 9 (December): 131–54.

Corden, W. M. 1968. "Australian Policy Discussion in the Post-War Period: A Survey." *American Economic Review* 58, no. 3 (June; supplement): 88–138. (Also published as *Australian Economic Policy Discussion: A Survey*. Melbourne: Melbourne University Press, 1968.)

Garnaut, R. 1989. *Australia and the Northeast Asian Ascendancy*. Canberra: Australian Government Publishing Service.

Harding, A. 1992. "Policy and Poverty: Trends in Disposable Incomes." *Australian Quarterly* 64, no.1: 19–48.

Kelly, P. 1992. *The End of Certainty: The Story of the 1980s*. Sydney: Allen and Unwin.

Lloyd, P. 1988. "Protection Policy." Chapter 5 In F. H. Gruen, ed., *Surveys of Australian Economics*, vol. 1, chapter 5. Sydney: Allen and Unwin.

Martin, V., et al. 1984. *Australian Financial System Report of the Review Group* (the Martin Report). Canberra: Australian Government Publishing Service (December).

Walters, A. 1992. "Fighting Back." *Australian Quarterly* 64, no. 2: 107–14.

# New Zealand

ALAN BOLLARD

## A Summary of the Reforms

New Zealand underwent a period of radical economic liberalization between 1984 and 1991, during which a wide range of reform measures were put into place. The first section of this paper lists the major measures introduced, discusses the chronology of their adoption, and summarizes their interim effects on economic performance and on the political standing of the government. The second section examines the political and economic preconditions for carrying out this reform. The third section investigates the new views on government and the implementation of the program. I conclude with what I perceive to have been the key elements that allowed the reform program to proceed. Note that the emphasis is on the implementation and consolidation of the reform program, not on its ultimate success.

Economic liberalization in New Zealand has to be viewed in the context of the country's geographical and resource position. New Zealand is a group of large islands, the size of the British Isles but with a population of only 3.35 million. It is geographically isolated in the South Pacific. It relies on its fertile land and climate to be a major primary producer of temperate agricultural products, particularly wool, meat, dairy products, and horticultural and forestry products. Until the postwar period, most of New Zealand's primary production (between 60 and 70 percent of exports) was sold with minimal processing in the British market. New Zealand achieved considerable prosperity by

*Alan Bollard is Director of the New Zealand Institute of Economic Research in Wellington. He is also Chairperson of the New Zealand Institute for Social Research & Development.*

exploiting its comparative advantage in this way and with preferential access to Britain. The country enjoyed one of the highest standards of living in the world, which allowed a generous system of universal social security, together with state provision of almost all education and health services, and a wide range of government involvement in utilities and financial and other services.

This enviable position changed with Britain's accession to the European Community in 1973: access for New Zealand exports to the European market has been increasingly restricted ever since. In addition, New Zealand's efforts to sell into third-country markets have been made difficult by the subsidization of EC agriculture under the Common Agricultural Policy, by East Asian and US agricultural protection (e.g., dairy industry agreements on importing and beef import quotas in the United States). Not only has market access to all these regions been difficult, but commodity products have suffered from a low income elasticity of demand, and demand has been volatile, with large terms-of-trade shocks occurring from time to time. These conditions have had a major effect on the domestic economy, because trade represents a high proportion of GDP.

New Zealanders have been increasingly frustrated by these access problems for agriculture in the international trading system, and they have made considerable efforts, together with Australia, to encourage agricultural reform through the Uruguay Round of the General Agreement on Tariffs and Trade (GATT). There is also a sense of realism that the country remains inevitably exposed to large price shocks unless it can improve the extent of its domestic processing.

Even as it was seeking out new markets, the New Zealand economy was hit by the oil price shocks of 1974 and 1979 and by the government's response. The government sought to insulate New Zealand from world oil prices through a major state-funded investment program in energy and related industries, known as "Think Big." This was an era of large fiscal deficits, high inflation, and strategic currency devaluations in an unsuccessful attempt to improve trading competitiveness. To finance the increased government spending and to pursue the traditional New Zealand concerns of income equality and state provision of services, high rates of income tax were levied. Largely as a result of borrowing for the Think Big program, total public debt rose from NZ$4 billion to NZ$28 billion during the decade following 1975.

The traded-goods sector in New Zealand had long been insulated from world price movements. Import protection took the form of import quotas and high tariffs on most goods that could be manufactured domestically. Many industries were subject to tight controls on entry and operating conditions. Price controls covered a wide range of products. Special protection was in place for some industries considered strategically important (e.g., steel production and automobile assembly). The agricultural sector also received significant assistance through a supplementary minimum price for livestock and concessional financing.

There were tentative moves toward economic liberalization in the late 1970s. However, faced with rising inflation, the government's response was to put in place a universal wage and price freeze and tighten financial market and capital regulations. During the early 1980s, government interventions were becoming increasingly selective and arbitrary.

The signing of the Closer Economic Relationship (CER) accord with Australia in 1983 was an important step toward economic integration for New Zealand. This agreement calls for free trade between the two countries in goods and services, and in practice there is also free movement of labor and capital. It has resulted in a big increase in intraindustry trade, particularly in manufactured goods.

In the 1970s and early 1980s, New Zealand's productivity rates were poor compared with industrial-country (OECD) averages, as a result of poor-quality investment. Similarly, New Zealand's growth rate over the period has been significantly below its trading partners' average. Recent economic indicators are shown in table 1.

The result has been a period of relative economic decline in the postwar years. In 1950 New Zealand's GDP per capita was 26 percent above the OECD average; forty years later it had dropped to 27 percent below the average.

## Major Policy Changes

Following the election of a Labour government in 1984, New Zealand commenced a program of rapid economic liberalization. The measures undertaken are listed here according to the "Washington consensus" classification (Bollard and Buckle 1987; O'Dea 1989; Bollard 1992; Walker 1989; Spencer and Carey 1988).

### Fiscal Discipline

The Labour government came into office professing the need to balance the government's budget, but without a clear agenda for doing so. New Zealand has had a central-government fiscal deficit since the early 1970s, indicating a persistent problem of adjustment. It was felt that fiscal balance should be attainable through revenue reform and expenditure restraint, but no formal targets or mechanisms were set. Fiscal balance was delivered in 1988–89 with the help of government asset sales, but this was a temporary achievement that has been put under further pressure by the growing level of overseas debt and debt servicing payments. The structural deficit problem has continued, with the financial deficit before asset sales in the range of 2 to 4 percent of GDP.

## Table 1 New Zealand: selected economic indicators, 1983–93
(percentages)

| Indicator | 1983 | 1985 | 1987 | 1989 | 1991 | 1993 (forecast) |
|---|---|---|---|---|---|---|
| Inflation[a] | 15.4 | 8.6 | 14.6 | 5.2 | 5.5 | 1.3 |
| Unemployment[b] | 5.4 | 3.8 | 4.1 | 7.4 | 9.9 | 10.6 |
| Interest rate[c] | 13.8 | 21.0 | 27.4 | 13.5 | 12.1 | 6.3 |
| Trade competitiveness index[d] | 0.70 | 0.72 | 0.98 | 0.95 | 1.0 | n.a. |
| Budget deficit as share of GDP[e] | −6.9 | −7.2 | −5.6 | −1.7 | −3.6 | −3.3 |
| Trade deficit as percentage of GDP | −6.2 | −8.5 | −5.3 | −1.3 | −3.4 | −2.6 |
| Effective rate of assistance[f] | | | | | | |
| Manufacturing | 39.0 | 37.0 | 26.0 | 19.0 | 14.0 | n.a. |
| Agriculture | 49.0 | 34.0 | 19.0 | −1.0 | −6.0 | n.a. |
| GDP growth rate | 0.4 | 5.0 | 3.6 | 1.0 | 0.4 | 2.6 |

n.a.= not available.

a. Annual percentage change. The rise in the consumer price index (CPI) for 1987, excluding the goods and services tax, was 11.5 percent; by December 1991 the rise in the CPI was 2.6 percent.

b. For 1983 and 1985, figures reflect registered unemployment; figures for subsequent years are Household Labour Force Survey measurements.

c. Interest on 90-day treasury bills, measured in March.

d. Figures drawn from the New Zealand Institute of Economic Research (NZIER) relative unit-labor cost index (where 1978–79 = 1.00). A decrease in the index implies improved competitiveness.

e. Excludes revenue from state asset sales.

f. Some of the data do not match these fiscal years exactly.

*Source*: New Zealand Institute of Economic Research.

## Public Expenditure Priorities

There have been two attempts at government spending reform. The first, from 1984 to 1987, involved reductions in administration and industry spending. These reductions were achieved principally for microeconomic rather than stabilization reasons. It was also felt that a small government sector was less likely to impose a fiscal burden or crowd out private investment. Core government departments were reorganized along corporate lines with outputs being specified, a "user pays" principle was introduced for many government services, a number of quasi-governmental advisory and operating organizations were abolished, and industry assistance was reduced.

These moves were partially successful in reducing the rate of growth of government spending in the mid-1980s; however, as the growth rate fell and unemployment rose, attention had to be refocused on social services spending. This area has a long history of government involvement in New Zealand, and there is considerably less public enthusiasm for reform. Education was reformed by passing more control to parents through boards of trustees. In 1990, eligibility criteria were tightened and overall expenditures were reduced for a range of social benefits including unemployment relief, housing assistance, and other social transfers to save money and limit incentives to rely on government benefits. New Zealand has a generous, nonfunded pension scheme that consumes 17 percent of public spending. The eligibility requirements have been tightened, but no new contribution-based funding system has yet been organized. In the health care area, public hospitals are being converted to state health enterprises to compete with the private sector for government contracts to offer health services.

The general objectives of these spending reforms have not primarily been to achieve stabilization, but rather to increase efficiency in the provision of market services, to reduce the role of the public sector, and to achieve a neutral fiscal policy.

## Tax Reform

Tax reform has been carried out reasonably successfully. The tax base was broadened through a universal goods and services tax on final domestic consumption. The tax was introduced in 1986 at 10 percent and increased in 1989 to 12.5 percent. Personal income tax rates were flattened and reduced in line with corporate rates, to avoid any incentive for shifting income between the two categories. A range of other indirect taxes and tax concessions have been eliminated.

The aim has been to set up as neutral as possible a tax system without identifiable incentives or disincentives for particular types of saving or spending, and to sharpen incentives to earn and invest. The flattening of rates and the broadening of the tax base had the effect of causing many more businesses to register for tax. The individual and corporate income tax burden, which had grown very high due to successive years of inflation, was reduced, so that by 1992 only 63 percent of revenue was from taxation of income. However, as the recession worsened in 1989, returns from income tax, especially from corporations, became disappointingly low. There have been attempts to restructure the international tax regime on similarly neutral grounds, but this has proved more difficult.

## Financial Liberalization

The financial sector was an important early focus of the economic liberalization program. The government viewed financial market deregulation much as it did other factor market deregulations. The program involved a range of reforms, in particular the removal of market entry restrictions, operating limitations, price controls, and regulatory monopolies. In contrast to the more cautious reforms in Australia, New Zealand abolished credit growth guidelines, interest rate controls, and official export guarantees in 1984. In 1985, banking was deregulated by removing separate requirements for trustee banks, building societies, finance houses, stockbrokers, and trading banks. Ownership restrictions have been removed, as have most traditional formal financial controls such as reserve ratio requirements. Entry is open to all comers who can convince the Reserve Bank of New Zealand (the central bank) of their ability to operate a financial institution prudently.

## Monetary Reform

Monetary policy was significantly simplified: the principal objective of monetary policy was to be price stability, with a single target, that of confining annual inflation to between 0 and 2 percent by a specified date. This policy was further institutionalized in 1989 by making the Reserve Bank independent from the government, with a formal contract to achieve price stability. The effect of these reforms was a generally tight monetary policy coupled with a loose fiscal policy through the reform period.

## Exchange Rates

Exchange rate regulation was removed. In 1984, a financial crisis followed the general election, and the incoming government devalued the New Zealand dollar by 20 percent. The following year the currency was freely floated on foreign exchange markets without direct control. Regulation of the foreign exchange industry was eased, and the market responded with the introduction of new foreign exchange hedging instruments. Despite some pressure from exporters during periods when the currency was strong, there has been no formal direct intervention to devalue the currency since 1985 (although the Reserve Bank has entered the markets to influence the currency's level in the pursuit of price stability).

## Trade Liberalization

The import-competing sector of New Zealand has, for many years, sheltered behind a high protective wall of tariffs, import licenses, capital controls, and fixed exchange rates. A crucial aspect of microeconomic reform has been the removal of this insulating barrier to drive domestic prices toward international levels. Import licensing was phased out over a period of four years, exposing for the first time the underlying high nominal tariff structure. This tariff structure is currently being rationalized following a "Swiss formula," whereby the highest tariff items are reduced by the highest percentage. As the program continues, nominal tariff rates will have been reduced to an average of 10 percent (expressed as a percentage of value) by June 1993, with a further one-third reduction planned by 1996. This will reduce tariffs to the OECD average. However, New Zealand's tariff structure still varies greatly by product, with significant (over 30 percent) tariffs on footwear, clothing, textiles, and assembled automobiles.

Coupled with the reduction in agricultural and industrial subsidies and the removal of export assistance measures, this reduction in import protection has decreased the effective rate of assistance to New Zealand producers quite noticeably. The effective rate of assistance to agriculture has declined from 50 percent to less than zero in under a decade. The manufacturing sector has also suffered (less harsh) reductions. Simulation results now show a true rate of assistance of 2 percent for import-competing sectors, and of −6 percent for the export sector (Duncan et al. 1991).

## Foreign Direct Investment

New Zealand has traditionally had tight regulations on the inward and outward movement of capital. This regulation has now almost totally been removed: foreign investment in or out of New Zealand in almost any form—direct, portfolio, or equity—is virtually free of restrictions. Similarly, since the 1984–85 reforms there have been no discriminatory restrictions on the establishment of foreign-owned companies in New Zealand or on the repatriation of profits.

## Corporatization and Privatization

A cornerstone of the New Zealand liberalization program was the reform of state trading activities. The first step was corporatization of central-government trading activities under the State Owned Enterprises Act of 1987. Thirty-one state trading organizations have now been corporatized; this procedure involves setting up a board of directors, a complete revamp of management, a general reduction in staff, and a renewed investment program. Ports, airports, electricity authorities, and other local-authority trading enterprises were corporatized in this manner. In addition, the government has used the corporate framework for its reorganization of state research and development, health services, and local government services.

Privatization was the second part of this program. It proceeded on a more hesitant basis. Between 1988 and 1992, 22 enterprises were sold for a total of NZ$12 billion. Almost all the proceeds were used to reduce the public debt. Little distinction was made among buyers, with foreigners as welcome as domestic investors (Duncan and Bollard 1992).

## Deregulation

There have been a number of further deregulatory measures in factor and product markets. Most market entry restrictions, price controls, regulatory monopolies, and operating restrictions have been eliminated. An early focus, beginning in 1984, was on key input markets such as transport, finance, and energy.

The only important factor market that was not seriously addressed early on was the labor market. Minor reforms in 1984 and 1987 did not directly tackle the question of labor flexibility, although they had some indirect effects. In 1991, the new National Party government enacted the Employment Contracts Act, a more radical piece of legislation deregulating employer-employee bargaining arrangements.

In contrast to the input markets, product markets have never been as heavily regulated in New Zealand, so reform there has been less critical. The main focus was the agricultural sector, which had enjoyed some price support and concessional financing. This was removed, as were regulated domestic marketing arrangements, but compulsory producer export marketing boards were retained.

Other reforms affected industry more broadly. These included the end of the general wage and price freeze in 1984 and the removal of price control on a long list of products. State-regulated monopoly rights (e.g., on electricity, telecommunications, and postal services) were almost all eliminated. Occupational licensing in a range of professions and trades was terminated. Tight restrictions on shop trading hours were liberalized. The intention of all these reforms was to allow businesses to respond in an unfettered manner to market signals.

There is a particular problem of natural monopoly in New Zealand, due to the small size of the industrial sector. Removing regulatory barriers to entry and reducing import protection narrowed the range of industries considered to comprise true monopoly problems. In some industries such as electricity, the natural monopoly core was split away from the more contestable operations. The remaining natural monopoly operations have been left subject to the dominant-firm provisions of the Commerce Act.

## Property Rights

While these deregulations were proceeding, legislation defining the rules by which businesses should operate within the new deregulated environment were revised. The main instrument was the 1986 Commerce Act, which governed mergers and trade practices on an efficiency rather than an equity basis. There is now little specific direct industry regulation apart from the Commerce Act.

The intellectual property regime was reformed on a similar basis. There is still debate on securities legislation, takeover laws, and planning legislation, centered on two opposing approaches: an efficiency-based test versus an equity-based test.

A fuller list of these reforms is given in the appendix table. Figure 1 indicates the phasing of these reforms and compares the sequencing with that recommended under a more standard reform process.

## Summary of Results

There were three main pricing mechanisms through which these structural reforms were signaled to the domestic economy: high interest rates, high real exchange rates (i.e., an appreciated domestic currency), and depressed demand conditions.

After the early years of reform, the fiscal deficit began to grow again because of high levels of social spending and poor revenue returns. The government therefore continued its strong demand for funds to finance its deficit, which kept real interest rates high. At the same time, the combination of tight monetary policy and loose fiscal policy encouraged high interest rates, particularly short-term rates. In New Zealand's case, real rates also remained high because of the perceived exchange rate risk, the country premium, and high world rates. The government had repeatedly told New Zealand businesses that they should follow market signals. High interest rates represented market signals to invest only in projects with high rates of return, and from 1987–92 there was a correspondingly low rate of market-sector capital formation.

After devaluation in 1984, the New Zealand dollar was floated. The widespread view was that there was a likelihood of further depreciation. Instead the currency rose strongly on a trade-weighted basis, mainly because of the high domestic interest rates, the government's demand for finance, overseas perceptions of investment opportunities in New Zealand, and the newly deregulated financial sector attracting capital flows from abroad.

During 1988 the Reserve Bank appeared to change the focus of its monetary policy to include exchange rate stability among its criteria. Initially New Zealand's inflation rate stayed high, and there was a marked rise in the real valuation of the currency from 1985 to 1988. (That has now abated.) What occurred appears to have been a classic exchange rate overshoot. With the strong currency, pressures from imported inflation were reduced, and this was mirrored by tighter domestic cost control. The main signal to the traded-goods sector, however, was the rising exchange rate, which together with tight monetary conditions put harsh competitive pressures on the sector.

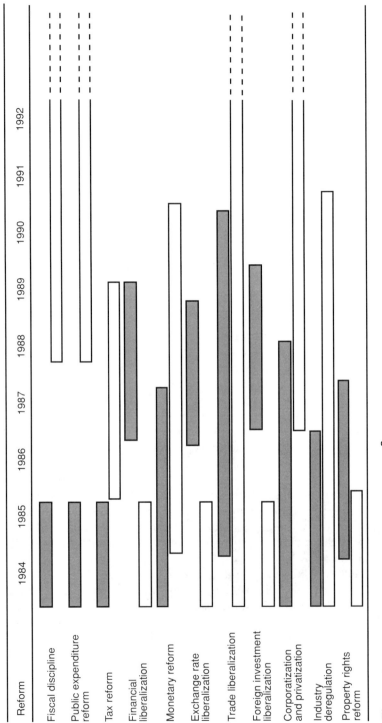

**Figure 1 New Zealand: phasing of reforms, 1984–92[a]**

a. Shaded bars indicate approximate recommended path for "big bang" reform, derived from the generalized proposal in Genberg (1991). Open bars indicate the actual reform path followed in New Zealand. Dashed lines indicate ongoing reforms.

How did business respond to these pressures? A series of structural surveys of firms during the period gives a picture of a business sector that on the whole welcomed the reform program but underestimated the size of the shocks and its own ability to trade throughout the adjustment period (Harper and Malcolm 1991). In the early years, there was new investment with some minor rationalization. By 1987 more serious attempts were being made to cut costs through layoffs and plant closures, falling profits, and cutting margins. Many firms did not survive this period. By 1992, most of the adjustment process was over, but firms had yet to return to profitability. Major improvements in labor productivity were experienced during restructuring. The survivors are more efficient and competitive but also bear the scars of the process: most firms are reluctant to reemploy workers and are cautious about reinvestment (these are the so-called hysteresis effects).

The first sector to be hit was agriculture. Many farmers incurred big increases in debt. Most New Zealand farming is still household-based, and banks found it politically very difficult to foreclose on debts of family farms. As a result, many farmers did not go through the financial restructuring process that the corporate sector was later subjected to.

The manufacturing sector was the next to be hit. This sector's share of the economy had grown (it accounted for 25 percent of employment in 1982) thanks to decades of protection and incentives, and was clearly ripe for restructuring. The industry scaled down notably during the reform period (employment fell from 330,000 to 240,000 from 1986 to 1991), with some sectors such as consumer electronics and ceramics disappearing altogether. Some of these firms had owed their existence solely to protection and had little hope of becoming internationally competitive.

The growth in financial services and government-sector reform led to a buoyant stock market and a construction boom from 1984 to 1987. The world stock market crash in October 1987 was especially damaging in New Zealand, however. Quoted companies lost more than half their value and have yet to recover this value. This has denied the corporate sector a source of equity funds, put considerable pressure on property markets, and brought recession to the construction industry. From 1987 to 1990, the construction sector lost 40 percent of its work force.

By 1988, the non-traded-goods sector was starting to feel the effects of reform, intensified by declining asset prices, corporatization of state-owned enterprises, government spending cuts, and decreasing prosperity in the household sector. By 1990, there were pressures on the financial sector to reform.

Throughout the program of reform, New Zealand exports have grown and remained strong—a consequence of the increased access to Australia under the CER agreement, the depressed domestic market, and the improved competitiveness of New Zealand business. As protection has been removed, there has been a marked increase in import penetration, but because of weak trading conditions this penetration has probably not yet peaked. The size of the imbalance has resulted in a rising foreign debt through the early period of restructuring, with the total foreign debt servicing ratio (servicing costs as a percentage of exports) reaching 47 percent.

The government sector was not spared the turbulence of adjusting to these reforms. The administration of reform put a major burden on civil servants. Employees of state trading activities had to undergo corporatization, declining employment, and, in half the state enterprises, privatization. During the years from 1984 to 1990, lip service was paid to the need to reduce government spending, and in the event industry assistance was cut to one-tenth its earlier levels. Administrative spending was tightened, but social spending continued to grow. During the 1980s, spending on health, education, housing, and social welfare, including universal retirement benefits, grew at an annual average rate of 15 percent. In the meantime, net public-sector debt (including that of the state-owned enterprises) rose to about NZ$48 billion.

Whereas capital bore the brunt of the early restructuring pressures, by 1985 labor layoffs were becoming common and unemployment was growing. Traditionally, unemployment has been very low in New Zealand, averaging around 2 percent in the 1970s, but the process of corporatization and declining competitiveness from the mid-1980s on brought a wave of unemployment, which by 1992 had risen to 11 percent. This above all else threatens the political viability of the reform process.

The National Party government that came to power in 1990 viewed radical labor market reform as a way to increase international competitiveness, increase adjustment flexibility, and possibly also reduce unemployment (through real wage reduction). Following the enactment of the 1991 Employment Contracts Act, labor market adjustment has been significant. Union membership, traditionally high in New Zealand, has dropped considerably, and wage determination has evolved from a relatively inflexible, centralized process to a more flexible system of individual employer-employee bargaining. In the early days of reform, wage increases continued despite declining profitability. Annual nominal wage growth has now dropped, from 18 percent in 1985 to about 2 percent in 1991.

One consequence of unemployment, wage restraint, and reductions in government social service payments has been to put the household sector under considerable pressure. Financial liberalization led to an increase in household debt, and the asset price reductions following the 1987 stock market crash left some households badly exposed. In addition, the tax reforms in 1987 meant those with lower incomes were relatively worse off. Disposable incomes did not grow from 1987 to 1991.

Considerable progress has been made with price stabilization. New Zealand has been plagued with 10 to 20 percent annual inflation for over two decades. A price freeze in the early 1980s provided temporary relief, but once free from restraint, prices rose rapidly again. The introduction of the goods and services tax in 1986 temporarily worsened inflation. The strong currency, tight monetary policy, and stagnant economic conditions have achieved near stability of prices: the annual increase in the consumer price index has fallen from 15 percent in 1986 to 1 percent. In line with this reduction of inflation, there have been other asset price declines, and by 1991 nominal interest rates were at last falling.

The overall picture is of a traded sector hard hit by economic liberalization, considerable contraction in production, and a torpid output response. Annual GDP growth has averaged from 1 to 1.5 percent since 1984, in contrast to the 4 percent average of New Zealand's principal trading partners. Given the rate of population increase, New Zealand has had no net growth in GDP per capita since reform commenced. This poor performance is illustrated in figure 2.

Forecasts are now for improved medium-term performance with a pickup in investment, but only a gradual decline in unemployment. This improvement has taken eight years to come about since economic liberalization commenced. Table 2 summarizes the achievements of the program of economic liberalization and compares them with the implied targets.

## The Preconditions for Reform

### Political Institutions

The origins of the New Zealand reform program may be traced far back historically. The country has a tradition of political radicalism within the relatively newly established European society of New Zealand, and a political structure prepared periodically to throw out old ways of doing things, while operating within a democratic and in some ways conservative framework.

In 1891 the first Liberal-Labour government came to office during a period of long recession and carried out a program of radical social reform, including some of the world's first labor legislation and suffrage for women. In 1935, during the Great Depression, the first Labour government was elected and proved equally radical: it put in place the remaining foundations of the social welfare state, introduced some Keynesian macroeconomic policies, and set up a structure of market intervention and industry protection. James (1986) points out that in each case these were newly elected, reform-minded governments that were committed to new ways of governing and were able to carry out these

Percent

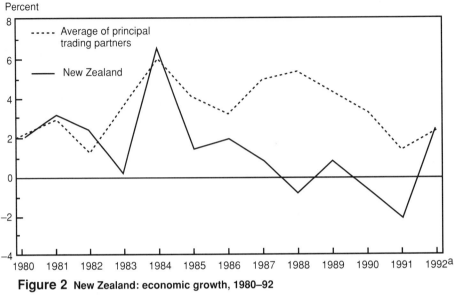

**Figure 2** New Zealand: economic growth, 1980–92

a. Estimated.

Source: New Zealand Institute of Economic Research.

changes. He sees the 1984 Labour government as acting squarely within this historical tradition, and therefore not the historical oddity that it might otherwise appear to be.

New Zealand political institutions lend themselves to such a reforming approach. There is a single legislative chamber in the Parliament (the House of Representatives), with 95 members in 1984, each of whom is elected as the sole representative of a constituency. Almost all members of Parliament belong to one of two parties, National and Labour. In most respects both parties have traditionally been centrist in their standing. Each has its own traditional support groups, but there are no huge differences in economic policy or inseparable gaps between supporters. Third parties have been generally small and weak. A strong Westminster-style system of whips means the elected representatives toe the parliamentary party line. Until recently there have been no important party splinter groups.

There is no upper house to act as a check on the House of Representatives. There are no state or provincial governments. There are territorial local authorities, but they have very limited economic powers beyond planning duties and provision of local utilities. There is no written constitution.

Governments are elected on a first-past-the-post system for a term of three years. This gives significant power (albeit for a short term only) to the party winning the most seats. There have been times in recent years

## Table 2 New Zealand: progress in economic liberalization by 1992

| Sector | Implicit target[a] | Actual progress |
|---|---|---|
| **Stabilization effects** | | |
| Public sector | | |
|   Revenue reform | Broader base, low marginal rates | Achieved |
|   Expenditure reform | Balanced budget | Not before 1996 |
| External sector | | |
|   Price adjustment | International competitiveness | Achieved |
|   Production response | International competitiveness | Achieved |
|   Reduced country risk | Lower external debt | Not achieved |
| Prices | | |
|   Interest rates | International levels | Partially achieved |
|   Consumer prices | Stability | Achieved |
|   Wages | Restrained growth | Achieved |
| Efficiency effects | | |
| Traded sector | Internationally competitive | Achieved |
| Nontraded sector | Efficient | Largely achieved |
| Public sector | Private sector efficiency levels | Partially achieved |
| **Distribution effects** | | |
| Household income | | |
|   Upper-income group | Neutral | Relative gains |
|   Lower-income group | Neutral | Relative losses |
|   State beneficiaries | Reduced fiscal burden | Partially achieved |
| Production | | |
|   Consumers | Improved purchasing power | Generally achieved |
|   Employers and shareholders | Neutral | Relative losses |
|   Employees | Neutral | Relative losses |

a. These implicit targets were rarely explicitly stated and have been interpreted subjectively.

(e.g., in 1981) when a party has won a majority of seats and has formed a government despite having received fewer popular votes than the opposition.[1]

The judicial system is completely separate from the legislative system. New Zealand has not followed the litigious US approach, and the courts are not generally used to review or slow legislative reform.

---

1. In the general election this year, there will be a referendum to determine whether New Zealand changes to a mixed-member proportional representation system, and at this stage it looks very likely.

The cabinet and ministers are appointed by the governing party and make the key decisions. A system of cabinet policy committees, with a smaller number of key ministers and attendance by key departmental officials, is used as the channel for decision making on important issues.

New Zealand has also traditionally followed the Westminster system of government departments headed by departmental secretaries appointed by their peers, rather than the American system of political appointees. Therefore departments do not change personnel following a change in government, which has meant a momentum in departmental decision making that contrasts with politicians' relatively short terms in office.

## The Key Politicians

Thus, New Zealand operates with a thin set of political institutions, which an effective government can use either to maintain the status quo or to drive through radical change. Robert Muldoon, prime minister from 1975 to 1984, exploited this by amassing considerable power in his hands and using it to intervene continually in the economy. Muldoon was a skilled politician, adept at playing off interest groups, and took a short-term, pragmatic approach to many issues. He consolidated power in his own party by removing dissenters and retaining the key portfolio of Minister of Finance for himself.

Faced with shocks to the economy, Muldoon's response was to distrust market forces and to intervene increasingly at a personalized level. The OPEC oil price rises were met with a program of public investment in energy industries. The growing problem of inflation was dealt with through price controls, and ultimately a national freeze on prices and wages. Growing unemployment was handled by instructing government operations such as the national railways to take on more workers, and through direct employment schemes. Falling farm incomes brought price supports for livestock production. Financial market imbalances brought a plethora of controls on reserves, lending, and interest rates. The outcome was that the signals of falling competitiveness were disguised and the economy was temporarily partially insulated from world price trends.

The key personality in the New Zealand reform movement was Muldoon's successor as minister of finance in the Labour government from 1984 on, Roger Douglas. Douglas came from a traditional, politically active Labour family. His father was a unionist and member of Parliament. Douglas himself was educated as an accountant and had some limited business experience in a carpet company, also running a family business. He entered Parliament at an early age and in the 1972–75 Labour government served as a junior minister.

In opposition, Douglas began to formulate more radical views about reducing the role of government. When these views clashed with traditional Labour policies, he was dismissed from his shadow ministerial position. As a backbencher he continued to articulate his line of thinking, and in 1980 he published his ideas in a brief book entitled *There's Got To Be a Better Way* (Douglas 1980). This was a comprehensive if nonintellectual view of what Douglas felt needed to be done to the New Zealand economy. It has been pointed out (Easton 1989) that the recommendations in the book were not entirely consistent with the later reforms (e.g., the book called for a tight competition policy). However, the book does give a picture of the way in which Douglas's views developed and provides a clearer signal of the reforms that were to follow than did any of the subsequent Labour Party manifestos.

During its long period in opposition, the Labour Party had had considerable time to rethink its traditionally interventionist policies. Douglas used the time to build up his knowledge on new microeconomic thinking and his views on how to apply it to the economy. During this time he was receiving advice from Treasury economists seconded to the Opposition Research Unit, and their influence is discernible. By 1984 Douglas had a personal vision of what he wanted to achieve with his reforms. This is the set of policies that later became known as "Rogernomics."

Douglas was, however, not a strong traditional politician. He was a poor speaker and a poor debater and was without a traditional support base. He also had no long-term commitment to a political career. In his book he states that members of Parliament should resign after a maximum of six terms in government. He himself tried to resign in 1981, disillusioned with the political process, but was talked out of this action by his electorate (Douglas and Callan 1981).

Eventually, the Labour Caucus shed its old leader and elected a new parliamentary head, David R. Lange, and a new deputy head, Geoffrey W. R. Palmer, both former lawyers. Douglas was appointed shadow minister of finance.

When the Labour government was formed in 1984, Douglas was confirmed as minister of finance. He was given two key associate ministers of finance as support. Nominally such associates are relatively junior and ineffective. In this case, however, they were very senior and very effective operators, and together with Douglas became known as the "troika." David Caygill, another ex-lawyer, was the more intellectual, able to present the case for liberalization in its theoretical terms. Richard Prebble, yet another ex-lawyer, was forceful and streetwise, able to argue the case with dissenting groups within and outside the party. The ministers proved to be a most effective trio.

During their first term in office, they were assisted by their fellow lawyers Lange and Palmer. David Lange played the role of "chairman of the board"—a deliberate contrast to Muldoon's domineering stance within his own cabinet. Lange did not have much interest in or knowledge of economics. He did have an interest in equity issues, but initially accepted the troika's views that much of the reforms could be expected to assist the lower paid, as well as other groups. Lange appointed a Royal Commission on Social Policy to investigate these questions, and until it reported in 1987 there was effectively a breathing space on equity issues. Lange therefore supported the troika during the first term (although he watched some policy developments with increasing unease), and lent the reforms some legitimacy among traditional Labour supporters. In addition, Lange was diverted at the time by another issue about which he felt very strongly, namely, the access of nuclear-powered ships to New Zealand, and ultimately the ostracism of New Zealand from the ANZUS Pact.

Deputy Prime Minister Palmer also had no economic training, but he too played a key role in the reforms. As a constitutional lawyer he had in the past criticized the tendency of the legislature to overlegislate, and the excessive control exerted by the executive in New Zealand (Palmer 1987). In office, he provided important help in putting many of the crucial reforms into law and in setting up a system from which there was no easy return.

Another important step was the change in the committee structure of the cabinet, in which influence was shifted to a Policy Committee, with the Treasury as its chief source of advice. With the minister of finance, the prime minister, and the deputy prime minister as its core members, the Policy Committee wielded strong influence within the cabinet.

## Other Key Institutions

Outside the political arena, the key institution in the political reform process was the New Zealand Treasury. This is a powerful department because it both exercises departmental control and provides economic advice to the rest of government—in other words, it is also a Ministry of Finance. The Treasury employs most of the government's public-sector economists and dominates departmental economic advice (Boston 1989). During the late 1970s and early 1980s, the views of Muldoon as prime minister and minister of finance increasingly conflicted with the Treasury's advice, and he effectively ignored this institution on certain important issues, taking some pleasure in appealing to the general public over the Treasury economists' heads.

The Treasury spent much of this time reexamining economic alternatives and eventually came up with its own views about New Zealand's economic requirements. The economists in the Treasury were heavily influenced by new microeconomic thinking from certain US universities, especially Demsetz and Coase on the nature of the firm, Williamson on the theory of transaction costs, Baumol's contestability theory, Alchian on property rights, and Buchanan and Tulloch on the political process. A number of key officials received postgraduate training at US universities, especially the John F. Kennedy School of Government at Harvard, the Harvard Business School, and the University of Rochester economics department. In addition, the Treasury called on a number of US experts to act as policy consultants (Bollard 1988).

Many of these ideas were relatively new and had had little exposure in US policy, and not much filtering for New Zealand conditions in New Zealand universities. In general, the role played by New Zealand universities was a minor one. Insofar as relevant policy research was done there, it was generally critical of the liberalization program, or at least of its sequencing or timing. One notable and heated debate between Victoria University economists and the Treasury took place in 1985 (Zanetti et al. 1985).

In general, however, the Treasury's ideas were not much debated with the economics profession outside the department. The department held a coherent internal position and was impatient with dissenting views. In such debates, the Secretary to the Treasury repeated Margaret Thatcher's dictum that "there is no alternative" to the reform program.

Two other key institutions were important to the reforms, namely, the Reserve Bank and the State Services Commission. The Reserve Bank of New Zealand administers monetary policy. It had been an early advocate of reform, both within government and among economists. In 1989, the Reserve Bank was formally reestablished as an independent agency, with a contract to supply services (in particular, price stability) to the government. Roderick Deane, the deputy governor of the Reserve Bank, moved to head the State Services Commission, the departmental organizing unit, to support and initiate reform there. This move was typical of a small group of key civil servants who staffed important agencies. Whereas the traditional New Zealand civil service had not been mobile, these people came from a range of backgrounds (many of them holding economics qualifications), and they moved among key institutions, putting reforms in place and preventing bottlenecks.

The reforms were broadly supported by a wide range of civil servants. One reason for this was that they had themselves experienced a decade of increasing intervention by politicians and had seen at first hand the costs of the system. In particular, those involved in the "Think Big" energy programs of 1978–84 were offended by the huge sums committed on noneconomic grounds. Thus, when the time came to downsize the involvement of the civil service, the Labour government found that it could draw on the support of key departmental employees. In time, important departments such as the Ministry of Commerce and the Ministry of Agriculture and Fisheries were reorganized to carry out and enforce deregulation.

A number of key business people also expressed enthusiasm for the program of economic liberalization. Some performed important roles by heading newly created state-owned enterprises, government investigating committees, and think tanks.

The 1980s saw the development of financial markets in New Zealand, and with financial liberalization came their attendant advisers. These market analysts were generally very supportive of reforms and had the power to influence the market response to the program. After some years of reform, a number of key Treasury economists themselves moved out of the public sector and into these private financial institutions, where they continued to support the reforms.

Overseas financial institutions were also interested in the reform program, principally because of New Zealand's large funding requirements and the liberalization of its financial markets, in which some of them played a part. Roger Douglas was voted Top Finance Minister of the Year by *The Banker* magazine in 1985, an indication of the extent of international financial-sector support. The two principal credit rating agencies, Moody's and Standard & Poor's, took a particularly keen interest in New Zealand's restructuring because of the country's large debt and because of the relevance to other countries' reform programs. These agencies were supportive of the changes, and although they downgraded New Zealand's credit rating during the ensuing recession, they have remained sympathetic to the reform policies.

The reform process relied also on support from international institutions. The IMF had been devoting considerable attention to New Zealand for some years, as debt rose to high levels in the 1980s (total overseas debt reached 83 percent of GDP). The OECD had been promulgating a similar approach in its regular reviews of the New Zealand economy. Once the reform process got started, these two agencies supported and reinforced the approach through continued reports. The OECD in particular viewed New Zealand as an important test case for reform in a Western developed country.

Postwar New Zealand governments of both parties had generally paid considerable attention to special interest groups, in predictable ways. National governments were supported by and supportive of farmers, manufacturers, and employers. Labour governments were assisted by and consulted with the labor movement. These groups formed close relationships with politicians and were regarded as "clients" of the departments of agriculture and industry.

## Supporters and Opponents

The 1984 Labour government was swept into office with a large majority: it received 20 percent more votes and 50 percent more seats than the National Party. The left wing of the party was relatively weak. The party had been out of office for nine years, and traditional industry lobbyists had weak relations with them. The new Labour government therefore commenced its term relatively free of interest group encumbrances or political promises, and with a view of such groups as self-centered rent seekers operating against the wider public interest.

Labour commenced its term in government with an economic summit conference, to which a wide variety of sectoral groups were invited. These groups were asked to commit themselves to the wider public interest. Within the following three years, farming groups were hurt by the removal of agricultural support, manufacturing groups by the reduction of import protection, pensioners by a superannuation surcharge, and labor groups by labor market reform and increasing unemployment. Some of these groups (e.g., the pensioner groups, the union movement, and the Manufacturers Federation) remained entrenched if relatively ineffectual opponents throughout the period of reform; others (e.g., the Federated Farmers and the Employers Federation) gradually embraced the reforms: having borne the pain of restructuring themselves, they argued that other sectors should undergo the same treatment.

The new policies were very strongly supported by a number of "reformist" think tanks, of which the most organized and effective was the NZ Business Roundtable. Directed by a former Treasury economist, it produced a range of reports that sought to lead the government through its agenda of reforms.

What of the typical voter? As already noted, the 1984 Labour government received a large proportion of the popular vote, although, as Colin James (1989) points out, most were clearer about what they were voting against than what they were voting for. Labour was seen as offering a new approach to government, although many voters were not clear what this would involve. The electorate gave the Labour government an unusually long political honeymoon, even when initial results were less than had been promised. In 1987 the party was rewarded for its political bravery by reelection.

Labour has traditionally drawn its support from the lower-income groups. In 1984, much of this traditional support continued, but the party also attracted a significant number of higher-income voters. With its tax cuts, Labour held the support of the latter group in the 1987 election, throwing awry traditional patterns of political support in New Zealand.

The media generally reflected this popular support. The higher-quality news media in New Zealand are usually relatively neutral in their views. Many reporters and editors had felt their independence under attack from the Muldoon government and were glad to support a new approach, although gradually this support grew more critical.

The National Party, its long period in office at an end in 1984, was left in some turmoil. Muldoon had purged the party of some possible successors, and it was only after considerable infighting that new leaders and revamped policies could emerge. Consequently, during its first term in office, the Labour government encountered little serious criticism from the opposition.

Roger Douglas records that during this time the nonparliamentary Labour Party represented the strongest opposition to its own government. Indeed, the Labour Party, led by more traditional left-wing presidents, was increasingly critical of its own ministers during Labour's term in office (Wilson 1989). The party's own support base declined from about 100,000 to about 10,000 members from 1984–88.

## The Ideas and Their Implementation

### New Views on Government

As explained above, the economic ideas of Roger Douglas were developed during his time in opposition and as a junior minister. Oliver (1989) argues that in 1983 Douglas's views shifted notably further toward a free-market approach. However, the Labour Party manifesto for the 1984 election (issued after the election) did not reflect these ideas to any degree and did not signal to the public the reforms that lay ahead. Easton (1987) maintains that the real manifesto was disclosed after the election by the Treasury. In the two months following the election, Treasury officials wrote a postelection briefing for the government, titled *Economic Management* (New Zealand Treasury 1984). This was probably the first comprehensive and consistent outline of the envisaged changes. The document took a broad economic determinist view on most aspects of government.

Douglas and the Treasury were both driven by the same aim: to improve the manifestly substandard performance of the New Zealand economy and the ineffective nature of recent government intervention. But whereas Douglas saw the problem in terms of a practical need for economic liberalization—a freeing up of enterprise in the economy—the Treasury's theoretical views went deeper. The Treasury economists were interested in the range of theoretical microeconomic developments of the preceding decade and anxious to try them in practice. They shifted their focus away from macroeconomic policy (for several years the Treasury cut its macroeconomic divisions and ceased formal forecasting). This also coincided with a change in policy focus from traditional New Zealand ones of stabilization and equity to a primary focus on efficiency.

The Treasury argued that the government should rethink all its traditional economic roles:

- The traditional framework that had guided New Zealand policy decisions on public funding was the market failure approach. The Treasury now argued that this was an unnecessarily restrictive framework and needed to be widened into a general discussion on transactions governance. Their model incorporated bureaucratic failure and sought organizational forms that would allow transactions to be carried out in a cost-minimizing way.

■ The new paradigms rejected traditional equity or nationalistic arguments for why government should own trading activities. Instead they used principal-agency theory to point to inefficiencies resulting from incentive and monitoring problems in the case of public ownership and to support the view that more efficient and dynamic investment decisions would be taken under private ownership.

■ The Treasury economists questioned the traditional approach of direct government provision of many traded services, arguing that supply-side and public-sector crowding-out theories suggested that a deregulated private sector should prove more capable and efficient in providing the same services.

■ The Treasury's approach also questioned the traditional views on regulation regarding the consumer effects of dominant firms, and they used contestability theory and modern theories of regulation to argue the case for a lighter-handed role for government. The role that these changing theories played in altering the view of government is summarized in table 3.

These views represented a major change from the traditional Labour Party support for the social market and paternal government to one of more laissez-faire, while within a system that provided some continued social services. As might have been expected, reducing the role of government in social services was to prove more difficult both conceptually and in practice.

The political economy of microeconomic reform is more complicated than the political economy of macroeconomic reform. The former, which was the focus in New Zealand from 1984, requires a strong commitment by the Treasury and the Finance Ministry, to the extent of overriding objections from the other government departments concerned with policy, their ministers, and the relevant industry groups. During the 1984–87 period, with the strong troika of ministers in place, this proved possible in New Zealand.

The belief (primarily held by microeconomists) was that this policy of structural change should in itself be sufficient to drive a change in economic performance. It was felt that, in some undefined way, the individual elements of an economic liberalization program would add up to a systemic improvement in performance. However, the general equilibrium implications of the reforms were never fully explored—for example, the effects of structural imbalance in the government sector on the

**Table 3   New Zealand: changing views of the role of government**

|  | Funding | Ownership | Provision of services | Regulation |
|---|---|---|---|---|
| Theoretical basis |  |  |  |  |
| Pre-1984 | Market failure theory | Equity and nationalistic arguments | Direct provision | Direct controls |
| Post-1984 | Public-choice theory, property rights theory | Principal-agency theory | Supply-side thinking | Contestability, transaction costs, light-handed regulation |
| Policy basis |  |  |  |  |
| Pre-1984 | Direct funding by parliamentary vote | Widespread public ownership of utilities, etc. | Widespread public provision | Many regulatory monopolies, and price, import, and entry controls |
| Post-1984 | Only for "public good" areas and social services | Corporatization, some privatization | Contracting out, private-sector crowd-in | Commerce Act and market competition (except social services) |

private sector, and the interrelationship of flexible and inflexible markets. The theory of the second best warns of such problems, saying in effect that partial policy reforms cannot be assured of yielding a general improvement. The implicit model in New Zealand was also deficient in assuming away important problems to adjustment such as sunk costs, and in focusing on investment and growth rather than on disinvestment and resource allocation.

The framework thus represented a relatively unsophisticated, comparative static view, which envisaged the economy moving from one low-performance growth path to another, high-performance path (O'Dea 1989). The framework appears to have taken relatively little consideration of such transitional issues as the loss of output during the transition, the flexibility of adjustment mechanisms, the timing and sequencing of measures, and the hysteresis effects. It also paid little attention to distributional issues, such as the costs of adjustment and whether there should be compensation for the relative losers in the transition process in the longer term.

## Views on Implementation

In practice, given the urgency of the situation, there was a certain impatience with such questions. The Treasury economists and other advisers appear to have recommended to the government that, with an elected term of only three years, they should make maximum use of any political honeymoon and cram in as much reform as legislatively possible. Given other postwar New Zealand governments' inability to maintain a consistent long-term policy stance, the Treasury clearly doubted that a gradualist program could be sustained as long as would be necessary. They also doubted their own bureaucratic abilities to identify and carry out the specific managed interventions necessary for such a gradual approach. In addition, they felt that a speedily implemented program was necessary to maintain credibility in the reforms, because there were pressing problems such as the mounting debt. It was also felt that rapid liberalization would reduce adjustment costs, prevent interest groups from regrouping, and give politicians less time to turn their backs on reform.

The government itself seems to have accepted this advice. Its political leaders knew that some of the reforms would be unpopular, and consequently that there was a danger they would not be reelected. They accepted this risk, which was a real one in view of the fact that no Labour government had been elected to two consecutive terms since 1946.

It is difficult to judge what both the politicians' and the Treasury's expectations were regarding the length of the adjustment period and the return to growth afterward. This is partly because the Treasury had ceased its formal macroeconomic forecasts at this time. It is likely that the Treasury anticipated some significant transitional disruption to the economy, although probably not as severe or as long as actually occurred. It is also likely that the politicians anticipated some significant interest group opposition, as indeed did occur. Certainly both groups anticipated an eventual step up to a long-term growth path at a rate of growth that would be significantly higher than New Zealand's historical average.

As a consequence, the government launched itself onto a fast-track reform program. Its speed was constrained by the ability of departments to analyze policy alternatives, of the Crown Law Office to write law, and of Parliament to enact it. The pace of reform was not, however, constrained by any self-imposed requirements to consult with industry or other groups, or by major concerns about correct sequencing. The established principles of sequencing as existed in the literature at the time were to:

■ stabilize before attempting structural reform, to ensure balance in the government sector

■ deregulate product markets and labor markets before financial ones, to ensure that commodity and not capital flows determine the real exchange rate

- deregulate domestic markets before external ones, to allow local interests to absorb any economic rents and to retain internal balance before liberalization.

All of these rules were broken in New Zealand, although sometimes for considered reasons. Some attempt at control of the fiscal deficit was made by reducing industry assistance and reforming government revenue, but the increasing problems of social spending through the period had left an enduring deficit that fueled government funding requirements.[2] Because external capital markets were liberalized, an inflow of foreign funds caused a strengthening currency and a loss of competitiveness in the traded-goods sector. Because labor markets were not fully deregulated and no account had been taken of other inflexibilities in markets, these firms were frequently faced with trading situations that they could not adjust to fast enough, with significant loss of capacity. The Treasury and government view was that such firms might not have survived in competitive markets anyway, implying that officials had paid little attention to the presence of sunk costs.

There was relatively little practical experience in other countries that the proponents of reform in New Zealand could point to in the early 1980s.[3] The reform experience in the Southern Cone countries was not seen as relevant to New Zealand, given the problems of hyperinflation, political instability, and capital flight that existed there. Margaret Thatcher was putting into place some microeconomic reforms and spending restraints in Britain at the time, and there were certainly lessons to be learned from the British restructuring recession of the early 1980s. Ronald Reagan meanwhile was preaching the virtues of small government, enacting tax reform, and espousing supply-side theories in the United States, and this also had some impact. In Australia, Paul Keating was advocating some microeconomic reforms, but these mostly had not been put in place. In practical terms, therefore, there was no close role model for New Zealand to follow at that time.

## Crisis as Catalyst

New Zealanders in 1984 recognized that their economy had major problems. The realization was dawning that there had been a long-term decline in the country's terms of trade. Having put off reform throughout the 1970s, it was now clear that New Zealand could not insulate

---

2. Once the economy slowed down during the restructuring, unemployment grew rapidly and placed an even greater burden on social spending.

3. An example of material commissioned by the New Zealand government was the report by Krueger (1985). However, at this time the main intellectual firepower of bodies like the IMF and the OECD had not yet been focused on these problems.

itself forever from these trends. There was less acceptance of Muldoon's interventionist economic policies and a willingness to consider new approaches, even untried ones. In February 1984 a leaked IMF report to the government appeared to attribute the blame for poor economic performance to government intervention.

This urgency was reinforced by a currency crisis in 1984. During the election campaign the New Zealand dollar came under threat in foreign exchange markets. The Treasury and the Reserve Bank advised Muldoon to devalue. He refused, and the attacks on the currency increased to crisis levels.

Following an election in New Zealand, there is a period of 10 days during which the incumbent prime minister remains in office but is expected to act on advice from the newly elected government. New Prime Minister–elect David Lange supported the officials' advice of an immediate 20 percent devaluation. Muldoon, however, still refused to act. A constitutional crisis loomed, with major losses in reserves and dire concern in the financial markets. Eventually senior ministers of his own party forced Muldoon to back down. In the meantime New Zealand had lost a large proportion of its external reserves.

The new Labour government immediately devalued the dollar, and stability returned to the markets. The following year the dollar was floated. The full details of this crisis were not revealed for some time, but nevertheless it left its mark. It was a final reminder to the public of the costliness of an interventionist prime minister and the need for swift constitutional reform. It was also a salutary reminder to the incoming Labour government of the power of the financial markets. Prime Minister Lange later claimed the crisis gave the minister of finance particular power.[4]

## The Distributional Outcomes

Labour Party manifestos had traditionally viewed distributional issues as important. However, in Roger Douglas's early writings, and to some extent in *Economic Management*, distributional considerations do not receive major emphasis. Rather there is an underlying supply-side argument that the government's role should be to create an environment within which individuals are responsible for exploiting their full potential.

---

4. Dalziel (1989, 67) notes the following quotation from an interview with the Prime Minister in the *National Business Review* dated 11 July 1986: "The circumstances of those first few days in government gave Roger the opportunity to do what he had always wanted to do anyway. But he wouldn't have been able to do that had we gone through the orthodox routine of an election in November, then a budget in June... When the crisis hit in July 1984 [when early elections were called] it was Roger Douglas who, above all, had thought through the economic issues—so when the Cabinet needed to fall back on an economic philosophy, it was Douglas who had one."

The prevailing welfare principles in the new framework seem to have been the following:

- in many of the envisaged reforms, equity and efficiency outcomes would be complementary
- there should still be a government-funded social safety net, but it should be set at a lower level to reduce dependence on the government
- social policies should be explicit, transparent, and targeted
- government industry policy should not have direct or indirect social objectives; hence, for example, antitrust law considering public interest concerns would normally not place greater weights on benefits to any particular class of the population.

The welfare implications of these reforms were not well thought out. The New Zealand approach seems to have expected the reforms to be distributionally neutral, with welfare generally improved across the board. Because transitional costs were not explicitly accounted for in this framework, there was little discussion of compensation for adjustment, and therefore no formal compensation principles were introduced. The fact is that very little compensation was offered to any particular groups for enduring transitional costs. Manufacturers were given a relatively long period during which to adjust to the reduction in protection, but that was unusual. Farmers, pensioners, public servants, and other groups were all faced with rapid change, relatively little consultation, and sometimes major costs to endure.

The government, under pressure from the prime minister, appointed during its first term in office a Royal Commission on Social Policy, which eventually issued its report in 1988. This commission represented a major blow to the economic reformers. It produced a scathingly critical report on the reforms, claiming major trade-offs between equity and efficiency outcomes. This report also marked a watershed in relations within the parliamentary Labour Party, and a growing rift developed between the prime minister and the minister of finance on the question of the distributional outcomes of reform.

Theoretically, the benefits of the liberalization were primarily designed to be felt not by producers but by consumers, who in New Zealand have a history of paying higher than international prices for manufactured goods of limited choice and variable quality. Although these goals were largely realized, they were never well-articulated and never generated much consumer support. Consumers have not been a well-organized lobby, and their chief mouthpiece, the Consumers' Institute, was lukewarm about many of the reforms. In particular, certain of the reforms involving the financial sector and state-owned enterprises were widely felt to disadvantage certain sectors of the public.

Both employees and employers were affected by the reforms and suffered through the transition from high unemployment and falling profits. Employees have also probably been put at a longer-term relative disadvantage by the labor market deregulations later put in place by the National Party government (it is still too early to state this definitively). The whole range of production sectors and the public sector has been affected at various times over the reform period. (Table 4 presents a summary of the main elements of the reform program, using the previous classification, and of its adherents and proponents.)

In hindsight one can see some major distributional effects of liberalization. In particular, the personal income tax reforms of 1987 and growing unemployment have meant that the lowest quintile in the income distribution has earned a decreasing share of income, while the highest quintile has gained in relative terms. Such changes in relative shares have not been unique in recent years, however. Ultimately it was Roger Douglas's proposal in 1987 for a flat income tax (probably about 23 percent) in 1987 that, after being rejected by the prime minister, led to the eventual split between the two, Douglas's resignation, and a slowing of the pace of reform. But these distributional effects were not foreseen at the start of the period.

## The Sustainability of the Reforms

The reform program remained firmly in place during Labour's 1984–87 term in office despite poor economic indicators and rising unemployment. Paradoxically, however, the speed of reforms meant that the full costs did not become apparent before the election. This is somewhat different from the traditional reformer's problem, where the benefits unfold slowly.

New Zealanders went to the polls in 1987 with the Labour government promising to finish its program of reform, and they voted Labour back into office with a reduced but still substantial majority. The reform program then ran into difficulty, initially within the Labour Party itself. After the dismissal of Roger Douglas, the program continued at a slower pace, and the more controversial decisions such as major privatizations were made tentatively. The government made little attempt to extend its reforms into the growing area of social services. The declining political popularity of the governments during this period is shown in figure 3.

In 1990, the government was beaten at the polls by the National Party, which then continued the reforms under the current minister of finance, Ruth Richardson. The National Party government has concentrated its efforts on reforming social services (education, health care, and social welfare) and reducing the fiscal deficit. This program has proved

**Table 4　New Zealand: constituencies for and against reforms and difficulties encountered**

| Reform | Proponents | Opponents | Time to put in place | Difficulties encountered |
|---|---|---|---|---|
| Public expenditure reduction | Financial markets, employers, investors | Unions, professional providers, superannuants, beneficiaries, unemployed, civil service | 9 years, uncompleted | Very difficult to achieve in social services |
| Tax reform | Financial markets, employers, investors | Low-income groups | 3 years | Technical difficulties with GST but introduced smoothly |
| Financial liberalization | Financial institutions, investors, shareholders, farmers | | 2 years | Relatively straightforward |
| Monetary reform | Reserve Bank, financial markets, investors | Some economists, union movement | 3 years | Relatively smooth implementation |
| Exchange rate liberalization | Financial markets, exporters, importers, foreign investors | Some economists | 2 years | Relatively smooth after initial crisis |
| Trade liberalization | Farmers, importers, consumers, exporters | Unions, manufacturers | 13 years until 1996 | Reduction continuing |
| Foreign direct investment | Financial markets, foreign investors | Some voters | 2 years | Relatively smooth implementation |
| Corporatization and privatization | Financial markets, investors, some customers | Some customers, some voters, unions, Maoris, rural groups | 5 years | Corporatization complete, privatization half complete, some complications |
| Deregulation of industry | Some businesses | Some customers, some businesses, unions | 6 years | Heterogeneous range of changes; some complications |
| Labor market reform | Employers, shareholders | Unions | 1 year | Occurred later |
| Social services reform | Taxpayers | Public sector, superannuants, unemployed, unions, other beneficiaries, health and educational professionals | 2 years | Not completed |

GST = goods and services tax.

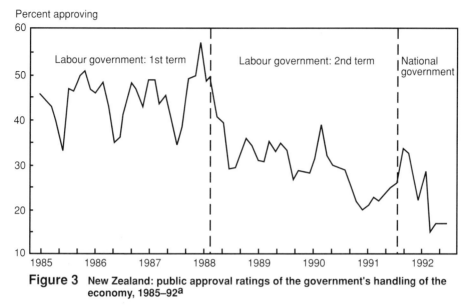

**Figure 3** New Zealand: public approval ratings of the government's handling of the economy, 1985–92[a]

a. Respondents were asked,"On the whole, do you approve or disapprove of the government's handling of the economy?"

*Source:* Heylen Research Centre.

increasingly unpopular with the electorate, which seems to be suffering from reform fatigue.

Also in 1990, a referendum on the electoral system delivered a blow to both major parties, with a resounding vote to change the voting system to a mixed-member proportional representation system. This might also be seen as representing a vote of no confidence in radical economic change.

The National Party government's attempts at completing the reform process continue but have run into growing opposition from the media and the public. In addition, there has been a fracturing of party loyalties and the formation of an alliance of third parties seeking to turn around the reform process. While there is now less appetite for major continued reform, many of the reforms in place are not easily reversed. For example, the repeal of the executive powers, the undertakings on trade policy to international agencies such as the GATT, the reduction in the strength and lobbying ability of many special interest groups, the reduction in union power, the deregulated financial markets, and the role of international money markets all make it difficult to undo the reforms.

## Conclusion: Determinants of the Reform Process

In summary, New Zealand from 1984 to 1991 instituted a radical and comprehensive program of economic liberalization. The timing was rushed and little attention was paid to sequencing. Consequently, despite some major achievements, a long transitional recession was encountered. The adjustment period was longer than envisaged, with beneficial results taking up to eight years to emerge. It is ironic that, in 1993, as the country is at last starting to feel the benefits of liberalization, the public appears to have lost its appetite for further reform.

In New Zealand certain unusual preconditions allowed these reforms to take place (although the same preconditions also allowed the reforms to be rushed and sometimes ill-considered). The more important determinants of the introduction of the program include the following:

- the emergence of a technocratic politician (Roger Douglas) with a clear vision of reform

- a strong core of cabinet ministers that allowed him to operate effectively

- a thin legislative system in New Zealand, permitting radical changes to be enacted

- supportive senior civil servants who promoted reform

- a committed and powerful Treasury dominating the policy debate

- the rise of new bodies of microeconomic theory giving the government's arguments theoretical respectability in the debate

- a belief that reform could be achieved quickly, without major adjustment costs, in a distributionally neutral way

- a recent history of excessive government intervention and poor economic performance

- a currency crisis at the time the reforming government took office

- and, finally, various political diversions in the form of the crises over the ANZUS Pact and the Rainbow Warrior affair.

## References

Bollard, A., ed. 1988. *The Influence of United States Economics on New Zealand: The Fulbright Anniversary Seminars.* Wellington: NZ/US Educational Foundation.

Bollard, A. 1992. "New Zealand: Economic Reforms 1984–1991." *Country Studies* 10. San Francisco: International Center for Economic Growth.

Bollard, A., and R. Buckle, eds. 1987. *Economic Liberalisation in New Zealand.* Wellington: Allen & Unwin.

Boston, J. 1989. "The Treasury and the Organisation of Economic Advice: Some International Comparisons." In B. Easton, ed., *The Making of Rogernomics*, chapter 3. Auckland: Auckland University Press.

Dalziel, P. 1989. "The Economic Summit: What People Were Thinking." In B. Easton, ed., *The Making of Rogernomics*, chapter 2. Auckland: Auckland University Press.

Douglas, R. 1980. *There's Got To Be a Better Way: A Practical Way to Solving New Zealand's Major Problems.* Auckland: Fourth Estate Books Ltd.

Douglas, R., and L. Callan. 1981. *Towards Prosperity: People and Politics in the 1980s, A Personal View.* Auckland: David Bateman Ltd.

Duncan, I., R. Lattimore, and A. Bollard. 1991. "Dismantling the Barriers: Evolution of Tariff Policy in New Zealand." *Research Monographs* 57. Wellington: New Zealand Institute of Economic Research.

Duncan, I., and A. Bollard. 1992. *Corporatization and Privatization: Lessons from New Zealand.* Auckland: Oxford University Press.

Easton, B. 1987. "Labour's Economic Strategy." In J. Boston and M. Holland, eds., *The Fourth Labour Government: Radical Politics in New Zealand,* chapter 8. Auckland: Oxford University Press.

Easton, B., ed. 1989. *The Making of Rogernomics.* Auckland: Auckland University Press.

Harper, D., and G. Malcolm. 1991. "Surviving the Change: How Firms Adjusted to the New Environment." *Research Monographs* 56. Wellington: New Zealand Institute of Economic Research.

James, C. 1986. *The Quiet Revolution: Turbulence and Transition in Contemporary New Zealand.* Wellington: Allen & Unwin.

James, C. 1989. "Overview." In S. Walker, ed., *Rogernomics: Reshaping New Zealand's Economy,* chapter 1. Wellington: GP Books.

Krueger, A. O. 1985. *Economic Liberalisation Experiences—The Costs and Benefits.* Wellington: New Zealand Treasury.

New Zealand Treasury. 1984. *Economic Management.* Wellington: New Zealand Treasury.

O'Dea, D. 1989. *The Economy in Transition: Restructuring to 1989.* Wellington: New Zealand Planning Council.

Oliver, W. H. 1989. "The Labour Caucus and Economic Policy Formation 1981-84." In B. Easton, *The Making of Rogernomics,* chapter 1. Auckland: Auckland University Press.

Palmer, G. 1987. *Unbridled Power: An Interpretation of New Zealand's Constitution and Government,* 2nd ed. Auckland: Oxford University Press.

Spencer, G., and D. Carey. 1988. "Financial Policy Reform—The New Zealand Experience 1984-87." *Discussion Papers* G88/1. Wellington: Reserve Bank of New Zealand.

Walker, S. 1989. "The Politics of Rogernomics." In S. Walker, ed., *Rogernomics: Reshaping New Zealand's Economy,* chapter 10. Wellington: GP Books.

Wilson, M. 1989. *Labour in Government 1984-87.* Wellington: Allen & Unwin.

Zanetti, G., et al. 1985. "Opening the Books : A Review Article." *NZ Economic Papers* 18: 13-30.

# Appendix: New Zealand economic liberalization program

| | Year |
|---|---|
| **Factor markets** | |
| Finance industry | |
| Abolition of credit growth guidelines | 1984 |
| Removal of separate requirements for trustee banks, building societies, finance houses, stockbrokers | 1985–87 |
| Removal of quantity restrictions and other entry barriers to banking | 1985–86 |
| End of formal financial controls (reserve ratio requirements, sector lending priorities) | 1985 |
| Removal of interest rate controls | 1984 |
| Abolition of export credit guarantees | 1984 |
| Removal of ownership restrictions on financial institutions | 1985 |
| Liberalization of stock exchange | 1986 |
| Energy industry | |
| Corporatization of state coal mines | 1987 |
| Financial restructuring of oil refinery | 1988–91 |
| Legalization of oil company ownership of service stations | 1988 |
| End of price controls (except on natural gas) | 1984–88 |
| Sale of Crown gas exploitation and distribution interests | 1988–90 |
| Sale of other Crown energy holdings | 1990–92 |
| Corporatization and restructuring of electricity generation, transmission, and distribution | 1986–91 |
| Transport industry | |
| Removal of restrictions on road and rail carriage | 1983–86 |
| End of quantity licensing of trucking | 1984 |
| Corporatization of state rail, air, and bus services | 1982–84 |
| Tendering of local-authority bus services and liberalization of licensing requirements | 1987–91 |
| Deregulation of taxi industry | 1990 |
| Opening up of domestic aviation industry | 1987 |
| Granting of a number of landing and on-flying rights to foreign airlines | 1989 |
| Corporatization and sale of airports and Airways Corporation | 1986–91 |
| Corporatization of ports | 1989 |
| Deregulation of stevedoring industry | 1990 |
| Removal of cabotage on coastal shipping | 1991 |

Research and development

| | |
|---|---|
| Removal of concessions for research and development, to put on equal footing with all investment | 1984 |
| Cost-recovery of public research and development work | 1985 |
| Establishment of a contestable pool of public funds (Foundation of Research Science and Technology) | 1990 |
| Corporatization of government research bodies (Crown Research Institutes) | 1992 |

Labor market

| | |
|---|---|
| Introduction of voluntary unionism | 1983 |
| More market-based bargaining under Industrial Relations Act Amendment: compulsory unionism reinstituted | 1984 |
| Some contestability in union coverage under Labour Relations Act | 1987 |
| Radical reform via Employment Contracts Act (Voluntary unionism, contestable unions of any size, any arrangements for employer-employee bargaining at joint or individual level) | 1990 |

**Industry deregulation**

Product markets

| | |
|---|---|
| Termination of supplementary minimum prices on agricultural products | 1984 |
| Agricultural tax concessions removed | 1985 |
| Termination of concessional financing of primary producer stocks held by producer boards | 1986–88 |
| Review of compulsory producer marketing board arrangements | 1987 |
| Termination of domestic boards for eggs, milk, and wheat | 1984–88 |
| Termination of export market development incentive schemes | 1984 |
| Phaseout of export performance tax incentives | 1984–87 |

Industry reforms

| | |
|---|---|
| End of wage-price freeze | 1984 |
| Termination of price controls and replacement by (unused) price surveillance powers under Commerce Act | 1984–88 |
| Removal of quantity licensing on almost all industries, and end of quality regulation on most | 1986–88 |
| End of all state-regulated monopoly rights (except postal service, air traffic control, and milk distribution) | 1984–89 |
| Removal of some occupational licensing | 1985–90 |
| Removal of producer cooperative tax advantages | 1989 |

## Appendix: New Zealand economic liberalization program
### (Continued)

| | |
|---|---|
| Termination of restrictions on shop trading hours | 1989 |

Business law reform

| | |
|---|---|
| Establishment of Commerce Act as liberal efficiency-based regime to govern mergers and trade practices | 1986 |
| Fair Trading Act to govern consumer rights | 1986 |
| Review of securities legislation and take-over law (extent of efficiency approach still under discussion) | 1988-91 |
| Review of whole intellectual property regime (patent, copyright, trademarks, and designs) | 1990–91 |
| Review of town and country planning | 1987–90 |
| Resource Management Act to govern more liberal planning and environmental legislation | 1991 |
| Crown Minerals Act to clarify property rights to mineral resources | 1991 |

### International trade and monetary reforms

Import protection

| | |
|---|---|
| Phaseout of import licensing requirements | 1983–89 |
| Reduction of import tariffs on Swiss formula from average 28 percent to 10 percent | 1986–92 |
| Further one-third reduction in import tariffs planned | 1992–96 |
| Removal of special protection features for 18 specific "industry plan" sectors and incorporation into general tariff reform program | 1984–92 |
| Slower reduction tariffs on two remaining "special" industries (motor vehicles and components, and textiles, clothing, and footwear) | 1987–96 |

International capital controls

| | |
|---|---|
| Removal of controls on outward investment and borrowing | 1984 |
| Free entry of foreign direct investment (rubber-stamped by Overseas Investment Commission, except for farmland, offshore islands, and fishing) | 1985, 1989 |
| Very liberal regime for portfolio investment and repatriation of profits | 1985 |

Exchange rates

| | |
|---|---|
| Deregulation of foreign exchange trading | 1984 |
| Devaluation by 20 percent against basket of currencies | 1984 |
| Free float of currency on foreign exchange markets without direct control | 1985 |

Monetary policy

| | |
|---|---|
| Devotion of monetary policy instruments to deflation, with target of "price stability" (0 to 2 percent price increase) by 1992–93 | 1989 |
| Tight monetary policy (M3 below rate of inflation) | 1987– |
| Independence of Reserve Bank from government, formalized through Reserve Bank Act | 1989 |

**Government sector reforms**

State trading operations

| | |
|---|---|
| Removal of almost all state-regulated monopoly rights | 1984–89 |
| Corporatization of 24 state-owned enterprises (in transport, finance, tourism, forestry, broadcasting, utilities, and service industries) | 1987–88 |
| Restructuring to isolate natural monopoly elements of state enterprises | 1989–91 |
| Full or partial privatization of Air New Zealand, Bank of New Zealand, Petroleum Corporation, Tourist Hotel Corporation, Shipping Corporation, Rural Bank, Government Life, Forestry Corporation, Post Office Bank, Telecom Corporation, and others | 1987–91 |
| Further privatization planned via divestment of asset sales, sale of rights, share sales, etc. | 1991– |
| Requirement for local authorities to corporatize local-authority trading enterprises and tender out services | 1990–91 |
| Encouragement to local authorities to sell holdings in airports, port companies, and local utilities | 1991 |
| Sale of other assets, e.g., irrigation schemes, fishing rights | 1983–88 |

Tax reforms

| | |
|---|---|
| Broadened tax base through goods and services tax on virtually all final domestic consumption (now 12.5 percent) | 1986 |
| Flattening and lowering of personal income tax rate, with top rate standardized to corporate tax levels, and aimed to minimize poverty traps | 1988 |
| Standardization and simplification of corporate taxation to minimize evasion and cut administrative costs | 1985 |
| Removal of most other indirect taxes | 1986–91 |
| Removal of tax concessions for savings, etc., to put on neutral footing | 1987 |
| Review of international tax regime | 1992 |

Expenditure control

| | |
|---|---|
| Attempts at reduction in government expenditure, especially in areas of administration and industry development | 1985– |

## Appendix:   New Zealand economic liberalization program
### (Continued)

| | |
|---|---|
| Assignment of proceeds of sale of state enterprise assets to repay public debt | 1987– |
| Public-sector management reform through Public Finance Act | 1989 |
| Reform of core government departments on corporate lines through State Sector Act of 1988, with separation of policy, provision, and funding | 1986– |
| User-pays principles for remaining state trading activity | 1986– |
| Redesign of government accounts on more commercial basis, accrual accounting, output-based monitoring systems through Public Finance Act | 1988 |
| Abolition of 50 quangos and quasi-governmental organizations | 1987 |
| Renewed attempt at reduction in social spending (education, health, social welfare, superannuation) | 1991 |
| Social services reform | |
| Reform of compulsory education system, based on elected boards of trustees | 1988–90 |
| Quasi corporatization and fee paying for tertiary education institutions | 1992 |
| Integration of state housing assistance into private-sector rental and mortgage provision | 1991 |
| Tightening of requirements and reduction of levels of unemployment benefits and other government social transfers | 1990 |
| Tightening of requirements, postponement of age of eligibility, and reduction of benefits for government-funded old age pension scheme | 1989–92 |
| Separation of funding from provision of state health services, establishment of Crown Health Enterprises, and expectations of private-sector crowd-in | 1992 |
| Likely development of private funding arrangements for health provision | 1992 |

# Comment

## W. MAX CORDEN

These two papers are very interesting. Let me first discuss New Zealand. There have been some remarkable changes, but the favorable results, other than that of getting inflation down, are slow to emerge. The interesting question is why these changes took place. After all, one used to think of New Zealand as a rather conservative country.

There seem to be essentially three reasons. First and perhaps most important, things have to get bad, really bad, before they get better. Second, New Zealand is a small country with a small, politically active community where a few individuals can really make a difference. It seems that there were in fact just three, namely, Roger Douglas and his two Treasury colleagues. They were determined, and they provided the necessary leadership. Third, the system of government, like that of Britain but unlike that of Australia, is quite centralized. It is not a federal system, and there is only one house of parliament. (In Britain the upper house hardly matters, but in Australia it certainly does.) The British parliamentary system also makes it possible for a determined leader to get her or his way, as Margaret Thatcher showed.

Another factor seems to have been the weakness of the opposition, which was discredited by the mess that Robert Muldoon left, and in any case, belief in Muldoon's ideas was melting away. Nevertheless, it is quite curious that three free marketeers, and notably Roger Douglas, chose to join and work through the Labour Party. Given its traditions and trade union basis, it was not a natural vehicle for such reforms.

*W. Max Corden is a Professor of International Economics at the Paul H. Nitze School of Advanced International Studies, The Johns Hopkins University.*

I know more about Australia. Here the reforms have been much less dramatic, and there is still quite a way to go. Although some steps have been taken, Australia still especially needs drastic reforms of its labor market. The reforms have been less dramatic than New Zealand's because things never got so bad: inflation did not rise so high, and considerable trade liberalization had taken place since the 1950s. Unlike in New Zealand, protection was almost wholly by tariffs and not by quantitative restrictions.

I have often wondered why it took a Labor government to bring about trade and other free-market reforms, rather than the Liberal-National (conservative) government under prime minister Malcolm Fraser that preceded it. I suppose the answer is that leading Labor people tend to be more ready to bring about changes if they believe they are necessary. They are natural reformers. In earlier days the changes they wanted were of the Fabian socialist kind, and now they are following newer ideas. To some extent their ideas—which were by no means supported right through the Labor Party—were shared by the conservative opposition. But Labor politicians were more prepared to act.

Also, Labor had an impressive team: the prime minister during the early reform period, Bob Hawke, is a well-informed, well-educated politician who understood what was required and was personally very popular in the community. The Hawke government also had a determined and decisive treasurer, Paul Keating, and a number of very competent ministers elsewhere in the cabinet.

I am not sure to what extent public opinion has been behind the changes in Australia. I suspect it is lagging. The recent recession has certainly revived protectionist thinking. Whenever I return to my home state of Victoria, I certainly hear and read plenty of old-style protectionism. Victoria has been a stronghold of the main protected industries.

Finally, the Industries Assistance Commission (IAC; it is now called the Industries Commission) also played a very important role in the Australian reform process and would be well worth emulating by other countries. Its history is actually a rather long and quite impressive story. The commission's origin was in the Tariff Board, which was converted into the IAC by the Labor government of Gough Whitlam in 1973, with a broadened mandate. The IAC and the Whitlam government laid the foundations for the more radical steps that the Hawke government took later. There was a unilateral, across-the-board reduction of tariffs under the Whitlam government. The conservative Fraser government that came between Whitlam and Hawke preached the virtues of trade liberalization and moved a little in that direction but was genuinely conservative in this and other respects.

The IAC was the first organization in the world to calculate effective tariff rates systematically and put an emphasis on them as distinct from nominal rates (they did this following on suggestions from me). A key role was played by Alf Rattigan, the IAC's first chairman, who had originally been put into the key position of chairman of the Tariff Board by a protectionist minister in the government that preceded Whitlam's. Rattigan was thought to be amenable, a practical bureaucrat. He turned out to be a man of principle—an idealist and a reformer—who was converted to "rational" (i.e., orthodox) economics, and he put the IAC onto its future path.

The IAC has produced many excellent, well-researched reports on microeconomic issues, among them analyses of protected industries, the cost of protection, subsidies, and microeconomic reform proposals, including reform in the public sector. It has been influential, its recommendations being debated and reported in the press, and providing the raw material for informed discussion. It has also had many enemies and critics in politics, business, and the trade unions. Several times its survival and integrity have been under threat. Even though its original purpose was to recommend appropriate levels of protection for products or industries, it has not been captured by interest groups, and it has been a consistent advocate of trade liberalization. One might say that it has been "captured" by professional economists.

# Comment

C. DAVID FINCH

My comments are based on a conviction that this conference, being primarily among economists, can contribute most by focusing on the lessons economists can learn from the history of countries adopting radical reforms under their guidance. That to me is a critically important task. I believe that the peaceful evolution of the world depends on gaining broad acceptance for the economist-generated principles that economic rewards between countries should be determined by markets, with strict limits on politically motivated interventions, and that monetary stability is an essential condition for long-term political stability. Consequently, it is our duty as economists to study the experience of economic reform closely, to reduce to a minimum the chances that our advice can lead to political failure. Any perception that following the advice of economists is politically dangerous inevitably strengthens the power of emotional nationalism and contributes to increasing world tensions.

What are the economic lessons from the experiences of Australia and New Zealand that have been so comprehensively and competently described to us in these two papers? Above all, although the paths taken by the two countries have differed, the present outcome in both as described by the authors is sobering. Growth, recently and in immediate prospect, has not been impressive. The danger of crisis has not disappeared, as external debt levels remain dangerously high. And the political rewards of instituting reforms recommended by economists, after some early strength, have come into question. In New Zealand, the

*David Finch was a Counsellor with the International Monetary Fund.*

party that initiated economic reform has been voted out, and in Australia the race is close. On the other hand, there does not seem to be any gathering of support for a reversal of the main thrust of the reforms. In fact, the public, and even more the leading political innovators now in both parties, have shown a tenacity to hold to long-term goals, and this bodes well for the power of the vision brought by economists and heightens the relevance of this reexamination of the record.

The first lesson seems to be that steady long-run growth at respectable rates, even rates significantly below East Asian levels, is more difficult to establish than we had led the political world to expect. That lesson in itself does not seem to be too helpful to reformers, but it does underline the need to improve the design of the reforms in any way that can deepen the drive to greater efficiency. Here, amid the myriad possibilities, I will try to focus on two lessons that I have not seen analyzed elsewhere.

In the circumstances of these two countries, to me it is clear that a stronger base for long-term growth could have been achieved if radical labor reform had been a successful part of the original program. Economic success in both countries was dependent on creating soundly based incentives for investment in export industries, yet labor reform was delayed and labor-management collaboration remained poor, with the result that potential investors in export industries held back. Action aimed at changing the situation substantially has recently been taken in New Zealand, but only after a change in government, and in Australia it seems much has yet to be done.

The problem, of course, is that labor reform needs the right political conditions to succeed. From Ross Garnaut's description, the political reasons for the Australian delay on labor reform are clear. There were considerable immediate benefits from union cooperation in wage level setting. Yet in Australia the government-run arbitration system, by overshadowing direct negotiations, had the crippling long-term effect of accentuating the adversarial aspect of labor-management relations. Faster growth of investment in exports would clearly be possible if Australia simply abandoned this system, provided that both sides were ready to cooperate freely. Unfortunately, it is all too easy for ending government intervention to look like taking sides against the workers, and to heighten rather than lessen tensions that reduce cooperation on the factory floor. Thus, if labor reform is to play a helpful role, there must first be much more effective public understanding of the central point, namely, that steady worker income growth can only be assured by direct collaboration to create the partnership needed for success in matching the growth in efficiency being achieved elsewhere.

The other issue I would raise involves capital inflows, and it involves a much more complex problem than political preparation. Generally speaking, reform is aided by its ability to mobilize foreign resources to fund a return to growth. One paradox from the experience of these two countries is, I would submit, that the welcoming response from abroad actually caused damage by facilitating excessive and misdirected capital inflows. For me this is an awkward lesson, because mobilizing resources and hence support for change has been the traditional basis for the defense of the IMF intrusiveness involved in conditionality. But clearly perverse effects are possible.

How can capital inflows be excessive? The answer is easy when it is the government that is borrowing for the wrong reasons. That is what created the debt crisis of 1982. And always lax fiscal policy, coupled with tight monetary control, can raise interest rates and can create an inflow that effectively finances the government, not export development. But at least until very recently, Australian developments did not fit that specification. The fiscal balance was under reasonable control by most standards, and the inflows seem to have gone primarily to the private sector. And it seems a good first principle to accept that, with open markets, the judgment of those involved in the capital inflow should be trusted. With the reforms, opportunities for successful private investment should have grown.

What then was the defect in the actual financial reforms? I think it lay in the failure, throughout the English-speaking world, to include in the wave of deregulation of banking sufficient provision for oversight to avoid excess. In the United States that failure led to the savings and loan collapse. In Australia, in my view, in the early years of reform, it promoted uneconomically high private borrowing abroad. Although much of the consequent loss was purely on private account, there were serious losses by state government development institutions and, in my view, excessive risks taken by the banking system, which damaged its later ability to support steady investment growth. These excess borrowings abroad also distorted the exchange rate, to the detriment of export growth.

The key issue is the role of regulatory oversight. In hindsight, the responsibility of the central bank to maintain financial order, including but not limited to the avoidance of bank defaults to depositors, should have meant that the opening of the system to new competitors, with its pressure to drop past inhibitions in the struggle to maintain profits, was accompanied by stronger supervisory oversight. That supervision should have involved more attention to the speed and extent of the rise in the external exposure of banks and, more particularly in this case, of their major clients. At the very least, bank oversight powers could have been used to collect and publicize information on the risks being incurred.

Consequently, from the experience of these two countries I would submit two issues for further debate: first, that future radical reform in market economies should place higher priority on labor reform whenever the existing system involves systematic government intervention, and second, that monetary liberalization involving intensified competition should be accompanied by a strengthening of regulatory oversight of all banking institutions so as to limit excesses in borrowing by the private sector.

Finally, we should take heart from the strong reassurance in the historical record presented in these papers that the ideas generated by economists, and featured in this conference, have the strength to continue to guide policymakers for extended periods, even in adverse conditions and with flawed implementation.

# Discussion

*Stephan Haggard* started by addressing what he called the counterintuitive issue raised by Max Corden, namely, why social democratic governments often proved ready to undertake sweeping economic reforms. He challenged Corden's reasoning on three grounds. First, by the time the labor parties had come to power in Australia and New Zealand, they had been fundamentally reformed: both parties had seen an extension of their electoral base toward the middle class (although that leaves open the key question as to why this had happened). A second hypothesis concerned the reorganization of interest groups at the time of reform, when the traditional sectoral union organization was superseded by an economy-wide labor council. A general principle of political economy held that a widening of the scope of an organization reduces the opportunities for particularism (this is a standard argument for a system of two broad-based parties rather than a multiplicity of parties). Had this been an important factor? A third hypothesis emphasized in the Australia paper (but not in the paper on New Zealand) was the apparent willingness of the Labor government to compensate the losers.

*Luiz Carlos Bresser Pereira* argued that there was nothing particularly surprising about left-of-center governments pursuing economic reforms. For example, in Portugal (as in Spain) stabilization had begun under a social democratic government in 1983; the Cavaco Silva government had merely continued the reforms. Why did politicians implement reforms? Because of *force majeure*: they acted when the scope for populism or interventionism (or, indeed, liberalism, for fashions are cyclical) left them with no alternative. Politicians who try to maximize their own interest embark on reforms when that seems the best hope of remaining in power.

(Bresser Pereira suggested that in Brazil there was currently no room for populism but that the president had not yet grasped this truth; when he eventually did there would be a new impetus to reform.)

*Jessica Einhorn* asked whether an attempt to keep up with the regional Joneses, notably Japan and Korea, might have influenced the behavior of Australia and New Zealand. This seemed to have happened in Eastern Europe, where countries had embarked on a path of reform with the clear aim of becoming modern "European" countries. Also, while the drive for reform surely stemmed primarily from domestic sources, to what extent was the hospitability of the international environment (such as the fate of the Uruguay Round of the General Agreement on Tariffs and Trade) important in influencing the will to reform? *Fred Bergsten* supplemented her first question by asking whether the two countries competed with each other or reinforced each other's reform efforts.

In replying to the debate, *Ross Garnaut* explained that the important ideas had developed in Australia over a fairly long period of time. He pointed to the crucial role of the Industries Commission in shaping a new climate of opinion from the late 1960s to the early 1980s, especially in drawing attention to the distributional and regional effects of protection. The commission's role had declined through the period when reforms were being implemented, partly because its agenda had gone on to other issues such as the reform of public enterprises. Referring to the need for labor market reforms mentioned by Corden in his comment, Garnaut remarked that there had been very little discussion among economists about labor market rigidities comparable to the debates about trade liberalization issues during the 1960s and 1970s. But a new public discussion, largely associated with nonuniversity think tanks, had been spurred by the government's reform programs, and this had been creating a climate for reform in this area too.

During the 1980s the relative importance of national as opposed to sectional trade union representation in Australia had become much greater. The same had happened in business, with the National Business Council becoming more important than the proliferation of sectional business groups. The National Economic Summit had invited representation from these broad groups and institutionalized them through further consultations. That had been very much a response to Hawke's style of consultation, which was a fairly deliberate attempt to curb the influence of sectional interest groups.

The reforms of the financial system had frequently been criticized as too ideological, and the charge had been made that the recession of 1991 was the result of financial deregulation. He agreed that the inflationary boom of 1987–88 (which took the form of asset price inflation, for reasons that were still not fully understood) had been caused by very rapid monetary expansion, and he conceded that this was a major cause of the recession in the sense that it required a subsequent monetary contraction. He also agreed that there was a link between financial deregulation and the subsequent monetary expansion, inasmuch as deregulation had distorted the interpretation of monetary growth (20 percent in 1987), and during this uncertainty the stock market had crashed, raising concerns about deflation. But such errors need not be repeated and provided no argument against financial market reform.

Had it been a mistake to proceed more quickly on financial market reform than on reform in other markets? Garnaut believed not: given the constraints on introducing reforms in other areas, there would have been no advantages in deliberately delaying financial deregulation. The removal of exchange controls in 1983 had in fact proved helpful to a number of real reforms. But he conceded that the weakness of Australian banking would ideally have elicited stronger central bank supervision.

Garnaut explained that for some years Australia had not taken New Zealand seriously because of differences on the defense issue and relations with the United States. But he confirmed that closer economic integration with East Asia had been a major theme for the Australian government, and in particular the success of outwardly oriented policies there had led to their embodiment in the reform model.

*Alan Bollard* confirmed the importance of international influences on domestic reform efforts in New Zealand. While Australia might have ignored New Zealand, the reverse was not true, and indeed New Zealanders took some pride in having implemented reforms that Australia had attempted but not consolidated. International financial markets and credit institutions had been very supportive, despite the high level of New Zealand's total overseas debt, which stood at 83 percent of GDP. The Uruguay Round was critical for both countries, and its failure might well have serious ramifications.

# 4

# THE EUROPEAN PERIPHERY

# Spain

## GUILLERMO DE LA DEHESA

Spain has probably experienced more fundamental political and economic changes in the fourth quarter of this century than any other country in Western Europe. To better understand the importance of these radical changes, a review of Spain's social, political, cultural, and economic background is appropriate.

Spain entered the contemporary era after having missed most of the major events and developments that shaped the liberal democracies and market economies of Europe. Spanish society was almost untouched by the French bourgeois revolution and the later development of liberal democracy. The Spanish economy missed most of the boost created by the industrial revolution. Capitalism penetrated the country only marginally through an industrial periphery in the Catalonian and Basque regions in the north. Spanish culture developed separately from the two dominant European currents: the Protestant Reformation and the development of the empirical sciences (Pérez Díaz 1987).

Thus, after suffering through a bloody civil war, Spain entered the second half of this century under a dictatorial political system; with a society characterized by anticapitalist sentiments based on a strong counterreformist Catholicism, with an authoritarian and absolutist system of values far removed from individual liberty and tolerance, with veneration of interventionism and the bureaucratic state; and with an

*Guillermo de la Dehesa is Vice Chairman of Goldman Sachs Europe Ltd in London and Vice Chairman of the Centre for Economic Policy Research. He was Secretary of Commerce (1982–86) and Secretary of Economy and Finance (1986–88) of Spain.*

economy that was basically rural and autarkic, based on state protection and intervention.

The differences between today's Spain and the Spain of only thirty-five years ago are striking. In a very short time the country has modernized and converted itself into a Western capitalist democracy, with an open economy integrated into European and world markets, and more tolerant and liberal values. As Pérez Díaz puts it, "Spain has applied a shock treatment in a very short time to the trauma of all her historical frustrations and repressions" (Pérez Díaz 1987). This change was possible thanks to highly skilled political maneuvering by its leaders, to a great deal of understanding and moderation on the part of the Spanish citizenry, and to a lot of luck, which is always needed in any successful reform.

This paper is divided into five sections. The first four sections describe in some detail the four major reformist periods, and the concluding section tries to single out the most important lessons to be learned from the Spanish experience.

## The Initial Breakthrough

The first important economic reform implemented in contemporary Spain came in 1959. After the civil war and continuing after World War II, Generalissimo Francisco Franco developed an autarkic economic policy based on import substitution, direct government intervention in prices and quantities, and nationalistic industrial development under the impulse of the state. This policy was not only a consequence of Franco's initial fascist ideology but also a necessary result of the isolation imposed upon his political regime by the industrial democracies.

After more than a decade of these wrongheaded economic policies, the Spanish economy found itself in an extremely difficult situation. In spite of widespread price controls, inflation was very high, and in spite of a huge panoply of trade restrictions (through licensing, quotas, import taxes, and export subsidies), the trade deficit was very large, the peseta was overvalued, and foreign currency reserves were exhausted. Franco was reluctant to accept the necessity of a stabilization plan, a devaluation of the peseta, and a liberalization of price controls, import duties, and quotas. Finally, however, the threat of international insolvency made him accept reform.

Three key elements made that reform possible. First, a group of high-level civil servants working at the Ministry of Commerce and the Bank of Spain, under the leadership of Manuel Varela and Juan Sardá, were able to convince other key people in government and in business of the need to change Spain's economic policy (Varela 1990; Sardá 1970). The second element was pressure from the Organization for European Economic

Cooperation (the forerunner of today's Organization for Economic Cooperation and Development) and the International Monetary Fund (IMF) to introduce a stabilization plan as a condition for joining both international institutions. The reports of the economic teams that visited Spain from both institutions, together with those elaborated by the Bank of Spain and the Ministry of Commerce, were enough to convince the more enlightened members of the government, notably Alberto Ullastres, the minister of commerce, and Mariano Navarro, the minister of finance, who both belonged to the new breed of "opus dei" technocrats that had just joined Franco's government. When these ministers explained to Franco that the situation was one of total insolvency, that there were no foreign currency reserves left in the Bank of Spain, and that, just to pay the entrance fees to the IMF, the World Bank, and the OEEC, a loan by three American banks was being negotiated, he finally gave in to the need for stabilization (Viñas et al. 1979; González 1979).

The main measures introduced by the 1959 stabilization plan had been recommended in the memoranda drafted by the OEEC and IMF teams and consisted basically of a devaluation of the peseta, the introduction of a single exchange rate, a program of monetary and fiscal restraint, and a liberalization of price controls and trade restrictions (de la Dehesa et al. 1991).

From that time until his death in November 1975, Franco slowly loosened his regime's grip on the Spanish people. It was clear that the country was destined to move, gradually, toward an open economy integrated into world markets. A large part of the rural population became urbanized, almost 2 million unemployed workers migrated to other European countries, and millions of foreign tourists invaded the Spanish coasts. Industrialists were able to import more foreign machinery, and consumers were able to buy more foreign goods. Foreign investors started to invest, cautiously, in Spain. The Spanish people started to learn to be Europeans, and finally to admire and to identify themselves with European institutions and the European way of life. Most citizens realized that the paleocorporatist, authoritarian, counterreformist, and autarkic ideals that Franco had reinforced after the civil war had been a total failure (Pérez Díaz 1990).

In 1970, a preferential agreement with the European Community gave a second boost to trade liberalization, which had stalled in 1966 after the initial thrust of 1959. Here again the high-level team of economists at the Ministry of Commerce played a major role in negotiating a very beneficial trade agreement for Spain (de la Dehesa et al. 1991).

## The Transition to Democracy

Spain's opportunities to become a democracy have come at inopportune times economically. The first attempt, in 1931, coincided with the Great

Depression. The second, successful attempt came when Franco died at the end of 1975, at the height of a recession provoked by the first energy crisis. On both occasions unfavorable economic conditions interfered with politics and complicated the transition (de la Dehesa 1991a). The first democratic experiment ended in a horrendous civil war, whose one positive result was that its traumatic historical lesson encouraged political and social forces to seek consensus in 1975 and avoid another such disaster.

The economic situation at the beginning of the transition to democracy in 1975 was grave. The energy crisis had hit the Spanish economy harder than others in Europe, since oil represented 70 percent of Spain's total energy demand, and all of it had to be imported, while the average of the EEC was well below 50 percent. Meanwhile Franco's ailing health had paralyzed all government decision making, and no adjustment measures were taken in 1974 or 1975 to react to the oil crisis. Part of Spain's industrial production was already quite obsolete because of its autarkic origins, and much of the rest was developed under an energy-intensive pattern. The weakness of the last administrations of the Franco regime and their commitment to avoiding social unrest translated into steep wage increases and more inflation. The emergent democratic trade unions, which had never had the opportunity to fight for better wages and working conditions, were purely ideologically minded and revolutionary, and in any case there were no business organizations to negotiate with.

Franco's best economic legacy was his fiscal conservatism. He left Spain's public finances in a very healthy condition, with a very small public debt and a relatively light tax burden.

If the economic situation was difficult, the political and social situation was even worse. The death of Franco gave rise to three important destabilizing factors that had to be confronted: the revival of peripheral nationalisms in Catalonia, the Basque country, and Galicia, all of which had been oppressed by Franco for many years; terrorism by the Basque nationalists and the extreme right; and, finally, the permanent threat of a military takeover. Adding to these political problems were severe social tensions. These derived, first, from the rapid increase in unemployment, due not only to the recession but also to the return of hundred of thousands of emigrants who had been laid off in other countries of Europe, and, second, by the huge and unmeetable expectations on the part of the population at large that democracy would bring a solution to their problems.

Franco had always thought that the institutional machinery of his dictatorship, the *democracia orgánica*, would survive after his death (Pradera 1989). In 1974, he passed a Law of Succession by which Spain was turned into a monarchy and he himself was appointed head of state for life. Previously, in 1969, he had decided to appoint as his successor

Prince Juan Carlos de Borbón y Borbón, son of Juan de Borbón and grandson of King Alfonso XIII, who had been exiled in 1931 when a republican form of government was chosen in a referendum.

The succession mechanism worked as planned when Franco died on 20 November 1975: Juan Carlos was proclaimed king of Spain by the Cortes (the Spanish parliament) on 22 November. Franco appointees remained as president of the government and president of the Cortes. King Juan Carlos's first move was to put his longtime tutor and professor of politics, Torcuato Fernández Miranda, at the head of the Cortes. Fernández Miranda, a very skilled politician who had been a minister under Franco, was able to get Adolfo Suárez, a young but very able politician with an impeccable Francoist past, appointed president of the government.

King Juan Carlos, Fernández Miranda, and Adolfo Suárez were all three convinced that Spain had to restructure its political system to conform with those of the European democracies, and they worked hard and skillfully toward that objective. They were able to convince the Francoist members of the Cortes to approve measures that legalized the existence of political parties and provided for the first democratic elections under the new regime. Those elections, held in July 1977, were won by Suárez's new party, the Unión de Centro Democrático (UCD). The new democratic parliament prepared a new Constitution, which was approved by a large majority in a referendum in December 1978.

Such a peaceful transition was only possible thanks to a consensus among the majority of the political forces—including the conservative right and the Communists, with the almost unanimous backing of the citizenry (Pradera 1989)—to forswear violence. Only the extreme right and the extreme left and part of the military establishment tried to stop the democratization effort through terrorism and the attempted coup of February 1981.

In view of the serious political and economic situation, the first democratic government under President Suárez had to make an important strategic choice between shock therapy and gradualism. Any attempt at rapid economic adjustment through radical structural changes and restrictive monetary and fiscal policies would risk further increasing social and political unrest; on the other hand, a more moderate and gradual economic reform aimed at avoiding social tension in the short term could jeopardize the incipient political transition (Maravall 1991).

President Suárez chose the second option. He gave priority to solving the country's urgent political and social demands over the need for economic adjustment. He realized that everything could not be done at once, especially when democracy was still very fragile, his center-right political party did not have a majority in the parliament, and its competition with the Spanish Workers' Socialist Party (PSOE) was fierce. Suárez tried, understandably, to ensure not only the survival of the new democracy but also the survival in power of his own political party.

Nevertheless, Suárez's policy of concluding political, social, and economic "pacts" (*acuerdos*) with the opposition did introduce some discipline in the economic sphere. In 1977 the Acuerdos de la Moncloa were signed by the government and the opposition parties, with the implicit consent of the socialist (UGT) and Communist (CCOO) trade unions and the newly formed employers' association (CEOE). The main objectives of the Moncloa pacts were to moderate wages, ending their indexation to past inflation, and to obtain wide acceptance of a free-market economy and a more orthodox economic policy in exchange for the creation of an institutional framework for industrial relations ("the workers' statute"), the recognition of the principal trade unions and employer associations as the genuine representatives of those interests, and the conduct of a moderate monetary and fiscal policy of "gradual adjustment" to the existing economic disequilibria.

In 1979 another pact, the Acuerdo Básico Interconfederal, was signed by the CEOE and the UGT; another, the Acuerdo Marco Interconfederal, followed in 1980 between the CEOE, the UGT, and the CCOO; and in 1981 a pact called the Acuerdo Nacional de Empleo was signed by the government, employers, and trade unions. All of these three pacts were trade-offs between wage moderation and improvements in working conditions and unemployment benefits (figure 1).

The economic results of this "neocorporatist" policy of social pacts (Pérez Díaz 1987) were positive overall but had some shortcomings. On the one hand, the pacts favored the consolidation of a market economy and the legitimation of the capitalist system in the new Constitution of 1978. Capitalism had never been fully accepted by Spanish society, and the traditional Catholic culture had always been distrustful of the market economy. The Franco regime not only had failed to help consolidate capitalism, but had contaminated what little legitimacy capitalism enjoyed, since his was not a "competitive" but an "assisted" capitalism (Maravall 1991), where business success owed more to government favoritism than to satisfying consumers' needs. The Moncloa pacts and the new Constitution encouraged the acceptance by the population at large of the idea of capitalism and the market economy as the best option available, and helped make possible political negotiations at all levels of economic life through the elected representatives of different interest groups. The agreements also helped moderate the ideological stance of the trade unions and leftist parties and their attitudes toward the business community and their role in a market economy, as well as to adapt their aspirations to the will of the prospective voters and not to their more militant supporters. All these factors helped to moderate wage increases and to reduce inflation from near 25 percent in 1977 to 16 percent in 1982. Finally, the sharp devaluation of the peseta brought the current account into surplus in 1979, from a $3 billion deficit in 1976.

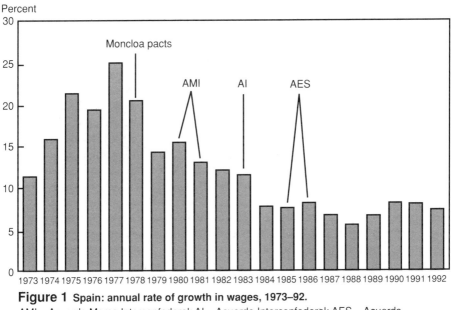

**Figure 1** Spain: annual rate of growth in wages, 1973–92.
AMI = Acuerdo Marco Interconfederal; AI = Acuerdo Interconfederal; AES = Acuerdo Económico y Social.
Source: Ministry of Labor, Madrid.

The two major problems of the pacts were their maintenance of the status quo in the labor market, with all the rigidities inherited from Francoism, and their contribution to a gradual increase in the fiscal deficit due to large increases in social expenditure. The deficit rose from 3 percent of GDP in 1975 to 6 percent in 1982, and the public debt from 24 percent of GDP in 1975 to 36 percent in 1982.

It is interesting that some of the same economists who had engineered the stabilization plan of 1959 were again behind the more orthodox measures agreed to in the Moncloa pacts, such as the devaluation of the peseta, the reduction of tariffs and quotas, the deindexation of wages, fiscal reform, and the deoligopolization of the banking system. Enrique Fuentes Quintana, a well-known professor of public finance, was appointed deputy premier for economic affairs and was the real intellectual force behind the Moncloa pacts (Fuentes Quintana and Requeijo 1984).

## Economic Reforms Under the Socialist Government

At the end of 1982 the PSOE won the general elections with a comfortable majority. Its leader and the new prime minister, Felipe González

Márquez, while in the opposition had attacked Suárez's policies for not being "social" and "progressive" enough and had asked for increased social expenditures and the nationalization of some productive sectors. Once in power, however, González behaved as a moderate social democrat and introduced some quite significant orthodox economic reforms. González was influenced by the German Social Democratic Party's revision in 1959 at the Bad Godesberg Congress, and by the moderation of social democrats Olaf Palme of Sweden, Tony Crossland of the UK, and Willy Brandt of Germany, who were his main mentors. The economic failure of the French Socialist government's radical expansionary and nationalizing policies in early 1982 further reinforced González's moderation in economic policy.

Modernization of the Spanish economy, full integration into the European Community, and "catching up" with the rest of Western Europe were the main thrust of the economic reforms that the Socialist government launched after 1982. Five of its 15 ministers were well-trained economists, and González put at the head of the powerful Ministry of Finance (which was responsible for the treasury, the budget, tax policy and tax collection, and foreign trade and investment policy) a group of economists known for their moderation and pragmatism. The team was led by Finance Minister Miguel Boyer, an orthodox economist from the Bank of Spain, who also played a key role in moderating the radical economic ideas of most of his Socialist colleagues and above all González himself. In 1986, Boyer left the government voluntarily and was replaced by Carlos Solchaga Catalán, another former Bank of Spain research economist trained at the Massachusetts Institute of Technology, who continued the line of moderation and economic orthodoxy begun by his predecessor.

Miguel Boyer's three years in total command of the economy were a period of hard adjustment to create the conditions for sustainable growth. The dramatic fall of the UCD and the huge capital outflows that followed the attempted military coup in February 1981 and anticipated the arrival of a socialist government had left a large current account deficit and a low level of foreign currency reserves, and had increased inflation and the budget deficit.

The new Socialist government attacked the problems on four fronts simultaneously: at the macroeconomic level through a mix of restrictive monetary policy and moderately restrictive fiscal policy, to regain basic equilibrium; through structural reforms in the labor market and in the financial and industrial sectors; through a continuation of incomes policy through pacts with the trade unions and employers' organizations; and through accelerated negotiations toward integration with the European Community.

The Socialists' first measure consisted of a new devaluation of the peseta, which, together with a strong dollar, helped increase the competitiveness of Spanish exports, reduce the current account deficit, and raise the level of reserves. The restrictive monetary policy brought inflation down by 6 percentage points in three years, to 9 percent. Moderation in fiscal policy reduced the budget deficit from 6 percent of GDP in 1982 to 4.6 percent in 1985.

On the structural reform front the main measures were the introduction of part-time and temporary labor contracts, the restructuring of major overbuilt industries (iron and steel, shipbuilding, and textiles), the liberalization of housing rents, the liberalization of retail shopping hours, the liberalization of foreign investment, and a program of privatization of state-owned companies. Some of these reforms were viewed as a prerequisite for joining the Community (de la Dehesa et al. 1991, 1992).

Finally, the continuation of incomes policy agreements gave birth in 1983 to a new agreement between the employers' associations and trade unions, the Acuerdo Interconfederal and in 1984 to a new pact between the government, the CEOE, and the UGT, the Acuerdo Económico y Social, which moderated wages in return for some government concessions, such as allowing trade union representatives to sit on the boards of state-owned companies.

The effects of these reforms were a major reduction in economic imbalances, an improvement in market flexibility, and the preparation of the country for EC integration. The treaty providing for Spain's accession was finally signed in the fall of 1985 and came into force in January 1986.

## The Effects of EC Integration

Spain's integration into the European Community was perceived by the rest of the world as a clear sign of the consolidation of democracy and the continuity of sound economic policies whatever the party in power. The new confidence on the part of the international community together with the effects of three years of adjustment, plus the fall in the price of oil and the depreciation of the dollar, gave a boost to the Spanish economy. Spain's GDP grew between 1986 and 1990 at an average annual rate of 5 percent, helped by the surge in domestic and foreign investment, which increased at an annual rate of 14 percent during the same period. Foreign investment was a major factor behind the modernization of the productive structure, since it accounted for an average of 2 percent of GDP, 15 percent of total investment, and 30 percent of industrial investment over the same period.

Through EC integration, Spain has continued its sweeping program of economic reforms. Trade liberalization has been almost total, since Spanish integration has coincided with the introduction of the single

European market and the creation of the European Economic Space through the Community's opening to the European Free Trade Association. The liberalization of long- and short-term capital outflows, together with the inclusion of the peseta in the European Monetary System and the European exchange rate mechanism, has been another major achievement of this period. The liberalization of short-term interest rates, the reform of the stock exchange and other capital markets, the liberalization of regulations on foreign banking, the compulsory establishment of pension funds and external auditing for medium and large companies, and, finally, the recent law establishing the independence of the Bank of Spain and the abolition of seigniorage have been the major reforms in the financial markets.

The government has announced for 1993 a new wave of privatizations of major state holdings, including Repsol (oil), Argentaria (banking), and Teneo (industry). It has pursued privatization even though the relative weight of state enterprises in the productive structure is already one of the smallest in Europe. A series of measures to reform the labor market was also announced, including a reduction in and increased control over unemployment benefits (implemented in early 1993); a reduction of firing costs; the abolition of regulations that limit functional labor mobility; an improvement of geographical labor mobility; and a new law providing penalties for illegal and wildcat strikes in essential public services.

This period also witnessed the rupture of the policy of concluding general pacts and agreements with trade unions and business organizations. Among the results of this change in policy was, for the first time since Franco's years, a general strike in December 1988 and a significant ideological break within the PSOE between the "pure" socialists and the social democrats or "liberal" socialists. This division has continued to create conflicts and strains between the party, its affiliated trade union (UGT), and the government. In the last two years the government has made strong efforts to reestablish consensus with the unions and employers by offering a new series of pacts, notably the "Social Progress" or "Competitiveness" pact in 1990, so far without any results. Prime Minister González sees very clearly that, in order to introduce flexibility into the labor market and moderation into wage demands, it is still necessary to negotiate a consensus with the other major economic agents, even more so now that the real challenge of the single European market and European monetary union (EMU) is the relative competitiveness of Spanish goods and services vis-à-vis the rest of Europe and the world. The loss of sovereignty in monetary and fiscal policy imposed by EMU leaves very little margin for political maneuver, except in so-called structural policies aimed at improving market flexibility and "horizontal" industrial policies to improve productivity through investment in research and development and enhancement of worker and management skills.

The Spanish government has also realized that the costs of a policy of disinflation and adjustment have been very high in terms of unemployment (Spain has the highest unemployment rate in the Community), mainly because of rigidities in the labor market and the increased burden of a greatly expanded welfare state. This is the reason why, in the "convergence program" that the government presented to the EC Commission following the agreements established in the Maastricht Treaty relating to the second stage of EMU, structural reforms of the labor market and the restructuring of government expenditure toward investment and away from consumption are the two main sets of measures proposed.

How to implement these reforms without losing the traditional political backing of the unions in the 1993 general elections is the most important dilemma facing the PSOE. Without those votes the Socialists could lose their elections or the governing majority, and without that majority the probability of these important reforms being implemented will diminish. Finally, in the 6 June election, many trade union affiliates and most people on the left of the political spectrum voted Socialist more to avoid a victory by the right (Partido Popular) than to support a Socialist platform they did not like. Nevertheless, although the Socialists won they did not get enough votes to retain the majority. This is the reason why the new government is trying to return to the policy of consensus and the conclusion of general pacts among the various political forces and economic agents. It seems that the young Spanish democracy is not able to advance in the process of economic reform if there is not a previous wide consensus.

## Lessons from the Spanish Experience

### The Importance of Political and Social Consensus

After a bloody civil war and twenty years of autarky and economic and political isolation, the Spanish people realized that this was not the right road to a better life. The arrival in Spain of European tourists and European enterprises and the experience of Spanish migrants in other European countries confirmed the suspicion that life on the other side of the Pyrenees was much more free and buoyant, and that Franco's regime was an obstacle to realizing that kind of life for the Spanish people. Of all of Franco's political slogans, "Spain is different" was the one that the majority of Spanish citizens hated most—they wished instead to be exactly the same as the rest of Western Europe. All those years of "being different" convinced the forces building the new Spanish democracy of the necessity of a common objective: to be European and to follow the model of the Western European way of life.

Moreover, while in some Western countries the idea of a "progressive" economic policy has been combined with strong intervention by the state to compensate for the imperfections of the market and to avoid monopoly and oligarchy, in Spain liberal democracy had only a single really progressive option: to try to liberate potential economic forces from an interventionist and inefficient system inherited from the previous regime. The liberalization of Spain's highly regulated markets was much more urgent and necessary than any other measure. This is why, in 1977, all the political parties from the Communists to the conservatives voted unanimously in favor of Spanish accession to the European Community and agreed to adopt, in the 1978 democratic Constitution, an economic model (the "social market economy") based on the predominance of market forces and the opening of the Spanish economy to the rest of the world.

The wish to belong to Europe was so strong that, in the NATO referendum of 1984, in spite of their traditional preference for neutrality, the majority of Spaniards voted in favor of remaining in NATO, since they thought that upon integrating with Western Europe they had a moral obligation to participate in its defense. The general consensus that Spain should be part of Europe has been, therefore, a major factor in achieving economic and political reform in Spain.

## The Need to Consolidate Democracy

The Spanish experience shows that, once the democratic rules of the political game have become established and accepted, economic reform is easier to implement. If they are not, political and social tensions may abort the adjustment measures for lack of political legitimacy or of credibility. In the Spanish case, it was only after the new Constitution was established, an elected democratic government was in place, the military threat overcome, and regional nationalistic claims calmed that it was possible to implement serious economic reforms without jeopardizing the whole democratic transition.

## The Importance of Broad Electoral Support

Governments that are supported by a broad electoral majority can undertake the necessary reforms and liberalizations with greater determination and rigor. The case of the Spanish socialist governments since 1983 is paradigmatic of this proposition.

In the process of transition from dictatorship to democracy there is a natural tendency for citizens to form a large number of fragmented parties and coalitions to express their different political and social points of view. This natural tendency conflicts with the necessity to concentrate voters' choices on a restricted number of options so that the government that finally comes to power represents a wide swath of the political spectrum and can push through the economic reforms that are always needed after years of political and economic inertia under the dictatorial system (Maravall 1991).

This is why it is so important to build a consensus on an adequate electoral system that supports the formation of a few wide-reaching political options. The choice of the "d'Hont rule" in the Spanish case has helped to concentrate the vote on a shorter menu of political options capable of winning the support of a majority. For example, as a result of this rule, in the first democratic parliamentary elections the UCD (Suárez's center party) won 34 percent of the vote but 47 percent of the seats, while the PSOE won 29 percent of the vote and 34 percent of the seats. The third and fourth parties (the right-wing Andalusian Party and the Communist Party) received fewer seats relative to their polling results.

## The Use of Social and Political Pacts

In countries in transition toward democracy, or even in young established democracies where "civil society" is still very weak and political life is not well institutionalized, a policy of broad social consensus through political and social agreements among a spectrum of economic and social agents seems to allow for greater efficiency in the implementation of economic reforms. Sometimes it is more efficient to implement reforms that are less radical than would be optimal for economic reasons but that enjoy consensus among political and social forces and therefore high credibility. It is not much use for the government to prepare measures that are never implemented because they are not accepted by large parts of the citizenry. Efficiency in implementation is much more important than efficiency in elaboration and approval. This is why the help of the intermediate social institutions that form the core of the civil society is necessary to convince the citizens of the need to accept short-term sacrifices for the sake of long-term benefits. This is the key difficulty facing transition governments that have to change the status quo and hurt a lot of entrenched interests and groups that were benefiting therefrom.

This kind of "liberal neocorporatist" (Pérez Díaz 1986) style of policymaking, although it may imply a gradualist approach, may still be a second-best, workable solution for economies in transition to achieve economic reform.

In the Spanish case, general public opinion was favorably inclined toward liberalizing and opening up the economy and reaching a consensus on certain economic reforms. The long history of government interventionism and regulation of markets under Franco was perceived

**Table 1  Spain: government social expenditures, 1975–91**

| Year | Billions of pesetas | Percentage of GDP |
|------|--------------------|-------------------|
| 1975 | 558.2 | 9.2 |
| 1976 | 723.9 | 10.0 |
| 1977 | 954.1 | 10.3 |
| 1978 | 1,345.7 | 11.9 |
| 1979 | 1,565.7 | 11.9 |
| 1980 | 1,860.7 | 12.3 |
| 1981 | 2,335.3 | 13.7 |
| 1982 | 2,647.5 | 13.4 |
| 1983 | 3,109.8 | 13.8 |
| 1984 | 3,513.0 | 13.8 |
| 1985 | 4,045.2 | 14.3 |
| 1986 | 4,503.6 | 13.9 |
| 1987 | 4,972.9 | 13.8 |
| 1988 | 5,558.2 | 13.8 |
| 1989 | 6,273.6 | 13.9 |
| 1990 | 7,311.8 | 14.6 |
| 1991 | 8,385.4 | 15.3 |

*Source*: IGAE.

as a failure, but, naturally, its reversal came at the expense of additional social expenditure (table 1) and greater political representation.

As Maravall (1991) puts it: "The Southern European experience does not conform to the argument that new democracies based on pacts will leave very little room for reform and that transition will be at the cost of socioeconomic changes. The only problem is that due to the pacts those economic reforms became very expensive in terms of social policies and public expenditure. This may be one of the distinctive differences between reforms in the new Southern European democracies (Spain, Portugal and Greece) and reforms in Latin America and Eastern Europe. After the transitions, Southern European reforms not only sought to improve the performance of economies but to increase the protection of social citizenship rights."

## The Importance of International Obligations and Compromises

A common characteristic of all postwar episodes of Spanish economic reform has been the contracting of obligations and compromises with international or multilateral organizations, who have imposed, reinforced, or maintained the reform and liberalization measures adopted by the government, giving them greater credibility. In the first attempt at reform under Franco in 1959, Spain's agreements with the OEEC and the IMF contained all the measures that would be taken later with regard to trade and price liberalization, exchange rate policies, and opening up to foreign investment. In the second effort at trade liberalization in 1970, the preferential trade agreement with the European Community contained the liberalization program that was later developed.

In the third period of economic reforms, under the democratic Suárez and González governments, no international agreement was followed, but the expectation of integration with the European Community and, above all, the choice by the Spanish people to follow the European model influenced to a great extent the decision to continue liberalizing and reforming. Finally, in the fourth period of economic reforms, under the socialist government (1986–92), first the treaty of accession to the Community and later the Single European Act, and EMU, allowed for some of the most important measures that have ever been taken to reform the Spanish economy. What is also important about these integration compromises is that they have been ratified by both the Spanish and the EC parliaments, with no possibility of revocation, which gives them even greater credibility.

## The Decisive Role of the "External Constraint"

Another feature of Spanish economic experience has been the enormous influence the state of the current account, the level of reserves, or both, have had at the moments when critical economic decisions were made, involving structural reforms and adjustments as well as decisions regarding the liberalization of the economy. The "golden rule" (de la Dehesa et al. 1991) of recent Spanish economic history is: "Only when the level of reserves was sufficiently low and/or the current account balance was in large deficit have necessary economic adjustment and structural reform measures been taken, and only when the level of reserves was sufficiently high and the current account in surplus or equilibrium have necessary trade economic liberalization measures been taken." It seems that the Spanish experience has followed the motto, "Liberalize when you can, and adjust when you must" (figures 2 and 3).

Other important imbalances such as high unemployment, large budget deficits, and high inflation have never been as decisive in moving policy in one direction or the other as has the external constraint. Franco accepted reforms only under the threat of external bankruptcy. Adolfo Suárez introduced adjustment reforms when the current account deficit was extremely large. Felipe González adjusted when the level of reserves fell to less than $3 billion.

## Adjustment First, Liberalization Later

During the last thirty years, Spanish economic policy has always adhered to the sequence of macroeconomic adjustment followed by

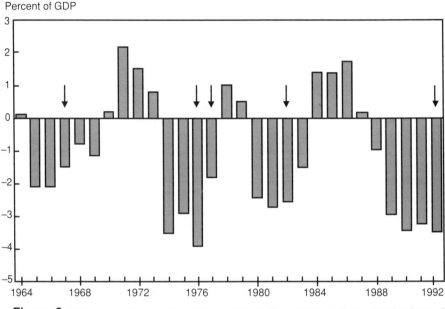

Percent of GDP

**Figure 2** Spain: current account balance, 1964-92. The arrows indicate devaluations of the peseta.

*Source:* Bank of Spain.

structural reform and liberalization. This sequencing can be summed up as follows.

First, the initially bad economic conditions (a low level or reserves, a growing balance of payments deficit, or both) require a process of macroeconomic adjustment. This adjustment usually consists of an orthodox stabilization, that is, a strong devaluation followed by a restrictive fiscal and monetary policy mix. Only when the balance of payments improves are internal and external economic liberalization measures initiated. The latter usually consists of a reduction of trade barriers and exchange controls and a liberalization of domestic markets.

After some years of economic liberalization there follows a worsening in the external sector and a slowing down or a halt (there has never been a clear reversion in the case of Spain) of the reform and liberalization process, and the sequence begins again. It is important to point out that the lack of retrogression in external economic liberalization is the result of always having used the exchange rate to balance the external deficit rather than introducing quotas or increasing import duties. "Protection" through the exchange rate has always replaced direct import protection.

There has been only one exception to this sequence since Spain won membership in the European Community. The decisive liberalization both of foreign trade and of capital flows beginning in 1986 has been

Billions of dollars

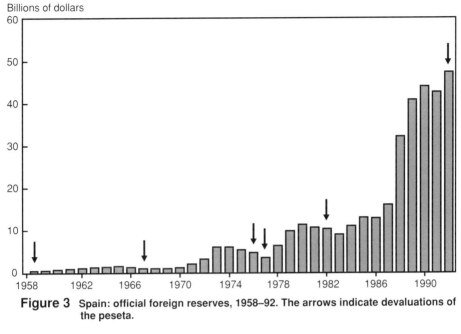

**Figure 3** Spain: official foreign reserves, 1958–92. The arrows indicate devaluations of the peseta.

Source: Bank of Spain.

realized not under a depreciation but instead under a growing revaluation of the peseta; finally, however, two sequential devaluations within the ERM in the fall of 1992 were needed to regain lost competitiveness.

## The Role of Economic Technopols

Two different breeds of economists have played a key role in the evolution toward economic rationality in recent Spanish economic history (Fuentes Quintana 1991, Varela 1990). On the one hand there was the group of "técnicos comerciales y economistas del estado"—high-level economic civil servants who, starting at the Ministry of Commerce in the 1950s and 1960s and later finding their way to other ministries (finance, industry and energy, agriculture, labor, etc.) introduced an element of economic rationality into most political decisions. At times these officials have risen to cabinet positions as ministers or secretaries of state and even, in two cases (Enrique Fuentes Quintana and Juan Antonio García Díez), became economic vice presidents under President Suárez.

On the other hand was the group of economists emanating from the research unit of the Bank of Spain, who have not only filled key posts at the central bank but also, under Prime Minister González, have accepted cabinet posts such as minister of finance (Miguel Boyer and Carlos Solchaga) or governor of the Bank of Spain (Mariano Rubio and Angel Rojo).

The role of these two groups of technocrats and technopols was also extremely important in the EC integration negotiations, in the achievement of a wider international credibility for Spanish economic policy, and in the creation of climate of public opinion favoring economic reform, through their writings in both academic and nonacademic journals such as the *Información Comercial Española* of the Ministry of Commerce, the *Boletín Económico* of the Bank of Spain, and the *Papeles de Economía Española*, among others, and through the specialized press and other printed media.

# References

de la Dehesa, Guillermo. 1988. "El Big Bang español." España Económica, Madrid (June).
de la Dehesa, Guillermo. 1991a. "Spain." In *The Transition to a Market Economy*, vol. 1. Paris: Organization for Economic Cooperation and Development.
de la Dehesa, Guillermo. 1991b. "Trade Policies in Spain." In Dominic Salvatore, ed., *International Handbook of National Trade Policies*. New York: North Holland.
de la Dehesa, Guillermo, José Juan Ruiz, and Angel Torres. 1991. "The Timing and Sequencing of Trade Liberalization: The Case of Spain." In Michael Michaely, Demetri Papageorgiou, and Armin Choksi, eds., *Liberalizing Foreign Trade*. London: Basil Blackwell.
de la Dehesa, Guillermo. 1992. "Privatization in Europe, the Case of Spain." London: Centre for Economic Policy Research (mimeographed). Forthcoming in *Moneda y Crédito* (Madrid).
Fuentes Quintana, Enrique. 1991. "Economía y Economistas Españoles." *Revista de Economía*, Madrid.
Fuentes Quintana, Enrique, and Jaime Requeijo. 1984. "La Larga Marcha Hacia una Política Económica Inevitable." *Papeles de Economía Española* 21 (Madrid).
González, Manuel Jesús. 1979. *La Economía Política del Franquismo*. Madrid: Tecnos.
López Claros, Augusto. 1988. "The Search for Efficiency in the Adjustment Process: Spain in the 1980s." *IMF Occasional Papers*. Washington: International Monetary Fund.
Maravall, José María. 1991. "Economic Reforms in New Democracies: The Southern European Experience." *Working Papers* 22. Madrid: Centro de Estudios Avanzados en Ciencias Sociales, Fundación Juan March.
Pérez Díaz, Víctor. 1986. "The Double Face of Neocorporatism." *Journal of European Sociology* 2, no. 1.
Pérez Díaz, Víctor. 1987. "El Retorno de la Sociedad Civil." Madrid: Instituto de Estudios Económicos.
Pérez Díaz, Víctor. 1990. "The Emergence of Democratic Spain and the 'Invention' of a Democratic Tradition." Madrid: Centro de Estudios Avanzados en Ciencias Sociales, Fundación Juan March.
Pradera, Javier. 1989. "Transición en España." *UNO* (January).
Sardá, Juan. 1970. "El Banco de España 1931-1962." In *El Banco de España: Una Historia Económica*. Madrid: Bank of Spain.
Varela, Manuel. 1990. "El Plan de Estabilización como yo lo Recuerdo." *Información Comercial Española* (Madrid) December 1989-January 1990.
Viñas, Angel, Julio Viñuela, Fernando Eguidazu, Carlos Fernández Pulgar, and Senén Florensa. 1979. *Política Comercial Exterior de España (1931-1975)*. Madrid: Banco Exterior de España.

# Portugal

FRANCISCO TORRES

On the eve of Portugal's accession to the European Community in 1986, a newly elected minority government of Partido Social Democrata (PSD), led by Aníbal Cavaco Silva, identified the completion of the European single market in 1992 as a renewed opportunity for economic reform.

To meet this challenge, the government proposed a reformist strategy entailing a very gradual liberalization of the economy and greater attention to the cost of government intervention. The PSD election platform, however, had focused on sustained growth rather than on liberalization.

The PSD government needed to demonstrate that the economy could grow again in order to garner broader support for economic reform. Cavaco Silva had been elected as the new leader of the PSD in 1985, and promptly led the PSD out of the Socialist-led coalition, which he severely criticized for not delivering sustained economic growth.

In the July 1987 election,[1] the landslide victory of PSD, which had become more focused on liberalization during the electoral campaign,

*Francisco Torres is Professor and Director of Centro de Estudos Europeus at Universidade Católica Portuguesa in Lisbon and Economic Adviser in Portugal's Ministry of Finance. The views here expressed are personal and reflect neither those of the Ministry of Finance nor those of the Bank of Portugal, with whom he has been affiliated since 1983. This author benefited from many of the contributions to this volume, especially those of John Williamson and Nancy Bermeo.*

1. The short-lived minority government of PSD faced a vote of no confidence in Parliament that led to new elections.

paved the way for a second amendment to the Constitution in 1989.[2] After the experience of 1983–85, in which the two major parties—the Partido Socialista (PS) and PSD—had to respond to an acute crisis and concentrate efforts on membership negotiations with the European Community, it became easier to reach consensus. And, despite the defeat of the presidential candidate of PSD and its former small coalition partner of 1980–83, Centro Democrático Social (CDS), this time by a very narrow margin, the PSD government and the new president, Mário Soares, developed a solid collaboration.

Anticipating the difficulty of instituting the necessary constitutional amendment, the government in 1987 initiated a privatization program by selling up to 49 percent of the capital of state-owned enterprises.

Apart from that imposed by the Constitution, there was another major constraint to liberalization. The PSD's reform strategy stressed social cohesion, and most political forces, including the trade unions, were still very much opposed to liberalization. This contributed greatly to the slow pace of reforms.[3]

As a result of these constraints and of some other institutional and government factors discussed below, liberalization of the economy was delayed for several years.

In 1992 the Portuguese escudo entered the exchange rate mechanism of the European Monetary System. Joining the EMS consolidated the change of economic regime initiated with Portugal's accession to the European Community in 1986. Nevertheless, it was not until the complete liberalization of capital controls in December 1992—just before the start of the European single market—that the protracted basic macroeconomic reform was finally accomplished.

## Government Policy in the 1980s

Current Prime Minister Cavaco Silva, formerly an economics professor and head of the research department at the central bank, had in 1980 been finance minister in the first government of Aliança Democrática—a PSD-led coalition with the Christian Democratic CDS. He then was responsible for an anti-inflation program that delivered the government's electoral promises of price stabilization.

In this respect, Cavaco Silva, although regarded as a technocrat by many, may be labeled a technopol: he identified the political constraints facing the government and orchestrated the timing of reforms to address

2. It was not until 1989 that there was a qualified (two-thirds) majority in Parliament, reached through an agreement with the Socialists, to amend the Constitution of 1976 to allow privatizations.

3. As Macedo (1990) puts it, the government was anxious to avoid being branded as probusiness.

electoral concerns and thus to secure the necessary majority to over-come both constitutional constraints and vested interests.

The PSD-CDS coalition had won the elections in 1980 and increased its parliamentary support, but in December, Francisco Sá Carneiro—the charismatic prime minister and leader of PSD and Aliança Democrática—died in an airplane crash. His presidential candidate subsequently lost the election to the incumbent, General Ramalho Eanes, despite fierce opposition from the government.[4] After the sudden death of the prime minister, Cavaco Silva refused to stay on as finance minister under the new party leader, Pinto Balsemão. Instead, he remained in opposition within his own party and distanced himself from the new leadership and government economic policies.

The PSD-CDS coalition governed the country until 1983. It proved unable to control growing macroeconomic imbalances, resulting from deteriorating external conditions and a countercyclical macroeconomic policy,[5] that led to a serious balance of payments crisis. At the same time, there was a political impasse due to tensions within the alliance (which lacked a clear leadership), between the government and President Eanes,[6] and over proposed changes to the constitution.[7]

In April 1983 new general elections gave the Socialists (PS) a plurality, which materialized in a PS-led coalition with PSD, known as *bloco central*. Prime Minister Mário Soares headed an emergency cabinet whose major tasks were restoring the external balance through an International Monetary Fund adjustment program and completing negotiations with the European Community concerning the accession of Portugal and Spain.

In 1985, after the severe adjustment program, inflation was reduced by 10 percentage points to 19.3 percent, and the current account was again in surplus. Public-sector imbalances, however, were not tackled:

---

4. As in 1985, and despite good results in the parliamentary elections, the PSD was not successful in getting its own presidential candidate elected. Unlike 1985, however, the defeat of 1980 proved very costly with respect to the pace of liberalization and reform.

5. While the rest of Europe was stagnating, Portugal grew at an average annual rate of 3 percent between 1980 and 1982. At the same time, however, the terms of trade deteriorated 3 percent a year.

6. The fierce opposition between the poles of the executive was very damaging indeed for the success of any reform attempts. Eanes had been elected by a grand coalition of all major non-Communist parties in 1976; in 1980 he was reelected with the support of Communists and Socialists (with the exception of their secretary general, Mário Soares, who had already served twice as prime minister—and would serve a third time in 1983–85—under Eanes's presidency) against the candidate of Aliança Democrática. The 1982 amendment to the Constitution abolished the blocking Revolutionary Council chaired by Eanes and reduced the powers of the president.

7. Despite its first amendment in 1982, the Constitution remained socialist in character until 1989.

public debt, as a percentage of GDP, kept rising until 1988 (to a peak of 74 percent). Domestic recession improved the external accounts but failed to curb the public-sector deficit and its inflationary consequences. The acute economic crisis had not triggered reform.

## The Pace of Macroeconomic Reform

After the emergency response to the 1983 balance of payments crisis, Portugal's governments pursued a strategy of gradual convergence toward EC standards. Formally, the strategy comprised a sequence of adjustment programs. The character of each of those programs and the extent to which they were implemented reflect the evolution of factors such as the amendment to the Constitution, external economic conditions, and integration with the European Community, the model of integration the government adopted, and the electoral cycle.

### Fiscal Adjustment and Structural Reform

The first adjustment program, prepared by the PSD minority government elected in October 1985 and approved shortly before the party got a parliamentary majority in 1987, was dubbed PCEDED. Its successor, P2, featured added fiscal adjustment and privatization of state-owned enterprises to stabilize the ratio of public debt to GDP.[8] The programs were aimed at redressing main macroeconomic imbalances but did not modify the exchange rate regime.

In 1986 and 1987, relatively high economic growth and substantial progress in reducing the inflation (from 19.3 percent in 1985 to 9.4 percent in 1987) characterized the Portuguese economy, mainly due to the decline of both the dollar and the price of oil and to world economic growth. Entry into the European Community at the end of the period of Eurosclerosis and the beginning of EC 1992 optimism was also a factor in Portuguese economic growth and the moderation of inflation.[9] At the same time, domestic fiscal transparency[10] was significantly increased, and curbing inflation (with specific annual targets) became a clearly stated policy objective.

By 1988, however, the anti-inflation efforts came to a halt. This was partly due to a clearer perception by the private sector of the inflationary

8. This was only possible thanks to the second constitutional amendment of 1989. It was then decided that 80 percent of privatization revenues would be used to stabilize public debt.

9. Due to its greater openness, the Portuguese economy benefited substantially from this effect. Between 1985 and 1988 Portugal's terms of trade improved by almost 6 percent a year. This in turn allowed for the pursuit of an expansionary policy without a major adverse impact on inflation.

10. Meaning both greater fiscal discipline and a more open reporting of fiscal decisions.

effects of a high public debt (equal to almost three-quarters of GDP) and to the lack of a clear-cut strategy for disinflation in the face of slowing global growth.

This deemphasis on fighting inflation was underscored by a stated shift in policy objectives focused on the need not to "slow down the catching-up process" with the rest of the European Community. Less control of domestic capital markets, large capital inflows, a postponed transition to a system of indirect credit control, coupled with the lack of a clear strategy for exchange rate policy and the slow pace of fiscal adjustment[11] further weakened the anti-inflation credibility of the authorities. In 1989 the inflation rate turned out to be almost 8 percent above the initial (successively revised) target.

The ambiguous Portuguese response to the need for institutional reform and European integration was mirrored by complete discretion regarding the future course of exchange rate policy and the timing of monetary reform.[12] For many years (well into the 1990s) the Portuguese government, although firmly committed to European integration, sided with the United Kingdom, its traditional Atlantic ally, in its skeptical attitude toward rapid institutional reform in the European Community.

On the other hand, capital controls, credit ceilings, and administratively set interest rates gave the authorities the illusion that monetary autonomy would last for ever.[13] Miguel Cadilhe, the minister of finance and the one responsible for the PCEDED and P2, felt very uneasy about a swift European monetary integration because of its perceived potential costs in terms of economic and social cohesion and loss of national sovereignty (Cadilhe 1990).

## Price Stabilization with Escape Clauses

In 1990, a new minister of finance, Miguel Beleza, formerly a central bank board member, reestablished disinflation as a priority, this time

---

11. The 1989 reform of both personal and corporate taxes reduced the budget deficit significantly. The positive effects of tax reform are, however, still very dependent on the reform of tax administration.

12. The crawling peg regime had been suspended for four months in 1985 and resumed at a decreasing rate. The regime, coupled with capital controls, credit ceilings, and administratively set interest rates had allowed the government to collect implicit revenues from the productive sector (Beleza and Macedo 1991; Torres 1990). As pointed out by Macedo (1990) and Torres (1989), the crawling peg was no longer effective in altering relative prices or compensating for inflation differentials with Portugal's main trading partners. At a time of greater financial openness and closer monetary integration, this exchange-rate limbo was incompatible with a strong commitment to fiscal adjustment.

13. While the minister of finance was never an enthusiast for central bank independence and shared the initial skeptical view of the government on rapid European monetary reform, the monetary authorities, unlike their European counterparts, favored a national road to increased central bank independence—capital controls rather than EMS discipline.

embedded within a package of fiscal consolidation and preparation for membership in the exchange rate mechanism of the EMS as a step toward Economic and Monetary Union (EMU). The "National Adjustment Framework for the Transition to Economic and Monetary Union," dubbed QUANTUM, was approved in June 1990.

However, the scale of fiscal adjustment for 1991 remained small due, among other things, to the political cycle (elections took place in October 1991). Furthermore, while monetary policy faced some additional difficulties stemming from the ongoing liberalization, the anti-inflation reputation of the monetary authorities was taking time to build, despite the significant steps taken to increase independence, beginning in 1990, of the Bank of Portugal.[14]

At the same time, the monetary authorities became more clearly committed to fighting inflation, sticking to a tight monetary policy stance. Fearing to lose its monetary autonomy to the exchange rate mechanism, the central bank, contrary to banks in other EC countries, was never enthusiastic about subjecting its intermediate targets to EMS membership.

The pursuit of a nonaccommodating (anti-inflationary) exchange rate policy of keeping the escudo inside a nondisclosed band may be seen as an attempt of the monetary authorities to reduce inflation through a hard-currency policy while leaving open the possibility of discrete and sudden changes in its value. One of the stated aims of not unveiling the band was indeed to create enough uncertainty concerning escudo fluctuation to reduce the amount of capital inflows (especially those of a speculative nature), which, if not fully sterilized, would torpedo the effects of tight monetary policy.[15]

On the other hand, it was customarily argued that joining the EMS, even with a large fluctuation band, was not a feasible option given the inflation differential between Portugal and the other EMS members. The then-prevailing inflation differential was, according to that view, incompatible with the oscillation of the escudo inside the large fluctuation band of the EMS. The argument went that such a policy would cause a

---

14. The new statutes of the Bank of Portugal, approved in October 1990, gave the central bank a high degree of economic independence while maintaining an average degree of political independence compared with other OECD countries. See Torres (1993) for a discussion and Grilli, Masciandaro, and Tabellini (1991) for the criteria of political and economic independence.

15. This sudden inflow of capital in Portugal bears similarities to the experience in Spain and Italy. A positive nominal interest rate differential together with a relatively credible nonaccommodating exchange rate policy generated substantial inflows of capital. Like Italy and Spain, Portugal introduced controls on inflows of capital following strong speculation in favor of the escudo. In line with controls on outflows since mid-1986 (Macedo and Torres 1991; Torres 1991), controls on inflows proved to be ineffective: capital inflows amounted to $10 billion between 1989 and 1992.

real appreciation of the escudo that in turn would provoke a halt or a slowdown in real economic convergence by putting at risk the competitiveness of the tradeable sector and by triggering speculative attacks against the escudo.

This contradictory justification proved to be unfounded: the escudo did fluctuate inside a shadowing EMS band, and speculation on the possibility of an early entry of the escudo into the exchange rate mechanism of the EMS, following declarations by the prime minister in June 1990, led to a substantial run in favor of the Portuguese currency, obliging the Bank of Portugal to intervene by selling escudos. Such interventions by the Bank of Portugal, which were common from June 1990 until September 1992, kept the escudo almost always within a narrow fluctuation band ($\pm 2^{1/4}$ percent) against the ECU.

Given the amount of foreign exchange reserves held by the monetary authorities[16] and the inflationary impact of these reserves, what were the underlying reasons for postponing entry of the escudo into the exchange rate mechanism? One likely explanation lies in the implicit possibility of discrete adjustments in the exchange rate, without the incurred political costs of doing so, by means of unilateral realignments of the escudo in the ERM.

While pursuing this discretionary policy inflicted high costs in terms of realized high real interest-rate differentials, it was counterproductive, given that controls on capital inflows were easily circumvented.[17] The ensuing inflows of capital complicated the already-difficult task of monetary control. The effect of capital inflows was indeed similar to that of the lower interest rates authorities so much feared—rates that had been kept high in the hope that controls on capital inflows worked properly.

In his widely cited critique of the EMS, Walters (1990) argued that EMS membership *cum* capital mobility would lead to a rapid nominal interest rate convergence across ERM members. The resulting low or negative real interest rates for high inflation members would generate inflationary tensions that would undermine the credibility of anti-inflation policy—the EMS was anything but a disciplinary device. As argued by Rebelo (1993) in the context of a modern version of the Scandinavian model, it is only the nontradeables sector's real interest rate that may fall to very low levels. This is not a source of inflation, nor is it incompatible with capital mobility. The biggest drawback of the noncommitment exchange rate strategy was, however, its cost in terms of

---

16. According to the *World Development Report 1992*, only Taiwan had higher foreign reserves, as measured by the number of months to finance total imports.

17. One possibility for resident banks to circumvent these controls was through their branches in the Madeira and Macau offshore markets.

credibility, particularly in regard to wage inflation in the Portuguese nontradeable sector.[18]

## A Global Political Strategy of Reform

It was only after the general elections in 1991, with a new PSD government based on an enlarged majority, that full participation in the EMU became a stated policy objective. The new adjustment program, which was very similar to QUANTUM, was named Q2 to stress continuity. However, it should be noted that the new program embodies a new, global approach to economic reform and to the process of European integration.

Building on previous achievements, the objective of the Q2 convergence program is to bring inflation under control by 1995 and thus to lay the groundwork for sustained economic growth and for the third phase of EMU (Ministry of Finance 1992). Q2 seeks the elimination of the inflation differential vis-à-vis the EC average while maintaining the positive differential with regard to rates of economic growth.

The budgetary process rests on the principle of nonaccommodation. The principal targets of the convergence program for 1992–96[19] are decided along with the respective annual budgets. The program lays out the projected macroeconomic framework under which convergence requirements for full participation in EMU can be met.

The transparency of budgetary procedures has been increased by multilateral supervision, which, contrary to the usual programs for balance of payments adjustment, is based on review of fiscal adjustment and financial stability. Besides the structural elements that the European Commission and the Committee of Governors of European Central Banks take into account when issuing their opinions, the evaluation of the various national convergence programs includes a political dimension introduced by the EC Council of Ministers of the Economy and Finance, the ECOFIN.

The judgment of representatives of the various national tax-payers thereby joins the institutional collaboration between the respective treasuries and central banks as a means to defend the specificity of the real and financial sector of each economy. Thus, the Community has helped to enhance the credibility of the convergence program.

---

18. In 1991 the monetary authorities announced that the escudo could be subject to a discrete devaluation at any time. Such a statement, made after a meeting of the Committee of Governors in Basel, was intended to deter capital inflows. While that warning was ignored by the financial markets with no effects on the amount of capital inflows, it did jeopardize the disinflation strategy.

19. Initially designed for the period 1992–95, the convergence program has recently been revised in order to take into account both common time horizons and underlying macroeconomic assumptions for all EC members.

As part of the convergence program, the escudo joined the ERM on 6 April 1992. A few months later, the turmoil in the European exchange rate markets began, and the momentum for EMU was lost amidst the recession (Torres and Giavazzi 1993). Paradoxically, it was during this period of turbulence that the government, especially due to the determination of the new finance minister, Jorge Braga de Macedo,[20] was able to overcome the remaining resistance to economic reform of the overly cautious (protectionist) monetary authorities.[21]

Capital controls were completely liberalized by December 1992, giving nonresidents full access to the Portuguese money market.[22] This was before the beginning of the European single market and well before the derogation granted to Portugal and Greece until 1996. The roles of institutions in monetary and fiscal policy became better defined, improving what had been an ambiguous and conflicting relationship between the treasury and the central bank.

Besides the inconsistency of the policy of capital controls, the ensuing high interest rates were also responsible for a higher debt service of the treasury, significant losses by the central bank, and significant distortions in the functioning of the economy (implied by the unwarranted transfer of resources from the productive sector to a sheltered financial sector). The capital controls policy was also undermining the political consensus needed to pursue reform because blame for high interest rates was being placed on exchange rate stability (there were the usual calls to devalue the currency in order to deal with the recession in the traditional Portuguese export markets) and on nominal convergence (responsible, according to that view, for a lower rate of growth). Consequently, the government tried to persuade the monetary authorities to accelerate the dismantling of the capital controls. In a public speech, which was widely believed to signal displeasure with the central bank, the minister of finance warned of the possible impacts of international recession; he also reminded monetary authorities of the implications of the exchange rate regime to which Portugal was committed, given that exchange controls had been abolished. One vice governor, known to have a strong preference for liquidity control, resigned, sparking a speculative attack against the escudo on 12 March 1993. Vested interests complained loudly for a couple of weeks, but as the government remained firm amidst the European currency crisis throughout which Portuguese interest rates continued to fall, the episode was soon forgotten.

---

20. Clearly a technopol, Jorge Braga de Macedo is the only minister of finance to have been elected (in 1991) as a member of Parliament.

21. At the same time, inflation came down from 9.8 percent in May 1992 to 5.6 percent in June 1993 while interest rates fell about 6 percentage points during the same period.

22. Outflows were liberalized in June 1992.

It was a classic struggle for power[23]: without controls on capital movements, the central bank would basically have to conduct its monetary policy like any other ERM country—that is, it would have to keep its currency within a band vis-à-vis the deutsche mark. As a consequence, monetary policy had to conform to the new exchange rate regime.

## Structural Policies and Social Consensus

The liberalization of capital markets has brought about significant microeconomic benefits. Interest rates have fallen, alleviating the debt service burden on the state and, to a lesser extent, on households and business. However, much remains to be done to eliminate regulatory distortions and enhance competition among financial institutions so that economic agents in Portugal may benefit from the emerging single European market for financial services.

The government is now insisting that wage and financial moderation is the only means to achieve sustained economic growth and macroeconomic convergence. Convergence improves the macroeconomic environment and thus stimulates modernization of the economy and society. While it was impossible to pursue structural reforms without the liberalization of the economy, it is very important to have a broad, consensual model of society manifested in a complementary economic and political strategy. The delays of the reform in 1988–89 and 1990–91 were in part due to the lack of such a clear economic strategy: it was not enough to reassert a commitment to stabilization. Without well-defined goals, it becomes even more difficult to resist antireform interests, especially during recession.

In Portugal there is consensus among the major political forces[24] (PSD, PS, and trade and business groups) on two major goals: increased economic and social cohesion, which includes an active employment and social policy in order to avoid "dependent federalism,"[25] and participation in the major institutional reforms of the European Community as a means of securing political and macroeconomic stability while preserving Portugal's universal tradition.

The objectives of inflation reduction and improved efficiency of labor, product, and financial markets continue therefore to feature in the

23. Miguel Beleza, the previous finance minister, was now governor of the central bank.

24. PCP, the Communist Party, has remained opposed to any liberalization of the economy and to European integration. The CDS, a former Christian Democratic party that has now adopted the name CDS-PP (Partido Popular), has become very much opposed to further European integration and much less concerned with social cohesion. Each party commands well below 10 percent of the vote.

25. Of the sort found within Europe, as in the Mezzogiorno, Ireland, or the five new German Länder, or with respect to any particular sector of an economy or social group that comes to depend on fiscal transfers.

adjustment effort, in line with the understanding that the most useful structural policy measures are those that reinforce the role of market mechanisms in resource allocation. Sustained growth and macro-economic stability are expected to provide better organization, improved work productivity, and new employment opportunities.

Fiscal reform included introduction of the value-added tax (VAT) in 1986, reform of direct taxation in 1989, and adjustment (in line with EC harmonization) of the VAT rate structure in 1992, which increased total revenue as a percentage of GDP. Budgetary adjustment between 1989 and 1992 was facilitated by the proceeds from privatization (which amounted to almost 6 percent of GDP in 1992) and EC transfers (which increased from 0.6 percent of GDP in 1986 to 3.3 percent in 1992). Thereby Portugal has managed throughout the period of reforms here considered to live up to its commitment to converge in real terms while gradually reducing public-sector imbalances.[26]

EC transfers have been mainly geared toward infrastructure development and human capital formation. The implementation of the European single market directives has greatly contributed to the quickening pace of other reforms (as diverse as environmental quality and consumer protection). Those transfers, to be complemented in 1993 by the European Cohesion Fund, have exerted pressure for internal reform in the sense that they required a a definite establishment of long-term priorities in Portugal because the transfers had to be matched by national public expenditure.

Unemployment figures throughout the reform period (around 4 percent in 1992) have compared very favorably with the rest of Europe. This development has to do with what Nancy Bermeo (see comment in this volume) called trading wage increases for job security, since it was impossible to liberalize firing practices. Low unemployment compensation benefits also increased the cost of being out of work. But there has been a consistent active employment policy to ensure social cohesion.

## Some Concluding Remarks

Portugal benefited significantly from European integration. This was due not so much to the amount of transfers involved (although these were an important contribution to the Portuguese process of catching up with the rest of Europe and the expression of social cohesion at the European level) but rather to the challenges posed by the European single market and EMU—both corresponding to the model of economic and social development that most Portuguese supported.

---

26. Public debt as a percentage of GDP was not only stabilized but has been steadily declining since 1989.

As the commitment to European integration strengthened, the government obtained the necessary support to change the Constitution and bypass vested interests in its pursuit of economic reform.

It was not until there was a global political and economic strategy of reform, however, that all the ambiguity (and some of the institutional distortions) of the past was removed. The technopols' job may now be done; good politicians may be entrusted to continue the process of continuous reform.

## References

Beleza, L. M., and J. B. Macedo. 1991. "Implicit Taxes and Credit Ceilings: the Treasury and the Banks in Portugal." In Beleza and Silva-Lopes, eds., *Portugal and the Internal Market of the EEC.* Lisbon: Banco de Portugal.

Cadilhe, M. 1990. "Luzes e Sombras da UEM." *Revista da Banca* 16 (October): 199–214.

Grilli, V., D. Masciandaro, and G. Tabellini. 1991. "Political and Monetary Institutions and Public Financial Policies in the Industrial Countries." *Economic Policy* 13 (October): 341–92.

Macedo, J. B. 1990. "External Liberalization with Ambiguous Public Response: the Experience of Portugal." In C. Bliss and J. B. de Macedo, eds., *Unity with Diversity in the European Economy: The Community's Southern Frontier.* Cambridge: Cambridge University Press.

Macedo, J. B., and F. Torres. 1991. "Interest Differentials, Financial Integration and EMS Shadowing: A Note on Portugal with a Comparison to Spain." In J. Silva-Lopes and M. Beleza, eds., *Portugal and the Internal Market of the EEC.* Lisbon: Banco de Portugal.

Ministry of Finance. 1992. "Portugal from P1 to Q2: A Strategy of Sustained Regime Change, 1986–1995." In F. Torres and F. Giavazzi, eds., *A Single Currency for Europe: Monetary and Real Impacts.* London: Centre for Economic Policy Research.

Rebelo, S. 1993. "Inflation in Fixed Exchange Rate Regimes: the Recent Portuguese Experience." In F. Torres and F. Giavazzi, eds., *Adjustment and Growth in the European Monetary Union.* Cambridge: Cambridge University Press.

Torres, F. 1993. *A Política Económica em Portugal: Da Ambiguidade Institucional à Integração.* Lisboa: Biblioteca de Economia, Publicações Dom Quixote. Forthcoming.

Torres, F. 1990. "Portugal, the EMS and 1992: Stabilization and Liberalization." In P. De Grauwe and L. Papademos, eds., *The EMS in the 1990s.* London: Longman.

Torres, F. 1989. "Portugal's Monetary Integration into a Changing Europe: A Proposal." *Economia* 13, no. 3, 395–405.

Torres, F. 1991. "The Persistence of Inflation in Portugal: Binding Political and Credibility Constraints." Universidade Católica Portuguesa, mimeograph.

Torres, F., and F. Giavazzi. 1993. "Introduction." In F. Torres and F. Giavazzi, eds., *Adjustment and Growth in the European Monetary Union.* Cambridge: Cambridge University Press.

Walters, A. 1990. *Sterling in Danger.* London: Fontana.

# Poland

## LESZEK BALCEROWICZ

## The Historical Background

After World War II, Poland fell under Soviet domination, with two resulting fundamental changes in its institutional system: first, the establishment of an authoritarian political system of a party-state type centered around the Polish United Workers Party (PUWP), and second, the replacement of private property and the market by central planning and state ownership. One major exception to state ownership was agriculture, which after the attempt at forced collectivization in the first half of the 1950s remained largely private.

The centralized economy of Poland, similar to that of other socialist countries, initially grew fast, thanks to the very low point from which it started and very high rates of investment. However, as time went on, the efficiency of investment and of the economy as a whole continuously declined because of the decreasing ability of the centralized economic system to cope with progressively more complex economic problems. As the efficiency of investment declined, there was a tendency to try and compensate for it by increasing the rate of investment. This in turn increased the complexity of the economy, and so on. The overall result of this vicious circle was declining rates of growth of national income

*Leszek Balcerowicz was the Deputy Prime Minister and Minister of Finance of Poland from September 1989 to December 1991. He is presently a Professor at the Warsaw School of Economics. The author is indebted to Ewa Balcerowicz, Marek Dąbrowski, Marek Jaśkiewicz, Jerzy Koźmiński, Peggy Simpson, and Edward Wnuk-Lipiński for comments on the first draft. The author acknowledges that he is responsible for the views expressed and also thanks Robert Koński and Małgorzata Sędziak for their help in editing this paper.*

and almost stagnant consumption, already witnessed as early as the late 1960s.

Against this background, there was a forced change of political leadership in 1970 after the brutally suppressed protests in Gdansk. The new leadership under Edward Gierek promised an improvement in the standard of living. The key to it, as it turned out, was massive foreign borrowing, which partly financed increased consumption and partly new investments in Western technology. The underlying assumption was that these investments would increase Poland's export potential to such an extent that the country would be able to service the debt and still achieve a higher level of GDP and consumption. However, this did not happen. The foreign borrowing proved excessive, and the related investments on the whole proved misdirected and inefficient, largely because they were undertaken within the framework of a basically unchanged centralized economic system. After rapid growth of the national income and consumption in 1971–78, Poland entered a long period of economic crisis with a huge and growing foreign debt. The drastic cuts in imports, due to the balance of payments difficulties, had brought about a decline in net material product of 27 percent between 1978 and 1982.

An extraordinary change in Poland's sociopolitical system then occurred: after a wave of massive strikes in August 1980, the authorities agreed to the creation of an independent trade union, Solidarity. This ran against the basic rule of the communist system, that there are no organizations independent from the party-state. Trade unions in this system served as "transmission belts" from the party to the masses. The form of a trade union was chosen largely because the leaders of the opposition rightly considered the proper organization— that of an opposition political party—totally unacceptable in the then-existing geopolitical situation. But Solidarity was a trade union only in name; in fact, it was a massive political movement for reform, which at its peak had 10 million members out of an adult population of 21 million. Despite this size, the presence of a common opponent—the authorities—and the common danger—Soviet invasion—produced a remarkable degree of unity and explained the self-limiting nature of Solidarity's demands, which may appear modest from today's perspective. In the area of economics, the principal demand was to replace central planning with market mechanisms without, however, privatizing the state enterprises.

The period of uneasy coexistence between Solidarity and the Communists ended with the introduction of martial law in December 1981 by General Wojciech Jaruzelski. The role of Soviet pressure is undoubted, although historians might quarrel about how large was the risk of Soviet invasion in the absence of the repressive measures the Polish authorities themselves took.

Solidarity was first suspended and then declared illegal. It continued, however, to work underground. The authorities launched an economic reform in 1982. It was even more modest than the one officially envisaged in 1980–81, and it preserved, among other things, a large measure of central allocation of inputs and the bureaucratic organizational structures necessary to operate such a mechanism. The authorities heavily relied on the increased output of coal, achieved by a radical strengthening of incentives for miners to work on Saturdays. This raised the relative wages of miners, the single most powerful industrial group, with about 450,000 people in 1985, but this increase in wages only accentuated their later drop during the transition to a market economy.

The autonomy of the state enterprises was, however, increased, and the workers councils, introduced in the second half of 1981, were gradually restored. Limited in scope and heir to many economic burdens, the reform failed to improve the performance of the economy. In this respect, it was not much different from the slightly more radical Hungarian economic reform.

Amongst the growing economic and social tensions, 1988 emerged as the initial year of accelerated change, as it turned out, in the final period of Communist rule in Poland. The last Party-dominated government of Mieczyslaw Rakowski, formed in October 1988, introduced substantial economic liberalization with respect to the private sector and foreign trade. This was, however, accompanied by very lax macroeconomic policy, accommodating the growing wage pressures. As a result, both inflation and shortages caused by price controls increased rapidly. In February and March 1989 the "Round Table" negotiations between Solidarity, led by Lech Wałęsa, and the authorities took place and culminated in an agreement signed on 5 April and approved by the Party-dominated Parliament a few days later. The agreement provided for political liberalization, including the legalization of Solidarity and other independent associations, and quasi-free elections.[1] The results for the economy were rather mixed. The private sector was to be given equal rights to develop, but there was no mention of privatizing the state enterprises. Besides, the opposition managed to get approval for indexation of wages[2] and many wage and social benefits for the largest social groups.[3] This was

1. The elections were totally free for the newly created Senate, but curial for the Sejm; that is, Solidarity was permitted to contend for only 35 percent of the seats.

2. The wages had to be increased by 80 percent of the price increases in the preceding quarter in excess of normal, spontaneous wage increases.

3. The largest groups—miners, railways workers, farmers—had their own negotiation groups, which acted only in weak coordination. The representatives of these groups usually pressured for commitments that wages in their respective sectors be, for example, 200 percent of the average wage in the economy. (Farmers demanded equivalently high guaranteed prices.) All these concessions were scrapped when the radical economic program was launched, but they were a source of conflict with the respective groups.

partially due to the "trade-unionist" nature of the opposition's economic negotiators and advisers, to the still-perceived political constraints, and probably to the conviction that it would be up to the government to implement these concessions. Another reason was the lack of overall coordination of the negotiations.

The results of the June elections surprised both sides. The Party suffered a crushing defeat, and Solidarity scored an unexpected victory. As a part of the political compromise, General Wojciech Jaruzelski was elected by the new Parliament to a newly formed post of president of Poland. His designated prime minister and closest ally, the former Minister of Interior Czeslaw Kiszczak, failed, however, in forming a government. After two months of hesitation, Solidarity decided to take the responsibility for the government by creating a coalition with two parties that used to be the junior parties of the PUWP. This government, led by Tadeusz Mazowiecki, was formed between 24 August and 12 September 1989. The author, after short but strong hesitation, accepted the dual job of deputy prime minister, responsible for the economy, and of finance minister.

## Initial Conditions in 1989

The economic conditions in Poland in early September 1989 can be broken down into those that were similar to the structural conditions prevailing in other socialist countries and those that were specific to Poland at the time. The former set of conditions comprised the economic legacy of the socialist economy, for example:

- an economic structure with an oversized industry and under-developed service sector;
- a heavy industrial concentration at the plant level, with many plants larger than optimum and some in poor locations;
- an industrial structure shaped during many years of import substitution;
- a heavy dependence on the Soviet market for exports in such sectors as machinery, textiles, electronics, and pharmaceuticals;
- a destruction of the environment in regions with a concentration of heavy industry and mining.

These problems were very serious in Poland but less severe than in some other postsocialist countries. For example, the dependence on the Russian market was less pronounced than in practically all the non-Russian republics of the former Soviet Union and Bulgaria. And the industrial structure was less distorted by the presence of the military-industrial complex and heavy industry than, for example, were Russia, Ukraine, and Slovakia.

The most important specific feature of the initial Polish economic situation was the dramatic state of the macroeconomy. Wages in the first quarter of 1989 were 120 percent higher than a year earlier. However, the real explosion happened in the following months. The growth of wages quickened, followed by the increase in prices. Sharp increases in the state purchase prices of agricultural products and the continued controls of the consumer prices of foodstuffs produced an explosive budget deficit, increasingly financed by the creation of money. In this situation, after freeing of food prices in August 1989, consumer prices jumped in that month by 40 percent and wages by 90 percent. The free market rate of exchange in early September 1989 was eight times the official one. Poland was entering hyperinflation, accompanied by massive shortages. There was also a heavy burden of foreign debt.

The Polish economic system had the following main features:

- domination of the state sector in the economy—this constituted the basic difference between the initial conditions of the postsocialist countries and those of other countries introducing market-oriented reforms (for example, East Asia, Latin America, and the transition from the war economy to the market economy in the West after World War II);

- heavily distorted prices due to price subsidies and controls, and this included the regime of multiple exchange rates and sharply negative real interest rates;

- absence of, or underdevelopment of, institutions needed in the market economy, such as a competitive banking system (separation of the central bank from the commercial banks had occurred only a couple of months earlier), a stock exchange, a system of government bonds to finance the deficit, genuine local government, etc.;

- a weak public administration that specialized in activities that had to be curtailed (e.g., detailed state intervention) and was weak in areas important in the market economy (i.e., analytical skills, macro-management, tax administration) but that nonetheless had to start the economic reform given the shortage of skilled bureaucrats;

- a "socialist welfare state," which was extensive relative to the level of economic development but increasingly inefficient and financially insupportable and which included, among other things, public provision of health services and education, relatively generous family benefits, easily obtainable disability pensions, long maternity leave, relatively long holidays, heavily subsidized sanatoria, access by the employees of larger state enterprises to holiday facilities for them, and summer camps for their children, largely financed by these enterprises.

It must be stressed, however, that the Polish economic system differed in important respects from the typical centrally planned economy. Agriculture was largely private, and there was a small but growing private sector outside agriculture. Within the dominating state sector, central allocation played a much less important role than, for example, in the centralized economies of Bulgaria or Czechoslovakia. In this respect, Poland was much closer to Hungary. (For more on the Polish economic system, see Balcerowicz 1989.)

The sociopolitical conditions prevailing in Poland at the start of economic reform were rather peculiar. There was a sense of a newly gained freedom, but there was no euphoria because the economy was in bad shape and there was still some uncertainty with respect to the Soviet Union. Solidarity achieved an unexpectedly great victory, and the Communist Party was, on the whole, ready to cooperate. But there were some more radical opposition groups, which did not participate in the Round Table discussions. Some of them later became more and more active, accusing the participants of a conspiratory deal with the Communists and propagating an extremely populist economic program.

Solidarity, with its idealistic ethos of a movement for the general good, was again legal and expanding, and was strongly represented in the Parliament. It was widely expected that Solidarity would provide an umbrella for the economic reforms. However, helped by hindsight, one remembers that Solidarity was united mainly by the presence of the common opponent: the Soviet Union and the Communist Party. There was no elaborated, shared positive program of how to organize the political and economic life after communism, and once these unifying elements disappeared, splits were inevitable.

There was also a peculiar social structure from the point of view of the transition to a capitalist market economy. The numerically largest group—the industrial workers—was the product of socialist industrialization; paradoxically, it was they who organized the strikes, supported and co-organized by intellectuals from the opposition, and undermined socialism. This gave the workers (and this was probably partly their own perception) a kind of romantic aura, superimposed upon the Marxist propaganda of the proletariat as the avant-garde. The Solidarity period also enshrined and popularized various forms of workers' protests, even hunger strikes, usually accompanied by a display of the national flag. These were the workers who had to face the negative consequences of the transition to a market economy, the first being actual or potential unemployment.

Another large social group, the farmers, were generally considered, and likewise considered themselves, as the preservers of private property. The average size of the 2.7 million private farms was only 7.2 hectares, and 30 percent of the farmers had less than 2 hectares (they usually had the status of farmer-workers). They had functioned for many years in a nonmarket environment characterized by a mixture of discrimination and tutelage from the state. The former consisted mainly of much lower administrative allocations of inputs compared with those obtained by the state farms and restrictions on enlarging the size of private farms. The latter took the form of subsidized credits and guaranteed purchases of agricultural products by the parastatal organizations. Moreover, in 1989 the farmers achieved large windfall gains, thanks to the freeing of the prices of foodstuffs by the last Communist government. Also, the hyperinflation in 1989 practically eliminated the real burden of taxation of the farmers, which was low in any case. The complementary liberalization of the prices of inputs to agriculture to be introduced in 1990 and the adjustment of tax rates took these windfall gains away from them. This sequence was politically unfortunate, but it was unavoidable because of the initial conditions in the country.

The existing interest groups were relatively strong on the labor side, which included the trade union Solidarity and its main rival, the Polish Confederation of the Trade Unions (OPZZ), which was organized after the introduction of martial law and the proscription of Solidarity. By contrast, the employers' organizations were very weak, and the same was true of the consumers' movement. There were several organizations fighting for influence among the farmers, both former allies of the PUWP and linked to Solidarity.

## The Economic Strategy: Concept and Launching

This strategy was elaborated piece by piece during late 1989 and launched, as a comprehensive package, in early 1990. While working on the comprehensive economic program, we also took measures aimed at coping with the current situation in such a way as to prepare the ground for the decisive operation in 1990. For example, there had been a series of devaluations preceding the unification of the exchange rate in 1990, interest rates were increased, and the wasteful system of subsidizing coal mining was replaced by a more rational one. Also, the excessive indexation of wages was abolished, and a much more modest system was introduced, to be replaced by a tough wage restraint in early 1990. Two successive budgets for the remaining part of 1989 were prepared. All this was done while negotiating with the International Monetary Fund (IMF) and lobbying the Western governments for a $1 billion stabilization fund.

The economic strategy dealt with the transition from the initial conditions described above to an efficient market economy, defined by domination of the private sector, market-type financial institutions, outward-looking orientation, stable money, and so on.

The economic strategy was designed to cure two economic illnesses: macroeconomic and structural. The macroeconomic problem was near-hyperinflation, combined with massive shortages. Stabilization and, to some extent, liberalization components of the economic program were the relevant cures. The structural problem was low and declining efficiency, which was responsible for the low standard of living. The relevant part of the economic program here was the transformation of the economic system, comprising the removal of unnecessary restrictions (liberalization) and fundamental institutional change—that is, building and rebuilding various institutional segments of the economy: enterprises (privatization), local government, financial sector, tax system, and so on.

The peculiar feature of the Polish economic program (and later that of other programs in the postsocialist countries) was that, in view of the initial economic system, the systemic transformation had to be far more comprehensive and radical than in any previous cases of market-oriented reform. Another characteristic of the Polish program was that the systemic change had to be combined with radical economic stabilization because of inherited hyperinflation and massive shortages. This distinguished the Polish situation from that of Czechoslovakia and Hungary, which were macroeconomically much more stable, and made it similar to the situation in some Latin American countries and to the initial conditions in the former Soviet Union as well as Bulgaria, Romania, and Albania two years later.

The Polish economic program had, since its earliest incarnation, devoted special attention to dealing with the foreign debt.[4] The goal here was to achieve a radical debt reduction, in the first place from the official creditors (who hold about two-thirds of the total debt). We assumed that the pioneering role of Poland in the political transformation of Eastern Europe and the radical nature of its economic program made such a goal realistic. The debt reduction was viewed in turn as a factor that increased the chances for success of economic stabilization and transformation.

Relating the Polish economic program to the "Washington Consensus" (Williamson 1992), I note that the program included practically all its elements but also many others.

Stabilization included fiscal discipline, moving toward positive real interest rates and a tough, tax-based wage restraint. In 1990 the budget was in surplus. Despite the continued fiscal discipline, the fiscal situation considerably worsened in 1991 because of a substantial decline in

---

4. Jeffrey Sachs was especially helpful in working out this part and in presenting the Polish case to the Western public.

real revenues related *inter alia* to the collapse of trade with the Soviet Union. Other reasons for the fiscal difficulties in 1991 and the later years included the fall in revenues from the state sector due to its slower-than-expected adjustment to a tougher market-oriented environment and the pressure to increase social expenditures, especially subsidies to the pension system. The expenditures for defense and price subsidies were radically reduced, but this was not sufficient to be able to increase the spending on health care, education, and infrastructure. These expenditures had to be cut in 1991, too, with the exception of telecommunications and environmental protection, which were increased considerably.

Liberalization and deregulation included these elements:

- removal of the few remaining restrictions with respect to private activity;
- liquidation of the remnants of the central allocation of inputs;
- price liberalization—the share of free prices (in terms of the volume of sales increased in early 1990 from 50 percent to about 90 percent;
- foreign trade liberalization—that is, removal of the bulk of the quantitative restrictions on exports and imports, practically in one step, in early 1990;
- unification of the exchange rates and introduction of the convertibility of the Polish zloty for current account operations;
- financial liberalization—that is, moving toward positive real interest rates and reduction of the volume of preferential credits, although some of them—with respect to housing and agriculture, for instance—remained.

The program of institutional change was very comprehensive and included the following, among other things:

- privatizing the bulk of the state sector in a couple of years;
- removing the bureaucratic barriers to foreign investment and ensuring the full repatriation of profits (the relevant law was passed in June 1991);
- breaking up domestic monopolies and introducing tough anti-monopoly legislation;
- strengthening the institutional independence of the central bank;

- reforming the financial sector—that is, "marketization" of the banking sector, the establishment of the stock exchange, reform of the insurance system, and so on;

- introducing tax reform—that is, removing the initially widespread tax preferences, introducing comprehensive personal income and value-added taxes, and strengthening tax administration;

- streamlining the budgetary procedures and institutions (this included, among other things, the liquidation of many extrabudgetary funds);

- creating genuine local government;

- setting up a social safety net to deal *inter alia* with the new problem of open unemployment and to replace the previous system of massive price subsidies for basic goods and social services, which were granted to employees by the enterprises employing them.

The economic strategy dealt not only with the type of measures to be taken but also with their timing. There were two basic options: trying to change the system first and subsequently to stabilize the economy, or rapidly launching the stabilization and transformation programs at about the same time, knowing that, because of the inherent differences in the speed with which parts of the plan could be put in place, stabilization and liberalization would have to be accomplished before the fundamental institutional structures of the economy could be transformed.

The first option was never seriously considered by the economic team in Poland. It would have implied tolerating hyperinflation for a longer time, thus increasing the difficulty and costs of its eventual elimination. It also appeared highly doubtful whether meaningful institutional change was possible in the midst of macroeconomic chaos. It seemed to us to be almost a hopeless strategy (although it may well be that this strategy—"privatization before stabilization"—will be tried in Russia). The alternative strategy of stabilization and liberalization before the economy could be privatized was thus selected. The risk of this strategy was that the supply response of the public sector to the tough stabilization-liberalization package was likely to be worse than that of a largely private economy. But this risky strategy had to be compared with the almost hopeless option.

Besides timing, the economic strategy had to determine the speed with which the selected measures would be implemented. Here, the radical strategy of fast stabilization and liberalization, combined with unavoidably slower but still rapid institutional transformation, had to be contrasted with the gradualistic options of stabilization and/or of liberalization. These gradualistic strategies were rejected in favor of the radical variant. Trying to stop hyperinflation gradually was perceived as a hopeless task. Gradual liberalization, in turn, would have resembled the previous failed attempts at economic reform. The slow liberalization of prices especially would have precluded a radical elimination of shortages, which was perceived as one of the basic necessary changes, both for consumers' welfare and for the more efficient operation of the respective enterprises. Radical liberalization of prices had to be linked to the radical elimination of quantitative and other administrative restrictions in foreign trade. This was necessary in order to increase the competitive pressure upon the domestic enterprises.

Political acceptance of the radical economic program required special mobilization on the part of the government's economic team. In the second half of November 1989, the team set up a special task force to coordinate the preparation of the final version of the basic 11 laws and related regulations. After a series of consultations in Parliament, I obtained approval of the idea by a special all-party parliamentary commission to work on the government's draft laws. This enabled a radical acceleration of the legislative process to take place, as compared with the normal procedure of sequential discussion of draft laws by several parliamentary commissions. A similar special commission was set up in the Senate, which normally would discuss the draft laws only after they had been accepted by the Lower House (the Sejm). But this time the Senate's commission agreed to work in parallel with the Sejm.

The draft laws prepared by the special working groups were first discussed by the Economic Committee of the Council of Ministers, of which I was chairman. These discussions went rather smoothly.[5] Then, the laws were submitted to the entire Council of Ministers. All this happened in the first half of December 1989. Given the amount of the proposed legislation and the time pressure, these debates had some dramatic moments.[6] But all of the draft laws and the budget for 1989 were accepted before the agreed deadline for the opening of the parliamentary debate, 17 December, which happened to be a Sunday. This speed underscored the extraordinary nature of the whole undertaking and gave some additional drama to my introductory speech on behalf of the government.

The special commissions of the Sejm and the Senate worked extremely intensively and in close collaboration with the government's

---

5. Some of the sessions of the Economic Committee in December 1989 were chaired (while I was negotiating with the IMF mission or conducting political consultations) by Deputy Prime Minister Jan Janowski, who stemmed from the party that used to be a junior partner of the PUWP and represented artisans and small entrepreneurs. Janowski turned out to be a close ally of the economic team during his service in the Mazowiecki government.

6. An important role in these crucial moments was played by Waldemar Kuczynski, an economist who acted as the chief adviser to Prime Minister Tadeusz Mazowiecki and supported the radical economic program.

experts. Any attempted major deviation from the government's proposals was quickly reported, and the economic team intervened. The legislative package was adopted by the Sejm on 27 December and two days later by the Senate, in both cases by a very wide margin. Just before the end of 1989, the package was signed by President Wojciech Jaruzelski, and it became law. The major legislative phase was over.

## The Developments of 1990–92

In early 1990 a radical, comprehensive stabilization-liberalization program was launched. Initial inflation turned out to be higher than expected and the fall in output deeper. Open unemployment started to emerge. But the inflation rate quickly started to go down,[7] and shortages and queues rapidly disappeared. The supply of goods improved dramatically. The newly convertible zloty held stronger than expected. Exports to the West surged.

On the institutional front, in May 1990 there were elections to new, genuine local governments, and in July 1990 the Parliament passed, after five months of deliberations, a comprehensive law on the privatization of state enterprises. Meanwhile, privatization of shops and restaurants (so-called "small privatization") was proceeding very quickly. Other important laws were passed, too, such as a law disbanding the compulsory "quasi-statist" associations of cooperatives, a law on insurance, an anti-monopoly law, a telecommunications law, a bankruptcy law, a law abolishing some 50 extrabudgetary funds, and a social safety law.

On the social and political front, after the initial calm between January and April 1990, the situation started to get more complicated. At the congress of Solidarity in April, many delegates were very critical of the economic program. In June, farmers blocked important roads demanding measures that would enable the dairies (formally farmer cooperatives) to pay higher milk prices. The government ordered the police to unblock the roads, provoking furious attacks in Parliament from the deputies of the peasant parties.

But most importantly, deeper and deeper splits appeared in the Solidarity movement itself. They were largely related to the growing conflict between its leader, Lech Wałęsa, and then–Prime Minister Tadeusz Mazowiecki. Wałęsa accused his opponent of being too slow in effecting political change but, on the whole, he refrained from criticizing the economic reform. In May 1990 Lech Wałęsa declared his intention to become the president of Poland, a post still occupied by Wojciech Jaruzelski. The conflict culminated in the open split in the Solidarity movement into two camps: one supporting Lech Wałęsa and the other Tad-

---

7. It was almost 80 percent in January, 23.8 percent in February, 4.3 percent in March, 1.8 percent in August, but then it increased to 4.6 percent in September.

eusz Mazowiecki. In the election campaign, which dominated the mass media in the autumn of 1990, the economic program came under attack from the three non-Solidarity candidates. The most demagogic critic, Stanislaw Tyminski, a Polish émigré not quite faithfully representing himself to the Polish public as a successful Western businessman who knew how to quickly turn the Polish economy into a thriving business, unexpectedly won second place. Wałęsa was first, and Mazowiecki, who was third, resigned together with his government.

The year of 1990 ended, therefore, in a complicated political situation. In the economy, after the rapid decline from 80 percent in January to below 2 percent in August, the inflation rate increased to between 4 and 5 percent monthly in the second half of the year. This was due to increased wage pressure, stimulated by the overall political climate, and to the monetary policy, prematurely relaxed during the summer. (It was tightened in the autumn of 1990.) But the budgetary situation during the year as a whole was better than expected: foreign reserves more than doubled, exports to the West increased by 43 percent, the shops changed beyond recognition, and privatization of the smaller units, especially in trade and services, rapidly advanced. Unemployment stood at over 6.1 percent, and the official statistics registered a substantial decline in GDP.

In early 1991 a new government led by Jan Krzysztof Bielecki was formed; the author continued as a deputy prime minister and minister of finance with overall responsibility for the economy. The year started with massive attacks by the trade unions on the wage controls. But after tough negotiations, the government did not give any significant concessions. Private enterprises, including the privatized ones, were released from wage controls altogether by the revised law of December 1990 on the assumption that the self-interest of private owners would prevent excessive wage increases. But this fueled accusations from the state enterprises that they were discriminated against by a "doctrinaire" liberal government keen on "destroying the state sector."

However, by far the largest source of problems in 1991 turned out to be the collapse of trade with the Soviet Union and the terms of trade losses due to the move to world prices and hard currency payments. This was mostly responsible for the higher-than-expected inflation in the first months of the year, the decline in output, and falling profitability of state enterprises. The two latter factors, together with forecasting errors, made the budget for 1991 obsolete after a couple of months. In the revised budget, 80 percent of the shortfall of the nominal revenues was made up by expenditure cuts and 20 percent by an increased deficit. This drastic revision had to be formally confirmed by the Parliament just before parliamentary elections in October 1991.

The institutional reform in 1991 included, among other things, a new securities law and establishment of the stock exchange, a new liberal foreign investment law, a law on a comprehensive personal income tax, and a law on fiscal policy. The new import tariff was introduced in August 1991 with a higher average rate, but it was more uniform and in line with the EEC classifications.

Privatization of larger state enterprises was slow, but the autonomous growth of the private sector was extremely fast and the privatization of smaller units and of assets of state enterprises rather rapid. As a result, the value added generated in the private sector increased in 1991 by 33.3 percent, and this growth occurred across the economy: in manufacturing by 42.2 percent, in construction 64.0 percent, in domestic trade 61.7 percent, agriculture 10.2 percent. In contrast, the GDP produced in the public sectors declined by 26.3 percent (*Rzeczpospolita*, 2 December 1992, III).

In May 1991 the zloty was devalued by 14 percent after 16 months of a fixed exchange rate and pegged to a basket of currencies, instead of the previous peg to the dollar. In October a crawling peg was introduced with a monthly devaluation of 1.8 percent.

In April 1991 Poland signed an unprecedented agreement with the Paris Club, whereby 50 percent of the official debt (two-thirds of the total Polish debt) would be reduced in two stages.

The parliamentary elections in October were preceded by two months of campaigning in which 65 political parties took part. Most of them were very critical of the government's economic program and presented radically different proposals. To the extent their economic programs were defined at all, they usually included relaxation of monetary and fiscal policy, increased protectionism, and more active involvement of the state bureaucracy in the affairs of specific industries and enterprises. The elections produced a very fragmented parliament, composed of almost 30 political groups. As a result, a coalition of five to seven parties was required to form the government. The new government of Jan Olszewski was formed at the end of December 1991, after over two months of intensive negotiations. (The author ended his public service in December 1991.)

The new government started claiming a sharp break with the past but gradually toned down its revisionist declarations and basically continued the disciplined fiscal policy. But privatization of larger state enterprises was practically brought to a halt, and political debate on privatization got more and more demagogic. The Polish zloty was devalued in February 1992 by 11.6 percent.

In June 1992 the government collapsed after a clumsy attempt at disclosing the former regime's "secret agents" in the state institutions, and, after more than a month, the new government of Hanna Suchocka was formed (still in power at this writing). The new government, based on a coalition of two clearly proreformist parties with a fundamentalist Catholic party and two small peasant parties, basically continues the program started three years ago: that is, it tries to strengthen macroeconomic stabilization, to maintain the liberal character of the economic system, and to speed up privatization. The major changes were concessions to the farmers (promises of increased protectionism, one-time subsidies on fuel for the farmers following a severe draught) and a "social pact" with the trade unions centered on modifying wage controls and on privatization. The government had to deal with a wave of strikes in December 1992, mainly in the coal mines. The strikes ended with an agreement, but its financial implications are not completely clear.

After three years, the Polish economy is macroeconomically much more stable and substantially transformed. The inflation rate, as measured by the consumer price index, had fallen from the annual rate of 2,000 percent in the second half of 1989 to 44.3 percent in 1992. Producer prices in manufacturing increased by 31.3 percent in 1992. Prices were freed, and therefore the price structure has been fundamentally improved; shortages and queues are gone, and the supply of goods is incomparably better than three years ago. The private sector employs 60 percent of the labor force and generates 50 percent of the GDP, by far the highest ratios in the postsocialist countries. Thanks to the continuous rapid growth of the private sector across the economy and to the improved performance of some state firms during 1992, Poland was the first postsocialist country where GDP stopped falling. As a matter of fact, it is estimated to grow at a rate of between 0.5 and 2 percent. The official GDP figures showed a cumulative drop in 1990–91 of 18 percent, but the recent estimates are in the range of 5 to 10 percent.[8] Both exports and imports increased rapidly, which sharply raised their share in the GDP. This happened despite the collapse of trade with the Council of Mutual Economic Assistance (CMEA). Foreign reserves almost doubled.

But some serious problems remain. Unemployment increased from practically zero in early 1990 to 13.6 percent at the end of 1992. Heavy industry and coal mining required unpopular restructuring. The budget deficit had to be contained, which demanded, first of all, measures aimed at reducing the growth of subsidies to the pension system. The liberal foreign trade regime is under attack from the farmers' lobby, and rapid, unconventional privatization of state enterprises, based on free distribution of shares, has been delayed for a year and half because of the elections and the political conflicts in the Parliament. All in all, maintaining macroeconomic stability and completing the transition to capitalism largely depends on a rather fragmented political system. But the economy is now much more independent from the political scene, and despite the fragmentation of Parliament, a tough budget for 1993 was passed in February 1993.

---

8. These estimates were made at the Research Institute of the Main Statistical Office and the Polish Academy of Sciences (Rajewski 1992, 133–40).

# Lessons from the Polish Experience

## Circumstances Leading to the Launch of the Economic Program

The Polish program was prepared and launched under a double crisis: a long-term structural problem of low and falling efficiency and a macroeconomic catastrophe. It was the latter that gave the Polish situation a dramatic dimension. This crisis both required radical measures, especially with respect to stabilization, and increased the people's readiness to accept such measures. But there was an important complement: the newly gained external freedom due to the collapse of the Soviet bloc. Otherwise, the radical institutional program, especially privatization, would not have been possible. Liberalization and a massive Solidarity victory probably motivated people to accept the radical reforms. In this special situation of "extraordinary politics," there was a stronger-than-usual tendency among the political actors to act in terms of the common good. This and the government's speed of action explain the overwhelming acceptance of the economic program.

The special motivation of the people at large would not have lasted very long and was probably cut short by the growing conflict within Solidarity and the rather unpleasant way in which it split in 1990. Indeed, people for whom Solidarity represented an idealistic movement for the common good might have felt cheated and thus were willing to look elsewhere to invest their political sympathies. This and the related presidential elections in the autumn of 1990 certainly shortened the honeymoon period.

Poland in 1989 cannot be regarded as a testing ground for a rival hypothesis that "the scope for reforms would be greater where an incoming government won a mandate for change by the substance of its preceding election campaign, rather than where it surprised its supporters after winning power" (Williamson 1992). For Solidarity at the Round Table represented, rather, "trade unionist" demands, and it did not expect then nor during the election campaign that it would be forming the government in 1989. Certainly, Solidarity did not present anything that resembled the radical stabilization-transformation program launched half a year later. This shift might be explained by the changed macroeconomic situation (price eruption in August 1989) and by the fact that the government's economic team was composed of people not present at the Round Table who had a critical view of the economic part of the agreement reached there. A different composition would probably have meant a different—most likely less radical—economic program.

Given these circumstances, notably the "third-way" elements in the Solidarity tradition and the speed with which the program was launched, the Polish public could not have been psychologically well-prepared for the radical economic measures. It is, however, highly doubtful whether the delay would have brought about much more understanding, and it definitely would have worsened the macroeconomic situation.

As to the opposition in Parliament, it formally consisted of the PUWP. But because it partly comprised disguised (or open) liberals and because there was a general atmosphere of national unity in late 1989 and the PUWP had suffered a crushing defeat in June 1989, it did not seriously challenge the program. There was much more opposition from the United Peasant Party, formally a coalition partner. In general, the distinction between the ruling parties and the opposition was not very pronounced, as far as the attitude toward the economic program was concerned. And although the parliamentary debates on the economy got more and more critical over time, until August 1991 (just before parliamentary elections) it was possible to persuade Parliament to adopt all the major economic legislation proposed by the government and to block any initiatives that would constitute a major deviation from the government's economic program.

## The Economic Team

An economic team with coherent views was an important factor in the Polish case. Here, I think I have to say a few words about myself. In August 1989 I still did not imagine for a second that I might be responsible for free Poland's stabilization-transformation economic program. But I had worked for almost 15 years on economic reform and institutional issues,[9] and in a paper written in April 1989 for a conference in Poland, I sketched out what I thought were the necessary elements of a radical and comprehensive economic package for Poland: price liberalization, convertibility of the Polish zloty, tough macroeconomic policy, privatization. In 1978 I formed a group of 10 young economists to work on economic reform. After August 1980, our work was given much publicity, and the group was often called the "Balcerowicz group." (It was probably because of this that I was offered the position in the government nine years later.) After the introduction of martial law in December 1981, the group's members and some sympathizers continued to meet at my institute for seminars to discuss various problems of the economic system, including the importance of property rights and privatization. When I accepted the job in Mazowiecki's government, it was agreed that I would be responsible for the makeup of the economic team (with Mazowiecki's final approval, of course). This applied without caveats to

---

9. This included the study of the South Korean economy I made as a visiting fellow at the Institute of Development Studies at the University of Sussex in 1985 and the research of Ludwig Erhard's reform, which I made in Germany in 1988.

my deputies in the Ministry of Finance and also to the main economic ministries. This was also true of the formation of the second government in early 1991.

In 1989 some of the members of the "Balcerowicz group" or other participants of the seminar became my closest associates.[10] Besides, I happened to know personally from my student days at the Central School of Planning and Statistics (now once again the Warsaw School of Economics) some of the people who were already in high positions in the Ministry of Finance and remembered them as capable and energetic individuals.[11]

The shared background, commonality of purpose, similar age (around 40), and the common pressures created what quickly became known as the "Balcerowicz team." This applied, first of all, to my deputies in the Ministry of Finance who had to defend the tough economic measures within the government structures, in Parliament, and against the public. An important intellectual support was offered by some advisers.[12]

Throughout my service in the government, there had been good cooperation with the central bank, headed in 1989–90 by Władysław Baka and in 1991 by Grzegorz Wojtowicz. This seems to be in sharp contrast with the situation in Russia in 1992. More generally, issues related to the central bank and its relationships to the government's economic team are important in the context of radical stabilization-transformation programs.

It was also of importance that as a deputy prime minister I was chairing the sessions of the Economic Committee of the Council of Ministers, which comprised economic ministers and chiefs of other economic agencies (including the governor of the central bank). The committee acted as a vehicle for coordination and the preparations of decisions to be taken by the Council of Ministers.[13]

---

10. For example, Marek Dąbrowski, who was my deputy in the Ministry of Finance until the summer of 1990, and Stefan Kawalec, who was first my chief adviser and then my deputy in the same ministry, responsible for financial institutions.

11. This applied to Janusz Sawicki, my deputy at the Ministry of Finance, responsible for foreign debt negotiation, and Andrzej Podsiadło, who was overseeing the state enterprises in the Ministry. Grzegorz Wojtowicz, first deputy chairman of the Polish National Bank and its Chairman in 1991, graduated the same student year in my faculty of Foreign Trade of the Central School of Planning and Statistics. Wojciech Misiąg and Ryszard Pazura, my other two deputies in the Ministry of Finance, also graduated from the Central School of Planning and Statistics.

12. This group included both foreign advisers—Jeffrey Sachs and David Lipton, Władysław Brzeski, Stanislaw Gomułka, Jacek Rostowski, and Stanislaw Welisz—and Polish ones: Karol Lutkowski, Andrzej Stanislaw Bratkowski, Antoni Kantecki, Adam Lipowski, Andrzej Parkola, Andrzej Ochocki. Most of the foreign advisers were of Polish origin.

13. The secretary of this committee was Alfred Bieć, one of my closest associates.

As deputy prime minister I had created a special section of overall coordination that focused on political aspects of the economic program—that is, contacts with the respective political parties, with the Parliament, and with the mass media. This section was directed by Jerzy Koźmiński, who used to be one of my best students of international economics. He played an important role in devising and sustaining political support for the economic program, as well as its overall coordination, especially in the crucial moments of December 1989.

## Political Leadership and Economic Reform

The relationship of political leadership to economic reform was not clear because the issue of political leadership itself was not completely clear. In late 1989 and the first months of 1990, Lech Wałęsa, leader of the victorious Solidarity, stayed in the background in Gdansk, and the prime minister, Tadeusz Mazowiecki, became the most popular Polish politician (he reached popularity ratings of over 80 percent). Mazowiecki, a man of deep principles, certainly had a vision of history. (Elections at that time were in any case not in sight.) But for a number of reasons, the program was not identified with him but was known already in October 1989 as the "Balcerowicz program." One of the reasons was the tacit agreement that I would take overall responsibility for the economy.[14] Another reason might have been the speed with which the economic program was launched and the visible role the economic team played in it. The economic team thus assumed an important political role.

Since May 1990, there had been a growing conflict within Solidarity, mostly on noneconomic and personal grounds. I tried and largely managed to keep the economic program outside this dispute. Wałęsa himself declared in his short presidential address in December 1990 that he would "support the Balcerowicz program," and he largely kept his word.

The new government formed in January 1991 displayed similar composition and orientation with respect to Poland's economic problems, and new Prime Minister Jan Krzysztof Bielecki, an economist by profession and one of the leaders of the Liberal Party, was courageously defending the tough economic program. But the political situation grew more and more complicated, especially after August 1991, when the coming parliamentary elections dominated the political scene. The election campaign was dominated by ever more virulent attacks on the economic program, and in the new, fragmented Parliament, formed in November 1991, groups opposing the program had a stronger representation than in the previous one.

---

14. During my first meeting with Mazowiecki, he said he was looking "for his Ludwig Erhard."

The issue of the political leadership's attitude toward the previous economic program became almost schizophrenic under the third government, headed by Jan Olszewski. He and some of his ministers were very critical of this program and came to power under the heading of "breakthrough"—that is, a radically different strategy. But with respect to fiscal policy, they largely continued the previous line.[15]

The situation became much clearer under the present government of Hanna Suchocka, since both she and some of her ministers are representing the reform parties that participated in the first or in the second government. The fact that the new forces of development turned out in 1992 to be stronger than declining tendencies also made it easier to identify in public with the economic program started three years before.

## Dynamics of Political and Economic Reform

The economic strategy in Poland was based mostly on economic principles but was supplemented by some psychological and political constraints. The economic rationale behind the radical economic program has already been discussed: hyperinflation and massive shortages called for tough stabilization measures, the previous unsuccessful attempts at partial reform spoke in favor of launching a comprehensive and radical transformation program, and so on. But I also remembered from Leon Festinger's (1957) psychological theory of cognitive dissonance that people are more likely to adapt internally to quick, radical changes in their situations if they consider them irreversible than they are to adapt to gradual changes. Finally, I also sensed that the period of "extraordinary" politics was short-lived and that one should use it to introduce tough economic measures. The full significance of that became obvious only in the second half of 1990 when the political situation deteriorated considerably.

The timing of political events, including the elections, was not planned in advance by any strategic center because of the conflicts and lack of efficient communication among Solidarity elites. For economic policymaking, the elections were a given—not fully known in advance and, clearly, not with a fortunate outcome. The two successive election

15. This government started operation at the end of December 1991, when a tough provisional budget for the first quarter of 1992 and some other accompanying laws, prepared by the previous government under my direction, were already in Parliament. The Olszewski government upheld these laws and the budget, claiming that they did not like them but that they had inherited them. Later, probably better understanding the constraints and thanks to Minister of Finance Andrzej Olechowski, the Olszewski government prepared a tough budget for the entire year. Another reason for this continuity was also that the budget department in the Ministry of Finance had been directed since September 1989 by the same person, Deputy Minister Wojciech Misiąg.

campaigns in the first and the second year of implementation of a tough economic program probably magnified public discontent and certainly contributed to wage pressure and to a slowing in state enterprises' adjustment to the realities of the market economy. In this respect, a contrast can be drawn between Poland and Hungary where, after free elections in early 1990, the next elections are due in 1994. The change of Parliament and even more frequent changes in the ministerial positions have slowed down some important reforms, especially the mass privatization of larger enterprises.

But given this unplanned and uncontrollable sequence of political events and the equally uncontrollable external shocks, it is highly doubtful there could have been a radically different economic strategy that would have made more economic sense and would have been politically more acceptable. The main reason for the success of the Polish economic reform seems to be the great speed of its early phase, when fundamentals of a liberal economic system and macroeconomic stability were established. It was easier for the supporters of the market-oriented reforms to defend them as fait accompli than it would have been to build reforms gradually in the face of strong populist opposition in Parliament after the elections of October 1991.

Besides this general explanation, there are related, more specific reasons for the sustainability of Polish economic reform. One of them is the independence of the central bank, introduced as an element of the comprehensive reform package in December 1989 and strengthened in 1991. This independence has allowed the bank to act as a constraint upon an irresponsible budgetary policy. Another reason has been the convertibility of the currency for current account operations, another element of the first reform package. In the absence of convertibility, it would have been easier to engage in populist macroeconomic policies. In this respect, convertibility plays a similar role as a check upon government policies, as does export-oriented growth. Third, the rapid elimination of shortages in a country plagued by them for over 40 years provided a strong, popular justification for free prices and, to some extent, for the overall economic program. The disappearance of queues and the significantly wider range of goods available in the shops constituted the most important forms of popular compensation for the radical economic reform in its early phase.

The fourth reason for the sustainability of economic reform has been the growth of the private sector. True, the privatization of larger enterprises has been delayed for political reasons. But other processes of the overall privatization of the economy—the spontaneous growth of the private sector, small-scale privatization, and privatization of the assets of state enterprises—have been fast. As a result, the share of people employed in the private sector, outside the already largely private agricultural sector, increased from 13.2 percent in 1989 to 34.4 percent in

1992.[16] Surveys show that those employed in the private sector are typically much more in favor of the market-oriented reform than employees in the public sector. Privatization has therefore an important political dimension.

The failure to introduce mass, unconventional privatization in 1991 and in 1992 based on the free distribution of shares probably thus entailed some forgone gain in political support for market-oriented reform. But the introduction of this privatization could not have positively influenced the economic situation in these years because of the lags between privatization and the change in the economic performance of affected enterprises.

## Communicating with the Public

There have been constant and justified complaints that the "information policy" of the government—that is, the explanation and prediction of the consequences of economic change—was inadequate. There were a number of reasons this was so. As far as policymakers—including myself—were concerned, there was a perennial problem of how to divide the limited time between making economic policy and explaining it. Since the number of problems to be tackled was rather unusual, the time spent on the latter was clearly insufficient. I also found it psychologically and intellectually difficult to make firm predictions. I was reasonably sure of the direction of general developments but could not predict their exact timing and magnitude. But there was the constant demand to commit "the fallacy of misplaced concreteness": to say when exactly things were going to get better, when the standard of living would rise. The economic reform was helped by the support of practically all the major national newspapers, which published articles and commentaries by a small group of very good economic journalists.

On the other hand, a number of factors served to counter attempts at explaining radical, market-oriented reform to the Polish public. Most of these factors could be regarded as by-products of the transition to democracy. First, in the newly freed mass media and especially in television, which was subjected to especially stringent political control under communism, there emerged a strong tendency to focus on the negative and the sensational. The same was true of most local newspapers. Part of the opposition press constantly presented various conspiracy theories as explanations for the economic difficulties.

---

16. These figures refer to a narrow definition of the private sector that excludes cooperatives. On a broader definition, including the cooperatives, the share of the private sector outside agriculture increased from 31.2 percent in 1989 to 44.4 in 1992 ("Informacja o sytuacji spoleczno-gospodarczej kraju. Rok 1992," *Glowny Urzad Statystyczny*, 1993, 51). This shows that a part of the growth of the narrowly defined private sector came from the privatization of parastatal cooperatives.

Second, the decisive majority of Polish economists were very critical of the program. This might have conveyed to the public the impression that Polish "experts" were, on the whole, against the reforms. To some extent, this impression was probably counterbalanced, particularly in 1990, by the echoes of favorable Western opinion.

Third, and by far most important, there were two election campaigns in the first and second years of economic reform. Election campaigns nowadays always have elements of propaganda or psychological "warfare," given the power of TV and radio. This raises the interesting empirical question of how the election campaigns influence the economic views of the public. In Poland, especially in 1991, the media bombarded the Polish public with messages that the Polish economy had been struck by economic catastrophe and that there should be a radically new program to improve the situation quickly. This proposed program had three familiar elements: relaxation of monetary and fiscal policies, protectionism, and state intervention at the industry level.

Fourth, under the previous regime there was a large apparatus for propaganda and information. The democratic revolution involved the abolition of this structure, and it took time to build a new government information structure to deal with the independent mass media and with the public at large.

## External Influences

One should distinguish between external influences with respect to the content of the economic program and those factors that affected internal support for the program. In the Polish case, the latter was much more important than the former. In negotiations with the IMF, multilateral banks, and Western governments, there was very little pressure with respect to economic strategy and its crucial details because the Polish program was basically in line with the goals of these organizations.

Within the government and in parliamentary debates, I used conditionality only as additional argument in favor of the economic program. In other words, I stressed that the program was motivated by our internal considerations, but in addition, its implementation meant the support of the IMF (and of other international organizations), and this support was needed to make the program internationally credible and to obtain sizable debt reduction. This was not only truthful but also probably politically more effective than trying to push through tough measures on the pretext that the IMF had imposed them. This view of conditionality also helped recently to push through the tough budget for 1993. Of importance in increasing the support for the radical stabilization-liberalization package discussed in December 1989 was the prospect of obtaining the $1 billion stabilization fund. This was interpreted as a sign of the private assessment of the program by Western governments, and the fund increased the confidence of the reformers in the feasibility of convertibility of the Polish zloty. Without the stabilization fund, convertibility would not have been launched.

## General Remarks

### Characteristics of the Reformers

Based on introspection and on observations, I cannot help but agree with John Williamson's assertion in his paper that there are policymakers whose characteristics and actions are at sharp variance with the stylized, self-interested politicians of public-choice theory. There are, in my view, two basic differences between "technopols" and the stereotypical politician. First, his or her economic knowledge may give a "technopol"—an economic technocrat in a position of political responsibility—a better picture of the available options and their economic and social consequences than is typically the case with career politicians. Second, there are motivational differences. One does not need to speak of altruism in the case of technopols (although it cannot be ruled out), but one may simply state that they attach different "motivational weights" to economic options than do typical professional politicians. These differences may be partly caused by differences in perception: for example, technopols may more clearly see the danger of populist strategies than other politicians do. Another motivational characteristic is differences in the need for self-esteem. The self-esteem of a technopol suffers if his economic reform is implemented and then fails from an economic standpoint. His self-esteem would probably suffer less if reforms that could have been successful if implemented were socially or politically rejected, costing him a job. The self-esteem of a career politician suffers the most if he loses in the political game. It is also probably of importance that technopols have alternative careers (in the field of academia, business, international financial organizations), and their reputation in those fields depends on how they conducted political reforms. A professional politician usually has to stick to politics, and abandoning politics may mean a life failure.

### "Extraordinary" versus "Ordinary" Politics

I have used the concept of "extraordinary politics" to describe the Polish situation in the second half of 1989 and early 1990. But this concept can be generalized to some other historical contexts. "Extraordinary politics" by definition is a period of very clear discontinuity in a country's history. It could be a period of very deep economic crisis, of a breakdown of the previous institutional system, or of a liberation from external domination (or end of war). In Poland, all these three phenomena converged in 1989.

The new political structures, including political parties and interest groups, are fluid, and in a sense, there are usually no professional politicians during such a period. The older political elite is discredited, and the politicians representing the new order have not yet emerged or have not had enough time to become professional. Among the political elites and the population at large, there is a stronger-than-normal tendency to think and to act in terms of the common good.

In such a case, the period of extraordinary politics both calls for and creates especially favorable conditions for the emergence of technopols. There is no guarantee, though, that they will appear, for there is a large element of chance. Also, the countries that are in greatest need of domestic technopols because of the past devastation (foreign technopols not usually being admitted to high government positions), are the least likely, because of this devastation, to find them. Depending largely upon whether technopols appear on the scene or not, the increased chances for extraordinary actions inherent in extraordinary politics are used or wasted.

Extraordinary politics is a short period and gives way to "normal" politics: politics of political parties and of interest groups, a sharply reduced willingness to think and act for the common good, and stronger institutional constraints with respect to the individual political actors. In the period of extraordinary politics, these constraints are fluid or loosely defined.

During the time of normal politics, the appearance and/or the continued operation of technopols is much less likely than during extraordinary politics.

Public-choice theory, as posited by James Buchanan and Gordon Tullock (1962) and others, is much more applicable to normal than to extraordinary politics. The main reasons for the latter's inapplicability are the high frequency of technopols reaching positions of power and the fluidity of institutional constraints.

# References

Balcerowicz, Leszek. 1989. "Polish Economic Reform, 1981–88: An Overview." In *Economic Reforms in the European Centrally Planned Economy*. New York: United Nations.

Buchanan, James M., and Gordon Tullock. 1962. *The Calculus of Consent*. Ann Arbor, MI: University of Michigan Press.

Festinger, Leon. 1957. *A Theory of Cognitive Dissonance*. Stanford, CA: Stanford University Press.

Rajewski, Zbigniew. 1992. "Produkt krajowy brutto." In L. Zienkowski, ed., *Gospodarka polska w latach 1990–1992*. Warsaw.

# Turkey

YAVUZ CANEVI

The aim of this paper is twofold: to attempt to revisit the Turkish experience in stabilization, structural adjustment, and liberalization policies during the period from 1980 to 1992, and to draw some lessons from this experience and assess the sustainability of the Turkish program. The paper begins with a brief economic history of the prereform period.

## Historical Background

One can identify several distinct periods in Turkey's political and economic development process. The first period, from 1923 to 1950, witnessed the founding of the republic and the rebuilding of the war-torn country through "étatism" within a single-party political system. During the second period, which roughly covered the 1950s, democracy emerged, with a multiparty system and a first wave of liberalization in economic management.

The third period was inaugurated in 1960 with the first of two coups d'etat and the introduction of the concept of five-year indicative development plans, with heavy emphasis on import substitution. Since the first plan, which covered the 1963–67 period, there has been a continuous succession of five-year plans and annual programs. The current plan covers the period from 1990 to 1994.

The fourth period, from 1971 to 1980, saw a return to democracy, albeit an unstable one in which successive coalition governments were

Yavuz Canevi is Managing Director of the Euroturk Bank in Istanbul and is the former Governor of the Central Bank of Turkey (1983–86) and the former Undersecretary of Treasury and Foreign Trade (1986–89).

too weak to respond to economic difficulties both internal and external as well as political difficulties and changing circumstances. Particularly important were episodes of civil violence between left and right and severe labor strikes.

The fifth period was marked by the successful implementation of a new economic reform program in 1980 under a military-backed government (led by a technopol). In 1983 democracy was once again restored, under which the reform program continued uninterrupted and was even strengthened. However, during the rest of the 1980s the reforms met with gradually decreasing success even though the same technopol was in charge (in a higher office).

At the beginning of the current period, in 1990, a new, populist political coalition consisting of parties of the center-right and center-left (social democrats) came to power. The coalition government formed its own economic team, in which the management of the central bank represented the only continuity of the reform program. However, by this time some of the policy reforms of the previous government were effectively irreversible.

## The Gathering of Storm Clouds: The 1950s to the 1970s

Turkey's development strategy during the 1950s and 1960s aimed in particular at fostering agricultural and industrial production, improving basic infrastructure, and integrating the rural and urban sectors into a single market economy. Implementation of this strategy resulted in a period of steady and substantial growth. The economic programs, supported by IMF stand-by arrangements in every year from 1961 through 1969, aimed at moderating fiscal and monetary expansion so as to provide a framework of domestic and external financial stability in support of the development strategy.

A relatively well-to-do developing country, Turkey maintained annual growth rates averaging 6 to 7 percent from 1965 to 1977. This seemingly good performance, however, was realized by means of an import substitution strategy, which made the country critically dependent on imports of capital and intermediate inputs and on strong protection of the domestic market, to the neglect of the country's export potential. The inefficiencies and distortions that developed in the domestic economy as a result of growing financial repression, with increasingly negative interest rates and discretionary allocation of credits, deprived the economy of the domestic savings needed to perpetuate high rates of economic growth. The viability of this strategy eventually became critically dependent on external savings to fill both the domestic savings gap and the foreign exchange gap resulting from the country's extreme import dependence.

In this early period, there were two serious balance of payments crises, which ended in sharp devaluations of the currency rather than comprehensive reform packages. The first crisis came in August 1958. Since the response to the crisis lacked a sound macroeconomic basis and the populist government continued deficit financing, the situation soon transformed itself into a political crisis, ending in the May 1960 military coup.

Within two years democracy was restored, and the 1960s were years of close cooperation with the IMF and the OECD. However, by 1970 Turkey again faced a foreign exchange crisis, and since the underlying macroeconomic weaknesses continued to be ignored, another major devaluation was the only answer. Economic and political instability further increased when, in 1971, the military issued a written ultimatum to the political leadership. This ultimatum opened the way for the building of a national coalition in an effort to broaden the sharing of political power and responsibility. In fact, however, the succession of short-lived coalition governments only contributed further to political instability.

Two factors played a prominent role in this development. On the one hand, there was fragmentation of the two main centrist parties along ideological lines. On the other hand, the polarization of left and right inside and outside the parliament contributed to an increase in civil violence and erosion of government authority. This created an atmosphere unfavorable to economic development.

After a prolonged period in which the external balance was continually under strain, Turkey experienced a short period in the early 1970s during which there was a rapid improvement in the balance of payments, culminating in a current account surplus for the first time since the end of World War II. Of particular importance were the remittances by Turkish workers in Germany and elsewhere, which rose from an insignificant level in 1970 to about $1.2 billion in 1973, owing to buoyant world economic conditions. This transitory improvement in the balance of payments, however, only served to insulate the Turkish government from external economic realities.

The Turkish authorities failed to take any serious measures to adjust the economy to changed conditions in the aftermath of the first oil crisis. The massive adverse shift in the terms of trade in 1974, brought about by the huge rise in prices for oil and industrial imports, as well as the fall in demand for Turkish goods due to recession in the industrial countries, led to the rapid disappearance of the current account surplus. In 1975 and 1976, economic growth was sustained by large-scale short-term borrowing, and by 1977 substantial external payments arrears had begun to accumulate, leading to a drying up of external credits. The period of rapid growth came to an abrupt halt.

Thus, the basic inward-looking focus of the Turkish development strategy of the 1950s, 1960s, and early 1970s had promoted a production structure biased heavily toward supplying the domestic market, discouraging exports and resulting, toward the end of the 1970s, in increasing rigidities and distortions, which intensified pressures on domestic resources. At the same time, the stance of financial policies weakened considerably, and increasing resort was made to exchange and trade restrictions and multiple exchange rate practices to fend off pressures on the balance of payments. Political instability, an unmanageable public-sector deficit, unproductive state enterprises, runaway inflation, protected markets and domestic currency, and a serious balance of payments crisis due to ill-conceived policies, together with the inherent difficulties of the political system, and, finally, the government's delay in responding appropriately to the first oil shock and ensuing adverse world economic developments, left very little room for maneuver in the face of the second oil shock in 1979–80.

An attempt to redress the deteriorating economic situation was made as early as late 1977. In fact, Turkey was forced to make this attempt as a result of debt rescheduling talks with its creditors: both private and official creditors insisted on an IMF stand-by arrangement as a precondition for rescheduling. However, one should also note the importance of international political developments that had positively affected the Western countries' attitude toward Turkey. These were the years during which the Shah of Iran fell, early signs of the second oil shock were emerging, and Afghanistan was becoming unstable, and therefore Turkey was seen as the only potential island of stability in the area. This situation, in fact, triggered rescheduling negotiations in coordination with the OECD's and the IMF's technical, economical and political supports. A stabilization program mainly designed to improve the balance of payments was developed, which formed the basis of a two-year stand-by arrangement that went into effect in April 1978 and July 1979.

This program proved inadequate in relation to the severity of the economic crisis. Although some improvement took place in the current account, it was achieved by a drastic curtailment of imports and only a minor increase in exports. Moreover, public-sector finances continued to deteriorate, mostly as a result of a sharp rise in the operational losses of the state enterprises. Consequently, the government could not stay within the IMF ceilings and limits, and the program proved ineffective in eliminating the macroeconomic disequilibria.

This outcome was not surprising when one examines the then-prevailing political structure and the composition of the coalition governments: Süleyman Demirel was prime minister from 1975 to 1977 in two consecutive coalitions between the NSP (National Salvation Party) and the NAP (Nationalist Action Party). In these coalitions, the NSP strongly promoted the idea of government involvement in heavy industry—one of their slogans was "factories manufacturing factories." This stance, coupled with violent clashes between right- and left-wing groups, including acts of terrorism, did not leave Demirel much maneuvering room to tackle the real economic issues. In 1977, Demirel was forced to leave, and Bülent Ecevit took his turn as leader of a minority government. It fell to Ecevit to try to deal with the economic crisis of the late 1970s, which witnessed not only an escalation of terrorism but lengthening queues for increasingly scarce goods.

By the end of 1979, Turkey was in the midst of a severe foreign exchange crisis. The country was unable to import essential items such as crude oil, sugar, and even coffee. Inflation had accelerated, and unemployment was widespread and increasing. Moreover, there was political turmoil, partly due to the economic difficulties and partly to foreign subversion. During the years leading up to the crisis (1974–79), annual GNP growth had declined to an average of 4.4 percent. The public-sector deficit expanded rapidly from less than 2 percent of GNP in 1974 to more than 6 percent in 1979, averaging 4.5 percent from 1974 to 1979.

Thus, Turkey faced the second round of oil price increases with an extremely weak economy, a grossly overvalued currency, virtually no foreign exchange reserves, strongly negative real interest rates, a very high rate of inflation, widespread unemployment, stagnant output, political turmoil, and an external debt in excess of $13.5 billion, more than a quarter of which was short-term. This spelled the end of Ecevit's short-lived minority government,, and the beginning of Demirel's third Justice Party (JP) coalition government with the NSP and the NAP.

## Surviving the Storm: 1980 and After

Faced with the most severe economic crisis in the history of the republic, the government finally realized the need to undertake fundamental reforms that would alter the structure of the Turkish economy. On 24 January 1980, the government, another minority one, this time a right-wing one led by Süleyman Demirel, initiated a major change in the orientation of economic policy and introduced a major and comprehensive economic stabilization package. Behind the package was Turgut Özal, a powerful technocrat in the position of undersecretary of the prime ministry.

Simultaneously the government entered into negotiations with the IMF and other official and unofficial creditors. Negotiations with the Fund resulted in a three-year stand-by arrangement in the amount of SDR 1,250 million in June 1980. However, because of the political weakness of the minority government, which was not even able to elect a president of the republic in months-long sessions in Parliament, political and economic turmoil continued until the military intervened in September 1980. The military quickly formed a civilian government and put Özal in charge of continuing the implementation and further strengthening the already-introduced reform program.

Later in 1980, the stand-by arrangement with the Fund, and in particular the strength of the underlying economic program, helped convince the OECD governments to reschedule principal and interest payments falling due between 1980 and 1983, for 10 years. Eventually, in 1981, the banks agreed to extend for a seven-year period the maturities of the rescheduled bank debts to 10 years.

Özal served as deputy prime minister from September 1980 until a bank and brokerage house crisis in 1982 led him to resign. The military leaders blamed Özal's minister of finance, K. Erdem, for the crisis. But in fact, financial deregulation and interest rate liberalization were the main pillars of Özal's program, so he took the matter personally and resigned from office. Prime Minister Bülent Ulusu, a retired navy admiral, was asked by the military leaders not to appoint a new deputy prime minister but instead only to replace Erdem with A. B. Kafaoğlu, a former official in the ministry and chief economic and financial adviser to Kenan Evren, the military leader of the 1980 intervention. In fact, the Ulusu government consisted mainly of former technocrats and prominent nonpartisan figures and was considered a transitory government put in place until elections could be held.

In 1982, a rewritten constitution was submitted to a referendum and was approved by a vast majority. In the same referendum, Kenan Evren was elected president for a seven-year term, and the first general election under the new constitution was scheduled to be held in the spring of 1983. In this election, former politicians and their parties were banned from seeking any political post. Two new parties gained prominence: the Nationalist Democratic Party, established by retired army general Turgut Sunalp and publicly supported by the new president, and the Motherland Party, established by Turgut Özal.

Özal claimed his party would pool four factions under one roof: the center right, the center left, the nationalists, and the religious conservatives (previously the core of the NSP). This was very appealing to a public fatigued by years of political instability and violence caused by endless and useless fights among the various factions. Özal's team consisted of new, young, and promising figures, and its pleas for a free-market economy and administrative, financial, and economic reforms matched the society's desires. Moreover, the proven performance of Özal himself while in government during the 1980–82 period convinced voters that he could put the country's house in order. Consequently, despite Kenan Evren's open support of Turgut Sunalp's party, Özal's Motherland Party won the elections with a comfortable majority, and Özal resumed office in 1983 as prime minister. He immediately picked up the banner of the January 1980 reform program to push through some ambitious and major additional policy measures.

The January 1980 program was qualitatively different from previous reform plans in that it called for far-reaching structural changes in the

Turkish economy aimed at establishing the basis for outward-oriented growth. The new government was determined to attack the sources of the economic crisis, where previous attempts at reform had only sought to deal with the symptoms. This was one of the main determinants of Turkey's ability to negotiate and implement a successful debt relief plan with private, multinational, and official creditors. The policy reforms introduced in 1980 aimed not only at redressing the economic situation, but also at changing the development strategy Turkey had followed for several decades. That is why the program is commonly referred to as having dual goals.

Stability was the first and immediate goal. One of the fundamental pillars of a free-market economy is the ability to establish and maintain relative price equilibrium. To achieve this goal in Turkey, it was necessary to remove imbalances in relative prices in the commodity, labor, and financial and capital markets.

Imbalances in the commodity markets originated largely from the pricing policies of the state enterprises. These imbalances were aggravated by discrepancies and inconsistencies in import regulations. Imbalances in the labor markets derived from policies affecting taxation, income distribution, and wages. Finally, imbalances in the financial and capital markets stemmed from the extensive state intervention in the financial sector. Given that the public sector had at that time direct or indirect control over 80 percent of Turkey's financial sector, it is no surprise that every instance of inefficiency in the public sector rebounded on these markets, disrupting relative prices. Despite the abolition of price controls, including those on interest rates, as long as the public sector continued to dominate the economy, the system could never operate efficiently. Moreover, uncertainties in government policies, and even on occasion retroactive decisions, put an even greater strain on these balances.

Structural transformation was the second goal. As a developing country in need of regaining international credibility, Turkey opted for a program that sought to achieve balance of payments viability over the medium term. On the other hand, the ultimate target of the restructuring was to enter onto a path of self-sustaining growth.

Based on these two interrelated objectives, the government's policies were designed to correct distortions, inefficiencies, and supply rigidities in the domestic economy, developed during the long years of financial repression, by restoring market signals as a principal guide to economic policy decisions that would also allow rapid adjustment to external developments. The reforms chosen to achieve these goals fall into two categories: institutional (behavioral) reforms and policy-oriented reforms. (The reforms of the 1980s and early 1990s are summarized in table 1 and are measured against the hypotheses offered in John Williamson's introductory paper in table 2.)

## Table 1   Turkey: economic reforms under successive administrations, 1980–93

|  | 1980 to 1983: military-backed governments, Özal as deputy prime minister until June 1982 | 1983 to 1991: democratic governments, Özal as prime minister until 1989 | October 1991 to January 1993: coalition government, Demirel as prime minister |
|---|---|---|---|
| Fiscal discipline | Yes | No | No |
| Public expenditure prioritization | No | No | No |
| Tax reform | No | Yes | No |
| Financial liberalization | Yes | Yes | Yes |
| Exchange rate liberalization | Yes | Yes | Yes |
| Trade liberalization | Yes | Yes | Yes |
| Foreign direct investment liberalization | Yes | Yes | Yes |
| Privatization | No | Yes on paper, no in implementation | No |
| Deregulation | Yes | Yes | Yes |
| Property rights reform | No | No | No |

## Institutional (Behavioral) Reforms

The government's institutional reforms are aimed at achieving a better, more unified, efficient, coherent, responsive, productive, and timely process of economic decision making and execution throughout the economy, from the central government to the state enterprises to the private sector.

Efficient decision making was before the reforms one of Turkey's scarcest resources. As a first step, soon after Özal was elected, the traditional organizational structure of the Ministry of Finance was broken down, and the Treasury Department was subsumed into the Ministry of Finance in 1983. A new Undersecretariat of Treasury and Foreign Trade was created, reporting directly to the prime minister's office. In this way the prime minister consolidated under his direction all the major agencies of economic and financial management: the Undersecretariat of Treasury and Foreign Trade, the central bank, the Undersecretariat for State Planning Organization, and the newly established Extra-Budgetary Fund Administrations.

A newly established Money and Credit Committee was the technical forum set up to discuss policy issues. It is chaired by the minister of

## Table 2   Turkey: economic reforms and the Williamson hypotheses[a], 1980–93

| | 1980 to 1983: military-backed governments, Özal as deputy prime minister until June 1982 | 1983 to 1991: democratic governments, Özal as prime minister until 1989 | October 1991 to January 1993: coalition government, Demirel as prime minister |
|---|---|---|---|
| Crisis hypothesis | Yes | No | No |
| Honeymoon hypothesis | No | Yes | No |
| Demoralized opposition | No | No | Yes |
| Economic team | Yes | Yes | No |
| Leader with a vision | Yes | Yes | No |
| Comprehensive program | Yes on paper, no in implementation | Yes on paper, no in implementation | Yes on paper, no in implementation |
| Direct appeal to the public | Yes | Yes | No |

a. A "yes" indicates that the hypothesis is validated or that the condition was present during that period; a "no" indicates the contrary.

finance (at times by the deputy prime minister or the prime minister) and attended by at least three undersecretaries of the agencies mentioned above. The Economic Coordination Council was the corresponding political forum, headed by the prime minister and attended by some of the same key ministers and technocrats. These institutions were considered short cuts to the long political decision-making process.

## Policy-Oriented Reforms

**Trade liberalization**   The principal trade reforms included the elimination of quantitative controls on imports, such as the quota and licensing system; replacement of the positive import list (which specified those goods that could be imported, with all others proscribed) with a negative list (which listed only the imports proscribed, allowing all others); replacement of nontariff with tariff barriers; and a gradual reduction of levels of protection.

**Liberalization of the exchange control regime**   The country's conservative and rigid exchange control system dated back to the early years of the republic. Whereas as late as 1980 a Turkish citizen could be penalized for having a single US dollar in his pocket, today Turkish citizens are free to open savings accounts in any foreign currency at the domestic bank of their choice, and to transfer funds from those accounts anywhere in the world without restriction. (At least this is true for most cross-border transfers.) In addition, investors in the Istanbul Stock Exchange may freely move money in and out of the country. Investors in real estate are guaranteed the right to repatriate principal, profits, and rent.

**Exchange rates**    Reform of exchange rate policy was one of the key policy decisions of the reform program. A gradual process of freeing the exchange rate was applied, beginning with mini-devaluations and later moving to daily adjustments and, finally, market-determined exchange rates. Recognizing this progress, in April 1990 the IMF accorded Turkey Article VIII status, regarding convertibility of its currency.

**Export orientation**    A new set of tools and institutions were introduced for export promotion. Exporters were allowed to import their inputs at world prices in order to be able to compete worldwide. An export-import bank was established, and an export insurance scheme was introduced to cover country risks.

**Financial-sector deregulation and reforms**    Freeing of interest rates was the main policy decision aimed at boosting the rate of saving. In a depressed market with negative interest rates, this policy increased the monetization of the economy. However, without efficient regulation and supervision, this situation first prompted an oligopolistic reaction from the banking system and ultimately led to a financial crisis when a major brokerage house went under. In the wake of this crisis, financial-sector reforms were institutionalized in new legislation governing commercial banking, the central bank, and the stock exchange and other capital markets. For the first time a deposit insurance system was introduced. Elimination of entry restrictions attracted many foreign banks into Turkey, and this in turn enhanced competition in the sector.

**Fiscal reforms**    The introduction of a value-added tax in place of nine different taxes was the key reform in the fiscal area. Elimination of price controls applying to both state enterprises and the private sector, and elimination of subsidies in the public sector, were other important achievements.

**Foreign direct investment**    Although Turkey has had one of the developing world's most liberal foreign direct investment laws since 1954, its implementation was conservative. The bureaucracy's negative stance toward foreign investment was overhauled under the new economic program, and some new elements were introduced to attract direct investments. Recent figures reveal the dramatic results of this change in policy. Whereas *total* foreign direct investment received between 1954 and 1980 was only $230 million, today *annual* inflows are around $1 billion.

**Privatization**  The privatization program, which is still under way, is an indispensable element of the new economic policy and part of a wide-ranging program of structural transformation of the Turkish economy. The government's main goal in privatizing its state enterprises is to make the economy more responsive to market forces. The role of the government in the economy is to be confined to areas where the private sector cannot or will not enter because of profitability considerations, or where the services provided are in the nature of essential public goods (e.g., defense, health care, education, and infrastructure). This policy is viewed not merely as a solution to the problems of publicly owned corporations; it also is intended to increase competition and productivity throughout the economy, to increase the ownership base and improve the distribution of income, and to spur the development of the capital markets.

After eight years, the results of the privatization experience are at best mixed. First of all, the privatization process was slow to get under way. The amount of preparation required was frequently underestimated. Second, the institutional arrangements were unsuitable and inefficient in the early stages. What was needed was a single independent agency with strong political backing. With the unemployment rate still around 15 percent, people are not yet convinced of the merits of privatization, and therefore politicians are still skeptical about the electoral implications. Third, the legal system has to be fortified to inspire confidence in international investors.

Last but not least, the issue of privatization has been overpoliticized, both by the administration and particularly by the opposition, which continues to summon up the shades of past "capitulations" to the West by the Ottoman Empire. Thus, the privatisation issue, which is one of the key issues where national consensus is most needed, still has not been properly addressed. An effort to depoliticize the issue is called for, because the government's vulnerability to political attack is reducing its efficiency and creating problems for the successful implementation of the rest of the economic program.

**Infrastructure priorities**  There have been intensive efforts to address the inability of the existing infrastructure to serve the new economic program. Energy, transportation, and telecomunications investments were given top priority.

Although the whole idea of the reform process is more liberalization, deregulation, decentralization, and giving market forces more freedom to operate, policy interdependence and a medium-term macroeconomic strategy have proved to be extremely important.

Decisions affecting the private and the public sector are closely inter-dependent, as are measures influencing the generation of saving and investment and incentives to particular activities and sectors. For one thing, an increase in the availability of investible funds is required to develop efficient export performance and import substitution. Ratio-nalizing the system of incentives is also necessary to ensure the appro-priate choice of investments. Budget implications and the impact of these policies on the public-sector borrowing requirement are also to be considered. Correspondingly, the simultaneous implementation of the program's medium-term policy measures is necessary for each of them to have maximum effect.

At the same time, one should remember that, in the Turkish case, growth of output and employment in the process of stabilization and structural transformation required, first, a consolidation of the external accounts, and then a continuing flow of external resources to Turkey. These resources came in the form of private international loans, both for debt rescheduling and as new money; contributions by multinational organizations, such as IMF stand-by arrangements and World Bank pro-gram and structural adjustment loans; government-to-government arrangements, such as OECD debt reschedulings and fresh program loans from the Turkish Consortium; and private foreign capital. In this connection, it should be recognized that the shift from an inward to an outward orientation is a long process, necessitating considerable invest-ment that cannot be financed from domestic savings alone. Therefore, putting Turkey's house in order through a comprehensive and coherent set of policies is a key precondition for mobilizing the required external resources.

## An Assessment of Turkey's Reforms and Their Sustainability

I have tried to present a brief historical overview of the Turkish experi-ence of economic stabilization and restructuring. It is undoubtedly true that there is nothing novel about the policies I have described. The merits of these policies are well-known, they derive from sound eco-nomic theories, and they have been practiced elsewhere—with mixed results. Why, then, were these policies so much more successful in the case of Turkey, especially during the period between 1980 and 1987? I believe that some additional ingredients in the Turkish case played a catalytic role of harmonizing these policies and making them successful.

First was the commitment and the determination of the political authorities to carry the stabilization program through. Turkey was fortu-nate in having governments with the necessary political will to imple-ment and carry out painful stabilization measures and to reorient the economy on the basis of free-market principles. I should add that the end of political turmoil and chaos and the introduction of social peace in September 1980, as a result of the intervention by the Turkish armed forces, together with the commitment on the part of military authorities to maintain the recently implemented stabilization program with increased vigor, greatly facilitated the economic adjustment process with a "heterodox approach" during 1980–83. Trade unions and government employees were ready to make sacrifices in terms of an incomes policy; that is, real wages were suppressed during this period.

Second, the speed of implementation of the adjustment policies was crucial for their success. Since the policy measures were a bitter medicine, it is better that they were taken quickly rather than gradually.

Third, the confidence of the public in the country's economic leadership made the adjustment process acceptable, although the authorities made it quite clear that the results might be realized only after three to five years. This is the reason why the working class accepted a decrease in real wages in the early years of the program.

Fourth, the availability of economic and human resources to be tapped, of a potentially sound infrastructure to start with, and of idle industrial capacity (as much as 50 to 60 percent of total capacity) eased the adjustment problems when the crisis emerged. In addition, a wave of returning skilled Turkish workers and professionals—a "reverse brain drain"—after 1983 contributed to the adjustment process.

Fifth, the availability and relative ease of access to new export and construction markets, despite the world recession and heavy protectionism, greatly facilitated Turkey's adjustment.

Finally, Turkey was fortunate enough to owe a relatively small share of its total debt to the international commercial banks and a relatively large portion to foreign governments and official multinational bodies. This structure of the external debt eased the management of rescheduling. Even keeping these special features in mind, I believe that any developing country in the process of structural adjustment and in need of external financing must first display the political will and determination, working with the international financial community, to undertake the necessary steps to ensure a successful adjustment to a changing economic environment.

However, it is not my intention to suggest that the problem has only one dimension. Any attempt at reform has to be considered within the context of the underlying economic and financial policies and the developments from which the crisis has emerged.

When the country's domestic considerations are coupled with volatile international interest and exchange rates, the problem of stabilization, and especially of an external debt overhang, becomes rather unmanageable. It was such a combination that led developing countries in the 1980s to find themselves faced with capital outflows when they needed fresh inflows. Therefore, a significant reduction in the volatility of international interest rates and exchange rates should be considered crucial in achieving a workable set of measures to deal with the problem of sustainable stability and adjustment.

Finally, without the restoration of more favorable terms of trade for the developing countries, without a sustained improvement in the access of the developing world's exports to the markets of industrialized countries, and without an increasing level of private direct investment, all efforts of the developing countries to design and implement a coherent stabilization or austerity program are bound to be short-lived as well as politically and economically unbearable. Of course, there will always be special cases subject to special considerations.

The last decade undoubtedly has witnessed unprecedented and, even more important, irreversible changes in the Turkish economy. Nearly 70 years after the foundation of the republic, we can at last look forward to both healthy and sustainable free-market-oriented growth and a gradual integration of the Turkish economy into the European Community and the world economy.

Starting from this background and these expectations, the October 1991 elections led to a peaceful transition of government, confirming the growing maturity of Turkey's parliamentary democracy. This was followed by the relatively smooth formation of a coalition between Demirel's center-right and Head of Socialist Populist Party Erdal İnönü's center-left parties. Demirel, as a veteran politician, was welcomed by the industrialists. But as the coalition reached its first anniversary, it had to face increasing business skepticism about its economic record. Growth may be higher than in most countries, but inflation, still between 65 and 70 percent, has remained a thorn in the economy's side, and the coalition's economic program has been criticized both for its content and the slowness of its formulation. The irony is that this slow progress in carrying out election promises in line with the previous reform program is due more to a lack of commitment to those promises than to the delays inherent in governing through a wide-based coalition.

In fact, the structure of the coalition inspired in many circles exactly the opposite expectations with respect to the speed and efficiency of government performance on major social, political, and economic issues. Therefore, it appears that, having missed the honeymoon period for action, the current government must come up with a plan to restore the lost momentum. The most vital point in the search for a new set of complementary policies, in my view, is to fill the gaps in the previous program and to fine tune it. The new government also has to review the policy instruments and institutions in place, since some of those employed in the 1970s and 1980s are no longer valid in the context of the 1990s.

The most conspicuous characteristic of the 1980 economic program was its accurate diagnosis that one of Turkey's scarcest resources was neither foreign exchange, nor savings, nor labor, but rather an efficient mechanism for making macroeconomic decisions. The efficiency, speed, and flexibility imparted to the previously inert policymaking mechanism by such institutions as the Money and Credit Board and the Economic Coordination Committee go a long way toward accounting for the program's success up to 1985–86. Clearly it is a foremost priority today to get this decision-making mechanism functioning properly again, as it has been deteriorating since 1987. This deterioration, or "reform fatigue," accelerated in 1989 when Turgut Özal assumed the presidency, and reached its peak with the advent of the new coalition after 1991.

Similarly, the extrabudgetary funds introduced as an institutional reform have lost their original target of allocative efficiency in public funds and have become the major source of the financial disarray. That is why a movement has begun to put these funds back in the budget.

The foreign trade regime has been increasingly liberalized over the past decade. As there is no question of reverting to the quota system or export incentives in the form of tax refunds, the time has come to liberalize the system still further, avoiding unfair competition through the objective and effective implementation of antidumping and antitrust regulations, while simultaneously expanding export-import bank lending and export insurance services. Recent arrangements with the European Free Trade Association and a commitment to integration with the European Community in the form of a customs union by 1996 are the right steps to take in this area.

To capitalize on these developments, Turkey has to develop its own export markets, using new opportunities such as the Black Sea Economic Cooperation Zone and closer ties with the new republics in Eastern Europe and the former Soviet Union. Easily accessible markets like those in the Middle East in the early 1980s no longer exist.

It is crucial not to overemphasize the role of the monetary authority and monetary policy in Turkey's export-led market reorientation. In fact, since 1980, monetary policy has had to be concerned with both domestic stability and the balance of payments, to the extent that one can pursue two goals with one instrument. This means that more support from the fiscal side is urgently needed. Otherwise the central bank's credibility will be at risk for an unintended cause. New and consistent macroeconomic policies as well as better coordination in their implementation is required to restore and sustain credibility, and thus to achieve steady growth under conditions of price stability.

Foreign exchange regulations and policies have been deregulated to the point of no return, and integration with international markets is on the march. Consequently, the response to developments on foreign markets should not be to resort to artificial amendments and interventions such as exchange controls, but rather to adjust domestic economic policies, fiscal and monetary, to eliminate differences in inflation rates between Turkey and its trading partners. A realistic exchange rate policy is a tool for balance of payments adjustment, not for inflation control. It is also particularly important that the Turkish financial markets, which have been integrating with international financial markets since 1980, continue to do so and to keep up the process of self-renewal.

As the market economy has taken root, the buttons that the public authorities can press to achieve economic development and combat inflation are now fewer in number; this is the inevitable outcome of building a free-market economy. Moreover, their characteristics and functions have also changed. Against this limitation on the options available to policymakers, there is an important positive side of having market forces and institutions functioning. Today we can comfortably talk about a considerable improvement of the Turkish economy's ability to respond to external and internal shocks without any public authority's intervention by law or decree. Lack of such responsiveness was the leading cause of the economic crisis in the late 1970s. However, one should also remember that this phenomenon itself makes the whole system more vulnerable to any change. Developments in the area of currency substitution (foreign currency–denominated savings have increased to around 50 percent of total bank deposits) is a good example of this vulnerability.

One should bear in mind that the bitter flavor of a stabilization program cannot be disguised by any name. Whereas doctors shake the bottle before giving the medicine to the patient, in economics one has to shake the patient instead. Markets are attached to the status quo. They prefer to assume that the current situation will continue indefinitely because the players have adapted themselves to the situation and are reluctant to change. To break this resistance, the patient must first be shaken out of his comfortable expectations by convincing him that in the not-so-long term the system will work better under the new adjustment policies.

It is important to note that initiating a reform program depends on certain preconditions, but sustaining that program requires some additional ones. The January 1980 program is a case in point. Although it looked comprehensive, in its implementation stage one key segment was ignored or postponed: namely, public-sector finances. That is why inflation remains an unresolved issue. The cost of not addressing this problem directly and in time is that the credibility of the whole program is today being questioned, and reform fatigue has started to build up.

Assuming for a moment that the reforms are completed on all fronts, then the next concern is to avoid slippages by creating "guardians" within the new system: beneficiaries of the program, such as exporters, construction companies, savers, and importers on the one hand, and professional market representatives such as chambers of commerce, trade unions, academics, and media professonals on the other, who will lobby for sustaining the reforms. What we are observing today in Turkey is just the opposite. Thanks to the almost decade-long persistence of high inflation, a disguised pro-inflationary lobby has been created, which may be stronger than the reformist lobby.

Since there is no visible crisis on the horizon that would make it easier to initiate a new reform package, the current government is facing a real challenge to reverse this situation and push through a complementary reform package that includes reform of public finances.

On the other hand, the government might not have any alternative than to pursue fiscal discipline (i.e., a reduction in the public-sector borrowing requirement) for at least the following reason. As was explained above, even as reform of public-sector finance was being put aside or postponed, liberalizations and deregulations that promoted financial deepening, such as new capital market instruments and institutions and in particular convertibility of the currency, were carried out at full speed. This situation had a public-sector crowding-out effect in the financial markets, which now could easily lead to a short-term capital outflow in the event of a crisis. In short, the vulnerability of the liberalized and deregulated economy should always be a prime concern to public decision makers.

Last but not least, a key deficiency in Turkey's implementation of market-oriented reforms was the failure to establish an efficient, speedy, and just legal system, whether in the administrative, taxation, or juridical domain. While financial administrative reforms were given some degree of priority, the working of the legal system was taken as a given. In fact, the most important element of a successful free-market economy is an atmosphere in which there is little or no room for unfair competition. If some market players can easily get away with the reduced rules and regulations without being penalized either by the market or by the law, the new market system easily becomes self-defeating. When that happens, most observers are inclined to blame the market system rather than the determinants of that system: the tax and audit system, the state enterprise system, the subsidy system, the court system, and so on.

## Conclusion

Turkey's experience during the 1980s in implementing market-oriented reforms as part of a growth-oriented adjustment strategy suggests that a set of comprehensive and coherent reform policies backed by political determination and public support can make economic recovery leading to a sustainable growth possible.

Every country embarking on structural transformation will necessarily have a different set of policies and instruments to choose from. But whatever policies and instruments a country selects, the commitment and the determination of the political authority to carry the program through, and the confidence of the public in its economic leadership, are essential ingredients for success.

Furthermore, no country undertaking a major structural transformation through market orientation should adopt a static or fixed strategy. Given the dynamic nature of developing-country economies on the one hand, and the unstable but mostly progressive nature of international markets on the other, the initial set of reform policies will be and should be subject to continuous review. In fact, one of the most significant results of any market-oriented structural program is to increase and improve the economy's ability to respond to internal and external developments through market forces.

Economic growth is an imperative, not a choice. Without growth you cannot achieve anything else. But what is important today is a model of growth that links growth with the life of people. The problem now is how to survive, not how to grow sufficiently rapidly, for the new concept of sustainable development is based on structural economic, human, and environmental constraints.

In this context, the dimension of human development elaborated by the United Nations Development Programme appears to be a realistic way out, a means of salvation. Only well-educated human beings can seize the opportunities offered by the world economy and overcome the difficulties arising out of its continued integration. Only they can raise foreign saving and investment and import and adapt appropriate technologies. Only they can reach the global market.

Turkey is much luckier than many other developing countries in this respect. Paradoxically, the fact that it was one of the first to go virtually bankrupt in the late 1970s led it to a major policy shift in the early 1980s, thus gaining very valuable time. I would only stress one point. Success in a free-market economy depends squarely on private initiative. In this process, Turkey discovered that it had some very good entrepreneurs, a new breed of managers, disciplined and productive manpower, and a service sector highly adaptable to new technologies. In other words, the new era found Turkey quite ready, in terms of human development, for new challenges. Our structural adjustment and economic transformation program, now a decade old, was in fact intended to build on the achievements and learn from the mistakes of the past. Similarly, to impart a new element of dynamism and to inject a new momentum into the Turkish economy in which the problems are less severe and the fundamentals much stronger, all we have to do is look back and take stock of the developments and develop a skill for converting our mistakes into our assets. This does not mean that we do not have shortcomings. We still do, but one can easily identify them and reach the conclusion that neither are we short of solutions.

No one today challenges the achievements of market orientation in Turkey. The majority of the Turkish people agree that Özal did a great job in the 1980s.[1] But with the momentum acquired during the 1980s, people are looking for new dimensions, challenges, new visions, and new directions. Especially now that the Cold War is over, the question of Turkey's identity has reemerged with force.

At this juncture, on the way to full membership in the European Community, Turkey's challenge is to pursue uninterruptedly its adjustment and transformation into a market economy, and its democratization, to secure sustainable but rapid growth and provide the living standards that Turks have come to expect. The real challenge, it seems, is to keep the dynamism going. This dynamism looks solid and deep rooted, but it can be lost if it is mismanaged.

The Turkish people realize the importance of this transformation. To avoid marginalization of the country within the context of EC 1992 and the evolving world economy, reforms must be consolidated and new attempts to reform public-sector activities, including privatization, will have to be accelerated to take full advantage of global opportunities. There are reasons enough today to believe that these opportunities will not be missed.

---

1. Özal, who died 17 April 1993, was succeeded by Süleyman Demirel.

# Comment

NANCY BERMEO

The papers by Francisco Torres and Guillermo de la Dehesa offer sound explanations for the success of economic liberalization in the cases of Portugal and Spain. In this comment I will highlight the similarities and differences between the two cases and develop some general themes that might be applicable outside Iberia.

The factors that John Williamson asks us to consider when thinking about the politics of structural adjustment fall into two general categories: those over which a governing team exercises direct control, and those that derive from the political and economic environment that the government has inherited. The timing of reform initiatives, the composition of the policymaking team, the executive's weighting of electoral concerns, and the comprehensiveness and timetable of the adjustment programs are all the fruits of government decision making. Whether the government takes reform initiatives because of an ''economic crisis'' or because of a voters' mandate is more environmentally determined. Whether a government faces a ''weak and demoralized opposition'' (in Williamson's words) is environmentally determined as well.

The only factor that does not fit easily into one of these two categories is whether the government has the ''will and ability to bypass vested interests and go directly to the people.'' A government's will is internally determined, but its ability to bypass special interests has a great deal to do with environmental factors beyond its control.

This distinction between governmental and environmental factors is extremely helpful in comparing the Portuguese and Spanish cases. A

*Nancy Bermeo is Associate Professor at Princeton University.*

review of recent history quickly reveals individual governments in each country that were remarkably similar in terms of the factors subject to government control. There clearly *were* teams of technopols behind the more profound structural adjustment initiatives in each country. Yet, because of environmental factors, these governments emerged at different times. They also faced different adjustment tasks. Portugal and Spain are justifiably considered successful cases of structural adjustment, but their routes to success—and their starting points—are so dramatically different that it is appropriate to think of them as presenting two distinct models for structural reform. The Portuguese reforms were slow and labor-protective. The Spanish reforms, in contrast, were faster and labor-compensating. The similarities and differences between these models are discussed below.

## Similarities

The Portuguese and Spanish models are similar in that each involved a cohesive team of technopols who presented a comprehensive program for reform shortly after their party won an absolute majority in a national election. This occurred in Spain in 1982, with the election of the Socialist government and the naming of Miguel Boyer to head the Ministry of Finance, Economics, and Commerce. In Portugal, a similar team with a similar program emerged only in late 1989, after Miguel Beleza (and later Jorge Braga de Macedo) became minister of finance under the majority government of the Social Democratic Party (PSD).

In both countries, as John Williamson would predict, the prime ministers made concentrated efforts to explain the merits of structural adjustment to the voting public at large. These public appeals were aimed not simply at facilitating policy implementation but also at protecting each ruling party's support base. There is little evidence to suggest that either Felipe González or Aníbal Cavaco Silva was unconcerned with his electoral future. On the contrary, it is highly significant that government leaders in both countries waited until their parties had secured absolute legislative majorities before undertaking major privatization and industrial restructuring initiatives. This occurred later in Portugal than in Spain, which brings us to the substantial differences between the cases.

## Differences

### Differences in the Pace of Reform

Both of the Iberian structural reform programs were gradualist, but the Portuguese program was more gradual than the Spanish. Both countries instituted stabilization programs almost immediately after the collapse of their dictatorships, but Spain moved from stabilization to a fully comprehensive adjustment program in only six years. In Portugal the process took some 12 years and included (unlike the Spanish adjustment) three austerity programs involving the International Monetary Fund. Although the PSD's 1987 program promised massive structural reform, it was not until 1990 (as Torres correctly states) that industrial restructuring actually began.

## Different Constraints

The different pace of structural adjustment in the two countries underscores the importance of environmental factors in determining the ability of technopols to institute reforms. Securing an absolute electoral majority was helpful in both cases, but a more detailed comparison suggests that a team of technopols with an electoral majority is not a sufficient condition for reform. Electoral majorities have to be analyzed in the context of a country's constitutional system as a whole, and the Portuguese constitution provides higher barriers to economic reform than the Spanish. The most obvious of these was the prohibition on privatization enshrined in Part II, Article 83. This provision could not be amended without a two-thirds majority vote in the national legislature—something the PSD was unable to secure until October 1988.

A second example of the importance of constitutional constraints comes from comparing the two countries' attempts to liberalize firing practices. In Spain, the Spanish Socialist Workers Party (PSOE) changed protective laws and made a major move toward flexibilization through normal legislative channels in 1984. The PSD in Portugal tried to do the same in 1987, but the Constitutional Tribunal declared the bill unconstitutional. The amended bill that was eventually passed was described as "virtually toothless" (*Economist Intelligence Unit* 1993, 17).

The comparison of Portugal and Spain illustrates that electoral majorities only guarantee success if power is actually concentrated in the legislature. If power is diffused through a divided executive or a strong constitutional court, or through other specific constitutional provisions, even a strong electoral majority will not ensure structural reform.

## Different Employment Practices

Portugal's structural reforms have thus far not involved high levels of unemployment. Table 1 illustrates the dramatic contrast in this regard with the Spanish case.

The contrast has its roots in the very different nature of the two countries' transitions to democracy. Portugal's revolutionary transition

**Table 1    Spain and Portugal: unemployment as a share of total labor force, 1976–91** (percentages)

| Year | Spain | Portugal |
|------|-------|----------|
| 1976 | 4.7 | 4.0 |
| 1977 | 5.2 | 5.3 |
| 1978 | 6.9 | 6.6 |
| 1979 | 8.5 | 7.0 |
| 1980 | 11.2 | 6.5 |
| 1981 | 14.4 | 5.6 |
| 1982 | 16.2 | n.a. |
| 1983 | 17.8 | 8.6 |
| 1984 | 20.6 | 9.3 |
| 1985 | 22.1 | 8.6 |
| 1986 | 20.9 | 8.3 |
| 1987 | 20.4 | 6.9 |
| 1988 | 19.3 | 5.7 |
| 1989 | 17.0 | 5.0 |
| 1990 | 16.1 | 4.5 |
| 1991 | 15.9 | 3.8 |

n.a. = not available.

*Source*: Eurostat, *Basic Statistics of the Community*, various issues.

involved the expropriation and nationalization of all banks and basic industries as well as many other firms. By the end of the revolutionary period in 1975, an estimated 53 percent of the country's fixed industrial investment was under state control. In the face of recession and intense competition from abroad, these state-owned industries have provided a safe haven for excess labor.

Because privatizations (and flexibilization more generally) have come so late in the chronology of Portuguese reform, redundancies resulting from further liberalization will occur in an environment substantially different from that of Spain in 1983. Whereas Spain took its initiatives some three years *before* accession to the European Community, Portugal is launching its restructuring programs well *after* accession. This means that the transfers and investment associated with EC membership are already gathering momentum. Portugal moved toward restructuring while its economy was on an upswing. In Spain, the PSOE government implemented its program some three years *before* investment began to rise.

Although the economic costs of artificially maintaining high employment are reflected in Portugal's comparatively high inflation rate, the PSD enjoyed a political payoff the Spanish never achieved. Although Cavaco Silva's 1988 attempts to introduce labor reform legislation pro-

**Table 2   Spain and Portugal: strike rates, 1977–90** (percentage of the labor force)

| Year | Spain | Portugal |
|------|-------|----------|
| 1977 | 22.09 | 7.39 |
| 1978 | 28.82 | n.a. |
| 1979 | 42.54 | 6.24 |
| 1980 | 17.00 | 6.64 |
| 1981 | 14.40 | 9.32 |
| 1982 | 7.75 | 6.06 |
| 1983 | 10.74 | 6.01 |
| 1984 | 16.17 | 5.09 |
| 1985 | 10.84 | 4.41 |
| 1986 | 6.06 | 5.12 |
| 1987 | 12.94 | 1.78 |
| 1988 | 44.94 | 3.37 |
| 1989 | 9.42 | 6.33 |
| 1990 | 6.37 | 2.71 |

*Source*: International Labour Office, *International Labour Office Yearbook*, various years; Organization for Economic Cooperation and Development, *OECD Labor Force Statistics*, 1968–88.

voked a massive general strike (Graham 1992, 293), strikes and labor mobilization in Portugal have generally been remarkably low (table 2). The PSOE invested a great many resources in compensatory programs for the unemployed—this is why the model is called ''labor-compensating''—but the fact of unemployment itself and a series of dramatic conflicts over the nature of the government's compensatory schemes drove millions of Spanish workers into the streets. Resistance to restructuring in Spain was usually confined to certain cities, but it was intense and often violent. Eventually, the controversy over restructuring led to a formal split between the ruling PSOE and its own labor federation.

Whereas the Spanish government succeeded (to use Williamson's language) in ''going over the heads of special interests'' to gain general popular support for its reforms, Portugal took another route. In Portugal, reforms were delayed until the strength of the economy gave workers greater hope for future employment, and until the special interests themselves were willing to accept the change.

## Different Wage Levels

A related factor distinguishing the Portuguese from the Spanish case has to do with wage levels. Spain's industrial policy allowed unemploy-

**Table 3  Spain and Portugal: average gross hourly earnings of manual workers, 1980–91** (in current purchasing power standard)

| Year | Spain | Portugal |
|------|-------|----------|
| 1980 | n.a. | 2.22 |
| 1981 | 4.81 | 2.72 |
| 1982 | n.a. | 3.30 |
| 1983 | n.a. | 3.28 |
| 1984 | n.a. | 3.51 |
| 1985 | 6.45 | 3.21 |
| 1986 | 6.73 | 2.22 |
| 1987 | 7.17 | 3.55 |
| 1988 | 7.68 | 3.74 |
| 1989 | 8.10 | 3.65 |
| 1990 | 8.40 | 3.76 |
| 1991 | 8.59 | 3.88 |

n.a. = not available

*Source*: Eurostat, *Basic Statistics of the Community*, various issues.

ment to rise, but wages for those who managed to keep their jobs were relatively high. Portugal took another route and traded wage increases for job security. Table 3 illustrates the contrast between the two cases. It is clear that environmental constraints (related to, among other factors, the constitution) forced Portugal's technopols to accept the wages-versus-jobs trade-off, but the serendipitous result is that the country currently presents investors with both the lowest wages and the lowest strike rates in Western Europe. These are assets the Spanish can only envy (table 3).

## Different Crises, Different Mandates

The Portuguese and Spanish cases suggest that neither an electoral mandate for liberalization nor a profound economic crisis is required for the deepening of structural adjustment. The PSOE won a strong electoral mandate in the election that brought its technopols to power, but the party's platform and campaign never promised liberalization. The economy was widely perceived to be in crisis, but the solution the PSOE offered the Spanish electorate before coming to office was, if anything, more state intervention rather than less. The PSD campaigned openly for the liberalization of the Portuguese economy and won a strong mandate for structural reform, but in that country the most radical structural changes were made *after* the sense of crisis had subsided. In Portugal (again to use Williamson's terms) there was a clear mandate for liberalization but a diminishing crisis. In Spain there was a clear crisis but no clear mandate.

## Conclusions

The differences between the Portuguese and the Spanish models have less to do with what their respective technopols *sought* to accomplish than with what they were *able* to accomplish given different environmental constraints. Finding a team of technopols and drawing up a comprehensive program seem to be the least problematic aspects of the structural adjustment process. Indeed, for certain aspects of the reform process, a clearly identifiable, cohesive team of technopols does not even seem to be required. Both Spain and Portugal undertook several sorts of economic liberalization initiatives without the guidance of a cohesive team of technopols. Economic stabilization and trade liberalization programs were initiated during the early governments of both renewed democracies, and although well-known economists headed the ministries that took these initiatives, ministerial positions and politics in general were so fluid that images of durable and decisive teams of any sort were hard to project. The economic ministries changed heads 21 times in the first five years of Portuguese democracy and 14 times during the comparable years in Spain (figure 1).

The fact that a visible and lasting team of technopols was not a requisite for some types of liberalizing reform does not negate the importance of this factor for reforms of a different sort. Highly salient teams of technopols initiated the deeper and more politically difficult aspects of structural adjustment in both states. Prominent among these initiatives were the programs of industrial restructuring and privatization that have been the focus of the preceding comparison.

The comparison teaches us that the environmental constraints on adjustment initiatives are greatly affected by the timing and nature of reforms. In both Portugal and Spain, various reformist governments announced certain sorts of reform initiatives fairly early during their tenure—a substantiation of the "honeymoon hypothesis." However, neither state implemented industrial restructuring or privatization during the first electoral "honeymoon." Both waited to deepen the structural reform initiatives until several electoral cycles had run their course and democracy had been consolidated.

Taken together these cases lead one to believe that, in redemocratizing states, structural adjustment programs are more likely to be successful if they are initiated after the multiple political problems associated with

**Spain**

| | 1976 (July)* | 1977 (July) | 1978 (Feb.) | 1979 (Apr.) | 1980 (May) | 1980 (Sept.) | 1982 (Dec.) |
|---|---|---|---|---|---|---|---|
| Economic Affairs: | | Enrique Fuentes Quintana | Fernando Abril Martorell | | | | |
| Economy and Commerce: | | | | | | Juan Antonio García Díez | |
| Economy and Finance: | | | | | | | Miguel Boyer |
| Finance: | Eduardo Carriles Galarraga | Francisco Fernández Ordóñez | | Jaime García Añoveros | | | Ministry merged with Economics Ministry |
| Commerce: | José Lladó Fernández Urrutia | | | | | | |
| Commerce and Tourism: | | | | | Luis Gamir Casares | | |
| Trade and Tourism: | | Juan Antonio García Díez | | | | | |
| Industry: | Carlos Pérez de Brizio Olarriaga | | Agustín Rodríguez Sahagún | Carlos Bustelo y García | | | |
| Industry and Energy: | | Alberto Oliart Sausol | | | Ignacio Bayón Mariné | | Carlos Solchaga |

**Portugal**

| | 1976 (July)* | 1977 (Jan.) | 1978 (Jan.) | 1978 (Aug.) | 1979 (Aug.) | 1980 (Jan.) | 1981 (Jan.) | 1981 (Sept.) | 1983 (June) |
|---|---|---|---|---|---|---|---|---|---|
| Economics: | António Sousa Gomes | | | Fernando S. Martins | Carlos Carreira Gago | | | | |
| Finance: | Henrique Medina Carreira | | | José da Silva Lopes | António Sousa Franco | | | João F. Salgueiro | Ernâni Lopes |
| Finance and Planning: | | | Manuel R. Constâncio | | | Aníbal Cavaco Silva | João Morais Leitão | | |
| Trade and Tourism: | António Barreto | João Mota Pinto | Basilio M. Horta | | | Basilio M. Horta | Alexandre Vaz Pinto | | Alvaro Barreto |
| Commerce and Tourism: | | | | Pedro Pires Miranda | | | | | |
| Industry: | | | | | Fernando M. Videira | | | | |
| Industry and Tech.: | Walter Rosa | António S. Gomes | Carlos Melancia | | | | | | |
| Industry and Technology: | | | | | | Alvaro Barreto | Ricardo Baião Horta | | José Veiga Simão |

**Figure 1  Spain and Portugal: key economic policymakers 1975–83**

* Transition elections held June 1977 in Spain, and April 1976 in Portugal.
*Sources: Europa Yearbook, Statesman's Yearbook, Facts on File, Keesing's Contemporary Archives,* and Economist Intelligience Unit country profiles.

regime consolidation have been resolved. The political timing of initiatives is important, but timing vis-à-vis regime change may be even more important than timing within an electoral cycle.

In Portugal, the time that elapsed between regime change and profound industrial restructuring was greater than in Spain, and the political strife associated with adjustment was comparatively low. Technopols in other countries should find a strong argument for gradualism here.

Another argument suggested by this comparison is that successful adjustment in new democracies might involve an informal division of labor among political parties. It is probably not coincidental that neither of the parties that successfully deepened structural reforms in the Iberian peninsula actually had control of their respective states in the years immediately following the collapse of dictatorship. In Spain, the first government of the new democracy was led by the center-right Unión de Centro Democrático (UCD). In Portugal, it was led by the Socialist Party. The difficulties of presiding over the political transition left both parties weaker, and a "weakened opposition" (to return to Williamson's original list of variables) decreased the electoral costs of structural reform for both the PSD and the PSOE.

Which of these models is most applicable abroad? This is a question for future research. Certainly, the Spanish model is best-known. Its pact-based, compensatory approach has caught the imagination of many politicians in Latin America and elsewhere. But the lesser-known, labor-protective Portuguese model merits attention as well. From an economic standpoint, Portugal's inability to control inflation has been a serious liability, but the political benefits of providing nearly full employment to a once-radicalized working class have not been inconsequential. Portugal has been able to move from a situation of literally revolutionary instability to one of high social consensus and consolidated democracy in less than two decades. Social mobilization in the 1980s has been extremely low, and the economic ground lost in the past is being regained daily.

Portugal thus provides an especially important lesson for those who argue that democracy must be compromised for structural adjustment to proceed, for the Portuguese political elite worked successfully within the framework of an extremely egalitarian constitution. Promising socialism and giving substantial powers to a "Revolutionary Council," the constitution bore the marks of the social revolutionary period in which it was written. The constitution was gradually modified, but always within its own democratic parameters and never at a pace that provoked destabilizing popular mobilization.

For the Eastern European countries, the Portuguese story is especially revealing. Beginning with a revolutionary regime change, a comparatively large state sector, and strong constitutional constraints on policymaking, the Portuguese case comes closest to their own. Certainly, both the Spanish and the Portuguese cases hold important lessons for technopols everywhere.

## References

Economist Intelligence Unit. 1993. *Portugal to 1993*. London: The Economist.
Graham, Lawrence. 1992. "Redefining the Portuguese Transition to Democracy." In John Higley and Richard Gunther, eds. *Elites and Democratic Consolidation in Latin America and Southern Europe*. Cambridge: Cambridge University Press.

# Comment

ANNE O. KRUEGER

It is a great pleasure to comment on Yavuz Canevi's interesting and insightful paper on Turkish policy reforms during the 1980s. Turkey's success, in the face of a worldwide recession and a debt crisis that engulfed other developing countries, is well-known. Canevi, as governor of the central bank in a critical period during these reforms, is in an excellent position to provide an insider's analysis of them.

I would like, first, to elaborate a bit on some of Canevi's points. Certain phenomena on the Turkish scene, including especially some of the political-economic interactions in the reform process, need explaining for a non-Turkish audience. I would also like to comment on the current economic-political situation. Finally, I have been asked to comment on the relevance of Turkey's experience for other countries, and especially for the countries of Eastern Europe and the former Soviet Union.

Turning first to the Turkish experience, it is hard to convey the extent of the economic difficulties, and the sense of crisis, that pervaded Turkey late in 1979 and in January 1980. Inflation was accelerating and had reached an annual rate of over 100 percent, in a country where there are fewer indexation mechanisms than in other inflation-prone countries. The public-sector borrowing requirement (PSBR) was huge, fueled in large part by the enormous deficits of the state enterprises (in Turkey these produce a wide variety of minerals, manufactures, transport services, and other items and distribute many agricultural inputs and out-

*Anne O. Krueger is a Professor of Economics at Stanford University. She is also a non-resident Senior Fellow at the Brookings Institution.*

puts). These enterprises had, at the behest of successive governments, failed to raise the prices of their outputs proportionately with inflation, although there is every evidence that many of them were also high-cost producers. As inflation accelerated, their deficits rose, and central bank credits were automatically extended, thereby further fueling inflation.

In addition, official foreign-exchange receipts had been dropping for at least two years in response to an increasing overvaluation of the currency and buoyant demand in the domestic economy. Shortages of imports (including oil, of which Turkey imports all of its consumption) pervaded the economy. By the early winter of 1979–80, which was an unusually cold one in Turkey, many people were unable to heat their homes and businesses, as even the trucks that might have brought lignite were unable to obtain petrol. The crisis had been worsening for some time, and per capita income had been dropping for at least two years.

During the 1977–79 period, there had been two stabilization programs agreed upon with the IMF. Each had been confidently announced but then abandoned before the end of the program, as the authorities were unable to remain within the credit and budgetary ceilings previously agreed to.

Canevi notes that the 1980 program was different. He is correct, but if anything he underemphasizes the differences. Whereas earlier stabilization programs (both those of the 1970s and the two earlier, reasonably successful ones also discussed by Canevi) had focused almost entirely on inflation and balance of payments difficulties, the January 1980 reforms were, from the beginning, intended to change the relationship between the private and public sector, on the one hand, and the incentives facing import-competing and export production, on the other.

After almost fifty years of adherence to import substitution and a large role for state enterprise in the economy, both of which had been initiated under Atatürk, this was a profound and startling change. Several things should be noted. First, the January 1980 reforms were developed by a small team of technocrats working under the direction of Turgut Özal, who had been appointed deputy prime minister late in the preceding autumn. It is reported that various members of the team putting the program together took decrees for signature to their ministers one by one, without informing them as to the entire set of changes being made. It was only the depth of the economic crisis that permitted this suspension of normal Turkish political processes. Second, the reforms undertaken prior to September 1980 were undertaken by decree; they were not approved by Parliament. Indeed, in the summer of 1980, the reform program appeared to be in difficulty because of parliamentary opposition, as Prime Minister Demirel was head of a weak coalition government.

Third, the military intervened in September 1980. This intervention appears to have been prompted by a variety of concerns, preeminent among which was the state of civil unrest at the time. The fact that the economic program appeared threatened may also have been a factor. Whatever their motives, the military promoted Özal to be deputy prime minister, signaling their strong support for the program.

Fourth, the traditional components of a stabilization program—cuts in fiscal deficits, credit ceilings, and nominal exchange rate changes—were undertaken in Turkey and were initially highly successful. Inflation fell from its peak of over 100 percent to an annual low of less than 35 percent by 1982. State enterprises were not only permitted to raise their prices, but were told that they could no longer finance their deficits through automatic access to central bank credits; state enterprise deficits as a percentage of GNP fell from the 8 to 9 percent range in 1980 to below 2 percent by 1983. In addition, export growth spurted immediately, and real GNP growth accelerated even in 1980. The crisis had been so deep that, while the reforms inevitably were associated with dislocation, benefits could be seen in some arenas very quickly.

Fifth, and perhaps most interesting, in 1983 the military wanted a return to civilian rule. They authorized two parties to contest the election, refused to permit the former politicians to resume political activity, and actively supported one of the candidates. Özal, who had been fired by the military government a year earlier in favor of a much more expansionary economic program, announced that he would form a political party and oppose the military and their candidate. Özal's party not only won the election but received over 40 percent of the popular vote, a very large plurality by Turkish standards.

Thus, Özal received a fairly strong mandate to continue with the reforms, and he proceeded to do so. Canevi has correctly stressed the need for, and the extent of, reforms in the financial sector. The government also removed all import quotas, moved to a lower and more uniform tariff structure, and greatly liberalized exchange controls. It even announced that full convertibility was the ultimate objective, and by the late 1980s, the remaining exchange controls had little effect. Although a program of privatization was announced, it was less successful than other aspects of the program, at least through the 1980s.

By the late 1980s, the Turkish economy was achieving an average annual rate of growth of over 6 percent, and the structure of the economy had been truly transformed: exports, which had been around 5 percent of GNP in the late 1970s, were over 20 percent by 1987. Imports had, of course, risen almost commensurately. Prior to the change in incentives associated with the 1980s reforms, Turkish businesses had focused on the domestic market. After the reforms took effect they demonstrated that they were capable of competing internationally as well. Indeed, if there is a point on which I would question Canevi's views, it is his statement that Turkey had an advantage in making reforms work because of its large supply of capable entrepreneurs. Although that is certainly true, no one in Turkey recognized it prior to the reforms. One of the lasting contributions of the reform program is that Turks have learned that their businessmen are competent and capable of functioning in international markets.

However, by the late 1980s support for Özal and his party was diminishing. Before each election, government expenditures had increased significantly, and the inflation rate had risen. By the late 1980s it had peaked at 60 to 70 percent several times but had fallen somewhat after each election. In 1991 the Motherland Party, which Özal had formed, lost the election, and a coalition government, again led by Süleyman Demirel, assumed power.

As Canevi hints, at present there are some real questions about the Turkish economy's prospects. The fiscal deficit is again prospectively in excess of 10 percent of GNP, and the inflation rate is in excess of 60 percent. As Canevi notes, many of the reforms that were undertaken have permanently altered the structure of the Turkish economy and cannot be undone. Nonetheless, there are many questions about the sustainability of Turkish economic policy at present.

Much more could be said: Turkey achieved these results at a time when most developing countries were experiencing stagnation or slow growth, due in part to the severe worldwide recession in the early 1980s and in part to problems associated with their own inward-oriented economic policies and prior buildups of debt. Turkey benefited from flows of new money to support reforms, receiving strong support from the international community. From the perspective of political economy, the most interesting lesson seems to be the support garnered by Özal in 1983 despite, or because of, his identification as architect of the reform program.

Let me turn now to the relevance of this and other countries' experiences with policy reform for the countries of Eastern Europe and the former Soviet Union. I started with the perception that the similarities were few and that the initial situations were entirely different. I have become increasingly less convinced of that viewpoint.

The first basis for belief in major differences is the fact that the former Communist countries now striving toward market economies necessarily must put in place commercial codes where they did not exist before and find ways of privatizing formerly state-owned assets. At first glance, that constitutes a clear difference. However, when it is recognized that, in many developing countries, private ownership has been surrounded by a labyrinth of government regulations and controls that determine the profitability of economic activity, the difference blurs. Whether it is easier to privatize from a position in which there is no tradition of private economic activity (and even in the former Communist countries there were gray markets), or to change enterprises' behavior from reliance upon governmental favors to reliance upon markets for profitability is, it seems to me, an open question. On the one hand, the fact that privatization is difficult makes the transition to a market economy more challenging; on the other hand, the fact that the step must be taken and is a highly visible change in a country's economic structure may make reform easier. In that regard, it should also be noted that state enterprises in Turkey and in other countries have operated at high cost and inefficiently, and it has proved, at least in Turkey to date, impossible to shut them down or make them into privately profitable economic activities.

Moreover, in many countries including Turkey, there have built up entrenched bureaucracies whose existence hinges upon control of private economic activity. One can think of a variety of arguments on either side of the proposition that breaking the grip of those bureaucracies in countries where there is a continuity of government may be more difficult than in countries undergoing conscious, radical changes in governmental structures.

Finally, there is the question of the collapse of trade in the former Communist countries. There is no doubt that such a collapse creates great short-term dislocation and is equivalent to a large terms-of-trade loss. The available evidence suggests, however, that much of that trade was highly uneconomic. How different is that from the situation in developing countries where firms sheltered by import prohibitions have produced low-quality goods for the domestic market? The terms-of-trade shocks no doubt complicate the political problems of leaders in countries attempting to shift toward market economies; whether it is also a qualitatively different challenge strikes me as much more problematic.

The good news from the Turkish experience seems to be how fast individual producers can respond to altered incentives. To the extent that there is the same sort of drastic shift in incentives in other reforming countries, there is considerable basis for optimism that the same sort of response may be forthcoming.

# Comment

DANI RODRIK

It is a rare privilege to discuss these papers on the political economy of policy reform, written by individuals who actually made the reforms happen. At the risk of gross oversimplification, I will try to summarize the experiences described to us in terms of several syndromes that I think these cases illustrate.

## The Honeymoon Syndrome

In the midst of a deep crisis, an incoming government often experiences a temporary autonomy from the push and pull of short-term political pressures. At such moments, it may be possible to implement relatively radical reforms—reforms that are unlikely to be adopted in normal times.

The surprising thing about the honeymoon period is not that it exists, but that it lasts for such a short period. In Poland it lasted about nine months, even though the Polish crisis was the deepest among the countries represented here, and the new Solidarity-led government had more legitimacy than the reform governments in any of the other countries. The team of Finance Minister Leszek Balcerowicz exhibited remarkable farsightedness in drawing the correct conclusion from the very beginning: the narrow window of opportunity open to the new government necessitated fast and radical action. The Polish "big bang" effectively rendered irreversible certain reforms that could have become

Dani Rodrik is a Professor of Economics and International Affairs at Columbia University.

controversial later on. For example, although there were some relatively minor reversals on the trade policy front, it would have been considerably more difficult to institute radical trade liberalization at the beginning of 1991 than at the beginning of 1990.

In view of the ephemeral nature of the honeymoon effect, what these cases also reveal is the importance of demonstrating early success in some key dimensions of reform. In Poland the elimination of shortages practically overnight, and in Turkey the stupendous and largely unexpected export boom, were critical in endowing the broader reform programs with legitimacy. Nothing entrenches and sustains the reforms like success of this kind. Successful reforms have many parents; failures must remain orphans. The political opposition will be quick to rally around reforms that it previously attacked when it turns out that the reforms are popular. In Turkey, for example, it is surprising how few of Turgut Özal's reforms (which were heavily attacked by the opposition at the time) were renounced once the opposition came to power.

## The Nixon-in-China Syndrome

It is a truism that only President Richard M. Nixon, with his impeccable anti-Communist credentials, could have made the overtures he did to Mao Tse-tung's China. Since Nixon was a trustworthy character to the American right, he could be relied on not to sell out US national interests. The translation of this principle to reform strategy is that it may take a labor-based government to undertake reforms that would be otherwise unacceptable to labor and other popular groups. And for the same well-founded reason: it is easier to convince organized labor that the changes are needed ones that will pay off in the long run, even if they hurt a bit now, when the argument is put to them by a government that *prima facie* has their interest in mind.

As an example, the Polish program decontrolled all important domestic prices save one: the wage rate. And the amended wage indexation rule (the *Popiwek*) virtually guaranteed a reduction in (statistical) real wages from the base of December 1989. The acceptability of this element of the program to the Solidarity rank and file must count as one of the greatest paradoxes of the Polish program. One wonders whether workers would have been equally farsighted if the party in power had been one based predominantly on middle-class interests (whatever that means in the Polish context). Similarly, it has fallen to Socialist Prime Minister Felipe González in Spain to consolidate openness and liberalization, and to privatize. Argentina may represent the most extreme example of this syndrome, with Carlos Saúl Menem the Peronist leading the charge against populist policies.

# The Promised Land Syndrome

When policymakers can articulate and communicate a sound vision of their model for society *and* there is widespread consensus in society about the desirability of this vision, it becomes easier to undertake and sustain comprehensive reform programs. In Poland, the clear rejection of the socialist system and the strong desire to become just like any Western European society provided clear beacons for the direction that economic policy would take in the transition. The reformers skillfully used this consensus about the country's ultimate goals to promote the reforms they called for. I call this ability of a society and its leaders to focus on a clear final goal for its reforms the "promised land syndrome."[1]

To appreciate the difference that the lack of such a vision can make, consider the contrasting experiences of Turkey and Spain in the mid-1970s. Both countries were severely hit by the first oil shock in 1974, not only through the direct terms-of-trade effect but also through indirect effects in the form of reduced workers' remittances from Europe and reduced export demand in recession-stricken EC countries. The political systems were superficially similar also. In Spain, a new and fragile democracy had followed on the heels of the Franco regime, and a weak minority government depended on the support of other parties in the parliament. Similarly in Turkey, a fragile democracy had been recently reestablished after a period (1971–73) in which the military had effectively been at the helm, and a coalition government was in power. But the policy reactions were quite different.

In Turkey there was no adjustment to the shock. Indeed, the effect of the shock was exacerbated by expansionary fiscal policies and unsustainable external borrowing. This culminated in a debt crisis in mid-1977, which lasted until Özal took charge of the economy in early 1980. Spain, in contrast, after some delay adjusted to the shock: the currency was devalued, macroeconomic policies were revised, and wages were restrained. A series of social pacts (the Moncloa pacts) brought together political parties, unions, and the employers' associations around a common plank of reform.

The difference, I think, is well-explained by Guillermo de la Dehesa's emphasis on the consensus that existed in Spain regarding two important things in particular: the fear of a return to dictatorship or civil war (which all political parties naturally wanted to avoid), and the strong desire to become like the rest of Europe (and to join the European Community). Hence there was consensus over a vision of both what was to be avoided and what was to be sought. This environment allowed the social pacts to be negotiated. In Turkey, in contrast, there

---

1. With thanks to Barbara Stallings for supplying a better label than my original one.

was no such convergence. Even if EC membership had been a realistic possibility, one of the parties in the governing coalition was adamantly opposed to it. Each of the political parties had a distinctly different image of the way in which Turkish society and economy should be organized. This rendered a social pact and a coherent economic reform package impossible: economic policy became hostage to the day-to-day pressures arising from the need to keep a very diverse coalition together.

## The Road-Not-Taken Syndrome

These generalizations take us only so far. In the end each case is different, and with the benefit of hindsight, we can almost always find missed opportunities.

This is particularly true of the Turkish case. In some sense, Turkey's real political economy story is its failure to deal adequately with the public-sector deficit (and with the problem of state enterprises in particular) when the government had a real window of opportunity. The first such window came in 1980–81, when the military regime insulated policies from short-term political pressures. But generous capital inflows from abroad obviated the need for fiscal adjustment, and Özal did not go much further than to make some long-delayed public-sector price adjustments. In late 1983 there was a second window, when, thanks to a change in electoral rules, Özal came to power with a crushing majority in the parliament. This time, however, he spent too much energy on microeconomic reforms such as trade and financial sector liberalization. He did put a value-added tax in place, but this was insufficient. The consequence is that the Turkish macroeconomy remains rife with instability, with the public-sector borrowing requirement hovering above 10 percent of GDP and inflation at an annual rate of around 65 to 70 percent.

What this story illustrates is that policymakers often do have room to maneuver. Sometimes they make the right choices, other times the wrong ones. Often there is a road not taken, and opportunities are missed. Hence, it is not correct to think of policy choices as always being predetermined by broad social and political factors. Policymakers do matter. Of course, this is a lesson for academics only, and not for the authors here.

# Discussion

*William Cline* contrasted the 5 percent to 10 percent decline of GDP in many Latin American countries after economic reforms had been introduced with the 20 percent to 30 percent contraction in output in Eastern Europe, which he interpreted as implying that standard austerity programs were not well suited for Eastern Europe. Did this not show the need for a different design of the transition for that part of the economy that remained under central control? Would it not have been possible to run the Polish program with a smaller decline in output? Furthermore, given that up to 60 percent of Polish employment was in the private sector, Cline argued that policymakers should be cautious about extrapolating the Polish experience to Russia, where nearly 90 percent of workers were employed in the state sector.

Given the influence of the Spanish economic model on Latin America, *Miguel Urrutia* sought to clarify the role of the Spanish social pact. Had its purpose been to control inflation once the labor unions had been freed from the Franco regime, or to increase real wages? The political implications were very different depending on which objective was sought.

*Carol Graham* recalled the strikes in Poland in the summer of 1992, which seemed to have forced the government to try to establish a social pact. She wondered whether, if the issue of compensation had been addressed earlier, there might be less opposition to the program now.

*Luiz Carlos Bresser Pereira* remarked that the four cases seemed to have been very different: two (Spain and Portugal) were clearly successful, Turkey less so, while Poland remained doubtful. In the two successful cases there had been a very substantial growth in welfare expenditures since democratization, with the tax burden rising to pay for it, from about 25 percent to 40 percent of GDP in the case of Spain. Was this large but responsibly financed increase in welfare spending an important element in explaining the success of the reforms?

*Vladimir Mau* referred to the political role of private and public enterprises. He challenged the "primitive thesis" that the former invariably support privatization and economic liberalization while the latter continuously try to impede the transformation to a market economy for fear of the consequences of competition. He argued that the position of an enterprise was determined by its economic interests: firms, public or private, that are weak and incapable of adjusting to competition will support inflationary policies, while competitive enterprises will support stabilization, tight monetary policy, and the liberalization of international economic relations.

*Ross Garnaut* discussed the question raised by Anne Krueger as to why in some polities public servants had supported but in others opposed economic reform. He suggested that the contrast was much less clear if one looked at the different categories of civil servants. In Australia and New Zealand only a small minority of officials, most of whom were in the central coordinating agencies, had supported the reform programs. The real question was why the relative balance of power between the different groups of officials had changed over time, with the officials in the central agencies gaining power in some countries but not in others. The answer had to be that this depended on which sort of bureaucratic advice was sought by the political leaders.

*Joan Nelson* voiced her impression that Spain, and probably Portugal, had been in a much better position to afford an increase in social expenditures than were the Eastern European countries in transition. She expressed some discomfort with the notion of compensation being a single-shot (or at most a repeated but ad hoc) issue. Experience with social pacts in different countries had suggested that the real issue was whether machinery for ongoing consultation with at least the more moderate elements of labor could be constructed, so that they feel they have a voice in ongoing decisions. There might be a trade-off between immediate compensation and longer-run institutional arrangements that give labor a voice at the table.

*Gustav Ranis* mentioned that in many developing countries social expenditures had been captured by the middle class, even where the intention had been to address the problems of lower-income groups, and he wondered whether Spain and Portugal had escaped this danger. If so, had that required a restructuring of social expenditures?

Turning to Poland, Ranis noted the advantages of having had the privatization of agriculture precede the other reforms. Could one assume that growth in the small-scale informal sector had partly offset the recorded output decline that so concerned Cline?

*Barbara Stallings* suggested renaming one of the syndromes on Dani Rodrik's list, to call it the "promised land syndrome." She thought that this vision of Europe as the promised land was important in all four cases and that it had both an ideological and a material component. At the ideological level, people in all four countries wanted to be *regular* Western Europeans. At the material level, EC transfers to Portugal and Spain had helped to subsidize the social policies undertaken there. Stallings emphasized the contrast with Latin America, where there was neither any ideological desire to be like the United States nor any suggestion of the United States giving financial support, even to Mexico. Rather, the US concern was with what it could gain for itself if the NAFTA were approved.

*Leszek Balcerowicz* started his response to the discussion by defending his assertion that the needed adjustments were vastly greater in the postcommunist countries. Even if the gulf were not big in every pairwise comparison, it was large on average; just think of the vastly larger scope of the privatization that was needed. As for the decline in output, the latest figures showed that this had been only in the range of 5 percent to 10 percent of GDP in Poland for 1990–91, rather than the old figure of 18 percent. One also needed to distinguish between a decline in output that increased welfare by reducing waste, on the one hand, and a welfare-decreasing contraction on the other; in Poland this component, he surmised, was much less than 5 percent. Three factors could account for it: the shock of stabilization, external shocks, and political instability, which tended to delay the adaptation of enterprises to the new conditions. In any event, this decline of GDP should be compared not with the initial situation but with what would have happened under the alternative strategy of no (or only gradual) reform, and one needed also to consider what the prospects for future growth would have been under the alternative strategy.

Balcerowicz argued that the establishment of a social pact in Poland in 1989 would simply have taken too much time during a crucial period. He had been required by law to consult with the trade unions, but they had been given only three days to respond! What would be the purpose of such a pact today? It could not afford to give compensation, because that would conflict with the fiscal program; the real compensation had consisted of the rapid elimination of shortages, which has been increasingly appreciated as time has passed.

Balcerowicz concluded by remarking that private agriculture in Poland had been a mixed blessing. Economically it was positive, because on average private production was more efficient than that of state farms. But politically it was a liability, because the number of Polish farmers was equal to the total in the entire European Community!

*Yavuz Canevi* started his reply by discussing the role of the central bank in stabilization programs in Turkey. A major problem was that the bank's policies had to be directed to both price stabilization and the balance of payments. Canevi argued that management of the balance of payments could not be a permanent policy concern of a central bank. Without stringent fiscal reforms the credibility of the central bank, which had been built up during the past decade, would be lost.

Canevi agreed with Krueger that Turkey's real crisis had started in 1976. The most striking feature of public policy in that respect had been the very slow response to internal and external disturbances. The first oil shock elicited no reaction for six years, until 1978–79. In 1983 it took the government more than six months to respond to a major financial crisis; in 1987 it took six weeks to respond to a foreign exchange crisis; the 1990 Gulf crisis provoked a reaction within six days; and today Turkey was flexible enough to react to any external shock within six hours. Nevertheless, internal imbalances such as the huge fiscal deficit (some 14 percent of GDP) have persisted, largely because the public enterprises accounted for half of it. For that reason privatization was a dominant policy concern of the government.

In 1980 Turgut Özal had correctly realized that the scarcest resource in Turkey was decision-making capacity. New economic decision-making centers were built up, in particular a four-person Money and Credit Committee, consisting of key under secretaries and chaired by the Ministry of Finance, and a four-minister High Economic Coordination Committee, chaired by the Prime Minister; these committees were concerned with practically all economic issues of the reform. (Ministers were even required to sign decrees in advance, only discovering after the meetings of the committees what they had agreed to!) Unfortunately this innovative structure was abandoned by Özal, in the belief that he could handle things personally, when he returned to power for the second time in 1987.

The third issue raised by Canevi was the growth in confidence of Turkish business in the wake of the export boom that had developed after 1980. The composition of exports had changed to one in which manufactured goods predominated, and new markets were gained. This had triggered a reflux of well-trained personnel into the country, reversing the previous brain drain of high-skilled, engineering, and white-collar workers.

Had Özal missed an opportunity to deal with the fiscal deficit in 1981–83? In 1981 he had planned to introduce a value-added tax, which he presumably thought would go a long way toward dealing with the problem, and in any case the public-sector borrowing requirement (PSBR) had been quite moderate at that time. In 1983 politician Özal focused on the microeconomic issues but was beginning to develop a populist reluctance to risk unpopular macroeconomic measures. By 1987 he had become a distinctly populist politician and made no effort to keep the PSBR under control.

Although Turkey was a potential candidate for EC membership, Canevi queried whether the financial benefits of membership would be particularly large. He asked how important the contribution of EC funds had been to reform in Portugal and Spain, not only with respect to welfare transfers but also for infrastructure projects.

*Francisco Torres* started his response by discussing the notion that a state of crisis was a precondition for successful reform. In Portugal there had been two balance of payments crises, in 1978 and 1983–84, which were followed by price controls and other short-term policies rather than basic reforms. It was only after the short-term crises had been resolved, in 1985, that a change in the political situation led to the beginning of gradual reform.

The commitment to monetary stability had been encouraged by external factors and institutions, including the International Monetary Fund and the Community. The convergence program committed the government to a number of targets concerning deficits, debt, and inflation. But in the first place this had been a commitment to the electorate, and only secondly did it involve the partners in the Community, who essentially offered monitoring services following the program's legitimation by democratic procedures.

In Portugal the commitment to monetary stability had been very important, in particular by ruling out the discrete devaluations that had been so common previously. Devaluation had actually been rather successful in reducing real wages without causing social turmoil. The only compensation had been increases in social expenditure (which, unlike in Spain, were not initially financed by tax rises), but even these were directed in large part at the middle class.

In response to the question posed by Canevi, Torres responded that the financing from the EC cohesion fund for infrastructure programs had been quite significant in helping Portugal to catch up. This was, however, a very recent development. Torres argued that it was important to define clearly what model of European integration the member states preferred; one could not rely forever on a vague promised land syndrome, and Portugal was currently importing instability rather than stability through its membership in the Exchange Rate Mechanism. It would be disastrous to get trapped like the Italian Mezzogiorno in some form of "dependent federalism," reliant on transfers from Brussels. To avoid this it was important that external cohesion funds be subject to proper conditionality and transparency requirements.

*Guillermo de la Dehesa* suggested that the crisis syndrome, and in particular the external constraint on the balance of payments, had more relevance to Spain than to Portugal because of Spain's long international isolation during the Franco regime. He ascribed an important stabilizing function to the Spanish social pact as a means of introducing gradual economic and political reform. When Prime Minister Felipe

Gonzalez abandoned the pact after winning a third absolute majority, he was faced with a general strike and social turmoil. De la Dehesa speculated that young democracies might need some form of institutionalized bargaining structure in order to integrate the working class into the decision-making process.

He confirmed that Finance Minister Miguel Boyer had played a key role as a technopol. One of his most important accomplishments had been to help modify Gonzalez's early economic views, for example by taking him on trips to the Soviet Union and to Eastern Europe, and by showing him the failure of the French nationalizations of the early 1980s, shortly before Gonzalez came to power.

Why had the level of reserves rather than the level of unemployment been the trigger for crises in Spain? This related to the points raised by Bresser Pereira and Joan Nelson about public expenditure, which had indeed provided substantial compensation through increased social spending, especially on unemployment benefits—something that was possible because the democratic government had inherited from Franco a strong fiscal position and scope to increase the tax burden. Furthermore, the government had chosen to overlook substantial social security fraud in order to buy social peace. One should also remember that the role of the family in providing social security was still very large in Spain.

Urrutia had asked for a description of the role of social pacts in Spain. Their purpose was indeed to keep real wages down. A large devaluation accompanied by monetary restraint and incomes policy (the pact) had led to a fall in the real wage. This had been traded off against increased trade union power, improved working conditions, and higher social expenditure on the unemployed. Both employers and employees had been helped by this in defining their role within the market economy.

De la Dehesa disagreed with Francisco Torres on the contribution of EC funds to domestic reforms. Although they were productively used, total structural funds from the EC accounted for less than 5 percent of Spanish social expenditures and less than 4 percent of total Spanish public expenditure, so their role was welcome but marginal.

# 5

# LATIN AMERICA I

# Chile

## JOSÉ PIÑERA

The military government that came to power in Chile after overthrowing the Marxist regime of Salvador Allende had little idea of what to do with the collapsing Chilean economy. The country's economic situation in 1973 was indeed desperate, with inflation accelerating and output withering—the result not just of three years of socialism but of more than 40 years of interventionist and protectionist policies. Soon after General Augusto Pinochet's accession to power, therefore, the generals who were his chief advisers assembled a group of respected businessmen, lawyers, and economists to obtain their advice on how to restore the economy to health.

The businessmen, who represented a variety of industries, each insisted that the key to renewing the country's prosperity was to promote, protect, and subsidize his particular industry. The lawyers, too, offered as many different answers as there were lawyers in the room. The economists present, in contrast, were in basic agreement among themselves on the main points on the agenda: cut the fiscal deficit to reduce inflation and stabilize the economy, free prices to be set by the market, sell off the state-owned enterprises, open the economy to trade with the rest of the world.

The generals not only accepted this radical counsel almost unreservedly but charged those who had offered it with carrying the plan to fruition. Thus, at a time when the doctrines of structuralism, import

*José Piñera was Minister of Labor and Social Security. He is currently Chairman of José Piñera and Associates. This article first appeared in July/August 1991 issue of* International Economic Insights.

substitution, and statism were still firmly enthroned in most Latin American capitals and universities—indeed, well before Margaret Thatcher or Ronald Reagan administered similar medicine to their economies—Chile returned to the classic open, market-economy model. The outcome, more than 17 years later, is well-known: although Chile suffered with the rest of the region in the debt crisis of 1980s, it was the first to recover from that setback, and since then it has enjoyed robust growth while holding inflation to low double digits and sharply reducing its external debt.

Some years after that initial meeting, I asked one of the generals who had been present why they had taken the advice of the free-market economists and ignored that of the other groups. He replied, "Because you agreed with each other and gave us simple answers to our questions." And indeed it was not that these generals were secret admirers of Adam Smith and Friedrich von Hayek. Rather they were sensible men who saw that the group of economists before them constituted a team that could work together to get things done without becoming mired in endless debate and infighting.

The fact that this team of like-minded and similarly trained economists was available to take the reins of policy during this crucial period in Chile's history is, I believe, the principal reason Chile was able to launch and sustain its ultimately successful economic reforms. It is certainly not the case that the Chilean reforms succeeded because they were undertaken under a military government. As the history of Latin America shows only too amply, virtually all military governments have been dismal failures economically. In almost every case they have increased the power and extended the reach of the state, while incidentally also enriching the ruling junta itself.

Rather, what was different about the Chilean case—and this is one of several factors that makes it a model for developing countries in similar circumstances—was its team approach to policymaking. Indeed, I would go so far as to say that the presence of such a leadership team is an essential factor in the political economy of any country that wishes to make the transition away from statism and socialism. Without the cohesiveness and single-mindedness that only a team can provide, any attempt at comprehensive reform, if it does not fail through simple lack of coordination, is sure to fall prey to factionalism and special interest politics.

## The Making of the Team

The presence in Chile of this group of like-minded economists does not spring from any natural unanimity in the economics profession. In most universities in Latin America, faculties have for decades been more heavily weighted toward the leftward end of the spectrum and away from the mainstream of classical, liberal Anglo-Saxon economic philosophy.

Chile, on the other hand, was fortunate in that, for more than a decade beginning in the 1950s, some four or five of the best economics students in each class at the Universidad Católica in Santiago would go on to graduate study in the United States, most of them at the University of Chicago. There they absorbed the fundamental principles of classical economics. When they came back, these students associated with scholars who had made the journey before them and taught other talented individuals. As a result, by the mid-1970s a core group of some 50 to 100 of Chile's best economists were thoroughly conversant with and convinced of the need to adopt a free-market approach to economic policy.

Because of the Chicago connection, the Chilean team has often been referred to as "the Chicago School." However, the training they received there, or the parts of it that mattered for our later purposes, could as easily have been received at any American university where the great tradition of Anglo-Saxon economics was taught—indeed, anywhere that Samuelson's *Economics* was used in the introductory course. I encountered the very same ideas at Harvard, where I later did my doctoral study.

The players on the Chilean team were not, after all, sophisticated monetarists *à la* Milton Friedman. We simply applied the basic laws of supply and demand, of an open economy, of the efficiency of competition and free enterprise. This, and not the more esoteric tenets of monetarism, prompted us to reduce tariffs, to deregulate, and to privatize.

The uniqueness of the Chilean team, then, was not so much the doctrine that we shared as the fact that we shared it. It may seem only common sense that those who share responsibility for making economic policy should agree on the fundamentals. Yet all too often one sees the opposite. Whether to satisfy the demands of various factions for representation in the cabinet, or because the head of the government thinks he needs (and is capable of judging among) opposing views, economic policy in many if not most countries is managed by coalition. For example, early in his administration one South American president told me that he was appointing a minister of economics who shared the views of the Chilean team, but to keep him in line and to have the benefit of their opposing views, he was naming to the labor ministry someone of a very different orientation.

I believe that such a coalition approach is doomed to failure for a simple reason. The results of many worthwhile reforms lie on a J-curve: they tend to make things a good deal worse before they get better. Under these circumstances, when a reform-minded finance minister attempts to put through reforms that bite and tries to ride out the J-curve, he soon finds his adversary, the planning minister, whispering in the president's ear. If the president does not understand where the economics minister's policies are leading, that minister is likely soon to find himself out of a job.

## The Element of Surprise

Other factors besides the team were critical in getting sensible policies implemented in Chile and making them stick. One of these is the radical reform approach.

Under the Allende regime and its predecessors, it was as easy for an industry to obtain tariff protection as to mail a letter. The result after 40 years was that most of Chilean industry was frankly addicted to tariffs. We often heard businessmen complain that it would take a generation to make their industries competitive in world markets. We gave them five years. From the highly differentiated tariff system we inherited in 1974, with rates as high as 500 percent or more, we moved to a single uniform tariff of 10 percent by 1979.

It is well-known that extending trade liberalization over 20 years distorts investment decisions and all too often leaves matters at the end no better than at the start. But there is also a political economy motive for swift action: giving a reform's opponents time to adjust also gives them time to orchestrate a political counterattack.

It is all too true that the adjustment costs of a sudden policy about-face are high. It is also true that those most severely affected are the poorest members of the society, who likewise suffered the most from the inequities of the old regime. But it is possible and desirable, according to my values, to subsidize those with low incomes during the turbulent period of transition when resources are being reallocated. When looked at in present-value terms, the summed adjustment costs of a few years of rapid transition are surely less than the costs of an adjustment spread over decades during which severe distortions and inefficiencies are allowed to persist.

The detoxification of a state-hobbled economy not only must be swift but must advance on all fronts simultaneously. It is no use freeing trade and opening up the capital markets if one is going to leave the labor markets untouched. Yet all too often the enormous power of the trade unions determines just such a strategy. Liberalizing an economy is, after all, a matter of changing the allocation of resources toward a position of greater efficiency, and one simply cannot finish the job if rigidities are allowed to remain in so important a part of the economy as the labor market.

## The Media and the Message

A third critical element in the political economy of radical reform is the effective use of the media. It is absolutely dangerous to think that, just because the measures one is applying are theoretically sound and internally coherent and consistent, they will work their effects silently and automatically. You must make your case to the people even if your policies are adopted by military decree rather than by referendum. At a minimum, economic actors must be informed about the new rules under which they must operate. Policies will not work if they are not understood and, more or less grudgingly, accepted.

This means that one must go over the heads of the vested interests, and for this the media are indispensable. Powerful vested interests are always present. Every authority wants to believe that they are pursuing wise policies that also have the support of the population—not even the worst despot likes being unpopular. They are therefore susceptible to the flattery of the special interests, who monopolize the leaders' time with assurances that what benefits their group is what the people want and deserve. To counter such sycophancy, one must encourage the people to speak for themselves.

There came a time in Chile when we had implemented most of the major elements of our reforms: we had stabilized the economy, freed most of the markets in goods and opened them to foreign competition, and sharply curtailed the power and intrusiveness of the state. The special interests affected by these reforms accepted them with more or less good grace because the economic team retained the confidence of the military leadership. Yet I and others on the team wanted to go further and extend the discipline of the market to the social sector: the pension system, health care, education, and the rest. We foresaw that leaving these activities in the hands of the state would only increase its power as the economy became wealthier, undoing much of what we had so far accomplished toward shortening the state's tether. We therefore argued, if private enterprise and the market are good for producing steel, should they not also be good at producing pensions?

In making this case we were well aware that, in those days at least, privatization of these activities was not well-accepted even among economists in the developed countries. We were not surprised, then, when our proposals met with sharp resistance from the special interests, first among them the leaders of the business community and the trade union organizations.

It must be understood that the majority of businessmen in every inert, state-ridden Latin American regime are really quite content with the status quo. As Adam Smith himself recognized, these people are hardly natural champions of free markets. In an economy that is growing by only 1 or 2 percent a year, businesses can still make profits. All the better if, as in prereform Chile, they are insulated from foreign competition by high tariffs. The more cynical among them will tell you privately, "The best thing is to be well off in a poor country. You can afford maids, servants, meals in the best restaurants. Who needs 7 percent growth?"

The answer, of course, is that the poor, the vast majority, need 7 percent growth. Yet they were no better represented in the privatization debate by their self-proclaimed Robin Hoods, the trade unions, which in Chile comprised only a cossetted subset of the population. We therefore set out to bypass the special interests and take our case to the people, via the mass media.

As minister of labor, I began to go on television to promote our pension privatization scheme. Once a week for six months I appeared with a short comment. I took care to limit my remarks to three minutes, using simple language and setting out no more than one idea at a time.

In the first session I asked the viewers, "Do you have any idea how much money you have to your name in this sinkhole of a bureaucracy that is our country's pay-as-you-go social security system? Go ask your grandfather, or your uncle or your father-in-law, how much they get to live on for their retirement. Then tune in again next week."

One week later the viewers had all done their research, and so they were not entirely unprepared to believe what I had to say to them next. I told them that 70 percent of all pensioners in Chile were receiving the minimum pension. All those years of hard work and miserly payroll deductions, and so little to show for it!

A few programs and simple ideas later, I showed up on TV holding in my hand a handsome, simulated leather passbook such as one of the better banks in Santiago or San Diego might issue to its depositors. I asked, "Are you content to have to spend hours in line just to get a vague answer about your social security entitlement? Would you rather have your retirement savings recorded every month in a beautiful passbook that you can open at night and say, 'As of today I have invested $50,000 toward my golden years.'?"

After several weeks of this, one of the generals came to me and said, "Everyone I see is talking about your pension proposals. They want to know when they are going to start getting their passbooks. So when are you going to present the proposal to us?"

When we first conceived the idea of privatizing pensions, we had suggested to the generals that the matter be put to a referendum. Not surprisingly, they rejected that idea; who could say where such a precedent might lead? Yet our media campaign worked more effectively than any referendum. Once we had presented our ideas in the most straightforward language possible, there was no question which side the people were on.

## Leaders, Not Politicians

One final, crucial ingredient in the political economy of any country making the difficult transition to a free, open economy is the presence at the top of people who are real leaders rather than politicians. This element is no less necessary for military regimes than for parliamentary democracies. The individuals who make the ultimate decisions must base them on what is best for the country, not on what will win them the next election or help them survive the next coup d'état. It is permissible for them to be concerned with how they will look in the history books: history consigns to oblivion those who are only good at getting endlessly reelected.

What I am asking for may seem at best a cliché and at worst something that is not of this world, but I believe that this kind of disinterested, or nationally interested, leader exists. Surely among those strong-willed enough to struggle their way to high political power are some who are also strong-willed enough to fight for a principle. This may even be the easier approach: not even Mikhail Gorbachev could calculate to the last decimal place the political costs and benefits of his every decision. There is a significant aleatory element to the best-laid political calculus. Better to rely on one's instincts and one's conscience—and on the off chance that the coming to fruition of the sound policies one has ordained will coincide with the next election. In the end, good policy is good politics.

# Mexico

JOSÉ CÓRDOBA

During the last ten years, Mexico has experienced a sustained process of macroeconomic adjustment and a rapid transformation of its microeconomic structure. Mexico shares this experience with other countries that have undertaken profound changes to stabilize their economies and compete in the new international environment. Yet many of those countries, at comparable levels of development, have not been able to hold to the path of change as Mexico has; others have endured, but at an extremely high cost, in terms of either social conflict and disruption or the loss of personal and political liberties.

What has enabled Mexico, within a climate of freedom and with significant popular support, to implement a lasting and consistent process of economic reform? To bring some partial answers to this question, I will examine three features of Mexico's reform program: the design and implementation of the general strategy of economic reform; the policies Mexico has followed to gather the support of various sectors for specific structural reforms; and the use of a deliberate social policy to build a broad consensus behind the overall transformation process. I will conclude with some general remarks on the political economy of reform in Mexico.

## The Reforms: Why, When, and How?

In the early 1990s, the debate in Mexico, as in many other parts of the world, about economic development strategies resulted in a certain con-

*José Córdoba is the Chief of Staff to the President of Mexico.*

sensus on the country's policy goals in an interdependent and competitive world. The consensus view saw economic stability as a necessary condition for structural change and increased efficiency of production as the only means to restore sustained growth. This consensus came about during a radical world transformation in which political arrangements created after World War II disappeared, the bureaucratic central planning systems of the socialist countries collapsed, and new financial, trade, and technological centers emerged through freer worldwide competition. Under these conditions, attaining financial stability and promoting structural change are an economic imperative for all countries, whether industrialized or developing.

From this consensus view have followed some relatively standard policy prescriptions that apply, with some important conceptual differences, both to the developing countries that went through the debt crisis of the early 1980s and to the former socialist countries that have engaged in market-oriented reforms during the early 1990s. Both suffered from large budget deficits, high inflation, balance of payments difficulties, and, ultimately, enduring economic stagnation. The standard approach to economic reform recommends a two-tiered strategy: on the one hand, macroeconomic stabilization, which involves balancing the budget, tightening control over credit, and, frequently, setting guidelines for prices and wages to curb inflationary inertia; on the other hand, structural change, which requires liberalizing trade, privatizing publicly owned companies, and deregulating economic activity, including financial markets.

One cannot, however, overlook the fact that today's consensus view about development strategies emerged only slowly during the course of the 1980s; it was not fully shared, at the beginning of the decade, by all decision-making circles in government, to say nothing of the different groups within society at large. Moreover, even if the overall policy objectives are clear, how are the steps toward change going to be defined? Where are the guarantees that these steps will not go beyond what is acceptable to the most significant social groups and tolerable to the population as a whole? How, on the other hand, can one be sure that these steps are not short and shy ones that will eventually erode people's patience and their trust in change itself? In an economy undergoing structural transformation, the costs of needed measures accrue immediately, while the benefits generally materialize only over the medium and long run. In these difficult circumstances, who are the allies of change and how are such alliances to be built?

Mexico's economic reforms in search of stability and competitiveness have come about, as one might have predicted, in stages. The first was defined by the harsh economic crisis of 1982, characterized by the increase in international interest rates and the sharp reduction in world oil prices. The macroeconomic imbalances and distortions that resulted from those shocks were dramatic. The seriousness of the situation generated a basic interest in macroeconomic stability across all sectors and made the government keenly aware of its duty to restore discipline in public finances. The second stage was defined by the Mexico City earthquake of September 1985 and the collapse of world oil markets in early 1986. The profound impact on Mexico's economic structures clearly showed their inefficiencies, the shortcomings of macroeconomic adjustment taken by itself, and the need for deeper microeconomic change: widespread trade liberalization and some initial privatizations were then launched.

The economic adjustments of the 1980s undoubtedly carried social costs. Suffice it to say that, from 1982 to 1988, the Mexican population grew by 10 million (about 15 percent) and GDP was stagnant. Yet despite the costs and difficulties of the changes that were introduced, the reform process had to be intensified at the beginning of the 1990s. In December 1988, at the inauguration of the administration of President Carlos Salinas de Gortari, a difficult political situation provided the setting for major structural changes and social programs, stepping up the general process of reform.

The outcome of the crisis and the results of the reforms undertaken to overcome it are well-known. Mexico redressed its public finances, converting large deficits to surpluses; it curbed annual inflation from triple to single digits; it fully opened its economy to international competition, negotiating agreements to ensure access to foreign markets, in particular those of the United States and Canada; it privatized state-owned enterprises on a large scale, keeping public ownership only in those sectors defined by the Constitution as strategic; it created a new regulatory framework for economic and financial activity, removing barriers to entry, streamlining bureaucratic procedures, and ensuring fair competition. All of these policies have allowed Mexico to stabilize its economy, putting it in a position to return to more rapid growth on a sustained basis as the efficiency of its productive sector increases.

In this section, I will review briefly how the standard two-tier strategy of reform defined above, embracing both macroeconomic stabilization and structural change, was implemented in Mexico. I will not stress economic arguments per se, but instead will emphasize the political and institutional considerations relevant for the design of policies, the timing of change, and the mechanisms used for implementation—in other words, the why, when, and how of the reform process.

## Balancing the Budget

In Mexico, the diagnosis of the crisis at first (1983–85) stressed the macroeconomic imbalances and the relative price distortions that emerged in the face of the collapse of world oil markets and the increase in international interest rates. At that time, the need for drastic structural changes, such as a redefinition of the role of the state, extensive dereg-ulation of markets, and a direct opening to the world economy, was recognized in certain important circles but was not generally acknowl-edged. This meant that the initial priority was to balance the budget and strengthen the economy financially. Unlike in many other countries, the central government absorbed, from the outset, all parafiscal capital losses (exchange rate losses on guaranteed deposits, losses or arrears on loans granted to public enterprises, etc.): this made clear to all the mag-nitude of the required fiscal adjustment. Across-the-board cuts in the budget then proved to be a swift way to eliminate nonpriority spending, as ample room for improvement could be found within the public sector. More-selective measures followed after 1986, requiring intensive pres-sure and extensive negotiations, as bureaucrats opposed item-by-item revision of their expenditures and the new zero-based budgeting princi-ples. It proved much easier politically to compress overall public spend-ing and freeze hiring than to cancel specific programs and suppress the activities of public entities.

The earthquake of September 1985 and the fall in oil prices in Febru-ary 1986—which together implied a loss of revenues of around 6.5 per-cent of GDP—made a strengthening of the economic reform program necessary. Only then were the country's structural problems and micro-economic inefficiencies emphasized. The attempts of previous years to stabilize exclusively through orthodox macroeconomic policies had led to a downward overadjustment of public investment (by around 50 per-cent) and real wages (more than 30 percent for the average wage and more than 50 percent for the minimum wage). This opened up signifi-cant room to maneuver and allowed structural reforms (trade liberaliza-tion, privatizations, deregulation) to be conducted later in an orderly way and within a relatively stable macroeconomic environment.

One reason for the success of the policy of fiscal consolidation and, ultimately, of the Mexican stabilization program as a whole is the fact that many of the officials responsible for planning the reforms of the 1980s had held staff positions in government during the 1970s. They had lived through, without being able to block, the consequences of irre-sponsible fiscal management. They had become conscious of the need to maintain strict discipline over public-sector finances, regardless of the internal pressures from the bureaucracy and the short-term social costs.

The operational deficit of the public sector (the financial deficit minus the inflationary component of domestic debt service), which reached 10 percent of GDP in 1981, was eliminated within two years (table 1). From 1984 onward, the operational balance of the public sector fluctuated between −2 and 2 percent of GDP, while the real component of domes-tic debt service rose from −1 to over 6 percentage points of GDP between 1983 and 1989. This reflected the fact that, as expectations lag behind inflation, real interest rates are negative when inflation goes up

## Table 1   Mexico: selected macroeconomic indicators, 1982–93
(percentages)

|  | 1982–88 | 1989–92 | 1993[a] |
|---|---|---|---|
| Annual average change in: |  |  |  |
| Gross domestic product | 0.1 | 3.5 | 2.0 |
| Consumer price index | 88.4 | 20.1 | 7.5 |
| Real wages[b] | –5.3 | 6.7 | 6.2 |
| Public-sector operational balance as a share of GDP[c] | –1.5 | 1.4 | 2.1 |
| Real component of domestic public debt interest payments as a share of GDP | 5.2 | 5.5 | 2.7 |
| Public-sector primary balance as a share of GDP[c] | 3.7 | 6.9 | 4.8 |

a. Estimates.
b. Includes total labor compensation payments in the manufacturing sector.
c. Excludes the receipts from privatization.
Sources: Banco de México; National Institute of Statistics, Geography, and Computing (INEGI); and Secretariat of Finance and Public Credit (SHCP).

and strongly positive under successful disinflation programs; after 1990, the inflationary component of domestic debt service fell to around 3 percent of GDP as the permanence of low inflation gained credibility. The primary balance (the financial deficit minus total service of the public debt) had to be increased systematically to offset increasing real interest payments: thus, it went from a deficit of 11.9 percent of GDP in 1982 to a surplus of 7.2 percent in 1989 and was stabilized at a slightly lower level thereafter. This development highlights the fact that it is more difficult to sustain a fiscal balance over time than to reach it as a target during the initial stage of a stabilization program: a constant fight within and outside the bureaucracy is required to keep under control the many pressures that often have been repressed but not eliminated.

In Mexico, in order to control and eventually eliminate the fiscal deficit, a major administrative effort was made, at the macroeconomic level, to establish comprehensive accounting for the consolidated public sector (the central government, the central bank, state enterprises, and public-sector banks), and, at the microeconomic level, to provide timely follow-up to the financial accounting of public-sector companies. Public financial planning in a transition characterized by sharp imbalances and high inflation differs quite substantially from budgeting in normal times. Traditional accounting is insufficient, as the International Monetary Fund has now acknowledged. An appropriate measurement of the economic imbalance of the consolidated public sector is needed to estimate the inflation tax and reveal the zero inflation-equivalent deficit: this requires distinguishing flows from stocks, separating nominal from real concepts, and having a clear economic accounting of central bank operations. This task can be complex both in analytical and in institutional terms, but it is an important priority in order to define and control the magnitude of the required fiscal adjustment.

The largest source of fiscal deviations was not located in the central government itself, but among the state enterprises, which frequently faced soft budget constraints. For this reason, it proved vitally important to have timely and complete accounting statements for those companies (including especially all items corresponding to nonbank credits, such as suppliers' credits, tax arrearages, etc.) and to give these statements a periodic follow-up (in Mexico this is done quarterly). The same problem appeared in the case of state-owned development banks, as hidden financial subsidies often had disruptive fiscal effects. Soon a conflict emerged between two objectives: control over the global public-sector deficit and independence of management of the state companies. During the critical moments of the stabilization process, priority was given in Mexico to the first objective. In retrospect, that was the correct decision.

The Mexican experience suggests that, in those countries with a sizable presence of the public sector in production, fiscal disequilibrium does not arise so much from direct overexpenditure as from official prices lagging behind inflation. This provoked a staggering increase in subsidies. Repeated public-sector price adjustments cause more political wear and tear on the government than do budget cuts. For this reason there is always a reluctance to increase prices, especially the most sensitive ones (on gasoline, foodstuffs, electricity, etc.). As a matter of fact, the reemergence of subsidies after a first attempt to reduce them is often the source of failure of stabilization programs. On the other hand, frequent discrete hikes in prices introduce cost shocks that feed back into the inflationary process. Facing this situation, the government drastically curtailed the universe of prices that it set directly (privatizations contributed to this), and carefully planned the relationship between the political cycle and the timing of public-sector price adjustments in order to avoid long lags and sudden increases.

It is almost impossible to stabilize without an efficient tax system: this requires a broad base, low marginal rates, and vigorous enforcement of compliance. The tax system in Mexico has been revamped along those lines since 1986 (mostly since 1989). The purpose of the reform was to make Mexico's tax structure more efficient and fair, while providing the government with increasing revenues. Although marginal personal income tax rates were reduced from 50 percent in 1988 to 35 percent, and corporate tax rates from 42 percent to 35 percent, the tax base was substantially broadened to compensate for the revenue lost from these lower rates. The number of taxpayers (excluding dependent workers who are captive taxpayers) was raised from 1.9 million in 1988 to nearly 4 million in 1992.

The value-added tax rate was lowered from 20 percent and 15 percent to 10 percent. Other indirect taxes have been lowered, such as those on automobiles, tobacco, and beer. The total number of federal taxes has been brought down from 18 to 6. To compensate in part for the reduction in revenues from the value-added tax, gasoline taxes were increased, and the price of gasoline has gone up by more than 60 percent since 1989. As a result, gasoline prices are today above US levels in spite of the fact that Mexico is an oil-exporting country. The results of tax reform are encouraging: between 1988 and 1992 tax revenues increased by 28.8 percent in real terms, while GDP increased by 14.5 percent.

Strong emphasis has been placed on enforcement. Between 1929 and 1988, there were only two indictments for tax fraud. During the first four years of the Salinas government, there were more than 380 indictments for tax-related crimes.

In Mexico, reducing tax rates has proved to be an effective means of increasing compliance: public opinion easily understands that one cannot simultaneously enjoy first-world tax rates and fourth-world compliance standards.

To sum up, the best way to measure the scope of fiscal consolidation and the extent of the privatization program over the last ten years is to trace the changes in public debt indicators, as shown in table 2. The reduction in the size of the public debt, and thus the improvement in the financial strength of the government, is undoubtedly impressive.

## Curbing Inflation

Unlike most other Latin American countries, and Israel, Mexico enjoyed two favorable conditions that reduced the temptation to index the economy. On the one hand, there was no inflationary memory in Mexican society, and there were no generalized social practices in place to protect against inflation; this allowed financial policies to be managed in nominal terms. On the other hand, Mexico has an organized labor movement that is capable of negotiating general wage policies and, because of its representativity and control over its members, of enforcing its agreements. Without a doubt, indexing is a temptation for a government and indeed often arises from the recommendations of theoretical economists. Nevertheless, a policy of structural change implemented under an indexed wage regime brings about rigidities, increases the vulnerability to supply shocks, and always leads to an inflationary explosion. Moreover, as wages tend to be indexed initially at too high a level in real terms, an outburst of inflation is required to adjust them down to a sustainable level: it is well known that, for a given indexation formula, real wages remain constant only when inflation is stable. Paradoxically, indexation ends up being economically more disruptive and socially more painful than nonindexation. This would be especially so in

**Table 2   Mexico: public debt indicators, 1982–93** (percentage of GDP)

| Indicators | 1982 | 1988 | 1992 | 1993[a] |
|---|---|---|---|---|
| Outstanding public domestic debt | 36.6 | 29.3 | 12.1 | 10.9 |
| Outstanding public foreign debt | 34.5 | 47.5 | 23.6 | 21.7 |
| Net outstanding public foreign debt[b] | 34.5 | 47.5 | 21.2 | 19.2 |

a. Estimate.

b. Total public foreign debt less foreign assets of the central bank.

*Sources*: Banco de México; National Institute of Statistics, Geography, and Computing (INEGI); and Secretariat of Finance and Public Credit (SHCP).

a country like Mexico, where large segments of the population (the unemployed, retirees, and peasant farmers, among others) are not wage earners.

The policy of not indexing either wages or interest rates is one of the fundamental reasons for the success of the Mexican stabilization program. Nevertheless, the fiscal system (personal income tax brackets as well as the deduction by firms of nominal interest payments) was indexed, to avoid an inflationary erosion of public revenues. This may be one of the few cases where ''selective indexation'' has proved politically manageable. In Mexico, although these policies were introduced later than necessary because of public opposition to their apparent complexity, they contributed in a significant way to creating the conditions for stability.

From the start, controlling inflation was a priority objective in Mexico: this was the variable that most powerfully generated economic uncertainty, social irritation, and political frictions. For this reason, the fiscal deficit had to be brought down as fast as possible to a level at which the inflation tax was not needed. This is fundamental to avoiding the acceleration of inflation, although, as experience has shown, it is not sufficient to reduce it. Once inflation has penetrated into the economic system, inertia-producing factors emerge. As a result, trying to lower inflation through exclusively orthodox policies has a severely recessive impact on the economy and involves a prohibitive social cost. Hence, there is a need to complement the policies of fiscal and monetary discipline with an incomes policy that breaks inertial factors in the process of price and wage determination.

Incomes policy in Mexico involved basically the joint adoption by government, labor, and business of nominal guidelines to anchor the exchange rate, wages, and key prices. With these guidelines, it was feasible to conduct very restrictive budgetary and monetary policies that could curb inflation without inducing too severe a recession. The social agreement implicit in an incomes policy may give it an apparently "heterodox" overtone. Strictly speaking, however, the heterodox elements only serve to increase the efficacy of an orthodox fiscal policy. This is why it is so important to make explicit the macroeconomic conditions required for an incomes policy to be effective. Three conditions should be emphasized: fiscal overadjustment, strong external accounts, and realignment of relative prices. If these conditions are not met, the inconsistency between the growth of monetary aggregates and the nominal guidelines gives rise to price distortions that become unsustainable over time. The resulting inflationary outburst would create a more unstable situation than the one existing beforehand.

In the case of Mexico, it is well recognized that, from the beginning of 1987, the necessary conditions for a successful incomes policy were in place. At the end of 1987, when the stock market collapsed and the induced foreign-exchange speculation forced a devaluation, the proper political moment was found to convince all participants of the benefits of a concerted adjustment. Before then, the private sector had been reluctant to follow such a policy course because of the greater responsibility that would accrue to business, and because of the failure of the heterodox economic programs previously adopted in Argentina and Brazil; the government was also concerned about risking the credibility it had accumulated over several years of orthodox adjustment in an initially uncertain experiment. This is why additional adjustment measures were front-loaded to increase the margin of safety.

On the fiscal side, the primary surplus, which had already reached 4.7 percent of GDP in 1987, was increased to 8 percent in 1988, and to more than 10 percent during the first semester of that year; the budget was severely tightened despite the fact that general elections were to be held in July. On the external side, foreign-exchange reserves were $13.7 billion in December 1987, the highest absolute level ever recorded up to then. As for relative prices, the peso was devalued by 22 percent before being temporarily fixed. Public-sector prices were overadjusted upward: the index of public-sector prices (with a base of 100 for 1984–85) reached 115 in January 1988; aggregate subsidies through public or publicly administered prices, which had reached 10.9 percent of GDP in 1981 and had already been reduced to 6.1 percent in 1983 and 6 percent in 1987, were cut to an average of 3.6 percent for 1988.

Against this background, the private sector made specific commitments, sector by sector, to absorb part of the increased costs through reduced profit margins; labor unions accepted general guidelines for wage moderation. The initial agreement, called the Economic Solidarity Pact (or simply "the Pact"), was made for one and a half months; it was then renewed for three months, six months, and nine months as its credibility became more firmly established. With some adjustments, it remains in place today.

The experience with high inflation in the 1980s made Mexicans skeptical about the capacity of the government to bring inflation down. Opinion polls show that the public gradually became conscious of the need for the Pact and eventually accepted it as a useful tool to control inflation (table 3). After the Pact was announced in 1987, people felt it was helping to reduce inflation rates. The persistence of price adjustments for many goods caused a decline in the credibility of the Pact in the years that followed, until the public assimilated the decline in the yearly inflation rate. Inflationary expectations have clearly changed over time: whereas in 1990 only 15 percent of the public believed that the inflation rate for the adjustment year would be less than 20 percent, 48 percent thought so in 1993.

Three elements were crucial for the success of the Pact. First was a sense of fairness: for the first time since the adjustment process began, the distribution of social costs involved among the different sectors was made explicit and discussed openly; the fact that each sector knew the contributions being made by the others—starting with the public sector—facilitated the acceptance of painful measures.

The second element was flexibility: although many prices were frozen through different periods, adjustments were allowed whenever necessary to avoid scarcity. In that sense, price controls in Mexico were significantly less rigid than in the Brazilian or Argentinian programs and were supported over time with less resistance from producing firms: their basic purpose was much more to control inflationary expectations than to reduce profit margins.

The third element was the creation of strong mechanisms for follow-up and compliance: weekly meetings between the secretaries of the economic cabinet and top business and union leaders have been held systematically since the beginning of the Pact to evaluate the state of the economy and the degree of compliance with the various commitments: the various sectors have become more sensitive about the country's economic dilemmas and have behaved in a more socially responsible manner. The fact that union and, to a lesser extent, business leaders authentically represent their memberships has enabled commitments to be disaggregated from the top down and enforced through the several stages of the program. And the fact that the government stuck very strictly to fiscal discipline was key to building the moral authority required to keep the participants together within the Pact.

The Pact has attained great political importance, such that it can be invoked by one ministry to induce other ministries and even state governors and producer groups to take appropriate action. It also generates strong incentives to participate, because all participants in the Pact are provided with precise and valuable weekly information on the state of

**Table 3  Mexico: public assessment of the Pact, 1987–93** (percentage of population)

| | 1987 | 1988 | 1989 | 1990 | 1991 | 1992 | 1993 |
|---|---|---|---|---|---|---|---|
| Do you believe that the government should maintain the Pact? | | | | | | | |
| Yes | n.a. | n.a. | n.a. | 56 | 69 | n.a. | 69 |
| Do you think the Pact is helping to bring down inflation? | | | | | | | |
| Yes | 60 | 45 | 52 | 38 | 43 | 40 | 52 |
| Inflationary expectations | | | | | | | |
| 0–10 percent | negl. | negl. | negl. | 3 | 16 | 14 | 43 |
| 11–20 percent | negl. | negl. | negl. | 19 | 31 | 46 | 34 |
| 21–30 percent | negl. | negl. | negl. | 32 | 19 | 18 | 11 |
| 31–40 percent | negl. | 27 | 10 | 16 | 11 | 9 | 3 |
| 41–50 percent | 3 | 38 | 28 | 30 | 23 | 14 | 8 |
| + 50 percent | 97 | 35 | 62 | negl. | negl. | negl. | negl. |

n.a. = not available; negl. = negligible.

Source: Polling and Survey Unit, Office of the President .

the economy and of specific industries. Finally, the assured presence of the key people in each sector, the absence of bureaucracy, and the possibility of discussing differences at the highest levels represent proof of the Pact's usefulness and explain its endurance beyond the immediate objective of reducing inflation.

In the first four months of the program, inflation was reduced from 15 percent per month to just over 3 percent, and after six months it was down to around 1.5 percent. The effects of such rapid disinflation were similar to those observed in other countries. Real interest rates became highly positive because of initial credibility problems as well as lags in the time structure of deposits: the financial system was never indexed, and no conversion formula was adopted to reduce nominal rates. After a very brief recession, a transitory burst of consumption and investment took place. Since then inflation has declined steadily, reaching an annual rate in single digits in June 1993, for the first time in more than two decades. This achievement had a strong psychological impact and was widely perceived as the reward for joint action by all groups in society.

Essential to the social acceptance of the Pact and, ultimately, to the success of economic reform has been a de facto link between wages and productivity. True, the Pact has established strict guidelines for the revision of minimum wages—something that is key to dampening inflationary expectations and to limiting the excess supply of unskilled labor. But the Pact has also left workers and employers free to engage in contractual bargaining, in a context of declining inflationary expectations and rising productivity. Since 1989, during a series of renegotiations of the Pact, the average real wage in Mexico has risen steadily, especially in the manufacturing sector, as shown in table 4, albeit from levels that were severally depressed by the crisis of the 1980s.

## Liberalizing Trade

Trade liberalization is fundamental to induce microeconomic efficiency and consolidate macroeconomic stability. Little will be gained by delaying its implementation once the timing is right. In the case of Mexico, by 1981 all imports were subject to quantitative restrictions, and the average tariff was above 50 percent, reaching in some cases 100 percent. This high level of protection was the result of the import substitution model that had been followed since World War II, compounded by the additional restrictions introduced in 1982 as an emergency measure to control the external deficit. After a gradualist phase from 1983 to 1985, trade liberalization was basically achieved within a three-year period, from 1986 to 1988, after Mexico made the decision to join the General Agreement on Tariffs and Trade (GATT). The full panoply of protection, involving a complex system of official prices, import licenses, and quan-

**Table 4    Mexico: real wages and labor productivity in the manufacturing sector, 1989–93** (annual percentage increase)

| Year | Real wage | Labor productivity |
|------|-----------|--------------------|
| 1989 | 8.9 | 7.0 |
| 1990 | 3.6 | 6.3 |
| 1991 | 6.1 | 5.8 |
| 1992 | 8.1 | 5.9 |
| 1993[a] | 6.2 | 7.0 |

a. January-June.

*Source*: National Institute of Statistics, Geography, and Computing (INEGI).

titative controls, was dismantled (these now apply to less than 3 percent of imports by category), and the average tariff was reduced to less than 10 percent and the maximum fixed at 20 percent. In a few short years, the Mexican economy evolved from one of the most closed to one of the more open in the world.

Speed is effective in making trade opening irreversible: faced with liberalization as a fait accompli, viable firms introduce changes and raise productivity much faster than they argue they can. This is why it is almost impossible to negotiate trade liberalization measures with the business community: they have to be imposed and sustained, over businesses' protests. Credibility is key: when businessmen become convinced that there is no chance of reversing trade liberalization, they quickly try to adjust to the new production patterns. Therefore, a credible trade liberalization program tends to be executed rapidly, and it often concludes ahead of schedule. When a government embarks on trade liberalization for domestic economic purposes, measures cannot be announced ahead of time, and they tend to be unilateral. As a consequence, it is difficult to get credit for them in bilateral or multilateral negotiations. This, at least, has been the case for Mexico.

Accelerated trade liberalization does tend to motivate businessmen to form coalitions against the government in a more radical fashion than under a gradual program. However, this pattern did not emerge in Mexico, because of the clear and firm stance of the government and because of the establishment of a pro-liberalization lobby, composed of exporters who needed unhampered access to imported inputs to raise their level of competitiveness. In fact, the sustained growth of nonoil exports took place only after the trade liberalization program gained speed: from 1983 to 1986 nonoil exports increased from $6.6 billion to $9.7 billion, reaching $14.9 billion in 1989.

Nevertheless, when initiating trade liberalization one must be sure that firms are financially healthy, so as not to induce the bankruptcy of companies that are structurally viable. One must also take care that the currency is adequately undervalued to provide a reasonable margin of protection; that foreign-exchange reserves are at a relatively high level; and that aggregate demand is relatively low, to minimize the temporary surge of imports that trade liberalization always provokes and that generates criticism and pressures for policy reversal. If liberalization is not credible, imports of durable consumer goods will increase as consumers anticipate a reimposition of restrictions; but if it is credible, imports of capital goods will increase as investment steps up for industry modernization. In the case of Mexico, the volume and structure of imports have considerably changed since 1987. The volume has increased from $12.2 billion in 1987 to $23 billion in 1989. The share of consumer goods—6.3 percent of total imports in 1987—reached 15 percent two years later. As the share of capital goods in total imports has remained relatively constant, the share of intermediate goods has dropped from 72 percent in 1987 to about 64 percent by 1989.

In Mexico, the effect of arbitrage in aligning domestic prices with world prices was much greater at the end of the stabilization process, when the degree of currency undervaluation, and thus of exchange rate protection, fell. In this sense, trade liberalization served to moderate the residual inflationary inertia in the economy, once the reduction of the fiscal deficit had eliminated the fundamental causes of inflation. Hence, trade liberalization was an instrument to consolidate more than to generate price stability. Likewise, the influence of world prices intensified as the deregulation of the economy advanced: the monopoly of many importers in certain trademarks and patents—a legacy of the old economic model—was reduced, and domestic oligopolistic practices that limited the trading of imported goods at low cost were gradually eliminated. In fact, profit rates have fallen significantly in some sectors only since 1989, at the end of the stabilization effort, when trade liberalization imposed a stricter pricing discipline.

Two additional factors proved crucial to the success of trade liberalization: rules against dumping and programs for export promotion. At first, a low level of aggregate demand and a high degree of currency undervaluation limit imports and give a competitive edge to exports. However, this situation cannot be permanent, since it soon becomes inconsistent with a stable recovery. Putting in place, at the microeconomic level, the regulations and institutions suited to an open trade regime then acquires a very high priority.

In the case of Mexico, under the old import-substitution model, the legal framework and the administrative apparatus designed to guard against unfair trading were extremely weak: thus, from 1986 on, they had to be created almost from scratch. Standard international practices in this area were an obvious point of reference. However, in the implementation process, three elements proved important. First, the customs service needed to be completely overhauled and agents retrained if operations were to proceed expeditiously; in particular, vigilance against underinvoicing practices, often used to avoid the full payment of tariff duties, needed to be increased. It is impossible to liberalize trade without an efficient customs system. Second, the timetable for the steps involved in antidumping procedures needs to be realistic: their unavoidable complexity and the initial lack of administrative experience tend to create delays that irritate the affected industries. Third, although complaints against dumping are filed by individual enterprises, it proved convenient to establish administrative monitoring of sensitive sectors of the economy and to alert, if necessary, the corresponding industries, which may be slow to react and ignorant of how to proceed with a formal complaint.

Unless exporters have access to infrastructure, services, and tax regimes that are equivalent or close to international standards, they will constantly press the government for a devaluation of the currency. This can jeopardize stabilization efforts. To overcome it, it is necessary to reduce the direct and indirect costs to exporters throughout the economy. In Mexico, after trade liberalization, some important measures were introduced to promote the deregulation of transportation (in particular, increased efficiency of seaports and railways), swift movement of goods through customs, expeditious drawbacks of taxes on imported inputs, and special administrative measures for intensively exporting firms.

## Privatization

In Mexico, the privatization of public enterprises had two main goals: to increase economic efficiency by focusing management objectives, and to strengthen public finances both through the revenues raised from the sale of these enterprises and through the elimination of subsidies. More broadly speaking, this policy increased the participation of society at large in corporate ownership, unleashed creative forces, eliminated a cause of distraction of the government's political attention, and did away with a source of friction between government and the public regarding the low quality of the goods and services supplied.

Part of the public sector in Mexico was created under a constitutional mandate to ensure state monopoly of certain "strategic" industries; however, many public firms had in fact been rescued from the private sector to maintain employment, and others had been created to ensure an adequate supply of basic goods or the production of import substitutes. Thus, the public sector had grown rapidly: already in 1970 there were 391 entities, and by 1982 there were 1,155 (many of these, how-

**Table 5   Mexico: privatization receipts, 1989–93** (billions of dollars)

|        | 1988 | 1989 | 1990 | 1991  | 1992 | 1993[a] |
|--------|------|------|------|-------|------|---------|
| Banks  | n.a. | n.a. | n.a. | 3.94  | 7.85 | n.a.    |
| Telmex | n.a. | n.a. | n.a. | 5.90  | 1.36 | n.a.    |
| Other  | 0.19 | 0.13 | 0.06 | 0.25  | 0.64 | 0.67    |
| Total  | 0.90 | 0.13 | 0.06 | 10.10 | 9.85 | 0.67    |

n.a. = not applicable.

a. January-June.

*Source*: SHCP.

ever, were trust funds rather than productive enterprises); the share of the public-sector-owned enterprises in GDP was 17 percent in 1982.

In Mexico, privatization has been pursued in a gradual way, bowing to the political need to foster a favorable climate for privatization among labor unions and the public at large. A more compact timetable would have contributed to strengthening confidence and public finances sooner: undoubtedly, the delay of some important privatizations was not without drawbacks. Nevertheless, the initial postponement of the large privatizations has had some favorable effects: from an administrative viewpoint, privatizing smaller firms first allowed the accumulation of a learning experience that later proved useful to reduce errors and costs when privatizing larger companies; from a macroeconomic viewpoint, it has allowed public revenues to increase. From 1983 to 1985, nonviable entities were closed down; from 1986 to 1990, small and medium-sized firms were privatized. Through February 1990, 891 companies were declared under privatization or liquidation. The government has pulled out of entire industries, especially banking and telecommunications, realizing in the process more than $20 billion in revenues, as shown in table 5.

The state of the economy directly affected the privatization of public enterprises, especially the larger ones. In Mexico, the ratio of the selling price to the book value of privatized firms has risen consistently as the program of economic stabilization has been consolidated and the repatriation of capital increased. In particular, a qualitative change was seen with the end of the foreign debt renegotiation process. Since that time, the number and the value of bids for firms put on the block have increased significantly. For example, two months before an agreement in principle on the debt was reached, the government attempted to auction off the largest Mexican airline, but there were no takers; two weeks later, there were eight bids over the minimum price. Privatizing to consolidate a stability that was already under way proved to be an appropriate strategy, to the extent that the additional revenues curbed the public debt and strengthened government finances, thus allowing an increase in public investment and social welfare spending—two expenditure items that are under strong pressure after a long period of austerity.

In Mexico, several concrete institutional aspects of privatization have proved extremely important:

■ Not all public companies could be privatized, since some of them were not viable. These had to be shut down in order to allocate public resources more rationally and signal the political commitment of the government to control the public-sector deficit. From the standpoint of credibility, closing a plant down is often much more valuable than selling it off. In some cases, a public-sector company is financially bankrupt and its operations are sustained only through government subsidies. Going through a formal bankruptcy procedure with generalized layoffs and overall restructuring has frequently proved to be the most efficient way to privatize.

■ Often the firms to be privatized needed to be modernized: their managers always argued that, given time to undertake their investment programs, the firms could be offered for sale under more favorable conditions. In Mexico, this argument has generally gone unheeded; as a result the asking price for firms has been lowered and more flexibility in investment decisions accorded to the new owners.

■ Prior to announcing the privatization procedures, it proved worthwhile to have studied each firm at length and evaluated its possible buyers: nothing creates more administrative uncertainty within firms and more political friction outside them than privatization processes that become excessively drawn out.

■ Once the political decision to privatize a given firm has been made, the secretary of finance (whose major concern is to maximize revenues) always becomes the chairman of its board, substituting for the secretary of state industry (who cannot as easily resist pressures from within the bureaucracy). Direct responsibility for the privatization process is always assigned to a commercial bank. This procedure has worked effectively to avoid or remove bureaucratic obstacles along the way. Nothing is more frustrating than the situation—not infrequent in many countries—where those nominally in charge of a privatization are silently opposed to it.

■ There is often a conflict between the rules of a public auction to the highest bidder and the objective of ensuring that firms are bought by sound investors. This is especially true when capital markets are thin and a public offering would not guarantee that an acceptable structure of ownership would emerge. When this problem has arisen, a two-step procedure has been followed: inadmissible bidders have first been eliminated according to subjective and qualitative criteria, and then a public auction governed exclusively by objective and quantitative rules has taken place. This scheme has functioned adequately.

■ A clause has generally been introduced into the sale contract that prohibits the winning group of investors from selling a controlling share of the company before a prespecified time: this practice has been useful to rule out speculative behavior and to secure significant stakes and long-term commitments.

■ In some cases, public managers have tried to organize their own investors' groups to purchase their firms ("management buyouts"). In most instances, this option has not been permitted, in order to avoid conflicts of interest during the privatization process; in some cases, however, such schemes have been allowed provided they adhere to a strict code of ethics.

■ The experience with selling public firms to trade unions or cooperatives has been mixed: in the most successful cases, the workers have hired management expertise; the most severe difficulties have been encountered when a lack of working capital has distorted the firm's decisions. A clear commitment not to provide government subsidies induces rational management on the part of the workers.

■ In many cases, the privatization procedures required the sale of a given percentage of shares (on the order of 5 percent) to workers, on credit terms and an individual allocation basis (even though the labor union may have organized the overall purchase). This method has performed well to overcome workers' opposition to privatization and to promote productivity increases. The most conspicuous case is that of the telephone company, where the labor union bought 5 percent with a line of credit; as the price of stock has gone up, the union has repaid its debt and has now a net worth of around $800 million.

## Deregulation, Competition Policy, and Financial Liberalization

An extensive process of deregulating economic activity has taken place in Mexico over the last several years. As a result of trade liberalization, the retrenchment of the state, and the anti-inflation pact, a maze of regulations became outdated. The businessmen whose profit margins were affected by the dead hand of these regulations were the first to argue for their elimination to be able to compete and survive. This pressure represented the best vehicle for overcoming the resistance of special interest groups.

The deregulation efforts initially followed certain pragmatic principles: to deregulate those processes that affect all sectors of the economy; to give priority to those activities in which the benefits of deregulation would be realized more rapidly or where the cost of not acting at once was high; to break up monopolies and small cartels that mainly injure those with low incomes. Thereafter a more systematic revision of the environment in which economic activity takes place was undertaken. Numerous changes in laws and regulations have created a more modern, open, and competitive environment for all participants in the marketplace, conducive to productivity gains and more rapid growth.

A modern regulatory framework should provide legal security to market transactions, protect consumers and the environment, and safeguard intellectual property rights. Regulation should provide adequate incentives so that free-market decision making results in socially desirable outcomes. The regulatory environment should ensure that the rules of the game are clear and permanent, uniformly applied, and subject to monitoring at reasonable costs. Recent changes in the electric utilities industry, mining, health care, the airlines, the ports, and antitrust—different yet interrelated issues—illustrate how regulatory reforms have been introduced in Mexico, with profound effects on industrial structure and competitiveness.

Before December 1992, the line between public and private provision of electricity was unclear, and opportunities in this area were hampered. Now the law clearly defines the frontiers, allowing for private investment for self-consumption, cogeneration, and independent power production as long as all surplus electricity from these sources is sold to the publicly owned grid. As a result, private investment is expanding, allowing for the needed expansion of the infrastructure without undue pressures on the federal budget.

Old regulations governing mining created incentives for land to remain idle by charging higher rates on extraction rights than on land surface rights. Regulatory reform reversed this situation by eliminating the former. This has resulted in mining companies unblocking large tracts of land for exploration or exploitation. In all, 7 million hectares (more than 17 million acres) had been withheld; of these, 4 million hectares have already been released, and shortly the same will happen to another $1^1/_2$ million.

Old regulations greatly increased production and distribution costs in the health care and food industries, through direct controls, without achieving the goal of protecting consumers' health. A new law, passed in 1991, changed this situation. According to a survey conducted by the Confederation of Chambers of Industry, over 84 percent of the firms affected by the new law consider it clearly beneficial, as it involves reductions in costs by eliminating bureaucratic paperwork while providing clearer rules and less direct controls by the government.

Mexican ports were also the victims of overregulation, leading to elevated costs for shipping companies and a general deterioration of Mexican competitiveness. In fact, rather than using Mexican ports, importers and exporters often relied on nearby foreign ports such as Houston, even at the cost of longer trips by land. The reforms involved the temporary requisitioning of the port of Veracruz in 1991 and its subsequent restructuring, eliminating exclusive areas of influence by trade unions and granting permits for three new competing companies to provide the whole range of port services. Productivity increased by 80 percent. A new law allows the complete operation of a port by a private corporation along with privatization of the associated infrastructure, coupled with regulatory provisions that promote competition between providers of port services.

Excessive regulation had also been an obstacle to the development of competition in the airline industry. A series of reforms in recent years have resulted in the creation of seven new airlines, serving mostly regional markets not previously attended by the larger companies. Service has increased from 43 to 61 cities, and traffic has increased from 12 million to almost 20 million passengers per year.

Reform has also focused on reducing the government's discretionary powers to issue new regulations that affect economic activity. Now, by law, all new regulations must be discussed with affected groups in the private sector, consumers as well as producers, who are entitled to comment, criticize, and suggest revisions. Moreover, before being issued, all new regulations must be subject to an economic analysis designed to ensure that the benefits exceed the costs.

This wide-ranging process of deregulation has faced resistance from many quarters. Probably the full economic impact of some of these measures has been delayed by the slower deregulation of factor markets, both financial and labor. Difficulties have emerged in coordinating deregulation among ministries and with autonomous state and municipal governments. The greatest obstacles remain in the agricultural and services sectors, since industry is now for practical purposes deregulated. But, without a doubt, the release of the productivity potential formerly inhibited by pro-oligopolistic regulations, especially with regard to goods and services in the nontradable sectors, has been a very important factor in absorbing the effects of trade liberalization and in consolidating low inflation levels without waves of bankruptcies or massive unemployment. In the longer run, these reforms are key to ensuring higher rates of growth and sustained price stability in a market-driven open economy.

The move toward greater reliance on market forces had to be complemented with a framework that ensured that market power would not be abused, and that monopoly rents would not accrue to a few individuals. With this in mind, a new antitrust law, the Federal Law on Economic

Competition, was approved in December 1992. The law takes a strong stance against anticompetitive practices: price-fixing arrangements, horizontal market division, and bid-rigging are considered unlawful per se. Other practices such as refusal to deal, vertical price maintenance, and tied sales are subject to a rule-of-reason approach. In evaluating mergers, the main criterion is not so much the size of the firms involved as the impact that the merger might have on competition; there is no rigid use of concentration indices. To promote an integrated competition policy, the law applies to public as well as private companies.

Five commissioners designated by the president for a 10–year renewable term are charged with enforcing the law; they cannot be removed from their posts. The head of the commission reports only to the president, so that his decisions cannot be affected by the interests of individual ministries. If the commission, by a majority vote, decides that a violation has taken place, it can impose stiff monetary fines, order those involved to cease from the offending practice, and even require divestiture. Thus, the new competition law has not only created an independent authority in charge of enforcement, but granted it sufficient powers to pursue its tasks effectively.

Mexico's financial reforms have comprised two distinct stages: market liberalization and institutional reforms. Mexico completed its financial liberalization in 1989: banks and other financial intermediaries are now free to set deposit and lending rates. Reserve requirements—which at times had been set as high as 80 or 90 percent of total deposits—have been eliminated, and the traditional system of compulsory credit channelling to priority activities at preferential rates has been abolished.

Financial market liberalization has proved to be very important for macroeconomic management and resource allocation. Since the government's deficit is financed through the market, the cost of servicing domestic debt has been made totally transparent. Monetary policy is now conducted through open market operations. In addition, with the elimination of the special investment regime for banks and compulsory finance to the government through reserve requirements, credit funds are allocated more efficiently.

The transition from a system of administered interest rates to one in which rates are market-determined was remarkably smooth. But this was only possible because certain necessary conditions were previously met: the reduction of the public-sector deficit, the existence of a deep market for government securities, and the removal of the segmentation between commercial and investment banking in the late 1970s. Fiscal consolidation proved to be key for financial liberalization: when the fiscal deficit is large in relation to the size of financial markets, interest rates must remain controlled or else they may become extremely volatile. The temptation to proceed to full financial liberalization in the absence of control of the fiscal situation and of adequate supervision must be resisted. There have been several examples in Latin America of financial crises prompted by premature liberalization in the context of weak supervision: Argentina, Chile, and Uruguay in the 1970s and Chile again in the early 1980s.

With financial market liberalization complete, Mexico has undertaken significant institutional and legal reforms to adapt the financial system to a more open competitive environment, developing a framework for an efficient operation of financial intermediaries. The more important changes include the updating of capital requirements in accordance with exposure and risk; a thorough deregulation of insurance companies and other nonbank financial intermediaries; and strengthened supervision.

In 1991, a constitutional amendment was approved to enable the government to privatize the banking system, which had been nationalized in 1982. A new banking law was enacted, implementing the strategic decisions necessary to shape the Mexican financial system in the future: the separation of banks and other intermediaries from industrial and commercial firms; the decision to move toward universal banking; and the gradual opening of the financial sector to foreign investment.

Special care was taken with the privatization of banks. In addition to the establishment of an appropriate regulatory and supervisory framework, banks were privatized in healthy financial conditions, ownership was distributed among a much greater number of shareholders than was the case before the nationalization of 1982, and competent management was assured. The price paid for the banks in open public auctions, close to three times book value on average, reflected great confidence in the future prospects of the Mexican economy. A balance was sought between the convenience of allowing foreign banks to operate (contributing technology and knowledge of international operations) and the need to allow time for the newly privatized banks to adjust. Minority participation of foreign banks was initially preferable to allowing full branch operations: in the years to come, 100 percent foreign ownership will be permitted, subject to a constraint referring to the foreign owners' share of the global market. This will impose a serious challenge to the domestic banking system to increase its efficiency.

The last major element of the institutional reform of financial markets has been the full autonomy granted to the central bank, by constitutional amendment approved by the legislature in April 1993. Henceforward, the only objective of the central bank will be price stability. No authority will be allowed to order the central bank to print money, and its governor, appointed by the president and approved by the Senate, may not be removed from office. The central bank also has significant responsibilities, shared with the Ministry of Finance, in conducting credit and exchange rate policies and regulating the banking system and financial markets. The reforms will institutionalize and give the force of law to the autonomous behavior of the central bank, which has been a de facto practice in recent years and has contributed significantly to the confidence now prevailing in the financial markets. Interestingly enough, the autonomy of the central bank, although a rather technical issue, was widely supported by public opinion, as it was perceived as a way to lock in economic reforms and avoid future episodes of the high inflation that proved so socially costly to overcome in the very recent past.

## Reaching Agreement on Structural Reforms

Mexico's experience through the economic adjustment process of the mid-1980s demonstrated the need for agreement and commitment among the main sectors of society on the measures to be undertaken. The Economic Solidarity Pact clearly established that inflation could not be reduced through government policies alone but required a social dialogue and active support by labor, business, and peasant organizations. That lesson profoundly impressed policymakers, and from then on much greater effort was made to build consensus and promote the direct involvement of those sectors in society that would be affected positively or negatively by the reforms. This was the case in the design and implementation of three of the most important structural reforms of the early 1990s: rural reform, educational reform, and the North American Free Trade Agreement (NAFTA).

### Rural Reform

In recent years, profound structural changes aimed at promoting productivity and increasing the welfare of peasant farmers have taken place in the Mexican rural sector. The new rural policy has been the result of an intense dialogue between the government, peasant organizations, and other private producers. Recognition of the challenges facing the Mexican economy during the 1990s was crucial to generating the political and social support necessary to implement the reforms. The establishment of a clear legal framework regarding property rights, the redefinition of the role of the state, and the implementation of new agricultural support and trade policies were widely perceived as necessary despite the related transitional and adjustment costs.

The reforms to Article 27 of the Mexican Constitution and the Agrarian Law, approved by the legislature in 1992, created a completely new legal framework for land tenure and property rights. One of the principal causes of the 1910 revolution had been the poor living conditions of the landless rural population. Before the revolution, less than 5 percent of the Mexican population owned more than 90 percent of the land: freedom for peasants and justice in rural areas were the banners under which the revolution advanced. The 1917 Constitution established that the government had to distribute land to any group of peasants that sought it; to comply with this provision, the government could expropriate land and, through endowments, constitute new *ejidos*, or communal farms. Furthermore, to protect the endowed *ejidatarios*, the law did not permit the sale, rent, or mortgage of plots, and inheritance was regulated by numerous legal stipulations. *Ejidatarios* could enter into contracts with other *ejidatarios* and, under stringent conditions and with state approval, with private farmers or firms. *Ejido* land could not be used as collateral for loans, and corporations could not own or manage land for agricultural, livestock, or forestry activities. In addition, all labor on the *ejido* had to be performed by the *ejidatarios* and their families, since the hiring of farm labor was prohibited by law to avoid the formation of a landless rural class.

Although these restrictions were originally established to protect *ejidatarios*, they ended up restraining them and hindering factor mobility and economic efficiency. Land distribution in itself became an important source of economic insecurity given the fears of expropriation. Under current conditions of economic and social stability, these regulations became excessive, limited producers' decision making, failed to guarantee property rights, and did not provide the necessary certainty for investment and extension of credit. The results were limited opportunities, low investment levels, stagnant productivity, and technological backwardness: although 27 percent of Mexico's population lives in rural areas, agriculture accounts for only 8 percent of GDP.

Perhaps no single issue in modern Mexico is more controversial than that of agrarian reform, given its historical, political, and social dimensions. It therefore took three years of dialogue and negotiation among the principal actors to reach a diagnosis on the causes of the agricultural crisis and some measure of consensus on the principal strategies needed to overcome it. Each of the various constituencies had its say regarding the proposed legal modifications. This effort at consensus building proved to be a key factor in the successful enactment of the reforms into law. Opinion polls have shown that, despite the initial importance of ideological objections, 57 percent of the public supported the proposed constitutional amendments, with only 17 percent opposed (the remaining 26 percent did not voice an opinion on the matter; table 6). Surveys conducted among those directly affected show that the reform enjoys support among the *ejidatarios* and private producers as well. More than 50 percent favor allowing *ejidatarios* to associate with private landholders and to convert their collective tenure into private property. For the public at large the issue was not so much whether collective forms of property were better than private, but how to promote security of land tenure, increase agricultural output, and assure the peasant farmers of higher incomes. Although the new policy is still in the implementation

## Table 6   Mexico: public assessment of rural reform (percentage)

|  | 1991 | 1992 |
| --- | --- | --- |
| Do you agree or disagree with the constitutional amendments? | | |
| Agree | 45 | 57 |
| Disagree | 21 | 17 |

|  | Population in general[a] | Private landholders[b] | Ejidatarios[c] |
| --- | --- | --- | --- |
| Which of the following would be better: to make all the land private property or *ejido*? (1992) | | | |
| Private property | 33 | 50 | 16 |
| *Ejidos* | 17 | 5 | 31 |
| Indifferent | 15 | 42 | 46 |
| Don't know | 33 | 3 | 7 |
| Would you agree with the possibility of association between private landholders and *ejidatarios* to produce? (1992) | | | |
| Agree | 79 | 63 | 52 |
| Disagree | 12 | 27 | 33 |
| The government asserts that there is no more land to distribute. Do you think this is true or false? (1992) | | | |
| True | 18 | 59 | 45 |
| False | 58 | 29 | 46 |

a. Based on direct household interviews with 3,500 adults (age 18 and up) in Mexico City, Guadalajara, Monterrey, Tijuana, Mérida, and Tuxtla Gutiérrez (cities accounting for 67 percent of total urban population).
b. Based on direct household interviews with 750 private landholders in the rural areas of 10 states.
c. Based on direct household interviews with 2,500 *ejidatarios* in 250 ejidos in 10 states. The sample unit is the *ejido*.
*Source*: Polling and Survey Unit, Office of the President.

stage and the direct benefits have not yet been felt, *ejidatarios* and private producers alike have high expectations for the near future. This shows that a reasonable social consensus has already emerged in favor of the reforms.

The amendments to Article 27 of the Constitution formally ended Mexico's land reform distribution system, which had been in place for more than 70 years. There was simply no more land to distribute, so to keep the system alive would no longer serve the interest of justice. In contrast with the previous legal framework, the new Article 27 and its regulatory law provide security in property rights for *ejidos*, communities, and private landholders alike. Excessive government intervention in farmers' decision making was limited, and the freedom of *ejidatarios* to organize and produce as they see fit was fully recognized: this includes the right to buy, sell, or rent land, to hire labor, and to associate with other producers and investors. The new law also establishes a secure framework within which renewable contracts of up to 30 years can be agreed, as well as joint venture schemes with private investors. Both domestic and foreign corporations will now be able to acquire land for agriculture, livestock, and forestry. With these reforms, the first step toward the sustained development of agriculture has been taken, namely, the establishment of clear-cut and firm property rights.

To complement the legal reforms, a comprehensive land titling program has been launched. Because property transactions of differing types had been carried out under the previous legal regime, *ejidatarios* at present lack a legal instrument that certifies their rights to the land. The land titling program seeks to cover all of the nation's 29,000 *ejidos* and each of the 3.5 million *ejidatarios*; $700 million will be spent to carry out this ambitious program, which will embrace 102 million hectares, more than half the national territory. This program is key to facilitate the land transactions that the new legal framework allows.

Support of agricultural production is another area subject to a major overhaul. Until recently, the government maintained a policy of guaranteed prices to producers. This policy was workable only in the context of a closed economy: prices exceeded international levels and did not reflect the structure of relative prices in world markets. One unfavorable result was economic distortions of decisions regarding what to produce. Another was that part of the implied transfers to producers came from consumers, who often had low incomes themselves. There were still other ill effects: some types of agricultural producers, for example, cattle growers, faced high costs for their inputs; many subsistence producers failed to get any subsidy; and, given the pervasive role of the government in buying up crops, disincentives were created for private, efficiently run, trading and marketing processes.

To overcome these shortcomings, a new program is being implemented whereby prices will be gradually reduced to international levels, and direct payments will be made on a per-hectare basis to all producers of basic foodstuffs (grains and oilseeds) to compensate for the reduction in guaranteed prices. This program will cover 3.2 million producers—the same number, coincidentally, covered today by support schemes in the whole of the European Community. For the first time, 2.2 million subsistence producers will be incorporated into agricultural support schemes. The program will also allow a shift of resources from traditional crops into those in which Mexico has greater comparative advantage; lower the cost of basic foodstuffs for consumers, especially those in the lower income brackets; and provide for a better use of

Mexico's natural resources, in keeping with the idea of sustainable development.

Trade policies have also been revised. The NAFTA is the first free trade agreement in the world that liberalizes completely—with no exceptions—trade in agricultural goods. Comprehensive free trade will be achieved only after long transition periods for the most sensitive products, to give producers time to adjust to a new environment of increased competition. For example, a 15-year transition period was negotiated for maize, beans, and powdered milk.

These reforms were conceived and shaped within an active political process. Government agencies have played a leadership role, but the direct dialogue between government officials and producer organizations has been at least as important. The reforms of agrarian legislation are one outcome of these dialogues and consultations. A similar consensus surrounds the significant changes pursued in agricultural support schemes and trade policy. A new, constructive attitude is gradually emerging: peasant organizations, previously structured around the demands of land redistribution, have had to engage in a profound process of internal reshaping to face the new challenges of association, joint ventures, and increased productivity; the unionization of agricultural workers is a newly emerging reality in the countryside; producers are in close contact with the government, searching for new ways to improve competitiveness and gain access to foreign inputs and foreign markets. All this has resulted in a new outlook among all who live and work in the Mexican countryside, and in a new environment of stability and certainty that will inspire confidence and permit farmers and peasants to plan for the long run.

## Educational Reform

Mexico has made tremendous strides in educational achievement in the last 70 years. In the early 1920s, more than 70 percent of Mexico's adult population was illiterate, and the average level of schooling was slightly over 1 year. Today, the illiteracy rate has dropped to less than 12 percent, and average schooling has risen to $6^1/_2$ years. All this has been accomplished even as the total population increased from 14 million people in 1921 to around 85 million today. However, given the country's new challenges and looking ahead to the 21st century, it had become obvious by the mid-1980s that the country's educational effort had to be reinforced substantially.

Spending in education by the federal government has increased by 80 percent in real terms since 1988. Combined public and private spending on education has increased from 3.6 percent of GDP in 1988 to an estimated 5.5 percent in 1993. Yet more spending on education is not enough. Competitive participation in the global economy will mean higher productivity and higher earnings for the Mexican population only if the quality of human resources is raised. And that can be attained only by improving the quality of education at all levels from the elementary schools to the universities, by upgrading workers' training, and by boosting research capabilities. For these reasons, President Salinas decided to undertake a sweeping educational reform.

To engage in such an important task, it was first necessary to acknowledge that the most severe problem with Mexico's basic educational system, and the main obstacle to any reform, was its extremely centralized and bureaucratic structure. Until 1992, the federal government directly managed 75 percent of the country's elementary schools. Such a highly centralized system was inappropriate for a country with such a complex geography and rich cultural diversity; moreover, the system was unresponsive to nearly all forms of innovation and lacked public accountability. Consequently, it was decided to transfer the responsibility for managing elementary education from the federal to the state governments. A change of such magnitude—which in fact had been attempted unsuccessfully in the past—posed a complex set of legal, financial, political, and administrative problems. It was necessary to negotiate during almost three years with all 31 state governments and the national teachers union, which has a membership of 1.2 million and is the largest labor union in Latin America.

Opinion polls showed that educational reform had a high degree of public support. There was a widespread belief that educational standards and teachers' wages needed to be improved, that primary and secondary school systems could be run efficiently by state governments, and that educational quality could be improved through decentralization. But many believed reform was impossible, given the enormous opposition it would face from the teachers' union.

Indeed the reform could not have been carried out without the support of the teachers themselves. Because past misconceptions still prevailed, including the belief that decentralization was a political measure geared to weaken the teachers' union, the government had to undertake an extensive public relations effort to explain the global nature of the reform and dissipate fears. Most teachers were in favor of the government proposals, mainly because they expected greater participation in the design of education plans, increased classroom resources, and more pay. Surveys conducted when the reform was announced showed that teachers supported decentralization, although by not as wide a margin as the population as a whole (table 7).

After a long and intensely complex negotiation process, a national agreement was signed in 1992, setting the decentralization process in motion. It involved 100,000 schools and 13.5 million students—one of the largest decentralization operations ever undertaken anywhere in the world. Yet it was fully implemented in only seven months, without a

**Table 7   Mexico: public assessment of educational reform, 1992**
        (percentage)

|  | Population[a] | Teachers[b] |
|---|---|---|
| Do you think education will improve with decentralization? | | |
| Improve | 52 | 34 |
| Remain at same standard | 34 | 36 |
| Worsen | 7 | 17 |

a. Based on direct household interviews with 3,500 adults (age 18 and up) in Mexico City, Guadalajara, Monterrey, Tijuana, Mérida, and Tuxtla Gutiérrez (cities accounting for 67 percent of total urban population).
b. Based on direct interviews with 6,500 teachers in a national sample of 1,025 schools in 30 states.
*Source*: Polling and Survey Unit, Office of the President.

single class day being lost. Although decentralization is the essence of the new framework, one of its main features is that a mandatory national curriculum and performance standards were retained. Thus, Mexico has opted for a pattern that balances efficient local administration of schools with national rules and standards. A further benefit of the decentralization program has been its role in stimulating participation by parents and the society at large. A constitutional amendment establishing compulsory education for all children and youngsters up to the secondary level was also promoted.

Simultaneously, the first major reform of the national curriculum since 1973 was undertaken. All textbooks for primary and secondary education will be new, including the 90 million free textbooks that are distributed annually by the government to all students in primary schools. The underlying philosophy of the curriculum reform consists of making sure that all students learn basic, fundamental skills. The emphasis will be on language and basic mathematics, with a significant increase in the number of hours in class devoted to these subjects.

Other key elements for maintaining high quality standards in education are the motivation and the academic capability of teachers. This means giving them higher salaries, a clear set of rules for their promotion, good initial and subsequent training, and community recognition for their work. Since 1988, teachers' salaries at the primary level have increased by 70 percent in real terms. But perhaps the most important factor at work to improve teacher proficiency is a new system for promotion. After long and complex negotiations with the union, a new national merit-based promotion system for elementary school teachers was adopted in early 1993. The system includes periodic teacher testing and systematic classroom performance evaluation. The acceptance of this system by the teachers themselves can be appreciated by the fact that, in its first year of implementation, about 450,000 teachers will have enrolled in it after complying with the established requirements.

The reform also seeks to achieve equal opportunity of access to the educational system. To this end, the federal government is implementing special programs aimed at raising educational levels in the neediest areas. A set of compensatory programs has been adopted to support the most disadvantaged social groups and geographic regions. These include programs to boost primary education in the four poorest states, to improve performance in the neediest schools, to address the specific educational requirements of rural poverty areas, and to enable under-privileged children to attend school by providing them with scholar-ships, health care, food allowances, and other benefits.

Reform is not limited to basic education, but also embraces adult basic education, vocational training, higher education, and science and tech-nology. A determined effort is being made to reduce the number of adult illiterates by one-third by the end of 1994. Another program, imple-mented under a special agreement with Mexico's principal business organization, is offering primary and secondary education in the work-place. Simultaneously, a complete reform of the country's vocational edu-cation institutions is about to be launched. It will emphasize the teaching of basic work skills, the raising of academic standards, the retraining of unemployed workers, the support of firm-sponsored training programs, and the adoption of modern technology by trainees. This program is in tune with the reality of modern industrial society, which requires flexible capabilities for problem solving and decision making in high-quality jobs.

Regarding policies for public higher education institutions, a distinc-tion has to be made between the autonomous universities and strictly government-run institutions. In the first case, the Mexican Constitution clearly establishes that universities enjoying academic autonomy should govern themselves according to their own individual regulations. Given this constitutional mandate, reform is basically the responsibility of the academic community of each autonomous public university. The gov-ernment has indirectly encouraged reform of these institutions through a process of intense dialogue and by implementing an optional program of supplementary financing for projects that would lead to better admin-istration, higher—and objectively measurable—academic standards, and stronger links with the productive and social sectors of the country. In the strictly government-run higher education institutions, reform is pro-ceeding at considerable speed. A thoroughgoing academic reform was launched in the system of 104 technological institutes. The reform involves a complete restructuring of the fields of study offered and their curricula, as well as a new policy to ensure a clearer link between these institutions and the needs of the labor market. Reform will also involve a comprehensive program to raise the training and proficiency of the aca-demic personnel of these institutions.

Finally, Mexico's new science and technology policy is the direct result of the shift from an inward-looking to an outward-oriented development strategy. The reform includes an increase in public spending for R&D by nearly 70 percent in real terms since 1989; the reorganization of public science and technology institutions under a single coordinating agency to achieve policy consistency and avoid duplication of efforts, while at the same time ensuring freedom of choice for research projects; the introduction of competition in the allocation of public funds; and the systematic use of a peer review process to assign funds among competing projects and evaluate their progress. The new science and technology policy also encourages the application of the matching-funds principle—especially in technology projects, the improvement of economic incentives for researchers, and the strengthening of the infrastructure of research centers and universities.

## The North American Free Trade Agreement

The countries of North America, sharing a rapidly growing and mutually beneficial trading relationship, must be prepared to face the new challenges arising in the international arena. As trade liberalization has spread, the world has become a more competitive place. The European Community is becoming an integrated market, benefiting from the proposed economic area with the European Free Trade Association and, ultimately, from the profound changes taking place in Eastern Europe. The Asian Pacific countries, on the other hand, offer a vivid illustration of the tremendous competitive advantages that can be derived from shared production processes among nations. These are dramatic transformations occurring in different regions of the world, and North America must respond to them.

It is against this background that a free trade agreement between Mexico, the United States, and Canada should be analyzed. An evaluation of the most successful postwar economic experiences confirms the fact that international trade and strategic linkages with other economies are basic elements to establish five sources that define the countries' competitiveness: clarity and permanence of economic policies, technological flexibility, scale economies, specialization, and efficient market operation. Mexico's new strategy is closely related to all these sources of competitiveness. The creation of a free trade zone in North America will allow Mexico to face, under better conditions, the acute competition for capital, technologies, and market share and to be part of the new dynamics of the international economy.

A North American free trade area will permit the more efficient use of the region's resources. It will imply a trade zone of more than 360 million people, with a combined GDP of more than $7 trillion. Such a market would be larger than that of the European Community, in terms of both population and output. The NAFTA will translate into greater economies of scale and new business opportunities, as a whole range of new production fields materialize. Perhaps one of the most important factors is the complementary nature of the economies: that of the United States is increasingly high-technology-based, capital-intensive, and services-oriented; Mexico, on the other hand, is a labor-abundant manufacturing economy. In addition, the United States is a society that is aging rapidly; Mexico, on the contrary, is populated overwhelmingly by young people. Thus, it is clear that the labor short-ages that will inevitably appear in the United States over the next few decades could be offset by sharing some production processes with Mexico.

The NAFTA is the most advanced agreement of its kind in history. It acknowledges growing globalization and economic interdependence by linking the exchange of goods and services and capital movements. It strengthens rather than weakens the multilateral trading system, for it envisages the creation of an open economic space vis-à-vis the rest of the world. The program for trade liberalization of goods defines a timetable for the elimination of tariff and nontariff barriers, establishes rules of origin (more stringent for those sectors that are overregulated world-wide), and speeds up customs operations. As the services sector consti-tutes more than two-thirds of the regional economy, the agreement establishes rules for trade in services among the three countries, mostly referring to cross-border and financial services. The agreement includes provisions that will make Mexico even more attractive in the world competition for investment through strategic alliances, exchange of technology, and other types of partnership. General provisions applica-ble to trade in goods, services, and investment deal with standards, public-sector procurement, unfair trade practices, safeguards, tempo-rary mobility of individuals, and intellectual property rights.

An agreement of such complexity calls for a number of mechanisms and procedures to supervise its implementation. Therefore, the agree-ment itself provides for the necessary management structure through the creation of a North American Trade Commission. In an economic relationship as intense as that among Mexico, Canada, and the United States, which will in fact be deepened by the agreement, it is only natural to anticipate that frictions and differences of criteria and inter-pretation will arise from time to time. Therefore, it was necessary to establish an expeditious mechanism to settle controversies and to ensure for all three parties neutrality, legal security, and protection against uni-lateral action.

The side agreements on cooperation with respect to labor and the environment seek to improve the living standards of the region and protect the environment. The agreements set up procedures that will guarantee the effective application of domestic labor and environmental legislation. The agreements fully respect the sovereignty of the three countries, are consistent with the free trade agreement itself, and do not contain protectionist measures. Basing themselves on these principles, both agreements established clear objectives and obligations for the newly founded labor and environmental commissions, as well as consultation and arbitration procedures.

Concluding such a wide-ranging agreement with neighbors with whom Mexico has shared a difficult and, at times, painful history has required a concerted effort at consensus building, as well as measures to disseminate information and establish channels of communication with all sectors of society. The Mexican Senate held a consultative forum to hear various opinions about trade liberalization from all walks of the country's economic, political, and social life. At its conclusion, the Senate issued recommendations with regard to Mexico's trade relations with other countries, including the NAFTA.

There were also a number of hearings before the Chamber of Deputies, as well as academic forums promoted by trade unions, business groups, peasant organizations, and experts and intellectuals from around the country. At the beginning of the negotiations, an intersecretarial commission was set up, along with an advisory body made up of representatives of businessmen, workers, and peasants, as well as specialists and academics. In 18 months, more than 200 meetings were held by the NAFTA working committees and by the advisory groups. Opinions were sought from every branch of industry to support Mexico's position. The legislature was kept informed, and the mass media reported regularly on the progress of the negotiations.

Most Mexicans have favored the NAFTA ever since the intention to negotiate it was announced: it was perceived as an integral part of a general reform process that has received broad public support. Nevertheless, opinion polls reveal that the level of approval has slightly diminished (table 8): as the accord comes closer to realization, uncertainty about its effects has grown. Because of their deeper integration with the US economy, people living in the border area are more inclined to take a stronger stand for the agreement. But it is hard to find a citizen anywhere in Mexico who has not heard anything about it. Mexicans support the NAFTA because they are convinced that with it there will be more exports and better pay and jobs in Mexico. Despite the economic differences between Mexico and its North American neighbors, a large majority (75 percent) of the Mexican people believe that Mexico will be able to increase the quality of its goods and to compete abroad. In Mexico there is no worry about negative cultural influences from the United States. For most people, stronger links with the United States do not threaten their nationalism, family loyalties, or moral values. In other words, the NAFTA is not perceived as affecting the cultural roots of Mexican society.

## Table 8  Mexico: public assessment of the NAFTA,[a] 1990–93
(percentage)

|  | 1990 | 1991 | 1992 | 1993 |
|---|---|---|---|---|
| Do you favor or oppose a free trade agreement between the United States, Canada and Mexico? | | | | |
| Favor | 69 | 55 | 56 | 52 |
| Indifferent | 13 | 18 | 24 | 20 |
| Oppose | 12 | 13 | 12 | 19 |
| Do you think that with the NAFTA wages will increase? | | | | |
| Increase | 18 | 26 | 38 | 45 |
| Remain the same | 54 | 44 | 34 | 27 |
| Do you think that with the NAFTA there will be more jobs? | | | | |
| More jobs | 48 | 53 | 59 | 56 |
| Remain the same | 16 | 14 | 19 | 16 |
| Which effect do you think the NAFTA will have on future generations of Mexicans? | | | | |
| More pride for Mexico | 39 | 52 | 42 | 48 |
| Remain the same | 45 | 38 | 41 | 36 |
| Better family life | 39 | 36 | 41 | 40 |
| Remain the same | 40 | 44 | 43 | 42 |
| Better moral values | 29 | 26 | 27 | 27 |
| Remain the same | 50 | 48 | 48 | 42 |

a. Based on direct household interviews with 3,500 adults (age 18 and up) in Mexico City, Guadalajara, Monterrey, Tijuana, Mérida, and Tuxtla Gutiérrez (cities accounting for 67 percent of total urban population).
Source: Polling and Survey Unit, Office of the President.

## The Social Basis for Economic Reform

Any successful economic reform program must include a clear and effective social policy. The urgent need to solve economic problems, some times of a critical nature, must not entail the neglect of those groups in society most affected by reform. On the contrary, deliberate social programs are of key importance to give immediate benefits to those most vulnerable, bridge the time gap between the introduction of reforms and the widespread distribution of their benefits, and thus gain the popular confidence and support needed to maintain the momentum for change. Thus, in Mexico, enhanced social policies have been put into practice simultaneously with deeper economic reforms.

Beyond these deliberate policies for the benefit of the weaker groups of society, other important reforms have helped enlarge the consensus in support of change by addressing the direct concerns of citizens, mostly in the middle classes: the reform of the electoral legal framework, the protection of human rights, and the strengthening of environmental policies. Economic reforms were thus part of a much wider modernization process that involves a reform of the state, the creation of a new legal and institutional framework, and much more active mechanisms of social participation.

The Salinas government put forward a two-tier social policy: it sought to strengthen the existing social security network, and it put in place a nonbureaucratic program of community mobilization to fight poverty, called Solidarity, subject to new rules for the allocation of resources. The most important features of the new social policy were that it would be subject to the fiscal discipline required by the stabilization program (thus ruling out populist initiatives); that it would promote the grassroots organization of rural communities and low-income neighborhoods to allow for greater autonomy and a permanent improvement in their situation (thus ruling out paternalism); and that a close link would be established between the general policies of structural change and the direct benefits for the communities, in order to lay the groundwork for new social bases of support of the reform process.

## The Social Security Network

The dynamism of Mexico's economy in the 1970s significantly broadened the population's access to health services, education, and subsidies for basic foodstuffs. The budget crisis of the 1980s, however, reduced government investment in these areas and set limits on the maintenance of high levels in the provision of services. The goals of reform, therefore, were to free public resources for social policies by curbing the share of interest payments in the budget, through privatization-induced reductions in the stock of public debt and by broadening private participation in constructing infrastructure, thus ending the state's exclusive participation in these activities; to rebuild health and educational facilities under a new alliance with communities; and to replace general subsidies hidden in distorted prices with direct income support programs targeted to the poorer groups in society. The changes in the composition of the budget since 1987 show that these objectives have largely been reached: today, more than half of total public expenditures are channeled to social programs, as table 9 shows.

A significant effort has been made to reduce infant mortality. During the 1990 United Nations World Summit for Children, Mexico made several commitments for the year 2000, most of which have already been fulfilled. Universal vaccination covers more than 98 percent of Mexican children. Since 1988, rural health centers have doubled in number; the campaign to provide drinking water, which originally covered only

## Table 9 Mexico: social public expenditure, 1982–93 (percentages)

| Social program | Percentage of GDP | | | Share of total budget | | |
|---|---|---|---|---|---|---|
| | 1982–88 | 1989–92 | 1993 | 1982–88 | 1989–92 | 1993 |
| Health and social security | 3.0 | 3.4 | 4.3 | 14.3 | 20.3 | 24.0 |
| Education | 2.9 | 3.0 | 4.0 | 13.2 | 18.0 | 22.4 |
| Solidarity | 0.2 | 0.5 | 0.8 | 0.8 | 3.3 | 4.4 |
| Other | 0.6 | 0.3 | 0.5 | 2.6 | 1.4 | 2.8 |
| Total | 6.8 | 7.3 | 9.5 | 30.9 | 43.0 | 53.6 |

*Source*: SHCP.

some 200 communities, now covers more than 25,000; and there are now reliable facilities throughout the country to detect and combat outbreaks of epidemic diseases. As a result, there have been no new cases of poliomyelitis since 1991, and the incidence of other diseases such as diphtheria and whooping cough has been reduced. Diarrhea, one of the world's main causes of infant mortality, was reduced in 1992 alone by 15 percent through information campaigns, the introduction of drinkable water in remote communities, and the distribution of more than 13 million oral serums. UNICEF recently identified Mexico as the Western country that has seen the most rapid decline in infant mortality and noted that it had met its commitments before the announced deadline.

The National System of Social Security provides protection to nearly 11 million workers and their families. It comprises health insurance, coverage for job-related accidents, child care, and pensions. Detailed studies have revealed a serious problem of unfunded entitlements, mostly for old age pensions. Although because of Mexico's demographic trends (a relatively large proportion of the work force is young) the social security system has a surplus every year, it shows a very large deficit from a long-term actuarial point of view.

A two-stage strategy has been adopted to address this problem before it turns into a crisis. The first step was taken in 1989 by modifying the social security legislation to establish a series of new financial and accounting practices in the social security institutions. This step also contemplates a gradual increase in employer and worker contributions. The purpose of this reform is to guarantee transparency and advance each of the branches of the social insurance system toward financial independence. In spite of these changes, as Mexico undergoes its demographic transition, it is estimated that the social security system will begin to face liquidity problems before the end of this century.

The second step was taken in 1992, with the creation of the National System of Savings for Retirement (known by its Spanish initials SAR), which is designed to parallel the national social security system. Under the SAR, savings accounts managed by commercial banks are opened for every worker. Eighteen million new accounts have been opened, equivalent to the total number that existed previously, for people that never before had access to the financial system. Employers must deposit in these accounts 7 percent of total payroll every month (2 percent introduced by the new law plus the existing 5 percent contribution to the workers' housing fund). On reaching retirement age, and then only, workers can withdraw funds from their SAR accounts to complement their social security pensions. All SAR proceeds are invested in inflation-indexed government securities.

It must also be stressed that, in addition to nominal wages, every Mexican worker is entitled to a minimum set of benefits, paid in money or in kind, which traditional international comparisons do not take into account. Housing and pension allotments are included in social security benefits; for these, companies pay the equivalent of an extra 25.5 percent of salary. The employer must also pay every worker a year-end bonus and wages for official holidays (including Sundays); together these additional payments amount to 30 percent of the daily wage. There is also mandated sharing of profits, and there are additional benefits for workers participating in collective bargaining agreements.

To prevent opportunities during the country's economic recovery from being concentrated among larger enterprises, Nacional Financiera, a development bank, has channeled resources totaling more than $4.5 billion to assist 100,000 small and medium-sized companies; during 1993–94 the bank will provide financial support to a total of 500,000 enterprises. Now these companies can access bank credits in less than 24 hours by means of a small-business credit card. More than 250 new firms are joining this program every day. A special taxation regime designed for these firms also allows overall instead of itemized deductions and simplified accounting systems.

## The Solidarity Program

The program that is having the greatest social impact, the Solidarity program, is also one that has close ties with the privatization, deregulation, and restructuring of public spending that are at the heart of the Mexican reform process. The program highlights the new profile of the Mexican state, with less involvement in managing productive assets and a much greater commitment to attending social needs. The fundamental principle behind Solidarity is community participation in all stages of the projects undertaken. It takes advantage of local traditions of community work and organization and indeed requires community involvement, so that priorities are set democratically, by direct citizen participation, and are chosen according to the actual needs of the community.

Government resources are used for programs chosen by the community itself and are directly managed through a monitoring committee, to ensure honesty and transparency; public works projects are made the responsibility of each community, which provides the labor and materials needed. The program offers nothing for free, nor are the subsidies unilateral or for an indefinite period of time; thus any relationship of dependence is eliminated. In fact, community participation has made Solidarity a highly efficient means to provide public goods in poor communities.

Solidarity is a strategy to help low-income groups (slum dwellers, peasants, and Indian communities) overcome poverty through the improvement of their living and working conditions. Solidarity has two broad objectives: to attend to basic social needs and to promote productive activities. To achieve these goals, total investment, state and federal, in the program during 1989–92 was equivalent to $8.7 billion. During 1993, an additional $3.2 billion was allocated. The principles of Solidarity are participation, organization, joint responsibility, and transparency in the allocation of public funds. This has allowed the birth of a new attitude toward public institutions and toward the community. Community life, cooperation, mutual respect, dignity, and self-confidence are the expression of Solidarity. The realization of these principles has already allowed many Mexicans to make major steps toward overcoming poverty, as table 10 shows.

President Salinas has been directly involved not only in the design of the program but also in its management. He keeps in touch with local Solidarity committees during regular trips through the country, two days every week as a norm, since the very beginning of his administration. Solidarity is perceived as clear evidence of President Salinas' commitment to the needs of low-income groups and is probably an important factor in his high popularity, especially among the poor. In fact, when compared with former governments, the Salinas administration is perceived as being much more concerned with the poor.

A nationwide media campaign has sought to explain the new rules of the program, the channels for participation, and the link between the privatization of state enterprises and the resources being made available for the communities. An annual national evaluation system has been established to mobilize millions of people to report on the program's progress, problems, and limitations.

Opinion polls show that most Mexicans, 68 percent of the total population, support Solidarity and view it as an effective program against poverty (table 11). Its contribution to maintaining social stability is also widely appreciated. The credibility that the Solidarity program enjoys is due to its effectiveness, since more than half of Mexicans polled say they have actually seen some of its results.

Survey data from the communities where Solidarity is working show that the core of this public approval lies in the actual involvement of

**Table 10   Mexico: achievements of the Solidarity program, 1989–93**

| Problems identified in 1988 | Actions taken during 1989–93 |
| --- | --- |
| No net additions to health infrastructure for 6 years. | Improvements in services benefiting 8.5 million people. |
| Deficit of 82,000 classrooms nationwide. | Construction of 74,000 new classrooms and major maintenance of 103,000 schools. |
| High dropout rate from elementary school. | 740,000 scholarships provided to help keep children in school. |
| Supply of potable water, facilities, electricity grows more slowly than social demand. | Water provided to 13.5 million new customers; sewage to 11.5 million; electricity to 16 million. |
| Limited access to credit for peasants and family-owned businesses. | Creation of 8,700 new family-owned businesses, adding 42,000 new jobs. Creation of 132 separate regional development funds adding 41,000 jobs for Indian workers. Assistance for more than 1,000,000 peasants on 2.9 million hectares. |
| Local governments received inadequate resources for provision of social services. | More than 95 percent of all municipalities now  receive Solidarity funds. |

*Source*: Secretariat of Social Development (SEDESOL) .

citizens in the decision-making process. For instance, in a survey conducted in the poor neighborhoods of Merida in Yucatan, most of the people interviewed said they knew about the activities of Solidarity, 66 percent knew about the meetings at which representatives of the community were appointed to the Solidarity committee, and 71 percent said that those representatives had been appointed by the community in a transparent process, and thus really represented them. Consequently, most of the respondents (60 percent) considered that the public works approved by the committees were those that their communities most urgently needed and that would bring significant benefits.

These social programs have already had a measurable impact on poverty. The commonly accepted method for measuring structural poverty establishes different levels of poverty for households according to how many of their basic needs are unsatisfied; these needs are defined in terms of the quality of the construction materials used in housing; the provision of basic services, such as water, electricity, and sewage; living conditions (i.e., the number of persons per room); the ability of children to attend school; and the relationship between the number of income earners and the size of the family. This measurement of poverty is called structural because the selected indicators correspond to stock variables,

## Table 11    Mexico: public assessment of Solidarity, 1990–93
(percentage)

|  | 1990 | 1991 | 1992 | 1993 |
|---|---|---|---|---|
| Have you heard about Solidarity? | | | | |
| Yes | 85 | 92 | 88 | 94 |
| No | 15 | 8 | 12 | 6 |
| Do you agree or disagree with Solidarity? | | | | |
| Agree | 52 | 63 | 66 | 68 |
| Partially agree | 18 | 15 | 19 | 21 |
| Disagree | 18 | 16 | 10 | 7 |
| Do you think Solidarity truly helps the poor or is just propaganda? | | | | |
| Helps the poor | 48 | 53 | 51 | 57 |
| Just propaganda | 12 | 14 | 15 | 18 |
| Both | 29 | 26 | 21 | 16 |
| Neither | 2 | 5 | 4 | 3 |

a. Based on direct household interviews with 3,500 adults (age 18 and up) in Mexico City, Guadalajara, Monterrey, Tijuana, Mérida, and Tuxtla Gutiérrez (cities accounting for 67 percent of total urban population).
*Source*: Polling and Survey Unit, Office of the President.

that is, to the more permanent features of a given household. These are, by the way, the variables that can be more directly improved by direct governmental social programs. A household is said to be in a situation of extreme poverty if it has three to five of these identified basic needs unsatisfied, and in a situation of intermediate poverty if one or two basic needs are unsatisfied. Using information collected by the National Institute of Statistics, Geography, Computing (INEGI), structural poverty trends in the Mexican population can be mapped, as is done in table 12.

Summing up these data, we can construct an index of structural well-being (scaled from 1 to 3, with 1 representing extreme poverty). The value of the index was 2.10 in 1984, 2.23 in 1989, and 2.50 in 1992. Thus, the index increased at an annual rate of 1.3 percent from 1984 to 1989 and at an annual rate of 3.8 percent from 1989 to 1992. These data confirm that, despite the deep economic crisis of the 1980s, the social safety net provided by the government offered some shelter to poor households from the degradation in their structural environment, and that a gradual improvement has already taken place with the economic recovery and the advent of the Solidarity program in the early 1990s.

We can also trace the evolution of poverty using the more traditional poverty line method. This approach relates the income of a given household to the cost of a basic consumption basket as defined, in this case, by the United Nations' Economic Commission for Latin America (ECLA). A household is said to be in extreme poverty if its total income is insuf-

## Table 12  Mexico: structural poverty, 1984–92

| Poverty level | 1984 | 1989 | 1992 |
|---|---|---|---|
| Extreme | | | |
| Percentage of population | 21.7 | 17.6 | 15.5 |
| Millions of people | 15.5 | 13.8 | 13.1 |
| Intermediate | | | |
| Percentage of population | 46.5 | 42.3 | 42.5 |
| Millions of people | 33.1 | 33.5 | 35.9 |
| Total population | | | |
| Millions of people | 71.2 | 79.1 | 84.3 |

*Source*: National Institute of Statistics, Geography, and Computing (INEGI).

ficient to acquire a consumption basket adequate to support the members of the family, and in a situation of intermediate poverty if the household's income represents between one and two times the cost of family's consumption basket. This is a short-term measurement of poverty since, instead of emphasizing the household's assets, it focuses on current income levels. Again using information collected by INEGI, poverty trends based on income in the Mexican population can be mapped, as was done in table 13.

Summing up these data, we can also construct an index of income-based poverty (scaled from 1 to 3, with 1 representing extreme poverty). The value of the index was 2.41 in 1984, 2.33 in 1989, and 2.39 in 1992. Thus, the index decreased at an annual rate of 0.67 percent from 1984 to 1989 but increased at an annual rate of 0.85 percent from 1989 to 1992. These data are consistent with the fact that income per capita went down at an annual rate of 1.31 percent from 1984 to 1989 and went up at an annual rate of 1.04 percent from 1989 to 1992; simultaneously, the Gini coefficient, the standard index for measuring the equality of income distribution, deteriorated from 0.43 to 0.47 from 1984 to 1989 while it remained constant between 1989 and 1992.

## The Electoral Legal Framework

After the disputed election of 1988, electoral reform, along with renegotiation of the external debt, was among the top priority issues of the new administration. In 1990, after more than a year of dialogue among political parties and social groups, a new legal framework for federal elections was enacted by the legislature, with the support of five of the six major

## Table 13 Mexico: income-based poverty, 1984-92

| Level of poverty | 1984 | 1989 | 1992 |
|---|---|---|---|
| Extreme | | | |
| Percentage of population | 15.9 | 18.8 | 16.1 |
| Millions of people | 11.4 | 14.9 | 13.6 |
| Intermediate | | | |
| Percentage of population | 27.4 | 28.9 | 28.0 |
| Millions of people | 19.4 | 22.9 | 23.6 |
| Total population | | | |
| Millions of people | 71.2 | 79.1 | 84.3 |

*Source*: National Institute of Statistics, Geography and Computing (INEGI) and the UN Economic Commission for Latin America ( ECLA).

political parties and the approval of 85 percent of the votes. The new legal framework involved a constitutional reform and new laws designed for an era of intense political competition. The fundamental changes under this electoral reform were a new voter registration list; the creation of a Federal Electoral Institute; and a new Electoral Court. The key members of the Federal Electoral Institute are the so-called Civil Councilmen; selected by a two-thirds majority of the Chamber of Deputies, their role is to represent society in the organization of the electoral process. All political parties are to be entitled to public financing, tax exemption, and free use of radio and television time.

A new voter registration process, unique in its scope and efficiency, was implemented in 1991. It was made possible by door-to-door visits to each household by 70,000 students and young professionals over a seven-month period. The new voter registry covers 39.5 million Mexicans, or more than 92 percent of the eligible population. Studies by independent consultants (Nielsen and McKinsey, for example) confirmed the accuracy and impartiality of the process.

Despite the considerable improvements already made, and the fact that, in every legislative body at the federal and the local level, minority parties were fairly represented, President Salinas proposed further measures of political reform. In 1993, a series of amendments to the Constitution and the Federal Code for Electoral Institutions and Procedures were introduced.

Regarding the Senate, there will be an increase in the number of senators per state, from two to four: three will be elected by majority vote and one allotted to the party obtaining the leading minority vote in each state, thus assuring at least 25 seats in the Senate to opposition parties. Regarding the Chamber of Deputies, adjustments were made to ensure that no single party can amend, by itself, the Constitution. Also, the so-called governability clause, which allowed any party obtaining 35 percent of the national vote to hold the majority of seats in the Chamber, was eliminated. Furthermore, parties that fail to obtain the minimum number of votes (1.5 percent of the total) can keep their registration up to one subsequent election, with the government providing additional economic support for these and for newly established parties.

In the area of political funding, new regulations bar government agencies, religious organizations, and foreigners from contributing to Mexican political parties. The reform also provides new standards for the preparation of parties' financial reports and establishes new authorities in charge of reviewing them. The financial committees of each party, not the candidates, are to receive and process contributions. Limits are established on expenditures in election campaigns at all levels; these limits are based on such factors as the geographic area of the state or district and the number of voters in it. Also, in addition to the time allotted for free to all parties in the broadcast media, the reform gives all the parties freedom to purchase newspaper and magazine space and, especially, radio and television time as they see fit; a special multiparty commission will monitor the media to ensure they do not discriminate for or against any political organization.

Other important considerations are the following:

- the Federal Electoral Institute will select citizens to be trained in electoral matters, with the aim of their becoming career electoral professionals;

- over 40 million voter registration cards with photographs will be issued throughout the country before 1994, at a cost of over $1.5 billion;

- a total of 700,000 citizens, chosen by lottery, will serve as presidents, secretaries, and observers at polling places;

- the publication of opinion poll results less than eight days prior to an election will be prohibited;

- a new Court of Appeals will be established to resolve, as a last resort, disputes involving electoral certification; the court will be made up of the chief justice of the Federal Electoral Court and four members of the judiciary (for the first time since the 19th century, the Supreme Court will be directly involved in electoral matters).

## Human Rights

In 1990, the National Commission for the Protection of Human Rights was created as the pillar of a renovated institutional framework with the specific mandate to contribute to the protection of human rights. In 1992, the Constitution was amended to ensure the permanence of this commission. During its first two and a half years the commission received more than 15,000 complaints and solved 11,600 of them. This level of effectiveness is well above international standards. The commission also imposed more than 700 sanctions on public officials, particularly among the federal police corps and the Attorney General's office. More than 300 officials are under indictment or have been tried for violations of human rights.

The Constitution was also amended to give full protection to the rights of Indian communities. It now includes precise and clearer dispositions to secure respect for their traditions, languages, and practices. Other laws were likewise modified to enhance the protection of human rights: the penal code and its procedural law were reformed to assure defendants of their right to a lawyer, and to invalidate confessions not made before a federal attorney. A new law was passed providing strict sanctions against torture. These reforms and other operational changes account for the dramatic decline in claims of torture and reflect the government's determination to eradicate this evil from the country once and for all.

## Environmental Policy

For many years, as in many countries around the world, the Mexican government paid little attention to the environment: the first priority was economic growth, and its adverse ecological impacts were not explicitly taken into account. Partly as the result of a new social awareness, and partly as the result of the dire need to reverse the extensive damage inflicted in the past, environmental policy is today a top issue on the public's and the government's agenda. Mexico has learned, the hard way, that it is much more costly to correct than to prevent environmental degradation. That lesson has resulted in a stepped-up commitment for action.

Since 1988, Mexico has a new Federal Law for the Protection of the Environment. Within this legal framework, the federal government has issued 83 environmental technical norms and will issue 80 more during 1993. In addition, 29 out of 31 Mexican states have issued their own environmental laws meeting federal standards. During 1992, the National Institute for Ecology, the agency responsible for the development and updating of these regulations and standards, conducted 1,269 environmental impact assessments—more than a 500 percent increase from 1988.

To ensure full compliance with the law, a Federal Attorney's Office for the Protection of the Environment was created in June 1992. The office has 505 inspectors, 200 of them working along the Mexico-US border.

During its first six months, the office conducted more than 3,000 inspections, 20 percent of them along the northern border, and during the first six months of 1993 there were 9,314 industrial inspections. The introduction of special charges based on pollution emissions and toxic waste levels by each industry is under study: such a regime has already been approved for industries in Mexico City and at the federal level regarding water pollution. A joint governmental investment program targeting the northern border region began in 1991; the Mexican government has already allocated $400 million for municipal waste water treatment, solid waste disposal, urban transportation, road system development, and land reserves in that part of the country.

The Program for the Protection of Natural Zones has incorporated hundreds of thousands of acres, for a total of 4.8 million acres, or close to 4 percent of the national territory. These reserves have been established with the active participation of various Mexican nongovernmental organizations, to ensure that they do not become ''paper parks'' in the future. Several programs for the protection of species have been implemented. Of particular interest are the bans on the exploitation of 37 species. There are in Mexico a total of 55 protected hatcheries for sea turtles, operated by government ministries and academic and research institutions. It is estimated that this effort results in the release of more than 1 million hatchings every year. There has been a decrease of almost 70 percent since 1989 in the mortality rate of dolphins associated with tuna fishing. A protected sanctuary has been created for the gray whale.

Furthermore, in 1992 Mexico participated fully as a member of the International Convention for the Prevention of Trade of Endangered Species (CITES). In 1991 and 1992, with international support, 25,000 wildlife specimens of Mexican origin were confiscated around the world. Mexico is also operating seven rehabilitation centers for the reintroduction of these specimens to their habitat. In 1988, the Mexico-US Joint Committee for the Protection of Wildlife supported 15 research and recovery projects; in 1993, the committee supported 67 projects. Most of the financial resources distributed by the committee are directed to nongovernmental conservationist groups.

Some $4.6 billion has been allocated to improve the air quality of the Mexico City metropolitan area. One of the country's main refineries was closed down at the beginning of 1991 because of its contribution to the capital's air pollution, even though the plant employed 6,000 workers and contributed $500 million in annual federal revenues. The use of unleaded gasoline is being expanded, and a program has been implemented to restrain the use of private vehicles at least one day per week. In all, during 1992 and 1993, federal resources equivalent to 1 percent of GDP will have been allocated for the protection of the environment.

# The Political Economy of Mexican Reform

Some global conclusions about the political economy of reform can be derived from the process of widespread change in Mexico that this paper has described. It is clearly the case that economic reform must be the result of a firm but flexible decision-making process: reformers must be able to learn from their mistakes and be ready to face new conditions; they must take advantage of existing institutional resources and establish links between diverse government activities; and they must learn to incorporate society at large in sharing the responsibility for decisions. Reforms must be built on a broad and deep-rooted social policy that pays attention to timing and pacing, so that change neither advances more quickly than the population can tolerate, causing fear and resistance, nor proceeds so slowly as to create impatience for results. Achievement of the goals of reform must open opportunities for people, who in turn must recognize those opportunities. In this final section, rather than merely elaborate on these global conclusions, I will address, from the perspective of the Mexican experience, some concrete questions and hypotheses that have been raised in this volume.

## The Speed and Sequencing of Reform

What is the correct balance between change and continuity, between flexibility and firmness, between gradual and radical implementation of new policies? Some recommend shock therapy, arguing that delay only increases the welfare loss that inevitably occurs in the process of reaching a new, postreform equilibrium and increases the risks of reversal of the reforms as the old political arrangements are slow to decline. Probably the overall thrust of the new reform orthodoxy today favors shock treatment strategies. Others, however, recommend gradualism because of the difficulty of doing everything at once without creating even greater economic disarray, social disorder, and even political nostalgia for the ancien regime.

There are probably no general prescriptions or abstract answers in the debate over the pacing of reforms. A reform program will be successful if there is economic rationality in its design, political sensitivity in its implementation, and, most important, close and constant attention to political-economic interactions and social-institutional factors, so as to determine in each case the dynamics to follow.

Mexico has adopted a mixture of gradual and radical policies: broadly speaking, a relatively rapid macroeconomic stabilization process, based on fiscal consolidation and incomes policies, has been combined with more gradual measures of structural change, phased in over time: trade liberalization first, followed by privatizations, then financial liberalization, and finally a comprehensive process of deregulation. Most of the stabilization process was completed from 1982 to 1988, whereas most of the measures aimed at structural change were undertaken after 1988. However, neither of these two major thrusts of reform followed a linear trajectory. Three drastic adjustment episodes were necessary to bring about fiscal consolidation and low inflation: an initial effort in early 1983, a renewed attempt in mid-1986, and the definitive launching of the Pact in late 1987: thus, macroeconomic stabilization was not as rapid as it might have been. On the other hand, most of the trade liberalization was accomplished in a single campaign in 1986, and most of the privatizations were carried out over a three-year period from 1990 to 1992; thus, structural change was not as gradual as it might at first appear.

If the Mexican reforms proceeded, all in all, more gradually them one would have expected *a priori*, this was basically because of the stability and the strength of the institutional framework within which the reforms were carried out. This is probably a distinctive feature of the Mexican reform process, whereas in other countries economic reforms have run parallel to the collapse of existing political institutions and even social arrangements. Mexico has enjoyed political stability and social peace for more than sixty years. The revolution of 1910 brought about great social changes, such as agrarian reform and the creation of a social security network. These, in turn, led to a stability that is unique in Latin America and outstanding by historical standards worldwide. It must be added that, because of its history and geography, and considering the persistent strength of its northern neighbor, Mexico has constructed a solid framework of institutions and social organizations with a clear sense of the national interest. This, in turn, makes it possible to ask all groups to sacrifice, something that in other circumstances and in other countries is not always possible.

The Mexican Constitution and political system place the president in a privileged role, with powers to arbitrate between different social and economic groups and to call upon, reconcile, and finally bring together the diverse interests at stake. This role is expanded by the broad political preeminence of the Institutional Revolutionary Party, or PRI, which gathers within its ranks the majority of the most important social organizations. For instance, Mexico's trade unions, confederated in central labor organizations, have developed a great capacity for mobilization and have maintained a historic alliance with all governments since the 1930s; they have a strong sense of internal discipline and, being representative of labor as a whole, have been able to contain the centrifugal tendencies that reforms can generate. Thus, the unity of Mexico's nationwide labor organizations, far from being an obstacle to change, made change possible, and in the process shaped it in accordance with their interest to the extent their bargaining power allowed. Ultimately these elements of political stability and institutional strength explain the sequencing of economic reforms, how they were implemented, and why they have worked.

The case of Mexico shows that, the stronger the institutional framework, the greater the chances for effective reform—but also the greater the need to negotiate. In those areas where there has to be mediation with those groups with sufficient power either to interrupt the flow of reform or to hasten its pace, the process must be gradual and pursued through clear agreements. But once their support has been assured, implementation can proceed expeditiously.

## The Honeymoon Hypothesis

It has been suggested that fruitful use of a new administration's honeymoon period, with the emergence of new faces in the decision-making process, is important in the launching of economic reforms. Yet, unlike its counterparts in other reforming countries, the Salinas administration did not base its reform initiative either on criticism of the outgoing administration or on an overwhelming electoral mandate for change. The fact that the same party remained in power and that Salinas himself had been a key member of the previous administration ruled out what is common in other countries when political power changes hands, namely, blaming present difficulties on past mismanagement and creating, through that criticism, hope for the future, a window of opportunity for radical decisions, and an impulse for reforms. Moreover, in the presidential election of 1988 the PRI won only 52 percent of the vote—a relatively low level of support by historical standards—in the midst of diverse allegations by the opposition parties. Thus, Salinas' victory was not a landslide mandate. For these reasons, the circumstances under which the Salinas administration took office did not lead naturally to a honeymoon.

The new president had to take political measures to create a basic truce between opposing factions and strengthen his personal capacity to govern. If words and promises may be sufficient in a favorable environment, in an adverse one actions and results are necessary to gain wider popular backing. This is why, in a sense, the honeymoon period and the initiation of reforms were inverted in the case of Mexico. The honeymoon really began in 1991, two years after Salinas' inauguration, after the approval of the new electoral law, the creation of the human rights commission, the solution to the debt overhang, a significant improvement of economic performance, and the widespread social impact of the Solidarity program. Significantly enough, the midterm legislative elections of 1991 showed a strong political recovery of the PRI, which won 63 percent of the votes with an extremely high turnout and no significant claims of fraud from opposition parties. It was only then that major and controversial structural reforms requiring a broad national consensus were undertaken: the reform of the constitutional framework for churches, the reform of land tenure, and the reform of education.

In summary, political processes are not linear, and although the honeymoon hypothesis undoubtedly has some value, it cannot be generalized as a simple rule for all reforming countries. True, introducing radical reforms requires finding a proper opportunity, seizing the moment, and framing the debate: the honeymoon period that tends to characterize the start of a new administration is a natural catalyst for change. But what the Mexican experience also proves is that a government can create, by deliberate action, a window of opportunity for radical reforms well beyond its inaugural phase.

## The Political Alliance Hypothesis

It has been advanced, as a general hypothesis, that a government undertaking reform has to seek support first from the groups that will benefit from the reforms, and from there enlarge its influence to other groups in society. More specifically, it has been argued that, when an economic reform contemplates liberalization of trade, state retrenchment, and privatization of public enterprises, the natural opponents are those who profit from the old system: the business groups that serve the domestic markets and enjoy access to import license allocations, along with the bureaucrats who administer the existing policies and run the state companies. Conversely, the expected first beneficiaries of the new policies are the exporters, since protection of imports means discrimination against exports. However, if curbing excessive government intervention is expected to improve the allocation of resources and enhance the overall performance of the economy, the corresponding benefits will be widely diffused, and thus many of the eventual winners cannot easily be identified *ex ante*. Thus, according to this hypothesis, a reforming government should initially build a privileged political alliance with the business groups in the export sector of the economy.

In the case of Mexico, the political alliance hypothesis has some validity, but its relevance should not be overemphasized. It is true that the Mexican export sector was the group that stood to benefit most directly from reform. However, at the outset of the reform, this sector was small and lacked sufficient influence on its own to ensure adequate political support in the country as a whole. Moreover, the largest exporters were also the most important suppliers of goods to the domestic market, since, under the prevailing import substitution strategy, these firms used to export their excess production, especially in the downturn of the economic cycle, rather than seek permanent access to foreign markets.

Thus, when the government sought to engage in broad trade liberalization in 1985, it had to convince most of the largest industrial groups in the country that, in the long run, they would benefit more from a liberalized than from a restricted trade regime. The task was not so much to play one group of businessmen (the prospective winners) against another (the probable losers), but to explain to the most important representatives of the business community as a whole the rationale for the new trade policy. In any case, that policy was implemented in the initial stage rather unilaterally, and, as the results of reform were slow to ripen, it was not easy to win unambiguous support from the sectors most likely to benefit. As time passes, exportable production and exports expand and the political influence of exporters increases as well. That, in turn, creates greater momentum for reform and permits further liberalization of the economy. To a large extent, then, the political role of the export sector is more important for sustaining a reform process already well under way than for creating a support base from which to launch it.

As already stated, building sectoral alliances is important to gain support for specific structural reforms: key reforms cannot be designed or implemented without full involvement of the people who will benefit from them or against the will of those who will suffer from them. The reforms may impose severe adjustment costs on different social groups, but they cannot, without being doomed to fail, leave them without options. For that reason, the proponents of reform have to conduct a dialogue with all affected groups—not only with the winners to gain their backing, but also with the losers to pacify a potentially violent opposition.

However, no single social group, however significant it may be or become, will ever be strong enough to provide on its own the support necessary to launch a general reform process. A much wider consensus has to be sought and built in society. This requires careful management of governmental institutions and a dedicated process of negotiation and coordination of reforms across all social groups. That, in essence, is a political task, and it calls for the direct intervention of the president, through personal negotiations with the representatives of interest groups, through regular trips and meetings around the country, and through an intensive use of the media, to appeal to the unorganized sectors of society, explaining the proposed reforms to all and calling on all to participate. This also accounts for the important role played in Mexico not only by the economic team, but also by the labor secretary (who is in charge of the management of the Pact), the secretary of social development (who is in charge of the Solidarity program), and the secretary of government (who is in charge of domestic politics). General policies have to be developed to attend to the population's needs as a whole, as part of a comprehensive reform program and not as a mere adjunct to it. The government's action in domains such as the environment, the status of the church, human rights, and electoral laws won extremely valuable support for the reforms and provided a solid foundation for the hopes of the majority of the population. The task of persuasion and of binding the will to reform is little recognized, but it is of the utmost significance for the success of any general process of change.

## The President and His Team

It has been argued that a homogeneity of views on the part of the economic cabinet is a key element for the successful management of reform. It is surely a very useful attribute, and possibly even a necessary one, for a reforming government to have, but it is undoubtedly not a sufficient condition for success. In order to proceed with reforms, a president and his economic team must have a shared vision of the future and a clear overall policy design. Otherwise, precious time will be wasted in internal discussions, and political problems can arise from the clash of mutually incompatible economic lines of action. Vision, drive, and commitment are necessary to introduce radical change. Thus, in the initial stages of a reform process, the risks derived from excessive cohesion of the economic team in government (for example, the danger that, absent any significant internal dissension, the team might overlook the downside of some of its actions) are less than the costs associated with a permanent divergence of views (primarily, paralysis of decision making and the sending of conflicting signals to economic agents trying to discern the new rules of the game). In such a situation, unity is preferable to diversity within the government.

In Mexico, the economic team of President Miguel de la Madrid (1982–88) was less philosophically homogeneous than that put together by his successor President Salinas. As a consensus on economic strategy emerged within the government over the course of the 1980s, especially regarding the role of the state in the economy and the scope of trade liberalization, both the homogeneity of the economic team and the effectiveness of its policies increased. Since 1988, the team has dedicated its energies to the implementation more than to the conceptualization of the reforms. The long tenures (over ten years) of the current labor secretary and the director of the central bank are clear examples of the importance given to continuity in Mexico's economic strategy. Since 1998, the economic cabinet has met over 200 times, or once a week on average, and is always chaired by the president himself. Evidence of this effective teamwork are the more than 1,600 agreements that have been issued after these meetings, of which 95 percent have already been put into practice. Even more compelling evidence is the fact that no confidential discussion on economic matters has ever been leaked to the press.

The importance of having a president with an economic background lies not so much in his technical grasp of the subject as in the time and the resources that can be saved: most of the energies of the government can then be directed toward the difficult political issues at stake in the detailed design and careful implementation of the reforms. A noneconomist president would probably have to grant too much independence to his economic team and then devote more attention to arbitrating their differences and monitoring their activities. Paradoxically, President Salinas, having been trained as an economist, dedicates less time to economic affairs and more to politics and to social problems, which is key to staying the course and sustaining the pace of reform.

In 1988, a profound and comprehensive policy of change was launched in Mexico to further the Mexican people's historic goals of sovereignty, justice, liberty, and democracy. Even though international economic conditions have not been favorable, structural reforms have already reached every aspect of Mexican life. Progress has come about because the government has devoted time and resources to explain at length the proposed reforms to Mexican society; because the reforms have not been imposed on but rather designed and implemented in concert with the various social groups; and because, where possible, their obvious impact on the political, economic, and social structure of the country has been mitigated and their benefits incremented, especially for those least able to bear the burdens. Notwithstanding the structural importance of each reform and the general relevance of the program as a whole, the principal change achieved during this short time has to do with attitudes and mentalities. In short, it has to do with a clear vision for the future, a vision of hope, initially articulated by the government but soon largely supported by the population. President Salinas has been the main architect of this vision, matching a clear understanding of world events with a most efficient social leverage, in order to communicate its meaning and its potential to the Mexican people.

What is this vision about? It means deeper integration with international flows of trade, investment, and technology. It means closer political and economic ties with those regions that are emerging, as the century ends, as the world economy's most important, and with those countries with which Mexico has always had strong historic and cultural affinities. At home, it entails a profound reform of the state to strengthen its social commitments and open a wider space for the economic initiative of the private sector; comprehensive policies to raise education standards and protect the environment; full support to Mexico's peasants, by widening their liberties regarding their own land and meeting their financial and technological requirements; an open and mature relationship with the religious establishment, full respect for human rights, and a permanent revision of electoral regulations in accordance with the increased political plurality and social diversity of modern Mexico. In short, it means change in harmony with Mexico's history and values, but also with world trends. It means facing every challenge and, far from running away from it, turning it into an opportunity to strengthen the nation.

Obstacles have not been scarce, the most important being the natural resistance of those who benefited from the old order of things: from protected industries, from patronage in the countryside, and from political populism—but also from those of good faith who are simply afraid of change, whatever direction it may take. However, important as they may be, the views of the past have not taken hold of the imagination and will of most Mexicans. Too much effort in the process of change has opened up people's experiences to a new and wider approach to public affairs and private expectations. Hope is sustained by a sense of voluntary, self-made destiny. The vision that Carlos Salinas proposed to the nation in 1988 has managed to transform itself into a wide-ranging social determination to seize the moment, look into tomorrow, and build a greater future for Mexico.

# Colombia

MIGUEL URRUTIA

As so often is the case, liberalization of Colombian trade, foreign exchange, and capital control liberalization do not fit the standard Latin American pattern. Colombian liberalization did not take place as a reaction to an economic or foreign exchange crisis, nor at the start of an administration, when its popularity would be at its highest. There was no great coherence or unanimity within the government in favor of liberalization. Nevertheless, the reforms, after an initial tentative start in the Barco administration, became coherent and radical in the first two years of the Gaviria administration (1990–94).

One of the distinguishing features of Colombian economic policy in the last two decades is its continuity and the lack of enthusiasm of policymakers and economists for economic experiments. The depth of the liberalizing reforms of 1989–91 is therefore surprising.

This paper is divided into three sections. The first shows the depth of the reforms, the second discusses the political and social basis for support of the reforms and for the pressures that made putting the reforms on the policy agenda necessary, and the third section draws conclusions about the likelihood that the economic liberalization will become permanent.

*Miguel Urrutia is now the Governor of the Central Bank of Colombia and was a member of the board of the central bank when this paper was written. He is also a past Director of the Colombian Planning Department.*

# The Reforms

The most noticeable area of liberalization has been that of trade policy. Sebastian Edwards (1992) has an illustrative table on the economic opening in Latin America, presented here as table 1. The first column shows that tariffs plus paratariffs[1] in Colombia averaged 83 percent in 1985, the highest level of protection in the region. In 1992 these had been reduced to 6.7 percent, the second lowest in the region. Nontariff barriers went from 73.2 percent coverage, the highest in the region, to 1 percent. The range of the tariff rates also shrank dramatically.

Another area of liberalization was foreign exchange transactions. Since 1967, Colombia had had foreign exchange controls that covered all foreign transactions. The sale of foreign exchange income from exports of goods and services was mandatory within a short period of the export being made and at an official exchange rate, and all purchases of foreign exchange had to be made and justified at the Colombian Central Bank. It was illegal for Colombians to have accounts or investments abroad, except when specifically approved, case by case, by the Planning Department. Foreign currency for travel abroad was limited to a fixed yearly amount, and all payments abroad had to be backed by an import license or service contract. By 1992, Colombians could freely buy foreign currencies for investment abroad, and there were no restrictions on foreign investment in Colombia.

The restrictive foreign investment legislation in place since 1967, and even more limiting legislation in existence since Colombia accepted Andean Group Foreign Investment Decision 24 in the early 1970s, was also reformed, and all foreign investment was authorized with almost no restrictions. In particular, Congress allowed foreigners to buy and invest in Colombian banks. All limits on profit remittances, royalty payments, and payments for know-how were also eliminated.

As a complement to the general trade liberalization, the Gaviria government also led an ambitious regional integration effort in the Andean Group. By 1992, free trade with zero tariffs was achieved with Venezuela and Ecuador. In addition to the direct benefits they expected this trade integration to bring, government officials believed that free trade with Venezuela would make it necessary to maintain a more general trade opening if Colombia wanted to avoid very serious economic distortions.

Liberalization of trade and foreign exchange transactions was accompanied by legislation to free the labor market. Complete job security after 10 years was abolished and replaced with a steeper severance pay schedule, and companies were given the alternative of hiring skilled and managerial workers with contracts that excluded fringe benefits. The

---

1. In Colombia the major paratariff was the opportunity cost of deposits frozen until an import payment could be authorized.

# Table 1 Reduction of barriers to trade in Latin America, selected countries, 1985–92 (percentages)

| Countries | Tariff protection (tariffs plus paratariffs, unweighted averages) | | Coverage of nontariff barriers (unweighted averages) | | Range of import tariffs | | | | | |
|---|---|---|---|---|---|---|---|---|---|---|
| | | | | | 1980s | | | Current | | |
| | 1985 | 1991–92 | 1985–87 | 1991–92 | Year | Minimum | Maximum | Year | Minimum | Maximum |
| Argentina | 28.0 | 15.0 | 31.9 | 8.0 | 1987 | 0.0 | 55.0 | 1991 | 0.0 | 22.0 |
| Bolivia | 20.0 | 8.0 | 25.0 | 0.0 | 1985 | 0.0 | 20.0 | 1991 | 5.0 | 10.0 |
| Brazil | 80.0 | 21.1 | 35.3 | 10.0 | 1987 | 0.0 | 105.0 | 1992 | 0.0 | 65.0 |
| Chile | 36.0 | 11.0 | 10.1 | 0.0 | 1987 | 0.0 | 20.0 | 1992 | 11.0 | 11.0 |
| Colombia | 83.0 | 6.7 | 73.2 | 1.0 | 1986 | 0.0 | 200.0 | 1991 | 0.0 | 15.0 |
| Costa Rica | 92.0 | 16.0 | 0.8 | 0.0 | 1986 | 1.0 | 100.0 | 1992 | 5.0 | 20.0 |
| Ecuador | 50.0 | 18.0 | 59.3 | n.a. | 1986 | 0.0 | 290.0 | 1991 | 2.0 | 40.0 |
| Guatemala | 50.0 | 19.0 | 7.4 | 6.0 | 1986 | 1.0 | 100.0 | 1992 | 5.0 | 20.0 |
| Mexico | 34.0 | 4.0 | 12.7 | 20.0 | 1985 | 0.0 | 100.0 | 1992 | 0.0 | 20.0 |
| Nicaragua | 54.0 | n.a. | 27.8 | n.a. | 1986 | 1.0 | 100.0 | 1990 | 0.0 | 10.0 |
| Paraguay | 71.7 | 16.0 | 9.9 | 0.0 | 1984 | 0.0 | 44.0 | 1991 | 3.0 | 86.0 |
| Peru | 64.0 | 15.0 | 53.4 | 0.0 | 1987 | 0.0 | 120.0 | 1992 | 5.0 | 15.0 |
| Uruguay | 32.0 | 12.0 | 14.1 | 0.0 | 1986 | 10.0 | 45.0 | 1992 | 10.0 | 30.0 |
| Venezuela | 30.0 | 17.0 | 44.1 | 5.0 | 1987 | 0.0 | 135.0 | 1991 | 0.0 | 50.0 |

Source: Edwards (1992).

expensive *cesantia*—a yearly bonus indexed to pay increases that could be withdrawn periodically without loss of indexing and be paid in full upon severance—was deindexed and made investible in private pension funds on a yearly basis. This last measure greatly decreased the cost to employees of changing jobs and to employers of having low turnover rates.

A financial reform law was also passed in 1990, and in 1989–90 many forced investments and interest rate ceilings in the financial sector were abolished or phased out.

As a complement to the liberalizing reforms, two revenue-enhancing tax reforms were carried out which, among other things, compensated for the decrease in customs taxes caused by trade liberalization.

Although Colombia had fewer public enterprises than other Latin American countries, during the Barco and Gaviria administrations some of the banks the government absorbed in the financial crisis of the early 1980s were reprivatized, and the state stake in the automobile manufacturing companies was sold, as well as other companies owned in whole or in part by the state industrial corporation (IFI). Legislation was passed privatizing the ports and the railroads, at the cost of paying workers in those enterprises generous severance settlements and creating endowed funds to guarantee their pensions.

A successful strike in 1992 on the part of telecommunications workers froze the privatization of public services in 1992, and this included state enterprises in water, electricity, and telephones. In addition, many of these enterprises belong to the municipalities, and it is not clear that local politicians are prepared to give up this source of clientelistic support. Nevertheless, the private sector has been allowed to build new electricity generation capacity and cellular phone networks. Oil production will remain in the hands of joint ventures between foreign companies and the state oil company. In the Barco government, it was also decided that private foreign companies could exploit coal and other minerals without having a state company as a partner.

The constitutional reform of 1991, along with enabling legislation passed in 1992, has given the Colombian Central Bank complete independence from the government and authority over monetary and foreign exchange policy. The five permanent members of the bank's board are appointed by the president for four-year terms, but any one administration can change only two members. The minister of finance is the sixth member of the board, but he does not have a qualified vote or veto power. The president of the central bank is appointed by the board, also for four-year terms, with a maximum term of 12 years. The bank was made responsible for monetary, credit, and foreign exchange policy.

In addition, the constitutional reform of 1991 accelerated the decentralization of social services toward local governments, and in the last decade, after 100 years,[2] appointed mayors and governors have been replaced by elected officials.

Most of these reforms occurred during the last two years of the Barco government (1986–90) and the first two years of the Gaviria government, which started in August 1990. Eduardo Lora (1991a) gives a good description of the economic reforms carried out in 1989–90: trade liberalization, labor reform, exchange controls reform, the first tax reform, reform of the foreign investment regime, financial sector reform, and privatization of the ports and railroads. In 1991 and 1992 the tariff reductions were accelerated, exchange controls were further liberalized, the central bank was made independent, and the second tax reform was passed in Congress.

Few outside observers realize the depth of the reforms that took place in Colombia in these four years. In Colombia, there has also been no feeling of having lived through a major economic revolution probably because the reforms had become inevitable, and in some ways, legislation simply recognized the reality that economic actors were increasingly having to address.

## The Politics of Trade Liberalization

For most of the postwar period, Congress has delegated to the executive the power to change tariffs and nontariff barriers. Therefore, the politics of trade and tariff policy have not involved Congress in a major way. This section, therefore, describes the capacity of the executive arm of the state to change a policy for which it is solely responsible. Congress only intervenes in the approval of international treaties that involve special trade aspects, but even then it gives the government wide powers to change tariffs within the parameters established in the treaty. Congress intervened in the process of ratification of the Andean Pact and the Foreign Investment Decision 24 of the Andean Pact in the early 1970s but has not intervened in many of the major changes made within the pact during the last two decades.

Although there was an aborted liberalization episode in 1966, we start the story of trade liberalization one decade later. In 1975, on the initiative of Rodrigo Botero, then minister of finance, meetings were held between the technocratic economic team in the cabinet[3] and President Alfonso Lopez. The decision to liberalize trade was taken. Despite the fact that the decision was made at the highest level, and with presidential support, almost no liberalization took place.

2. The constitution of 1886 allowed for elected municipal and state assemblies, but with mayors and governors appointed by the elected president. Both houses of Congress were elected.

3. This included Botero; Jorge Ramírez Ocampo, minister of development; and Miguel Urrutia, then director of the Planning Department.

The announcement that some goods produced nationally were going to be put on the free import list generated very substantial opposition from the National Association of Industries, and in particular by the industrialists of Medellin, the traditional industrial city of Colombia, who were quite critical of the government after the 1974 tax reform. The opposition from industrialists was strong and unanimous, since most saw a protected national market as the source of growth. In addition, Antonio Urdinola was then head of the Foreign Trade Institute (INCOMEX), and he was a convinced interventionist. A brilliant economist who had pursued graduate studies at Harvard, he believed then and still believes now that industrial policy must be dealt with case by case. He therefore liberated imports of irrelevant items and maintained nontariff barriers when local industrialists complained of unfair competition or of potential displacement of local production by imports. By then, the opposition to the Lopez administration on the part of industrialists and the upper classes in general was substantial due to the effects of tax reform, which included confiscatory death duties and capital gains taxes without inflation adjustment. In that environment, Lopez allowed Urdinola to calm things down by not implementing the trade opening, a position that his pragmatic bosses, Ministers of Development Jorge Ramirez and Diego Moreno, found politically attractive.

Around 1980, Jaime Garcia Parra, as minister of finance, also announced a trade liberalization in the government of Julio Cesar Turbay. Opposition by the Colombian private sector was again substantial, and the bureaucracy of the Foreign Trade Institute and the minister of development (who was from Medellin and closely allied to the region's industrialists) again liberalized only what did not create undue competition for national producers. In addition, in the early 1980s the peso was clearly overvalued, and when international reserves started to decline as foreign credit dried up after the debt crisis, the enthusiasm for trade liberalization disappeared.

The liberalization policy of the early 1980s contained many mistakes common in the frustrated liberalization episodes in other countries. The currency was overvalued, and tariffs and nontariff barriers were decreased where they were highest: in consumer goods. The result was a rapid increase in the import of consumer durables, especially automobiles, and this makes it difficult to sustain liberalization, both due to the rapid drawing down of international reserves and to the difficulty of justifying a policy that diminishes investment in machinery and equipment and that seems to benefit primarily wealthy consumers. Add to this the Latin American debt crisis, and the return to controls was inevitable.

A return to import controls was part of the Betancur government's adjustment to the balance of payments crisis. In addition to the reintroduction of import controls, Minister of Finance Roberto Junguito

**Table 2   Colombia: products on free import list and average tariffs, 1950–91** (percentages)

| Year | Liberalization index[a] | Average tariff | Year | Liberalization index[a] | Average tariff |
|------|------|------|------|------|------|
| 1950 | 65.00 | 17.02 | 1971 | 28.30 | 13.90 |
| 1951 | 75.00 | 25.01 | 1972 | 28.20 | 14.70 |
| 1952 | 80.00 | 19.42 | 1973 | 31.20 | 15.70 |
| 1953 | 85.00 | 21.01 | 1974 | 43.60 | 12.70 |
| 1954 | 90.00 | 21.75 | 1975 | 42.80 | 14.70 |
| 1955 | 85.00 | 23.76 | 1976 | 39.80 | 14.90 |
| 1956 | 77.84 | 21.07 | 1977 | 41.20 | 15.60 |
| 1957 | 70.91 | 16.67 | 1978 | 42.80 | 16.00 |
| 1958 | 57.76 | 18.27 | 1979 | 44.40 | 18.00 |
| 1959 | 61.02 | 18.47 | 1980 | 44.00 | 17.80 |
| 1960 | 59.91 | 17.78 | 1981 | 52.20 | 18.10 |
| 1961 | 60.61 | 16.43 | 1982 | 54.70 | 18.40 |
| 1962 | 52.65 | 15.51 | 1983 | 41.40 | 18.40 |
| 1963 | 37.62 | 13.68 | 1984 | 21.10 | 17.60 |
| 1964 | 37.30 | 12.70 | 1985 | 14.80 | 21.10 |
| 1965 | 15.12 | 15.83 | 1986 | 42.40 | 25.70 |
| 1966 | 56.36 | 22.74 | 1987 | 45.30 | 27.00 |
| 1967 | 3.78 | 16.05 | 1988 | 40.50 | 26.20 |
| 1968 | 17.00 | 14.40 | 1989 | 40.40 | 24.40 |
| 1969 | 17.20 | 15.00 | 1990 | 58.00 | 23.50 |
| 1970 | 19.00 | 16.00 | 1991 | 100.00 | 18.00 |

a. Percentage of items on free import list.
Source: National Accounts-DANE.

accelerated the crawling devaluation to produce a substantial real devaluation and got Congress to pass a tax reform that brought down the fiscal deficit to manageable levels. The Junguito adjustment was successful in discouraging imports and promoting nontraditional exports, and it received the blessing of the International Monetary Fund (IMF) and the Federal Reserve, which in turn made possible the negotiation of "voluntary" loan packages from the international commercial banks and fast disbursing loans from the World Bank. The Colombian foreign exchange and debt crisis was thus solved in less than 18 months.

The index of liberalization in table 2, which measures the proportion of products on the free import list, shows the story of import licenses and import controls since 1967: the slight liberalization of 1974–75, the Garcia Parra liberalization of 1981–82, and the return to controls in 1984–85.

The IMF and World Bank's "certificate of good behavior," however, was conditioned on a move toward foreign trade liberalization. Colombia, therefore, negotiated with the World Bank a large, fast-disbursing trade adjustment loan, which included the commitment to liberalize trade. The policy, designed by Luis Jorge Garay, the adviser to the minister of finance and trade negotiator, turned out to be too clever. He put on the free import list a large portion of the items in the trade list but was careful not to liberalize imports of items that were produced locally. (Note in table 2 the increase in the index of trade liberalization in 1986.) The World Bank's conditions for disbursement of loans were therefore duly met, but when the World Bank staff realized what had happened, relations between that institution and the Colombian technocrats seriously deteriorated. The World Bank became very difficult with Colombia, despite the fact that it was the only major country in the region that was servicing its external debt. It was also the only country that was not even rhetorically supporting the conditionality of the emerging "Washington consensus." Since for political reasons President Belisario Betancur had publicly made it a point of honor not to sign a stand-by agreement with the IMF, this possibility was also closed to the Barco government, and for this reason the World Bank loans and reports to the commercial banks were crucial for Colombia's management of its foreign debt problem.

World Bank pressure for trade liberalization built up considerably as the Barco administration entered its second year, and obtaining commercial bank finance became harder and harder as the international debt crisis dragged on. In addition, some Colombian exports were running into protectionism in the United States, and US customs agents were harassing Colombian exporters in apparent retaliation against Colombian illegal drug exports. As a result of these problems, a trade discussion mechanism was set up with the Office of the US Trade Representative, and in those discussions additional pressure was brought to bear for trade liberalization in Colombia. In addition, the Barco government proposed trade preferences for Colombia as compensation for the human and economic costs the country was experiencing due to its war on the drug cartels, and the US government was surprisingly receptive to the idea, which later became the Andean Trade Initiative. These trade negotiations seemed to promise important benefits in the export area, but some measure of trade liberalization seemed to be the prerequisite.

By the late 1980s, exporters had become a very strong pressure group that included some industrialists (textiles, leather products, shoes, cement) but also the progressive members of the landed gentry who exported flowers and fruits and agribusinesses that exported bananas and the products of shrimp farms. In addition, there was a consensus among politicians and technocrats that the growth of nontraditional exports was a prerequisite for sustained economic growth. In the late '80s, even Cepalinos such as Antonio Urdinola had become convinced that, due to the pressure of international creditors and developed-country trade negotiators, Colombia could not handle its foreign debt and expand export markets without some liberalization of imports.

In addition, the slow growth of the economy during the 1980s had convinced many industrialists that the internal market was no longer a dynamic source of growth. Furthermore, they had realized that one cost of protection was the necessity to produce an excessively diverse range of products. If no textile imports were allowed, the large mills had to produce any sort of cloth demanded by clothing manufacturers. If they did not, the latter could effectively pressure the government to allow the import of products not produced locally, and there was no way of controlling contraband once the first textile licenses were given. The result was that a company such as Fabricato had to produce more than 3,000 types of cloth in the early 1980s, and these short production runs raised costs substantially. Around 1981, the management of the large textile companies in Medellin calculated that 30 percent of all textile consumption in the country was contraband.

Contraband has been an important activity in Colombia since the 18th century, but the illegal drug trade of the 1980s facilitated it, since contraband is the natural way to launder dollars. Merchandise paid for in cash in Miami or Colon is sold for pesos in Colombia. Because of contraband, the Colombian economy has always been to some extent open. Two anecdotes illustrate the contraband phenomenon (Urrutia 1982). By comparing household surveys and statistics on imports and production of color TV sets, I estimated that in 1982 at least 61 percent of all sets had been brought into the country illegally. Contraband of items with high value per kilo is understandable, but at one point there appeared to be contraband of construction steel from Venezuela, a product that can only be transported on the largest flatbed trucks. It was also found that in 1980, air travelers to the United States carried an average of 20 more kilos on the return trip. I estimated that this "quasi-legal" contraband may have been worth $500 million, compared with $1,627 million of declared nontraditional exports in that year. Traditional protection seemed to have lost much of its effectiveness.

For all these reasons, when the Barco government started to discuss trade liberalization, there was no unanimity at the National Association of Industrialists. Although its president and the Medellin chapter remained protectionist, the Bogotá and Cali chapters seemed to have a majority of members who were for economic liberalization in general and less state intervention. The latter were joined by industrialists who sold both in the local and foreign markets. Some local and transnational corporations also saw the possibility of improving profits by distributing imported products together with locally produced goods through their local sales networks.

The Barco government also decreased opposition to liberalization by setting up an infinitely complicated auction *cum* quota system for the import of products that had been on the prohibited imports list.[4] With the argument that nobody had any idea what the tariff equivalent of the nontariff barriers was, a system was developed in which import licenses would be awarded to the bidder willing to offer the highest tariff equivalent for goods previously on the forbidden or "difficult license" list. The system gave industrialists assurance that there would not be a flood of imports, and this disarmed some private and academic opposition to the new policy. Furthermore, Finance Minister Luis Fernando Alarcon accelerated the rate of devaluation via the crawling peg in 1989–90 to accompany the liberalization with a real devaluation (table 3).

The first auctions were complicated and took place with a significantly undervalued currency. There were few bidders that proposed higher tariffs than those on the books, and the pressure to import the auctioned items was often below the limited quotas established by the cautious trade bureaucracy. Given the limited bidding at the auctions and the evidence that there had been a lot of water in the tariffs and nontariff barriers, the new government of President Gaviria was able to eliminate the auctions and carry out a straightforward elimination of all import licenses and a gradual reduction of tariffs. This further policy step was encouraged by the fact that international reserves were growing rapidly (since the central bank was obliged to purchase all foreign exchange), and creating what appeared to be a dangerous increase in the monetary base.

During the presidential campaign, the team of economic advisers to candidate Gaviria had agreed that the new government should deepen trade liberalization, but it was to be a gradual process. This policy obtained the support of the economists on the interventionist wing of the Liberal Party who were working in the campaign, such as Antonio Urdinola and Eduardo Sarmiento. Even Rudolf Hommes and Armando Montenegro, future ministers of finance and of planning, were not thinking of radical trade liberalization.

In 1988, before the start of trade liberalization, 38.9 percent of tariff positions were on the different types of free import lists. At the end of the Barco government, 55.6 percent of tariff positions were on the free import list (either formally or informally, in cases where the the granting of licenses was virtually automatic). The rest were subject to auctions and various degrees of strictness in the granting of import licenses. In November 1990 the new government of César Gaviria eliminated import licenses on 97 percent of tariff positions. Soon after, liberalization was extended to agricultural goods, but within a scheme of flexible tariffs that increased protection in times of low international prices and decreased protection when these prices increased above a trend level.

---

4. The liberalization was scheduled to take five years. The complex auction system is described in Maria Mercedes de Martinez, *Memoria al Congreso Nacional: 1989–90*.

**Table 3  Colombia: selected economic indicators, 1970–92**

| Year | GNP in millions of dollars | Nonoil exports as a share of GNP | Nontraditional exports as a share of GNP | Real exchange rate index (1986=100) | Percentage change in index | International reserves in months of imports of goods | International reserves in months of imports of goods and services |
|---|---|---|---|---|---|---|---|
| 1970 | 7,199 | 9.77 | 3.13 | 88.60 | -0.09 | 1.0 | 0.6 |
| 1971 | 7,821 | 8.61 | 3.31 | 88.52 | -4.88 | 0.9 | 0.5 |
| 1972 | 8,672 | 10.36 | 4.47 | 84.20 | 0.88 | 3.6 | 2.0 |
| 1973 | 10,287 | 11.46 | 5.50 | 84.94 | -1.57 | 5.6 | 3.2 |
| 1974 | 12,369 | 10.89 | 5.41 | 83.61 | 3.95 | 3.0 | 1.9 |
| 1975 | 11,385 | 14.13 | 7.14 | 86.91 | -8.00 | 3.9 | 2.3 |
| 1976 | 12,269 | 17.50 | 6.84 | 79.96 | -5.89 | 7.9 | 4.8 |
| 1977 | 14,646 | 17.67 | 6.75 | 75.25 | -0.33 | 10.7 | 6.6 |
| 1978 | 17,452 | 17.76 | 6.25 | 75.00 | -5.83 | 11.3 | 7.4 |
| 1979 | 19,736 | 17.21 | 6.20 | 70.63 | 3.44 | 16.2 | 10.6 |
| 1980 | 24,450 | 17.16 | 6.82 | 73.06 | -3.31 | 14.8 | 10.0 |
| 1981 | 25,712 | 13.08 | 6.25 | 70.64 | -7.21 | 14.0 | 9.1 |
| 1982 | 25,550 | 12.01 | 5.37 | 65.55 | 2.64 | 10.8 | 6.9 |
| 1983 | 26,068 | 10.41 | 3.95 | 67.28 | 6.84 | 8.3 | 5.1 |
| 1984 | 27,503 | 11.56 | 4.00 | 71.88 | 28.48 | 5.4 | 3.1 |
| 1985 | 32,236 | 10.46 | 3.49 | 92.35 | 8.28 | 6.9 | 3.7 |
| 1986 | 34,943 | 13.49 | 3.90 | 100.00 | 2.49 | 12.6 | 6.1 |
| 1987 | 36,264 | 10.79 | 4.29 | 102.49 | 0.12 | 11.2 | 5.6 |
| 1988 | 38,307 | 11.37 | 4.85 | 102.61 | 2.00 | 10.4 | 5.7 |
| 1989 | 41,526 | 11.15 | 5.16 | 104.66 | 12.23 | 10.7 | 5.6 |
| 1990 | 47,106 | 10.89 | 5.65 | 117.46 | -2.90 | 11.0 | 5.9 |
| 1991 | 45,733 | 13.22 | 7.74 | 114.05 | -4.80 | 17.3 | 8.9 |
| 1992 (est.) | 49,476 | 11.65 | 6.91 | 108.58 | | 17.0 | 9.5 |

*Source*: Banco de Republica.

At the same time, a gradual schedule of tariff reductions was established. The flat supplemental tariff of 16 percent on all goods was reduced to 13 percent in 1990 and was to decline to 8 percent in 1994. The differential tariffs, which had 14 levels and ranged from 0 to 100 percent, were reduced to 9 levels and would end up with only 4 levels in 1994. The average tariff, without the supplemental flat rate, was to decline from an average of 16.5 percent in 1990 to 7.0 percent in 1994. The largest reductions would occur in consumer goods, where the average tariff would decline from 47.6 percent in December 1990 to 22.2 percent in 1994.

This cautious reduction in tariffs, combined with the elimination of import licenses, again generated private-sector opposition, but it was not overwhelming. Imports were not growing, and international reserves continued to increase. The trade liberalization clearly was not affecting the demand of Colombian producers negatively.

The minister of finance and the governor of the central bank continued to allow the nominal exchange rate to rise faster than the rate of inflation throughout 1990 in preparation for the expected import surge generated by the elimination of import controls and tariffs. In December 1990, however, the consumer price index showed inflation to be above 30 percent per year, a threshold above which inflation could be considered out of control in Colombia (see table 4 for the historical record of inflation in Colombia). In January 1991, therefore, on the initiative of the minister of finance, the Monetary Board took radical action and established a 100 percent reserve requirement on the deposits of most financial institutions. The object was to curb the growth of credit and of the money supply.

Minister Hommes, in discussions with the author, has explained that he was aware that a reduction in credit would accelerate the inflow of foreign capital and that this would compensate in part for the decrease in the supply of money resulting from the control of bank reserves. At that point, however, he felt the increase of reserves would give credibility to and guarantee trade liberalization. At the time, however, no mention was made of the potential impact of the credit squeeze on international reserves, since all government pronouncements emphasized the need to control inflation and the money supply.

Monetary authorities seriously underestimated the amount and speed of capital flows. Despite an attempt to stem this flow by having the central bank buy the additional reserves via central bank certificates with 90-day maturity (a de facto revaluation and a way of postponing the monetary impact of the increases in international reserves), capital inflows continued, while imports decreased (table 5).

By the middle of the year, on his return from a trip to Ecuador, President Gaviria called the minister of finance and told him that, in his opinion, there was no alternative to accelerating the trade opening, given the need to control inflation. There were no more options. After a night of consultations, the economic team agreed to bring forward all the tariff reductions planned for 1991–94, despite the reluctance of Ernesto Samper, the minister of development and the politically most influential member of the cabinet (he controlled the largest number of Liberal Party members in Congress).

The public justification given was that without the acceleration nobody would import until all the announced tariff reductions had taken place. In addition to a sincere belief in the advantages of liberalization, the economic team was desperate to stop the increase in international reserves, which by then covered 17 months of imports (table 3). The belief in the need to promote nontraditional exports in Colombia was so widespread that floating the exchange rate and the revaluation this implied was unthinkable. In a sense, exporters had become the most legitimate pressure group in Colombia and therefore the most influential. The devaluation of 1984–85, plus the further devaluation of 1989–90 in preparation for trade liberalization, produced a current account surplus that required a deeper trade opening than originally envisioned, as revaluation or inflation were not considered acceptable options.

Rudolf Hommes described the administration's position to the author in the following terms: opening the economy put Colombia within the mainstream of economic thinking and international trends, and revaluing would have been shameful. It went against what officials had all been saying for years about the need to promote nontraditional exports.

One can also consider the hypothesis that although the president gave strictly economic arguments for his initiative, he might also have felt that, given the very comfortable level of international reserves, a once-and-for-all liberalization would be less costly politically than the possibility of a long, drawn-out debate about liberalization during the whole four years of the programmed tariff reductions. In a conversation with me, the president confirmed this hypothesis and added that he considered it politically unlikely that he would be able to execute the large tariff decreases scheduled for the last year of his administration.

Three additional comments on the politics of trade liberalization are in order. First, all four liberalization episodes were initiated in the Ministry of Finance and the Planning Department, at times in which the growth of international reserves was making money supply management difficult within the crawling peg regime. Unlike in other countries of Latin America, trade liberalization was only considered when there was no balance of payments crisis, and it was stimulated by a desire to control money supply and inflation without an export-destroying revaluation.

Second, in most episodes, there was no consensus on the policy among the economic team. In most of the cases, the Ministry of Finance and the Planning Department were checked by the Ministry of Development,

**Table 4 Colombia: inflation, GNP, and investment, 1950–92**

| Year | Annual inflation rate[a] | Real GNP (millions of constant 1975 pesos) | Change in GNP (percentage) | Private investment (millions of 1975 pesos)[b] | Change in private investment (percentage) | Public investment (millions of 1975 pesos) | Change in public investment (percentage) |
|------|------|------|------|------|------|------|------|
| 1950 | n.a. | 118,655.7 | | 22,568 | | 1,669 | |
| 1951 | n.a. | 122,340.8 | 3.11 | 21,898 | (2.97) | 2,170 | 30.02 |
| 1952 | n.a. | 130,069.1 | 6.32 | 25,041 | 14.35 | 888 | (59.08) |
| 1953 | n.a. | 137,966.7 | 6.07 | 29,333 | 17.14 | 5,746 | 547.07 |
| 1954 | n.a. | 147,516.6 | 6.92 | 35,918 | 22.45 | 4,917 | (14.43) |
| 1955 | n.a. | 153,282.6 | 3.91 | 37,104 | 3.30 | 6,054 | 23.12 |
| 1956 | 7.82 | 159,498.4 | 4.06 | 34,310 | (7.53) | 6,644 | 9.75 |
| 1957 | 20.23 | 163,046.6 | 2.22 | 29,114 | (15.14) | 1,592 | (76.04) |
| 1958 | 8.10 | 167,063.4 | 2.46 | 27,248 | (6.41) | 1,946 | 22.24 |
| 1959 | 7.86 | 179,126.8 | 7.22 | 27,725 | 1.75 | 3,646 | 87.36 |
| 1960 | 7.22 | 186,779.7 | 4.27 | 32,867 | 18.55 | 4,082 | 11.96 |
| 1961 | 5.90 | 196,277.6 | 5.09 | 37,382 | 13.74 | 2,707 | (33.68) |
| 1962 | 6.41 | 206,901.8 | 5.41 | 34,181 | (8.56) | 6,059 | 123.83 |
| 1963 | 32.56 | 213,709.7 | 3.29 | 27,997 | (18.09) | 4,074 | (32.76) |
| 1964 | 8.92 | 226,887.7 | 6.17 | 37,985 | 35.68 | 3,673 | (9.84) |
| 1965 | 14.55 | 235,050.9 | 3.60 | 36,548 | (3.78) | 2,769 | (24.61) |
| 1966 | 12.98 | 247,358.8 | 5.24 | 30,144 | (17.52) | 4,881 | 76.27 |
| 1967 | 7.30 | 257,587.0 | 4.13 | 29,533 | (2.03) | 8,569 | 75.56 |
| 1968 | 6.55 | 272,873.4 | 5.93 | 33,305 | 12.77 | 10,048 | 17.26 |
| 1969 | 8.60 | 289,525.8 | 6.10 | 35,616 | 6.94 | 11,841 | 17.84 |
| 1970 | 6.78 | 307,497.0 | 6.21 | 37,730 | 5.94 | 15,471 | 30.66 |

| Year | | | | | | | |
|------|------|-----------|------|--------|--------|--------|--------|
| 1971 | 13.62 | 325,828.2 | 5.96 | 38,056 | 0.86 | 17,730 | 14.60 |
| 1972 | 14.01 | 350,812.2 | 7.67 | 34,515 | (9.30) | 20,172 | 13.77 |
| 1973 | 23.53 | 374,397.6 | 6.72 | 38,991 | 12.97 | 20,452 | 1.39 |
| 1974 | 26.04 | 395,908.1 | 5.75 | 46,185 | 18.45 | 18,419 | (9.94) |
| 1975 | 17.70 | 405,108.0 | 2.32 | 41,109 | (10.99) | 21,020 | 14.12 |
| 1976 | 25.68 | 424,261.5 | 4.73 | 44,909 | 9.24 | 13,130 | (37.54) |
| 1977 | 28.37 | 441,905.9 | 4.16 | 38,664 | (13.91) | 29,854 | 127.37 |
| 1978 | 18.77 | 479,335.8 | 8.47 | 49,589 | 28.26 | 25,334 | (15.14) |
| 1979 | 28.80 | 505,118.7 | 5.38 | 51,233 | 3.32 | 26,542 | 4.77 |
| 1980 | 25.96 | 525,765.0 | 4.09 | 51,267 | 0.07 | 36,754 | 38.47 |
| 1981 | 26.35 | 537,736.2 | 2.28 | 54,598 | 6.50 | 38,941 | 5.95 |
| 1982 | 24.03 | 542,836.6 | 0.95 | 51,684 | (5.34) | 44,623 | 14.59 |
| 1983 | 16.64 | 551,379.8 | 1.57 | 54,899 | 6.22 | 42,545 | (4.66) |
| 1984 | 18.28 | 569,854.9 | 3.35 | 49,226 | (10.33) | 49,430 | 16.18 |
| 1985 | 22.45 | 587,560.9 | 3.11 | 44,679 | (9.24) | 48,826 | (1.22) |
| 1986 | 20.95 | 621,780.8 | 5.82 | 52,184 | 16.80 | 48,466 | (0.74) |
| 1987 | 24.02 | 655,163.8 | 5.37 | 59,228 | 13.50 | 42,243 | (12.84) |
| 1988 | 28.12 | 681,791.0 | 4.06 | 66,440 | 12.18 | 44,321 | 4.92 |
| 1989 | 26.12 | 705,032.0 | 3.41 | 65,318 | (1.69) | 46,161 | 4.15 |
| 1990 | 32.37 | 734,250.0 | 4.14 | 67,372 | 3.14 | 42,570 | (7.78) |
| 1991 | 26.82 | 751,246.0 | 2.31 | n.a. | n.a. | n.a. | n.a. |
| 1992 | 25.13 | 776,037.1 | 3.30 | n.a. | n.a. | n.a. | n.a. |

n.a. = not available

a. Percentage variation in consumer price index.

b. Public and private investment comes from national accounts.

## Table 5  Colombia: imports, 1970–92

| Year | Total imports (millions of dollars) | Changes in imports (percentage) | Imports as share of GNP (percentage) |
|------|------|------|------|
| 1970 | 796 | n.a. | 11.1 |
| 1971 | 892 | 12.06 | 11.4 |
| 1972 | 843 | −5.49 | 9.7 |
| 1973 | 976 | 15.78 | 9.5 |
| 1974 | 1,502 | 53.89 | 12.1 |
| 1975 | 1,415 | 5.79 | 12.4 |
| 1976 | 1,654 | 16.89 | 13.5 |
| 1977 | 1,969 | 19.04 | 13.4 |
| 1978 | 2,552 | 29.61 | 14.6 |
| 1979 | 2,978 | 16.69 | 15.1 |
| 1980 | 4,283 | 43.82 | 17.5 |
| 1981 | 4,730 | 10.44 | 18.4 |
| 1982 | 5,358 | 13.28 | 21.0 |
| 1983 | 4,464 | −16.69 | 17.1 |
| 1984 | 4,027 | −9.79 | 14.6 |
| 1985 | 3,673 | −8.79 | 11.4 |
| 1986 | 3,409 | 7.19 | 9.8 |
| 1987 | 3,793 | 11.26 | 10.5 |
| 1988 | 4,515 | 19.04 | 11.8 |
| 1989 | 4,558 | 0.95 | 11.0 |
| 1990 | 5,108 | 12.07 | 10.8 |
| 1991 | 4,548 | −10.96 | 9.9 |
| 1992 est. | 5,598 | 23.09 | 11.32 |

n.a. = not available.
Source: Banco de la Republica.

which has been in charge of the trade bureaucracy and industrial policy. At the start of liberalization under President Barco, opposition came from German Montoya, the very influential chief of staff of the president and former industrialist from Medellin who later became a crucial advocate of the gradual and targeted liberalization finally approved in early 1990. It would appear that the start of successful liberalization did occur in Colombia on the one occasion in which the economic team was united behind the idea. The story of how this came about is of interest.

The first detailed studies of how to liberalize were carried out in the Ministry of Finance, and by early 1989, studies were being carried out at the Planning Department and the central bank on the macroeconomic effects of liberalization. When he found out about this, German Montoya called in the minister of finance and the head of planning to find out exactly what they proposed to do. Although an enemy of eliminating import controls, he was aware of the international pressures for liberalization. He therefore told them this was a very delicate issue, with serious political repercussions. He suggested that such a reform had to consider many ramifications, that the program would have to be very carefully crafted, and that an analysis should be carried out of why the previous liberalization attempts had failed. He then sounded out the other members of the economic team, including the head of the central bank and the minister of development. Although the minister of development was not deeply committed to defending such a reform, he favored it in principle. The president was then informed about the general ideas being studied, and the decision was taken to prepare a first proposal, which was then taken to the Council of Economic Policy, which was chaired by the president.

The minister of finance defended this proposal, but otherwise it was received coldly. German Montoya suggested that this was simply the initiation of a process, and the council decided that the issue should be studied further, although the president warned that the timing of the reform should be considered very carefully, given all the other political problems the government faced.

In the following weeks, the economic team continued to flesh out the proposal, in permanent contact with the chief of staff. By then, Maria Mercedes de Martinez had moved from head of the Planning Department to the Ministry of Development and made common cause with the minister of finance. For the first time in decades, the minister of development supported trade liberalization. Things came to a head after a call from the governor of the central bank to the chief of staff in which the former urged an immediate decision, given the favorable international reserve position and the apparent acceleration of the inflation rate. The governor insisted that the liberalization proposal, as it had been drafted, implied a gradual reform. A meeting was arranged for the following Saturday with the president, at which the ministers of development and finance, the head of the Planning Department, the governor of the central bank, and the chief of staff were present. At the meeting, the economic team took a common position, and it was agreed that the program of liberalization would be gradual and targeted. By then César Gaviria, the Liberal party presidential candidate, had been consulted and had given his blessing, and German Montoya had sounded out executives from the textile and steel industry, particularly vulnerable sectors, and had not received very negative feedback. There was the feeling that reform was inevitable and that the political costs would not be major.

The liberalization program was then presented to the full Council of Economic Policy, where it was made clear that the agricultural sector would not be included. Very early on, the minister of finance had judged that the minister of agriculture was unlikely to support the reform, so he decided to exclude the agricultural sector from the program. The details of the Barco liberalization program can be found in Lora (1991b).

Over the issue of accelerating liberalization under President Gaviria, the economic team split in the traditional way. Finance and Planning were in favor of accelerating the process, and the minister of development opposed the policy. The president, however, was a convinced partisan, and he overruled his politically powerful minister of development, Ernesto Samper. In the case of Colombia in 1990, the hypothesis that opposition to trade liberalization can only be overcome by a unified front for it within the government seems to be valid.

Joan Nelson's idea that weakened opposition is critical in facilitating liberalization does not apply. The Conservative Party opposition was weakened, but it was in favor of liberalization. The protectionists that had to be defeated were what one could call the traditional ideological wing of the Liberal Party. This defeat was gradual. Criticism of protectionism and import substitution started in the Lopez wing of the party in the 1960s and became respectable in his presidency (1974–78). The generational change that took place when Gaviria became president—the first elected chief executive in his early 40s since the war—increased the influence of the new school of thinking in the government and within the Liberal Party.

Another interesting feature of the Colombian process is that it was started at the end of the Barco government, when support for liberalization was quite low. How could an unpopular government initiate a process that had been repeatedly blocked in the previous decade and a half? Clearly, the influence of private-sector groups in favor of protection had declined, and the new influential pressure groups, including exporters, were beginning to see that protectionism was incompatible with exports in a world more and more unwilling to allow Colombia to maintain trade policies no longer accepted anywhere else. Traditional protectionist practices also seemed to be less effective, and the national market was no longer a dynamic source of growth.

Another reason, however, is that trade reform was not an important subject in a society in the middle of a violent war on drugs, a violent struggle with some guerrillas and peace negotiations with others, and a politically and legally complicated process of organizing the Constituent Assembly, which would reform in a major way a constitution in place for 100 years. In those circumstances, it was not wise for the private sector to mount major opposition against the government. Nevertheless, the hardest part of the discussion concerning trade liberalization did take place at the end of the Barco government, when the first tentative steps were taken. This made it easier for the Gaviria government to radically accelerate the process at the height of its popularity in its first year.

The acceleration of liberalization in 1991 also took place when the Congress was not meeting and the Constituent Assembly had decided that elections for a new Congress had to be held within the new rules established in the 1991 constitution. The first major debate of the new Congress, however, was organized by opposition groups to criticize the trade liberalization. The government and the minister of finance were much criticized by some of the more radical members of the opposition and by old-line interventionist Liberal Party congressmen. A commission was created to evaluate the economic and social costs of the *apertura*, or opening, but it came to nothing. By then the *apertura* was popular, and criticism of it appeared not to produce political dividends. Toward the end of 1991, polls were showing that the public liked the idea of opening up the economy.

It could be argued that in Colombia it was not difficult to decide at the highest administrative level that liberalization must take place. What was difficult was to get it implemented. The implementation took place at the beginning of the Gaviria government, when the bureaucracy could not easily oppose administration policy. In addition, Minister Hommes, who had seen how the bureaucracy had frustrated the Lopez liberalization when he was a young adviser at the Ministry of Finance, closely monitored the behavior of the Foreign Trade Institute. The elimination of all import licenses also did away with the possibility of the case-by-case approach so beloved of the INCOMEX bureaucracy. This was a fortunate strategic decision and shows the advantages of radical reform over any attempt at gradualism. The gradual dismantling of import controls gives the trade bureaucracy the power to frustrate a trade liberalization effort.[5]

## The Role of Technocrats

Maria Mercedes de Martinez, then–head of the Planning Department, recounts that after a trip to Washington in early 1989, in which the World Bank had made clear that its future loan program with Colombia depended on the country's progress in trade liberalization, she asked the deputy governor of the central bank to study the impact of such a policy on the Colombian economy. He enthusiastically set some recently graduated PhDs at the bank to the task, and they soon produced good

---

5. There has been little evidence of open corruption at the Foreign Trade Institute (INCOMEX). Nevertheless, officials of the institute did become nationally known because of their posts and upon leaving became well-paid advisers to private industry or found attractive jobs with industrialists they met while working at the Institute.

reasons for carrying out such a reform. The macroeconomists at the Planning Department produced macroeconomic models showing that such a policy would accelerate growth, and the Ministry of Finance economists were also dedicated partisans of the idea. Among the young economists in government in the late 1980s, there were no structuralists or Cepalinos.

Due to low salaries in the Colombian government, there is a rapid turnover of highly qualified personnel. By 1989, there were no economists in government trained in CEPAL (Comisión Económica para América Latina) or who had studied development economics at the time in which planning and state-led growth were fashionable in academia. Most of these young PhDs had studied macroeconomics or monetary and fiscal economics with scholarships from the central bank, and free markets and free trade were the bias of the programs in the US universities where these people studied.

In the Colombian universities and think tanks, an older generation of economists still defended protectionism, but even there, a growing majority favored free trade. Even Salomon Kalmanovitz, the dean of radical economics, declared himself favorable to opening the economy in the late 1980s. There was therefore a growing consensus in the economics profession for an *apertura*. This was important, since in Colombia the private sector and the government listen to academic economists, who often have had previous policy experience.

Since the early 1970s, most ministers of finance and all heads of the Planning Department have been professional economists, and this has given Colombian economic policy a bias toward orthodoxy. In addition, President Virgilio Barco, an engineer with a degree from Massachusetts Institute of Technology, had been Colombian executive director at the World Bank and ambassador in Washington, and was well aware of the growing consensus at the international level on the advantages of market-based policies and free trade. President Gaviria was an economics graduate from Los Andes University, which had the best economics faculty in the country, and he was personally convinced of the necessity of liberalizing the economy. He encouraged the Barco economic team to start the liberalization process when he was a presidential candidate.

Without question, then, the liberalizing reforms were led by government officials who were professional economists and were convinced that such reforms would be necessary if the country were to resume rapid economic growth. This suggests that the political economy literature should take into consideration in policy analysis the scientific perspective of politicians and technocrats involved in policymaking.

Economists were particularly worried about slow productivity growth in Colombia in the 1980s. It appeared that the economy needed a major shake-up in order to start achieving greater productivity growth and efficiency. This was the official justification for trade liberalization (Departamento Nacional de Planeación 1990). Even José Antonio Ocampo, the best-known structuralist economist, declared in 1990 that trade liberalization was the Schumpeterian shock the economy needed, although he was also of the opinion that the liberalization should be gradual to allow industry to carry out its conversion.

The role of the young generation of economists in government was important, but the growing professional agreement on the need for liberalization, as reflected in the writings of economists in journals and newspapers, probably also influenced the political establishment and managers in the private sector. The influence of international economic opinion of the time and *The Economist* newspaper went in the same direction and helped to give respectability to the reforms the government proposed.

Rudolf Hommes also suggested to me that a major difference between the liberalization episodes of the 1970s and the 1990s was the changing nature of the executives in the private sector. In 1974, companies were in the hands of the men who had entered industry and the financial sector in the 1930s, usually from law faculties or local engineering schools. They had lived through the successful import substitution of the '40s and '50s and therefore found government protection natural. In 1990, private-sector enterprises were often in the hands of a new generation of economists, engineers, and MBAs with foreign postgraduate degrees. To them, the government economists' arguments were more familiar and fitted the ideas they had absorbed in their training.

## The Politics of Exchange Control Liberalization

It is easier to understand why there was political support for dismantling exchange controls. The crawling-peg policy started in 1967 had kept the peso-dollar exchange rate at reasonable levels most of the time, and controls were not needed for rationing foreign exchange. Exchange controls increased the cost of trade transactions. They also harmed the middle and upper classes, who had to pay large transaction costs in order to diversify their portfolios without running into trouble with the Superintendency of Exchange Control. By the late 1970s, thousands of Colombians had foreign accounts, and many went to the parallel market to get dollars for travel abroad, for paying foreign services, or even for underinvoicing imports. (Since the mid-'70s, due in part to taxes and delays in the monetization of foreign exchange and to an adequate supply of foreign exchange in the parallel market, the official exchange rate has tended to be above the parallel rate, except at the time of the exchange crisis of 1983–85.)

It is hard to see who benefited from exchange controls. Policymakers often justified the regime as a means of diminishing the instability created by short-term capital flows. There was also a moral justification, in so far as it was believed these controls could keep away drug profits generated abroad and hinder capital flight. The former argument backfired when the Colombian and US press, and even the US embassy, started to claim that the central bank bought dollars from illegal drug dealers. This was inevitable since, according to the law, all foreign exchange, including remittances, had to be sold exclusively to the central bank.

The strongest argument for maintaining exchange controls, however, was the fact that Colombia had had only one balance of payments crisis since 1967, when those controls were introduced. Not too many people fully understood that you could maintain the crawling-peg mechanism and a realistic exchange rate, which were the real reasons for the stability in the foreign exchange front, without such a detailed exchange control system.

The Gaviria administration wanted to adopt legislation that would diminish the need for so many otherwise respectable citizens to enter into illegal activities and to allow some foreign exchange transactions to be carried out in a free exchange market. Since this was a major change in the existing regime, the matter had to be taken to Congress. The exchange control law (Decree 444 of 1967) gave the Monetary Board, dominated by the executive, wide powers to modify the exchange control legislation, but major changes in the general framework of the exchange regime had to be taken to Congress.

When the Congress opened after the Gaviria inauguration, the central bank had convinced the government to present legislation it had drafted that implied a less radical change. It emphasized making the regime more flexible by decentralizing foreign currency operations to financial intermediaries other than the central bank. When opposition congressmen presented an alternative reform, which involved complete elimination of exchange controls and a floating exchange rate, the minister of finance negotiated a law that closely resembled the scheme he and his colleagues had designed before the inauguration. By shifting the discussion on the exchange regime from the Monetary Board, where the governor of the central bank was very influential, to the Congress, the partisans of exchange controls were greatly weakened.

Once exchange controls were liberalized, the only opposition came from exporters, who thought tough controls would diminish the inflow of repatriated capital in 1991, both legitimate and drug-related, and this would diminish the pressure for revaluation. Since most exporters had illegal accounts and investments abroad, however, they did not pursue this line of reasoning too vigorously. Banks, on the other hand, were enthusiastically in favor of liberalization, since they now handled all foreign exchange transactions, previously the monopoly of the central bank, and their foreign currency departments started to account for an ever-higher proportion of profits.

In the case of exchange controls, the surprising thing is how long it took to dismantle them. There were only two groups interested in their maintenance: central bank officials who thought the controls made the management of monetary policy easier, and politicians identified with the 1967 exchange control legislation. The central bank, however, did not have a solid basis for support of exchange controls. Control of short-term capital flows is probably desirable but not easy, even with the complete array of exchange controls existing in Colombia after 1967. The resource costs of the controls were probably higher than the benefits provided in terms of effective control of short-term capital movements. These controls also created many enemies for the central bank, and the costs started to be viewed as outweighing the presumed benefits in the area of monetary policy.

Also, the old-guard interventionist Liberal Party politicians were out-numbered in Congress by a new generation, which easily had the major-ity to pass Exchange Reform Law 9 of 1991. This majority knew that legalizing private foreign currency accounts abroad was popular.

There was also no bureaucracy to defend the controls. The governor of the central bank wanted to move the controls out of the central bank and into the financial sector. Furthermore, the prosecuting arm of the government, the Superintendencia de Control de Cambios, was a weak agency. Prosecuting people for exchange control violations was not pop-ular and had become dangerous as the illicit drug traffic increased. Few people wanted a job in the Superintendencia de Control de Cambios.

## The Labor Reform

Labor reform was also a reform waiting to happen. For over two decades, employers had been complaining about the legislation on job security. Fringe benefits and the *cesantia* bonus were becoming intoler-able burdens for companies with an aging labor force.

In Colombia, labor legislation is the responsibility of Congress, and there has been a tradition of not diminishing previously legislated labor rights. Dismantling the legislation on job security was therefore consid-ered very difficult.

In the 1980s, however, academic research showed that employers tended to fire workers before they obtained any rights to job security. It turned out that Colombia had passed from being a country with sub-stantial job stability in the 1960s to having one of the highest labor turnover rates in the world. The job stability legislation appeared to have had an effect exactly opposite to that desired. This academic research was important in convincing many progressive congressmen that reforming this aspect of labor legislation was not a reactionary thing to do.

During its last session before the Constitutional Assembly, Congress wanted to demonstrate how enlightened, efficient, and courageous it could be in order to diminish the pressure for congressional reform at the Constituent Assembly. It therefore passed the government initiative on labor reform despite spirited opposition from the labor movement.

The political strength of the labor movement has historically been its capacity to threaten the government with politically disruptive strikes. This last tactic was not a realistic tool to use on the eve of the Constituent Assembly, when both the public and the government were concentrating on other political issues. Politically, labor has become weaker. There are about the same number of union members now as in 1967, but the union confederations are now completely dominated by Communists and have therefore little influence in the major parties and Congress, where there are only a handful of Communist or radical members. Furthermore, the unions have no funds to use in support of congressional elections.

The potential for disruption and violence from a general strike dissuades most governments and congresses from passing legislation strongly opposed by the unions. However, the special circumstances leading to the Constituent Assembly and the mood of reform of the first year of the Gaviria government, plus the argument that without labor market flexibility the trade liberalization could harm some industries and create unemployment, made the reform politically possible. In this area, the deep commitment of the president to reform was important. He had prepared the projects for reforming the labor legislation before taking office, and these were among the first that the congress received from the new government.

## Tax Reform

Tax reform in Colombia is the responsibility of Congress, although discussion of tax changes can only take place at the government's initiative. Tax reform projects are therefore always initiated by the executive branch.

All the literature on trade reform suggests that the liberalization process must start with a realistic or undervalued exchange rate and fiscal accounts in balance. Colombia followed the orthodox scenario. We saw that the real devaluations of 1984–85 and 1989–90 had made Colombian production quite competitive, and the Junguito adjustment of 1985 had reduced the fiscal deficit to 1 or 2 percent of GNP (table 6).

Trade liberalization, however, created a serious fiscal problem, since import taxes were as high as 25 percent of total central government revenues in 1989. Trade liberalization therefore could potentially have had disastrous fiscal effects.

## Table 6   Colombia: consolidated government fiscal deficit as a proportion of GNP

| Year | Not including National Coffee Fund | Total |
|------|------------------------------------|-------|
| 1980 | -2.64 | -2.31 |
| 1981 | -5.14 | -5.50 |
| 1982 | -6.16 | -5.98 |
| 1983 | -7.43 | -7.44 |
| 1984 | -5.51 | -5.94 |
| 1985 | -5.70 | -4.38 |
| 1986 | -2.68 | -0.29 |
| 1987 | -1.63 | -1.94 |
| 1988 | -2.40 | -2.48 |
| 1989 | -2.14 | -2.29 |
| 1990 | -0.31 | -0.33 |
| 1991 | 0.66 | 0.16 |
| 1992 est. | 0.35 | -0.45 |

*Source*: Consejo Superior de Política Fiscal: Programa Anual de Caja del Gobierno Nacional y Panorama del Sector Publico no Financiero 1992-1993 (Bogotá: Documento Asesores 030/92, Dic. 30, 1992).

In 1990 the Congress passed its first tax reform legislation, which enhanced fiscal revenues by increasing the value-added tax from 10 to 12 percent and increased the base of the tax. It also included rules governing a tax amnesty for the repatriation and declaration of capital held abroad, the rationalization of taxation of foreign investment, and tax incentives for the development of the capital market, such as the elimination of capital gains on the sale of stocks through the stock market. This tax reform passed relatively easily in the activist congress of 1990 as part of the package of measures meant to open up the Colombian economy.

When the government implemented all the tariff reductions planned to take place in five years in 1991, it announced it would present to Congress a tax reform to compensate for the loss of revenue. Initially, most of the revenue to be generated was to be raised by increasing the rates of the value-added tax and increasing coverage of that tax by extending it to services. Some congressmen criticized the regressiveness of the VAT, and so the government agreed to raise those rates by less and increase income tax rates instead. Congress, against the government's wishes, also increased taxes on oil exports and did not decrease the dividend remittance tax for foreign companies. Clearly, foreign companies have little influence on congressmen.

The tax reform generated strong and vocal opposition from the private sector. The association of retailers went as far as to pay for radio and newspaper advertisements, as well as roadside billboards, against a tax increase. The only president of a business association who spoke for the reform was the president of the Association of Exporters. Some weeks before, President Gaviria had explained to him and the board of directors of the association that there were only two alternatives for the control of inflation: a tax reform that would eliminate the fiscal deficit or a revaluation. The opposition of the press to the reform was also very strong, and private lobbying against it was intense.

The president put all his political skills to work and met daily with groups of congressmen to convince them of the need for the tax reform. He was fortunate in having the support of Minister Hommes at Finance, who in addition to being technically very knowledgeable, turned out to be a very skilled negotiator with an easygoing personality that made him popular in Congress. The reform was in fact passed, with the help of Victor Renan Barco, a congressman who, with more than two decades of legislative experience, has become the leader in the Senate on most economic legislation by creating a complicated series of political alliances based on ideology. This time around, the government was unable to maintain discipline in the Liberal Party, and the income tax part of the reform was voted through by a combination of Liberal and M19 (the former guerrilla movement) congressmen, who were for an increase in the income tax on equity grounds. The increase in the VAT was voted by a coalition of Liberals and the Andres Pastrana wing of the Conservative Party, which favored trade liberalization and the substitution of trade taxes by a VAT.

Throughout the debates, in the press and in upper-class circles there was widespread criticism of the president and his minister of finance for including in the budget funds for projects close to the heart of congressmen that needed persuasion and for appointing supporters of other congressmen to middle-level administrative positions. In the moralistic ambience of Colombia in 1991, the press acted as if these practices were not usual in most democracies, and these allegations of favors rendered were used as arguments against the reform and the government.

However, in Colombia, as opposed to other Latin American countries, Congress does pass tax reforms. The political class is not closely related to or influenced by the private sector, and so private-sector opposition to tax reforms is not effective. The business of congressmen is politics, and they do not like inflationary fiscal deficits because inflation is not popular with the electorate. I will not go more deeply into the politics of tax reform in Colombia because I have analyzed the subject in detail elsewhere (Urrutia 1989) using the tax reforms of the 1970s as case studies. The 1991 tax reform followed the same pattern and required a deep commitment on the part of the president and his minister of finance.

The reform of 1991, as was the case in 1974, had a clear cost in terms of popularity for the president and his government. It is also significant that all of the revenue-generating tax reforms in the last two decades have been passed by technocratic ministers of finance who have no future political ambitions.

## Conclusion

Apparently, the economic liberalization of 1989–92 will not be reversed. On 10 January 1993, a newspaper (*El Tiempo*) poll of 500 enterprises showed that there was no longer much opposition to trade liberalization. While 21 percent of industrialists considered the *apertura* to be negative, 60 percent thought it positive, and 19 percent were indifferent. Taking all economic sectors together, only 14 percent of respondents were against the trade liberalization. On 19 January 1993, the newsweekly *Semana* published a survey of 1,000 citizens in which 39.6 percent of respondents declared that the *apertura* was somewhat good for the country, and 16.1 percent declared it had been very good for the country (9.7 percent answered they did not know).

International reserves continue to grow and cover about 19 months of imports, so there is little danger of a balance of payments problem that would stimulate a new episode of import controls. In addition, at the end of 1992 it was confirmed that there was a very major oil field in the Llanos area, and this guarantees that there will be no balance of payments problems in the next decade. The challenge is, on the contrary, to avoid a Dutch Disease problem.

Consumers are also beginning to be aware of and enjoy the opening of the economy. The unpopular part, the tax reform, was passed and will not again be on the agenda for a few years. Programs for financial reform and central bank independence have now passed Congress, and the latter cannot be reversed without a difficult process of constitutional reform. Inflation has been decreasing for two years in a row, and there is no reason to think it cannot continue to decrease gradually until it reaches single-digit levels. The independent central bank, now responsible for exchange rate management, has declared that it will not allow a significant real revaluation, and most economists in the country, as well as policymakers, consider such a policy a prerequisite for economic growth. The avoidance of an overvaluation of the exchange rate will be a crucial ingredient for the survival of the recent trade and exchange liberalization.

In 1992 there was a budget surplus for most of the year, and the deficit was probably close to zero in December. There is, however, the danger that in the following years the deficit may increase. This must be closely watched in order to maintain the macroeconomic balance that will be necessary if economic liberalization is to persist. The reform agenda of the future must therefore give priority to making public services more efficient and to the targeting of public expenditure in favor of the poor in order to build a just and peaceful society.

With respect to the politics of the economic reforms of 1989–92 in Colombia, the first enabling circumstance was the mood for change that has existed in the society. The violence generated by the war on drugs and the guerrillas in the second half of the 1980s had led to a generalized feeling that major institutional changes were required. The murder of three presidential candidates, most of the Supreme Court, a minister of justice, and other high government officials and members of the judicial branch, as well as terrorist attacks in the cities and against economic infrastructure, were all circumstances that put into question some of the basic institutions of society. The governments of Presidents Barco and Gaviria therefore supported and finally were able to gain support for the calling of a Constituent Assembly. Originally, the objective was to change voting rules to give greater access to the political process to political minorities that felt excluded and to make the judicial system more efficient and operational. By 1991, however, the Constituent Assembly received a mandate to consider all of the institutional arrangements in society, and the government created venues at all levels for popular discussion of what reforms the Constituent Assembly should discuss.

The elections for the assembly produced a body with a political profile quite different from the traditional profile of the Congress. There were representatives of the small Indian population in the country, representatives of the growing Protestant sects, intellectuals, and the more ideological members of the traditional parties. In addition, 27 percent of the assemblymen belonged to M19, the party created by a former guerrilla movement. In this general mood for change, the economic reforms seemed tame, but there was also a greater willingness to experiment with reform than in the past.

The constitutional reform of 1991 strengthened the Congress in many ways but also reformed it. In general, the executive lost leverage over Congress, and this may have made the passing of the 1992 tax reform more difficult than in the past. On the other hand, the mood for change created by the calling of the Constituent Assembly facilitated economic reform.

With this background in mind, the following considerations about the sources of support for the reforms may be useful.

## Trade Liberalization

- Trade liberalization became possible when, after two decades of consistent export promotion policies, exporters had become the most legitimate and influential pressure group in the country.

- The conversion of the majority of highly trained economists in the country, and particularly in the government, to economic liberalization was an important ingredient in the reform.

- In the first stage, the pressure of the World Bank and US trade negotiators forced consideration of the first steps toward trade liberalization. In 1990, on the other hand, the shift in the position of the World Bank, and its reluctance to support the trade liberalization scheme developed by the government with loan commitments that would facilitate trade liberalization, almost killed the program.

- The radicalization of trade liberalization occurred when substantial current account surpluses threatened a revaluation in the absence of trade liberalization.

- In all cases, except in 1989, the agencies in charge of industrial policy and trade opposed liberalization, and the reforms were pushed by the Ministry of Finance and the Planning Department, which are responsible for macroeconomic policies.

- The deep commitment to economic liberalization of a president who was also an economist was crucial for the implementation of the reforms.

- Technocratic ministers with no future political ambitions were crucial in the process of economic liberalization and the fiscal reforms it entailed.

## Foreign Exchange Regime

- The effectiveness of the foreign-exchange control regime put in place in 1967 had decreased significantly. A great number of Colombians had illegal foreign exchange accounts, and many influential people and entrepreneurs found exchange controls costly and dangerous. A constituency against them had built up.

- Many economists in middle levels of the government and the central bank were doubtful about the usefulness of the controls.

- A shift in the discussion from the Monetary Board to Congress weakened the influence of the central bank's defenders of the policy. In Congress, the interventionist wing of the Liberal Party had been seriously weakened between 1967 and 1990.

## Labor Reform

- There was growing evidence that the job security legislation was in fact decreasing job security.

- In the generalized crisis and violence of 1989–90, the labor unions could not frighten the government with the threat of a general strike, and the violence these usually generate. The major reforms being discussed in the country as the Constituent Assembly was being organized put labor opposition to the labor reform at the bottom of the agenda of the government and of the society.

- At the Constituent Assembly, labor representatives attempted a counterreform but were defeated.

## Tax Reform

- The tax reform was difficult to pass in 1992, but the Congress once again showed its independence from private-sector pressure groups.

- The fact that tax reform must be an initiative of the government and that in order to pass it the president has to commit himself totally to its defence identifies tax reform with the executive. The political cost of increasing taxes costs the executive much more popularity than it does individual congressmen. A deep commitment and identification of the executive with the reform therefore makes it possible in Congress.

- As has been mentioned, congressmen fear inflation, since it makes the traditional parties unpopular and favors new movements not identified with economic management. At the same time, congressmen favor public expenditures. This makes the desire for low fiscal deficits translate into support for tax increases.

- Public expenditure not financed by taxes (money creation) strengthens the political factions that control the executive and decreases the bargaining power of congressmen. This also makes for fiscal orthodoxy on the part of Congress.

- Technocratic ministers of finance with no future political ambitions have been responsible for all the major revenue-enhancing tax reforms of the last two decades.

# References

Departamento Nacional de Planeación. 1990. "Programa de Modernización de la Economía Colombiana." *Revista de Planeación y Desarrollo* 12, nos. 1 and 2 (Enero-Junio).

Edwards, Sebastian. 1992. "Trade Policy, Exchange Rates and Growth." Paper presented at Stabilization, Economic Reform and Growth Conference. Sponsored by National Bureau of Economic Research and Inter-American Development Bank, Washington, D.C. (17 December).

Lora, Eduardo, ed. 1991a. *Apertura y Modernización: Las reformas de los noventa.* Bogotá: Tercer Mundo-Fedesarrollo.

Lora y Catalina Crane, Eduardo. 1991b. "La Apertura y la Recuperación del Crecimiento Económico." In E. Lora, ed., *Apertura y Crecimiento: El reto de los noventa.* Bogotá: Tercer Mundo—Fedesarrollo.

Mercedes de Martínez, Maria. 1991. *Memoria al Congreso Nacional: 1989-90.* Bogotá: Banco de la República.

Urrutia, Miguel. 1982. "Una Política nueva para combatir el contrabando." *Coyuntura Económica* 12, no. 1 (Mayo).

Urrutia, Miguel. 1989. "The Politics of Fiscal Policy in Colombia." In M. Urrutia, S. Ichimura, and S. Yukawa, eds., *The Political Economy of Fiscal Policy.* Tokyo: The United Nations University.

# Comment

## COLIN BRADFORD

The papers on Mexico and Colombia discuss two very interesting cases, well-articulated by two people involved in the process. First I wish to discuss the framework within which these two cases come up. John Williamson has said that the objective of this volume is primarily to ask how one can strengthen the political muscle of those politicians (not technocrats or technopols) who are most driven by concern for the general good rather than a particular good, and that the technocratic agenda is one based on normative economics, which posits that the objective of economic policy is the promotion of the general good. So the volume, like the conference on which it is based, is to be focused on the politics of furthering the general good.

There seem to be lurking here four theories of the politics of economic reform. One is the new political economy, which is a kind of neoclassical economic theory of politics in which agents rationally pursue their self-interest within a political framework. This theory goes a long way to explaining rent seeking and what Williamson calls the favor-granting state.

There is also a pluralist theory of politics in which policy is driven by competition among interest groups. Competition in the political marketplace drives the agenda toward policies that promote the public interest, in analogy with competition in the economic marketplace, which leads to efficiency.

The third theory is Williamson's own, which one might call the technopol model. This theory seems to say that if there is a crisis; if there is a

*Colin Bradford is Head of Research Programme at the OECD Development Centre, Paris.*

window of opportunity (a honeymoon); if the opposition is fragmented; if the regime type is favorable (the nature of a favorable regime is a bit unclear); if there is a mandate (or an opportunity for surprise?); if there is a leader with vision; if there is a consensus among the team; if the reforms are radical and comprehensive; if there is public support; and if external influences are positive, then the conditions are ripe for an economic policy reform directed to the general rather than a particular good. In this model the state pursues what mainstream economists assume should be the objectives of government policy, and accordingly the state becomes an umpire rather than a favor-granting mechanism. This causes the state and the political actors to become detached from the political process and technopols to become detached players for the common and general good.

The fourth theory is Robert Bates's partisan theory, in which the motivation of politicians is to implement policies in the interest of certain sectors of society. This implies that market-oriented reforms are not apolitical. This theory of partisan delegation is consistent with Merilee Grindle's chapter in Meier (1991), which offers an alternative model of politics to the neoclassical approach that dominates the Meier volume. Her model rests much more on historical and contextual factors and focuses much more on dynamics and interactions within the state (such as relations between the executive branch and the Congress, within the legislature, between parties, or between agencies), between the state and society, and between elements within society such as interest groups and their constituents or the media. In other words, she focuses on the the dynamics of politics—its flux and flow—rather than on a set of static conditions in which interests are being maximized.

Meier concludes from that conference, in the final chapter of the volume, that the new political economy is limited because it rests too much on instrumental rationality rather than on procedural rationality. Given this limitation, he argues for the need to:

> seek a more eclectic approach that combines the old and new political economy. From the perspective of the older political economy we should give special attention to the influence of historical tradition, social structure, ideologies, and institutions. An explanation of the motivations of policymakers is then too mixed to be understood only by rational choice models of the new political economy. (Meier 1991, 307)

What I derive from this alternative approach of Bates and Grindle is a more inclusive focus that avoids isolating technopols from the political process, and instead embeds them as political actors in the political process with interests like those of everyone else, including the desire to survive. Jeffrey Sachs has given us (in chapter 11) some insight into how intense the political struggle in reforming countries is. However much the general welfare may be advanced by a particular set of reforms, there is still going to be a deep-seated power struggle, in which the reformers are involved as a part of the flux and flow of the historical process.

All three countries examined in this chapter are ones in which democratic politics were subject to various forms of constraint, regulation, or control. There has been a prearranged sharing of power between the two principal parties in Colombia during much of the recent past, there exists a modulated form of democratic politics in Mexico through the dominance of the PRI, and of course there was a severe interruption of the democratic process in Chile under Pinochet, which has resulted in a more constrained political process in Chile even in the post-Pinochet period. In each case there have thus been structural limits placed on open political competition, which I suggest lie at the heart of understanding the path of policy reform in the three countries.

Miguel Urrutia's paper on Colombia describes a deliberate effort on the part of government reformers to build a reform constituency around the export sector. That was crucial for generating support for the reforms, and in particular for establishing the political linkage (which is perfectly logical from our perspective as economists) between tax reform, trade reform, labor market reform, and exchange rate reform. What I found missing from the paper was some explanation of the institutional context in which the reforms occurred and how the legislature was involved. Urrutia's remark about the media and the limited ability of the government to communicate with the public at large was quite revealing. Incidentally, drug dealers are also exporters. To what extent were their interests involved?

José Córdoba's paper on Mexico depicts the current Mexican president as an arbitrator, or indeed an umpire, and one who happens to be endowed with considerable powers of persuasion and brokering. But this mediating role occurs within the context of what can only be described as a constrained political setting, in which labor unions and the corporate sector are very much included within the overall process. The comment that President Salinas is an economist and therefore needs to spend less time on economics and can spend more time on politics was interesting. I would have liked to have heard more, however, about how political coalitions were formed in Mexico, and about how the interactions and the dynamics within the political process and institutional structure worked to further the reforms.

The paper by José Piñera on Chile contains some statements that reveal once again the view of the technopol as someone isolated from politics. He says, ''It is certainly not the case that the Chilean reforms succeeded because they were undertaken under a military government,'' and notes that there have been a lot of military governments that never undertook any reforms. But that does not prove that in Chilean circumstances the presence of a military government was not absolutely crucial. He claims instead that "what was different about the Chilean case, and this is one of the several factors that make it a model for developing countries in similar circumstances, was the team approach to policymaking." I think what was different about the Chilean case was the fact that the political process had been brutally massacred, and political competition had been wiped out. What was crucial was not so much agreement within the team as the fact that the team had no opposition or criticism to contend with. The flux and flow of competition and the dynamics that most reformers have to deal with in a normal political process were largely absent in Chile.

Everyone knows that every good conference leads to another conference. The papers for that next conference, of political scientists, should look at the broader political processes within which these reforms are embedded and include more insight into the dynamics of the political process.

## Reference

Meier, Gerald M., ed. 1991. *Politics and Policy Making in Developing Countries: Perspectives on the New Political Economy.* San Francisco: ICS Press.

# Comment

RICHARD E. FEINBERG

The rich and stimulating papers by José Córdoba and Miguel Urrutia underscore the importance of the economic team, of having a sizable group of like-minded economists and social scientists designing and implementing policy reforms. In all three countries discussed in this chapter—Mexico, Colombia, and Chile—the economic teams have demonstrated the coherence and consistency bred of years of working together in think tanks and bureaucracies. In some cases the individuals also studied together. Out of these shared experiences came common perceptions and the *esprit de corps*, the trust, that make for effective teamwork.

Not only are these three cliques cordial and coherent, they are also of superior quality. The Mexican and Chilean economic teams of recent years stack up very well against their counterparts in the industrial countries; they are world-class. Colombia has also had a tradition of very good economic policymakers.

The motives of policymakers are impossible to know with certainty. We cannot peer into their hearts and minds. Thus, the debate over motives cannot be brought to closure. Inevitably, the motives of technopols are mixed and may include the desire to aggrandize their agencies and perhaps their own careers, and in some cases to gain personal wealth. But I am personally convinced that many of the technopols in

*Richard E. Feinberg prepared this commentary when he was President of the Inter-American Dialogue, Washington. He has since become the Special Assistant to the President for National Security Affairs and Senior Director for Inter-American Affairs at the National Security Council. The views expressed here are solely his own and do not necessarily reflect the policy or views of the US government.*

the cases in question were strongly motivated as well by ideals. At issue are not merely occasional ideas, but rather an ideology, in the sense of a set of values and ideas that make up a full-blown world view. Some technopols are so passionate about their ideology, and their desire to remold their countries to conform to their ideas is so evident, that they exude a charismatic mystique. That mystique can be an important rallier of public support behind reform. The very absence of such a mystique around the troubled presidency of Carlos Andrés Pérez in Venezuela is evidence of the importance of image and commitment in forging public backing for reforms.

Where does this ideology originate? Many of the ideas of the technopols derive from global currents of thought, a source given inadequate attention in the implicitly closed, nation-state models in the public choice or "new political economy" literature. The international transmission of ideas is occurring through education at elite universities in the industrial countries, electronically transmitted media and entertainment, and travel, including that of the diaspora of Latin American intellectuals who fled political repression in the 1970s. The result is a cultural convergence of values and ideas in the United States and in Latin America. I speak of convergence rather than consensus so as not to overstate the case, in the hope that we will continue to be enriched by cultural diversities. But this adaptation of ideas in Latin America is producing a paradigmatic shift toward more liberal economics and pluralistic politics. As they make this shift, Latin American technopols very much want to integrate into the global system by joining the club of open democracies, both as individuals and as citizens of reformed nation-states. They use international agreements—IMF stand-bys and World Bank structural adjustment loans, bilateral investment treaties, free trade accords—not only to lock in economic standards but, more important, to render the liberal paradigm the only one imaginable in the minds of their fellow citizens.

The transmission belt linking these reforming countries with the international financial institutions (IFIs) operates in two directions, however. The IFIs have recently begun to speak of the need to address the social agenda in order to consolidate liberal reforms and to improve governance. Several years ago, leading Latin American technopols (especially in Mexico and Chile) had already started to devise programs to target the needy and to increase the efficiency and honesty of the state. Indeed, the IFIs are now coming to accept that economic development is an undertaking in political economy, and they owe this insight to the Latin American technopols.

To win their populations to their ideology, the technopols have been using the mass media, which can be democratizing insofar as it imparts information that allows citizens to make more-informed decisions, but which can also be used in a heavy-handed manner to manipulate malleable minds. In his article in this volume, José Piñera makes reference to a media campaign orchestrated during the Pinochet era to sell the idea of privatizing pensions: "Yet our media campaign worked more effectively than any referendum. Once we had presented our ideas in the most straightforward language possible, there was no question which side the people were on." Contrast that top-down attitude with this commentary on the good technopol by the current Chilean Minister of Finance, Alejandro Foxley: "Economists must not only know their economic models, but also understand politics, interests, conflicts, passions—the essence of collective life. For a brief period of time you could make changes by decree; but to let them persist, you have to build coalitions and bring people around. You have to be a politician."[1]

Mexican political culture lies somewhere between the paternalistic impulse of Piñera and the democratic passion of Foxley. Obviously Mexico is not a fully open, pluralistic political system, but the paper by José Córdoba does display the clashes of interest and the interplay of organized associations within and around the PRI government. At the same time, Córdoba gives us some candid insight into the constraining roles of the ministries of interior and labor in maintaining political stability.

Another interesting characteristic of the Salinas government is what we might term its fiscally sound populism. In his solidarity program, his weekly trips to the interior, and his extensive use of the mass media, Salinas is reaching over the heads of organized groups and leaders to the masses. But unlike traditional Latin American populism, Salinas' social programs are responsibly financed within the context of an impressive fiscal surplus.

The NAFTA is accelerating political change in Mexico. Indeed, the NAFTA may be more important for its democratizing impact than for its stimulus to trade and investment. The NAFTA is tightening the cultural ties between the United States and Mexico, and by sensitizing the Mexican government to American political opinion, it is erecting a protective umbrella over the mushrooming community of activist nongovernmental organizations working in Mexico on behalf of such causes as human rights, free elections, labor representation, and environmental protection. I am pleased to notice that Córdoba considers progress on human rights to be one of Salinas' three major reforms.

Córdoba and Piñera both provide evidence that technopols can act decisively in pursuit of their economic ideals. The rapidity with which both Mexico and Chile opened their economies to foreign imports was calculated to liquidate noncompetitive firms before they had time to organize against trade liberalization. In contrast, Colombian reformers, judging that they lacked the political strength to behave so ruthlessly,

---

1. Published interview in *The State of Latin American Finance* (Washington: The Washington Exchange and the Inter-American Dialogue, 1992), 22.

opted instead for gradual liberalization. These three anecdotal cases do not provide enough evidence to conclude that democratic governments are incapable of rapid trade liberalization but do suggest that governments constrained by democratic passions need a sophisticated strategy to overcome political resistance.

Even in the Chilean case, however, it would be a mistake to conclude (as Piñera implies) that radical reform was a simultaneous affair. During the Pinochet years, the Chilean economic teams may have possessed a comprehensive vision, but implementation of their program occurred gradually over a period of 15 years, and indeed the generals left privatization of the copper industry to their successors. Both Córdoba and Urrutia make it clear that reforms have been paced in their countries to take account of political realities.

Finally, technopols North and South are aspiring to integrate their countries into global markets and culture. The United States may be the source of some of this culture, but the self-conscious adaptation of the American economy to global change is coming to Washington only with the advent of the Clinton administration. In this sense, the United States has been lagging behind Latin America, and the Clinton administration signals the belated coming to power of the technopol culture in the United States.

# Discussion

*Luiz Carlos Bresser Pereira* argued that the turning point in the Mexican reforms had not been the Brady Plan, as often assumed in the United States, but the domestic stabilization program launched in December 1987. Did Córdoba agree that the incomes policy had been absolutely crucial?

In the paper on Colombia Miguel Urrutia had rejected some of the hypotheses of the background paper by Williamson. *Gustav Ranis* asked how he would then explain the occurrence of reform in Colombia. Could it be that, despite the absence of a major crisis, the desire to keep up with its reforming neighbors had encouraged Colombia to follow their lead? On Mexico, Ranis requested some clarification about the procedural rules of the Solidarity program, for example whether it was decentralized in the same way that education had been decentralized, and how it had been institutionalized. Ranis also commented on Córdoba's lack of any treatment of the influence of Mexico's accession to the GATT and of the impact of the maquiladora program on trade liberalization. Finally, he asked what reforms were next on the agenda.

*Steve Parker* wondered why the growth response to reforms had been so much less in Latin America than in Asia—growth remained well below 5 percent, while in Asia growth rates had been in the range of 5 to 10 percent.

*José De Gregorio* commented on the role of the state in the transformation process. When Augusto Pinochet came to power in Chile, and when reforms started in Colombia and Mexico, those countries had working governments and reasonably efficient public administrations. This had been an extremely important precondition for the success of the structural reforms, the absence of which would not be compensated by any number of Chicago boys. De Gregorio also noted that the mass media had been manipulated by the Pinochet regime in a way that would not be possible under a nonauthoritarian regime.

*Nora Lustig* referred to Córdoba's discussion of the importance of having the proper institutions to implement reforms. In Mexico, history had played a fundamental role by providing the institutions that allowed implementation of a program that, although controversial, never precipitated political discontent or resistance of the proportions witnessed in other Latin American countries. In countries without this "benefit of history," what were the requirements for the sequencing of reforms, and in particular should institutional reform precede liberalization or not?

*Francisco Torres* commented that to him Mexico seemed a much more successful case of reform than Portugal, but he added that foreign perceptions of one's success could be important in reinforcing the determination to persevere. He remarked that there seemed to have been much more intellectual agreement on the content of desirable reforms in Mexico and Chile than there had been in the Iberian countries.

Torres added that the North American Free Trade Agreement (NAFTA) did not call on the United States to play the same role as the European Community had played in providing financial aid to its reforming members, nor was it associated with a monetary union. In light of these differences he found it difficult to see the NAFTA playing the sort of role in nurturing Mexican democracy that Richard Feinberg had suggested. Torres also suggested that reforms were often easier at early stages of adjustment than later on; for instance, it was easier to reduce inflation from 50 percent to 10 percent than to bring it down from 10 percent to 2 percent, where the nominal anchor was fundamental. At that point it made no sense to have a crawling peg of 2 or 3 percent per year as in Mexico.

*Allan Mendelowitz* noted that a country like Mexico, in which a large share of the work force was employed in an inefficient agricultural sector, could either proceed with economic modernization of the rest of the economy and wait for economic opportunities there to siphon off the surplus labor from the rural sector, or target agricultural reform directly and thereby push labor out of the rural sector. Mexico had chosen the latter strategy, and he was curious to know why.

*Guillermo de la Dehesa* commented that Domingo Cavallo once lamented the absence in Argentina of a technocratic structure as strong as that in Mexico. He also noted that, as in Spain, the Mexican government had dramatically increased social expenditures in order to stabilize the social consensus needed to support reform. At the same time the budget balance had moved into surplus, and the ratio of public debt to GNP had fallen from 83 percent in 1986 to 37 percent in 1991. De la

Dehesa asked what the role of tax policy had been in bringing about this remarkable shift in fiscal position.

Finally, de la Dehesa challenged Jeffrey Sachs' assertion (see chapter 11) that social consensus was always and everywhere unnecessary to the success of reforms. He speculated that greater institutionalization of civil society implied a greater need for any reform program to be grounded in social consensus.

*Fred Bergsten* added several questions. First, Jeffrey Sachs had emphasized what he called the decisive role of foreign assistance in all the reform programs. Did Córdoba agree that the Brady Plan had really been so central in the Mexican case? Second, in the early days of the debt crisis, Brazilian policymakers had often told Bergsten that the free press in Brazil made it hard to take the same tough measures that were possible in Mexico, where the press was controlled. Did Mexican policymakers see their more quiescent press as an advantage? Third, the regular conventions of business leaders, labor, and the government appeared to have been a highly effective mechanism for discussing and promoting reform in Mexico. Germany had at times also had some success with such a corporatist bargaining structure, but it was still unclear to what extent such institutions were transferable to other systems and countries. Finally, Bergsten remarked that he had been stunned by Córdoba's claim that some reforms ''like fiscal policy'' could be introduced quickly because they did not need consultation; that was certainly not true in the United States!

In replying to the discussion, *Miguel Urrutia* attributed a significant role to the illegal drug trade in helping to shape reform in Colombia. The aim of eliminating illegal activity (of which the drug trade is only part) had helped spur constitutional reform. In economic terms the drug trade generated perhaps 10 percent of foreign exchange proceeds and might thereby have facilitated liberalization. Furthermore, as society came to place increasing weight on minimizing illegal activity, it seemed more attractive to eliminate the pervasive controls and regulations that had driven much of foreign trade (for example) into the black economy.

Ranis had asked what could explain the timing of reform in Colombia. Urrutia speculated that the presence of technocrats did have some importance in explaining this. Once convinced of what needed doing for the sake of welfare and efficiency, they then considered whether it was politically acceptable. They started putting their feet in the liberalization pond, and repeatedly found that the water was too cold. But once a constituency for reform had emerged, perhaps as the result of other policies, the water might turn out to be as warm as the Caribbean, as had happened in Colombia in 1989.

A strong incentive for liberalization had been the weakness of the Colombian bureaucracy, which meant that many of the controls were not really functioning. Hence Urrutia questioned the extension of De

Gregorio's argument that an efficient government and public administration were a key to successful reform beyond Chile (where the bureaucracy did work).

Whether national consensus was important, according to Urrutia, depended on the strength of the different actors. If there was no one to talk to in Poland, then it made no sense to seek consensus. In Colombia one could never reach a consensus with labor because the trade unions were both weak and communist-dominated, so it was pointless to invest a lot of effort in talking to them. It was better instead simply to walk through any legally mandated consultations (for example, on the minimum wage) and then promulgate a decree. On the other hand, import-substituting industry was a significant force in society, and accordingly it was necessary to seek a measure of understanding with it.

*José Córdoba* first addressed the question as to whether the social pact or the Brady Plan had been the key to Mexican reform. He thought that both had been important, but that the momentum of reform had been triggered by the introduction of the pact and the resulting sharp decline in inflation. The decision to resort to a pact had not been easy, despite the fiscal consolidation that was already in process, because many felt that a pact was a "heterodox" policy instrument and contradicted the objective of moving to a full-fledged market-oriented economy. Had it not been for the stock exchange crash and the subsequent downturn of expectations, the government might not have risked making the pact. Despite these initial reservations, however, that policy had succeeded in bringing inflation down, mainly because the fiscal adjustment had been done, and also because in Mexico there were social organizations (trade unions, business representatives, peasants' groups) with which one could meaningfully consult and which were able to deliver what they promised. The reduction in inflation had then opened the way for further reforms.

The role of the Brady Plan was very different. Its first impact had been psychological, removing the issue of debt from the policy agenda and the public consciousness and refocusing discussion on such factors as productivity, investment, and competitiveness. Second, it had released policymaking resources for more forward-looking purposes, such as deepening structural reforms.

How was the Solidarity program organized? Solidarity was a highly decentralized program that relied on the extensive involvement of all social groups at the grassroots level; these characteristics have been the source of the program's effectiveness. Well over 100,000 community committees had been created for specific projects all across Mexico. Funds were made available to all of them and to local authorities that satisfied the requirements for the decentralized procedures and transparent use of resources, as set out by the Solidarity program. Some opposition groups had charged that the program was politically biased, but their complaints were somewhat contradictory: it was claimed both that funds went only to districts controlled by the ruling PRI, and at the same time that the PRI was trying to buy votes by funnelling funds to opposition-controlled areas! Córdoba inferred that it was impossible to avoid the politicization of debate on such a high-profile program.

Had accession to the GATT and the maquiladora program helped build momentum for trade liberalization? The maquiladora program was economically helpful (it provided half a million jobs and close to $4 billion annually in foreign exchange), but it was largely detached from the domestic economy (less than 5 percent of the material inputs to the program came from Mexican industry) and had always been something of a side issue. Accession to the GATT, on the other hand, was a major event and had triggered much of the easing of trade barriers. Formal entry into the GATT in 1985 had involved introduction of a wide range of trade liberalization measures. Businesses had feared that membership in the GATT would impose unsustainable competitive pressure on domestic industry, causing large-scale bankruptcies. But the costs of adjustment in terms of output and employment had proved less than expected, which, Córdoba argued, provided a hopeful omen for the impact of the NAFTA.

As to what remained on the Mexican agenda, Córdoba stated that the process of structural reform had to be consolidated, especially in agriculture and education. Responding to Steve Parker's observations about the slower growth rates in Latin American reforming countries than in Asia, he commented that in the case of Mexico a wide range of structural reforms (privatization, economic and financial deregulation, trade liberalization) had been introduced relatively recently, so that their effects had not yet been fully felt.

Córdoba confirmed that there was still a sizable productivity gap between the average of the Mexican economy and the agricultural sector, which employed 25 percent of the active population but produced only 7 percent of GNP. This consideration had been crucial in the timing of rural reforms: these reforms had been introduced relatively late in the general reform process, so that other sectors of the economy would by then have the capacity to generate employment and to absorb the outflow from agriculture. But the effect of the reforms in pushing jobs out of agriculture should not be exaggerated. First, rural adjustment tends to be slow. Second, the government was pursuing a strategy of creating nonagricultural employment in rural areas, mainly in upstream services such as technical assistance and downstream industries such as food processing.

Does the NAFTA have implications for Mexican monetary policy? Will Mexico peg to the dollar? All Mexico was negotiating was a free trade area, not even a customs union or a common market, let alone coordination of monetary policies or common social policies. Foreign exchange policy was still guided by trying to balance the need to remain competitive against the aim of reducing inflation. Fiscal consolidation had lent credibility to the government's commitment to anti-inflationary policies so as to lessen the role of the exchange rate as the basic nominal anchor of price movements, but exchange rate policy still remained in a transitional phase with a wider band and, if necessary, a somewhat faster crawl than before.

# 6

## LATIN AMERICA II

# Brazil

## LUIZ CARLOS BRESSER PEREIRA

Economic reforms will succeed or not depending on their efficiency and on the political support they elicit. In recent years, the second factor has been emphasized by economists, political scientists, and policymakers, but it should not be forgotten that many reforms fail simply because they impose unnecessarily high transition costs and are thus politically infeasible. In certain cases, even inefficient reforms eventually succeed because the government—usually an authoritarian one—is able to go ahead with them despite their costs.[1] That was clearly the case in Chile, particularly in the 1970s. But under usual circumstances, inefficient reforms that are not part of a comprehensive and sensible economic program will fail, even if the government initially enjoys strong political support, because the transitional costs involved or its sheer economic inconsistency will cause it to lose that support.

In his background paper for this conference, Williamson proposes some hypotheses to explain how successful reformers have been able to mobilize and maintain political support for their reforms. His list can in fact be reduced to two main factors: political support for reforms depends on the perception of a crisis, and their success depends on the efficiency and quality of the economic program, which in turn requires a competent economic team and a statesman at the top. To these could be

*Luiz Carlos Bresser Pereira was the Finance Minister of Brazil in 1987. He is presently a Professor at the Getúlio Vargas Foundation and President of the South-North Institute, São Paulo.*

1. Inefficient reforms are those whose costs are disproportionate to their outcomes. Besides being inefficient, a reform may also be ineffective, that is, unable to achieve its objectives whatever the cost. Here I am speaking only of inefficient reforms.

added two other factors: the sensitiveness of the society in question to economic disarray and sheer fortune. The positive impact of the crisis will depend on the society's responsiveness to economic distortions. A society like Germany that is extremely sensitive to inflation will easily support anti-inflationary measures without waiting for a real crisis. On the other hand, some political events, such as the emergence of a statesman, and some economic ones, such as a sudden improvement in the terms of trade, are blessings that only chance can explain. In this extended context, Williamson's "honeymoon hypothesis" is a special case, and the presence of a fragmented opposition is only a positive factor if it results in a strong government. But we know that in democracies strong governments—that is, legitimate governments, which can count on support from the society at large—are usually accompanied by strong opposition parties.

I have been working with a model for explaining the success of economic reforms that is close to Williamson's. The basic idea of the model is, first, to gauge the seriousness of the crisis and the sensitiveness of society to it, and second, to compare the costs of muddling through the crisis with the transitional costs of reforming, to determine the net transitional costs. It is quite a different matter to discuss successful reforms in normal times, when economic distortions are just emerging, than to discuss them in abnormal times, when the economy is approaching hyperinflation.

Political support for economic reforms depends on the society's perception of the need for reform and of the net costs of transition. Reforms are not always perceived as necessary. When the inflation rate is still at a modest level, certain societies, such as the Brazilian, that are not sensitive to inflation, are content to live with it. Other reforms, such as trade liberalization, may take a long time to become viewed as necessary because they threaten certain special interests.

Once the need for reform has been perceived, it is necessary to consider the net transitional costs. These are calculated as the short-run difference between the costs of reform, in terms of higher taxes, unemployment, and restructuring of business enterprises, on the one hand, and the costs of postponing reforms or muddling through the crisis, on the other. Net transitional costs tend initially to be positive and high, since the costs of not reforming—of living with inflation, balance of payments problems, protectionism, the inefficient use of resources, and so on—are still small, while the costs of reform—of stabilizing, getting prices right, and orienting enterprises and consumers toward the market—are high. As reforms are delayed, however, the costs of muddling through the crisis increase and eventually become greater than the costs of adjusting. The "costs of not reforming" curve eventually crosses the transitional costs curve, making them negative. In the extreme case the distortions lead to an acute fiscal crisis and hyperinflation. Net transitional costs will be highly negative. When this happens, society ceases to doubt that the costs of muddling through are much greater than the transitional costs.[2]

Yet it may take a long time before a country gets to hyperinflation. Before it does, what can induce a society to support necessary economic reforms? Even when the net transitional costs are already negative, society may remain resistant to reforms. This collectively irrational behavior may have several explanations. First, society may not have perceived that the balance has shifted. The previous growth strategy may have been so successful in the short run that it is difficult to admit that it has now failed. Second, some powerful groups within the economy may still be gaining from the status quo even though the economy as a whole is losing.[3] If we were to draw the two sets of curves for each group, we would probably find that for some groups the curve representing the costs of muddling through the crisis crosses the transitional costs curve early on, while for others this intersection occurs much later, if ever.

Reforms may also be delayed for lack of institutions able to facilitate the negotiations between these groups on how to adjust the economy and guarantee their implementation. If labor unions do not really represent workers, if business associations do not really represent business owners, if political parties are weak and disorganized, or if the government is disrupted by a severe fiscal crisis, it will be much more difficult to implement reforms successfully.

Finally, even when the crisis is serious and society perceives the need for reforms, they may still be delayed for lack of political leadership or for lack of a competent team of economists capable of defining a comprehensive and efficient program for the transformation of the economy. At this difficult moment, fortunate societies will have political leaders with the vision and the courage to challenge vested interests, conservatism, and fear of change—which are usually disguised as common sense or conventional wisdom—and take the radical and risky economic reforms that the situation requires.[4] If these leaders are served by competent economic teams, capable of understanding the

---

2. For a more complete analysis of the efficiency of economic reforms and their net transitional costs, see Bresser Pereira (1993). For a more detailed analysis of the net transitional costs see the commentary of Jairo Abud (1992).

3. This last case was analyzed and formalized by Przeworski (1991) and by Alesina and Drazden (1991).

4. In Portugal, for example, President Mário Soares twice lost elections (in 1977 and 1984) because he implemented unpopular economic reforms; in the second episode he was voted out even though adjustment had already been achieved. Socialist President Felipe González of Spain broke with his party's populist views and was able to promote reforms without betraying his leftist beliefs. President Miguel de la Madrid of Mexico embarked on fiscal adjustment and structural market-oriented economic reforms in 1985, at a time when most of Latin America remained prisoner to old national-developmentalist views.

particular dynamics of their country's abnormal times and of defining comprehensive, bold, market-oriented reforms, the chances of success are greatly enhanced.

The last observation suggests that it is important to distinguish economic reforms in normal from those in abnormal times. States have grown too big all over the world since the 1930s; their economies have become distorted and have fallen into crisis and now are in need of reform. But just as the crisis of the state varies in intensity from case to case, so the depth of the required reforms also varies. The present crisis of the economy—which is essentially a crisis of the state—broke in the 1970s. Most of the developed countries and some developing ones, particularly in Asia, faced the crisis early on, when the net transitional costs were still positive and avoided a deeper crisis. Others, particularly in Latin America and Eastern Europe, refused to incur short-term transitional costs, postponed adjustment and got trapped in huge foreign debts and still greater domestic distortions. These countries faced a deep crisis of the state, defined by a fiscal crisis—the state had lost its creditworthiness—and a crisis of the mode of state intervention—the state-led development strategies that had been so successful had become distorted and inefficient. A major crisis defines abnormal times. If normal times allow conventional economic policies to succeed, abnormal times will require heroic and sweeping ones. The objective is the same: to stabilize, to get prices right, and to implement market-oriented reforms. But the strategies will be different.

I will discuss here the economic reforms I tried to implement in Brazil in 1987. I was finance minister of Brazil for less than eight months, from 29 April to 20 December. Thus, I did not have much time to implement reforms. Yet if I were asked what was the basic reason why I did not succeed, I would not say it was lack of time, but rather faltering political support from the president and from Brazilian society. That lack of support turned into outright opposition on the part of some interest groups. It was this lack of support for the fiscal adjustment to which I and my team were committed that led me to resign in spite of the president's attempt to insist that I stay.

Five years later, after several more attempts to stabilize and reform the Brazilian economy, the country remains in deep crisis. This suggests that the forces opposing reform were and remain very powerful and that political support for reforms was faltering as the society continued to show a low sensitivity to inflation and economic disarray, and failed to perceive that the net transitional costs were turning negative. It is also an indication that Brazil lacked either the political leadership or a competent and stable economic team capable of formulating and implementing a comprehensive and efficient reform program. On several occasions Brazil failed to stabilize the economy for this last reason. The 1986 Cruzado Plan and most of the first phase of the administration of Fernando Collor de Mello (March 1990 to May 1992)[5] are examples of inefficient economic reforms undertaken when the political conditions were favorable for serious reform.

In the first section of this paper, I will describe the economic and ideological environment that prevailed when I took office. In the second I will present the "Bresser Plan," the heterodox part of the stabilization program implemented during my tenure, and in the third the "macroeconomic control plan," which was the orthodox part of the program, besides containing my first diagnosis of the fiscal crisis as the basic cause of the Brazilian crisis. In the fourth section, I will discuss how my administration tried to manage Brazil's foreign debt and how that problem related to macroeconomic adjustment. In the fifth section, I attempt to describe the planned second phase of the stabilization program, which was to include a new heterodox shock, preconditioned upon the conclusion of the foreign debt negotiations, a redefinition of Brazil's external commitments and their fiscal aspects, and a strong fiscal adjustment, including expenditure reduction and tax reform. In the concluding section, I will evaluate the reasons for my decision to resign and thus abort this second phase of the stabilization program; in this section I will use as reference the reasoning I have briefly developed in this introduction.

## A Populist Environment

I took office as finance minister at a crucial moment in the economic and political history of Brazil. The Cruzado Plan, a well-conceived but poorly implemented heterodox stabilization plan, which came to be known as the last populist episode in Brazil (Sachs 1988), had just broken down. Inflation was exploding, sales and real wages were falling vertiginously, firms were going bankrupt, and international reserves were vanishing. Yet behind the acute short-term crisis was a much more serious one, which Brazilian society eventually started to acknowledge by 1987.

This deeper crisis was both political and economic. The political crisis was defined by the collapse of the 1977 democratic-populist pact, which marked the transition to democracy in Brazil from 1977 to 1987. This collapse was a direct consequence of the failure of the Cruzado Plan. The structural economic crisis was essentially a crisis of the state. To the popular acknowledgment of the severity of this crisis I, while finance

---

5. The political crisis that led to the impeachment of President Collor in December 1992 began in May of that year. Already by that time two opportunities had been lost: the first at the inauguration of the new administration and the second during the first four months of 1992, when the economic and political conditions for a decisive stabilization plan were present.

minister, gave a significant push. My warning to the nation that Brazil was facing not just a short-term crisis but a structural one was perhaps my most important contribution to the country during my short time as finance minister.

As long as Brazilian society remained unaware of the crisis, the democratic-populist coalition that commanded the transition to democracy tended to make the political environment adverse to economic reforms. The transition to democracy started in 1974, when the party that opposed military rule won the senatorial elections, and particularly in 1977, when President Ernesto Geisel's authoritarian "April package" aroused indignation throughout the society. Beginning in that year the business elites in Brazil, which had up to then supported the military regime, deserted the old alliance and entered into a new one with the democratic forces that had been defeated in 1964. This is the historical fact that explains the emergence of a democratization process in Brazil. But it also explains why, when the transition was complete and José Sarney took office as president in March 1985, a populist coalition found itself in power.

National-developmentalist views on how to run the economy, which had been successful from the 1930s to the 1950s, entered into a crisis in the 1960s. The 1964 military coup was in large part a consequence of this crisis. Once in power, however, and particularly in the 1970s, the military regime was able to postpone adjustment and artificially resume populist policies, based on foreign finance. Only in 1981 did the authoritarian government embark on an adjustment program, and then in a hesitant and incompetent way. From then until the end of 1984, the authoritarian regime tried to stabilize the economy with the adoption of orthodox policies—including an IMF program in 1983—but without success.

The new democratic government that took over in 1985 was based on a broad coalition between the entrepreneurs, who had definitively broken with the military, and the middle- and working-class pro-democracy groups, which had opposed authoritarianism from the beginning. The democratic-populist coalition's critique of the military regime included opposition to the "orthodox economic policies" that characterized the 1981–84 period. All evil was attributed to the IMF's orthodox policies and to technocratic rule. The implicit idea was to return to the good old days of the 1950s—to accelerate development together with some degree of income redistribution and moderate inflation, as had prevailed in the Vargas-Kubitschek years (1930–59). In other words, the climate was ripe for a new populist experience, with the difference that the country now faced a fiscal crisis. Moderate populism, of which the national-developmentalism of those years was a form, may work well when the initial fiscal situation of the country is sound and when there is a sector of the economy from which income can be transferred without major distortions.[6] But neither condition prevailed in 1985. The inevitable result was "populism with empty hands" (Faucher 1991). If populism in general is not workable in the long run, populism without some fat to burn is not viable even in the short run.

The first two years of the "New Republic," ending with the Cruzado Plan, were populist years. Populism had returned in full force, using democracy as a disguise. The right wing, which had been basically developmentalist and populist during most of the military regime, converted to economic austerity in the early 1980s, when the pressure from the international banks became unbearable. Given its basic commitment to free-market ideology, it was relatively easy for those on the right to switch to a rhetoric of fiscal discipline and support for structural reforms aimed at reducing the size of the state. They remained, however, tied to protectionism and to a web of subsidies that favored certain industries and regions. For those on the left and the center-left, such as myself and my team, this change was more difficult, because it also had an ideological aspect. My party, the PMDB (Partido do Movimento Democrático Brasileiro), was the core of the democratic opposition and was strongly populist.

My own change to nonpopulist views—which did not extend to embracing an orthodox economic approach—had taken place in the early 1980s, while I was studying and teaching inflation and stabilization theory and fiscal adjustment theory at the Getúlio Vargas Foundation. Drawing on the neostructuralist theory of inertial inflation, to whose development I and my associate Yoshiaki Nakano had contributed,[7] I remained strongly critical of the gradualist and conventional strategies advocated by the IMF to fight the type of inflation prevailing in Brazil, which was driven by a high level of indexation throughout the economy. I also remained critical of the way the creditor countries and the multilateral financial institutions were managing the debt crisis for the benefit of the creditor banks. But it was clear to me that fiscal discipline and market-oriented reforms aimed at increasing the market's role in coordinating the economy and reducing the role of the state were essential to any rational economic policy in Brazil. This conviction would cost me a great deal when I was later nominated finance minister.

---

6. During this period, agricultural export goods, particularly coffee, benefited from high international prices. That made it possible to transfer income from the old primary-exports oligarchy to the new industrialists and the urban workers. This was the basis of the "populist pact." When prices, particularly coffee prices, fell in the last part of the 1950s, the populist pact became unworkable .

7. At that time we published together a collection of essays on inertial inflation, titled *Inflação e Recessão*. Inertial inflation (i.e., high inflation autonomous from demand) is a type of inflation that lies between moderate inflation and hyperinflation. It is defined by its level and its highly indexed character (the indexation may be formal or informal). It is also possible to speak of an "inertial component" in all three types of inflation.

When my predecessor and friend Dilson Funaro fell in disgrace after the failure of the Cruzado Plan and the cold reception abroad and internally to the foreign debt moratorium of February 1987, President Sarney had to choose another finance minister. Besides being a well-known economist in the government party, I had experience as chairman of the State Bank of São Paulo and as chief of staff of Governor of São Paulo André Franco Montoro. The condition PMDB had imposed on the president was that the new minister should come from within the party. Sarney did not know me. I was not a person of his confidence. But after a troubled process, I was finally invited to head the finance ministry.

The crisis that followed in the wake of the Cruzado Plan was serious and acute. A lot of people were therefore surprised that I accepted the job. In the days following the announcement, two friends—Celso Furtado, then culture minister, and Olavo Setubal, a banker and former foreign minister—told me separately that Brazil had not faced such a grave crisis since the 1930s at least. Yet I was prepared for the job and knew I would be able to assemble a good economic team. What I did not foresee was the resistance that I would face once in the job, from the left and the right, from the populists and the orthodoxists, and from the clientists (or ''physiologists'' as we call them in Brazil), the corporatists, and the rent seekers.

## A Heterodox Program

On the morning of 29 April, as I was preparing my acceptance speech, I received the visit of the departing country division chief for Brazil at the World Bank, Roberto Gonzalez Cofiño. This was my first interview as finance minister. I was not known in Washington. Thus, he was agreeably surprised when I told him that Brazil needed an urgent fiscal adjustment and the elimination of all subsidies so as to permit the recovery of the state's savings capacity, positive internal real interest rates, a new stabilization program combining orthodox and heterodox policies, the regularization of the foreign debt through a realistic agreement with the commercial banks, and an export-led development strategy. These goals, plus trade liberalization and privatization, which I included in my program a little later, guided my actions in the finance ministry.[8] These ideas were the source of continual conflict with my party, the political staff of the president, and the Brazilian business community, to whom I made it clear that fiscal adjustment involved not only reducing state expenditures but increasing taxes as well. My decision to leave the government seven months later derived from the lack of political support for a tax reform that increased taxes and made them more progressive

---

8. Privatization was not my direct concern, since it was not the province of the finance ministry, but I strongly supported it.

and for a program of public expenditure reduction that involved the elimination of several departments and sections of the state apparatus.

When I assumed the ministry, it was clear to me that the transfer of real resources due to the debt crisis was a major cause of Brazil's high rates of inflation. The debt crisis also made net foreign saving negative and, through the heavy burden of interest payments, reduced public saving. The consequence was a dramatic reduction in the rate of growth of the Brazilian economy in the 1980s. A solution had to be found to this central question. It was also clear that Brazil could not prolong its moratorium on debt service indefinitely, and that an agreement with the commercial banks and with the Fund was urgent. But I wanted a debt agreement that, while implying internal sacrifices, proved to be at least consistent with price stability and the resumption of growth. The scheme offered by then–US Secretary of the Treasury James A. Baker III (the so-called Baker Plan), with its menu approach and the pledge of additional financing (which never materialized), seemed to me insufficient, but at that moment I did not see any alternative. Schemes of debt reduction or debt relief were not on the Brazilian agenda at that time simply because no one imagined Brazil's creditors would accept them.

In the next three months I would learn a lot about the debt crisis. As a consequence I was eventually able to propose the securitization of the debt (with the creation of a debt facility to manage it) and a relative delinkage between the IMF and the commercial banks in the debt negotiations. These two proposals initially were branded as a "nonstarter" by Secretary Baker but later became the cornerstones of the plan proposed by Baker's successor Nicholas F. Brady: the Brady Plan.[9]

My main concern in office was macroeconomic stabilization. I needed to put together a program immediately: a short-run stabilization plan, to stop the inflation that was exploding in the wake of the Cruzado Plan's failure,[10] and a medium-run stabilization plan, based on a sound assessment of the Brazilian crisis and laying out the basic policies that would orient my future actions. At the same time, it was essential to introduce institutional reforms in the state apparatus in order to make fiscal and monetary policy more effective.

The short-run stabilization program, which came to be called the Bresser Plan, consisted of an emergency price freeze coupled with institutional reforms and some fiscal adjustment measures.[11] The objective was to reduce temporarily inflation and to regain a minimum degree of

---

9. A history of the Brazilian debt negotiations was published in the work of mine cited above (Bresser Pereira 1992), an English version of which will be published as part of The World Bank History Project, sponsored by the Brookings Institution.

10. Inflation rose from around 2 percent in the month of November 1986 to 26 percent in June 1987.

11. For a comparison of the Bresser Plan with the Cruzado Plan see Bresser Pereira (1988).

control over the economy, so as to permit, in the second phase, a definitive stabilization program. This heterodox shock was consistent with my neostructuralist views on inertial inflation. As it was an emergency policy, the freeze was intended to be very short. We did not deindex the economy, nor did we undertake a monetary reform or attempt to use the exchange rate as a nominal anchor. The objective of these measures was not really to stabilize the economy, but rather to stop the explosion of the inflationary process. My forecast was that within six months inflation would still be around 10 percent a month because of the insufficient fiscal adjustment and the imbalance in relative prices at the time of the freeze. Thus, a second and definitive plan would be required some months later.[12]

Inertial inflation is an asynchronous process of phased price increases through which firms and workers try to protect themselves from prevailing inflation by indexing their prices. In this process, which lacks a basic coordinating mechanism, relative prices are constantly shifting between balance and imbalance. Conventional monetary and fiscal policy, although a necessary condition for the success of the stabilization program, are ineffective by themselves to control this type of inflation. The only way to put an end to it is to combine orthodox fiscal and monetary policies with a heterodox direct intervention on prices so as to establish a mechanism for coordinating expectations (Lara Resende 1991). As inflation accelerates and price changes become more frequent, there is less asynchrony and thus a tendency for relative prices to stay close to balance. When the economy reaches a state of hyperinflation, price decisions become practically synchronous, and it is enough to impose and sustain a nominal anchor, usually the exchange rate. This, coupled with a stern fiscal policy and a tight monetary policy will stop the inflation. But until inflation reaches this level—that is, as long as inflation is merely inertial—only a price freeze, as was adopted in Israel in 1985 and Mexico in 1987, will work. Even a price freeze, however, will not be successful if relative prices are extremely unbalanced, or if prices charged by state-owned enterprises and/or the exchange rate have been artificially kept behind inflation. An abrupt price correction at the moment of the freeze (a *tarifação* and a maxi-devaluation) will not be a solution because economic agents will feel injured and will try to recover their losses (or supposed losses) at the first opportunity once prices are again free. If inertial inflation is a continuous process of balancing and unbalancing relative prices, a reasonable price equilibrium (it can never be perfect) at the moment of the freeze is essential.

---

12. Obviously I did not transmit this prediction to the press. Instead I shared it only with the two economists who directly collaborated with me in the definition of the plan, Yoshiaki Nakano and Francisco Lopes.

On the other hand, to impose a heterodox shock without adopting strong fiscal measures is useless. In June 1987, relative prices were very unbalanced, and I had neither the time nor the authority to adopt a full-fledged fiscal adjustment. Thus, my plan called for two short price freezes. The first, of an emergency character, was implemented immediately, and the second was to follow six or seven months later, after public prices and the exchange rate had been corrected and a fiscal adjustment program had been enforced. The first freeze would be provisional, the second definitive.

The Bresser Plan went into effect in June and was successful in normalizing the economy: in achieving a minimum of macroeconomic balance, in halting the precipitous decline of real wages coupled with the skyrocketing rate of inflation, in coping with the record number of bankruptcies of small and medium-sized enterprises that had borrowed and invested during the euphoria following the initial success of the Cruzado Plan, in stabilizing the interest rate, and in recovering a minimum level of government control over the economy. The fiscal and institutional measures that were introduced along with the plan made it possible to recover some control over the budget deficit, which had gone out of control during the Cruzado Plan and in the first months of 1987.[13] But, as expected, the plan was not able to solve the fiscal crisis or to neutralize completely the inertial component of inflation. The rate of inflation, after falling from 26 percent per month in June to around 3 percent in August, increased in the next several months at a slightly faster rate than expected. In December it reached 14 percent instead of the expected 10 percent.[14] The resurgence of inflation even as aggregate demand remained shaky was essentially due to economic agents attempting to reestablish relative price balance as soon as prices were liberated. It also indicated the state's lack of creditworthiness—the essential characteristic of all real fiscal crises—which expressed itself in the overnight maturity of treasury bills and the lack of confidence in the currency.

---

13. The first projection of the operational public deficit for 1987 was 7.2 percent. This projection was almost exclusively based on already realized or definitively committed expenditures. We officially planned to reduce it to 3.5 percent, but we knew that this would be practically impossible. The final figure for 1987—the result of our strict control over new expenditures, which created a lot of dissatisfaction, particularly among the other ministers—was 5.2 percent.

14. The 6 percent "inflationary residuum" after the freeze showed that relative prices had been highly unbalanced at the moment the stabilization plan was implemented. I knew that, besides an effective fiscal adjustment, the other condition for a successful heterodox program was to have relative prices reasonably balanced at the time of the imposition of the freeze. That is why I expected a 10 percent rate of inflation in December.

## An Orthodox Program

The Bresser Plan was the heterodox part of the stabilization program. The medium-run stabilization plan—the macroeconomic control plan— was the orthodox part. It was prepared by my staff between May and early July. The plan, which drew on a macroeconomic model of the Brazilian economy, sought to define the parameters for the negotiation of the foreign debt, establishing Brazil's capacity to pay. My guidelines to the excellent staff of economists[15] who drew up the plan were quite clear and had been advanced in a paper that I had presented to a seminar at Cambridge University on 5 April, 24 days before taking office (Bresser Pereira 1987). The diagnosis should emphasize the fiscal crisis of the state: that the budget deficit was high; that public saving, which had been highly positive in the 1970s, was turning negative, forcing public investments to be financed through the budget deficit; that the public foreign debt was very high, demanding extensive financing; and that the internal public debt was increasing at a dangerous rate.

I wanted the macroeconomic control plan to look as much as possible like a letter of intent to the IMF. These letters, usually drafted by the staff of the Fund and signed by the local authorities, define certain strategic targets (the nominal and the operational budget deficit, domestic net credit growth, variations in the basic monetary aggregates, etc.). I planned to sign an actual letter of intent with the IMF, but first I had to prepare Brazilian society for the idea because at the outset actually signing an agreement with the Fund was out of the question politically. The previous conflict with the Fund, due to its one-sided position on the debt crisis and the failure of the IMF–sponsored stabilization program of 1983, was aggravated by the populist views that dominated Brazil after the transition to democracy was completed in 1985. But I knew that a stabilization plan could not diverge substantially from the basic recommendation of the Fund in the fiscal arena. The only possible divergence, which I believed would be a minor and merely formal one, would be on the need for a heterodox shock. As a prudent international bureaucracy, the IMF does not propose shocks, but it accepts them quite easily. I remember very well my first meeting with Thomas Reichmann, the IMF's chief economist for Brazil, in May 1987. I had already decided to impose a price freeze, but I did not tell Reichmann that; nevertheless, in our conversation he came close to proposing a move in that direction.[16]

---

15. Among others, the macroeconomic control plan benefited from the participation of Yoshiaki Nakano (head), Fernando Maida Dall'Acqua (coordinator), Adroaldo Moura da Silva and Enio Kadota (developers of the macroeconomic simulation model), Gustavo Maia Gomes, João do Carmo, and Sílvio Rodrigues Alves.

16. Later Reichmann told Yoshiaki Nakano that he was convinced that a price freeze was necessary at that moment.

I needed a program that would orient my later actions and those of my team, and that could be understood by both Washington and New York—by the multilateral institutions and the American government, and by the commercial banks, since I planned to visit both groups as soon as the plan was announced. On this same trip I would start the negotiations on the foreign debt. Thus, I also needed a plan that would define Brazil's ability to pay. For that purpose, my staff, using the macroeconomic model already mentioned, was given two basic financial parameters: Brazil would receive finance for 60 percent of the interest coming due on its commercial bank debt, while paying the banks the remaining 40 percent;[17] on debt to the multilateral institutions and the Paris Club Brazil would maintain an even cash flow: interest plus amortization would equal new disbursements. For the multilateral and official loans the even-cash-flow assumption seemed fair, given the interest of the creditor governments in solving the crisis.

I also proposed a growth parameter: future real GDP growth would be assumed to be 5 percent per year. The model had its own additional parameters, including a saving function (including public saving), a function for the tax burden, a consumption function, an investment function, and parameters for the internal and the foreign debt, the level of international reserves, and so forth, which to a certain extent could also be considered as variables.

After running the model, my staff came to the conclusion that the two debt parameters and the growth objective were feasible but implied the need for an increase in total saving. In order to increase public saving, a substantial increase in taxation and a reduction in state expenditures were necessary so as to reduce the operational public deficit to 3.5 percent of GDP in 1987, 2 percent in 1988, and zero in 1989. In this way public saving, which had been sharply reduced in the early 1980s, would be restored. The alternative would be to try to increase private saving by reducing wages and consumption. Yet there was no assurance that reducing wages would increase private saving. On the other hand, by increasing public saving, which had fallen from higher levels in the past, rather than private saving, which had not, the burden on workers and consumers would be smaller. But they would have to carry some additional burden, since even a progressive tax reform would not leave the lower middle class untouched.

The model showed that a 5 percent growth of GDP would require an increase in public saving of 5 percent of GDP. I was not happy with this result: the target was too tight. The sharing of burdens between Brazil and its foreign creditors did not seem fair. The creditors were, after all,

---

17. Although the banks did not like to speak in terms of "refinancing of interest" but instead of "new money," they showed some disposition to finance between one-third and one-half of the interest coming due. I was asking for just a little more.

as guilty as we for the debt crisis, and the only thing they were offering to do was to refinance part of the debt. But, again, at that moment I was not considering any other alternatives. In order to recover foreign confidence and domestic business confidence, the essential thing was to suspend the moratorium and regularize Brazil's foreign payments. Thus, I decided to publish the plan with those constraints, to submit it to the president and the National Development Council—and to take it to the United States.

## The Foreign Debt

In mid-July 1987, two and a half months after taking office, I finally traveled to Washington with my macroeconomic control plan. My second appointment, after a courtesy visit to the Inter-American Development Bank, was with Senator Bill Bradley (D-NJ). On the way to his office, Marcílio Marques Moreira, the Brazilian ambassador in Washington, told me that both houses of Congress had already approved resolutions asking the administration to provide some form of "debt relief" to heavily indebted Third World countries. I was very surprised and asked Marcílio to repeat what he had just said, since I, like practically all Brazilians, had never heard the term. Marcílio repeated the words and informed me that this was already a familiar issue in the creditor countries. This was for me a revelation, and one that I immediately connected with the talks about securitization of the debt that I had had with some bankers and economists during the previous two months in Brazil. I became convinced that something should be done in this direction. The climate in the creditor countries, it seemed, was favorable to new ideas.

Once back in Brazil, I started to prepare my proposal, helped by Fernão Bracher, the chief Brazilian negotiator, by Yoshiaki Nakano, my closest fellow economist, and by many others. I also asked for technical help from two international investment banks—First Boston Inc. and S. G. Warburg—particularly on the securitization deal.[18]

Local resistance to the unconventional proposal I was preparing soon emerged. To begin with, I faced some difficulty in convincing my own staff. They liked the idea but thought it dangerous because it could elicit a strong negative reaction from Brazil's creditors. Indeed it did. I remember very well Edwin Yeo, the secret representative of Paul Volcker for Latin America, on his second visit, telling me that "after Funaro decided on the moratorium, Washington concluded that he could not remain the finance minister of Brazil." The internal debate ended when I said, somewhat dramatically, that I was in the finance ministry to face and solve these problems, even at the risk of losing my job. I was ready to compromise, but only on minor things, not on the essentials.

---

18. The two banks produced a joint memorandum regarding the "Partial Securitization of Bank Debt," dated 16 November 1987.

Much more serious was the resistance of the staff surrounding the president. A very able diplomat, Rubens Ricúpero, was Sarney's international adviser. He obtained the support of Ambassador Moreira and Jorge Murad, the conservative son-in-law of the president. Together they developed the argument that, domestically, Sarney already faced an economic and a political crisis and therefore should not risk an international crisis as well. Therefore Brazil should make a conventional proposal to the banks.[19] I argued that the risk was not as great as they thought, since there was an increasing conviction in the creditor countries that the Baker Plan had failed to solve the debt crisis. Besides, some risk is part of the game when the national interest is involved. After a difficult debate, part of which took place during Sarney's visit to Mexico in August, the president accepted my reasoning.[20]

The strongest resistance, however, would come from the commercial banks and the US Treasury. Toward the end of August I received a call from Secretary Baker. He had been informed that I was preparing a debt proposal and asked me to visit him. An invitation from the US secretary of the treasury to a Latin American finance minister is tantamount to an order. I said I would visit him on 8 September.

My visit to Baker was initially a disaster but eventually a breakthrough. The first part of the meeting was a private talk. Baker rejected the obligatory partial securitization of the debt that I had intended to include in my proposal. In exchange, he accepted the idea of voluntary securitization and delinkage of the IMF and the commercial banks in the debt negotiations. However, pressed by his staff, which during the formal meeting that followed the private one expressed its opposition, Baker issued one hour later an aggressive note to the press, saying that the Brazilian proposal was "a nonstarter" and ignoring the concession he had just made privately. Yet two weeks later, when the IMF–World Bank annual meeting began in Washington, the "nonstarter" turned into a "starter." Securitization was now the word of the day. Eighteen months later the Brady Plan would incorporate both Brazilian proposals: securitization and delinkage.

---

19. Brazil signed a conventional agreement with the commercial banks eight months after I left the ministry, in August 1988. It was a failure. One year later Brazil was again in arrears.

20. An interesting episode during this visit was my talk with Carlos Salinas de Gortari, then the planning minister of Mexico. My old friend Gustavo Petriciolli, then Mexico's finance minister, took me to see Salinas and Pedro Aspe Armella. My comments during the meeting concerned exclusively the advantages of a heterodox shock to control the Mexican inflation. Salinas, who was already being talked about as a future president, listened very attentively but made no comments. Four months later the Mexican inflation would end with the conclusion of a social pact and a heterodox shock, which complemented the fiscal adjustment and the structural reforms President de la Madrid had initiated.

In spite of the clear and quite reasonable proposal that Brazil finally made on 24 September, which accorded with what had been agreed with Baker, the negotiations with the commercial banks, permanently intermediated by the Treasury, advanced slowly. Soon Bracher and I realized that the 29 January deadline for the signature of the agreement—the so-called "term sheet," established with the banks when Brazil signed an interim agreement in October, would not be met. The commercial banks were confused, not knowing how to behave. They probably sensed that they were living through a transition period in the debt crisis.

## Adjustment as a Condition for the Second Phase

Brazil could not and would not allow itself to rest dependent on the banks' decision indefinitely. As already noted, inflation was accelerating. In November it was already more than 10 percent, above the figure that back in June we had projected for December. According to our team's initial plans, it was time to start preparing the second phase of the stabilization program, which would include a heterodox shock. But this could not be an emergency stabilization program, as the Bresser Plan had been.

The new plan, scheduled to be implemented in the first months of 1988, would have to be well-planned and obtain the assent of Brazilian society. First, relative prices should be well-balanced, so that on the inaugural day of the plan we would not have a maxi-devaluation or large increases in public prices (*tarifações*). According to the theory of inertial inflation, a shock coupled with a *tarifação* and a sharp devaluation of the local currency would be doomed to failure. Second, a fiscal adjustment should precede the plan. Heterodox policies are necessary when inflation is high and inertial but not yet at the level of hyperinflation.[21] However, their scope is necessarily limited. They are not intended to replace but rather to complement orthodox fiscal and monetary policies. Third, I had to have a precise assessment of what Brazil would be committing itself to regarding the foreign debt. This was important for projecting the balance of payments and for the fiscal adjustment plan. I knew that Brazil would be able to pay around one-third of the interest coming due and none of the amortization.

President Sarney was informed and agreed on the need for a new plan at the beginning of the year. I had been preparing this second phase of the stabilization program from the outset. Relative prices were basically bal-

---

21. In open hyperinflation the asynchrony of price increases ends. Thus, to stabilize under such circumstances it is enough to promote a credible fiscal adjustment and to use the exchange rate as a nominal anchor. To do that, the country must have sizable international reserves and the support of the international community.

anced. At the cost of accelerating inflation in the short run, in the last few months of 1987 I had consistently increased public prices at a rate faster than inflation in order to avoid the need of a *tarifação* on the day the new plan was launched. The currency was initially devalued and thereafter kept steady. Wages were still being indexed on a monthly basis. Thus, if the launch of the new freeze came in the middle of the month, wages would not need any special conversion formula but would be automatically consistent with other prices. As for the foreign debt, Sarney agreed that, if we did not come to an agreement with the banks by 29 January, Brazil would have to decide unilaterally how much it would pay and make plans and set budgets accordingly while continuing to negotiate. Sarney also agreed that a fiscal adjustment plan was necessary and urgent, but it was in this area that he eventually withdrew his support in December. My decision to resign would be a direct result.

Toward the end of November I made another trip to Mexico, this time to participate with Sarney at a meeting of eight Latin American presidents in Acapulco. The foreign debt was the major topic. I had little opportunity to talk with Mexico's finance minister at that time, Gustavo Petriciolli. He was deeply involved in negotiations with the unions that would lead, a few days later, to the heterodox stabilization plan, involving a price and wage freeze that, coupled with the fiscal adjustment and the structural reforms, marked the stabilization of Mexican inflation that has held to the present day. I did, however, have an important conversation with the other finance minister of the Latin American G-3, Juan Sourrouille of Argentina. We agreed that we would continue until the beginning of February 1988 to seek a reasonable agreement with the banks. Absent an agreement, we would decide in a coordinated way an Argentine moratorium and a unilateral Brazilian policy of paying about one-third of maturing interest obligations to the commercial banks. In this we were not creating a debtors' cartel—such an entity is not viable— but defining a minimum level of coordination of our policies.

The second phase of the stabilization program and the coordination of actions between Brazil and Argentina terminated with my resignation from the finance ministry 20 days later. Following my return from Washington at the end of September, I had defined as my absolute priority a fiscal adjustment plan involving a sizable reduction of expenditures and subsidies, and a tax reform that would increase the overall tax burden. Relying on the support of my team, I worked incessantly on this project for two months.[22] Meanwhile I kept President Sarney informed of the progress I and my team were making. But when the plan was com-

---

22. The tax reform project was headed by my director of revenue, Antônio Augusto Mesquita; the expenditure reduction, involving a mini-administrative reform, was headed by my vice minister, Mailson da Nóbrega, who I would later recommend to Sarney as my successor. Yoshiaki Nakano, Fernando Dall'Acqua, and Antônio Ximenes also made important contributions.

pleted, in the third week of December, and I presented it to the president, I did not win his support. He cited strong political forces as the reason for his decision. Thus, in spite of his insistence that I stay in my post, I decided to resign. Sarney said more than once that "next year" he would approve the expenditure and subsidy reductions and the tax reform, but that made little sense to me. Why next year, if it could be done this year?

I left the finance ministry without having been able to stabilize the economy. The overall situation was much better than when I took office. Inflation was around 14 percent a month but accelerating slowly. Real wages and consumption had been kept well below the Cruzado Plan highs and were stable. The wave of small-business bankruptcies had been stopped. Financial markets were calm. The exchange rate was realistic, and the balance of payments had been balanced. The moratorium on the foreign debt had not been suspended, but an interim agreement to resume payments existed. The premium on the dollar in the parallel market remained stable at around 25 percent over the commercial rate, without any need for central bank intervention in the gold market.[23] Confidence in public bonds had been partially restored. Brazilian society was beginning to listen to the stern warnings I had been making about the seriousness of the Brazilian crisis, and of its essentially fiscal character. The economy was fully indexed, but practically all private-sector prices were free. The economy was not growing, but a worsening of the recession had been avoided.

Several important institutional reforms had been implemented meanwhile, separating the treasury from the central bank, unifying the fiscal budget, establishing more strict and formal controls on disbursements by the treasury, creating a public servant bureaucratic career track for the treasury and the budget office, and reducing the power of the National Monetary Council to create credit (and thus money). These were preparatory measures for eventual independence of the central bank, which I had planned to achieve in the second stabilization program. Structural reforms had also been initiated. The agricultural credit system had been fully restructured: subsidies had been eliminated, and as a trade-off farmers got more realistic minimum prices. Studies paving the way for tariff reform—the essential condition for the elimination of all nontariff barriers—had been completed, preparing the way for trade liberalization.[24] A new industrial policy, under study at the ministry of

---

23. Given the tax on exchange rate transactions of 25 percent, this premium was actually around zero.

24. The need for trade liberalization was far from universally endorsed in Brazil in 1987. Nevertheless, during my administration the first objective steps in this direction were accomplished. José Tavares de Araújo, head of the Comissão de Política Aduaneira (Customs Policy Commission), accomplished a complete revision of the Brazilian customs

industry and commerce, would independently complement trade liberalization. Privatization was marching ahead slowly, but some progress had been made.

Yet this was not enough. The budget deficit was no longer increasing, but it remained high, and without the fiscal adjustment plan, the chances of reducing it were limited. Inflation was, as already noted, on a moderate but clear acceleration trend. Thus, when I decided not to go ahead with the second stabilization program and resigned, I was proud of the advances I and my team had made, but I also knew that, in the final analysis, I had failed to adjust and stabilize the Brazilian economy. I had succeeded in defining the real nature of the Brazilian crisis—the fiscal crisis of the state and the bankruptcy of the developmentalist strategy—and I had been able to tranquilize the economy and initiate the institutional and structural reforms that were required, but I had not been able to implement the fiscal adjustment that was the precondition for a definitive stabilization, and I had not implemented the second phase of my stabilization plan.

## Conclusion

In the introduction, I presented my views on the conditions for successful economic reforms. These in many ways coincide with or complement those in Williamson's introductory paper. First, many stabilization programs, or economic reform programs more broadly, fail because they are inefficient, because they do not take the peculiarities of the current economic situation into account, or because they do not have behind them a competent and cohesive economic team. In my judgment, which is admittedly not unbiased, none of these factors characterized the Brazilian reforms proposed in 1987. The stabilization plan explicitly took into consideration the inertial character of Brazilian inflation and the abnormal times Brazil was experiencing.

Second, economic reforms need political support. And political support depends on the seriousness of the crisis and the sensitivity of society to economic disarray. Lack of political support for my economic program was clearly the central problem. I did not get support from my president, nor from my party, nor from the broader society for the fiscal adjustment that was necessary. The crisis was already serious, although it had not reached the hyperinflation level, but it was not perceived as serious. And the sensitivity of Brazilian society to inflation is low.

---

system—an essential condition for the planned trade liberalization. Meanwhile, our negotiations with the World Bank toward a structural adjustment loan were well-advanced. Armeane Choksi and Demitrus Papageorgiou, both of whom have extensive experience on the subject, were directly involved in the negotiations with Yoshiaki Nakano and Tavares de Araújo.

I have stressed how populist views were particularly strong in Brazil in the first two years of the new democratic regime. The Cruzado Plan's failure weakened this vision of the economy, but it was still strong in 1987. President Sarney was not able to provide the support I was seeking for several reasons. First, his own views of economic policy are essentially (although not purely) populist. The failure of the Cruzado Plan was no accident but resulted from Sarney's refusal to modify the price freeze. Second, Sarney was deeply involved in getting support from the Congress to stay in the presidency for five years instead of four (the provision of the new constitution defining the president's term had not yet been decided). To obtain it, he needed to please the "Centrão"— the populist and conservative group in Congress that had been formed in the last quarter of 1987 to give him political support. Third, a conservative group within the president's staff, led by Jorge Murad, Mathias Machiline (a businessman friend of the president), and Antonio Carlos Magalhães (a powerful politician from Bahia), was unhappy with my domestic and foreign policies and pressed the president not to accept my fiscal adjustment plan. They knew that if Sarney did not accept the plan I would resign.

My party, the PMDB, was also unable to provide support because national-developmentalist views remained dominant within it. I did receive the support of some political leaders, but they were the exception rather than the rule.[25]

Finally, I did not win the support of Brazilian society. When the Bresser Plan was announced, the reaction against a supposed "wage squeeze" (arrocho salarial) was enormous throughout society. Resistance came not only from the unions but also from the print media, which mostly represent the middle class in Brazil. That group felt threatened by a possible further reduction of wages and salaries.[26]

Yet the real resistance to reform came from the business community. In December, when I proposed the tax reform, the nine most important business associations in São Paulo, whose presidents held regular informal meetings, issued a communiqué repudiating the tax increase I was proposing.[27] I had very good relations with Brazilian businesspeople,

25. On several occasions, the president of the PMDB, Ulysses Guimarães, and Fernando Henrique Cardoso, the party's leader in the Senate, had to intermediate between me and the party, which did not accept my views on the country's fiscal problems, on the need for a positive real interest rate, on the negotiation of the foreign debt, and on other matters.

26. The acceleration of inflation that marked the Cruzado Plan's failure caused an average real wage reduction of nearly 30 percent between November 1986 and June 1987. With the stabilization plan, real wages stabilized a little above a somewhat lower level than the 1985 average real wage (real wages had increased sharply during the Cruzado Plan).

27. The meetings of the Fórum Informal were attended by, among others, the presidents of the Federação das Indústrias do Estado de São Paulo, the Federação do Comércio do

who were feeling more secure with me as finance minister. When I resigned, the president of the most important Brazilian business association called it "a tragedy for the country." But these positive views did not prevent him and his associates from writing their antitax communiqué. Their populism and conservatism, respectively, prevented their acceptance of a tax increase and of some progressivity in that increase.

The net costs of adjusting the Brazilian economy were still positive at the time of the plan—or at least so most Brazilians perceived. Only two years later, when the first hyperinflation episode struck the Brazilian economy, this view was profoundly shaken. It was then realized that the crisis that I so strongly warned of in 1987 was indeed serious and that some sacrifice had to be shared among all. The incoming administration, headed by President Collor, would profit from this change of mood, but the inefficiency of the policies that were tried in the following two and a half years would waste that opportunity.

Given that the net transitional costs were still positive or were so perceived, and that the workers were not ready to accept wage reductions, nor the capitalists tax increases; and given the classical lassitude of Brazilian society toward inflation, the unawareness of the Brazilian élites of the severity of the economic crisis, and the continued strength of populist and national-developmentalist views in 1987, only a statesman in the presidency, endowed with vision and courage, could have confronted society, anticipated the costs of adjusting the economy, and proceeded with the necessary economic reforms. Statesmen, however, are a rare species, which societies are only fortunate enough to find leading them once in a while. That is probably why Berthold Brecht once said, "Sad are the nations that need a statesman." Sadder still, I would add, are the nations that need a statesman but don't have one, whose people are not yet ready to perform collectively the role that would be his.

# References

Alesina, A., and A. Drazden. 1991. "Why Are Stabilizations Delayed?" *American Economic Review* 81, no. 5 (December).

Abud, Jairo. 1992. "Interpretação Gráfica dos Custos de Programas de Ajustamento." *Revista de Economia Política* 11, no. 4 (October).

Bresser Pereira, Luiz Carlos. 1987. "Changing Patterns of Financing Investment in Brazil." *Bulletin of Latin American Research* 7, no. 2. Glasgow: University of Glasgow.

Bresser Pereira, Luiz Carlos. 1988. "Brazil's Inflation and the Cruzado Plan, 1985–1988." In Pamela S. Falk, ed., *Inflation: Are We Next? Hyperinflation and Solutions in Argentina, Brazil and Israel.* Boulder, CO: Lynne Rienner, 1990. (Originally presented at a seminar at Columbia University, March 1988, as "The Two Brazilian Price Freezes.")

---

Estado de São Paulo, Associação Comercial, the Federação Brasileira de Bancos, the Federação da Agricultura do Estado de São Paulo, and the Sociedade Rural Brasileira.

Bresser Pereira, Luiz Carlos. 1992. "Contra a Corrente: A Experiência no Ministério da Fazenda." *Revista Brasileira de Ciências Sociais* 19. (Translated into French as "Experiences d'un Gouvernement." *Problèmes d'Amérique Latine* 93, no. 3, 1989.)

Bresser Pereira, Luiz Carlos. 1993. "Economic Reforms and Economic Growth: Efficiency and Politics in Latin America." In Bresser Pereira, A. Przeworski, and J. Maraval, *Economic Reforms in New Democracies*. Cambridge: Cambridge University Press, 1993.

Bresser Pereira, L., and Y. Nakano. 1987. *The Theory of Inertial Inflation*. Boulder: Lynne Rienner.

Faucher, Philippe. 1991. "The Improbable Stabilization and Inconceivable Popular Market Capitalism: Argentina, Brazil, Mexico and Peru." Paper presented to the XVth Congress of the International Political Science Association, Buenos Aires (July).

Finance Ministry of Brazil. 1987. *Macroeconomic Control Plan*. Brasília: Finance Ministry of Brazil.

Lara Resende, André. 1991. "Para Evitar a Dolarização." *Exame* (26 June).

Przeworski, Adam. 1991. *Democracy and the Market*. Cambridge: Cambridge University Press.

Sachs, Jeffrey. 1988. "Social Conflict and Populist Policies in Latin America." Paper presented to a conference on "Markets, Institutions and Cooperation," Venice (October).

# Peru

RICHARD WEBB

In October 1968 Peru's President Fernando Belaúnde Terry was ousted and exiled by a military coup. The generals cited corruption and nationalist indignation over an oil contract, but their more convincing justification was economic mismanagement. After almost two decades of dynamic growth and price stability, a devaluation crisis in mid-1967 had brought the economy to a standstill, while inflation that year had reached a then-shocking 19 percent.

Over the next 11 years the military regime carried out deep social, institutional, and economic reforms, many of them applauded by the Washington consensus of the time. Indeed, much of the reform agenda, in particular the land reform, the educational reform, and the reinforcement of planning mechanisms, seemed to come straight from the books of the earlier Alliance for Progress and from standard World Bank prescriptions of the time. Despite initial difficulties with a US aid cutoff mandated by the Hickenlooper amendment, which extended to lending by the international financial institutions, the regime also received considerable external financial support in the form of major direct investments and large credits from commercial banks, development agencies such as the Inter-American Development Bank and the Agency for International Development, and suppliers, notwithstanding its nationalist rhetoric and large-scale expropriation of foreign-owned assets.

*Richard Webb is a non-resident Senior Fellow at the Brookings Institution in Washington, DC and is President of the Cuanto Institute in Lima, Peru. He was the Governor of the Central Reserve Bank of Peru, 1980–85.*

When it came to macroeconomic management, however, the military government was even less successful than Belaúnde. From 1975 to 1979 inflation broke all previous bounds, rising to annual levels of 60 and 70 percent, foreign exchange reserves evaporated, and both production and real incomes fell. An energetic and lucky stabilization program in 1978–79 (commodity prices soared and new oil finds came on stream) nevertheless arrived too late to save the regime; the price hikes and wage freezes, which to economists were commendable adjustment measures, to the average citizen were merely further evidence of mismanagement. By 1978 riots, a strike by the police, a general strike, and strongly adverse public opinion finally led the military to admit defeat: a constituent assembly was called, elections were scheduled, and a new constitution was approved by a freely elected Congress. In the spring 1980 presidential election, Belaúnde was returned to power for a five-year term with a comfortable majority in both houses of Congress.

The electorate was in fact split into four large groups: an opposition made up of a conglomerate of factionalized leftist parties, Acción Popular Revolucionaria del Peru (APRA)—a disciplined, left-leaning, populist party created in the 1920s on an industrial union membership—a majority coalition dominated by Belaúnde's own centrist Acción Popular party, and also including the more ideological, rightist Partido Popular Cristiano. This party structure held through Belaúnde's term, but it became increasingly unrepresentative of popular opinion. In the November 1983 municipal elections, for instance, Belaúnde's party dropped sharply in the national vote, with most of the gain going to the left-wing conglomerate and to APRA. Stresses and defections in the coalition majority also weakened and, for many purposes, eliminated Belaúnde's initial majority in the Senate. By 1984, public opinion polls were showing a collapse in support for Belaúnde, threatening an electoral disaster in the spring 1985 general election.

Notwithstanding his slide in popular support, the 1979 constitution provided Belaúnde with sweeping powers to enact emergency legislation in economic matters, with the ambiguous proviso that Congress be informed. As his legislative and popular support weakened, and as the debt crisis gave increasing legitimacy to the use of emergency powers, Belaúnde resorted more and more to this constitutional authority.

Belaúnde's initial stance on economic management leaned to caution and responsibility. He continued to dream of, and press his ministers and foreign lenders for, massive dam, road, housing, and other infrastructure projects, but the lessons of the fiscal mismanagement behind the 1968 coup and the 1978–79 collapse had not been lost on him. Moreover, he had spent most of his years in exile teaching at universities in the United States, including a long spell in Washington where several close associates worked in the multilateral organizations. It came as no surprise, then, that early in 1980, several months before his inauguration, Belaúnde chose Manuel Ulloa for the Ministry of Finance, reinforcing Ulloa's power by appointing him premier as well. A lawyer and sophisticated international financier with a grasp of economics, and part of Belaúnde's inner circle, Ulloa was respected across the political spectrum as a wunderkind who had carried out a far-reaching program of financial, fiscal, and administrative reforms during a brief spell as minister of finance in 1968. Those orthodox reforms had been sensibly preserved by the leftist military government of General Juan Velasco Alvarado, although Ulloa himself was forced to leave the country. Ulloa's appointment in 1980 was taken as a signal that, contrary to the adage, Belaúnde had indeed changed his stripes; although he continued to stress public investment and social welfare objectives in his speeches, his choice of finance minister was a strong indication that the regime would be committed to economic stability and reform.

Ulloa assembled what was seen as a model economic team, consisting mostly of political independents with top technocratic pedigrees, including IMF and World Bank experience. Working with Ulloa, the team had no difficulty in quickly agreeing on a program that combined stabilization with structural reforms, consisting mostly of trade and financial liberalization, but including deregulation of labor and land markets, privatization, and tighter administrative and financial controls over public enterprises. Drafting these plans was made easier by the fact that, for the most part, the agenda consisted of a continuation of the stabilization and reform efforts that had been under way since 1978, with considerable IMF and World Bank technical and financial support. The new program was thus blessed by strong agreement within the team, by continuity with their predecessors' program, and by advice and approval from Washington. Little-noticed at the time was the fact that the economic team was working in isolation under Ulloa, with no direct contact with the president, members of Congress, or private-sector leaders.

Overspending and monetary expansion had been the Achilles' heel of both previous governments. How then did Belaúnde and Ulloa define the central bank's role in the coming administration? In part, this had been predetermined by the 1979 constitutional congress. Under the new constitution, the central bank would enjoy an unusual degree of autonomy: its governor and the other six board members could only be removed from office by Senate impeachment for nonpolitical misbehavior. The loophole, however, was that the governor and board majority were to be presidential appointees. Perhaps the clearest signal of Ulloa's stabilization intentions, therefore, was his handling of these appointments. He began by inviting me to become the governor, knowing that I had no political loyalties, and that having served for six years in the 1960s as the central bank's chief economist I was likely to take a blinkered view of my obligations. He then gave me total freedom to choose the remaining board members. Concerned that an image of excessive political independence could backfire for the bank, I handed Ulloa a list that had a majority of independents but included his two vice ministers, arguing that their presence on the board would ease coordination. He returned the list and strongly advised me to go for total independence, meaning no government officials or persons with political loyalties on the board. In the end we compromised by including one vice minister. In defining the bank's role, Ulloa had thus proved himself more purist than the new governor.

The central bank episode provided another good signal: Belaúnde, closely attentive to appointments, chose not to intervene in the selection of board members. Although Ulloa was the only link between the team and political power, his close relationship with Belaúnde promised that it would be a strong link.

At the time of Belaúnde's inauguration, on 28 July 1980, the betting was very much in favor of an avoidance of the macroeconomic mismanagement that had torpedoed the two previous administrations. Furthermore, for those who put great store in the advantages of freer markets, there was reason to expect an increase in economic efficiency. Moreover, Peru was in the middle of a commodity price boom, reinforced by rapid expansion in the volumes of oil, mineral, and nontraditional exports. Finally, the successful adjustment efforts of the outgoing military regime and the quality and stated intentions of the new one produced enthusiastic offers of support from both official and commercial sources of foreign finance. In short, there were strong grounds to expect that Belaúnde's second term would be a period of successful economic management and reform.

Looking back, the period proved a terrible disappointment, all the greater given the high expectations that prevailed in 1980. The fiscal deficit rose, output fell, debt went into arrears, and reforms were only partial, with some backpedaling. Although a severe adjustment was in fact carried out, much of this was completed in the last months of the regime, and those who now classify economic experiences as either "reformist" or "nonreformist" do not hesitate to assign Belaúnde's second term to the latter category. From that perspective it makes sense to ask why Belaúnde failed to achieve reform, as defined broadly by the Washington consensus.

I will first provide an account of the policies carried out between 1980 and 1985 and will then offer some interpretations of that record, including a discussion of several factors suggested by John Williamson's introductory paper to explain successful reform. I will take several backward looks at the crisis and reform experience of the preceding military administration, especially between 1987 and 1990, since that experience was a major input into the decision making of the Belaúnde government. One distinction should be borne in mind, namely, that between inputs and results. The discussion of reform becomes confused when reform measures (an input) are equated with successful performance (an output). The Peruvian economy clearly suffered a disaster over the Belaúnde years: GDP per person fell by 15 percent, and inflation rose from 59 percent in 1980 to 163 percent in 1985. It is less clear how much of the explanation lies in a failure to reform.

The account of policy will be in two parts, because a break occurred midway through the quinquennium. From the inauguration through December 1982 the government by and large followed its inaugural script, even if its execution fell short of targets on several counts. That script was drafted in the context of a balance of payments boom that looked robust because it was driven by both commodity and nontraditional exports, and sustained as well by a reformist image that seemed to justify Peru's access at that time to foreign credit. The domestic economy, moreover, had already undergone major economic reforms and was showing signs of growth and slower inflation. On the political side, a major consideration behind the Ulloa program was the need to safeguard a newly recovered democracy; above all this meant no frontal attacks on the more sacred symbols of the military government, including land reform, protective labor legislation, and oil nationalization. All of these considerations influenced the Ulloa program in the direction of moderation and gradualism in seeking both stabilization and reform. Although reforms were part of the agenda, and several were implemented through legislative decrees in the first months of the government, the priority was maintenance of discipline and an improvement in the quality of management rather than dramatic change.

An entirely different situation arose at the beginning of 1983, when Peru's policymakers were confronted by the sudden and coincidental appearance of the debt crisis and a devastating natural disaster, the recurrence of the "El Niño" weather phenomenon. The policy agenda adapted quickly, aided by another coincidence: in December 1982 Belaúnde decided to replace Ulloa. From early 1983 through the end of Belaúnde's term, policymaking was characterized by an almost exclusive preoccupation with stabilization and debt management, and by the zigzags associated with changing ministers and a rapidly changing political environment. The following account will describe the policy record in a few key policy areas in these two periods separately, each of which, by further coincidence, covered exactly half of Belaúnde's five-year term.

## Economic Policy: First Phase
## (July 1980–December 1982)

### Fiscal Policy

The initial situation called for deficit prevention rather than deficit reduction. The total public-sector deficit amounted to only 1 percent of

GDP in 1979 and was entirely financed by foreign credits. Nevertheless, end-of-term politicking by the military regime, through wage increases and subsidies to hold down food and fuel prices and public utility rates, had created the threat of an explosive growth in the 1980 budget, even before one included the spending initiatives that were expected from the new regime. The budgetary situation thus called for prompt measures to maintain fiscal discipline, but not for the major overhaul normally associated with reform packages.

Even before assuming power, Ulloa prepared public opinion for the removal of subsidies by describing the military's price policy in the early 1980 electoral period as an artificial damming up (*embalse*). That phrase became a centerpiece for public debate through the decade. To refer to price subsidies as an *embalse* was to imply that a *desembalse* was inevitable, that subsidized prices could not be held down forever. Despite the fiscal deficit in 1980, inflation had not fallen from its average 1975–79 annual rate of 50 to 60 percent. The initial plan included a package of corrective price increases and subsidy reductions—the *desembalse*—which was timed for the first weeks after the inauguration. The economic team saw the immediate price corrections as necessary because the widening gap between general inflation and government-controlled prices meant that subsidies were growing exponentially. Our (amateur) political judgment also told us that such unpopular measures should take advantage of the inaugural honeymoon, when much of the blame for any popular hardship could still be placed on the outgoing government.

Belaúnde overruled this reasoning on other grounds: municipal elections were scheduled for November of that year. He decided to postpone the fiscal measures until after those elections; given that delay, it then seemed proper to wait until after Christmas.

The *desembalse* finally occurred in January 1981. The five-month delay was damaging in several ways. For one, the initially calculated and politically approved price adjustments had become too small, and years would go by before the fiscal slippage was made up. Then, because the corrections were known to be coming, the opposition was able to register its opposition to them over a much longer period, multiplying the political cost. Also, in the public eye, the delay had the effect of attaching full responsibility for the unpopular measures to Belaúnde and Ulloa. On the other hand, Belaúnde was able to extend his honeymoon through the November elections, and his party won a majority of the provincial and district councils.

Fiscal discipline continued to slip during 1981 and 1982, as both Congress and the president pushed through new spending initiatives, and as monthly haggling with the president and the cabinet on the size of price increases on government-controlled goods and services failed to achieve the revenue targets needed to reduce subsidies. At the same time, the president was pushing his public investment agenda through the ministries of Transport, Agriculture, Industry, and Housing, pressing them, in effect, to overrule the spending and borrowing restrictions drafted by the Ministry of Finance and approved with his signature. Additional spending pressure arose when a border dispute with Ecuador—the Paquisha incident—suddenly increased the armed forces' budgetary bargaining power. The failure to control spending was also an effect of Ulloa's botched relationship with Congress, including members of his own party. On one occasion, all but three Acción Popular congressmen snubbed his invitation to a meeting at the ministry.

The rising trend in public spending was at first accommodated by the central bank's decision to apply the monetary brakes gently. With IMF approval under a stand-by agreement, the money supply was set to expand by 40 percent, moderately below the 1980 rate of inflation of 60 percent. Foreign credit provided a second source of finance.

By January 1982, the central bank reacted with alarm to the rising fiscal deficit, which had risen from 3.9 percent of GDP in 1980 to 6.7 percent in 1981: the bank flexed its independent muscle by closing its windows entirely to the government. All projected credit expansion during the year was assigned to the private sector. A flood of foreign credits, however, left the bank punching at air. Ulloa and the semi-autonomous state enterprises resorted to massive foreign borrowing during 1982, increasingly in the form of short-term loans from commercial banks. State enterprise spending was being driven by presidential prodding, by exaggerated forecasts of projected deficits in energy, water, and other services, and by the political cowardice of the state enterprises, which often ducked the need to make unpopular price increases. Foreign bankers filled Lima's hotels, and Ulloa, having shelved his own procedural controls to restrict foreign borrowing, was making almost daily calls to New York for additional funds. Supply outran demand: attending the 1982 World Bank–IMF annual meetings, one central bank official woke up to find half a dozen business cards thrust under his hotel room door by bankers desperate to obtain interviews. By the end of 1982, despite zero financing from the central bank, foreign borrowing had lifted the fiscal deficit to 7.3 percent of GDP.

## Financial Reform

Interest rates on bank loans were raised from 40 percent per year to over 60 percent in January 1981, while deposit rates also became positive in real terms. Between 1981 and 1982, required reserve ratios were reduced substantially, cutting the inflation tax and allowing banks to expand credit to the private sector. Regulations restricting entry into the financial sector were reduced, including those on foreign-owned banks. More radical reform was ruled out by the team, almost all of whose members had been persuaded by the Chilean experience in the late 1970s that financial reform should be gradual. Ulloa's program aimed at partial liberalization and deregulation during the first years of the administration. It was decided to maintain interest rate ceilings, to raise the capital requirements for new banks to high levels, and to continue to support state development banks using subsidized central bank and foreign credits and treasury grants. It was also decided that commercial banks should open a portion of their capital to the public through the stock market. The main reform target, however, was to achieve and maintain positive real interest rates.

Because legal maximum interest rates were set by law, the implementation of this policy required congressional approval. In this respect, financial sector policy differed from much of Ulloa's program, which could be achieved through executive decrees. At the same time, the need for legislative authority was especially urgent, because interest rates inherited from the military government were well below the inflation rate and were fueling inflation by raising monetary velocity and capital flight.

But Ulloa took his time on financial reform, and his evasive reactions to the issue during meetings of the economic team in the first few months suggested that he was unwilling, for the time being, to take on that political battle. The probable reason for Ulloa's reluctance was that his influence over the president did not extend to the party's congressional majority. In fact, the Senate majority leader, Senator Javier Alva Orlandini, was Ulloa's principal rival within the party.

By October 1980 the central bank had decided that, in view of Ulloa's procrastination, and because interest rates were vital to its own monetary responsibilities, it had to shoulder the responsibility for obtaining congressional approval. This decision was a deviation from the unstated procedural rules, under which Ulloa was the team's only political link. It was also a venture into the unknown. After a history of government dominance, especially during the preceding military regime, the bank lacked the political experience and the mechanisms for lobbying or persuading public opinion in the context of a very open democracy and vigorous media.

The bank's efforts produced a partial success: Congress approved a law delegating primary authority over interest rate levels to the bank, although it gave the Ministry of Finance a veto on rate changes. The strongest opposition to this law had come from the construction lobby and some bankers. Once the law was passed, Ulloa followed through in a manner consistent with his own program, giving immediate executive consent to interest rate adjustments, which then became positive in real terms, and remained so through December 1982. The new law became a critical instrument during the following years, particularly when inflation began to rise in 1983: if authority had not been transferred to the bank, Congress would certainly have evaded or delayed interest rate adjustments, allowing rates to sink to severely negative levels after 1982.

The bank's political apprenticeship in selling the interest rate law had major and unexpected effects on its capacity to act and, more generally, on the nature of the relationship between the economic team and political groups. Over the five-year term, the bank extended and expanded this initial political experience, eventually developing a political base that gave it a degree of independence from successive ministers of finance, and in this way put some muscle on the bones of strictly legal independence provided in the Constitution. By 1985, the bank had chalked up a remarkable legislative record, obtaining passage of close to a dozen laws that it had sponsored for reasons of monetary or balance of payments policy, while blocking several other laws that it considered harmful to its purpose. In addition, the bank received critical public support when its independence was directly challenged by President Belaúnde and his party during 1984. Between July and October of that year, the central bank was besieged by the executive and pressed by foreign bankers, demanding, unsuccessfully, that the bank hand over its foreign exchange reserves to pay arrears on the external debt. The executive's intent was also to use those funds to finance preelection spending. The siege included an effort to impeach the bank's governor. Foreign commercial banks, and in particular Citibank, which chaired the Debt Steering Committee, became knowing accomplices of the executive's attempt to infringe the Constitution by bullying the central bank, and to break the domestic credit limits of the IMF stand-by agreement which the banks themselves had required of Peru.

## Trade Policy

Trade policy was the most politically visible and sensitive item on Ulloa's reform agenda. More than the other components in his program, it had the appearance of a real reform, aiming at major, once-for-all changes in the rules of the game. In fact, this appearance was exaggerated by a confusion between the liberalizing measures of the previous regime and the additional measures proposed by Ulloa. Moreover, by the more radical standards of the current Washington consensus, Peru's 1979–81 trade reform was only a moderate and partial step, thus justifying the classification of Ulloa's entire program as a ''nonreform'' experience. At the time, however, and through the 1980s, the trade reform became the hallmark of Ulloa's program, causing him to be branded as a neoliberal and *aperturista* (antiprotectionist).

Considerable import liberalization had been carried out during the last two years of the previous regime: most import prohibitions and other quantitative restrictions had been eliminated, and tariff levels had been reduced to nonprohibitive levels. Ulloa took the process further, eliminating all remaining quotas, setting a maximum tariff rate of 60 percent (which was restricted to a small category of consumer goods), cutting most other tariffs to the range of 20 to 30 percent, and raising some tariffs on intermediate goods to reduce levels of effective protection. Most of this agenda was carried out during the first six months of the regime, and few further modifications were made through the end of 1982, the major exception being a 5 percent across-the-board surcharge on imports imposed in 1982 as part of a fiscal package.

An important "liberalization" measure was also taken on the export side: in January 1982, export subsidies on nontraditional exports were cut by approximately one-third. This measure, also part of the original Ulloa program, was justified on grounds of fiscal cost and administrative control; the subsidy had encouraged inventive corruption.

The timing of the export measure proved unfortunate, since the balance of payments deteriorated considerably during 1982. The daily rate of devaluation against the dollar had been accelerated, but the continuing strength of the dollar was a major offset to the devaluation gains, especially for manufacturers who had developed markets in Europe and Japan. The coincidence of import liberalization and export subsidy removal with a deterioration in the balance of payments created a strong *post hoc ergo propter hoc* accusation against the Ulloa "liberals." Liberalization, in fact, became the catch-all explanation for the deterioration of the economy after 1981, and a justification for the disastrous return to protection under the government of Alan García Pérez.

As would be expected, business groups waged guerilla war on the trade and exchange rate measures. Their effectiveness, however, was limited by the fact that both import and exchange rate policies were matters for executive and central bank decision; Congress intervened only in funding decisions and thus the level of export subsidies. Moreover, Belaúnde was an unsympathetic audience to the concerns of rich businessmen. Many had contributed to his campaign, and some were part of his court, but Belaúnde listened to their complaints with the Olympian disdain of a poor aristocrat. Nevertheless, congressional lobbying and media campaigns by business groups did have an inhibiting effect. Somewhat unexpectedly, the sharpest opposition came from ADEX, the nontraditional exporters' association, which did not forgive Ulloa for his reduction in export subsidies. The attacks by ADEX and other business groups largely coincided with those from the left, which objected, for instance, to the role of the IMF, to faster devaluation, and to higher interest rates. APRA and the leftist unions echoed these criticisms of economic policy in regular communiqués and during strikes and demonstrations. But the inhibiting effect of all this criticism peaked in the first year of the regime and then ebbed through the rest of Belaúnde's term. Much economic policy was legally in executive or central bank hands, and that authority was extended by an increasing use of constitutional powers: one provision allowed Congress to delegate its legislative capacity to the executive on a designated topic, while another allowed the executive to issue decrees in economic matters in cases of emergency.

## Other Reforms

Ulloa's second decree put an end to land reform, that is, to further expropriation, and in a limited way allowed the sale and mortgaging of land. A subsequent decree allowed members of farm cooperatives to subdivide and work the land as individual plots. These steps were not seen as major affronts to the 1970 Land Reform Law, but the decrees were daring at the time and went a long way to restoring a market economy in the modern agricultural sector. Ulloa also took immediate steps to initiate the privatization of numerous state enterprises. A third reform initiative taken in 1980 consisted of administrative steps that had the effect of sidestepping the restrictions on foreign direct investment agreed to in the international treaty that created the Andean Pact (Decision 24). A fourth reform consisted of a softening of the terms for foreign direct investment in the energy sector. All of these initiatives fared poorly once they had left the reformist hothouses of the ministries of Finance and Energy. The measures challenged popular ideas and political taboos, yet were announced with no prior search for a political mandate nor any effort to convince either key political players, even within Belaúnde's party, or the public at large. In addition, by their very nature these initiatives could not succeed without the zealous and often courageous support of the president, cabinet colleagues, other government officials, and congressmen. One important exception was the new Petroleum Law, which was sold to the public and to Congress through the almost single-handed and energetic lobbying of Pedro-Pablo Kuczynski, the minister of energy. In all cases, however, the measures required implementing legislation and ministerial resolutions, active bureaucratic problem solving, and lower-level day-to-day decisions that were open to public criticism. Congressional approval was required, for instance, for privatization, and for the liberalization of land and labor markets, and here the high level of public criticism did restrain the government's hand.

In summary, the reform component of Ulloa's 1980 plan was conceived less as a response to crisis than as a second-stage, mopping-up operation that sought to consolidate the earlier budgetary improvement, while taking the 1978–79 structural measures a stage further. Taken together, the military regime and Ulloa's plans over 1978–82 add up to an extensive and radical reform program, even though the critical fiscal improvement began to come apart toward the end of the period. Through 1981, Peru's economic program continued to rate high marks from the foreign financial community—even allowing for the relatively lax standards of the time.

## Economic Policy: Second Phase (January 1983–July 1985)

The assumptions behind the Ulloa program were suddenly invalidated at the end of 1982. As noted above, Ulloa's economic program had been designed in the context of easily available foreign exchange and an incipient recovery. These conditions were already changing by the end of the first policy phase: commodity prices were falling, nontraditional exports were stagnating, annual inflation had risen from 60 percent to 70 percent, and industrial production had begun to fall. The deterioration accelerated during the last quarter of 1982, when foreign commercial banks began to cut trade credits and refuse new lending. Even before the 1983 collapse associated with the debt crisis and with El Niño, the economic malaise had prompted debate within the economic team on changes in the program to reinforce the external sector and stimulate output, but the discussion was cut short when Ulloa resigned from the Ministry of Finance in December 1982. Although Ulloa's reform policies and the downward trend in the international economy had eroded Belaúnde's support for his prime minister, the principal factor behind the resignation was a difference of opinion regarding policy on internal security: Ulloa saw a need for a much more aggressive and centralized antiterrorist effort, and asked that he be put in charge. Belaúnde refused.

The next minister of finance, Carlos Rodriguez Pastor, seemed well chosen to deal with the severe balance of payments and stabilization crisis that began in 1983. Although a member of Acción Popular and a companion-in-exile of Belaúnde during the 1970s, Rodriguez Pastor was a seasoned technocrat, a former senior central bank official who, during the heady international lending boom of the 1970s had become a star salesman of syndicated loans for a US bank. Rodriguez Pastor was predisposed to the energetic and aggressive macroeconomic adjustment and debt management required by the new situation. On the other hand, he was even more dependent on Belaúnde for political backing than Ulloa had been.

Rodriguez Pastor immediately launched a program of accelerated devaluation, higher taxes (especially on fuels and imports), public spending cuts (which included salaries, subsidies, and military purchases), and renewed efforts to complete the original Ulloa reform agenda, which included deregulation in land and labor markets and institutional changes geared to improve the control and management of public enterprises.

After setting these changes in motion, however, Rodriguez Pastor began to dedicate an increasing proportion of his time to deal with the swelling foreign payments gap, at first through new loans and later through debt renegotiation. A large part of his year in office was spent traveling abroad. For all his efforts, however, the economy continued to deteriorate during 1983: inflation jumped to triple digits, and GDP fell by an unprecedented 12 percent. The recession and higher inflation were the main causes of a 30 percent fall in real tax revenues, which far exceeded the spending cuts. An ironic outcome was that, despite his notable commitment to budget balance, Rodriguez Pastor was eventually responsible for a record fiscal deficit, reaching 9.8 percent of GDP. The IMF, which had projected positive GDP growth for the year, evaded responsibility and abandoned their best ally in Peru, blaming the fall in tax revenues on "an administrative collapse" in the tax office. In the end, Rodriguez Pastor appeared to fail on both the domestic and the external front: his radical adjustment policies were increasingly blamed for higher inflation and the collapse in production, and by the end of the year he had nothing to show in terms of debt renegotiation, much less the fresh money for public works that Belaúnde had hoped for when he chose Rodriguez Pastor.

At the end of 1983, a political backlash forced Rodriguez Pastor's departure, opening the door to a period of backsliding under a new minister of finance, José Benavides, a civil engineer and loyal political jack-of-all-trades. Benavides increased import tariffs and export subsidies, reintroduced import restrictions, and raised price subsidies once again by holding back on monthly adjustments in fuel and other officially controlled prices.

In firing Rodriguez Pastor, Belaúnde may have been reacting to his party's electoral disaster in the November 1983 municipal polls. The United Left Party surged throughout the country as a truly and finally united organization, capturing Lima's town hall, while Belaúnde's Acción Popular party dropped from its first place showing in 1980 to fifth in the total count. The terrorist Sendero Luminoso (Shining Path) organization was also beginning to force itself on the public attention. During the year, the Confederación General de Trabajadores, a communist-controlled federation of unions that dominated the labor scene, organized a nationwide general strike. Opposition to reform became intense within Acción Popular, led by Alva Orlandini, a politician who controlled much of the party machinery, and who was targeting his party's 1985 presidential candidacy. Alva Orlandini, who had continually harassed Ulloa, objecting to the latter's reform efforts, now focused on the even more damaging—from his electoral perspective— adjustment agenda of Rodriguez Pastor. Toward the end of the year, a group of senior Acción Popular leaders and advisers, including several cabinet ministers, began to meet secretly to discuss policy alternatives to the Rodriguez Pastor adjustment program. In the midst of this intense political opposition and economic setbacks, it is hardly surprising that Belaúnde blinked.

This setback to reform was short-lived, however. Coming near the end of his term, scheduled for July 1985, Belaúnde seemed to be more concerned to avoid a repeat of the 1968 scenario, when financial chaos had opened the door to military intervention, than to manage the economic program with an electoral eye. At the same time, he still hoped for fresh funds from abroad that would allow him to complete and inaugurate a slew of unfinished public works. Shortly after pandering to the opposition by firing Rodriguez Pastor and taking several of the anti–Rodriguez Pastor plotters into the cabinet, one of whom became the new minister of finance, Belaúnde turned his back on his political followers and ordered his cabinet to proceed with an IMF agreement and the corresponding reform agenda. A short time later, Belaúnde attempted to break out of the political cul de sac created by the economic crisis by offering the premiership to Peru's highly respected man of letters, Mario Vargas Llosa, but failed to reach an agreement.

The upshot was that, starting in the third quarter of 1984, policy took an unexpected turn—back onto a reform track—with the appointment of Guillermo Garrido Lecca as Belaúnde's fourth minister of finance. An economist, former commercial bank officer working under Rodriguez Pastor, and former vice minister to Benavides, Garrido Lecca returned to a course of gradual but accelerating fiscal, balance of payments, and financial sector adjustment. With little personal or political weight outside his sector, he was unable to prevent some backsliding in other areas of the economy, in particular in the form of increasing trade interventions and protection, while Belaúnde shelved other components of Ulloa's original reform agenda.

However, over a relatively short span of time, from late 1984 to mid-1985, Garrido Lecca restored a large measure of fiscal discipline through a mix of hefty fuel taxes, elimination of almost all subsidies, and drastic expenditure cuts. The fiscal deficit was cut to zero during 1985, allowing the treasury to amortize part of its debt with the central bank. Although debt servicing to foreign commercial banks was interrupted, exchange rate and financial policy achieved a substantial degree of adjustment during this period. Accelerated devaluation pushed the real exchange rate to its lowest (most depreciated) level in the decade, while interest rates were raised significantly.

On balance, the degree of macroeconomic adjustment carried out by Garrido Lecca could be described as a major package of fiscal, external, and financial sector reform. These measures were implemented in the face of intense opposition from within Acción Popular, which was calling desperately for an electoral breather from adjustment efforts, and a frenzy of criticism from the media, business lobbies, and the communist-led union movement, which made repeated attempts to repeat the success of the 1978 general strike. Belaúnde stubbornly backed Garrido Lecca through this reform effort, but by the end of 1984 all hope of fresh money from abroad had evaporated.

## Political Economy

This section presents a more systematic effort to understand the politics behind adjustment and reform decisions in Peru over 1980–85. Some of that politics was referred to in the preceding review of policy. The discussion here will focus on the crisis, honeymoon, and weak opposition hypotheses suggested by Williamson.

First, however, it will be helpful to define what exactly we are trying to explain. As already noted, my starting point is the perception that Peru "failed" to carry out reform during the early 1980s. The preceding account of the policy record does not support such an unambiguous conclusion. Judged by Peru's economic performance over the five-year period—recession, higher inflation, and debt arrears—the reform effort appears to have lacked the vigor and continuity needed for success. A fairer test, based on results in subsequent years, is no longer possible because the program was turned upside down by President García in 1986; Belaúnde's program is now permanently tarred by García's brush. The analysis is also confused by the force of exogenous factors bearing on the timing and effects of reform measures, such as the initial foreign exchange boom, the effects of El Niño, the lack of a G-7 godfather in foreign debt negotiations, and the delayed effects of policies and circumstances under the military regime.

Also, results were not determined solely by dramatic orders coming down from the bridge; like that of a ship, much of an economy's performance turns on the quality of day-to-day administration, on the ship's company ethos, and on the continuity and authority of the captain's orders. When it comes to explaining the economic free fall that began in 1983—with loss of confidence, increased monetary velocity, higher inflation, capital flight, difficulty in controlling public spending, and falling production—it might be said that 15 years of increasing policy volatility and eroding administrative control in the public sector were as important as the precise arithmetic of the fiscal deficit or of tariffs. The right dosage might have been less rather than more adjustment and reform. It is not clear, therefore, whether the following discussion should attempt to explain why reform and adjustment were or were not carried out.

The crisis hypothesis was tested in Peru by two major stabilization crises over the decade between 1975 and 1985. In both cases, under General Francisco Morales Bermudez in 1978–79 and under Belaúnde in 1983–85, the government responded by imposing sharp stabilization and reform programs over vociferous opposition from organized labor, some business lobbies, and most of the media. Both regimes paid a high political cost. Although the first episode occurred prior to Belaúnde's term, I will review both, partly because the earlier experience helps explain Belaúnde's reactions, and partly because it is interesting to compare the two experiences.

The 1975–79 crisis was accompanied by greater civil unrest, in the form of riots and major strikes, than the later period, when economic indicators registered much deeper cuts in living standards. Although moderate by today's standards, the 1975–79 loss in household income and employment was felt as an unprecedented hardship by a large part of the population. By opening the doors to pent-up political frustration at the authoritarian regime, and to newly mobilized leftist unions, especially in the public sector, the crisis led ultimately to the demise of the military regime.

For the great majority of military leaders and their civilian supporters, the drastic reforms and adjustment carried out during the final stage of that crisis, in 1978–79, were unexpected, unplanned, initially postponed, and finally undertaken in grudging submission to the economic emergency. The crisis broke on the military government after four years of major achievements, and reform measures were first resisted, then initiated and dropped over three years before worsening economic conditions and pressures from external creditors forced the issue. Once begun, however, the reform program developed into an almost instantaneous reversal of the interventionist, loose-money, public-sector-driven model of development that had provided the blueprint for most economic and social measures carried out by the military over almost 10 years. In addition to forceful macroeconomic adjustment, the new program included drastic trade liberalization, some deregulation of the land and labor markets, and an opening to foreign investors. The about-face took place at the very top of the government, with almost no public debate nor pressure for such measures, and largely preceding a realization by the general public, and even a majority of the military leaders, that it was the least-cost course of action.

One may speculate about the leadership's personal reasons for the abrupt policy change. Certainly, the inadequacy of price controls and intervention to control inflation and restore production was becoming increasingly plain, and there was growing pressure from creditors. However, it may have been equally important that General Morales Bermudez was a closet conservative. He had served as minister of finance for six weeks towards the end of the first Belaúnde government, in 1968. He spent most of his time in office in all-day briefings given by a team of ministry and central bank economists. Toward the end of that period he secluded himself, returning with a detailed "war plan" consisting mostly of orthodox adjustment measures to fight inflation and recession. He took his plan to President Belaúnde and to Congress but found no support for the adjustment program, and promptly resigned. During the military government he swam with the interventionist current, partly hiding his views, and probably partly carried along by the early success of the radical model, serving as minister of finance during a high-spending period, and from 1975 as president. The crisis almost surely undermined his more radical colleagues and gave him the courage to return to earlier beliefs; those convictions, in turn, gave energy to the turnabout.

The crisis that broke in 1983 also occurred midway through a presidential term. By then, Belaúnde's political capital had been severely eroded by a worsening economy, a sense of drift, and criticism from both outside and within the governing party. As with Morales Bermudez in 1978, Belaúnde's January 1983 decision to give Rodriguez Pastor the green light for a vastly stepped up adjustment program was taken largely on his own. But it differed from his predecessor's decision in being much more timely, and therefore less supported by public awareness of a crisis situation. Although the economy had deteriorated during 1982, no one in January 1983 expected the free fall in production, incomes, and price stability that was to occur during the year. Even as late as March of 1983, the IMF projected 0.9 percent growth in GDP for the year, when in fact it was by then well on its way to a 12 percent collapse.

Another point of difference is that, for Belaúnde, the decision to adjust was more at odds with his personal intuitions than had been the case with Morales Bermudez. Belaúnde had an almost physical aversion to economics. He heavily discounted the preaching and warnings of his economist advisers, and during his entire political career he took every opportunity to push for vast schemes of public works. During his first two and a half years in office, he continually sought to postpone the adjustment measures and to dilute the reforms that he had originally approved. The most likely explanation for Belaúnde's about-face is miscalculation: he believed that adjustment in early 1983 would be rapid and once-for-all, and that it was the necessary and sufficient course to keep foreign money streaming in. The IMF and his new minister of finance, Rodriguez Pastor, certainly encouraged him in those beliefs. Once adjustment had begun, Belaúnde was trapped: the situation spiraled out of control with the devastations caused by El Niño and the panic created by accelerating inflation, devaluation, and the foreign debt crisis. Rodriguez Pastor and the IMF insisted that the only available course of action was to intensify the adjustment measures. Belaúnde acquiesced through the year, and although he rebelled and backtracked during the first months of 1984, he later returned to an even more austere reform program that was carried through to the end of his term. The paradoxical conclusion is that the crisis did indeed provide an opening and a motivation for reforms, but that, to a large extent, the speed and severity of the reform program itself was possible because Belaúnde, in his innocence, and his IMF and ministerial advisers, perhaps less innocently, vastly underestimated the magnitude of that crisis.

It could be argued that fiscal backsliding during the short-lived, in-between bonanza period, 1980–82, provides an additional, negative proof of the crisis hypothesis: adjustment was abandoned as soon as it became possible. Fiscal policy began to deteriorate in early 1980 when the military regime suddenly reversed its 1978–79 austerity, seeking to improve its predeparture image by granting public-sector wage increases, raising price subsidies, and signing large investment contracts.

Ulloa's program checked some of these expenditures during 1981, but the fiscal deficit rose anyway as public investment expanded and falling export prices cut tax revenues. The extraordinary recovery of the economy during 1979–80 is perhaps a sufficient explanation for the more relaxed stance on fiscal discipline between 1980 and 1982. A fairer answer would cite the widespread perception, in 1980, that it was time to attend to a backlog in public investment and social services, built up during the preceding crisis, and, more importantly, that the overriding priority, following the return to democracy in July of that year, was to avoid making waves that could become an invitation for a return to military rule. The president was extremely shy of anything that smacked of shock or a new crisis, and his guideline for economic policy during that period was ''yes, but gently.'' And there was a generalized urge to get on with the long-postponed task of physical construction. In tune with this spirit, for instance, the central bank (with the IMF's approval) opted for gradual rather than shock stabilization, meaning that annual monetary targets were set about 20 or 25 percent below prevailing inflation. The practical effect of this thinking was to justify lower price adjustments and deficit borrowing and spending.

President García's policy reversal in 1986–87 could be cited as another negative proof of the crisis argument. His interventionist and high-spending policies were made possible, at least, by Belaúnde's adjustments and accumulation of international reserves.

On the other hand, the negative argument breaks down with respect to Ulloa's sectoral reform agenda. Although pressure was taken off him by the balance of payments bonanza, and although the measures were accompanied by heavy political flak and negligible support from outside the economic team, Ulloa stuck to a reform course, extending the previous reform measures with additional trade and financial sector liberalization measures.

Part of the explanation for the uneven, stop-go character of policy reform in Peru, I believe, lies in the gradual and incomplete process of ideological conversion. From the late 1970s through 1985, with the exception only of part of 1984, the presidents in power and their economic teams were pushing an adjustment and reform agenda that was perceived as radical, exaggerated, insensitive, and technically flawed by a majority of the public. Most academic and professional "expert" opinion kept up a continuous critical barrage. Although the motivation was partly political, and partly linked to interest groups, much of the criticism was sincere. The media and the general public were even further behind in understanding the need for major reforms. Looking back from 1993, the extent of change in public awareness has been remarkable, and President Alberto Fujimori is now applauded from all corners of society for actions that are many times more radical than those that evoked intense criticism 10 years ago. This change in perceptions is surely a response to the crisis, but it has been reinforced by a broad flow of information on the experience, policies, and opinion in other countries. The Chilean experience has been particularly influential in Peru. That external influence is visible in the language used by journalists, politicians, academics, and businessmen in their daily commentaries on events.

One mechanism by which a crisis facilitates reform is through its effect on public perceptions. A second is the shift to a more authoritarian mode of government that occurs in an emergency. As each of Peru's crises developed, first over the late 1970s, then from 1983 through 1985, governments responded as they would in wartime or in any national emergency: decisions became increasingly concentrated in the hands of a few ministers, in particular those of the minister of finance and his economic team; more and more decisions were taken by executive decree, at times under explicit congressional delegation, and at times simply as a result of executive daring and arrogation of powers. Acts that in normal times would evoke democratic outrage, and that would often, in fact, be blocked or reversed by the workings of the democratic machinery, were accepted with little question by an increasingly resigned polity. As budgets tightened, ministers and other decision centers within government found themselves with less and less to decide, while de facto control of the purse tended to empower the economic team. Normally arrogant and commandeering ministers and state enterprise presidents found themselves increasingly at the mercy of technocrats in the economic team who could speed or delay payments or peremptorily block projects. As the crises developed, even presidents found themselves resignedly signing off, with fewer and fewer questions and objections, on the decrees and other papers placed on their desks for signature by unelected technocrats. In these crisis situations, democracy and normal hierarchy became as irrelevant as they are in any hospital emergency room.

Each crisis facilitated reform in Peru by curtailing democracy and empowering technocrats. This mechanism, however, is also part of the explanation for the difficulty that Peru has had in sustaining reforms. As crises receded, normal democratic scrutiny and checks and the precedence of elected over unelected officials reestablished themselves. Earlier decisions were questioned and revised, and noncrisis priorities came back onto the front burner.

The honeymoon hypothesis is much less helpful than the crisis hypothesis in explaining the 1980–85 experience. During the preparation of Ulloa's economic program, the economic team fully expected that much of it would be enacted during Belaúnde's honeymoon, during the second half of 1980. We had been drilled on the critical importance of using the honeymoon to the hilt by the friendly advice of more experienced colleagues from other countries. Indeed, the advice is standard technocratic lore.

Yet most of the adjustment and reform carried out in Peru between 1978 and 1985 occurred either before or well after the one honeymoon period that occurred in those years—the months in late 1980 after Belaúnde's second inauguration. Belaúnde's honeymoon was used for some trade liberalization measures, but those measures, although inherently difficult, were at the same time not revolutionary: they extended and deepened a process of opening up that had already taken far more radical steps under the preceding administration.

The simple reason for the irrelevance of the honeymoon to Peru's reforms over that period was unfortunate timing. The honeymoon period coincided with the one breathing space in a period of almost uninterrupted crisis since 1975. It was a period of commodity price boom, new oil exports, easy external finance, booming international reserves, and a sense that most of the difficult adjustment measures had already been taken by the outgoing regime.

In Belaúnde's case, the honeymoon was, potentially, an even greater opportunity for reform than a normal inaugural period. The sense of a new beginning was heightened by the fact that Peru was emerging from a 12–year dictatorship. The honeymoon was a double celebration, as much for the return to democracy as for the new president. Yet under the surface the opportunity for change was not as great as might appear. Despite the general repudiation of the outgoing regime, there was a large measure of legitimacy in many of the measures and, indeed, reforms carried out by the military. The new reform agenda drawn up by Ulloa meant undoing much that the military had done, but there was no clear mandate for the proposed counterreforms. In fact, a democratic decision process would probably have rejected much of Ulloa's program. By forcing through a counterreform during his honeymoon, Belaúnde would have affronted the democracy that, more than his person, the country was then celebrating. In the middle of an emergency, such as that inherited by Fujimori, such an affront might have been swallowed by the electorate, as indeed has been the case with Fujimori. At the time of Belaúnde's inauguration, however, it seems unlikely that the country would have tolerated the measures.

The argument thus far has stressed the role of presidents, economic teams, and an amorphous public opinion. By implication, organized groups with political clout, such as labor unions, political parties, business lobbies, and the military would seem to have played a minor and diminishing role. Perhaps the main exception, mentioned above, is that the latent threat of a return by the military acted to inhibit more drastic reforms, especially in the first part of the period, while the Paquisha border incident added to spending pressures. I believe that this is an accurate assessment with respect to key decisions regarding adjustment measures, although the opposition did inhibit farther-reaching institutional reforms. Despite the constitutional system, the left's capacity to mobilize strikes and demonstrations, the right's power to influence public opinion through the media, the ever present background threat of a coup, and the activity of a virulent terrorist movement, it was the personal agenda of Belaúnde, marginally influenced by a handful of advisers, that determined the timing and intensity of reform.

One reason was that the constitution gave the executive a remarkable degree of centralized decision-making power. Another was Belaúnde's own independent character and self-confidence in his political judgment. A third was the empowerment that resulted from the crisis, partly through the education of public opinion, and partly through the mechanics of decision making under circumstances of high inflation. A final reason is that, throughout this period, the power of traditional political, labor, and business organizations was waning. The military threat was felt to ebb as time went by. Unions were weakened by repeated failure to pull off major general strikes, despite or because of the deepening recession. Business lobbies were similarly weakened by recession, division, and a growing realization that their opposition to reform was not in their own long-run interest. Sendero Luminoso was too extreme and distant from real-life policymaking to have an input. New organizations, especially public-sector employee unions and regional movements, tended to cancel each other out in public perceptions, and also to reduce the power of traditional political organizations. The interests of these many groups were at cross-purposes and did not line up clearly with specific items on the reform agenda. By the end of Belaúnde's term, the opposition, including that from within the governing party, seemed in fact to have given up trying to influence the economic program. In the final months, Belaúnde himself seemed to shrug his shoulders at the coming political debacle for his party and to avert his eyes while the minister of finance, Garrido Lecca, and the central bank pushed through a draconian adjustment program in the midst of an election campaign.

# Comment

MIGUEL A. RODRÍGUEZ

Venezuela has been growing very impressively over the last three years, and yet, paradoxically, the political situation unraveled in 1992, with two failed coup attempts against the government of Carlos Andrés Pérez.

But before discussing the Venezuelan case, let me briefly address the objectives and the issues John Williamson has presented. I think it is an excellent idea to discuss the interaction between economics and politics, since the historical process that is taking place all over Latin America and around the planet evolves precisely from this dynamic. Everybody would agree that reformers must have a coherent team and a comprehensive program, that the reforms must proceed fast, that reformers must appeal to their populations through the media, and that substantial and timely contributions from the international financial institutions advance the reform process.

The point I want to stress is that, although these are important conditions for launching and sustaining a program of structural change, they are by no means sufficient. Of paramount importance is the specific political situation in each country. Chile and Mexico have been mentioned as the two biggest success stories of Latin America. To be sure, they are very peculiar by Latin American standards. The Chilean reform emerged almost full-blown during the Pinochet regime, and in Mexico, a very peculiar political and social system determines the dynamics of the

*Miguel A. Rodríguez is Senior Adviser and Vice President, Latin America and Caribbean, at the World Bank and he is a former Minister of Planning and President of the Venezuelan Central Bank. He is also a Professor of Economics at the IESA in Caracas.*

civil society. These cases—if we want to talk about success stories of reform—cannot be easily generalized to a single "Latin American case." Their political settings do not resemble those in the rest of the region.

In truly open democratic societies, we are going to see over the years a historic and lengthy transformation with forward leaps, successes, and setbacks, but unquestionably establishing a trend toward progress in the region. For each country, the relative speed of transformation is going to depend on its individual political realities and dynamics. Take, for example, the case of Brazil, a country with a great potential for economic growth, but where the political and institutional settings create a very difficult environment for change. At this particular historical crossroads, it is extraordinarily difficult to implement a comprehensive program of economic transformation in Brazil. Bresser Pereira attempted that in his short tenure; he had neither the time nor the political support to put such a program into effect. The Collor administration attempted some reforms, but Brazilian politics made it almost impossible (granted, there were some substantial "errors" made along the way). Without any detraction from the transformation efforts of countries such as Mexico or Chile, reform in the complex and active political and institutional settings of Brazil or Venezuela differs completely from that of countries where tighter control is possible.[1]

Chile and Mexico demonstrate that the process of reform is going to be, in general, lengthy and intricate. Chile began more than 10 years ago and Mexico after the debt crisis. José Córdoba explained today that Mexico is still reforming, that the microeconomic adjustments came a little later. It was launched only a few years ago, and many challenges lie ahead: financial sector reform, the creation of the pension funds, labor legislation, and other "micro" changes that are essential and have very important macroeconomic implications.

And this brings me to my second point: we have been talking about success stories (plural) in Latin America when the only true success story one can clearly identify in the region is Chile. The Chilean economy is the only one producing the type of results that have led us to believe that opening of the economy and structural transformation rather than import substitution are the *desideratum* in terms of economic development. Economists and policymakers in Latin America saw the per capita income growth of the Asian countries over the past 20 years and became more and more convinced that the opening of the economy was the best way to produce a real transformation in Latin American society, advance economic development, and rescue from poverty large segments of the population.

---

1. Where you can, for example, "approve" legislation at the cabinet level because there is a tight rein on Congress.

What has happened, despite the fact that a few countries have been managing reform for a long period, is that we are seeing very sluggish economic growth. GDP growth rates of 2 and 3 percent are not the orders of magnitude that will produce a true transformation in a backward society. Despite all the propaganda, all the media impact, all the "success" stories recounted about a few countries in Latin America, Chile is the only one showing sustained economic growth. In the last seven years, it has averaged more than 6 percent of annual real GDP growth (export-driven and increasingly investment-driven), a strong balance of payments—including the current account—a systematic reduction of inflation to low levels, a substantial reduction in debt, and a powerful surge in domestic saving, both public and private. Mexico will doubtless increase its rate of productivity growth over the next few years, but they have still a way to go. And Argentina, despite the astonishing reduction in inflation, is only a very recent story. And then, there is Venezuela.

In early 1989, Carlos Andrés Pérez began his second term as president of Venezuela. He invited a group of young technocrats to be part of his cabinet, and with them, the famed populist of the 1970s launched a massive program of structural change of the Venezuelan economy.

The program was comprehensive in its design. It included complete trade reform, elimination of all import restrictions, and reduction of tariffs to a narrow band; elimination of all exchange controls and adoption of a free float that would permit an exchange rate level compatible with the development of nontraditional exports; price liberalization; the restructuring of the public sector with widespread decentralization and privatization of parastatal enterprises; a comprehensive tax reform; a new policy to set public-sector prices at efficient levels; the restructuring of the financial sector, featuring liberalization, increased competition, and strengthening of the regulatory framework; modernization of labor legislation, including the creation of pension funds and the restructuring of the social security system; elimination of restrictions to foreign investment; restructuring of the external debt; an overhaul of the policy of external financing; and a new social policy that would eliminate the system of massive generalized subsidies (many of which went to the rich) in favor of targeted subsidies directed to the poorest segment of the population.

This effort was begun simultaneously with a massive program of stabilization to overcome the disastrous situation inherited from the previous government. The numbers speak for themselves. The fiscal deficit reached 10 percent of GDP in 1988. The current account of the balance of payments featured a $6 billion deficit (about 9 percent of GDP). The operational foreign exchange reserves of the central bank were negative by more than $6 billion (a mere $300 million in liquid reserves against $6.5 billion in short-term letters of credit due within a four-month period and guaranteed at the official, overvalued exchange rate), and this in an oil-producing country accustomed to a very high level of reserves. There were widespread controls in the exchange market, in interest rates, and in trade, leading to corruption, rent seeking, and totally inefficient resource allocation. The foreign exchange system, for example, featured three rates: the official ones, at 7.50 bolívars per dollar and 14.50 bolívars per dollar, allocated within a corrupted system known as RECADI,[2] and the parallel market at about 40 bolívars per dollar. There was an acceleration of inflation despite substantial real appreciation and widespread price controls. Public-sector prices were frozen at the world's lowest levels (for example, gasoline was selling at less than 10 cents per gallon, and fertilizers were sold at less than 5 percent of the cost of production).

Part of the program of macroeconomic stabilization and structural adjustment was launched in March 1989; this was a demonstration of courage—rioters had stormed Caracas in February only 26 days into the government term. The results were as expected: a sharp 8 percent decline of real GDP in 1989 but with a rapid rebound a year later, as real GDP grew 6.5 percent in 1990, 10.5 percent in 1991, and 7.3 percent in 1992. The fiscal deficit was reduced to 1 percent of GDP in 1989 (the cause of the contraction in real GDP of 1989), and the public sector was in surplus in 1990 and 1991. With the adjustment, the current account swung into a surplus of $2.5 billion in 1989. Inflation slowed down in 1990 and 1991 to about 37 percent and 30 percent, respectively, after a surge from 40 to 80 percent in 1989 due to the devaluation, the adjustment of public-sector prices, and price liberalization. Unemployment was reduced from 12 percent in 1989 to 6 percent in 1992, with the creation of more than 600,000 jobs, mainly in the modern sector of the economy.

Foreign exchange reserves recovered quickly, reaching $14 billion by early 1991. The external debt was restructured under the Brady Plan with an important reduction in debt and debt service. Major agreements were reached with the multilateral institutions: a $5 billion extended fund facility with the International Monetary Fund, and large programs to support structural change and finance projects with the World Bank, the Inter-American Development Bank, and the Japanese Export-Import Bank. A large investment program has been carried out by PDVSA in the oil sector, with participation—for the first time since nationalization—of the private sector in key areas of production (such as petrochemicals, heavy oil, and gas). A successful privatization program has been executed since 1990, including the telephone company (which fetched the highest price in Latin America), ports, one airline, hotels, a shipyard, and sugar mills. A huge influx of foreign direct investment started in late 1990 and reached more than $2 billion in 1991 (an important amount

2. After the name of the foreign exchange allocation agency of the Ministry of Finance.

was tied to privatization). There was a substantial repatriation of flight capital and recovery of external credit for the private sector.

In summary, at the beginning of 1992 we were witnessing one of the most successful adjustment programs in Latin America. To be sure, the complex reality of Venezuelan society was not as rosy as the economic statistics. In early February 1992, a military uprising almost toppled the elected government of Carlos Andrés Pérez. After the coup attempt, the political situation unraveled, and support for the president plummeted to record lows. The drive for reform stopped, and some backsliding took place. Although one cannot deny the impact of the political turmoil of 1992 on reform in Venezuela, the truth is that the reform program was already suffering from serious delays in key areas.

While the program announced in early 1989 was comprehensive, implementation lagged well behind. The tax reform, a cornerstone for fiscal and price stability, was presented to Congress in 1989, and it still has not been approved (keep in mind that in Venezuela the tax burden on the private sector is about 3 percent of GDP). Financial sector reform is also waiting for approval. The privatization program was seriously delayed in 1992 because of the political instability. The legislation to create pension funds and to modernize the social security system was also stalled in Congress. And labor legislation suffered a setback with the approval of an old-fashioned and costly approach. In other words, the Perez government advanced decisively in its "cabinet" agenda (trade reform, exchange rate unification, adjustment of public sector prices, social programs, and the like), but hit total gridlock in its parliamentary agenda, which was absolutely essential to consolidate the reform process and achieve more success on the inflation front and a stronger performance in the external sector.

In order to explain the sluggishness in the implementation of a reform agenda after the quick success at the "cabinet" stage and to understand the political crisis of 1992, one has to go beyond the complex political economy of change. Here, I will suggest only a few elements of analysis.

First and foremost, Acción Democrática, Pérez's party, became the main opposition to the whole process of reform. A very old party, with outdated notions among its leaders and a very traditional, clientelistic approach to politics, it never understood the need for change and felt threatened by the concept of reducing the size of the public sector and curtailing opportunities for discretionary policies. In pursuing wide-ranging reform, one expects to find strong opposition from many sectors of society affected by change, but one needs at least the backing of one's own political base.

The institutional deterioration at different levels of society was a clear factor precipitating the crisis of 1992. This included the four levels of government—the executive, Congress, and the judiciary, the political parties, in addition to (and crucially important, as we found out in 1992) the military. In the case of the latter, it has been clearly documented that the coup attempt was not a spontaneous reaction of the group that launched the "putsch," but a conspiracy hatched over almost a decade within a group that originated at the military academy and that took command of key garrison posts in late 1991. The undetected rise of a putschist group to key positions of command tells much about the weakening in this key Venezuelan institution that was supposedly committed to democracy.

Let me mention also the deterioration of the judicial system. Its partisanship and consequent leniency has represented a major source of instability for Venezuelan democracy. Persistent corruption has sparked complaints over the failure of the judiciary to check it.

A final word about the future. Despite the important setbacks of the last year, I am optimistic about the evolution of Venezuela. After many years and much suffering, Chile is starting to harvest positive results. Mexico, after many years of reform effort, is not there yet. In a historical perspective, the Venezuelan process has just begun, and extraordinary success has been achieved in a short period. The country will get its political act together sooner rather than later because that is the clear will of the majority of the population. Political and economic reform will continue at a relatively rapid pace, and despite the temporary setbacks, Venezuela will find its path to rapid growth and development.

# 7

## ASIA

# Indonesia

IWAN J. AZIS

## Indonesia Since the 1960s: Crises and Reforms

Discussion of economic reforms in Indonesia cannot be detached from the nature of the events and crises that prompted them. Unfortunately, no easy generalizations can be made as to whether any given shock, be it external or internal, constitutes a crisis. Furthermore, reforms have to be viewed from a historical perspective as well as in the context of the country's geography and resources.

The three episodes of economic crisis and response in Indonesia identified in this paper reflect this context. However, most of the discussion focuses on the period of the 1980s; the two earlier episodes of crisis and response will be discussed only briefly.

### The Political and Economic Crisis of the 1960s

The political collapse that accompanied the state of total economic chaos in Indonesia in the 1960s was unquestionably a major crisis. The events of those years resulted in a huge loss of life, placing them in the category of political, economic, and social crises of the first order. Runaway inflation, peaking at 595 percent in 1965, and the apparent decline of per capita income during the early 1960s, could easily have given way to

*Iwan J. Azis is a Visiting Professor at Cornell University and the Director at the IUC (Inter University Center) for Economics at the University of Indonesia. The author is indebted to Emil Salim and M. Sadli for insights into the role of technocrats. Special thanks to Sid Saltzman, Gustav Ranis, and Max Corden for suggested revisions, and to Erik Thorbecke and Wing Thye Woo for extremely helpful suggestions. Comments by an anonymous referee are also acknowledged.*

political upheaval and the resurgence of the Indonesian Communist Party, which was believed at that time to be the strongest Communist party outside the Communist bloc. Microeconomic distortions were myriad, and the corrupt administrative structure created serious economic disarray. The extent of macroeconomic imbalance was also extreme, making it impossible for even the most productive economic sector, the export sector, to grow.

The political and ideological climate during those days favored socialism, albeit of a non-Marxist variety, and a large number of the government's policies were still influenced by the idea of struggle against imperialistic and capitalistic forces and the quest for an egalitarian state. As one senior economist put it, ''. . . the ideological climate in Indonesia [at that time] was probably the same as what prevailed in bygone days in India.''

With the collapse of the old regime in the mid-1960s, new opportunities opened up, and the whole economic policy framework was changed. Having identified monetization of the budget deficit as the major source of the country's extremely high inflation, the new government, with its ''stabilization and rehabilitation'' program announced in 1966, replaced the policy of easy money with a policy of fiscal balance. This bold change was initiated by a group of economists most of whom graduated from the Faculty of Economics of the University of Indonesia and later became known as the ''economic technocrats.''[1]

Given the state of chaos that prevailed during the last few years of the old regime, the reforms introduced immediately after the new government took power naturally enjoyed considerable public support. In this respect, the Indonesian case confirms the ''crisis'' and ''honeymoon'' hypotheses in John Williamson's introductory paper to this volume. Serious resentments were practically never expressed, and the outcomes of the reforms were quite dramatic: the inflation rate dropped to less than 115 percent in 1967 and plunged further to double-digit rates in 1969 (17 percent) and 1973 (19 percent). The neoclassical influence on the reform program was reflected more in its rehabilitation aspects, where efforts were clearly made to allow at least some play to market forces. Output in both the agricultural and the manufacturing sector increased, and GDP growth revived, reaching 9.2 percent in 1970 and 14 percent in 1973.[2]

---

1. This group, under the leadership of Widjojo Nitisastro, was later labeled the ''Berkeley mafia'' by some observers because some of its members had been educated at that university.

2. Different figures for GDP growth may be found in other publications. These numbers are based on my own calculations using a somewhat different method; they are measured at 1983 prices.

## The Balance of Payments Shock of the 1970s: The Pertamina Crisis

Another, later shock, also often labeled a "crisis," stemmed from the overexpansion of nonoil investments by the state oil company Pertamina, following the first oil boom in the mid-1970s. Headed by General Ibnu Sutowo, a close confidant of President Suharto, the company borrowed heavily in the international credit markets, including many short-term loans. When the debt-service burden reached an intolerable level, forcing Pertamina to default, the crisis began to be felt nationwide. As expected, Bank Indonesia, the central bank, had to take over the company's debt; this resulted in a drawdown of foreign reserves, which by September 1975 amounted to only $0.5 billion.

Interestingly enough, the erroneous decision to borrow short-term in the international credit markets was said to be the result of the technocrats' persistence in persuading the president not to allow the company to borrow in the medium-term credit market because of its shaky financial position. The episode was thus the first sign of the president's support for the economic technocrats.

The Pertamina crisis itself was managed by a special team of economic technocrats, and the handling was considered a success. The aftermath of the crisis caused official borrowing to proceed very cautiously with regard to exposure in the short-term credit market.

This crisis was obviously different, both in nature and in scope, from that of the 1960s. Whereas in the earlier episode it was the severity of the crisis itself that, in keeping with the "crisis hypothesis," created the political backing for change, in the Pertamina crisis it was the president's personal support for the views of the economic technocrats that made the difference. This, coupled with the disciplined nature of the reform itself, apparently played a major role in the success of the maneuver. That success reinforced the president's trust in the team of technocrats, strengthening their hand even further.

Certainly, compared with the episode of the 1960s, the Pertamina crisis did not produce a major reform. Indeed, the only reform resulting from the crisis was greater control over Pertamina finances or, more generally, greater discipline of foreign borrowing. No changes in the management superstructure of the other state enterprises were made.

## The Crisis of the 1980s

The crisis of the 1980s was largely propelled by the worldwide economic recession of 1982–83 and by the plunge in oil prices in 1983–86, from almost $30 to less than $10 per barrel. Given that 60 to 70 percent of government and export revenues were generated from the oil sector, the price collapse dramatically affected the Indonesian economy almost across the board.

The government made an immediate and fairly forceful response to this external shock. A series of measures within a wide-ranging stabilization and structural adjustment (SSA) program was introduced, with spectacular results. The stabilization part of the program was reflected in a balanced budget policy, maintained mostly through such austerity measures as budget cuts and the postponement of major industrial projects. On the revenue side, the government moved quickly to mobilize nonoil revenues through a major tax reform.

A new income tax law, enacted in 1984, extended tax coverage and improved collection rates. The new system was designed to avoid excessive income tax rates while enlarging the tax base. The value-added tax (VAT) of 10 percent was introduced in 1985 in the manufacturing and construction sectors and on fuel oils; an additional tax of 10 to 20 percent applied to luxury goods sold in domestic markets. The new value-added tax basically replaced the old sales tax, in the expectation that it would avoid taxation of full value at each stage of the production chain. Excessive use of tax incentives to achieve particular objectives (e.g., tax holidays) was also discontinued.

The tax reforms dramatically reversed the shares of oil and nonoil receipts in the budget. In the first two years of the tax reform, the main increase in nonoil revenues was due to the VAT. In the following years, income and land tax revenues also increased, resulting in a dramatic jump in total nonoil revenues of around 30 percent from the 1987–88 period to the 1989–90 period. As can be seen in table 1, the annual rate of growth of nonoil revenues increased sharply, from 16.5 percent during the prereform period to more than 20 percent during the reform period. The VAT and the income tax remain today the two major sources of government revenues aside from the oil tax.

The tax reform was also meant to enhance the efficiency of the tax system. The government's efforts resulted in an increase in the number of registered taxpayers (doubling for VAT and more than doubling for the income tax), and an increase in the number of tax returns submitted.

Along with these steps, civil service employee salaries were frozen for at least three consecutive years. Obviously this move was politically very difficult, but it was implemented without serious resistance from any pressure groups.

Reforms within the context of the stabilization program were also made in monetary policy. During the oil boom, monetary policy had been based primarily on two mechanisms: credit ceilings and interest rate controls for state banks, which were major players in the financial market at that time. The government also had determined that subsidized interest rates were necessary for some high-priority sectors. While the policy was effective in limiting credit expansion in certain sectors, in general the banking system suffered from considerable excess liquidity due to the augmented net foreign assets prompted by the two oil booms,

## Table 1 Indonesia: selected economic indicators during periods of external shock and policy reform, 1980–90[a]
(percentages except where noted)

| | Prereform period, 1980–83 | External shocks and early reform period, 1983–86 | Active reform period, 1986–90 |
|---|---|---|---|
| Economic growth | | | |
| Gross domestic product | 3.2 | 5.1 | 6.4 |
| Oil | –4.3 | 3.3 | 2.5 |
| Nonoil | 5.2 | 5.6 | 7.4 |
| Gross domestic income | 4.1 | 3.7 | 6.1 |
| Growth by sector | | | |
| Agriculture | 2.6 | 3.7 | 3.4 |
| Mining | –4.4 | 0.4 | 1.8 |
| Manufacturing | 3.6 | 14.0 | 11.0 |
| Construction | 6.1 | 0.1 | 10.0 |
| Electricity | 18.9 | 11.0 | 14.0 |
| Services | 8.2 | 5.8 | 7.4 |
| Consumption expenditures | 7.2 | 2.7 | 5.3 |
| Private | 7.5 | 2.4 | 5.3 |
| Government | 5.5 | 4.6 | 5.2 |
| Gross capital formation | 6.6 | 3.2 | 11.6 |
| Private | 16.1 | 4.1 | 15.2 |
| Government | –2.9 | 1.9 | 5.0 |
| Exports of goods and services[b] | –8.8 | 4.2 | 7.8 |
| Imports of goods and services[b] | 9.7 | 0.5 | 4.3 |
| Merchandise exports[c] | –1.2 | –11.2 | 14.8 |
| Oil | 0.9 | –19.9 | 7.8 |
| Nonoil | –6.8 | 9.2 | 22.1 |
| Merchandise imports[c] | 14.7 | –13.1 | 17.4 |
| Oil | 33.3 | –35.6 | 15.0 |
| Nonoil | 10.3 | –7.6 | 17.7 |

# Table 1 Indonesia: selected economic indicators during periods of external shock and policy reform, 1980–90[a]
(percentages except where noted)   (Continued)

| | Prereform period, 1980–83 | External shocks and early reform period, 1983–86 | Active reform period, 1986–90 |
|---|---|---|---|
| Money supply (current prices) | | | |
| M2 | 23.9 | 23.5 | 32.3 |
| M1 | 14.8 | 15.4 | 19.6 |
| Claims by monetary authorities (current prices) | 26.9 | 20.7 | 13.8 |
| Government budget (current prices) | 13.8 | 9.9 | 18.9 |
| Nonoil revenues | 16.5 | 25.8 | 21.5 |
| Oil revenues | 10.0 | –2.5 | 13.1 |
| Loans | 26.4 | 14.6 | 23.9 |
| Development expenditures | 10.7 | 7.0 | 15.2 |
| Oil price (dollars) | 0.0 | –22.7 | 13.0 |
| Devaluation (rupiah per dollar) | 13.2 | 12.1 | 9.5 |
| Inflation | 11.2 | 4.9 | 8.3 |
| Share of population living below poverty line[d] | | | |
| Urban | 12.1 | 7.3 | 7.3 |
| Rural | 39.4 | 26.8 | 20.8 |
| Total | 33.0 | 21.7 | 16.7 |
| Gini coefficient[d] | 0.331 | 0.321 | 0.319 |

a. Figures are annual rates of growth except where noted.

b. In local currency terms at constant 1983 prices.

c. In dollar terms.

d. For 1984, 1987, and 1990.

*Sources*: CBS, Indonesian Central Bank, and World Bank.

and by uncontrolled liquidity credits (*kredit likuiditas*) to many high-priority sectors. The dominant state banks remained plagued by inefficiency and were unable to accumulate deposits from the private sector because of the controlled interest rate.[3] The excess of funds being created in the banking system had an adverse effect on the country's balance of payments position.

The plunge in oil prices led to a shortfall in government revenues and balance of payments deficits. This, in turn, constrained the interest spreads of Indonesian banks and forced the government to promulgate monetary and financial reforms in June 1983. These reforms were aimed at dismantling the old system of monetary control, replacing it with a more indirect approach based on reserve management through open market operations. In 1984, a new monetary instrument, the Sertifikat Bank Indonesia (SBI), was introduced, followed by the issuance of promissory notes, known as Surat Berharga Pasar Uang (SBPU), in early 1985. The SBI is a debt certificate that may be used by the central bank to reclaim its share of net foreign assets and to create government debt instruments, to secure greater control over reserves.

Although the new financial mechanism was able to cover only the equivalent of 20 percent of reserves, it did prove effective when the government needed to act quickly in response to a serious financial crisis. The "Sumarlin shock" of 1986 was a good example. Fueled by rumors of impending devaluation, signs of capital flight became visible during that period. The economic technocrats, led by Minister Sumarlin, took action by calling in SBPUs before maturity and persuading state banks to buy SBIs. Naturally, this move triggered a surge in the interest rate (upon the announcement, interbank rates soared to 40 percent), but at the same time it indicated that the government had policy measures other than devaluation at its disposal to discourage capital flight.

Meanwhile the government took a strong stance on maintaining the stability of exchange rates and domestic prices. This prudent and persistent policy has paid off. Inflation remains very much under control in single digits (table 1), resulting in a stable real exchange rate and greater competitiveness. Remarkably enough, control of inflation was achieved without giving up much in terms of economic growth: GDP rose on average by 5.1 and 6.4 percent per year during 1983–86 and 1986–90, respectively.

The structural adjustment aspects of the SSA program were designed to move the country toward a more outward-oriented development strategy. Using various deregulation measures, the government aimed at an improvement of national efficiency through greater reliance on market forces. The spirit of the deregulation policy was to promote the

---

3. Many of the state banks were dependent on captive markets, notably the state-owned enterprises.

fostering of internal dynamics in the domestic economy by removing structural rigidities.

One may wonder why, in a country as large as Indonesia, the technocrats emphasized the export-oriented strategy more than the reforms targeted at the domestic market. The usual argument stresses the nonproductive quality of the domestic market and lower domestic purchasing power compared with the international market. Another, no-less-common argument holds that competitive pressures from abroad are necessary to raise the efficiency of various sectors in the economy. Too many obstacles, including those of a political nature, persist when the ballgame is contained within the country (e.g., under a strategy based on import substitution).[4] But perhaps the strongest justification relates to the fact that the increasing debt payments left the government no option but to earn more foreign exchange.[5] Given the fall in oil prices in 1986 and the uncertainty of future prices, nonoil exports were the logical alternative.

Two major devaluations were implemented, in March 1983 (28 percent) and September 1986 (31 percent).[6] The resulting increase in nonoil exports has been dramatic. In only six years, nonoil exports almost tripled, from $5 billion in 1983 to $14.4 billion in 1990, and their share of total exports rose from 25 percent to 56 percent. This implies annual growth rates of nonoil exports of 9.2 and 22.1 percent during 1983–86 and 1986–90, respectively (table 1). It is believed that, at least for the 1987–88 period, the impact of the devaluations was greater than that of the trade deregulation promulgated in May 1986 (see Azis 1992b, 15).

Although the system of monopoly importing rights remained in place after the 1986 reforms, a series of measures to liberalize trade were adopted. A number of tariff categories were cut, and rates were reduced across the board. Import restrictions were lifted on a wide range of

4. Japan, for example, has a long history of using outside pressures to enhance the efficiency of the domestic economy.

5. By 1990, the total external debt of Indonesia reached $67.9 billion, $9.4 billion of which was "private nonguaranteed" debt (World Bank 1992). Debt-service flows in that year were already quite alarming: $4.1 billion for repayment of principal and $2.5 billion in interest payments for long-term public and publicly guaranteed external capital. For the private nonguaranteed debt the corresponding figures are $1 billion and $0.5 billion. These obligations, coupled with increasing deficits on current account and the expectation of increased scarcity of external funding, gave the export-oriented strategy much stronger leverage.

6. After 1978 the exchange rate was no longer fixed at 415 rupiahs to the dollar. The introduction of a "managed floating" system in that year inevitably required a major adjustment of the prevailing overvalued rate; hence, the devaluation in 1978 took place at the same time as the emergence of a more market-determined exchange rate system. Interestingly enough, the decision was unrelated to, and to some extent was not in accordance with, the advice of the IMF. In fact, since the 1960s, Indonesia has never had the need to submit to IMF conditionality.

products, and the import licensing system was revamped. Further relaxations of investment restrictions and other efforts to create a more favorable investment climate were made systematically.

The overall results of these efforts have been very encouraging. Along with the boost from other demand components, the liberalization measures accelerated economic growth, which reached more than 7 percent in 1989 and 1990. In fact, as already described, during the whole of the post-reform period the country has enjoyed an average growth rate of more than 6 percent (table 1).

Trends in other selected variables are also depicted in table 1. Table 2 lists the various reforms implemented in the 1980s and the purpose of each. In general, the SSA program, designed to respond to the external shocks of the 1980s, has been a success for Indonesia, at least as viewed from its repercussions upon macroeconomic trends.[7]

## The Preconditions and Reasons for Effective Reform

Many of the measures taken in response to the crisis of the 1980s were bold and drastic, and, as one would expect, the social impacts were enormous. Indeed, in the early period of reforms, open unemployment increased considerably, particularly in the urban areas, although this was due in part to rural-urban migration. The freeze on government employees' salaries and the austere budget constraints caused a drop in domestic purchasing power, one result of which has been a decline in manufacturing profits. The real earnings of urban workers have fallen, especially in the construction and services sectors, and including in the informal sector.

Although all these repercussions took place only during the early reform period, one may wonder how a series of pro-market reforms was able to survive in the mid-1980s and to the present day without serious challenge. To many observers, the success of the Indonesian economic reforms of the 1980s is even more puzzling, given that a number of economic nationalists, in the army and in civilian groups (including the business sector), hold influential positions both in and out of government, and would theoretically oppose a more liberal and open economic policy. Furthermore, Indonesia has a long history of separatism and regional rebellions. Although the history in each region is different, in general there is always a sense of alienation among regions outside Java,

---

7. Some observers view the Indonesian case as unique, in that liberalization did not follow the standard path of current account followed by capital account liberalization. In fact, since the end of the 1960s, Indonesia has had a free foreign exchange system, making it easy for badly needed foreign capital (investments in oil and other natural resources, as well as foreign aid and loans) to flow into the country.

## Table 2    Indonesia: summary of economic reforms, 1983–90

| Reform | Contents | Repercussions |
|---|---|---|
| **Fiscal** | | |
| 1983–84 | Postponement of large-scale and capital-intensive projects | Reduced pressures on government budget |
| | Reduction of subsidies on fuel and rice | |
| April 1984 | Introduction of value-added tax | Increased coverage, collection rates, and government revenues |
| | Rationalization of income tax | |
| | Additional 10 to 20 percent tax on luxury goods | Reduced tax bargaining |
| | Removal of withholding tax | |
| | Improvement of tax administration and apparatus | |
| 1986 | Introduction of new property tax at a single rate of 0.5 percent | Slight increase in property tax revenues |
| | Introduction of new law on stamp duties | Reduced number of transactions involving stamp duties |
| | Subsidy on fertilizers and pesticides reduced | Further reduction of pressures on government budget |
| | Efficiency of government agencies in implementing development projects increased | Increased efficiency |
| | Suspension of carrying unspent development funds over to next year (SLAP) | |
| 1987 | Further reductions in capital expenditures | Strong relief in budget constraints |
| | Restraints of subsidies and administrative cost | |
| **Financial** | | |
| March 1983 | Devaluation of rupiah by 28 percent | Improved export competitiveness |
| June 1983 | Credit ceilings removed | Rise in deposit rate |
| | Interest rate controls removed | Liquidity credits still increased |
| | Subsidized liquidity credit reduced | Fall in cost of intermediation |
| | SBI and SBPU introduced (see text) | |
| 1983–84 | Jakarta Stock Exchange activated | Trade in stocks occurs below par value |
| | Opening of bond market | |
| 1985 | Capital Market Executive Board (BAPEPAM) initiates further reformand reduces requirement for new  issues (to Rp 200 million) | Some commercial banks receive underwriting privileges for stock and bond issues |
| September 1986 | Devaluation of rupiah by 31 percent | Increased export competitiveness |

| Reform | Contents | Repercussions |
|---|---|---|
| October 1986 | Ceiling on swaps removed | Increased swap trading |
| December 1987 | Capital market deregulation | Increase in capital market activity |
| | Stock purchase allowed to foreigners | |
| | Establishment of a secondary over-the-counter market | |
| October 1988 | Lending limit regulation | Many banks and joint ventures emerged |
| | Reserve requirement lowered | Intense competition between banks |
| | Licenses for new banks and joint ventures | Interest rates soar |
| | More competition allowed between commercial and state banks | Signs of fall in interest rate spread |
| | Easier branching for existing domestic and foreign banks allowed | |
| November 1988 | Reform of the currency market | More market-based swap rate |
| December 1988 | Deregulation of insurance industry | Significant increase in market activity |
| | Further capital market deregulation | Increased market index |
| | Rationalization of financial services sector (including foreign) | Many companies going public |
| **Trade** | | |
| March 1985 | Reduction in number of tariff levels | Increased efficiency and import flows |
| | Reduction of tariff ceiling | |
| April 1985 | Swiss survey firm assigned to manage customs | Early positive psychological effects |
| | Port charges reduced | Reduced inefficiencies in shipping, port handling, and customs procedures |
| | Shipping industry opened to international competition | Increased export competitiveness |
| | Port administration simplified | |
| May 1986 | Introduction of duty drawback system to "producer-exporters" | Clear signs of export increase along with augmented foreign investments |
| October 1986 | Import licensing reduced | Further increase in export-oriented investments |
| | Tariffication | Increase in necessary (nonconsumption) imports |
| | Further tariff reduction | |
| January 1987 | Further reduction in import licensing | Same as in October 1986 |

# Table 2 Indonesia: summary of economic reforms, 1983–90
## (Continued)

| Reform | Contents | Repercussions |
| --- | --- | --- |
| July 1987 | Still further reduction in import licensing with no tariff increase | Same as in October 1986 |
| | System of textile quota allocation improved | |
| November 1988 | Inter-island shipping deregulated | Increased competition |
| | Removal of monopolies in imports of steel and plastic | Increased confidence in government efforts to deregulate the economy |
| May 1990 | Deregulation in pharmaceuticals and animal husbandry | Increased competition |
| | Adjustment in tariffs | Improved investment climate |
| | Reduction in number of surcharges | |
| | Further removal of nontariff barriers | |
| **Investment** | | |
| 1985 | Simplification of application procedures for foreign investment | Reduction in waiting period and number of documents |
| May 1986 | Allowance of 95 percent foreign ownership in export-oriented investments | Increased exports and further increased investment |
| | Local distribution opened to export-oriented firms | Japanese department store "SOGO" opened |
| | Export credit scheme opened for participation by joint ventures | Increased confidence in the economy |
| | Retail trade opened to foreign firms | |
| 1986 | One-year tax exemption on imported equipment | Enthusiastic response from foreign investors |
| | Visa requirements from 29 countries lifted | |
| | Investment from Eastern European countries no longer needs intelligence approval | |
| September 1986 | Maxi devaluation (More than 30 percent) | Increased export competitiveness |
| July 1987 | Deregulation of investment and capacity licensing | Improved investment climate |
| | Stock exchange opened to foreign investors | |
| November 1988 | Further deregulation in shipping industry | Increased competition |
| | Joint ventures allowed to distribute their own products domestically | |
| May 1989 | Replacement of priority list with negative list | Improved investment climate further |

| Reform | Contents | Repercussions |
| --- | --- | --- |
| June 1989 | Attempts to improve efficiency of state enterprises | Some state enterprises showed improved efficiency |
| | Encourage privatization | Increased signs of more "going public" |
| 1989 | Foreign portfolio investors allowed to purchase 49 percent of nonbank companies listed on stock exchanges | Improved foreign confidence in the economy |
| November 1989 | Steps to improve performance of state enterprises | 186 out of 210 state enterprises affected |
| | Specific steps to improve efficiency in 75 enterprises | Sales of equity in 52 state enterprises |
| | | Mergers of joint ventures in 59 state enterprises |
| 1990 | Up to 30 percent of shares of three large state cement enterprises offered to public | Increased expectations of further privatization |

not only because the economy's center of gravity is in Java, but also because the administration frequently has been dominated by the Javanese. Therefore, it is legitimate to ask how economic reforms affect interregional imbalances in a large, ethnically diverse, archipelagic country such as Indonesia.

Then there is the question of the type of reform being undertaken. Any crisis demands a response, but there is no general precept that the response will be of a pro-market type. In fact, unlike the economic reforms of the 1980s, the response to the two preceding crises, especially that of the 1970s, did not reflect a strong move toward reliance on market forces. The reaction to an economic crisis can go either in a pro- or an anti-market direction.

## The Key Role of the Technocrats and the President's Support

Political institutions in Indonesia are such that they can be used by an *effective* government to steer policy direction (including economic reform) in either of these two ways. There is no strong system of checks and balances between executive, legislative, and judicial powers. Serious ideological controversies are absent as well, and civil society is not organized to the same extent as, for example, in Latin America. On the other hand, there is a strong consensus on the need to put a priority on economic development.

Because of its longevity (from 1966 until the present), the government of President Suharto is unquestionably very effective. The policy direction proposed in the 1980s was to reform the economy using pro-market mechanisms. This recommendation came from a group of people that have also been effective in the political arena, namely, the economic technocrats. The analytical capabilities of this group are superb, and more importantly they possess a talent for selecting policy changes that recognize the political and other noneconomic constraints. The technocrats' approach is pragmatic, professionally based, and little influenced by party politics and ideology.

The shared views and persistent courage of the economic technocrats under the leadership of Widjojo Nitisastro, former economic and planning minister and now a senior government adviser, have been the economic team's primary source of strength and the reason why its reforms have gone practically unchallenged. The concrete outcomes of their strategy—a rising standard of living together with sustained rapid growth and low inflation, an evident reduction in poverty, and the enhancement of infrastructure throughout the country—have further strengthened the standing of the economic technocrats in the political arena.

However, to contend that the work of the technocrats is the only factor in Indonesia's success story would be an exaggeration. Without other supporting factors the story would undeniably have been different. The economic team has received the full support of the president since the very early days of the new government. In a heterogeneous and at the same time paternalistic society such as in Indonesia, this factor is of utmost importance. When very difficult economic decisions have to be made, it is only the president's blessing that allows them to be successfully implemented.

Many of the policy measures taken in the 1980s were certainly not easy to implement. Nevertheless, after conducting careful analyses, some with a fair degree of sophistication, the technocrats made their case to the president using straightforward economic arguments. These were often accepted by the president, and the proposals were subsequently put forth with no serious challenge in the Parliament. The full support of the president, as in the Pertamina crisis, has been the prime reason for the effective implementation of the reforms.

The drastic "Sumarlin shock" in 1986 and the fiscal austerity program implemented in anticipation of falling oil prices during the mid-1980s are examples of unpopular decisions that originated with the economic technocrats. It was difficult to bypass several vested interests, but the initiatives were believed necessary to stabilize the financial sector of the country. Here too the blessing of the president strengthened the implementation of some difficult decisions.

Another example was the courageous decision of the technocrats to devalue the currency in 1983 and 1986.[8] This decision originally encountered great resentment among some interest groups, but the devaluations were implemented anyway, and with only very minor disturbances. The economic consequences were positive: export growth accelerated while inflation was kept at the single-digit level. Robust export performance has also helped improve the living standard of many Indonesian farmers through greater competitiveness of their export crops. Hence, poverty was reduced and the anticipated worsening of the income distribution due to the reform was averted. The floating exchange rate regime has also been well-managed. From the time the first reform was introduced (in the banking and monetary sector in June 1983), the inflation rate has been kept below the two-digit level, except in 1984.

Then there was the Pertamina case. As previously discussed, a team of some influential economic technocrats, again with the president's support, undertook a bold financial rescue of Pertamina in 1975, when the company was on the brink of bankruptcy. It should be noted that the company was headed by General Sutowo, who is a close confidant of the president.

Thus, it is clear that the economic technocrats have enjoyed the president's full confidence, without which many tough economic decisions could not have been implemented. The backing of the president was also of crucial importance in implementing the SSA program during the 1980s.[9]

The basis of the president's confidence can be traced to a specific event: a 1966 seminar, called the Seminar Angkatan Darat, at which the economists who later would serve as technocrats were active participants. They managed to impress the president with their bold proposals, even though these made less of a bow to political susceptibilities than those broached by other groups, at least in the first stage. Although one could argue whether such an approach was indeed less political, the "straight economics" character of the technocrats' proposals is viewed even today as one of the group's hallmarks.[10]

---

8. Prior to each devaluation, the government would announce its forecast of the balance of payments position, and especially of the expected size of the current account deficit. Their predictions of large deficits on these occasions might permit one to argue that the technocrats were attempting to engineer a "pseudo-crisis."

9. At least three technocrats have directly confirmed this in separate private conversations with the author.

10. Emil Salim, Minister of Environment and Population and an economics professor at the University of Indonesia, is one of the most dynamic of the government's technocrats and is very popular among students, even those who are strongly critical of the government. Salim once told me that, in almost all cabinet discussions involving economic decisions, the technocrats have always tried to maintain the "straight economics" (his own term) approach.

Another illustration is worth mentioning. In the deliberations over the 1993–94 budget, there were extensive discussions about the possibility of eliminating subsidies for fuel. It was realized that such a move would likely induce an increase in domestic fuel prices and thus contribute to inflation. And, as expected, various interest groups have strongly opposed the proposal. However, by making their case in terms of "straight economic" arguments that are appealing to the public, the technocrats succeeded in making the 1993–94 budget the first to eliminate fuel subsidies entirely. Thus, another battle for the liberalization of the economy has been won.

The increase in the price level, it appears, however, was taken into account before the decision to remove the fuel subsidies was made. Indeed, the following argument was offered. The inflation rate for 1992 was at an all-time low (less than 5 percent). Further inflationary pressures from the fuel price hike in 1993 would, therefore, still enable the government to expect a one-digit inflation rate, a range considered harmless for pursuing prudent macroeconomic policy. However, judging from the sharp increase in the inflation rate for January 1993 (almost 3 percent, suggesting a yearly average well into double digits), special efforts to maintain low inflation are certainly needed. Thus, while there is no doubt that the technocrats are masters of the art of winning political arguments (in this case to remove subsidies), they often face a situation where, by winning one battle, they end up facing another problem.

Interestingly, the same budget also raised civil servants' salaries, providing another potential source of inflationary pressure. To offset these pressures, or at least those transmitted via expectations, the salary increase was disguised by calling it "changes in the salary structure." As deceiving a tactic as this may appear to be, and however limited the impact would be, past experience suggests that such a maneuver can be effective.[11] The removal of subsidies in fact is often found to be the best solution in a straightforward, unconstrained optimization exercise. Hence, a complex calculation and the corresponding economic analysis (not merely based on psychological and other noneconomic factors) was surely conducted prior to the decision. With foreign debt payments ballooning to almost half of all routine expenditures, and with stagnant inflows of foreign loans, it is only appropriate to slash all government-funded subsidies.

---

11. One cannot neglect the important role of the mass media and other forms of public relations in forming a favorable public opinion. As is easily observed, over time, more open and critical views toward monopolies and other types of distortions are increasingly expressed by growing numbers of media commentators. Intellectuals and scholars often voice similar concerns through various forums (seminars, conferences, workshops, interviews, etc). To a certain extent, this criticism can help alleviate the burden on the technocrats in their struggle to eradicate distortions and protection in some sectors of the economy.

From this review of the various policies taken in response to the economic crisis in Indonesia, John Williamson's hypothesis that "the existence of a team of economists with a common, coherent view of what is needed to be done and commanding the instruments of concentrated executive authority" seems unquestionably to apply in the Indonesian case. The pragmatic approach of Indonesia's team of economic technocrats has certainly won the support of the public and the president.

In fact, the same pragmatism can be detected in the early history of the Suharto regime. The regime has been faithful to the 1945 Constitution decree, which declared that the national economy should be organized in a cooperative way, in contrast to unbridled laissez-faire competition. And in fact the new regime has always deliberately avoided speaking in terms of "embracing capitalism and abandoning socialism."

## The Indonesian Reforms in Light of the Williamson Hypotheses

Several hypotheses have been proposed as to the preconditions for successful reform and to explain how a country can mobilize and maintain the necessary political support for reform. Naturally, none of these hypotheses can be either unambiguously confirmed or rejected in the case of Indonesia.

Although some may argue that the policy package introduced by the team of economists installed in the late 1960s already constituted "economic reforms," this is true only if "reform" is defined in a very broad and somewhat ambiguous way, as denoting any change in government policy designed to alter economic activity. The term could cover, for example, changes in administrative procedures and in institutional structure, in addition to standard economic policy changes. Such a definition fails to specify whether the reform is more focused on stabilization or structural adjustment, or both. Under such a broad definition, one can maintain without any hesitation that there was indeed a major reform in the late 1960s. It could be argued further that the reform was deliberately designed in response to a perceived crisis (economic as well as political), and hence is an illustration of the "crisis hypothesis" at work. In fact, the crisis of the 1960s was the most traumatic of the three examined here; it even threatened the existence of the nation.

The economic technocrats during that period were kept busy, and were even obsessed, by the goal of slowing the country's runaway inflation, which plagued the economy and depressed the living conditions of most of the population. They confronted the task by balancing the budget (inclusive of receipts of foreign aid) in order to prevent the budget from being a major source of money creation. However, given the absence of an appropriate institutional setting and effectively functioning administrative procedures, and given the enormous amount of capital required, the task was unquestionably very difficult.[12] Yet the record of the technocrats in controlling inflation was impressive. In a relatively short period of time, inflation dropped to low double digits.

The "crisis" that prevailed in the 1980s was different, and certainly much less severe. It was propelled by external shocks, inflation did not reach triple digits, infrastructure conditions were already better than in the 1960s, and a stable institutional structure and administrative procedures were in place, as were many other necessary conditions for sustained development. The severity of the worldwide economic recession in the early 1980s, followed by the plunge in oil prices over the 1983–86 period, certainly did not match the crisis of the 1960s. In this respect, acceptance of the "crisis hypothesis" for the 1980s events is still justified, but much less than for the phenomena of the 1960s.

What is interesting to observe is that, while the crisis in the 1980s was by no means of traumatic proportions, the nature and scope of the response were far more extensive, spawning a series of trade and industrial policy reforms. One speculation is that there was a pent-up pressure for comprehensive reform in the 1980s, and the economic technocrats had clearly undergone a learning process over the course of time.

It is less clear that the "honeymoon hypothesis" applies to the Indonesian reforms of the 1980s. There has been no "new team of economic policymakers" in Indonesia since the late 1960s. True, there was a period when a group of special advisers to the president, the "Aspri" (from *asisten pribadi*, which translated literally means "private assistants"), held a crucial role in shaping various strategies. These individuals were not always in agreement with the views of the economic technocrats, but the strategies they advised mostly, although not exclusively, pertained to the political arena. In economic matters the strategies they advocated were too general to reverse, or even affect, those championed by the economic technocrats. The Aspri are also known to be more inclined toward "operations"—that is, toward individual, ad hoc measures than toward articulating an alternative economic system.

There was, of course, something of a honeymoon between the technocrats and the political forces supporting the New Order, which included students, the media, and the armed forces (and in particular the army),

---

12. One of the technocrats who twice held ministerial positions (labor and mining), M. Sadli, who also designed the investment laws that prompted the inflow of foreign capital in the early 1970s, once indicated that the enormous problems faced by the former Soviet Union and other former socialist countries in transition today are quite similar to the Indonesian case in the late 1960s. Nothing could be done properly without immense flows of foreign capital. The main difference is perhaps that Indonesia, under the old regime, was not a completely centrally planned command economy. Private enterprises and other institutions characterizing a mixed economic system were already present in Indonesia, even during the early postwar period.

especially during the early stage. Yet, with the exception of the armed forces,[13] the relationship fluctuates. For example, the honeymoon between the technocrats and the 1966 students' movement petered out after the Malari affair in 1974. Some members of the media are also increasingly critical of the government's policy direction, although in general the relationship between the technocrats and the media has been mutually supportive.[14] The increasingly significant role of engineers in the cabinet (discussed in the next section) has led to a rather different view about development policy in general, and this has recently been reflected in media coverage.

The absence of opposition, however, should not be exaggerated. It is certainly not true that the SSA program went totally unchallenged by those inclined toward a populist macroeconomic policy. The usual allegation is that the SSA program favors growth at the expense of equity—a classic trade-off argument. However, this claim is unsupported by the data. Several studies found, at least during the early years of the SSA program, no sign of a worsening income distribution (Thorbecke et al. 1992a). A simple Gini coefficient actually shows a slight improvement in income distribution (table 1), from 0.321 in 1987 to 0.319 in 1990.[15]

The poverty figures also have been encouraging. The proportion of the population living below the poverty line declined from 33.0 percent in 1984 to 21.7 percent in 1987, and to 16.7 percent in 1990 (table 1; the figures are based on a head count index using World Bank estimates).[16] This achievement is primarily due to the persistent allocation of public expenditures to infrastructure and to other social overhead capital that surely benefit the middle- and lower-income groups, including the rural population.[17] A government program known as Inpres played perhaps the most important role in this regard. Despite the existence of ad hoc criteria for the allocation of some Inpres categories among the country's 27 provinces, implying the need for further improvement, this government program has become the major impetus for averting a worsening

---

13. The armed forces have always been given the responsibility of securing and protecting development policies and the outcomes of the New Order's initiatives.

14. There is perhaps only one exception, namely, the *Merdeka* daily newspaper. This is not hard to understand, since the paper is considered a remnant of the old Indonesian Nationalist Party (PNI), which has a strongly nationalist ideology.

15. However, this index ought to be read with caution, since the data source used (the SUSENAS socioeconomic survey) is plagued by a severe underestimation of incomes among the high-income group. See Azis (1992a).

16. However, using different assumptions, one can come up with a slightly higher number for poverty incidence for 1990 (see Azis 1992a).

17. An alternative political calculation that has worked to the benefit of reform in Indonesia is the fact that, in the wake of the traumatic events in the 1960s, the government has been continually careful to pay attention to the needs of the rural population.

of income distribution and poverty conditions during and after the economic reform. In a study utilizing the 1985 input-output table, I have found that Indonesia's outward-oriented strategy, compared with the alternative strategy of import substitution, is far more favorable to employment creation (Azis 1989b).

It has also been shown that the SSA program is capable of generating a wider dispersal of investments throughout the country. Thus, the fear of alienation among the regions outside Java has gradually abated. However, judging from the trend during the early years of the reform, the SSA program also appears to reinforce the concentration of export activities on the crowded island of Java, mainly because of the island's relatively superior infrastructure (Azis 1992b). It is expected that these conflicting outcomes will disappear as various deregulations begin to take effect in many regions outside Java. Moreover, the maintenance of a competitive exchange rate will strengthen further the position of the export-oriented farm sector in the outer islands.

Hence, while the point should not be exaggerated, opposition to the policy course is indeed fragmented and, in general, weak. Some of those who were regular critics in the past have even jumped on the bandwagon, militating for further deregulation and pleading for the removal of monopoly powers and other protectionist policies that remain. Cynical observers may charge that these people have merely been co-opted. Other opponents, some of whom attempted to amalgamate economic reform with greater political democracy, likewise receive no popular support, mainly because it is still fresh in everybody's mind that the economic strategy during the period of liberal pluralistic democracy (in the 1950s) was ineffective. The exuberance of the democratic politics of those years led to undisciplined and disorderly conditions that were inimical to development.

At present, the political parties other than the government party, Golkar, do not have an alternative strategy that can capture widespread popular support.[18] It is no overstatement to assert that the views of the various parties are converging—or at least are no longer diametrically opposed. In this respect, a sort of consensus has emerged.

Some have also maintained that an important part of the success of the Indonesian economic reforms relates to the fact that the reforms were undertaken before the actual crisis arrived (see, for example, Bourguignon and Morrisson 1992). If this is true, it is not too difficult to understand why the reforms were also easier to implement, since room to maneuver is more ample when reforms are taken prior to the crisis.

---

18. During the 1992 election, the Indonesian Democratic Party (PDI) offered a series of economic proposals that many believe were the result of serious and sincere effort. However, for whatever reason—perhaps the proposals' heavily microeconomic rather than macroeconomic agenda—the PDI's plan was never considered as an alternative to the SSA program.

However, I am not convinced that this was indeed the case. It is true, for example, that a range of policy reforms were implemented before oil prices hit their lowest level in August 1986. However, the decline in oil prices had begun in 1983, immediately following the worldwide recession. Indonesia's policymakers undoubtedly did anticipate still lower oil prices, but to assert that policy reforms were taken long before, or even independently of, the crisis is certainly an exaggeration. The hypothesis that the technocrats actually introduced a "pseudo-crisis" is perhaps easier to believe than the hypothesis of precrisis reform. Nonetheless, the unprecedentedly high quality of economic reforms in Indonesia cannot be discounted, whether the reforms were undertaken before or during the crisis.

Finally, the severity of the crisis certainly suggests some reasons why the reforms were effective and largely unchallenged. Whereas the financial rescue of Pertamina, in particular, was made possible through the president's support of the economic technocrats, the handling of the crises in the 1960s and 1980s unquestionably had something to do with the nature and extent of the deteriorating economic conditions during those times.

## Market Reform and the Role of Foreign Capital and Advisers

Although it is true that the economic technocrats were by no means free-market ideologues, the policy direction that emerged in response to the crisis of the 1980s was clearly pro-market. Some government interventions were condoned, as long as they were market compatible.[19] Hence, the technocrats' position on the role of the state is more or less clear. Maintaining such a position should, at least in principle, imply a certain degree of compatibility with the emerging ideas of market reform. It would also be difficult to envision the alluring performance of the economy without contemplating the role of external funding. Some of these issues are discussed below.

Ideas about pro-market reforms in Indonesia in fact began to spread long before such reforms were actually put in place. One former economic minister recalls that, in the late 1970s, the idea of market reform was already being discussed quite extensively, albeit privately, among economic policymakers. In their judgment, however, the timing was not propitious. It should be recalled that, in the 1970s, Indonesia experienced two episodes of oil boom (1974 and 1979), so that a sense of urgency for reform was not really present. The technocrats fully realized

---

19. The continued operation of Bulog, the government body that controls the price of rice and other basic commodities, as well as the presence of state-owned enterprises (*badan usaha milik negara*) in various sectors reflects policymakers' recognition of the need for state intervention in some areas.

that the choice would not be well received politically, and that support from the president also would be difficult to obtain.

## The Importance of Foreign Investment

The first and, perhaps, foremost idea is concerned with what, precisely, should be the role of external funding in the process of development. In this regard, the economic technocrats have fully recognized, from the beginning, the link between foreign aid and private foreign investment. The 1966–67 law on foreign investment strongly reflected that recognition. With the objective of attracting foreign capital inflows, a series of incentives (and disincentives) were introduced. In 1969, the system of foreign exchange controls was abolished, making the rupiah completely convertible at market rates. The idea was to attract capital repatriation by making capital transfers easier and lawful—tax authorities asked no questions about the origin of repatriated funds. In addition, a set of fiscal incentives and duty exemptions was introduced. To break the fear of nationalization, the provision of legal protection was made.

But perhaps the most interesting case was the implementation of an open capital account system as early as in 1969. Recognizing the need for foreign investment in oil and other sectors based on the country's abundant resources, Indonesia liberalized its capital account long before the SSA program was begun in the 1980s, and at a time when the current account remained full of protection and distortions. In this sense, Indonesia did not follow the usually prescribed sequence for liberalization. One consequence is that the government is constantly under pressure to maintain a competitive real exchange rate. This partly explains the persistently jittery policy toward inflationary pressure on the part of Indonesian policymakers.

At any rate, all the efforts paid off. Foreign direct investment inflows as recorded in the capital account turned positive after at least three years in a row of persistent outflows (1966–68). Other factors also attracted foreign investors, including the country's wealth of natural resources and, later, the low cost of labor. Following the first oil boom in 1974 (which of course was an oil crisis for neighboring oil-consuming countries), a strong import substitution strategy was implemented. All of a sudden, the domestic market became potentially attractive. To make sure this factor worked in the face of low purchasing power, the government mostly granted investors' requests for protection from competing imports. A similar practice was later extended to domestic investors, and thus began the heyday of infant-industry protection; so, too, began the process of industrialization.

There is no doubt that foreign investment helped propel the country's economic growth, which in turn allowed foreign financing to become available on easier terms. Indonesia's lack of ideological aversion toward foreign investment facilitated its continued inflow, which continues to the present. The requirement that the government control the country's natural resources and those economic activities considered important for the livelihood of society at large (as stated in the constitution) did not reduce the interest of foreign investors in many resource-based sectors, particularly petroleum, timber, and mining. The attraction of Indonesia'a large domestic market was recognized later, mostly by the Japanese. Then, through massive subsidized investment credits made possible by the oil bonanza in the mid-1970s (mostly via the state-owned development bank Bapindo), the domestic industrial class, consisting of both Chinese and indigenous peoples, came to the fore. This marked the start of the real process of industrialization.

The solid economic performance following implementation of the SSA program in the 1980s was also made possible by strong inflows of foreign capital, particularly those related to the relocation of many industrial investments from Japan (and later from the newly industrializing countries as well), that swept the ASEAN countries as a consequence of the appreciation of the yen in 1985 and after. Economic growth was very strong, the rate of increase of nonoil exports was at an all-time high, and the growth of manufacturing production accelerated. Some observers, rightly or wrongly, even referred to the late 1980s as an economic boom period. Another noted economist labeled the phenomenon "Japanese-led growth."

Obviously, however, the flood of investments would not have occurred had Indonesia not followed the policy course described earlier. The push factor from abroad directed investment flows to the ASEAN area, but these countries able to provide incentives and welcoming macroeconomic environment (pull factor) were those to whom the investment gravitated. Thus, the economic reform of the 1980s helped to attract these capital inflows, which in turn stimulated strong economic growth.

## The Role of Foreign Borrowing and Foreign Assistance

Another important external source of Indonesia's economic growth has been foreign loans. Both the old and the new regime recognized the importance of this source of financing for the country's economic development. But there were major differences in the sources and uses of this financing under the two regimes. More than 60 percent of the debt incurred under the old regime was owed to the Communist bloc. A considerable share of those funds was used for the purchase of military hardware. When Indonesia eventually defaulted, the new regime requested a special meeting to discuss a rescheduling scheme. Two important and historic meetings finally took place in Tokyo and Paris in the autumn of 1966. In terms of the substance of the relief program that was agreed upon by all parties involved, the meetings, especially the one in Paris, were considered an unprecedented success. They allowed the new economic team to start working on a new economic plan without being overly constrained by the debt problem.

The new regime also took a different approach to borrowing. The terms of the new loans, which came from the Western countries, were always set as soft as possible, and a special group known as the IGGI (Inter-Governmental Group on Indonesia) was formed. This group has become an important avenue for discussing the problems, challenges, and amounts of foreign aid required by the Indonesian government in order to undertake continuous development efforts. After the first IGGI meeting, the Indonesian government received $167 million in foreign loans. The amount has been consistently increased every year since then, and by the early 1990s annual lending (the bulk of it concessionary) through the IGGI was in the neighborhood of $4 billion.

Thus, like foreign direct investment, foreign loans have played an important role in the development of Indonesia. But the role of the latter dates back not only through the 25 years in which the present government has been in power, but to the old regime as well. It is difficult to imagine the stabilization and rehabilitation program of the 1960s succeeding without the massive foreign capital inflows the Indonesian government received during that time. In fact, some believe that foreign financial support played a central role in establishing the program's political acceptance.

However, many observers have mistakenly overstated the role of foreign loans. A counterexample may clarify this point. By the end of the old regime, Indonesia's debt-GDP ratio had reached more than 30 percent. Although this figure was lower than the 1990 ratio of approximately 70 percent, it nevertheless reflects the presence of massive flows of foreign assistance under Sukarno's government. Yet at that time the economy was in virtually total disarray. There was no prudent management of publicly guaranteed external debt, and consequently default was inevitable. Cases where massive flows of foreign assistance produced less-than-desirable outcomes can be easily found in other countries as well.

Hence, while foreign loans are an important support for the development process, by themselves they do not ensure healthy economic performance. How foreign loans are utilized is absolutely critical. The historical evidence of the public sector's development expenditures in Indonesia indicates a persistent intention to improve infrastructure conditions so as to achieve more rapid and sustained growth and, at the same time, maintain and protect important social programs (see Azis 1989a). Most foreign assistance is channeled to these programs.

Recently some of the government's technocrats have expressed concerns about the size of the country's foreign debt. It is absolutely necessary for the government to make productive use of budget expenditures, be it sectorally or regionally, if Indonesia is to avoid becoming a "debt-ridden" country. Efforts have been made to create a mechanism to secure the productive use of private foreign loans, while preserving the principle of accepting only concessional (soft) loans.

Another important pillar in the management of debt under the present government is the consistent policy of avoiding any move that might lead to a debt rescheduling. This strong stance is driven by the full recognition that the principle effectively puts a limit on budget expenditures (and keeps spending decisions relatively free of unbridled political lobbying). Furthermore, the country's invariably prompt payment has caused its creditworthiness to stay mostly in the upper tier.

## Foreign Advisers and Donor Agencies

Since the first oil boom in 1974, the number of foreign economic advisers in Indonesia has increased considerably. Indeed, their presence is obvious in various government offices. Some are under long-term contract, while others are engaged in short-term endeavors. The sources of funding for retaining these advisers vary: while some are funded by domestic sources, either budgetary or extrabudgetary, a number of others are funded by particular donor agencies or by foreign governments.

Unfortunately, not all of these advisers are of high quality, and some of their work and recommendations are quite trivial and show an inadequate understanding of local issues. Even when their suggestions appear to be the result of rigorous analysis, their conclusions seem to have been reached beforehand. Given the amount of resources involved, if funded by loans or other domestic sources, such cases are easily perceived as a financial waste to the country. It is to these kinds of foreign advice (and advisers) that increasingly negative critiques, including from members of the Parliament, have recently been directed. In the early stage of reforms, foreign advisers may have offered more concrete contributions to the design of policy reforms. But as part of their "learning process," economic policymakers should have developed a better grasp of the problems they face and of appropriate alternative solutions.

To be fair, there are a number of cases where foreign advisers have produced some truly innovative work. Many believe, for example, that the help of foreign advisers in designing the tax reforms of the mid-1980s was of great importance. Yet it is still often found that, even in cases where potentially valuable work is done, there is no effective dissemination of knowledge to the local staff, either because the latter are already burdened by a heavy workload, or simply because no mechanism has been created for transferring the knowledge. Of course, a few exceptions to this tendency do exist.

It is generally believed, rightly or wrongly, that the hiring of foreign advisers has few advantages. Foreign advisers often refrain from disclosing important data and information to the public that is considered confidential.[20] This is more difficult to guarantee when domestic rather than foreign consultants are involved. To many local experts and even academic researchers, this type of government (officials') attitude may cause a great deal of annoyance. As ironic as it may sound, of all possible explanations, this has been perhaps the most often cited. Moreover, foreign advisers are considered capable of making objective and more comprehensive analyses, since they are not tied to any local value system, nor are their schedules cluttered by other engagements (most, although not all, foreigners who are hired are supposed to allocate a considerable amount of their time to the assigned task). Whether they are indeed more capable than local experts remains, of course, a subjective matter. But the more recent complaints seem to be concerned more with the mismatch between the quality of work or advice that foreign advisers provide and the fees they earn (especially when those fees are taken from the public sector's budget), which are far higher than what local consultants could make.

Finally, foreign observers often criticize the independence of Indonesian policy reforms from the influence of donor agencies such as the IMF and the World Bank. Interestingly, domestic critics often make the opposite indictment: that the country's economic policymakers simply follow meekly whatever these international agencies prescribe. The truth, most likely, lies somewhere in between the extreme positions.

The independence of policy reforms in Indonesia is not entirely clear. Certainly, a "learning process" has taken place during the course of Indonesia's development over the last 25 years. Along the way, various sound ideas concerning market reform undoubtedly have had a considerable effect, which policymakers have eventually grasped and digested. Thus, the idea of market reform might have been in place even before donor agencies came up with their prescriptions. On the other hand, should a different kind of idea emerge in Indonesian policy circles, one that is diametrically opposed to those held by the IMF and the World Bank, it is difficult to imagine that as good a relationship and as strong support from these international agencies to Indonesia and its SSA program as we are witnessing today would be possible. One thing, though, is absolutely true. Unlike those of some other countries, the Indonesian SSA program in the 1980s never came under strong pressure from the famous IMF conditionality: there was never any quid pro quo situation in which additional funding was made contingent on further reforms.

---

20. However, in one case a foreign adviser got into trouble because he made some statements in a public forum related to the work assigned to him.

## The Coexistence of Liberalizing and Protectionist Policies

Despite the successes of Indonesian macroeconomic reform, it would be absolutely incorrect to assert that the economy today is free of protectionist policies. Besides the presence of strong protectionist lobbies (as in other countries), another important factor in the persistent mix of liberalizing and protectionist policies in Indonesia is the effective presence of two groups of presidential economic advisers: the economic technocrats and the "engineers." Many observers see the emergence of these two camps of contending advisers as a recent phenomenon, particularly since the appointment of B. J. Habibie as minister of science and technology. But the division of views between the two groups toward national industrialization and a broader range of development issues actually began much earlier.

Whereas in the past the engineers' group lacked a single influential leader and a common strategy was not easy to identify, in general the economic technocrats were much more focused on strategy and policy design, largely through the leadership of Widjojo Nitisastro. This group of very able and mostly low-profile technocrats has basically been given the responsibility for the country's major economic portfolio since the launching of the first Five-Year Development Plan (Repelita) in 1969. Today, even without a direct ministerial or executive position, Widjojo is still believed to be the key designer of economic policy and is even considered by many to be a major player of the country's portfolio of economic policies.

Talk about the roles of the economic technocrats and the engineers reemerged more intensively in the mid-1980s. In fact, more or less the same economic technocrats have been present since 1969, through several cabinets. Although different names may appear on the list of ministers, the consistency of their views is notable. Hence, at least in absolute terms, there seems no reason to believe that the technocrats' role is declining. If this is so, the recent talk must have been prompted by something that provides a strong boost for, and recognition of, the engineers' group.

At the outset, it does seem that the persistence and determination of Science and Technology Minister Habibie, backed by his internationally acknowledged capability, has made the role of the engineers in the Indonesian political arena far more significant. Some also point to his appealing personal style; perhaps more important, however, these attributes are also bolstered and sustained by his apparently strong support from the president.[21]

---

21. Recently, Minister Habibie was also assigned, with the blessing of the president, to head a very influential organization called ICMI (Ikatan Cendekiawan Muslim Indonesia),

While it may not always be true that the engineers favor a more protectionist approach than the technocrats, many believe this is not an exaggeration. Foreign scholars (e.g., Woo et al. 1992) also make this comparison. In fact, the positions traditionally held by engineers, or at least those that are largely controlled by them (e.g., the Ministry of Industry, the Investment Coordinating Board, and, in the past, the Ministry of Trade), are connected with aspects of policymaking where certain reasons for protection, such as for infant-industry purposes, seem natural. In many cases, this is true either because they share the interests of the lobby groups they represent, or because they simply see the importance of fostering high-technology industries that require support and protection from the government.

This tug-of-war between protectionist and liberalizing policies, with outcomes oscillating between the two poles, is found in other countries as well (for example, in Korea). Sometimes the economists' idea of market reform triumphs; at other times the engineers' and economic nationalists' view prevails. Which view prevails at any given time is most often determined by the state of the economy. During a booming economy protectionist notions receive widespread support, while in difficult times more prudent policies and pro-market reforms tend to gain stronger backing.

The identification of so-called strategic industries, all of which are under the control, directly or indirectly, of Minister Habibie, is also seen as deviating from pro-market reform.[22] Yet the president has given his full support to this undertaking. This, however, does not mean that the SSA program cannot be implemented. Certainly there is still ample room for further structural adjustment. As some senior politicians like to put it, "the coexistence of liberalizing and protectionist policy simply indicates the multitudinous objectives of development strategy."

The difficulties in completely eliminating monopoly powers and various forms of nontariff barriers are facts of life that cloud efforts to reform the economy fully. Notwithstanding these difficulties, Indonesia has now gone through a period where major reforms have been implemented with success. This certainly has required superb abilities on the part of economic policymakers in identifying areas where changes could be made and acknowledging those things that cannot or should not be changed. Cynics may call this approach opportunistic, but Indonesians consider it pragmatic.

---

whose members are largely Moslem intellectuals. A member of the economic technocrats' team, Emil Salim, was designated vice head of the organization.

22. The list of these industries has lengthened markedly over time and now covers no fewer than 10 industrial sectors: aircraft, steel, machinery (two separate industries), explosives, shipbuilding, telecommunications, arms, electronics, and the railway industry.

Besides being the result of the presence of engineers in the cabinet, many of the remaining protectionist policies today can best be understood in historical perspective. The strong flavor of government intervention that often leads to protection (and, in the past, has led to nationalization as well) has its roots in Indonesian political and economic nationalism, which emerged after independence. The Dutch legacy of a plantation economy, with its exploitation of resources and profit repatriation, was considered antithetical to prosperity. The natural response was, as might be expected, a drive toward industrialization.

To secure and maintain the new industrial investments, it was implicitly asserted, some forms of protection were needed. High trade (tariff and nontariff) barriers and restrictions on entry for foreign ownership were imposed. On the financial side, the required capital was largely provided by the government. Strong support for such an approach also came from a great number of intellectuals, who at that time were certainly not champions of the laissez-faire paradigm.

The emotional need to counter the colonial legacy was further combined with resentment against those Indonesians of Chinese origin who, as in many other Asian countries, often managed to hold economic power out of proportion with their numbers. Moreover, from the perspective of regional development (especially of the outer islands), the absence of infrastructure and the resulting low level of economic activity further justified government intervention.

Although the installation of able economists in the economic policymaking arena during the late 1960s led to many changes in the direction and nature of the country's development strategy,[23] some elements of protectionist policies prevailed throughout the 1970s and 1980s and even to the present day. Following a series of policy changes within the context of the SSA program, Indonesia has entered a different policy environment, although many undesirable outcomes are still easily observed. These outcomes are often associated with protectionist measures that are either no longer the direct results of, or have little to do with, deliberate new policies. Rather, many of them are tailwinded by historical circumstances or are the legacy of past policies. As a result, the 1980s saw the implementation of appropriate macroeconomic policies, but trade and industrial policies remained unliberalized.[24]

This situation was observed particularly in the early years after the decline in oil prices. For this reason, many analysts believe that the major thrust of reforms in Indonesia during the early period has been macroeconomic, oriented toward stabilization, and backed by the open

---

23. The most dramatic change was the promulgation of new investment laws clearly designed to allow (and attract) inflows of foreign capital.

24. By comparison, the situation in Korea during the 1980s seems quite congruous with this phenomenon, whereas in the case of India the export orientation did not prevail.

capital account system in place since the late 1960s. The structural adjustment phase, that of trade and industrial policy reform, came only after changes in industrial policy in an export-oriented direction had taken place. But even with an export-oriented strategy, economic nationalism and the urge to foster strategic industries remain great.

In summary, the SSA program has indeed worked quite effectively in Indonesia, because the various measures taken were either bold, bringing radical transformation, or simply timely and appropriately chosen. But to conclude that there are no protectionist policies in Indonesia would certainly be incorrect.

## Conclusions

In various respects, the three episodes of crisis and response in Indonesia since the 1960s differ from one another. The preconditions and reasoning for the effective handling of the crises, however, bear some degree of similarity. Each episode was marked by the presence of an able and coherent team of economic technocrats, under the leadership of Widjojo Nitisastro, supported by the stable and effective government of President Suharto.

This paper has emphasized the events of the 1980s. Overall, the responses to the crisis of those years were bold and drastic, resulting in dramatic improvements in macroeconomic conditions and robust economic growth. The Indonesian case is rather unique, however, since the achievement of macroeconomic equilibrium produced neither worsening poverty nor a deteriorating income distribution, at least in the years immediately following the reforms. This outcome was largely due to a strategy of budget allocation in which infrastructure and social overhead capital, particularly in the rural sector, were consistently given top priority. In part, the strategy has been preserved because the memory of the events of 1965–66 causes the government to continue to focus on the needs of the rural sector.

The neutral role of the military has helped to sustain the economic growth of the country in the last 25 years. This factor is often underestimated by many observers. Foreign assistance has also played an important role in the reform, but it would certainly be misleading to assert that external resources guarantee the success of the reforms. As noted above, unlike reform programs in some other countries, the Indonesian SSA program in the 1980s has never been associated with IMF conditionality.

Emerging ideas of pro-market reform have also contributed a great deal to the shaping of policy directions. In this respect, Indonesia's economic technocrats have undergone a "learning process." Over the course of time, various ideas about market reform have gained widespread acceptance, which policymakers eventually grasped and digested.

The absence of a strongly organized civil society and the dominance of a single party have made it relatively easy to reach a national consensus on giving economic development a high priority. The Indonesian system lacks strong checks and balances between executive, legislative, and judicial powers. Serious ideological controversy is also absent. The country's political institutions are such that they can be used by an effective government to steer policy (including economic reform) either toward or away from a pro-market direction. Given its longevity, the New Order government is unquestionably very effective, and the policy direction proposed in the 1980s was to reform the economy in a pro-market direction.

However, the present-day Indonesian economy is by no means free of protectionist policies. Besides the presence of strong business lobbies and the persistence of economic nationalism, the presence of two groups of presidential economic advisers with differing views helps explain the coexistence of liberalizing and protectionist policies. The result has usually been a seesawing between liberalization and protection: the hands of the technocrats were strengthened when serious problems were perceived, or when there was a scarcity of capital, whereas when the economy was booming or capital was in adequate supply, the engineers and the protectionists have often gained the upper hand.

It is worth mentioning in closing that the 1993 election has clearly led to the strengthening of the position of the engineers' group in the cabinet. Although a few of Widjojo's group remain in the cabinet, and Widjojo himself is still present in an advisory position, many perceive that the new cabinet reflects the coming of a new era. Consistent with the thesis that the engineers and nationalists gain strength in relatively prosperous times, this most recent cabinet restructuring occurs at a time when annual economic growth is in the neighborhood of 6 percent, nonoil exports are growing at better than a 20 percent annual rate, and the current account deficit is well under control. Whether this relatively healthy state of affairs can be preserved under the new cabinet remains to be seen.

# References

Azis, I. J. 1989a. ''Economic Development and Recent Adjustment in Resource Rich Countries: The Case of Indonesia.'' In T. Fukuchi and M. Kagami, eds., *Perspectives on the Pacific Basin Economy: A Comparison of Asia and Latin America*. Tokyo: Institute of Developing Economies.

Azis, I. J. 1989b. ''Export Performance and the Employment Effect.'' Paper presented at a conference on ''The Future of the Asia-Pacific Economies,'' sponsored by the Asia-Pacific Development Center and the Thailand Development Research Institute, Bangkok (8–10 November).

Azis, I. J. 1992a. "Regional and Social Impacts of Structural Adjustment in Indonesia: A Preliminary Analysis." *CRP Working Papers* Ithaca, NY: Cornell University.

Azis, I. J. 1992b. "Review of Regional Development: Equity and Foreign Exchange Accumulation." In T. K. John, G. Knaap, and I. J. Azis, eds., *Spatial Development in Indonesia: Review and Prospects*. London: Avebury.

Bourguignon, F. and Morrisson, C. 1992. *Adjustment and Equity in Developing Countries: A New Approach*. Paris: OECD Development Centre.

Nelson, J. M., ed. 1990. *Economic Crisis and Policy Choice: The Politics of Adjustment in the Third World*. Princeton, NJ: Princeton University Press.

Sadli, M. 1992. "Resources and Management, The Indonesian Case." Paper presented at a conference on "The Asia Pacific Region: Efficiency in Transition," organized by the Asian Association of Management Conference, New Delhi (1–4 November).

Thorbecke, E., et al. 1992a. *Adjustment, Growth and Income Distribution in Indonesia*. Paris: OECD Development Centre.

Thorbecke, E., et al. 1992b. "The Indonesian Adjustment Experience in an International Perspective." Washington: Institute for Policy Reform (mimeographed; reprinted in *Indonesian Economic Journal* 1 [April]).

Woo, W. T., et al. 1993. *Macroeconomic Policies: Crisis and Long Run Growth: The Case of Indonesia, 1965–1990*. Washington: World Bank (forthcoming).

World Bank. 1992. *World Development Report 1992*. Washington: World Bank.

# Comment

## GUSTAV RANIS

Both Indonesia and Korea have been highly successful developing countries by any international standard—even if both, when one uses the magnifying glass, exhibit substantial blemishes. There has been a continuing evolution toward economic reform, comprising macroeconomic balance and the sequencing of various structural adjustments at the microeconomic level. Although there is no approved boilerplate conforming to textbook or IMF or World Bank prescriptions in place in either country, the development experience in both has, in general terms, been very positive. This is what makes an examination of their experience particularly valuable.

Both cases appear to vindicate the crisis hypothesis presented in John Williamson's introductory paper. In the case of Indonesia, there can be little doubt that the major crisis of the late 1960s, marking the end of the Sukarno period, permitted major reforms to take place, accompanied by debt writeoff, and although the later crises were more modest, there are meaningful responses to record. Indeed, there is the clear record of a tug-of-war, continuing to this day and extending even beyond what Iwan Azis presents in his very interesting and instructive paper, between the economist-led technocrats under Widjojo Nitisastro and the engineering-led industrialists, spearheaded first by Ibnu and later by B. J. Habibie. Who was winning at any given time in this tug-of-war can be traced to the perceived presence or absence of crises and the decision by the president as to whose side to come down on. I would argue that one can trace a clear pattern: when oil prices were high and the macro-

*Gustav Ranis is Frank Altschul Professor of International Economics at Yale University.*

economic situation consequently seemed comfortable, the engineers and industrialists were likely to get the upper hand, whereas when there were lower oil prices or other problems arose, the Berkeley mafia had a better chance of gaining the president's ear. As Azis points out, in both 1974 and 1979, years of oil boom, there was less of a sense of urgency, and it was harder to get President Suharto to support reforms. The tug-of-war is today complicated by the fact that Indonesia now wants to move firmly toward the status of a newly industrializing country, even as it harbors a substantial volume of surplus labor, especially on Java.

Nevertheless, what is undoubtedly more relevant to other countries looking at Indonesia is that, despite these fluctuations, the overall policy trend has been persistently in the direction of continued reforms. This underlines the overwhelming importance of maintaining the credibility of policy trends. The average quality of the policy mix chosen, as between the deployment of markets and the deployment of government, is undoubtedly much less important than avoiding stop-go oscillations in policy, as has recently been pointed out in the work of Guillermo Calvo and Dani Rodrik.

The same sort of argument can be made for Korea. What constituted an oil bonanza in Indonesia after 1973 was, of course, an oil crisis in Korea. Initially, in sharp contrast to Taiwan, the response was a planned expansion of heavy and chemical industries, with an accelerated schedule for developing technologically more sophisticated industries. The government not only invested directly in industry, but also made extensive use of firm-specific allocative interventions, including differential credit terms and tax rates, in order to influence the precise direction of investment. I would, moreover, argue that part of the explanation for the difference in behavior between Korea and Taiwan is that in Korea the system failed to mobilize domestic saving to an equivalent degree through an agriculture-first strategy, and this failure in turn led to a relatively heavy reliance on foreign capital. This, I believe, had an impact reminiscent of that of natural resource abundance in the case of Indonesia and permitted the crisis to deepen initially rather than be alleviated.

Azis's paper, as well as most discussions of Korea, explicitly or implicitly, accepts the necessarily positive role of foreign capital, the basic premise being that increased flows are needed to help ensure the continuity of the liberalization program. One cannot but agree that properly conditioned—hopefully by the recipient—and properly utilized foreign capital flows are bound to be helpful. They add resources and may even add to the quality of the domestic policy mix. But one must also repeat the warning, which may perhaps be more relevant to concessional aid in Indonesia and to private foreign capital in Korea, that such inflows can be a two-edged sword. Japan's transition to modern growth was accompanied by very little foreign capital, and the major steps in the liberalization of the Taiwanese economy occurred with the announcement of the impending end of foreign aid, mainly from the United States, in the early 1960s. To a lesser extent, a similar case can be made for public capital in Korea. Thus, both public and private foreign capital can be used equally well to permit the continuation of inappropriate policies or to ease the transition to more appropriate ones. In that sense we may once again note the symmetry with the deployment of a country's natural resources.

It is becoming increasingly clear that any consideration of structural adjustment requires not just an examination of what belongs in any adjustment package, but also an understanding of the more subtle political economy–tinged processes, which must be examined along with the purely technical ones. After more than 40 years of a buildup in human capacity in the developing world, and more than 40 years of discourse between donor-creditors and recipients, the question has become more one of responding knowledgeably to relatively well-understood phenomena rather than attempting to reinvent the wheel every time. That is why this volume, focusing on the political economy dimensions of policymaking, is pointing us in the right direction. It is clearly my contention that a system's initial conditions, including its natural resource wealth as well as its ability to attract foreign capital "for the asking" over time—which is another kind of national resource—are likely to affect the opportunities and risks of policy responses over time.

Nevertheless, while there clearly exist important behavioral differences between these two countries, what marks them off from the more typical developing-country case goes deeper, to the fact that Korea and, to a somewhat lesser extent, Indonesia were able to retract and respond to crises by gradually depoliticizing their systems and returning each time to the essential linearity of their continuing liberalization trend. In other words, although shocks such as the oil crisis and the assassination of President Park Chung Hee initially did not get the "right" response, East Asia's famous pragmatism meant that corrections took place relatively quickly and, most important, that confidence in the sustainability of that trend could be maintained. A good example of this is provided by the gaining of control over the budget and of the pace of monetary expansion, the evolution of fiscal policy reform, and the gradual liberalization of import controls, while leaving to last the liberalization of international capital movements. Thus, the East Asian experience, especially in Taiwan but also in Korea, demonstrates a realistic liberalization trend resolutely maintained in the face of exogenous shocks.

Both Indonesia and Korea demonstrate that successful reform over time is possible even when political democracy lags. But I would argue that in both cases there resulted substantial economic democracy in terms of the achievement of popular participation. This was done through the redistributional and cross-regional impact of the INPRES program in Indonesia, and, belatedly, through the New Village Movement and follow-on efforts in Korea. This argues for the importance of informal pacts among contending interest groups, very much in the spirit of the more formal pacts that have been so valuable in Mexico, for example, in recent years. Such understandings, even in a relatively authoritarian context such as prevailed in Indonesia and Korea, may be as important as the trappings of Western political democracy focused on voting behavior.

One may also argue that, whether a country is relatively large, like Indonesia, or medium-sized, like Korea, the maintenance of a successful reform trend requires addressing not just the international transactions through the policy packages heavily emphasized in the Washington consensus, but the domestic economy as well. In particular, attention needs to be paid to the interaction between agriculture and the nonagriculture sectors, a process that is complementary to the enhanced international participation so strongly advocated in Washington. Even if there were constant relative oil prices in Indonesia over time, and even if physical and human infrastructure were allocated equitably across all the islands, one would expect Indonesia to focus heavily on increasing agricultural productivity and encouraging rural industry, especially on Java, and in this fashion to be able to participate internationally through labor-intensive industrial export expansion initially and through nontraditional industrial exports later on. On the other hand, Korea, which had already ceased to have a labor surplus during the early 1970s, was able to avoid premature increases in unskilled and semiskilled wages by, somewhat belatedly, turning its attention to the need to bring the rural economy into step with the expansion of industrial exports.

The intensity of the search for rents in different markets, which liberalization is intended to diminish, is an inverse function of initial cultural homogeneity, of the kind emphasized by Simon Kuznets, and a direct function of the size of these rents, whether they be natural resources–based, as in Indonesia, or based on the ample availability of foreign capital, as in Korea. The fact that reliance on foreign capital can be excessive is indeed one of the dimensions not really taken up sufficiently in the context of these two cases. Together with natural resource bonanzas, it certainly added to "Dutch disease" problems in Indonesia; in Korea it contributed to excessive capital intensity, a relatively large debt burden, an unduly concentrated industrial structure, and a deteriorating distribution of income. More recently, we have seen the creation of new rents, in the form of capital gains from land and stock market appreciation. These, counter to some people's notions, have had some real effects in terms of focusing large-scale urban interests on speculation at the expense of competitive productive activity.

Nevertheless, while the performances of both Indonesia and Korea are not unblemished, what sets them apart from the more typical developing-country case is that they both seem to have avoided, most of the time, a strategy of forcing growth beyond natural levels through the pursuit of activist policies. When inflationary pressures occurred, both countries tended to respond relatively quickly: they kept deficits in check; they maintained relatively low rates of money growth, usually but not always achieving positive real rates of interest; and they usually but again not always kept exchange rates realistically flexible. Thus, although neither country approached the textbook performance of Taiwan, one may nevertheless note a relative restraint of government expansionary tendencies in good times and of price flexibility in bad times.

Both the Korean and the Indonesian experience support the notion that macroeconomic stabilization must come first, that the dismantling of protectionism can come later, but that the timing of the freeing up of the capital account can vary substantially and, of course, has a lot to do with the perceived sustainability of the entire process. This brings us back to the initial point, that credibility is the key element in avoiding capital flight, the breakdown of the social consensus, and undue stop-go oscillations around a more or less universal liberalization trend.

Although both countries resorted to a typical import substitution policy mix early on, the intervention habits of that subphase were less deeply ingrained than in the typical developing-country case. Thus, the temptation to return to import substitution–like interventionism when the inevitable external shocks occurred, leading to crises that had to be responded to by another round of liberalization in a stop-go pattern, was less severe in these two cases, especially in Korea.

A final comment on the lessons of economic reforms in these two countries: both South Korea and Indonesia are unitary governments, even though one could argue that especially as diversified an archipelago as Indonesia calls for consideration of a federal system. But even if unitary governments are to be maintained, both systems undoubtedly require additional dosages of real public-sector decentralization than has thus far taken place. The Indonesian government, during the first 25 years of Suharto, understandably emphasized unity and the need to respond very cautiously to the demands of diversity. But as one looks toward the future and asks what is required in terms of further institutional amendments to the Washington consensus, it seems clear, at least to me, that increased economic complexity will force increased devolution of power to local governments. As labor-intensive output mixes gradually yield to skill-, capital-, and technology-intensive activities, along with the continued exportation of natural resource–intensive goods from the outer islands, the need for both vertical and horizontal decentralization in Indonesia will become more and more obvious.

It is understandable that developing-country leaders, in view of the current trends toward splintering and atomization in such more-advanced countries as Yugoslavia and parts of the Soviet Union, will be hesitant to move too quickly in that direction. But there is also the question of whether the pace of economic reforms can be sustained, given an overstretched central government, and given the increased complexity of the decisions that have to be made about infrastructural allocations and human capital formation. Both Indonesia and Korea have made substantial advances in trying to move additional resources toward laggard regions—something only the central government can do—through the INPRES program in Indonesia and through the New Village Movement and its aftermath in Korea. Nevertheless, one can foresee that a widening gap between enhanced economic and political participation will become an increasingly serious problem, unless administrative decentralization of the public sector is permitted to catch up with the inevitability of ever more decentralized private decision-making processes in both of these countries.

# Comment

SUBROTO ROY

Ever since Plato's *Republic*, it has been asked what role, if any, there is for experts in managing a country's affairs. The 1960s witnessed a lively debate between those who held Plato responsible for the elitist claims made by the European dictatorships of the 1930s and 1940s, and those who argued that questions of knowledge and expertise could be kept distinct from questions of democracy and dictatorship (see Popper 1962; Bambrough 1967). This debate has special relevance for many developing countries, where displacement of colonial rule by local elites often has not resulted in firm political institutions taking root. The potential for such elites to do good or harm remains disproportionately high in these countries.

In my own country, India, the devastating results of Sovietesque central planning in the 1950s continue to reverberate through the economy and the political system today. This was a "technocratic" initiative, sponsored by the political leadership and underwritten by Indian economists and pseudo-economists with the eager help of foreign academics. The single Indian economist whose courage compelled him to analyze and predict the results (correctly, as it turned out) was blackballed in the Indian profession and slandered as a traitor to conventional wisdom. Two foreign economists who did the same were left unpublished and unread.[1] On the other hand, it can be argued that the process of "nation building" following decolonization made a strong centralized govern-

---

*Subroto Roy is a Washington consultant.*

1. These were, respectively, B. R. Shenroy, and Milton Friedman and P. T. Bauer. The intellectual history is described in Roy (1984).

ment necessary above everything else. By this argument, the fact that a country like India has managed to survive at all as a more or less coherent nation-state, and indeed a large functioning democracy, is measure enough of success.

With the exception of Japan and possibly Korea, no Asian country has yet been able to combine a reasonably high standard of living for its people with a free civil society and responsible democratic institutions. But at the same time, with only a few exceptions such as Myanmar and North Korea, these national values have been publicly accepted all over Asia. From China, India, Indonesia, Pakistan, and Malaysia to Sri Lanka and Singapore, there is considerable agreement across Asia that a liberal polity and a market-based economy are the things to aim at over the long run—even if the power of local political or economic elites is such that the path seems tortuous and even impossible.

The ''Third World'' was a figment of the Cold War, when it was too easy for Asian elites to find it in their interest to equate Soviet-style economics with political nation building, since the departing colonial powers were too closely associated with market-based economics. The failure of Sovietesque experiments around the world has finally reached Asia's elites, whose awkward task now becomes one of seeming to be eager to dismantle systems they have found profitable to manage thus far.

Iwan J. Azis's paper attempts to describe the Indonesian experience of economic reform. He takes the view that, in his country, economic experts and technocrats have been in the vanguard of not only saving the economy since 1966 but placing it on a highly successful growth path. Although he may well be right that Indonesia's economists and civil servants, with the backing of the political leadership, have steered the economy clear of the rocks, his view that these are people whose ''analytical capabilities . . . are superb'' and who ''possess an exquisite talent for selecting policy changes'' is surely an exaggeration. Great power in a few hands can be used for great good or great harm, and a strong argument for decentralization and democracy is simply that it reduces the repercussions of political mistakes. Azis's view that the approach of technocrats is ''pragmatic, professionally based, and little influenced by party politics and ideology'' must also be constrained by the recognition that few bureaucracies anywhere contain more than a small fraction of selfless bureaucrats.

Other observers have described Indonesia's exchange rate policies as relatively prudent and outward-looking, for which Indonesia's economic policymakers deserve much credit. At the same time, trade policy in Indonesia has been for long periods inward-looking and protectionist, and it evidently remains so today even though there was considerable liberalization in the 1980s. The result has been an uneasy coexistence, caused by the fact that the two sets of policies emanate from different agencies with different economic perspectives (see Gillis and Dapice 1988). To the extent that this is an accurate description, it would have been interesting to learn from Azis's paper the precise nature and parameters of this internal dialogue.

Finally, in a paper on the politics of Indonesian economic reform, it is odd not to find mention of Indonesian politics except to say that there is an ''absence of a strongly organized civil society and the dominance of a single party'' without any ''strong checks and balances between executive, legislative, and judicial powers.'' Azis suggests that these conditions ''have made it relatively easy to reach a national consensus'' on economic development. Although he may well be right to endorse the economic priorities of the Indonesian government, these cannot really be considered the result of a national consensus—since consensus requires dialogue as a precondition, which in turn requires the kinds of institutions Azis suggests to be absent in the Indonesian polity at present.

# References

Bambrough, Renford, ed. 1967. *Plato, Popper and Politics: Some Contributions to a Modern Controversy*. New York: Barnes and Noble.

Gillis, Malcolm, and David Dapice. 1988. ''Indonesia.'' In Rudiger Dornbusch and Leslie C. H. Helmers, *The Open Economy: Tools for Policy-Makers in Developing Countries*. Washington: World Bank.

Popper, Karl. 1962. *The Open Society and Its Enemies*. Princeton, NJ: Princeton University Press.

Roy, Subroto. 1984. *Pricing, Planning, and Politics: A Study of Economic Distortions in India*. London: Institute of Economic Affairs.

# 8

## IMPLICATIONS FOR ECONOMIES
## IN TRANSITION

# Ukraine

OLEH HAVRYLYSHYN

Ukraine, like other countries of the former Soviet Union, has now had a full year as an independent nation to attempt the transition to a market economy. Much can be written about its travails, and the list of concrete lessons one could draw is long. I shall limit myself to three main lessons of political economy I see emerging from the experience of Ukraine and from the other former Soviet countries.

First, progress in reform is not hampered primarily by a lack of understanding about the objective measures of stabilization and adjustment that need to be taken. What is most lacking is a sufficiently large constituency that is both committed to implementing such measures and able to see them through the political process. Compare Ukraine and Russia in the spring of 1992, when the prevailing view was that Russia was far ahead of Ukraine on economic reform. The differences were not apparent on paper, for the 30 March Economic Reform Program of the Ukrainian Cabinet of Ministers was no less sensible or orthodox than the Russian Letter of Intent to the International Monetary Fund (IMF) of February 1992. In practice, the major difference was a reformist Russian cabinet, led by Yegor Gaidar, that was much more committed to implementing reform. But even this unquestioned commitment was not enough to make a lasting difference, for this group was unable to sell anyone on its program except for Western admirers. The Ukrainian government allowed a huge expansion of credits to the economy starting in mid-1992, revealing its lack of commitment to the stabilization goals set out in March. The Russian government did exactly the same thing, not

*Oleh Havrylyshyn is alternate executive director (Ukraine), International Monetary Fund.*

because it was uncommitted, but because it was unable to sell the body politic on the need for monetary restraint.

My second main lesson concerns the evolution of a new and very powerful interest group opposed to reform: rent seekers in the producing and trading sector. As signs of major weakening of the socialist camp began to show a few years ago, many analysts expected strong opposition from entrenched interest groups, including the plan bureaucracy, the party, plant managers, and the like.

Many of the individuals in these groups are indeed part of the opposition, but they have regrouped into a different kind of interest group. They favor decentralization of economic decisions essentially to the producer level and the virtual elimination of the old command structure. But a retention of considerable administrative controls on prices and licenses for trade (exports in particular) have dramatically altered the interests of these individuals. They are, of course, delighted to be free of commands from above, as this gives them even greater control over resources, perks, and personal gain. They have learned to profit hugely from the remaining administrative interventions of the state and to play the popular game of proclaiming "jobs will be lost" in order to obtain soft-budget credits that keep them in perks. They have also learned a new game, borrowed from the developing-country experience of distorted trade regimes: the difference between domestic and world prices can generate huge profits if the appropriate government agency is persuaded to give licenses to trade. (In the former Soviet Union, this consists almost entirely of export activities.) In a word, they have learned that the greatest private gain comes in a system somewhere between central command and a free market: a system of administrative interventionism.

That this is not optimal for society as a whole is well-supported by the political economy literature. A particularly virulent divergence between social and private optimality has prevailed in the former Soviet republics during 1992: barter trade. Breakdown of the old trading mechanisms and the lack of foreign exchange resulted in the popularity of barter, albeit as a second-best option, and its institutionalization in regulations for a while included exemption of barter operations from taxes. Not surprisingly, barter accounted for a huge share of Ukraine's hard currency trade. Its welfare costs have not yet been calculated but may turn out to be enormous. Under the barter system, each Ukrainian exporter has been free to set the terms of trade. In general, the deal most advantageous to the trader (including various forms of corruption, capital flight, personal perks) could be struck by offering the foreign buyer a very good deal. Hence, Ukrainian terms of trade deteriorated sharply.

I come finally to the third lesson, which follows directly from the second: opposition to further market reform is much stronger today than it was a year ago, and it will therefore be all the more important for the constituency favoring reform to be not only committed but also successful in dealing with this new opposition. It must do three things. First, when given the opportunity—as Ukraine's cabinet and prime minister have been, with emergency powers continuing until June 1993—the government must move quickly to remove as many price and regulatory distortions as possible, as they are the source of high rents. Second, it must engage the public in support of a battle against this new interest group. It is noteworthy that the first major action of Prime Minister Leonid Kuchma's new government in November 1992 was to institute a campaign to flush out those who amassed excessive profit from oil exports under government license. Third, realizing it cannot simply defeat such a strong lobby, the government must co-opt this group. One way to do this is to accept the political necessity of some form of special credit access for ''restructuring.'' The government's stubborn resistance to any form of industrial policy is likely only to ensure that it will soon be replaced by one that is favorable to such a policy. Within the overall macroeconomic goals of monetary restriction, some capped amount of special funds, at competitive interest rates and under restricted conditions, can be made available to industry.

Let me conclude by tying the above arguments to the issue of Western financial support for transition economies. It goes without saying that substantial support will only be useful if a country has a sensible stabilization and reform program, expressed in the kinds of numbers that typify IMF-led efforts. I concur with this approach and exhort the number-crunchers on both sides to continue their work. I would add that the underlying condition for the success of a Western support package is that there be in place a government team that is committed to reform, realistic about the problems, and politically astute enough to build a constituency for reform. Such a team will know better than anyone else what monetary and fiscal policies are consistent with a viable reform path.

# Russia

VLADIMIR MAU

Russia must perform three tasks in its transformation. The first, of course, is stabilization: Russia must confront the classic stabilization problems of a country with high inflation, soft budget constraints, and so on. The second is the radical structural transformation of the national economy, similar to that undertaken in some Latin American countries. The third task is the transformation of the social system itself, the basic values of the society, the creation of a new system of property rights, and much else.

I do believe, even though the problems and the internal contradictions in the Eastern European countries are similar to those in Russia, that the situation in Russia is unique. The communist regime to be overcome was not imposed on Russia, as regimes in Poland, Lithuania, and Czechoslovakia, for example, were; it was produced by Russian people and by Russian history. This has led to the situation faced by the Russian reform government, created in the autumn of 1991 and later called ''Gaidar's government.'' That government operated without any hope of arriving at a national consensus about values and a common vision for the society. That is why Prime Minister Yegor Gaidar, at his last session of the Congress of People's Deputies (December 1992), joked sadly that, while all the deputies and all the people were proclaiming themselves in favor of reforms, some of them were not against political prisons and concentration camps as the means to that end.

*Vladimir Mau is head of the Department for Political and Social Issues of Economic Reform at the Institute of Economy in Transition in Moscow and was until 1993 an adviser to the Chairman of the Russian Federation.*

What are the main political conditions for the radical transformation of Russian (or post-Soviet) society? These conditions were created during the years of perestroika. And only toward the end of 1991 could we observe, in the political process or in the economy, any signs that Russia was ready to undergo real economic reforms.

I would like to step back and offer a brief historical account of perestroika. Before 1992, Russia passed through two stages of political and economic transformation that were very similar to the stages of radical transformation (or indeed revolution) in other countries at different times, including Russia itself at the beginning of this century and, to my mind, even the French Revolution of two centuries ago. We passed through the "rosy" period of transformation, when the people united to overthrow the communist regime, which by then had come to be considered silly, weak, and foolish. The success of this union, of this political bloc of different forces, fostered the dangerous illusion that it would be an easy matter to overcome all the problems of society through the creation of a new social order.

The contradictions of the economic policy of that period were not the result of stupidity on the part of the political leadership; rather they were the result of this common illusion. One of these contradictions in Russia was the antialcohol campaign of 1985–89, which destroyed the fiscal balance of the country. Another was the idea that there could be a rapid increase in the standard of living while the share of consumption spending in national income was dropping drastically. And there were a lot of other contradictions between slogans of the Soviet leadership and actual policy, which in fact worsened economic conditions.

The second stage of development was one of political struggle, of the polarization of social forces, to which the country's economic problems and processes were held hostage. There was a powerful struggle for sovereignty between the Soviet republics and the central government, at that time epitomized in the fight over taxes; Russia here played a very important role. The Soviet and Russian governments both reduced taxes on enterprises twice, as each encouraged the enterprises to switch over to its side. This tax cutting was done without any regard for its effect on the fiscal budget.

There also occurred a "price battle," when the Russian government, in total disregard of the consequences, increased procurement prices for agricultural goods. Everybody—economists, politicians, and historians— knew from the history of 1917 under the provisional government of Russia that these steps, in a situation of shortage in the national economy, could only undermine agricultural sales to industry.

Industrial Soviet wholesale prices at the same time were partly liberalized by the Soviet authorities: state enterprises were allowed to double the prices they charged for their products, but retail prices remained fixed. This, too, was done to win the industrialists' support.

The dismantling of the Soviet Union, despite all the problems that arose from it, accomplished one extremely important thing: it left only one political entity with responsibility for economic reforms in Russia, namely, the Russian Federation. The same is, of course, not true of the other former Soviet republics, which have their own vision of the political prospects of their reforms. Some of them in fall 1991 were oriented to the Western form of market democracy, others to the Asian style of modernization; still others wanted to return to the status quo ante. But at last they could now afford to pursue their own economic policies independent of dominance by the center. Certainly, there were in Russia many problems, especially concerning the currency; nonetheless, the situation has become much more clear than it was during the political struggle over the economy.

There are two prerequisites for a positive outcome to Russia's economic reforms. First is the stance the general public takes regarding radical economic change: the most favorable condition for reform would actually be a neutral and even weary public, exhausted by the previous political struggle. The situation of 1921–23 offers a model: the economic situation at that time, in terms of inflation, unemployment, and the like, was much worse than in 1916–17, but a new revolution was impossible, not so much because the police powers of the communist regime prevented it (they were still weak), but because the majority of the people were exhausted. So they acquiesced in the stabilization policy of the early 1920s, which was very difficult and painful but nonetheless proved effective.

In late 1991 and the beginning of 1992, the Russian people were again exhausted. That is why the government was confident, on the eve of price liberalization, that a drastic social clash was impossible, that the government would not be overthrown by popular revolt, and that the democratic political regime would survive at least in the short term. From our own experience as well as polling results and much other information, we could see that the people, then and now, were concentrating on the yields of their private plots and in general on their individual economic circumstances.

We did notice a very important shift in political values. Asked in a public opinion poll whom they most relied upon and believed in, most Russians answered that they relied only upon themselves—almost no one believed in political parties, democratic or antidemocratic. When a 1992 poll asked, "Are you an adherent of any political party?" 78 percent replied no and only 9 percent yes. I am convinced that this attitude provides a very good basis for the implementation of radical and painful reforms.

The support for reform from the new, democratically oriented trade unions was another important element for all aspects of the situation, economic, social, and political. The following anecdote illustrates well the current political neutrality of the Russian people. During 1992 I paid close attention to the various political manifestations and demonstrations being held in Moscow, and in particular to their social makeup. I found this makeup to be the same whether the gathering was pro-communist or pro-democracy: pensioners dominated the gatherings (making up about 40 percent of those attending), followed by white-collar workers (25 to 30 percent). Students and laborers were less than 10 percent. Yet it is this last stratum that is considered in Russia to be the decisive force during any period of sharp tensions.

I do not think, however, that one should exaggerate this position of the bulk of the population. Various polls now display characteristic contradictions in the Russian people's understanding of the logic and purposes of market-oriented reform. For instance, according to polls taken by the Institute of Sociology in May and June 1992, about 50 percent of the Russian population was sure that the government's steps toward a free-market economy were correct, 71 percent that the government should allow full economic freedom, 64 percent that private ownership of land was to be permitted, and 48 percent that the growth of free enterprise would improve the economic situation. At the same time, 70 percent of respondents supported price controls, and 88 percent favored at least the fixing of price ceilings; 67 percent felt that the best method of privatization was to turn over enterprises to their workers, and 79 percent agreed with the proposition that the government was obliged to maintain full employment.

Another prerequisite of radical economic reforms is the existence of a dominant social and political force that is able to impose its economic interests on the rest of the society. There was no such force in 1992. Yet radical reforms could be launched after the August 1991 *coup d'état* because most of the industrial, agricultural, and other organizations were demoralized and without real influence. There was only an extremely popular president to champion the unpopular economic policy, and that is what he did. If mistakes were made, it was probably in pushing the transformation too slowly. Of course, the government's opponents raised exactly the opposite criticism—that the transformation was too radical and far too fast. But it was practically possible, and therefore necessary, to do something rapidly. For example, at the beginning of 1992, the government's economic adviser Jeffrey Sachs argued that it was better to liberalize all prices right away (including energy prices), because the government would not be able to do it two months later. The Russian leaders pledged to do so, but of course it was almost impossible later on.

Count Sergei Witte, a prominent reformer under the czars, used to say that there were two essential elements for radical reforms in Russia: absolute monarchy, because you need not pay attention to your critics if His Majesty supported you, and speed, because somebody might persuade the czar to change his mind before the reform could be made irreversible.

The latter danger arose in Russia's recent experience: the reform policy drew serious opposition in the summer of 1992. This was probably the most dangerous period, as producers in all sectors—industrialists, agrarians, trade unions, and managers of state enterprises—combined forces to fight against radical economic transformation. At that time the government did not have widespread support from the various groups of society, and in fact held to the view that seeking such support implied weakness and required giving in to lobbyists and rent seekers. Failure to seek broad support was probably a mistake, because the government was in fact weak, and had to furnish cheap credit to the enterprises not in accordance with any political criteria, but simply in proportion to the lobbying force of this or that firm (or region), without any other reasons for bias toward any of them.

Nonetheless, since the summer of 1992, through various tactical maneuvers, the government has been able to split the opposition. One can observe a division among the industrialists, with some of them sympathetic to the radical conservative (neocommunist) wing and the others to the radical reformers.

The advantage of an alliance with the industrialists in mid-1992 was that it enabled the radical reformers to enlarge somewhat their field of political action. It has allowed them to abandon a number of the bold promises they had made, for public relations purposes, in the fall of 1991 (for example, to bring a rapid end to inflation). Such an alliance might even increase, for a short time, the popularity of the executive. Finally, the appointment to the government of several leading representatives of the industrialist group made for a more open and legal working out of mutually acceptable measures and put an end to the influence of anonymous pressure of some industrialists and businessmen.

As with any political alliance, there have had to be compromises. For one thing, a fairly high monthly rate of inflation acquired respectability in autumn 1992, and this ought to suit both sides. The reformers were able to attribute this inflation to the activities of the industrialists (whose fierce opposition in the previous period had prevented the attainment of a "price plateau"). The industrialists, for their part, were able to some extent to "protect" their enterprises, which under a strict monetary policy would very rapidly have gone to the wall. Of course, it remained an open question whether inflation could be contained at a socially acceptable level, or whether it would jump to Bolivian heights of 200 percent or more. Such an outcome was entirely conceivable if the government turned a blind eye to the danger of hyperinflation.

Another potential area of compromise concerned privatization. The government now had to rid itself of the idea of rapid, full-scale privatization. A more realistic course might have been to hand over the major enterprises to their managers (directors) or senior administrators. Here, a variety of formal mechanisms could be employed. But whatever kind of privatization was adopted, we had to avoid a situation in which the principal motive of the new owners became the maximization of current consumption (that is, an increase in wages). We know that the propensity to consume is far less among industrialists and administrators than it is among their employees. If only for this reason, turning enterprises over to their managers might deliver socially (and in part economically) more acceptable results.

Finally, there was the problem of foreign economic relations. Measures to liberalize import-export transactions, to open the domestic market to foreign competition, and to introduce a single investment rate for the ruble have aroused considerable anxiety among many Russian industrialists. On the other hand, many managers, especially in the high-technology defense industries, reacted favorably to the opening up to world markets, where they hoped to make a considerable impact. Measures to open the economy were accepted with much more equanimity than could have been imagined several months ago, even if calls for protection have also become more pronounced. By following this strategy, the reformists in the government have been able to split the ranks of industrialist opposition and bring about a change of mind among a good number of Russian managers.

As an aside, the political organization Civic Union, once described as conservative, is now recognized as holding a centrist view. There was much speculation in the Western media about the power and influence of this organization. To my mind, Civic Union now seems too weak to wield significant power because of its role as the political voice of the so-called "Soviet middle class"—the managers of the state enterprises. This middle class, on which the centrally planned economy was built, is eroding, partly because of the privatization program launched in Russia last autumn. A number of managers view themselves as the future owners of their firms, and where these firms have any prospect of prospering under the market economy, their managers have become proponents of radical reform. The agreement with the directors of major factories was a triumph for Gaidar's "team." Their support gave the Gaidar government a crucial lever for influencing small and medium-sized enterprises, which cannot blackmail the cabinet with the threat of stopping their operations and are probably headed for bankruptcy. This is corroborated by their more loyal attitude to the government of Gaidar at the Russian Industrialists and Entrepreneurs Union conference on 14 November (especially in comparison with the conservative manufacturers' convention on 22 November, which went virtually unnoticed).

The principal danger for the government of pursuing radical reforms under these conditions has been its political (i.e., constitutional) vulnerability. Seeking to stay within the system of democratic values, the cabinet was compelled to function as a minority government, relying almost exclusively on the personal backing of the president. Meanwhile, the increasing political polarization obviously signaled an impending political crisis, which could result either in the president implementing a package of politically justified, but dubiously constitutional measures (such as restricting legislators' rights), or in the radical reform team stepping down.

# Bulgaria

## OGNIAN PISHEV

Ukraine and Russia, which are discussed by my fellow panelists, adopted both Orthodox Christianity and literacy from Bulgaria—the Church Slavonic (Old Bulgarian) language formed the basis of all East and Southern Slavic languages. Despite the fact that all three nations belong to a vast cultural area with a common history, they demonstrate distinctly different approaches to economic and political transition. Unfortunately, this diversity has not heretofore spawned substantial comparative analysis of the politics of economic reform in Central and Eastern Europe and the Commonwealth of Independent States.

This is a dramatic departure from the postwar experience of the region. In the not so distant past, experienced Communist politicians knew how to take advantage of cultural and historic arguments in their efforts at political and economic deal making.

In recent years, the Bulgarian political and government leadership made at least two attempts—in 1963 and 1973—to join the Union of Soviet Socialist Republics. In the end, it would have been a logical step, as Bulgaria was considered the most subservient Soviet satellite. But as it turned out, Bulgaria's effort to become a Soviet republic on both occasions was an exercise in blackmail—the Soviet leaders knew all too well that whenever Bulgaria was included in a bigger empire—Roman, Byzantine, or Ottoman—these empires always collapsed, so the offer was gracefully rejected. As a result, on both occasions, Bulgaria walked

*Ognian Pishev is Bulgaria's Ambassador to the United States. He was an Economic Adviser to the President of Bulgaria.*

away from these negotiations with promises of more credits and increased deliveries of crude oil and other raw materials.

The differential between CMEA and world oil prices, which had the significance of a formal and permanent subsidy for the Bulgarian economy, amounted to 12.1 percent of Bulgarian GDP (in the case of Czechoslovakia, it was 7 percent; Hungary, 5.9 percent; Poland, 5.0 percent [Gelb and Gray 1991, 38]). The small Bulgarian economy had additional advantages to offer in purely economic terms as well. Within the framework of the "international socialist division of labor," Bulgaria played the role of an intermediary, or *pays-relais* as the French call it, between the Soviet economy and the developed market economies, particularly in high-technology industries. This introduced two major, inherent weaknesses: the dependence on Soviet deliveries of raw materials for a number of resource-based and energy-intensive industries, the only ones capable of exporting to hard currency markets in the West, and high import intensity and technological dependence of its computer, telecommunication, machine tools, pharmaceutical, and other industries on inputs provided by Western suppliers for incorporation in products sold on the Soviet market.

Bulgaria was trapped in a vicious circle: it borrowed to serve CMEA customers, and it processed Soviet natural resources to service its external debt. The unilateral debt moratorium declared by the Communist government of Andrey Lukanov on 29 March 1990 underscored the crisis this pattern of trade and specialization had produced. Socialist internationalism turned out to be the bane of my country and one of the planned economy's longest-lasting legacies. Both institutional arrangements and the international macroeconomic linkages have made stabilization and structural adjustment extremely difficult. The lack of sufficient international support and the vulnerability of Bulgaria to external economic and political shocks remain the trademarks of economic and political transition.

Stabilization started in great style shortly after the creation of the coalition government of Dimitar Popov. The most important steps of economic reform in Bulgaria, undertaken in February 1991, included:

- sweeping and immediate price liberalization

- introduction of a market-based exchange rate for the lev (the national currency) being freely traded on the newly established interbank currency market

- export/import liberalization

- early agreement with the International Monetary Fund on a one-year program to contain inflation through deficit reduction and an austere incomes policy.

In February 1991 the coalition government led by Dimitar Popov put an end to the lengthy discussions about the need to secure national consensus before the start of the stabilization program. It created de facto national support for the first package of executive measures by simply implementing them. The almost immediate alleviation of some of the most acute shortages, and the redressing of domestic balances, thanks to the elimination of basic price distortions, overcame most of the political divisions in Bulgarian society. The experience of early 1991 clearly supports Mancur Olson's hypothesis that the crisis that had undermined the socialist political and economic system opened the door to the first phase of policy reform.

We need to introduce some additional explanations to shed more light on the Bulgarian experience. First of all, the collapse of communism was evident despite the fact that the Bulgarian Socialist Party (the renamed Communist Party) won the June 1990 parliamentary elections and political reform was far more gradual than in Central Europe. And second, Bulgaria was immediately perceived as being a part of a broader regional trend. As a result, the "reformed" Communists[1] tried to use their participation in the coalition government as well as their collaboration on the adoption of a new post-Communist constitution, to legitimize their political survival. The inefficiencies of the National Assembly led to the transfer of most of the checks and balances to the executive branch, whose work was defined by the intense competition among the "young Turks" of various political colors. This period of cohabitation roughly corresponds to John Williamson's definition of a political honeymoon, but this level of cooperation between parties will never be repeated.

The initial success of the reform was gradually eroded by the inherent weaknesses of the Bulgarian economy. GDP fell by 11.8 percent in 1990, 22.9 percent in 1991, and 8.1 percent in 1992. The inflationary expansion of consumption in 1990 (nominal wages and salaries were increased by the Communist government, and there was 0.6 percent growth of consumption) precipitated the crisis, and in 1991 and 1992, consumption fell by 11.9 percent and 10.4 percent respectively.

The lack of a comprehensive reform program to a great extent explains the inability to proceed quickly with structural reforms, namely public sector reorganization and privatization, completion of the banking sector reform, and land restitution, to mention but a few of the principal necessary elements. After the elections of October 1991, the Union of

---

1. I usually responded to the the Western public in its initial fascination with the so-called reformists in Central and Eastern Europe with a line of analogy: "There is no such thing as a reformed Democrat in the United States; they all become Republicans," although it may no longer be pertinent.

In Latin America we observe the case of recycled democrats (for example, Belaúnde and Carlos Andrés Peréz) who in a completely different historical setting attempt a political comeback with an economic program that has nothing to do with their original beliefs.

Democratic Forces (UDF) government, reflecting the political divisions in society, departed from the original 1990 economic platform in emphasizing restitution as opposed to large-scale privatization, which delayed the transformation of the public sector.

Despite the emergence of a strong and independent central bank capable of carrying out strict monetary policies and combating inflation, brought down from almost 300 percent in 1991 to less than 80 percent in 1992, banking and financial sector reform were further delayed. Moreover, the commercial banks, most of them state-owned, were the first to realize their particular interest in channeling credit for spontaneous privatization. A demonstration of this well-organized spontaneity is the establishment of a new circular pattern of economic behavior. For instance, a public enterprise guarantees a sizable bank loan to a private company set up by the next of kin of the public enterprise's managers. The private company's management in turn buys shares of the commercial bank that gave the loan. Because financial sector profits are the most reliable source of tax revenue, the Ministry of Finance was ready to tolerate such practices, even though they ran against the logic of economic reform. Instead, the government opted for more immediate control over the real economy through demonopolization and transformation of public enterprises into joint-stock companies with the state as the sole shareholder.

Such policies cannot eliminate CMEA-inherited dependence and structural rigidities. The pace of reform is quite uneven across sectors— the external sector is responding to market incentives and signals—price and trade liberalization, domestic convertibility of the lev, and administrative reform—quite well, though only after a significant decline in the volume of trade—with the ensuing drastic decline in output and GDP. Agriculture is also ready to take off again, now that the lengthy process of land restitution is gaining momentum. Service industries, tourism in particular, are adopting rational, free-market behavior, but their revival depends on attracting customers from abroad—a task not made easier by the war in Bosnia. The closing down of uranium mining was the first serious step of industrial rationalization, but manufacturing in general is still a largely ossified system of huge sunk costs, immobilized labor, and few incentives to change.

Administrative centralization can be justified by noting that economic reform always starts as a revolution from above. It is important to have, or to construct quickly, a government machinery—that is, a nonpartisan civil service. By definition, all East European revolutions led to the destruction of the existing public administration, which in Bulgaria took the form of massive replacement of Communist cadres by newcomers with no experience and no system of proper ethical checks and balances. In Bulgaria purges of pro-Communist loyalists took extreme forms after the October 1991 elections. But the last technocratic government of Professor Lyuben Berov is relying increasingly on seasoned, middle-level bureaucrats.

The need for public oversight and governance is urgent, but if these revolutions from above fail to create active constituencies interested in the radicalization of systemic transformation, they often abort as yet another example of failure of enlightened social engineering without unleashing widespread and irreversible changes in the political and economic system.

There are many examples of earlier modernization efforts in developing countries (Iran, Turkey, the Philippines). They show that public administrations emerge as the new political and business elites, but this does not necessarily assure the power base for continuing modernization.[2]

One of the issues all conference participants discussed is the consolidation of the power base of reforming governments and the emergence of new political elites. But rarely has a simple question been asked: where does the new elite come from? Most of the new politicians are people without any background in practical economic issues, managerial decisions, and teamwork. But do history and practical experience really matter in a situation of revolutionary upheavals? There is a continuous need to build coalitions and to co-opt elements of the old economic system, or at least to neutralize the old guard's resistance to change. So why do we need this practical experience? For a very simple reason—we should know the motivation of the people we want to change. Just a simple example. We have a colonel who runs a military factory in Bulgaria. A very lucrative deal is proposed to him. He refuses. Why? He is not interested in profit, high salary, or bonuses; he wants to become a general. And he will sit quietly and wait for three years until he gets there. If you do not know the noneconomic motivations of these people—both participants in the old system and the new business elite—then it is much harder to create coalitions, to engage them in the process of transition, to propose innovative deals, and to create this new political and business elite. Given the unclear demarcation line between political and business power groups, the temptation of direct involvement in each other's spheres of competence is very strong. Private sector groups create "business" parties and blocks, government officials and politicians, including elected ones, sit on various corporate boards, or participate in the management of enterprises that are under their regulatory authority. The elites themselves don't have the practical experience of

---

2. It is interesting to note the interaction between the international financial institutions—the IMF and the World Bank group—and the public administration in Bulgaria. At the very beginning of economic reform, the staff of the international organizations acted as a substitute for the vanishing public administration. As a result, the process of learning by doing on both sides is still going on, partly due to the exceptionally high turnover of people involved.

functioning under a democratic system as countervailing powers with well-defined parameters and interests.

The typical composition of the economic teams in Central and Eastern Europe, as well as in the Commonwealth of Independent States, defies the idea of the technopols as advanced by John Williamson in his model. Bulgaria witnessed the emergence of a powerful group claiming to be the new technocrats of the emerging market systems—but they were not "economists who use their professional/technical skills in government," so much as (to borrow another Williamson definition from three years ago) "ideologue[s] . . . someone who knows the answer before he has heard the context of the problem" (Williamson 1990, 36).

The emergence of technocrats and of free-market technopols in particular is conditional on a developed government infrastructure, which includes a number of new government bodies, as well as redefinition of the role played by traditional institutions (e.g., a new balance of power between the Ministry of Finance and the independent central bank). Otherwise, the recruitment of the new professional cadres takes place somewhat arbitrarily, with the most obvious candidates being economics professors and engineers. Eastern Europe has a long tradition of favoring technical education. That is why the ratio of technical people in the administration is disproportionately high; the only economists who were professional civil servants were the students and practitioners of central planning who had no prior experience and much less understanding of how markets work.

The economic team that started working on the concept of transition to market economy in Bulgaria comprised people from the research community and the universities: the first non-Communist minister of finance had taught political economy of socialism and econometric modeling of the centrally planned Bulgarian economy; the minister of industry presumably conducted research on socialist accumulation and investment planning (he was engaged in pseudo-research but was never held in high esteem by the economics profession). In Russia, Yegor Gaidar first became known to the reading public through his *perestroika*-type articles, published in *Kommunist* magazine during the second half of the 1980s. None of these activities presupposed any understanding of the practical workings of a business enterprise, bank, or ministry.

The dogmatic and ideological formulation of economic plans has been widespread in the entire East European region, and it led to a number of self-inflicted wounds. In the case of Bulgaria, the most significant example of misjudgment (supported, it has to be said, by the forecasting techniques of the IMF) was the considerable deviation of all actual macroeconomic indicators from the estimates included in the first stand-by agreement with the IMF. In the absence of a comprehensive model of institutional development, there are ad hoc, partial solutions to emergencies. The most successful and spectacular phases of economic transition are usually those that unleash free-market forces to fill the void left by the destruction of central planning of production and resource allocation. Political passions leave too little room for careful planning and execution of the many steps of institution building. There is a pervasive desire to discover the magic plan of uniform transition to a market economy—the centralized process of voucher privatization, which is a macroeconomic-policy answer to an essentially microeconomic problem, providing the perfect illustration of this point. But once adopted, this centralized approach forges political consensus and helps win elections. And maybe this is one of the criteria by which success of postcommunist transformation should be judged.

The differences in initial conditions, timing, and international environment make intraregional comparisons very problematic. From the point of view of economic stability, Czechoslovakia might have been a winner, but it is no longer a united country. Hungary has attracted the most foreign direct investment, but it still displays xenophobic tendencies, despite its elaborate and civilized political system.

Profound changes are taking place in Poland, the nation with the best chance of renewed economic growth. The coalition that brought down the communist system now bears the brunt of the pain of economic transformation. In the beginning of the 1980s, the mass movement, created by the unique alliance between intellectuals and workers (with the cementing involvement of the Catholic Church), had a very different social and economic agenda.

The mass movement lost. This is one of the paradoxes of the situation in Eastern Europe. Poland started with a well-defined coalition, where one would think it possible to extrapolate from the expectations of the coalition members to create a framework for political discussion and to support mobilization. All of a sudden, the program is changed and, *chemin faisant*, expectations also change. Intellectuals and workers lose the most as a result of transition, not only in Poland but throughout the region. Creation of left-of-center political organizations (Zbignev Bujak, one of the legendary leaders of the underground Solidarity, is leading the effort in Poland) as a balance to conservative economic and social policies was the natural response to the dissolution of the first mass movement in the region. And the price for stability in Poland may have been too high—the creeping loss of the secular character of the state signaled *inter alia* by the adoption of conservative anti-abortion legislation and the like.

Essential dimensions of civil society are slow to materialize. One of the disturbing features of postcommunist society is the virtual absence of significant public policy debate. There is no framework for such discussions outside the government—no think-tanks, professional publications, business organizations, or universities that provide this sort of forum.

The establishment of an organic link between the power elite and the masses is conditional on an odd mixture of outcomes or mere suggestions—that markets work but that they do not create excessive inequality. In response to one of the principal points in John Williamson's paper—on "the emergence of politically significant beneficiaries of the economic reform"—I would say that, rather, the politically significant in Eastern Europe, in Bulgaria in particular, become the main beneficiaries of economic reform.

Once again, there is a certain inversion in social evolution that is important to understand because it has a lot to do with the rent seeking mentioned by Oleh Havrylyshyn and Vladimir Mau, a common trait of delayed transitions in Eastern Europe.

The interaction between the administration and the business sector creates an "integrated circuit." The analogy with semiconductivity is compelling: you introduce regulations into the trade regime just as you introduce impurities imprinting paths onto the silicon chip—to direct the flow of information, as well as money and benefits from the quotas allocated to exporters. Administrative intervention increases, and new measures are introduced that direct rents toward the political elite, who want to derive immediate cash benefits from economic transition. This raises an interesting question: what is the fastest way of creating wealth—attaining political power or introducing and/or benefitting from economic reform?

The new capitalists in Bulgaria and elsewhere are being recruited from among the old *nomenklatura*, the new political elite, and the early beneficiaries of market reform—the vigorous private sector. The latter is subdivided into new businesses, and restituted property is being put back into commercial use. Reform in Bulgaria is building momentum. But concurrently it is also generating new obstacles:

- The delay in privatization, for example, is due not only to the ideological debates around the issues of "equal starting conditions and opportunities" versus "market-based privatization." It has a lot to do with the emphasis on physical restitution of property as opposed to large-scale privatization. On a broader scale, it is the larger contradiction between rent seeking and entrepreneurship and innovation.

- The symbiotic circular relationship between public and private industrial enterprises, which often have almost identical management teams, acts against the introduction of financial discipline.

- The relative unwillingness to accept and attract foreign direct investment is linked to old sensitivities about foreign domination and exploitation. Neither the administration nor the private sector is ready to compete or cooperate with big transnational corporations.

- Little attention is devoted to one of the principal issues of market reform: centralization versus decentralization. Local governments depend on the state budget for their survival and yet are reluctant to privatize municipal property. The system of centralized tax collection cannot provide the necessary incentives for local governments to accelerate this privatization.

- Equally insufficient are the efforts to foster a balance between public control and self-regulation or self-organization of economic life.

There are some notable examples of the uneven pace of economic transition in Bulgaria:

- The limited role for autonomous market institutions—stock and commodity exchanges, capital markets.

- The delayed appearance of automatic market-based feedback of economic performance. Both in the domestic economy and in international trade, competition is still heavily managed by the state, cases of bankruptcies of public enterprises are very rare, and there is nothing that might resemble consumer sovereignty.

- The dearth of market-generated information—on prices and economic performance, competitiveness and comparative advantages, etc.

In less than three years, Bulgaria lived through two inconclusive parliamentary elections, one presidential, and one local government election. It managed to preserve the peaceful character of the political revolution, but to a certain extent at the expense of speedy and efficient economic transformation. Inadequate international support, the succession of a number of external shocks,[3] and the persistent crisis on our western border explain most of the delay. And yet, some of the essential elements of a market economy have taken root and are increasingly determining the pace and direction of transition. A quiet revolution is occurring in people's minds. For the economics profession, it means a sweeping change of paradigms and a new generation of young professionals coming to maturity. Transition is not only an end; it is an important learning experience. Therefore, it is not only the goal that matters but also how we get there.

## References

Gelb, Alan H., and Gray, Cheryl W. 1991. *The Transformation of Economies in Central and Eastern Europe. Issues, Progress and Prospects.* Policy and Research Series 17. Washington: The World Bank.

John Williamson, editor. 1990. *Latin American Adjustment: How Much Has Happened?* Washington: Institute for International Economics.

---

3. The chief shocks are the collapse of the COMECON market, the Persian Gulf War, and the introduction of trade sanctions against Serbia.

# Discussion

*Steve Parker* drew some comparisons between the reforming socialist economies in Asia and those in Eastern Europe. First, agricultural reform had started very early in the programs in Asia, preceding industrial restructuring. Given the large proportion of the population employed in agriculture and the favorable land tenure arrangements, price reforms and improved property rights had generated rapid increases in farm output and incomes. This had enfranchised a large proportion of the population into the initial economic reform effort, and it had reduced the balance of payments burden by increasing agricultural exports and reducing food imports. In contrast, in most of Eastern Europe and Russia, agriculture has not been a focus of reform.

Second, privatization had played a minor role in Asia, where the basic approach has been to implement market reforms, allowing the private sector to grow around the state sector. This had led to rapid increases in output and exports by the private sector, as competitive forces that had been restrained by the previous policy regime were unleashed, while limiting the adjustment cost and resistance to reform by the state sector. Support of the latter, although often wasteful, had not led to significant budget problems as had occurred in Latin America. The sort of rents that were described as available in Ukraine would have stimulated a large influx of people into those activities in Asia. The relatively broad-based growth had created constituencies for sustained reform through gradual liberalization.

*Fred Bergsten* suggested that, in economies as highly monopolized as those in the former Soviet Union still were, it was inevitable that price liberalization would lead to the emergence of many rent opportunities.

*Nicolás Ardito-Barletta* followed up by asking what Oleh Havrylyshyn thought could be done in the Ukrainian situation to curb the rent seekers and thus permit continuation of the reform program. On Peru and Brazil, he remarked that in both cases external factors had actually impeded policy reform. In Peru, the international crisis of 1981–82 had created substantial problems, especially since President Fernando Belaúnde was not really interested in economic policy reform. In Brazil in 1964–67, Planning Minister Roberto Campos had introduced major reforms similar to those debated today, which had resulted in annual growth rates of up to 10 percent for six successive years (the "Brazilian miracle"). But the first oil shock had triggered policies of import substitution and foreign borrowing. Between 1974 and 1980 growth had remained in the range of 7 to 8 percent, and the population had got used to rapid growth. The second oil shock had then caught the military off guard, and Planning Minister Antônio Delfim Netto had been prevented from doing what the Chilean military did later, namely, turn over a well-functioning economy to the electorate as a practical demonstration that a market economy is superior to the kind of populist management that had been so pervasive over the past decade.

*Stephan Haggard* complained that the discussion of the sources of political support for the technopols had so far alluded either to interest groups on the one hand or to the executive on the other. The new democracies that had been most successful—for example, Spain and Chile—were those with strong party backing for their reforms. In contrast, reformers in those countries that had suffered the greatest difficulties, such as Peru and Brazil, had not received support from the party structure. Poland's problems in 1990–91 had been clearly related to the emergence of a fragmented and fractious party system, just as Boris Yeltsin's difficulties in Russia were being multiplied by his confrontation with a legislature that was totally out of sympathy with his objectives. A solid base of political support was one of the most basic prerequisites for successful reform.

*Yavuz Canevi* asked what value external assistance could have for the economies in transition in Eastern Europe in the absence of functioning payments and price systems. The Marshall Plan had not just provided aid, it had been instrumental in reestablishing a payments system (the European Payments Union). Unofficial barter was the only real mechanism of exchange in the former Soviet republics at the present time, and perhaps a first step should be its institutionalization.

*Kalman Mizsei* listed some of the major achievements of the Central European economies that had pioneered the transition from socialism. Inflation had fallen over the last three years to civilized levels; they had substantially liberalized prices and trade; exports, foreign investment, and the consumption of durables had increased dramatically; and there were hopes of positive economic growth in all three countries in 1993.

*William Cline* contrasted two possible reactions to recent developments in Russia. One considered an output decline in the range of 30 or 40 percent (the result of a traditional austerity program) to be unacceptable and suggested a policy of triage, allowing the most inefficient state firms to collapse, leaving the competitive enterprises alone, and concentrating help on maintaining production in marginally viable enterprises. The other, along the lines proposed by Jeffrey Sachs, was to ignore the collapse in output and reject any form of Keynesian expansion or industrial policy. Which of those two reactions would Mau and Havrylyshyn espouse?

*Guillermo de la Dehesa* suggested that capital accumulation by rent seekers might be a necessary condition for launching a transformation of a planned economy. Mediation between consumers and producers by rent-seeking traders might in fact be efficient, and the ''mafia traders'' might be the future entrepreneurs the countries needed.

*Shafiqul Islam* stated that Jeffrey Sachs believed that Yeltsin had made a great mistake in deciding not to form a political party of the reformers. Islam also argued that rent seeking was neither a dominant problem nor confined to the transition economies. Rents were used for something, which could be something constructive like developing private entrepreneurship. And both Japan and Korea had exhibited such behavior in response to the heavy regulation of their economies.

*Luiz Carlos Bresser Pereira* suggested that it would be appropriate to refer to the Eastern European countries before 1989 as statist rather than communist economies. The transition from statism to capitalism was so complex that it needed a lot of time to be done properly. Stabilization, in contrast, could and should be done quickly. So why had Russia chosen to give priority to the transition to capitalism?

*Vladimir Mau* replied that only the left-wing newspapers claimed that Russia was seeking to make the transition to capitalism in a single step. He went on to stress that the situation in Russia at the end of 1991 had combined hyperinflation with extreme shortages; Russia was a dying country whose people had no understanding of what was happening and no hope. Radical price liberalization had been essential to create some degree of understanding of the problems among the population and some hope that things might get better. But that was a first step and not the complete transformation process. Real stabilization is needed, but it will have to come along with other measures such as the establishment of property rights.

While Mau agreed with much of what Jeffrey Sachs had said, he did not share his understanding of the ''mafia problem.'' There was a damaging mafia in Russia, but it was not found only in the monopolistic state system. For example, since liberalization the price level in Moscow had been about 30 percent higher than a hundred kilometers away; that was not a result of the forces of supply and demand or of the state organizations, but of the ability of criminal trade organizations to exclude competitors. But it was pointless to complain about this, as the leftist politicians did, as a bad way to a market economy, because it was the *only* way to a market economy.

On the question of the output decline, Mau thought 40 percent was an exaggerated estimate of the fall in industrial production. The true average was probably closer to 20 percent. In any event, the average was not of much interest; there was actually increased output of some civilian goods, but this was more than offset by a radical decline in military output. In addition, the statistics did not cover the private sector, where output had been increasing. The real issue posed by industrial contraction was a political one: should the uncompetitive enterprises be subsidized or not?

Mau agreed that there was rent seeking in the monopolized markets. Part of the answer was to open the market to foreign competition. He agreed that the reimposition of price controls would not help. He also agreed that a well-structured party system was to be desired, but parties were extremely unpopular institutions in Russia. He therefore doubted whether a party system would be established in the medium term.

*Oleh Havrylyshyn* started his reply by outlining the basic structure of the Ukrainian government. Three main sources of power existed—the presidency, the cabinet with the prime minister, and the parliament. Very slowly the beginnings of party formations could be discerned. The government, together with the military-industrial complex, controlled the economy. The previous prime minister had been associated with certain trading interests (as opposed to producer interests). The severe deterioration of the economy had led to strong opposition by the minority democratic-front parties (which were powerful enough to obstruct government), and well-intentioned reformist elements in the government had indeed been blocked by the opposition for purely political reasons. The power struggle was finally resolved by putting a compromise candidate from the industrial lobby and the former elite into the premiership. His appointment was considered a victory for the leader of parliament over the president. It had rapidly transpired, however, that this compromise candidate was not what he had been assumed to be, namely, a Ukrainian equivalent of Volsky (the leader of the Russian industrial lobby): after his appointment he had quickly become a convert to reform, as exemplified publicly in his advocacy of a "big bang" on the Polish model after a meeting with his Polish counterpart Hanna Suchocka.

Havrylyshyn argued that parties and a political structure emerged from the historical process rather than being designed by governments or politicians. But one could not afford to wait until a good political structure was in place, and the best a government, or the leading figures in government, could do was to seek to build a constituency for economic reform.

With the discipline of the central plan having been dropped and the discipline of market competition not having been put into place, there was great scope for corruption and inefficient rent seeking. Barter was an excellent mechanism for furthering the private interests of the two parties directly involved, but it involved huge costs to society through terms of trade losses.

In reply to Canevi, Havrylyshyn argued that the best way of developing an internal and external payments system was to create one radically and swiftly, as, for instance, Estonia had done by introducing its own currency. Once the Ukrainian link to the ruble zone was broken, it would be possible to introduce a working payments system (e.g., via correspondent banking) rapidly. (Vladimir Mau interjected that he had recently seen an advertisement on Moscow television for making payments to Ukraine within two days; Havrylyshyn responded that he understood the fee to be 40 percent, but the example was nevertheless to the point.)

Responding to Cline, Havrylyshyn suggested that the availability of credits to maintain employment, with no monitoring to ensure that the people employed were producing anything, could help to explain the decline in output. He also agreed with Balcerowicz that much of the decline in production was of goods that had no economic value. There was also some increase in unrecorded output in the private sector (although less than in Poland). However, if Sachs could not convince this audience that the output decline was not a cause for concern, then it was hardly likely that the peoples of Russia and Ukraine were going to be persuaded to dismiss it, so the problem had to be addressed for political reasons. But the rough and ready industrial policy described as triage was also subject to inefficient rent seeking.

Havrylyshyn argued against taking a benign view of rent seeking, because it posed two major risks. First, much of the rent would flow out as flight capital. Second, economies that develop extensive rent seeking might get stuck in an intermediate regime (like that of Argentina or India) rather than develop a competitive market economy. And even if government intervention had worked in Japan and Korea, these were exceptional cases, and he thought the countries of the former Soviet Union were far more likely to go the route of India or Argentina than that of Japan or Korea. Hence he favored fighting rent seeking, which involved removing as rapidly as possible the distortions that nurtured it (monopolistic structures, price and administrative distortions, etc.). In order to be able to move quickly, policymakers needed either public support or public apathy. Another possibility was to coopt rent seekers, for example by creating legitimate investment opportunities with returns that could compete with those from rent seeking.

*Ognian Pishev* agreed with Steve Parker that the spontaneous emergence of new private enterprises was at least as important as the privatization of existing state firms, and this had been a promising feature of the transition process in Bulgaria, especially in agriculture. He also endorsed Havrylyshyn's view that opening the economy was an efficient means of curbing distortions and improving incentives.

How should one judge success? The introduction of market reforms was not the only thing that mattered, in Pishev's view; preservation of the nation-state was also at issue in many parts of Central and Eastern Europe. What will future historians say of the breakup of Czechoslovakia? Is it likely to provoke a chain reaction, with the dissatisfaction of the Hungarian minority in Slovakia being the next step in an intensification of xenophobic and nationalistic sentiments, whose reemergence has been the least welcome byproduct of the reforms?

Pishev expected the new government in Bulgaria to shift policy away from restitution and embark on a more ambitious privatization program. There were signs that the new government would devote more attention to microeconomic and structural issues in agriculture and manufacturing. Success depended not just on Bulgaria's own policies, which had already introduced free prices for over 95 percent of goods, had established a completely free trade regime, and had reduced inflation to 80 percent in 1992, but also on international conditions, and unfortunately Bulgaria faced a serious constraint (intensified by the war in neighboring Yugoslavia) from the limited supply of external finance.

# 9

**PANEL DISCUSSION**

# Panel Discussion

## NICOLÁS ARDITO-BARLETTA

I will attempt to identify some conditions under which economic policy reforms may be implemented and derive a few rules of action that may be useful to technopols to gain political support for such reform. This exploration assumes a concrete scenario in which the objective is to move from a framework of statist or dirigiste economic policies to one of policies based on an open economy with competitive markets, supported by a government that creates the policy environment for private economic activity and for human development.

Ideally, we would like to define a model of political and economic action that brings together ideas, social values, situations (both national and international), constituencies, and concrete positive results to sustain the stability of the new policies. These reflections fall short of that goal. Instead, I offer some approximations based on the experience of certain Latin American countries and illustrate a typology of situations in which successful policy reforms are often possible.

In broadest outline (I quote from a previous essay on the subject):

> Ultimately, elites that hold power or influence policy making consider trade-offs between the perceived national interest and their interest when evaluating policy options. If a new policy is favorable to both, then it is easily adopted. If a new policy entails losses to them, even though it may produce a national gain or prevent a future problem, they may postpone it. When the national problem worsens to the degree that it threatens the political power or the economic gains of the elites, they may change policies to cut their losses short. If a new policy implies short-term losses and a perceived long-term gain for them or for other

*Nicolás Ardito-Barletta is the Chairman and General Director of the International Center for Economic Growth. He was the President of Panama, 1984–85.*

groups, careful political coalition building may permit the change. The situation is most difficult when a new policy entails new ways of perceiving reality and a change in the value system. In such a case the national learning process needs to be complemented by a crisis or by persuasive, concrete evidence that a new scenario may indeed produce better results for the nation and for elite groups. (Ardito-Barletta 1991, chapter 11, 294)

## The Latin American Experience

This century records two major watersheds both in the models that dominated economic thinking and in the policies that put the models into practice. The first, initiated during the Great Depression and implemented from 1935 onward, was the movement from a liberal open trade model to a model largely based on import-substituting industrialization and a dirigiste state that would regulate the economy, create state enterprises, and fix key economic variables such as prices. The second, which started in the 1970s, gained momentum in the 1980s, and is still continuing, has moved away from that model toward one based on open economies working in competitive markets within a more stable macropolicy framework.

Both of these watershed changes were influenced by economic crises within a number of countries, the immediate causes of which were external. Both times, governments responded to the evidence of inadequate internal circumstances in the midst of a changing international economic environment. In both episodes there were new economic ideas that established a framework and rationalization for the policy changes. And in both cases the traditional political cultural values, defined as favoritism, clientism, and paternalism practiced by both the political right and the left, were strongly influential: in the 1935–55 period to support the import substitution model, and in the 1975–90 period to resist the movement toward a market-oriented economy.

An economic crisis may be defined as a situation in which there is a general awareness that most people in the society are worse off than before and want a change. It entails a realization that the existing rules of the game no longer produce the results desired by a majority of the people.

During the 1935–55 period, import-substituting industrialization in Latin America favored urban laborers, producers, and government employees and discriminated against the rural population and exporters through direct and indirect taxation. The favored urban groups were emerging new political constituencies and were strengthened by the new economic model. Since 1975, economic stagnation has increased unemployment, reduced standards of living, and diminished public social services. The debt crisis of the early 1980s accelerated the process and created the opportunity for policy changes.

But the seeds of the intellectual environment that would later support economic policy changes had been sown since the 1960s. A growing number of Latin American PhD's were being trained in the most modern economic theories at US and British universities. The Alliance for Progress had given political recognition to the importance of development and economic policy. This led politicians to appoint economists to important policymaking positions. The seeds for policy change soon began to blossom throughout the region. Noteworthy and partially successful attempts at policy change were made in several countries: in Brazil during 1964–67, Argentina during 1975–80, Chile in 1973–83, Peru in 1979–85, and Uruguay in 1975–82. With the exceptions of Chile and Uruguay, however, the policy reform effort was not sustained long enough to turn around people's expectations. In most cases the second international oil price increase of 1979–80 and the resulting international recession aborted the experiments.

Ultimately it was the debt and liquidity crisis of 1982–85 that created the circumstances that permitted the new economic thinking to take hold. This thinking has been introduced into Latin America by the significant number of foreign-trained Latin American Ph.D. economists and by the international financial organizations and has sustained economic policy changes in Chile, Mexico, Bolivia, Uruguay, Costa Rica, and Argentina. More recently it has influenced most of the remaining Latin American countries. In some countries, enough time has elapsed to show that the export-led growth model, accompanied by responsible fiscal and monetary policy in a market-oriented economy, produces a sustainable growth process, which is then supported by a majority of the people. Other countries are still in the midst of the transition, and expectations have not been sufficiently transformed to place the new policies on a more durable footing.

The change in economic model and in economic policies is bringing about a change in perceptions and in value systems concerning the rules of the game, and that change in turn is producing improved economic results. Perceptions have changed not only about the importance of export-led growth based on more open economies and a less interventionist state pursuing market-oriented policies, but also about the need to improve social welfare through better targeted human development programs. In country after country, politically and economically powerful groups are finding out, as is a majority of the general population, that their material well-being improves more quickly with sustained growth and more efficient social programs.

## A Typology for Successful Policy Reform

Sustainable policy reform obviously requires the presence of a combination of elements, some related to the political arena and some to the economic system.

## The Political Arena

Every government at any point in its tenure enjoys a certain level of support and credibility. Different social groups with particular interests and objectives may either support, be neutral toward, or oppose a government and its policies. The aggregation of support and credibility that a government may have at a given moment can be considered its stock of political capital. This can be maintained, spent, or increased during the life of that government.

The government constantly needs to reevaluate how its policies and actions affect the stock of political capital, which it needs to govern effectively. Policy reform implies, by definition, that groups that now benefit from the policy status quo may be affected adversely by having their privileges taken away, while other groups may benefit. We know that some economic policy changes may be detrimental to some groups at the beginning, yet beneficial to the majority after a while. Hence, the process of reform needed to introduce a new model of economic policy can be viewed politically as one in which a government spends political capital, but maintains a minimum level of it and replenishes it over time so as to retain power and sustain the policy change.

## The Economic Arena

As we know, the movement away from policies that restrict trade, control prices, sustain fiscal deficits that fuel inflation, and maintain negative interest rates, and toward policies that do the opposite, create for a while winners and losers in the economy. The change in direction and in the rules of the game implied by the new policies is substantial. It is not just tinkering at the margin of established policy to improve performance; rather it represents profound changes in incentives, benefits, and costs to well-established groups. It is not evident, either at the beginning or during the process of policy transformation, that the majority will gain from the policy changes. A policy change that results in an environment conducive to sustainable, more dynamic growth and improved human welfare eventually creates a situation that benefits even those who had profited from the initially restricted economic situation and had lost ground with the implementation of the reform. But this end point is not perceived by those who only see short-term losses from the policy changes. Their negative expectations lead them to oppose the policy changes and even to bet against them with their economic actions. A government embarking on reforms has to be in a sufficiently strong position, first, to make the policy changes, and then to sustain them long enough to make it evident to most groups in society that the new policy framework works better for them.

The policy transformation process recalls the biblical journey of the Israelites to the promised land. As long as the people are still wandering in the desert between the old and the new status quo, the process is unstable and may even be reversed. Once policies achieve their announced purposes and their benefits begin to be perceived by an increasing number of groups in the society, the policy framework enters a more stable and sustainable level. This stage is what I call the "motherhood stage": when a new economic policy framework finally comes to be regarded universally as something good and indeed almost sacred, like motherhood, then there is no turning back.

There is a national learning process that permits society to discover, through trial and error, how to arrive at new social rules of the game and policies that are beneficial to the majority. Once that learning is complete, people will stand ready to defend the new situation. For example, in most of the industrialized countries, governments are easily voted out of office if they permit inflation to increase beyond certain minimum limits. Such is not yet the case in many Latin American countries. This difference in perceptions about how much inflation may be tolerated illustrates that the industrialized societies have undergone a learning process about the causes and effects of a harmful policy.

## Conditions for Success

We may classify the conditions necessary to achieve sustainable policy changes as being either outside or inside the government. Others in this volume refer to certain outside conditions. One is the presence of a domestic crisis caused by national or international circumstances. Another might be the presence of a discredited opposition, under whose leadership the country has experienced economic worsening or stagnation. A third is the presence of neighboring countries that have successfully pursued different policies, as in East Asia and Europe: their success can have a persuasive demonstration effect. Another external circumstance could be the pressure of the international community in the midst of a difficult financial and balance of payments situation, whose solution needs the support of the international community as a complement to the internal effort for change.

Although those external circumstances create the possibility (or opportunity) for policy reform, perhaps only the first condition, the perception of a crisis, opens the door to rapid and thorough reform. The rest mainly add to or deplete the government's stock of political capital at the margin and build up the perceived need for change. In such cases a gradual evolutionary change process is prescribed.

What is elsewhere in this volume called the honeymoon period provides an opportunity for radical reform only in a situation of generally perceived crisis demanding prompt and sometimes heroic actions. Otherwise, the honeymoon begins to erode quickly, as different pressure groups sense that the policy changes are adverse for them and those that may benefit from policy changes are not sufficiently aware of the costs to them of existing policies.

Even an apparent electoral mandate for policy change is of doubtful value unless it occurs in a crisis situation. An electoral landslide may be perceived as the expression of a majority wanting to escape its present economic circumstances, rather than a mandate for specific policy changes that will create short-term losses for politically powerful pressure groups. There are clear examples of candidates for public office who lost support from labor groups, business organizations, public employees, and others when they announced policy positions that were detrimental to those groups' immediate interest, even though they may have been desirable to the silent, unorganized majority.

For reform to succeed, there must be a correlation between the severity of existing economic problems, perceptions of their causes, and the policy changes that powerful groups are willing to tolerate. If the regulatory environment favors special interest groups, and economic stagnation can be connected to that regulatory environment, then those groups can be weakened or discredited, stimulating majority support for reforms. If, instead, the highly regulatory environment is perceived as the natural way of doing business (for example, because of clientist traditions) and the economic problems are not sufficiently profound or cannot be traced back to the excessive regulation, then it will be difficult politically to bring about major policy changes quickly. In these circumstances, an evolutionary approach—tinkering at the margin—may be the only politically feasible one.

It is slowly being understood in Latin America that the closed economy model leads to increasing regulation that creates economic inflexibilities, inefficiencies, and a lack of adaptability in the economy, which produces slow growth and stagnation. This awareness is encouraging acceptance of a more open, competitive economic framework as a way to regain growth and economic welfare.

If the external conditions create the opportunity for policy change, the internal conditions—those that pertain to the character and structure of the government itself—are what make the changes viable. The internal conditions for successful policy change seem to be, at a minimum, strong political and administrative leadership and a team of policymakers with a coherent and convergent strategy for economic reform. Political leaders need to have a sense of history and a statesman-like view of the country and of how to harmonize divergent interests within a broadly defined set of national goals. The policy leaders may be made up either of technopols or of technocrats working with conventional politicians to develop the reform program. In the recent Latin American context, Chile and Mexico stand out as the most successful examples where technopols and technocrats have worked with politicians to establish a sustainable program of policy actions. These examples are repeated, to a lesser degree, in most of the other Latin American countries where policies are being transformed.

Ultimately, political power (i.e., political capital) is necessary to implement and sustain policy changes until their benefits become evident. Political power is derived from different sources: a strong political organization such as an institutionalized party, a majority in the legislature, support from the media, or credibility with the influential pressure groups whose well-being may be temporarily affected by the planned reforms. Such credibility was enjoyed by President Carlos Menem's Peronist Party in Argentina, the socialists in Spain, the PRI in Mexico, and the Australian Labor Party. The power bases of these parties, all of which initiated dramatic policy changes, are made up of groups that were initially affected by the change. Political power may also be increased by maintaining integrity and credibility in the execution of the reform program. It can also be strengthened by maintaining the broad guidelines of policy while retaining some flexibility and allowing many representative groups to participate in the policy negotiations. To maintain political capital, it may be helpful to mount a clear informational campaign for the general public, explaining the policy change and how different groups may benefit from it.

The dynamics of these factors may play out differently depending on whether the political regime is representative and democratic or authoritarian and centralized. Under the preferred mode, a democratic government, careful coalition building is an important condition for success. Often this takes the shape of a social pact in which government, business, and labor, for example, negotiate various aspects of a stabilization policy to break inflationary expectations and make policy application more effective, facilitating the dovetailing of results. Under an authoritarian government, the concentration of power sometimes makes reforms easier to implement, but obviously only if the government has the objective of transforming the economic model. Although an authoritarian government still has to educate public opinion and negotiate with divergent pressure groups, it may be able to act more quickly because it can negotiate from a position of power.

The conventional analysis of policy reform compares the initial costs of policy reform against the medium-term benefits. A government may spend political capital at the beginning, produce some early positive results that allow it to regain some of the capital it lost, and these in turn permit the government to continue with its program, incurring additional political costs in the expectation of subsequent positive results. That once again rebuilds political capital.

In the Latin American context, where both economic stabilization and structural adjustment have been necessary, the most successful policy sequence focuses on stabilization first, sustaining policy to maintain credibility and to make results effective. Careful harmonization of a devaluation with fiscal deficit reduction, price stabilization, and interest rate liberalization is itself a difficult technical accomplishment, requiring careful political management until the results are evident. Thereafter, the sequencing of adjustment policies builds upon those results. This will permit the positions of opposing interest groups, such as those of commercial and farmers groups against those of protective industrialists and labor unions, to offset each other.

In economies in transition from socialism, clear trade-offs appear when they move from centralized political power structures and command economies to market-oriented economies and democratic, representative governments. Some countries maintain centralized political power long enough to create economic structures. A final political opening may occur once new economic structures, private property, decentralized market organization, and policies are in place. Where the political status quo does not favor economic policy reform, political reform may be necessary to create a more favorable climate for economic change. Those seeking political transformation must then work to create the constituency for economic change. In so doing, however, they may diffuse political power to such an extent as to endanger the possibility of building the coalitions necessary to support economic reorganization and policy reform. High costs and a prolonged transformation may therefore result.

In either case, success depends upon a combination of appropriate knowledge, coalition building, the building of a team of technopols, the sequencing of actions in a way that maintains credibility through results, at least some political power, and the ability to define and sustain policies until gains are recognizable. In the environment of transitional economies more than in any other, the change in value systems about the rules of the game is critical for the eventual stabilization of policies.

A new policy framework can be sustained when the majority of people and leadership groups see that the new policies work. Often, however, the policies are not in place long enough to produce results because political commitment to reform itself cannot be sustained. Reforms can be interrupted by the election of a new government or a mid-term election of a new congress. The likelihood of such an interruption increases when voters turn against part or all of the reform program because a majority has not yet perceived benefits from the early stages of the policy reform process. Timing policy reforms and matching successes with election periods is one of the most critical aspects of targeting and sequencing. New policies become truly stabilized when an election in effect ratifies them. The reform process has progressed this far in Chile, Mexico, Argentina, Bolivia, and Costa Rica. In authoritarian governments such problems do not arise, and policy continuity is easier to maintain until success is widely perceived.

To achieve basic change in an economic model requires time to change expectations and behavior patterns. Such change will strengthen the results of improved growth, efficiency, and human welfare.

## Guiding the National Learning Process

As suggested above, there is a national learning process that permits nations to change their policies and constitutional rules. This can occur under a variety of governmental systems, but the Western democratic system seems better able to sustain it. The process does not normally move in a straight line or at constant speed; it moves more in a zig-zag fashion, with intermittent jerks. Sustaining this learning process is difficult because the normal competition among divergent pressure groups in a society is typically more amenable to tinkering around the edges of policymaking than to making basic changes in a given model or framework.

To fundamentally change the model and the rules of the game requires sustained leadership in producing knowledge about the inadequacies of the existing model and convincing evidence about the benefits of the new one. This is true not only for the nation at large but also for all the elite pressure groups that stand to lose at the beginning from the transformation of the economic framework. These are some key elements to strengthen that process: production of the relevant knowledge; effective dissemination and communication of that knowledge; creation of mechanisms by which to inform political parties and leadership groups about the benefits of the new system and policies; leadership to organize a coherent coalition for change that can multiply the support for policy change and neutralize the opposition.

At a given moment, one group may be able to provide the leadership necessary to bring all those elements together. However, the probabilities of success will be improved by creating an institutional basis for a more lasting guidance of the national learning process. Think tanks that produce and communicate knowledge, trained cadres of professionals to nourish it and form policy teams, and the linkage of these to political parties and other policy-influencing organizations such as the media are among the more useful institutional ingredients to accomplish this objective.

People are always looking for ways to improve their lot. It is not always evident how this can be done within a system that should be as fair in opportunities to all as is desirable, nor how changes can be implemented as free of cost to others as possible. The value systems, institutions, and rules of the game provide the mechanisms to sustain that exploration in a civilized manner. Knowledge of the merits of the model and the policies that follow from it, and about how certain policies maximize benefits to the nation and to the powerful groups that influence policies most, is useful to take advantage of the opportunities created by external or internal problems in order to improve the policy framework and change the value system. But in the end, such opportunities can be taken advantage of, and the actions taken made lasting, by coupling the knowledge of policy models and impacts with the evidence of results through which the lot of a majority of citizens may be improved.

## Reference

Ardito-Barletta, Nicolás. 1991. "Experiences of Policy Makers." In G. Meier, ed., *Politics and Policy Making in Developing Countries*. San Francisco: ICS Press.

# STEPHAN HAGGARD

As the adjustment record of the 1980s becomes more clear, we now look back with relief on the fact that many autocracies have poor records at economic reform, while a number of democracies managed to undertake quite comprehensive adjustment programs. We should not take too much comfort, however. The process of successful economic adjustment has not always been politically smooth, and unpleasant political facts should not be hidden behind euphemisms such as the importance of "strong leadership." Some of the widest-ranging reform efforts in the developing world were undertaken following military coups: this was true in Chile (1973), Uruguay (1976), Argentina (1966 and 1976), Brazil (1964), Turkey (1980), Indonesia (1966), Korea (1961 and 1980), and Ghana (1983). Although the reforms in some of these cases were technically misguided or were not sustained, we know that they would not have been launched without military rule; indeed, military governments came to power in each case precisely because previous democratic governments had failed both economically and politically. Another cluster of "successful" adjusters includes single- or no-party systems: Taiwan, Singapore, Mexico, and Hong Kong.

I do not wish to join the debate over whether reforms in these countries can be judged a "success" given their high political and human cost. I only wish to underline the sad fact that good things—such as democracy and market-oriented economic policy—do not always go together.

If our interest is in drawing policy lessons, the interesting cases fall into two different clusters. First are the democracies that initiated new reforms: in this book, these countries include Colombia, Australia, New Zealand, Spain, and Poland. The second cluster consists of those democratic governments that sustained or deepened economic reforms initiated by their authoritarian predecessors; Chile under Patricio Aylwin, Korea under Roh Tae Woo, and Turkey under Turgut Özal fall into this group.

To understand these cases, it is useful to draw a distinction between the initiation and the consolidation of reform efforts, because the political logic of the two phases is somewhat different (Haggard and Kaufman 1992). The distinction also helps explain the apparent paradox running

*Stephan Haggard is a Professor in the Graduate School of International Relations and Pacific Studies at the University of California, San Diego.*

through the chapters: that governments need both independence and support in order to achieve their reform objectives.

In the initiation phase there are typically groups in society benefiting from the policy status quo; this is the political reason why reform has been delayed. Moreover, there is disagreement about what should be done. Initiation of reform is thus more likely when executives and their teams enjoy a degree of independence or autonomy from constituent pressures, that is, when legislators and social groups *delegate* authority to the executive either actively or through acquiescence.

When we speak of "honeymoon" periods following elections, for example, we mean the delegation of a certain degree of discretionary authority to executives and their teams—a kind of willing suspension of disbelief. When John Williamson speaks in the introductory paper to this volume of the importance of a strong and coherent team, he means a team of key technocrats to whom politicians have delegated authority. Two points need to made about such delegation. First, it is a political choice on the part of politicians; technocrats do not ascend without political backing. Second, delegation does not imply authoritarian tendencies. Rather, delegation is a feature of all democratic politics, which would be absolutely impossible without it.

The key question is why politicians choose to delegate, but as Robert Bates has already offered a searching comment on this point, I will turn to the second problem: how reforms are consolidated. The answer is simple to state, but difficult to accomplish: as the current debate over President Clinton's economic program has demonstrated quite clearly, the consolidation of reform demands the building of legislative and interest-group bases of support.

One of the crucial debates at this conference centered on two contending models of how this consolidation is achieved. The first approach I will call the "market model" of adjustment. This perspective argues that good economics is good politics. Good policy enhances aggregate social welfare. Therefore, political leaders simply have to concentrate on the right policies, and constituent support will emerge automatically: from consumers enjoying an end to shortages and inflation, from managers of newly privatized firms, from new export interests, and so forth. Efforts to compensate losers or to sequence reforms for political reasons will only lead to delay, backsliding, and loss of credibility.

The second model, which I believe has more support from both theory and the cases, might be called the "strategic model" of adjustment. This model rests on the observation that there is a high level of uncertainty about adjustment outcomes, that there are often quite severe distributional consequences of adjustment, and that the successful consolidation of reform rests on providing some minimal forms of insurance against the risks associated with exposure to the market. The literature on the small European states has noted that the most open economies have highly developed welfare systems and even corporatist political arrangements (Cameron 1984; Katzenstein 1985; Bates et al. 1991). In this volume, the point is made most clearly in the paper on Mexico by José Córdoba. His account shows how extensive reforms were accompanied by a reordering of budget priorities to target negatively affected groups. Turkey presents an interesting contrast, where compensation was organized in ways that contributed to undermining the program.

Unfortunately, politicians do not usually enjoy the luxury of crafting the optimal strategy under circumstances of their own choosing. This brings me to the role of crisis in reform efforts. The cases in the book fall into two distinct groups in this regard. First are those countries in which there was a profound crisis involving severe policy distortions, high inflation or even hyperinflation, and the threat or actuality of a complete depletion of foreign exchange reserves. Poland, Chile, Mexico, Brazil, and Peru fall into this category. Second are those countries in which economic conditions may have deteriorated, but not to the same extent. Spain, Colombia, Portugal, Australia, New Zealand, and Korea in the 1980s fall into this category. These differences in initial conditions are important not only to the economic strategy but also to the politics of reform.

It has been noted frequently that, in crisis cases, technopols are likely to gain in influence and to pursue radical reform strategies. The precise reasons for this are not always clearly elaborated, however. First, in hyperinflation cases in particular, crises expand the group of potential winners. Our typical model of reform is one in which policy changes are difficult to make because there are high costs at the outset, but the benefits emerge only gradually. The political gains from stopping hyperinflation are immediate and broad, and far outweigh the distributive costs associated with such measures as trade liberalization. As Dani Rodrik (forthcoming) has argued, this is one reason why it is logical to *package* reforms in crisis settings.

The second reason why crises strengthen the hands of technopols has to do with access to foreign resources. The reason politicians are willing to delegate authority to technocrats is that such delegation enhances their credibility with crucial external actors, including the international financial institutions, foreign creditors, and potential investors. The Polish program provides a good example. Leszek Balcerowicz's utility to the new government, and its willingness to trust him, were enhanced by his standing in the international community.

The lesson to be drawn from this simple point is often difficult to make in practice. On the one hand, as Jeffrey Sachs argues eloquently elsewhere in this volume, it is important to provide adequate support for genuine reformers because their political position can be undermined otherwise. But it is also the case that politicians will not be inclined to make difficult adjustments if they know that they will be bailed out by external donors. This was the story in the Philippines at the end of the Ferdinand Marcos era, and it remains the case in many aid-dependent African countries today.

In this regard, I believe Sachs has somewhat mischaracterized the debate over assistance to Russia, although I ultimately side with his position. Those reluctant to provide support to Prime Minister Yegor Gaidar did not necessarily doubt *his* intentions. Rather, they did not believe that Gaidar had adequate internal support or the institutional wherewithal to carry through the reforms, even *with* an infusion of massive Western assistance. In this political and institutional setting, the assistance would be wasted. Whether this judgment was prudent or a tragic error remains to be seen, but it certainly seems to have delayed the adjustment effort in the short run.

When we turn from the crisis to the noncrisis cases, a different set of political considerations come into play. It is less compelling to move rapidly, and it may in fact prove disruptive to do so; the New Zealand case suggests this possibility. Second, there is more political and economic space to build consensus around policy reform prior to its initiation. Spain provides the most clear example of pact-like agreements facilitating reform efforts, but the reform efforts in Chile (under Aylwin), Australia, New Zealand, and Portugal were also carried out by social democratic governments sensitive to the needs of potential losers, particularly in the labor movement.

My final observation concerns the central role of institutions in the reform process. I have found the preoccupation with technocrats to be somewhat misleading, or only half of the story. The criticial question is not whether a technocratic team exists, but where it sits in the institutional matrix of decision making. It can be stated categorically that not a single reform effort in this group of cases was initiated and sustained without supportive changes in the institutional setting.

First, every case of reform was accompanied by a strengthening of the executive branch and, within the executive, a strengthening of what I call the "control" ministries vis-à-vis the "spending" or "constituent" ministries. This was true in Australia, where Hawke's Economic Planning Council played a crucial role; in Mexico, where ministries were consolidated or eliminated altogether; in Colombia, where important institutional reforms took place in 1968; in Korea, where the Economic Planning Board was created in the early 1960s; and in Turkey and Chile, where central banks were strengthened.

A second set of institutions that matter in democracies are legislatures, and perhaps my major disappointment with the papers is the failure to pay more attention to the legislative, partisan, and ultimately electoral dimensions of reform in the democratic cases. It appears impossible to sustain reform efforts without legislative backing, and thus the nature of the party system and executive-legislative relations are crucial elements of successful reforms. Governing parties in successful democratic cases—Spain, Portugal, Australia, New Zealand, and, more controversially, Mexico—enjoyed strong legislative majorities. Efforts were weaker or fell apart where the party system was polarized, as it was in Turkey in the late 1970s, where the executive and the legislature pulled in opposite directions; in Peru, as Richard Webb describes; and in Korea in the late 1980s; or where the party system was fragmented, as in Poland. Although constitutional change is historically infrequent, the recent wave of democratizations should raise the question of how the character of new democratic institutions will affect the prospects for market-oriented reform.

# References

Bates, Robert, Philip Brock, and Jill Tiefenthaler. 1991. "Risk and Trade Regimes." *International Organization* 45, no. 1 (Winter): 1–18.

Cameron, David. 1984. "Social Democracy, Corporatism, Labor Quiescence, and the Representation of Economic Interest in Advanced Capitalist Society." In John H. Goldthorpe, ed., *Order and Conflict in Contemporary Capitalism,* New York: Oxford University Press.

Haggard, Stephan, and Robert R. Kaufman. 1992. "Institutions and Economic Adjustment." In Stephan Haggard and Robert R. Kaufman, eds., *The Politics of Adjustment,* Princeton: Princeton University Press.

Katzenstein, Peter. 1985. *Small States in World Markets: Industrial Policy in Europe.* Ithaca: Cornell University Press.

Rodrik, Dani. 1993. "The Rush to Free Trade in the Developing World: Why So Late? Why Now? Will it Last?" In Stephan Haggard and Steven B. Webb, eds., *Voting for Reform: Economic Adjustment in New Democracies.* New York: Oxford University Press for the World Bank. (forthcoming).

# JOAN M. NELSON

How much political support can be expected, and how much is needed, for economic stabilization and structural reforms? I will argue that the politics of early stages of economic reform differ in predictable ways from those of later stages. Technopols need to take this shift into account in their political tactics and in the very design of their programs.

## Crisis as a Facilitating Factor

In his introduction to this volume, John Williamson, following Mancur Olson, posits that reforms that increase the general good but harm established interests normally will not be undertaken. An economic or political crisis may destroy political coalitions that had blocked reform and may also create a consensus on the need for fundamental change. A good deal of evidence broadly supports these propositions but also suggests some important caveats.

A relatively sudden shock, such as the crisis that emerged in Costa Rica between 1979 and 1982, is not likely to destroy existing coalitions, except in the superficial sense of destroying support for the government held responsible for the debacle. A long period of decline, such as occurred in Jamaica during most of the 1970s, in Ghana from the mid-1960s until 1983, or in several Eastern European countries beginning in the 1970s (or even earlier), will indeed erode established coalitions, since the government cannot continue to deliver the benefits the constituent groups have come to expect in return for their support. Despite the weakening of the coalition, however, important groups will continue to have vested interests in the old arrangements. The industries and sectors that benefited from protection, subsidies, and privileges normally prefer to revive the old system rather than tear it down and build anew.

Does crisis create a consensus regarding reform, and therefore the willingness to sacrifice in the interests of reform? An acute crisis—the drying up of reserves, shortages, capital flight, and above all rapid inflation or hyperinflation, with the accompanying political turmoil—predictably generates a strong popular desire for a take-charge government with a plausible plan to contain the emergency. Even draconian

*Joan M. Nelson is a Senior Associate at the Overseas Development Council in Washington.*

stabilization programs such as Bolivia's in 1985 can be accepted by much of the population as the painful remedy for an increasingly nightmarish situation.

But it is much less obvious that crisis generates acceptance of permanent structural reforms. Whether it does so depends in good part on the perceived causes of the crisis. Often economic crisis discredits the current government but not the economic system. If the crisis is widely blamed on mismanagement or corruption, then people understandably will view changing the management as an adequate solution. Economic failure hastened the exit of military governments in Argentina, Brazil, and Bolivia in the early or mid-1980s, but during the civilian governments that immediately followed them, the prevailing views blamed economic problems on military ineptness rather than the basic policies and structure of the system. Particularly in countries where economic performance has been strong until shortly before the crisis—as, for example, in Costa Rica in the late 1970s, or in Brazil in the early 1980s—public opinion is much more likely to blame the managers than the system itself.

Where much of the public is indeed convinced that fundamental changes are needed—as, for instance, in Eastern Europe in 1989—reforms are clearly facilitated. But, as Williamson notes, even with broad consensus on the need for and general direction of basic reform, there will inevitably be bitter disputes over the speed, sequence, design, and allocation of costs of specific measures. Willingness to sacrifice creates a climate generally receptive to change, but technopols must still confront intense opposition over specific structural reforms.

In short, consensus on most of the reform agenda will emerge—if at all—only after the fact. Moreover, as Jeffrey Sachs noted in his dinner speech at this conference, in an acute crisis, hard-pressed technopols cannot devote much time to seeking consensus. Initial macroeconomic stabilization measures and the first (often very major) steps toward deregulation and opening the economy have typically been taken rather autocratically, by executive decree, with legislatures pressured to act quickly to provide pro forma approval. This is inevitable, not only for technical reasons but also because of political realities.

Yet many of the case studies and much of the discussion at this conference has emphasized the need to generate support and consensus—to build coalitions. That challenge, I suggest, comes to the fore not at the beginning but in the subsequent stages of the reform effort.

## The Politics of the Different Phases of Reform

One particularly clear lesson of the 1980s is that basic market-oriented reforms take years to put in place and usually require still more time before they generate robust investment and growth. Many countries have launched promising efforts; far fewer have sustained those efforts long and vigorously enough to produce results.

It is often assumed that the hardest political hurdle for an adjustment program is the initial package, combined (as it almost always is) with austerity measures. If that is true, the high incidence of programs well launched yet then aborted is puzzling. I suspect that the conventional assumption is wrong: the most difficult political challenges come not initially, but somewhat later in a program, after the first months or year.

In part, this is a result of the changing nature of the reform measures themselves. Initial stabilization and adjustment packages typically include fiscal and monetary austerity measures, devaluation, and varying degrees of price and trade liberalization. These measures are administratively easy, in the sense that they can be decided and put into effect by a small circle of senior economic officials. Measures that are usually introduced later, such as financial-sector reforms, the rationalization or privatization of large state enterprises, opening of labor markets, and restructuring social services and social security, are much more complex. They entail extensive institutional and legal changes and involve the legislature, the courts, and a wide range of central and local government agencies. They are therefore far more vulnerable to dilution, delay, and derailing.

Not only the nature of the measures, but also the political context, changes from the initial to the later phases of reform. If the reforms are launched by a new government, that government's honeymoon will fade. If the reforms are launched in response to an acute crisis, and the results are good, the sense of crisis and willingness to sacrifice fades. If, however, the results are disappointing, then confidence in the government dwindles. If the country has a democratic political system, elections approach. If early stages of reform were facilitated by the fact that opposition parties and interest groups were in disarray (usually because they were held responsible for the crisis), then as time passes they will get their act together.

In short, both the changing nature of later-stage reforms and the shifting political context are likely to place growing pressure on the government, and specifically on technopols, to give increased attention to creating support.

## The Special Case of New Democracies

Especially after the initial stages, the need to generate support and consensus for reform is greater in democracies, particularly in countries that have recently turned or returned to democratic politics.

Far-reaching economic reforms have often in the past been carried out under authoritarian auspices (sometimes, as in Chile, Korea, and Taiwan, followed by political liberalization). Established democracies in economic difficulty have also been able to reform: examples include Colombia, Costa Rica, and currently (and still tentatively) India.

The global democratic wave of the past decade means that difficult economic reforms are now far more frequently launched and continued by fragile new democratic governments than has been true historically. In much of Latin America since the early 1980s, in Eastern Europe and the former Soviet Union since 1989, and increasingly in sub-Saharan Africa, a large and growing number of countries are attempting a simultaneous transition from authoritarian to more open political systems and from state-dominated and closed to market-led, open economies.

Where market-oriented economic reforms are carried out simultaneously with political opening, the two processes interact in complex ways that are in part complementary but in part also conflicting. The uncertainties of both transitions compound each other. The political transition normally disrupts and weakens the authority of already severely eroded state institutions, just as the economic reforms are generating extraordinary demands for state initiative and efficiency. The early effects of economic reforms increase insecurity, inequality, and apparent foreign influence, just as major sectors of the population begin to find themselves empowered politically. The point is not that economic and political liberalization cannot proceed in tandem but that the attempt does pose special problems.

## Tactics for Technopols

John Williamson's introduction invited authors to concentrate particularly on "achieving the initial breakthrough" from an unstable, statist, and closed economy to a more stable, market-led, and open one. That breakthrough is not accomplished by the launching, or even the sustaining, of initial stabilization and liberalization measures. It is a process that extends at best over several years and in many countries may require a decade or even longer. Especially in the first several years, and above all in new democracies, there remains a real possibility that the process will stall or be seriously diverted. Fairly shortly after the initial launch, technopols need to develop a political strategy as well as an economic program.

Several conference participants have stressed the importance of using the media to help explain the rationale for reform measures to the public. Persuasion may indeed ease the introduction of specific reforms, but in fairly short order people will judge reforms by their perceived results.

Some measures, if effective, benefit almost everyone. The clearest example is containing hyperinflation, as in Bolivia and Argentina. Where widespread shortages are relieved, as in Poland and New Zealand, the benefits may also be fairly widespread. (It would be interesting to examine how long, and under what circumstances, groups too poor to benefit from improved availabilities, especially of imported goods, nonetheless regard the improved supplies as an indicator of better times to come for them as well.)

Other reforms benefit narrower groups. Whether such benefits translate into useful political support for the economic reforms depends on the size, orientation, and organization of the groups that benefit and on the country's political institutions. For instance, reforms rather quickly benefited manufacturing or agricultural exporters, or both, in Turkey, Mexico, and Ghana. In Turkey, this translated into helpful political support, but José Córdoba suggests that this may have been less true in Mexico. In Ghana, the government of Jerry John Rawlings seemed unable to tap the potential support of cocoa growers without using procedures that would simultaneously empower deeply discontented urban groups.

Because privatization involves the direct reallocation of resources, it always entails explicitly political choices. Privatization has often been used to distribute benefits to established supporters (as in Mexico) or to reintegrate potentially alienated elements into the system (by tacitly accepting "spontaneous privatization" that benefits the ex-*nomenklatura* in several Eastern European countries). Such measures can also have a political backlash: widespread concerns that privatized enterprises might go to the already wealthy and powerful (thus further biasing informal power relations) or to foreigners have fed opposition to privatization. A clear example is the March 1993 rejection by the Polish parliament of the carefully designed "large" privatization bill.

A key political problem of sustaining support for reform programs is the long delay in reaping visible benefits for much of the population. That problem is compounded by the history, in many countries, of protracted fiscal crisis and the virtual disintegration of fundamental public utilities and services, from law and order to garbage collection to basic health care and education. The result is not only a greatly deteriorated quality of life, but widespread alienation from government and politics at all levels.

Economic reform programs might prove more sustainable if they were accompanied by a high-priority drive for rapid improvement in one or two selected basic services or utilities, particularly if they target the urban working and middle classes. The idea of rapid returns does not imply favoritism or subsidies, but rather heightened priority for doing whatever is required (including seeking external aid) to demonstrate concrete progress on some aspect of life that matters to most people. (This idea is quite distinct from that of buffering the social costs of adjustment for the most vulnerable parts of the population; such programs, while highly desirable on welfare grounds and sometimes politically useful, are usually both narrowly targeted and billed as special and temporary efforts.) The services or utilities chosen should probably be ones that can be significantly improved fairly quickly. Such a program might help to dissipate the widespread sense of hopelessness and alienation that has often slowed, and then derailed, reform efforts.

More generally, politicians and the technopols advising them must broaden their approach to sustaining reforms beyond the tactic of creating and securing the support of winners. Quite simply, in most cases there are not enough early winners to ensure the political sustainability of the program after the specific circumstances that facilitated its launching have faded. In nondemocratic settings, governments have relied on repression to sustain reforms. In democracies, leaders must offer both some modest tangible returns, plus a credible vision of the future.

José Piñera suggested as one crucial element for reform a leader with a vision of the future. John Williamson's rephrasing—a leader with an adequately long time-horizon—captures the technical dimension but misses the political point. In place of the discredited visions of communist, or populist, or African socialist societies, people need a credible image of a reasonably just and attractive society. In Central Europe, the plausible prospect of becoming like Western Europe serves that purpose. In Russia, that prospect appears neither as unambiguously attractive nor as plausible. And in a Bolivia or a Zambia, the marketplace looks less than magical to most of the population (including much of the middle classes). Technopols must offer a better developed vision of the society they hope to build in order to sustain support.

My initial ambition was to present here a 13 x 13 matrix summarizing the results of the conference. Along the horizontal axis would be the 13 case studies we have considered, and along the vertical would be the 13 hypotheses that either were contained in my background paper (chapter 2) or have been added to the agenda during the course of our deliberations. Each cell would contain either a yes or a no to indicate, respectively, that the hypothesis had been satisfied in the case in question or that it had been refuted, thus enabling one to inspect the rows to find which hypotheses worked and which did not.

Reality has proved too messy to be summarized so neatly. Not every paper has commented on every hypothesis, so there are lots of blanks. And many of the answers that are given are highly qualified ones. At this stage, at least, I have to limit myself to providing a less comprehensive summary.[1] What I have therefore constructed is a matrix with only 2 columns instead of 13 (table 1). The first column offers an overall judgment of whether or not the hypothesis seems to fit the facts, while the second gives counterexamples.

Consider first the crisis hypothesis. A number of countries were indeed stimulated to reform by crises, as the first column indicates. But there were also cases, such as Colombia and Portugal, where reform occurred without the stimulus of a crisis. Much the same is true of the honeymoon hypothesis: many reformers exploited honeymoon periods, but Colombia introduced its reform program at the tail end of one administration, and Mexico has not had a honeymoon in living memory, yet its reform program is among the most comprehensive of all. Similarly with the hypothesis that reform needs a demoralized opposition unable to offer effective resistance: it seems to have been fulfilled in the majority of cases, but again Colombia and perhaps Australia provide counterexamples.

The hypothesis that reform requires an authoritarian regime comes off much worse. It was satisfied in only about half the cases, and there are a string of counterexamples (Australia, Colombia, New Zealand, Poland, Portugal, and Spain). The hypothesis that reform is an inherently right-wing project is also inconsistent with the evidence: while the majority of

---

1. The summary paper in chapter 12 does make an attempt to construct the more comprehensive matrix that I was here visualizing: see table 1 of that chapter. A number of the preliminary judgments offered here were there revised, in the light of further information and deliberation.

## Table 1  The validity of 14 hypotheses[a]

| Hypothesis | General assessment | Counterexamples |
|---|---|---|
| Crisis | Many cases | Colombia, Portugal |
| Honeymoon | Many cases | Colombia, Mexico |
| Demoralized opposition | Usual in democracies | Colombia, Australia |
| Authoritarian regime | Invalid | Australia, Colombia, New Zealand, Poland, Portugal, Spain |
| Rightist government | Invalid | Australia, New Zealand, Spain |
| Voodoo politics | Most cases | Portugal, (New Zealand) |
| Visionary leader | Strong support | New Zealand |
| Coherent team | Strong support | Present also in Brazil and Peru |
| Comprehensive program | Most cases | Colombia, Indonesia, Korea, (Australia) |
| Use of media | Little support | Colombia |
| Compensation of losers | Little support | New Zealand |
| Acceleration of gains | Little support | None reported |
| External aid | Most cases | Australia, New Zealand |
| Political base | Strong support | Collapsed quickly in Poland |

a. Parentheses indicate qualification mentioned in text.

reforming regimes may have been right of center, three of them were self-consciously left of center (Australia, New Zealand, and Spain). The notion that a party that wants to reform needs to disguise that intent—play "voodoo politics"—in order to get elected seems consistent with the experience of most countries, but not of all: Portugal is perhaps the clearest counterexample,[2] with the reelection of New Zealand's Labour government also arguing against the hypothesis.

The need for a visionary leader to inspire the reform process seems to have been satisfied in most cases, with the clearest exception being New Zealand, where reform happened not because the prime minister wanted it, but because he was too busy worrying about denuclearizing the South Pacific to notice what his finance minister and his team were up to. Every case of successful reform seems to have benefited from an effective and coherent economic team; but clearly this is not a *sufficient* condition for successful reform, for Luiz Carlos Bresser Pereira's team in Brazil (and perhaps that of Manuel Ulloa in Peru too) also seems to have been pretty impressive.

---

2. At least, Aníbal Cavaco Silva's intentions were surely clear by 1987, when he first won an absolute majority, even if they were not in 1985.

The proposition that successful reform demands rapid implementation of a comprehensive program is another one that seems consistent with the bulk of the cases considered by the conference, but there were nevertheless prominent counterexamples (Colombia, Korea, and Indonesia, and perhaps Australia). There was rather little support for the hypothesis that conscious use of the media was a key to successful reform, with the original claim based on the Chilean experience backed up only by the failure of the Venezuelan authorities to use the media to sell their program to the public, which may have contributed to the derailing of reforms there, and the contradictory comment that in Colombia any similar attempt to use the media for propaganda purposes would be unconstitutional. Neither did there seem to have been many cases where the reforming government had made a conscious effort to compensate the losers or to accelerate the gains to the winners so as to nurture a constituency for reform, and indeed at least in one case (New Zealand) the government blatantly disregarded any such concerns yet was still reelected.

Most countries did receive some external help, both financial and intellectual, but again there were exceptions, notably Australia and New Zealand, neither of which received aid (although they did have access to the international capital market to lubricate the adjustment process) and both of which apparently felt something of a dearth of role models. In most cases, however, what Barbara Stallings called "linkage"—the transmission of intellectual ideas from abroad—seems to have been important, even if the effective use of "leverage"—meaning conditionality—was less important. Finally, the government had a solid political base in virtually all the countries where reforms took root (with Poland after the first nine months being the nearest to a counterexample), while the two cases of failed reforms were characterized by the lack of such a solid political base.

One's first reflection after examining such a list is that political science, unlike economics, does not seem to support many robust empirical generalizations. About all we are able to say is that economic reform needs an effective economic team with a coherent view of what needs to be done, backed by a sufficiently firm base of political support to give them the opportunity to implement irreversible changes.

Is it desirable that the team be headed by a technopol? Three interesting reasons have been given during the conference for answering this question in the affirmative. José Córdoba argued that an economist serving as chief executive could be more effective because he would not need to devote so much time to mastering his brief on many of the routine matters of the day, and therefore would have more time left over for the more important and creative parts of his job. Leszek Balcerowicz similarly referred to the significance of having someone in office who could determine for himself what the issues were and was not dependent on the briefs he received—a necessary condition for leadership in Balcerowicz's view. He also reasoned that an economist in high office drew his self-esteem from whether his policies worked, rather than (as with a professional politician) from whether he hung on to office, and was hence prepared to resign rather than to implement policies that would sully his professional reputation. A living example of the validity of this contention addressed our conference, namely, Luiz Carlos Bresser Pereira, who chose to resign as finance minister of Brazil rather than soldier on when his president refused to push for the fiscal correction that was needed, and is in consequence held by us in the highest esteem—despite the fact that we invited him to come here to discuss the failure of his reform attempt.

Indeed, those of us who have been socialized as economists tend to get our satisfaction from maximizing social welfare functions.[3] (This suggests that one might expect economists who wish to play a political role to join parties that have a rather wide conception of their constituency: to be more comfortable in Solidarity than in the fragmented parties that succeeded it in Poland, for example.) As Max Corden suggested at the beginning, what we really were doing in the conference was asking ourselves the Machiavellian question about how we can achieve that, given the "obstacles" posed by the political system. This poses profound questions about how one reconciles democracy and good economic policy, which we have at least put on the agenda even though we may not have got far toward resolving them. One thing we should always bear in mind is the dictum that power corrupts: however inconvenient democracy may seem in the short run, it imposes disciplines that should be taken unquestioningly as part of the background within which we operate.

---

3. It is not clear whether this is still true: it seems that nowadays some branches of the subject are elevating the pursuit of individual self-interest (greed) from a regrettable though realistic summary of human motivation into an ideal, and there is evidence (Frank, Gilovich, and Regan 1993) that economics students are becoming less altruistically motivated after studying such subjects as microeconomic theory.

# Discussion

*Bob Coats* started the discussion by pointing out that in some presentations, notably the one on Korea, the terms "technopol," "technocrat," "bureaucrat," and "administrator" had been used almost interchangeably, while in the Indonesian paper the term "technopol" had not been used at all. It was normally acknowledged that economic policymaking always involved some normative considerations: did this mean that all economists in policymaking situations were technopols? Some of the Councils of Economic Advisers in the United States (e.g., under Walter Heller) had been decidedly political. On the other hand, the Chicago boys had introduced into Chile a concept of economics as an impartial, neutral, and objective science that was self-consciously apolitical and asocial. It might thus be more constructive to identify who the technopols were and where they work in the governmental process. In a stable system they might be top civil servants who had previously been ineffective because of lack of political support. In more authoritarian regimes they might (like Córdoba) be in the office of the presidency, at the right hand of power. Hence Coats found Williamson's definition of technopols—"economic technocrats who assume positions of political responsibility"—in need of refinement.

*Leszek Balcerowicz* again emphasized the importance of initial conditions in explaining economic reforms and formulating normative conclusions. In the first place, the structure of the economy was important: the dominance of agriculture in China had meant that liberalizing that sector created the possibility of igniting a virtuous circle—that opportunity was absent in Russia. Second, macroeconomic conditions had implications for the necessary speed of reforms: mastering a hyperinflation might sometimes (rarely) be compatible with democracy, but only under conditions of "extraordinary politics." Third, the size of the public sector has implications for such areas as the operation of the labor market, credit markets, and the scope for privatization.

Balcerowicz turned to a discussion of the dynamics of economic reform. Reforms would generate both sources of satisfaction and sources of discontent. In Poland the elimination of shortages, privatization, and increased opportunity (something that appealed primarily to those most likely to succeed, notably the young) had been the main sources of satisfaction. It was not true that satisfaction depended just on changes in consumption, as in some naive political models; the widespread frustration in eastern Germany, where everyone had benefited from increased consumption, showed this clearly. He thought that the main sources of discontent were envy on the part of those who lost out and increased uncertainty (especially among those who moved from disguised to open unemployment).

These sources of satisfaction and discontent might be magnified by the political system. Two factors were especially important in that connection: the timing of elections, which was not always under control of the government, and the structure of the political system, in particular the number, the concentration, and the types of political parties. Balcerowicz argued that a large number of parties was not so bad if support were concentrated among a few of them (for example, if there were 20 parties, it was much easier if the two largest had half the vote rather than if the first five together could muster only 30 percent). In terms of types of parties, the important distinction was between parties of reform and parties of "frustration"; the latter defended populist programs and tried to exploit the frustration generated by the economic reforms in order to gain power. The relative strengths of these two types of party depended on the history of the country in question and had a critical influence on the political ability to further reform.

*Alan Bollard* suggested the desirability of paying closer attention to some of the East Asian countries, notably China and Vietnam, since these would provide some interesting counterexamples on the relationship between political and economic liberalization as well as provide cases of considerable economic success. As for the crisis hypothesis, one needed to think in terms of relative crises: in an established democracy, a long-term downward trend in the terms of trade and a conviction that the world trading system was stacked against the country could create the same feeling that there was no alternative to reform as would need a much more severe crisis under another type of regime. He thought that more attention should be paid to international capital markets as a source of discipline and support. *Fred Bergsten* cited Korea in 1984 as a case in point, where the freezing up of new credits had induced an adjustment in policy, but he argued that it was primarily the more advanced countries that were vulnerable to pressure from the capital markets.

*Luiz Carlos Bresser Pereira* commented on the issue of consensus. Consensual reforms were possible when the costs of adjustment were perceived to be less than the costs of muddling through, which was more or less the same as a situation of major crisis. Another case ("partial consensus") could arise where the winners and losers from a reform could be identified and it proved possible to assemble a majority coalition of winners. When Sachs had argued against the need for consensus, he was referring to a situation of acute crisis where rapid results were possible (e.g., stopping hyperinflation). But when the reformers were initiating reforms that had to be sustained in the long run, such as fiscal consolidation or structural reform, then adjustment had to build on full or partial consensus.

Bresser Pereira further suggested that the term "economic reform" ought to be used only with reference to reforms of the state. Stabilization meant reforming the (state's) money, while trade liberalization or privatization involved reforming the institutional structure of the state. The aim should be to build a small but strong state.

Finally, the need for a competent economic team arises from the need for economic policies to be "right." Brazil had recently implemented two programs that had won wide international support (from May to December 1990, and from December 1991 to the time of the conference), including that of the IMF, but both had failed because they were not technically good programs.

*Francisco Torres* urged the need to contrast radical with smooth reform programs and short-term with long-term reforms. The programs in Australia and New Zealand were examples of radical reforms, while Spain and Portugal (and Ireland) had done smooth reforms. Brazil was in his view a case for smooth reform, since radical reforms had failed, perhaps because institutions had adjusted to high levels of inflation. Concerning the distinction between short-term and long-term reforms, Torres pointed out that Portugal's reforms had occurred in two stages. In the first stage the government had responded to a payments crisis by consulting the IMF and negotiating a strict stabilization program, which was consensual in the sense that it was supported by the two major parties, which were in coalition. When Aníbal Cavaco Silva came to power he did not build a consensus; on the contrary he broke up the coalition and started the second stage of the reforms with a minority government and "voodoo" promises that reform would lead to the modernization of Portugal. In Spain, in contrast, Felipe Gonzalez had gone to the electorate with a promise of the blood, sweat, and tears needed to participate in European monetary union; he won the election.

Consensus was necessary for long-run reforms of the institutional system (to reform political as well as economic institutions, *pace* Italy), although Torres agreed with Sachs that in an acute short-run crisis one simply had to do whatever it took and hope that the public would come around to accepting it. He affirmed his belief in central bank independence, while arguing that it was a lower priority when, as nowadays in Portugal, the treasury shared the objective of achieving the Maastricht convergence criteria.

*Ognian Pishev* recounted how the Bulgarian reform efforts had been launched by a coherent team, in which some economists were designated as politicians to carry out the reforms. The team had collapsed when some of them allowed economic concerns to be superseded by political interests. Pishev discussed whether it would be better to consolidate economic and political reform on a national basis or within an international framework. Spain, Portugal, and Greece had been able to embed their reform efforts within the European Community (and NATO). Could the international community play a similar role in supporting the political transition in young democracies with economies that were not individually viable?

On the role of the state, Pishev explained that excessive state power had in the past caused transition leaders to give priority to curbing that power, by means of price and trade liberalization. But competition was relevant in the political arena too, and the search for strong governments to implement economic reforms in a parliamentary democracy should not lead to neglect of the need for checks and balances and the protection of minority rights. The most successful phase in the modernization of Bulgaria had been accomplished under the coalition government in 1991, when the communist party still held a parliamentary majority. The reason was the competition between the younger members of the communist party and the so-called democrats of the Union of Democratic Forces (UDF), which forced the coalition government to deliver promised policy changes within a relatively short time span. The assumption of complete power by the UDF after the second election produced a stalemate, which Pishev attributed to the lack of any such productive challenge from the opposition.

*Carol Lancaster* criticized Williamson's methodology. He had listed a set of hypotheses and then sought to identify which of them were not refuted in any of the cases considered by the conference. This typical economist's approach to seeking a bottom line had led him to conclude that a strong economic team and a solid political base were the crucial preconditions for successful economic reform. She thought this was both potentially misleading and uninteresting: the question should not be a crude either-or but a nuanced consideration of the conditions (the type of crisis, the characteristics of society or the economy, the different stages of reform, the political system) under which a certain factor could be helpful in achieving policy reform. She speculated that, because of basic differences in social and economic organization, the many cases of

African reform that had not been considered by the conference would have generated quite different findings. So the key question should be, where and under what circumstances are the various factors important?

*Shafiqul Islam* asked whether success was being defined as success in implementing reform or as successful economic performance. The importance of that distinction was highlighted by the fact that many of the East Asian countries, which had not adhered to a number of points of the "Washington consensus," were growing at 10 percent per year, while countries like Mexico, which had followed the rules of the consensus more strictly, had not achieved more than 2 percent growth rates so far. Similarly, it was important to distinguish the conditions for initiating from those for sustaining reform: *pace* Lancaster, the relevance of Williamson's hypotheses would depend on which of these two stages was involved. A strong economic team was probably more important for initiating than for sustaining a reform process, whereas a solid political base was more a condition for sustaining the reform.

Islam also asked whether the experiences of other countries—such as China, Malaysia, Thailand, and Singapore—were to be ignored, for their inclusion would surely have influenced the conclusions reached.[1] Finally, Islam offered the list of core prerequisites for a successful adjustment program that he had drawn from the conference: a strong leadership committed to the general good; a coherent team of economists with a consistent and credible policy package and authority bestowed on them by the political leadership; conditional foreign assistance, used to exert leverage; and public support.

*Barbara Stallings* expressed her surprise that Spain and Portugal, let alone Australia and New Zealand, had been included as countries making important structural reforms; perhaps it would prove helpful, but one did need to group countries in categories, and she wondered whether the problems of these countries were sufficiently similar to those of reforming developing countries to justify their inclusion. She also suggested that insufficient attention had been paid to the countries that had failed in their reform efforts. In particular, both Brazil and Peru had been analyzed at specific points in time: 1987 in Brazil, when Bresser Pereira had been finance minister, and the early 1980s in Peru, when Richard Webb had been governor of the central bank. But both countries had been consistently failing on the same issues over a long period of time. Both Brazil and Peru were deeply divided along a number of lines: the distribution of socioeconomic power was among the most inequitable in the world, a phenomenon that had been magnified by a political system and a party structure that enabled groups strongly

---

1. Bergsten and Williamson reiterated that the countries chosen were those that had embarked on comprehensive economic reforms starting from adverse conditions, rather than those that had never needed a comprehensive reform package because they had adopted appropriate reforms piecemeal over a longer time span.

opposed to any form of structural reforms to mobilize support. It was easy to mobilize such opposition because a large part of the two countries' populations believed, rightly or wrongly, that they would be hurt by reform. Their opposition had been nourished by the experience of neighboring countries, including Chile, where the 1973–90 period had produced a profound, regressive redistribution of income, made more offensive by a new tendency to flaunt wealth. (This was very different from the story in Korea and Taiwan, perhaps because they had implemented agrarian reforms rather than just the Washington consensus.) Furthermore, Chile had destroyed its industrial sector in the process of reform, which was an example that Brazil, with its aspirations to be a Latin American power, would certainly not want to emulate.

One lesson to learn from the case of Peru was the critical importance of having a state with the ability not just to devise but to implement reforms. The economic team could make decisions, but that was not much good if they were never implemented. Many African countries had the same difficulty.

*Jacques Polak* missed a treatment of the linkage between the preconditions for reforms and the contents of reform. A conference like this held in 1965 would have reached much the same conclusions regarding preconditions (a prime minister who was an economist, a strong team, broad support, and support from abroad) for the adoption of good economic policies, but what was rated good economic policy would have changed. While good monetary policy still meant much the same thing, in 1965 Nicholas Kaldor would have flown in to increase the progressivity of the income tax, the IMF would have improved the system of exchange controls, and the World Bank would have designed a new Planning Ministry. Anne Krueger's earlier emphasis on the importance of ideas was right.

*Catherine Gwin* commented that if one agreed with Joan Nelson that it was important to distinguish between the initiation of reform and its consolidation, and if one accepted that building a political consensus was more important in the latter phase, and if one accepted José Córdoba's imaginative point that it was desirable to have an economist as president so that he could get on with the job without spending all his time trying to master his brief, then Williamson needed to follow up his manual for technopols with one designed for politocrats. The consolidation and political reform that was now confronting these countries would need a different set of skills and visions.

In reply to the debate, *Stephan Haggard* sought to clarify the concept of "consensus." In democratic countries the formulation of policy was by its nature a competitive rather than consensual process: parties were in the business of differentiating their product and competing over policy. The problem arose when there was a fundamental disagreement over the basic policy model. Stallings was right to point to the fundamental cleavages over the model that prevailed under some social orders. This could lead not just to the implementation of bad programs but also to wide swings between policies, with attempts at decent policies being discredited and followed by populist episodes (in Peru, for example, Fernando Belaúnde had set the stage for Alan Garcia). One theme that had come out of the discussion repeatedly, and which economics did not handle at all, was the concept of learning (how preferences change). Haggard argued that countries where there had ultimately been a consolidation of economic reforms had witnessed profound changes in the ideological positions of the political parties, resulting in convergence toward a centrist position. Such a minimal convergence, which did not imply the elimination of conflict over details of the model, was what was meant by "consensus" in the context of this debate.

*Joan Nelson* endorsed Lancaster's strictures on Williamson's methodology. Indeed, if it were true that there were important differences between launching and sustaining economic reform, there was a risk that the study of past experience might be a case of fighting the last war. The examples of successful consolidation, especially under democratic auspices, were rather few. She agreed with Stephan Haggard on the importance of a fundamental consensus over the basic model, but she argued that such an agreement was likely to emerge in the process of reform rather than usually being present at the start of the program. Some countries in Eastern Europe, where policymakers and the population in general aspired to a model based vaguely on Western Europe, might be an exception. In general, however, there might be widespread agreement over the failure of the old order but great disagreement as to what the new model should look like.

While efforts to build support for reform through persuasion might be worthwhile, Nelson argued that people would ultimately not be persuaded by explanations about the benefits of reform if their personal experience ran counter. The reform process thus had to engineer gains for at least enough members of the population so that it was in their interest to go along with the reforms. Who would gain would depend on the structure of the economy and the initial conditions, so it was important for economists to think about how to design a program that would produce a minimum critical mass of beneficiaries. She reiterated her belief that restoring basic services was an efficient way of distributing the benefits of reform, and it had the advantages of being widely understood and valued. She also thought it important to introduce early on some controls on the worst abuses of "raw capitalism."

*John Williamson* agreed that today's consensual economic policy package differed substantially from that of 20 or 30 years ago, but he argued that it could not thereby be dismissed as just the latest fashion. He thought today's package was more likely to endure, partly because it no longer involved advising developing countries to do things that the developed countries did not regard as good for themselves too. This intellectual convergence was one reason for treating both categories of countries together in the conference, rather than taking it as axiomatic that no developing country could learn anything from Australian experience. One dared hope that the area of agreement might expand in the future, as evidence accumulated on (for example) how the social agenda could be addressed most effectively. But the combination of pluralist democracy and a market economy did seem to provide a rather stable, and therefore presumably satisfactory, order, which was why it was worthwhile trying to help countries make the historic transition.

One result of making the transition was likely to be increased social consensus. Haggard was right to say that this did not mean total consensus on everything, for democracy was about making choices, but democracy itself involved acceptance that the political system provided a set of rules of the game within which such choices could be made.

Williamson expressed sympathy for Lancaster's views that one might be able to provide useful guidance about what factors could help reform even if no absolute prerequisites could be identified, and that what was helpful was likely to depend upon circumstances. He conceded that it might have been a mistake to not to include any African case studies, since it was possible that the results of the conference would be more relevant there than elsewhere.

In response to Stallings's argument, Williamson agreed that economists should ask themselves whether the policies they recommended would enable a country to reach its desired outcome. However, he doubted whether the liberal policies that had hurt the industrial sector in Chile would have the same consequences in Brazil, a much larger economy. Furthermore, in Chile the liberal policies had been implemented by a right-wing regime, and much of the impact on the distribution of income had come about from factors (like the generous bailout of financial enterprises that ran into trouble in 1982) that were quite separate from the liberalization of the economy.

# 10

## ECONOMIC REFORM: A VIEW FROM LATIN AMERICA

# Economic Reform: A View from Latin America

ENRIQUE IGLESIAS

I would like to address five questions derived from my personal experience in the region where I have been living for many years, and which have been the focus of my work for the last five years as president of the Inter-American Development Bank. This position involved a very close working relationship with the Bretton Woods institutions and, on a more or less daily basis, with the countries of the region and their leaders—ministers and heads of government.

The first question is: why did Latin America undertake the change in economic policy that this seminar has set to analyze? There is, I would think, substantial agreement on the answer to this question. Of course, the ideas developed in the North during the Reagan-Thatcher era were very important in Latin America, but the Chilean experience was far more significant in so far as it provided a viable model. The Chilean experience encompassed different stages, and its success was very much noted by other regional leaders. While they made little mention of this success then, because it was not very fashionable to speak favorably about Chile in the 1980s, they could not but notice that the Chilean program was beginning to work.

The new generation of politicians that had emerged throughout the region was confronted with a major crisis and hyperinflation, which in turn caused substantial social commotion in the region. These developments had very significant impact on these new leaders and civil servants,

Enrique Iglesias is President of the Inter-American Development Bank. He was formerly Foreign Minister of Uruguay and Secretary of the Economic Commission for Latin America and the Caribbean.

including those that were part of the diaspora. In the case of Chile, the fact that so many of its experts, economists, and sociologists had gone abroad and were looking at the region from a foreign perspective was extremely important. They returned with views that were less ideological and more pragmatic. These factors help explain why the new national bureaucracies were able to relate to the new leaders and to implement new policies that were very fashionable in other parts of the world.

Southeast Asia also had some relevance as a model for Latin America, but it was viewed with some doubts because the Asian region was made up of many diverse countries with different social and cultural environments. Therefore, southeast Asia never was seriously considered a model for Latin America, whereas Chile presented a far more relevant example to emulate.

The second question is, what kind of change actually occurred? John Williamson invented the idea of the Washington consensus, and there is no doubt that international organizations have had a tremendous influence on the region.

Around 1984, when the debt issue was on the table, we came up with the so-called Cartagena consensus, which represented a critical moment in the life of Latin America. As first secretary of that group, I remember vividly the conversations that took place between the ministers of finance and the ministers of foreign affairs. There were two dissenting voices: one from Alan Garcia of Peru, who exerted very strong pressure on the group, and the other from Fidel Castro of Cuba. And the idea of pursuing their line was vigorously discussed. From the first, I advocated staying within the international club, and this was probably the prevailing view then. But a few others were saying, ''Why don't we make a club of debtors to upset the international club?'' This was a very important moment in the history of Latin America.

In order to remain in the club, Latin American officials began discussions with the International Monetary Fund and the World Bank and started the process of adjustment. It cannot be denied that the Washington consensus was an important factor in influencing our approach. The fact that the countries of the region had the courage to carry out the necessary fiscal reforms is to me one of the most impressive things that can be singled out today in Latin America; it is nothing short of a revolution. Today everyone is deeply aware that one cannot play games with fiscal policy and that fiscal accounts must be balanced.

Uruguay, for example, is now discussing how to achieve a zero fiscal deficit. That is, the people and the political parties are assuming that this should be the target—a very new development when considering our history and, indeed, a revolution in itself. Fiscal discipline is probably the most important reform that has taken place in Latin America.

The reform of the public sector is a second area that stands out in this picture, albeit with some nuances, due to a far lower level of public acceptance as yet. In Uruguay, for instance, two weeks ago, 72 percent of the people voted against privatizing utilities and the telephone company.

The opening of the economy is the third pillar of the Washington consensus. While it is now the accepted trend in the region and almost everywhere else, the pace of reform varies greatly across the region.

The third question relates to whether there is a cultural revolution as well as an economic one in the region. Here I refer to "cultural revolution" in the sense used by Andrés Bianchi. I personally believe a cultural revolution is under way in Latin America in terms of the values and concepts that the political leadership and the public are endorsing, and it is in that sense a genuine revolution. I have dealt with the issue since the early 1960s, so my opinion on this is backed by 30 years of experience. Specifically, what are the basic cultural changes taking place in economic management and thinking? The first is clearly a distrust of excessive government intervention in the economy. We all are aware of what institutions such as ECLAC proposed for many years on the role of the state. But now people have grown very suspicious of government, of its inefficiencies, of corruption, of their lack of control. Indeed, this explains why unions are backing privatizations in Argentina or Brazil. Thus, the first big change has to do with a shift from a state to a market-oriented management of the economy.

Another cultural factor I find extremely important is that countries are abandoning the exculpatory view that most of their problems originate outside their borders. We were always blaming external forces for things that were happening inside our countries. This is changing dramatically as people begin to see that many domestic factors were the cause of our problems. They also noted that the world was moving ahead, whether or not we were responsible for our problems, and that in any case our problems were not at the center of the world's concerns. It has since been recognized that action must be taken, even in an imperfect world, and this change in perspective explains the radically new attitude toward foreign investment and multinational corporations that prevails in the region today. In the 1970s Latin America had tended to resist both. In the past, discussions of Latin American issues typically began from a world perspective and only then would focus on Latin America. Of course, international events do shape our affairs to some extent, but we are distancing ourselves from the idea that they are the main determinants.

Another element, which has also very much to do with a cultural change, is the current shift from a closed economy to an open economy. When economist Raúl Prebisch (the leading thinker in the region in the postwar period) addressed the problems of Latin America, he thought of the countries as closed economies and then urged them to move toward integration. Later on, in 1964, he proposed the Generalized System of Preferences. The region, in reference to his early writings, followed very much his closed approach to the economy which prevailed for the last 20 years. Against this background, I cannot explain how the impressive reductions in tariffs happened so quickly and, indeed, I wonder whether they happened too fast in some cases. Nonetheless, there should be and there is a more open economy throughout the region, and this transformation is akin to another cultural change.

Let me move on to the fourth question—namely, what are the risks lying ahead of us? Allow me, in this regard, to share some of my concerns. The first risk is one that we can do very little about: the international situation. Clearly, there are some positive international developments today. For example, the interest rate reduction is a very favorable one for us. The confidence in the capital markets vis-à-vis Latin America is also good. We closed 1992 with $57 billion in capital inflows to the region, compared with $39 billion the previous year and $20 billion the year before that. So all this speaks well about the positive influences from outside.

The negative side is the still-sluggish growth in the world economy. In our capacity as exporters, we are suffering from declining prices and lack of access to markets. There could also be a reversal in investor confidence if current trade imbalances continue to grow. People are starting to look at the size of the trade deficits and ask whether they can continue to lend in the face of these uncertainties. Confidence will continue to be more important in securing our sources of funding until the world economy begins to grow again.

Other concerns were brought up during a recent seminar at the Inter-American Development Bank. One is the slow response of investment to stabilization, Bolivia being a good example of this. There are also difficulties in managing exchange rate policies due to the inflow of capital from outside, particularly capital that is attracted by high interest rates.

Then, there are concerns about what I call social fatigue and the growing expectations for reform in the region, especially among the most deeply affected group—the middle class. I do not think social fatigue is so much a low-income class phenomenon as it is a middle-class phenomenon because the interests of the latter are strongly entrenched in the public sector and thus are most affected by privatization efforts.

Indeed, I sense a certain revisionism or nostalgia in the region. I recently attended an important meeting organized by the Catholic Church in Santo Domingo. Let me quote what Manuel Camilo Vial Risopatrón, the bishop of San Felipe in Chile, said on the Chilean experience, which is again and by any measure the most successful one. His comments impressed most participants and are illustrative of the social fatigue I just referred to:

The macroeconomic reforms have been good. Almost all of the indicators are positive: the external debt has been reduced, inflation is down, and there is less unemployment; reserves have been built up, we are experiencing sustained economic growth, and markets and exports have been diversified.

A more modern, enterprising business mentality has emerged. No longer do we need to look to the state to provide for everything or wait for foreign handouts. Finally, there is a glimmer of hope: now there exists the possibility of eliminating the poverty around us.

It is not possible, however, to hide the negative side of this experiment—the high price that has been paid for this success:

1. The transformation of the productive apparatus has been an extremely difficult process that is hardly compatible with the democratic system of governance.

2. The heaviest burden has been borne by the poor. The deregulation of the labor market produced massive unemployment. Wages fell to very low levels, and labor was overworked.

3. The unions were broken up. All progress they had achieved was lost, and they were rendered powerless by draconian legislation.

4. The proposed system has produced social disparity so great that a deeply divided society has been created in terms of living standards and even cultural differences. This situation is explosive. The growing inequities in the distribution of income have been alarming.

5. The need to reduce the size of government resulted not only in the privatization of state-owned companies but also in the reduction in social spending for health services, education, and social security. Those most affected by this retrenchment have been the poor, and in many cases the damage has been irreparable.

6. The resulting inequities are flaunted in advertising, which encourages the consumer to spend by creating fictitious and unattainable needs that give rise to deep rooted frustration and the search for easy money through violence, prostitution, and theft.

7. Finally, the market economy has undoubtedly become an end in itself for which everything is sacrificed. Of serious concern in particular is the loss of any sense of community. The great social inequalities that exist in our countries have left many sectors of society on the margin.

I do not agree with the opinion expressed by the bishop, but it does give an indication of the growing impatience that could threaten the continuation of reform if something is not done, and it does provide a good synthesis of the issues the region needs to face in the coming years.

Another issue that is very much on the table is the whole question of governance. One underlying problem is that political timing does not coincide with economic timing. While democracies are already in place, economic changes need time to work and one consequence of this has been the extremely low popularity enjoyed by presidents in many countries today. In my country (Uruguay), which is growing by 11.5 percent, where unemployment and inflation are down, and where reserves are up, the popularity rating of the president is 12 percent. That's why the administration lost its bid to privatize the telephone company. It was not so much the question of whether to privatize that was at stake as much as the desire to punish politicians.

The question of governance involves more than the efficiency of the public sector alone. It encompasses the whole question of justice, of the lack of modernization of the political system, and corruption, which are very much to be blamed for the inequities in the system.

Based on the foregoing, my fifth and last question is, what are the issues we need to address? First, we must stress that there is no substitute for the type of reforms we have been undertaking; they must be deepened and continued in the coming years. There have been areas where reform has been lagging and others where reforms have not been put in place. Reform must continue, but an essential element is to introduce the social component into the process. This is precisely what we are trying to accomplish at the IDB now. We are trying to approach social reform in Latin America as a complement—a deeply rooted one— to the concept of economic reform. It would be a mistake to try to design social policies in isolation from the new economic model. We must learn to avoid the populistic approach of the past and make the system more efficient socially. That, of course, is not easy to accomplish, but we must try our best to help countries achieve this goal. My good friend Louis Emmerij has joined the IDB to give me guidance on this issue, and we are organizing an international forum in Washington in February to explore ways in which the IDB can help promote social reform as an essential part of overall reform.

Another important element, I am increasingly convinced, pertains to the political skills of leaders in the region. It is often difficult for economists to practice the art of politics, but some leaders in the region have demonstrated their ability to gain time and to convince people that things are changing for the benefit of the masses. People must not only see decency, honesty, efficiency, and the absence of corruption, they must also perceive that the political leadership is behind the process of change. A very good example of this is the current president of Mexico, who takes two days a week to travel all over the country, talking to the people and putting the Solidarity Program in place. This creates the perception that the leader of the country is really committed to change, even if it is not possible to give the people everything they would like. This is not something that technocrats can provide; only politicians can assuage public opinion in this way. This aspect, I believe, is crucial at a time when the most difficult challenge facing politicians is the crisis of the impatient middle classes of Latin America. And the more they see that things are changing, the more impatient and the more demanding they become.

For example, the issue arises of how to deal with the salaries of teachers or the military. Only real political leadership is able to deal with these issues, to gain time, and to give people the feeling that they are part of the process, without making promises that would wreck the economy.

Last but not least, I think we must get to some real redefinition of the role of the state. It is clear to me that the question of getting prices right, reducing the deficit, and liberalizing markets is not enough. Something else has to be done, and this "something else" has to be defined. How do we do this, giving the state a market-friendly role in the economy (as the World Bank phrased it in the 1991 *World Development Report*) rather than "interfering"? How do we gain time for these ideas to take root while giving people hope? Providing hope must be left to those with political skill; it is something economists, unfortunately, cannot do.

# 11

# LIFE IN THE ECONOMIC EMERGENCY ROOM

# Life in the Economic Emergency Room

JEFFREY SACHS

I have entitled my talk "Life in the Economic Emergency Room," or, even more aptly, the shock trauma unit, because I want to talk about cases of extreme economic instability, such as Russia is facing now or Poland faced in 1989. More countries have experienced hyperinflation in the 1980s and 1990s than in any other time in history, and we are not done with it yet. This great instability poses enormous challenges for us as economists and enormous pain for countries struggling to overcome past military rule, communist despotism, war, or revolution. And so my focus is on such cases, rather than on the equally interesting and important cases such as Spain's accession to the European Community and its shift from an inward- to an outward-looking orientation.

## International Role

I want to make one basic point about these emergencies. It is such a trivial point that it shouldn't require repeating, but it seems to be controversial in every case, forgotten in almost every case, and in need of relearning in every case. That is, the ability to succeed in reform has two critical components. One is the capacity of the country itself to reform. Successful domestic reform depends on vigorous political leadership. Equally important is the role of the outside world in helping the country to overcome the crisis. Even in the conference, the role of the interna-

*Jeffrey Sachs is a Professor at Harvard University and has served as an adviser to several governments, including Russia's, on economic reform. What follows is the text of a speech delivered during the conference.*

tional community in many of the countries that we are talking about has been very much downplayed. This is not to take away from the accomplishments of anyone who has presented a paper in this conference—many of them, such as Leszek Balcerowicz, former finance minister of Poland, are my heros. But countries cannot be transformed without the generous and farsighted involvement of the international community.

Despite the lessons of this century, the international community forgets this point again and again, at enormous risk to the world. We seem to be forgetting again—this time vis-à-vis Russia—and the stakes could not be higher. No matter how valiant, brilliant, and lucky are Russia's reformers, they won't make it without large-scale external assistance. This was true for Poland, as it was for Turkey, Mexico, and Chile. The papers in this conference fail to reflect this basic point, and so I feel the need to help set the record straight, or at least, to help put it clearly, because we are close to missing a historical opportunity in Russia.

I spoke on this topic recently at the Heritage Foundation. My talk was sparked by a letter sent to me by an analyst there, who believed strongly in Russia's reforms but not in foreign aid for Russia. This is a common view of free-market ideologues—of which I am one. It is plausible, but it is mistaken. The market cannot do it all by itself; international help is critical.

The International Monetary Fund's view, all too often, is also based on a misunderstanding of what its own role should be. The IMF officials say, "Prove it to us first that you can do it." This response reminds me of the British aristocrat walking by the pond one day. He hears a man screaming, "Help, I can't swim!" And he looks down at the man and says, "Sir, I can't swim either, but I don't make such a fuss about it." Clearly, when there is a cry for help, it is necessary to respond.

Of course, foreign aid is not the main factor in economic success. The reforms themselves are the key. My argument is that foreign aid is critical to helping the reforms themselves take hold. Of course, some people are on the other side of this debate, believing that external help alone is sufficient. Such arguments remind me of the poor man begging to God every night, "God, let me win the lottery." This goes on for a few months. One night he is again on his knees, begging, "God, let me win the lottery. I am a pious and good man." Suddenly, the heavens open up with a clap of thunder, and a voice from above pleads: "Give me a break; buy a ticket." Yes, a country has to buy its own ticket to success. Only then can external help can be fruitful.

Aid is crucial because reforms are inherently very fragile at the outset. There is typically little consensus on what should be done, pessimism is rife, and the reformers' hold on power and on policy is tenuous. But despite the urgency of timely assistance, the aid package for each country must be put together on an *ad hoc* basis. The IMF and the World Bank do not by themselves offer a reforming country an adequate international framework for viable reform and recovery. Leadership from key countries, particularly the United States, has almost always been behind a successful international assistance effort.

## Reform Without Consensus

The conference has failed to stress the fragility of reforms in the early phase. Many participants have suggested that reformers succeed by constructing a "social consensus" in favor of reforms. This is mostly not the case. In deep crises, there simply is no consensus to build upon, only confusion, anxiety, and a cacophony of conflicting opinions. Take the case of Poland, where it is sometimes suggested that the Solidarity-led government was able to carry out its "shock therapy" program because of a social consensus. In fact, there was no consensus on specific economic measures. From the start, Leszek Balcerowicz and his policies were enormously controversial—even though he will surely go down in history as a national hero.

While Poland did have a basic consensus in its desire to "return to Europe," this certainly did not translate into agreement on the specifics of economic policy. Poland was as likely as any country to succumb to rampant populism and wild, misdirected policies. That it found its way out of the crisis was heavily dependent upon the leadership of Leszek Balcerowicz and the critical involvement of the international community.

Let me describe what it was like when Poland was wheeled into the emergency room in 1989. Poland was in critical condition—with extreme and intensifying shortages, an incipient hyperinflation, and an extreme balance of payments crisis. And most of the doctors leaning over Balcerowicz's shoulder were screaming contradictory advice. Poland's economics profession was in disarray. Communist economic concepts (e.g., the primacy of industry over services, or the need for protectionism) still hung heavily in the air; stale arguments of the past continued to stir confusion; and many would-be "market economists" were distinguished by their attachment to a crude Keynesianism that had gone out of style in the West decades earlier. The stark fact was that almost no economists in Poland had professional experience with the problems of monetary destabilization or the implementation of macroeconomic policy reforms.

Consensus on many specifics (e.g., currency convertibility, price decontrol, budgetary discipline) has come to Poland, but only after three years of reform. Now many people are coming out of the woodwork to say they supported the Balcerowicz program from the start. But at the beginning, it was touch and go. The policy debate was not whether the exchange rate on 1 January 1990 should be pegged at 7,500 zloty per dollar or 9,500 zloty per dollar, a question that many Monday-morning quarterbacks continue to second-guess today. The question was far more basic and pivotal: Should Poland move quickly to convertibility? Leszek Balcerowicz will well remember late December 1991, on the eve of the reforms, when even the central bank governor threatened to walk out on the basic policy of currency convertibility at the start of the reform. The central banker's support for convertibility was contingent upon Poland's receipt of the $1 billion zloty stabilization fund at the start of the program.

The initial confusion, and the difficulty of forming a consensus, is fueled in most crises not only by inexperience and misconceptions but also by the extravagent fears that accompany a program of fundamental change, no matter how promising the program might be in objective economic terms. While the history of market-based reforms has repeatedly shown that free markets, open trade, and an economy fueled by private ownership are enormously powerful in stimulating rapid economic growth, the general public rarely knows it or believes it at the start. It is always crucial to make policymakers aware of this historical record, a point that Anne Krueger has properly stressed over the years.

The father of the "German economic miracle," Ludwig Erhard, has vividly described the confusion and pessimism that gripped Germany at the time that he was promoting market-based reforms in the late 1940s. Here was an economy minister whose government was sustained by a single vote in 1949 (it was Konrad Adenauer's own vote that made him chancellor). While Erhard is now rightly remembered as one of the great economic policymakers of the century, at the start of the German postwar reforms he was widely attacked as the cause of Germany's rising unemployment, and there was hardly anything miraculous in the situation, as most Germans saw it. In his memoirs, Erhard remembered the pessimistic, static outlook:

> It was calculated that for every German there would be one plate every 50 years, a pair of shoes every 12 years, a suit every 50 years, and that only one in every three Germans would have the chance to be buried in his own coffin. Few realized," Erhard writes, "that if the people could once more realize the value and worth of freedom, dynamic forces would be released. It was a time when public opinion seemed resigned to the ruin of West Germany. Opposition at home joined with international criticism. With prices rising every day and the foreign trade balance becoming more unfavorable, speaking of the future optimistically was only possible through a deep conviction in the market economy. It still took months before the change became apparent, but this turn toward salvation in 1950–51 was, as a result, all the more positive and lasting.

Confusion over economic crisis is multiplied by high inflation, a point eloquently stressed by Keynes in *The Economic Consequences of the Peace*. As Keynes so famously put it,

> Lenin was most certainly right. There is no subtler, no surer way of overturning the existing basis of society than to debauch the currency. The process engages

all the hidden forces of economic law on the side of destruction, and does it in a manner which not one man in a million is able to diagnose.

The Western economics profession has been spoiled rotten by rational expectations thinking, by diverting our attention away from the profound misunderstandings that are part of every deep crisis. Few Russians understand the source of Russia's current inflation, least of all the governor of the central bank, who, to combat what has become a 30 percent per month inflation rate, called again for wage and price controls on 14 January 1993, rather than for tighter credit policy. The central bank governor is largely innocent of monetary economics. But pity the rest of the Russian people. They may know a little bit more than the central bank, but not much. They do understand that the quadrupling of the money supply in the last six months is somehow part of the problem, but the confusion over the price of the ruble and the source of the problem is truly spectacular.

Keynes also stressed the particular insidiousness of the confusion over the causes of inflation. He said that inflation heightens society's antipathy to those who make profits in the turbulent market conditions. Businessmen are converted in the public's mind into "profiteers." But, said Keynes,

> these profiteers are, broadly speaking, the entrepreneurial class of capitalists— that is to say, the active and constructive element in capitalist society who, in a period of rapidly rising prices, cannot help but get rich whether they wish it or not. If prices are continually rising, every trader who has purchased stock or owns property inevitably makes profit. By reviling this class, therefore, the European governments were carrying a step further the fatal process conceived in the subtle mind of Lenin. The profiteers were a consequence, not a cause, of rising prices.

Much of the excess focus on the "mafia" in Russia today reflects this kind of thinking. There was a real mafia in Russia until recently: the Communist Party of the Soviet Union—a veritable mafia in every key aspect. It was an economically corrupt, thoroughly insidious organization, and a protection racket at the far reaches of society. But today, many of those who are called "mafia" are simply traders: Azeri traders, traders from Turkmenistan, traders from other places.

The confusion, anxiety, and the profound sense of bewilderment about market forces are inevitable when breadwinners must worry whether the income will be enough next week to feed the family. The anxieties created by high inflation underscore what several conference participants have said: at the beginning, it is essential to stop hyperinflation, before any other reform. You cannot think straight in the midst of hyperinflation. The society becomes unglued. What is needed is sufficient stability to permit the government to address other crucial economic issues, not to mention actions in other spheres, involving the constitution and the legal structure.

Many Western economists have also fundamentally misdiagnosed the macroeconomic situation in Poland and Russia. With a surprising casualness, they have jumped from the observed declines in industrial production to the conclusion that a demand expansion (such as in increase in money-supply growth) is warranted as a countercyclical "boost" to the economy. Such advice is naive in the face of the huge inflationary pressures in the region and is simply a misreading of the real economic situation. The industrial output decline reflects the profound structural imbalances of the Stalinist economies of the region, with their gross overemphasis of heavy industrial production, rather than a simple shortfall in aggregate demand. Output is declining because the factories lack real customers. Where there are customers, such as in food processing, consumer goods, or exportable production, output in Poland is rising, not falling.

In essence, these economies are undergoing the Schumpeterian "creative destruction" of old, moribund industrial sectors that was put off for 40 years or more. There is simply no reason why the economies of the former Soviet Union should produce 80 percent more steel than the United States, as the Soviet Union was doing in the late 1980s. A decline in heavy industrial production is inevitable, and desirable, as it frees resources for other sectors of the economy, including services, consumer industry, and new export sectors.

This is more and more clear to outside observers, although it was not clear to many Western observers and analysts in the first couple of years. What has made it clear is that every country of Eastern Europe has had an output decline of between 30 and 50 percent, whether the country is reforming or not reforming, doing it fast or doing it slow, doing it coherently or incoherently. Those whose reforms were the hardest and the fastest, like Poland, have actually had the smallest cumulative declines and the quickest return to growth. Hungary, which reformed more gradually than Poland, continued to have a decline of industrial output in 1992, even as Poland's industry started to grow, particularly in the new consumer goods and export sectors.

At the critical moment when reformers are fighting for financial stability, Western calls for allegedly more "humane" policies can seriously undercut the political support for the reformers. Just as there has been a casualness in interpreting the nature of the industrial output decline in the East, there has also been a casualness in judging the "harshness" of the reforms in terms of their effect on living standards. It was widely alleged that Poland's reform program caused a real-income drop of one-third. This led some outside observers to argue that the Poles should "ease up," or go more slowly, just at the moment that decisive stabilization measures were most necessary. We now know, on the basis of careful analysis, that no such sharp drop in living standards in fact took place. The calls for gradualism therefore threatened the hard work of financial stabilization, while being based on naive interpretations of shaky statistics.

When one examines what Poles have actually been consuming since the start of the reforms, the idea that living standards collapsed is clearly put to rest. One charge was that Polish pensioners were suffering terribly as a result of the reforms. The fact is Poland more than took care of its pensioners. If you compare per-capita meat consumption between 1989 and 1991 (which should be a sensitive indicator of monthly consumption) for retired persons and pensioners, it went up 11 percent in volume; for employee households, it went up 2 percent, and for the country as a whole, it went up 2.6 percent. For fruits, similarly, pensioners saw a 10 percent rise in fruit consumption per capita and employees an 11 percent rise. Taking into account a small drop for farm households, there was an 8 percent rise for the country as a whole.

Over the last three years, Poles have been buying the Western consumer durables that were out of their reach for decades. Perhaps the best indicator of this is VCR ownership in Poland. During this period of supposed ''great depression,'' VCR ownership among employees has risen from 1.9 per hundred households at the end of 1988 to 41 per hundred households at the end of 1991. Automobiles went from 30 to 38 per hundred households; stereo radios from 22 to 38; and color televisions from 41 to 82 per hundred households. And all of this was happening at a time when many or most economists were arguing wrongly that the reforms were too hard, too dangerous, too costly, too destructive—exactly what one hears about Russia today.

What does one do in these circumstances? If you are the reform team, I think it is absolutely clear. You lead; you press forward. The key reform input that is missing in most economic analyses is political leadership. Leszek Balcerowicz was not a household name in Poland three years ago. He had to earn the public trust through results. Alexander Hamilton, the first US Treasury secretary, faced similar difficulties in the early days of the American republic. He was very much influenced by Jacques Necker, the last French finance minister of the *ancien régime*, who wrote a Machiavellian guide for finance ministers. Necker said that a great minister must have five attributes: genius, regularity, prudence, firmness, and breadth of knowledge. Necker maintained that flexibility or willingness to compromise, which might be harmless or even advantageous in other ministers, was an unforgivable failing in a finance minister! A weak and compromising minister of finance was worse than a dishonest one. Toughness has been and continues to be an extremely important attribute in this position.

The reform team must make its reforms an accomplished fact. A key human attribute is attachment to the status quo. We even have detailed theories and empirical evidence of this bias, which Twersky and other economic psychologists have analyzed with great insight. When people are offered a choice between A and B, according to basic economic theory, that choice should be made independently of whether they start with A and are offered B as an alternative or if they start with B and are offered A. But what psychologists have found is that an individual who starts with A and is offered B is much more likely to choose to stay with A than he is to choose A if he started with B. This is the basis for the theories of loss aversion and status quo bias.

If reformers want free prices, they should not stand around and talk about it—they should do it, because everyone will be against freeing prices until it has been done, until it is an established fact. But once done, there is no going back, or, at least, little chance of going back. The Russians will probably not go back to price controls because Yegor Gaidar acted rapidly at the start of 1992 to free prices.

## Laissez-Faire Policies

Strategy in the shock trauma unit requires the use of radical, laissez-faire policies, for a reason that is rarely recognized: it is a political strategy, not just an economic strategy. I learned a great deal from the brilliant former minister of economy of Bolivia, Gonzalo Sanchez de Lozada, who used to say, "Thank God, I don't have to decide on the weather because if I did, the farmers and the city people would be at me every day." And he said the same thing about prices for bread and other things. A government facing political and economic collapse (the case at hand) must give up responsibility for market prices in order to focus on the core functions of government that are not being met: law and order, public security, a stable monetary system, and basic social welfare. Governments that have reached hyperinflation cannot, *self-evidently*, be expected to develop complex industrial policies or structural policies. After all, they aren't even carrying out their most fundamental tasks.

Nonetheless, many economists would have such governments also take on many ancillary responsibilities, for example, government-led restructuring of enterprises, or an industrial policy. In the case of Russia, such advocates of big government somehow believe that, even though the government cannot now even avoid a quadrupling of the money supply over the second half of 1992, it can somehow manage 200,000 firms in a politically sound, technically competent, and responsible way. It is a ludicrous supposition, of course. What radical laissez-faire policies entail, in circumstances of extreme crisis, is shucking off the secondary burdens of government so that the government can focus on its core functions.

The World Bank too is often on the wrong side of this debate. Too many World Bank programs are implicitly predicated on an honest, technically competent, smoothly operating, and market-friendly bureaucracy. World Bank programs for sectoral restructuring often build in new and heavy responsibilities for ministries that rather should be closed because of incompetence, corruption, and lack of need!

## Resorting to Self-Help

I return now to the main theme: international assistance in support of radical reforms. There are two kinds of assistance: self-help and real help. Self-help is what happens when a finance minister increases national income by stopping debt payments while appealing to the international community for understanding. Self-help is needed because our international financial institutions, particularly the IMF, simply don't operate fast enough or coherently enough to handle the financial crisis in the absence of self-help.

Consider the case of an overly indebted corporation in the United States that is unable to service its debts in the short run. Under Chapter 11 of the US Bankruptcy Code, the debtor enterprise can file for bankruptcy to obtain a ''standstill'' on debt servicing. Under the standstill, creditors must refrain from attempting to collect the debt, pending a collective solution to the indebtedness problem. Moreover, the law provides ways for the enterprise to borrow new working-capital funds even after filing for bankruptcy, in order to ensure the continued efficient operation of the firm.

No such procedures operate with heavily indebted countries in the grip of a balance of payments crisis. A country cannot file for an immediate standstill in an international bankruptcy court. Perhaps it can achieve one, following months of laborious negotiations with creditors, but usually only after tremendous damage has been done by capital flight, a withdrawal of trade credits, and other hostile creditor actions. Moreover, there is no routine way to obtain the working capital vitally needed to keep the economy functioning. It is literally the case that Macy's had an easier time raising $600 million in emergency working-capital loans after filing for bankruptcy than did Russia in 1992. Macy's got the loan three weeks after the filing of the bankruptcy petition; Russia's $600 million financial rehabilitation loan from the World Bank was not fully negotiated during the entire 1992.

The United States actually started with self-help in 1790, when Alexander Hamilton unilaterally cut the interest rate on the US foreign debt. He in fact gave the creditors a menu of options, in the time-honored fashion: the creditors could accept low interest and par bonds, or they could accept a cut in the face value by not converting, or they could keep with their 6 percent interest rate loan and expect servicing of that part of the debt to sink to the bottom of priorities. In effect, he unilaterally subordinated the debt of those creditors who were not willing to cut the debt burden. Interestingly, this was done in Paris, where most of the debt was held—an early and effective "Paris Club" rescheduling.

Now let's turn to real help: structured financial assistance to support a reform program. The point I want to make is that the traditional arguments against development assistance (for instance, the influential arguments made by Lord Bauer in past years) are largely irrelevant to the kind of financial aid needed by countries in acute economic crisis. The case for development aid in traditional thinking is that it helps countries to grow by filling the "savings gap" and/or the foreign exchange gap. We are after something else here, to help countries to reform, with growth coming mainly as a result of the reforms rather than as a result of the aid itself. The aid functions to bolster the social and political situation in the country and to help the government manage its strained finances in a noninflationary way.

Critics of traditional development assistance are usually right to point out that aid is almost too small, by itself, to make much of a direct dent on overall living standards or growth rates. (The $100 billion annual flows from West Germany to East Germany, however, offer a unique and conspicuous exception.) Even the famed Marshall Plan funds, at around 2 to 3 percent of recipient-country GDP, were surely too small to serve such a purpose. But revisionist historians are grossly mistaken when they conclude that the Marshall Plan therefore had only a tiny effect on Western European economies. The Marshall Plan had the effect that I am stressing: it allowed market-friendly governments to survive and to function long enough for their economies to recover, driven by market forces. Erhard's Germany was the case *par excellence.*

The conservative critique of foreign aid is that it bolsters governments. That might be undesirable in the case of corrupt authoritarian regimes not implementing economic reforms, but it is exactly the goal in the case of the radical reform governments of Eastern Europe and Russia. It is true that you cannot make bad governments do good things with aid— conditionality is not so powerful. But what you can do is help good governments to survive long enough to solve problems.

Sometimes aid cannot work when the government is uninterested in real reform. It is necessary to walk away from a lousy government, which is something that international institutions also have a hard time doing. But when the IMF walked away from Poland early in 1992—after Jan Olszewski came in as prime minister based on a highly populistic campaign platform and with recklessly populistic rhetoric—the IMF departure shook the place up tremendously and effectively. It was the IMF at its absolute best. It surprised the Poles. Quickly, Olszewski appointed Andrzej Olechowski as finance minister, giving the country a fighting chance of staying on track, despite difficulties posed by the rest of the cabinet. When the Olszewski government fell soon afterward on other grounds, the new government came in committed to a continuation of the reform path.

In the Polish case, the capacity of international financial institutions to walk away had an important and hugely favorable impact. The other case—the one that I have been lucky enough to be part of several times— is the case in which there is already a good government. We wake up one day, and Russia has a dynamic 35-year-old reform leader, dedicated to radical economic reform—something we could never have dared to expect. This is not the time to engage in a debate about whether foreign aid can help or not, or whether foreign aid props up bad regimes. This is an opportunity to seize. It is precisely the opportunity we failed to take in 1992 and must quickly take in 1993, if it is not already too late.

## Case Histories

Before going into the particulars of the Russian case, I would like to remind the participants of this conference that at some point almost all of their countries have required significant international help (for US participants, I have already alluded to the situation in 1790).

Adenauer would not have survived without the Marshall Plan; he barely survived *with* the Marshall Plan. And the Social Democratic Party was not exactly the moderate, market-friendly party that it became in the late 1950s after the proven success of Erhard's market reforms, which forced the party back to a mainstream position. Aid was absolutely fundamental to getting postwar Germany onto a healthy long-term path.

Many of my Japanese friends have been neglecting their own recent history in their consideration of aid to Russia. US assistance was absolutely fundamental between 1947 and 1950 in giving the Yoshida government the opportunity to put in place a real stabilization program to unify the exchange rate, create a market economy, carry out land reform, and the rest. When the Japanese shrink from helping Russia because of the truly nasty periods in their past relations, they must remember that the US decision to give large-scale aid to Japan three years after World War II was also not the most palatable policy for Americans as well. Yet it was surely the right thing to do and was vital for Japan's later magnificent success. On another point, some Japanese economists now say to the Russians, "Don't go with the IMF, don't go with stabilization: we have a different way." They also forget that the United States imposed a rigorous IMF-style stabilization plan (the Dodge Plan) in 1949 that was key to a decade of subsequent stable growth in Japan. Many leading Japanese politicians opposed the Dodge Plan because it forced a cutback in vote-getting public spending. Yet, the plan was carried through and was crucial in providing a stable financial base for Japan's growth in the 1950s.

Bolivia's successful stabilization and structural reforms, which enabled Bolivia to end hyperinflation and to achieve sustained economic growth (equal to Mexico's cumulative growth since 1986), similarly required self-help and real help. The self-help came early in 1986. I was called in Cambridge one day to come quickly to La Paz. The problem was most odd: after just two months of a fragile antihyperinflation effort at the beginning of 1986, Bolivia was being pressed by the IMF to devalue the currency once again! Without the devaluation, the IMF claimed, Bolivia would not be able to service enough of the debt that year.

Bolivia was drowning in debt. The debt service due was more than total government revenues, and debt reduction was surely going to be needed. But this was still early in the debt crisis, and the IMF and the creditor governments had not yet acknowledged the role for debt reduction. The IMF was still insisting on debt servicing, despite the obvious potential harm of such an approach. The Bolivian government eventually cut short the debate, saying, "Look, we can't pay, and we're not going to pay." Eventually, after heated arguments, the IMF acknowledged the need for a complete standstill on debt servicing and cancellation of a substantial part of the debt. In 1987 the IMF became the sponsor of Bolivia's debt buyback operation with the commercial banks. The success of the Bolivian buyback eventually contributed to an overall rethinking of the debt strategy, culminating in the Brady Plan.

International assistance has also played a key role in Mexico's economic reform and recovery. Mexico is the World Bank's second largest customer—with $19 billion in loans outstanding at the end of 1991. It is by far the largest US Export-Import Bank customer. The Brady Plan was designed originally for Mexico following an emergency bailout in 1988 that was crucial in helping Salinas to get off to a good start. The lesson from Mexico is that when the United States is focused, for foreign policy reasons, on managing a financial workout, the right things can happen.

The strength and coherence of Chile's economic reforms in the 1980s are well-known, but Chile's economic success also depended on external help. I have been criticized by one of Chile's erstwhile US advisers, Steve Hanke of Johns Hopkins University, for calling for foreign assistance for Russia, even though Chile itself was a major beneficiary of international assistance after 1982. Between 1983 and 1987, official loans to Chile went from $1.2 billion to $3.9 billion, an increase of 16 percent of Chile's average GNP over the four years, or an average of 4 percent a year. Did the aid provide the solution for Chile? No, the grapes did: the answer was Chile's trade liberalization, which began to show its full fruits, as it were, in 1985. But would the reforms have lasted until that point without the international help? In my view, not likely (and almost certainly not had Chile been a democracy in the early 1980s).

Let me turn to Poland. I cannot stress enough the heroism of the Polish economic team and its capacity to operate amidst profound confusion and intense political and economic difficulties. But here too, international help was crucial. The billion-dollar zloty stabilization fund for Poland, not actually even touched, was of principal importance in helping Leszek Balcerowicz to convince the rest of the government, and the general public, to accept his program. Many of Balcerowicz's closest advisers did not believe it was possible to move quickly to convertibility; international help was essential to get them to contemplate such a policy. Viewed through the optic of the Polish experience, the IMF's treatment of the ruble stabilization fund—to delay its mobilization until after stabilization is achieved—is a serious tactical misjudgment.

Also critical for Poland was the two-stage debt cancellation, which was engineered in 1991 by the Group of Seven with resolute US leadership. The strength of that deal lay not only in the financial lift that it gives Poland and in the hope that it offers to the Polish people, but in the key tactical fact that it comes in two parts. Part of the debts were canceled in 1991; the other part—a significant chunk—only is to be canceled in 1994, and only if Poland is still in compliance with its IMF program at that point. This is an enormously powerful and politically salient kind of conditionality; deep debt reduction is not something a government or country lightly walks away from.

Turgut Özal led very successful reforms in Turkey during the 1980s, following the financial collapse at the end of the 1970s. It is important to remember, however, that Turkey's financial recovery also owes much to timely international assistance. In 1979 Turkey's financial fragility was of enormous strategic concern to the United States, Germany, and NATO, especially with the Iranian revolution under way. The OECD countries coordinated massive financial assistance to Turkey, so that during 1979–82 Turkey never had to make net resource transfers to the rest of the world (in contrast to the major Latin American debtor countries, which were pushed initially into large negative resource transfers). The West cushioned the adjustment process during the critical early years. Official aid to Turkey averaged $623 million from 1975 to 1978 and then went to $1.1 billion in 1979, $2.7 billion in 1980, and $1.8 billion in 1981. There was an emergency OECD loan, a special $1 billion in short-term credits, and a very generous debt rescheduling.

Israel, which had a successful stabilization in 1985, also has had very extensive international backing. During the first year of stabilization, the United States gave an extra $1.5 billion in aid (above the usual $3 billion per year). This was grant money that amounted to about 6 percent of Israeli GNP.

Indonesia also was the recipient of an extremely generous debt cancellation deal in 1969 arranged by the German banker, Herman Abs, as head of the creditor committee. It was the second case of debt cancellation in the post-World War II period, after Germany itself in 1953. The cancellation allowed Suharto to end a very high inflation and begin a very successful period of economic stabilization and liberalization.

The point is that there are few miracles; reforming countries need help, no matter how good the reform team. If you look closely at successes, you will find that help was at hand. And if you look closely at the help, you will discover its *ad hoc* character. Either the US president was concerned, or there was a special strategic need, or there was a creditor government focused for some other reason. Mexico was an obvious concern because of its 2,000–mile border with the United States. Poland was of critical concern as the first postcommunist country, and the mother country of large numbers of Polish-American voters in Chicago. In Turkey, the key was NATO's strategic concerns in the midst of the Iranian revolution. And so forth.

## Reform in Russia

This pattern of assistance is dangerously accidental. It is too little based on conceptual understanding and a coherent analytical framework. There is no place where this lack of understanding and institutional response has been more evident than in Russia since the collapse of communism. The Western policy has been shocking in its neglect and in its incapacity to face the real economic issues in Russia. This incapacity was epitomized by Secretary of State Baker's thrust toward symbolism over reality in the formulation of Western aid, and in the IMF's failure to mobilize large-scale international support.

I have found the Western performance nearly unbelievable. I must say that my greatest personal mistake this year was to say to President Boris Yeltsin, "Don't worry; help is on the way." I believed deeply that the assistance was too important, and too crucial to the West, for it to be messed up as significantly and fundamentally as it has been this past year.

On 28 October 1991 Yeltsin made a remarkable speech in which he said Russia was to become a normal country and that it wanted to become a democracy with a market economy. The next morning, when I opened the *Financial Times*, I was reminded of one of Solzhenitsyn's famous characters in the *Cancer Ward*. The character is a party *apparatchik* who lies waiting in the cancer ward, anticipating the one-year anniversary of Stalin's death. He fantasizes about the big black rims that will run around the newspaper that day in commemoration of the Great Man to whom he dedicated his party service. When the paper arrives on that day, there is no black rim, and in fact not even a mention of Stalin's death. He knows that a political earthquake has occurred; his political life is finished.

I woke up on 29 October 1991—the day after Yeltsin's speech—similarly expecting red, white, and blue banners around the *Financial Times*, with Western leaders praising the speech and saying that a new day had dawned in international cooperation. But there was not one mention of Yeltsin's speech by anybody: not the World Bank president, nor the IMF managing director, nor any G-7 leader. It came and it went. One week later Yeltsin appointed Yegor Gaidar, and again, no reaction.

The G-7 finance deputies arrived in Moscow soon afterward. I assumed they would talk to Gaidar about his problems. The man, after all, had a rather large task: an empire falling apart, hyperinflation, fundamental system transformation, and the army. But the G-7 deputies only wanted to talk about one thing for three days: the foreign debt. It was really important to them to get the Russians to sign an agreement on the "joint and several responsibility for the old Soviet debt" and to get Russia to agree to continue to service all the interest and short-term debt as it fell due! The G-7 deputies did not spend five minutes with Gaidar actually discussing the overall economic situation, much less what the West might do to help.

The Russians, of course, had almost no international reserves. (The Communists were not ones to hold on to reserves in prudent safekeeping for the next government!) I wrote in *The Economist* a few weeks later that while countries normally should have reserves equal to three months of imports, Russia had only three days of import cover. The minister of foreign economic relations took me to task for "exaggerating" the financial soundness of the country: the truth was the Russians had only about three hours of reserves! And yet the G-7, without looking carefully at a single number, pressured the Russians to sign a debt agreement guaranteeing continued debt servicing. Under pressure, the Russians signed. The last reserves were paid to the G-7 creditors, and then the reserves hit rock bottom, and within weeks the debt agreement fell into abeyance.

The next milestone on the way to "saving Russia" was Secretary Baker's White House conference in January 1992. Secretary Baker forgot one thing—to invite even a single Russian. It was not exactly an oversight. The Russians were asking the United States to discuss the financial situation and the incipient hyperinflation. But the purpose of the conference was "humanitarian" rather than financial. A cynic might suggest that one goal was to orchestrate the landing of a C5A transport with food and medicine, with Baker and CNN in Moscow to greet it. The White House believed it was "too early" to discuss finance. And lest a Russian might have caused embarrassment by asking for financial assistance while in the White House, none was invited.

The IMF, meanwhile, told the G-7 in January 1992 that Russia did not really need much financial help. The balance of payments scenario that they had worked up showed that there was almost no financing gap.

This is because the IMF, after 45 years, still does not have sound standards for determining the financial gap. The IMF had simply assumed that imports would fall again in 1992 after falling by 45 percent in 1991. If imports shrink far enough, the financing gap is of course zero! The only sense in which a financing gap can be understood is in a normative sense: how much financing does a country need in order to be able to sustain an adequate flow of imports? But a senior IMF official rejected this view as naive, claiming that a financing gap "has nothing to do with need."

The Russians and their financial advisers put up a major ruckus and told the IMF officials they ought to look again at the import numbers. They considered it unacceptable to design a program for 1992 with imports falling several billion dollars below the collapsed level of 1991. Subsequently, the IMF decided that the financing gap was in fact somewhat higher. I suppose that the US Treasury decided it.

In the midst of the IMF discussions, the Russians and the IMF received a fax from one of the investment banks that was helping to manage the foreign debt. It said that a new calculation had been made that showed the amount of interest due was $1 billion more than had been expected. Given the previously determined target level of imports for 1992, the financing gap would have to be raised by $1 billion. The next morning the IMF produced a table that showed Russian exports now at exactly $1 billion more than they had estimated the night before, so that the financing gap remained unchanged. One of the Russians went to one of the top IMF people, and I went to the deputy, and we each asked what had happened. The senior man said, "We thought about it last night, and we think your export capacity is higher than we had estimated. We had erred." The fellow I went to said, "We got the fax on debt servicing; we had to do something since we had a cap on the maximum financing gap that we could acknowledge."

This is not the way to behave in these circumstances: it is deeply damaging to the process. Unless there can be an honest assessment of need, based on serious criteria, rather than calls to the Treasury to find out what it is permissible to admit, the world system will not make sense. And of course, this episode deeply poisoned the Russians' understanding of the whole nature of the IMF negotiations: they understood afterward that it was a highly cynical game and not a substantive discussion. If those are harsh words, it was a harsh situation.

Finally on 1 April—for reasons ranging from speeches and appearances by Richard Nixon, to Bill Clinton's speech that day, to German pressures on the United States, to the sitting of the People's Congress in Russia—Bush announced a $24 billion aid program of the G-7. I thought this was the breakthrough. It took me the following four months to understand fully that there was nothing in this at all—no program and no concept. The $24 billion figure was based on a loose estimate of what various countries might or might not contribute, through their export-credit agencies, in short-term credits. In the end, what materialized was dreadful, unconditional, corrosive of the political process in Russia, and thoroughly lacking in meaningful support of the reforms.

What happened? Without going into excruciating detail, it became clear that what was to be counted was anything that could be found. At one point, for example—and it is still a live issue today—the German payments for troop relocation found their way onto the $24 billion tally. The first day that the program was announced, I called the German finance ministry to learn exactly what would be in the $24 billion package. The German government made clear that troop relocation money had nothing to do with the $24 billion aid program. About two months later, it reappeared on the list after the G-7 realized they could not come close to any of their initial targets. I called Germany again to confirm my original understanding. The IMF again took it off. Then in recent days it has come back on the list, to justify last year's effort.

In the end, here is what happened. First, there was supposed to be $2.5 billion in interest relief. There has not yet been a debt rescheduling. Gaidar came and has gone, and the G-7 never got around to a Paris Club rescheduling! Paris Club rescheduling is not the most difficult thing in the world. It is what deputy finance ministers do routinely for around 40 other countries in the world, yet they could not manage it for Russia during an entire year. Second, there was supposed to be $4.5 billion from the international financial institutions. The World Bank managed loans of $670 million, but these loans came so late in 1992 that they were not disbursed in 1992. The World Bank also lent a few million dollars in very useful technical assistance, mainly for the privatization ministry and the employment service.

The IMF was even less timely. In effect, the IMF told the drowning man not to worry. After months of negotiation and at great political cost to Russia, the IMF came up with a scheme—and I can only imagine how Boris Yeltsin understands this to this day—in which, IMF Managing Director Michel Camdessus explained, the IMF would loan $1 billion to Russia, but the money could not be used in 1992 (it had to be held as reserves). This money was not touched during the balance of 1992.

There also was supposed to be $11 billion in grants and loans. In fact, there was $500 million in grants, and about $10 billion in commodity loans, almost all under four-year maturity. There were two investment loans of about a billion dollars or so: one from Germany, one from Italy. But basically all the bilateral money was unconditional, uncoordinated, and not linked to any reform, with $2.5 billion of it coming due in 1993. Almost all was short-term money at market interest rate: good for Iowa farmers and extremely costly for the Russian budget.

That was the sum total of the Western aid effort: no program, no conditionality, no linkage to reforms, no strategy, little interest. I have also had six times more permanent advisers on the ground in Moscow than the IMF has had. The IMF has had two, and I have had 12. That is not something of which I am proud. I find it extremely peculiar in these circumstances that in the area of technical assistance, the IMF, the World Bank, and others have relied almost totally on fly-in help, which simply cannot do the job, with the complex issues Russia faces.

## What Ought to Be Done?

The reformers are in an extraordinarily precarious situation right now. Gaidar was dumped, I think, partially because Yeltsin was besieged on all sides internally, and no support was forthcoming from the outside. Gaidar therefore left, and Viktor Chernomyrdin, an *apparatchik* of the Gorbachev cabinet, has become prime minister. Yeltsin found vigor at that point and fought to keep the reform cabinet intact, which he succeeded in doing. In fact, he also made two important additions. The first was Sergey Shakhrai on the political side—a young, vigorous constitutionalist—and on the economic side, Boris Fedorov, the new deputy prime minister in charge of the finance ministry and the economy ministry. That means that the ministries remain in the hands of the reformers.

The real balance of power and influence and the capacity to move forward, however, remain unclear. Yet, it is not much less clear than it was in Poland or other places in deep crisis. The reformers are the people that know what to do—the ones with the energy, ideas, and the capacity to operate, and they are in charge of the key ministries. There is little point in asking where the power "really" lies. Most likely it lies nowhere in particular; it is there for the taking. And if the reformers act coherently and aggressively, they have a chance to carry these reforms through.

Of course, there is a real risk that the reformers in Russia will get bogged down. With the constitutional referendum planned for April 1993, the reformers may come to be seen as a lame duck cabinet. So they must start acting, and acting fast and vigorously right now. Fortunately, Fedorov has done exactly that. He is a sharp, tough guy who fits Jacques Necker's description of what a finance minister should be: a strong man who knows what to do. His statements over the last few days have been clear and coherent, and he already has succeeded in getting Chernomyrdin to roll back a price decree announced last week before the new government had assembled for its first meeting. Next week, he will put on the table a program of financial stabilization that is wide-ranging, detailed, and professionally drawn. The plan will call for increased interest rates, cuts in subsidies, the unification of interest rates charged by the central bank, and a tight credit program and fiscal reform. In other words, it is a broad-based stabilization program. His capacity to implement this program, however, may well depend on whether the West is clever enough to act right now to back up Fedorov and the overall reform effort.

This is a difficult period for the United States, as the new administration will be in office in days; the timing could not be more precarious. The Paris Club issue is still unresolved; a successful Paris Club agreement would be an enormous boost for the reformers, and it would be an enormous vindication of the reforms in President Yeltsin's eyes. He, like President Wałeşa, is focusing on the issue of foreign debt and how to avoid utter bankruptcy and isolation. So debt rescheduling is something that can be done, but it must be done through coherent US Treasury policy action in a short period. For the longer term, I believe the West has to return to the concept of a $24 billion program—or thereabouts—and structure it in a politically and economically meaningful way that signals strong support for the reformers and helps them materially.

Consequently, I argue for a four-point program. The first would focus on Western support for social programs in Russia—mainly unemployment compensation and job retraining—both to serve as a political signal and to provide budgetary support, which is crucial to stabilization. The second point is a small-business fund managed by the European Bank for Reconstruction and Development, partly on the theory that supporting small businesses is an enormous political plus and partly on the theory that the EBRD needs a systemic role, and this would be an important one. Third, the G-7 export-credit agencies, World Bank, and EBRD should coordinate funds of several billion dollars for long-term industrial restructuring. This would go for real, bankable projects, not support for old industry. Fourth is *real* stabilization support: a ruble stabilization fund at the beginning of stabilization and not at the end, an IMF standby, and a deep debt rescheduling.

These are the things that can help the reformers succeed in Russia. It is not a question of peering into crystal balls or wringing our hands, wondering what might happen. To a very large extent, our own actions will determine how the Russian reforms fare in the coming weeks and months.

## Editor's Postscript

The IMF complained, after learning of the above speech, that Jeffrey Sachs had misrepresented its role in Russia. Since no current member of the Fund staff was present to respond on the spot, the director of the External Relations department, Mr. Shailendra J. Anjaria, wrote a letter explaining its concerns and requesting that they be conveyed to the readers of the conference volume. The relevant portion of his letter reads as follows:

The discussion by Mr. Sachs of the IMF's relations with Russia both understated and misconstrued what has been done. The IMF began meeting with the Russian authorities while the U.S.S.R. was still extant, dispatched a major mission to Moscow immediately after President Yeltsin's October 28, 1991 speech, and has worked intensively with his government ever since. In all but one of the past 18 months there has been a Fund mission in Moscow providing policy advice and developing the data base essential to providing financial support. The Fund office in Moscow has also been expanded to four resident representatives. The IMF relies primarily upon headquarters-based staff to do country analyses for the good reason that decisions on economic assistance require thorough preparation and discussion at headquarters, not just in the field. Also, of course, I believe it is important that international and other external advisors not unnecessarily monopolize the time of senior country officials.

The IMF is exerting every effort to help the Russian authorities to develop an economic stabilization and reform that would make large-scale financial support from the IMF and other international institutions and bilateral sources effective. The $1 billion standby arrangement approved in August 1992 was an important early step, intended to bolster Russia's rapidly disappearing reserves and to lead quickly to larger and longer term financial support as reforms took hold. Unfortunately, some of the key policy elements of the Russian economic program were abandoned or diluted almost as soon as the standby was approved. Despite strenuous exertions by all parties in the ensuing months, a new program was still not in place as of April 1993. The problem has not been a shortage of IMF staff in Moscow, nor the admitted difficulties in accurately projecting the Russian balance of payments (Mr. Sachs' statement confused and exaggerated this issue by relating off-hand conversations completely out of context). The central problem has been the inability of the Russian authorities to make or implement credible commitments to control money and credit expansion and the fiscal deficit.

I think all reasonable observers will agree that what has to be done is well known by now, and the decisions needed to put sound policies in place have to be taken in Moscow, by Russians not by advisors from abroad. This institution's responsibility is to encourage this sensitive consensus-building process, often in difficult conditions—a point that appears not to have been fully grasped by Mr. Sachs in his statement.

Jeffrey Sachs asked for the right to reply to these comments, and has submitted the following rejoinder:

The IMF vastly underestimates the importance of timing in successful reform. Despite working "intensively" with the Yeltsin government, it did nothing in November 1991 to head off a disastrous debt deal imposed by the G-7. It did nothing at the end of 1991 and the start of 1992 to warn the G-7 about Russia's urgent financial needs. It did nothing to make the $24 billion announcement in April 1992 into an operational program. It seriously misadvised Russia on the reorganization of the ruble zone at the start of 1992. And it apparently still believes that four staff members on the ground in Moscow can somehow fulfill its vast responsibilities in Russia.

The IMF's delays and inattentiveness contributed materially to the loss of momentum of Russia's reforms in 1992 and to Gaidar's fall by the end of the year. The IMF might reflect on the fact that when Macy's declared bankruptcy in January 1992, the same month that Gaidar launched Russia's radical reforms, the department store received an immediate standstill on debt service, and two weeks later received a working capital loan of $600 million. It took the West 18 months to grant Russia a debt standstill in the Paris Club, and the IMF money, remarkably, came with the condition that it be held in the bank and not actually used to finance imports!

The IMF's performance has not been properly scrutinized. Under current procedures, detailed and independent scrutiny is all but impossible. All IMF operational documents, including IMF advice as well as the terms of the loan agreements, are treated as confidential in perpetuity. Maybe the IMF's continuing involvement with Russia will be the occasion for *glasnost* on 19th Street.

# 12

## THE POLITICAL CONDITIONS FOR ECONOMIC REFORM

# The Political Conditions for Economic Reform

## JOHN WILLIAMSON AND STEPHAN HAGGARD

Since its inception, the Institute for International Economics has gone beyond the development of policy agendas to make a conscious effort to sell the resulting ideas to the policy community. We have not behaved like the model economist of the traditional literature, who confronts the policymaker with a menu of technically efficient choices, from which the latter's intuition of the general will permits disinterested selection of the option that maximizes a social welfare function. Nor have we assumed that we were dealing with the policymaker posited by the more simplistic public choice literature, the politician or official whose every action is dictated by a narrow conception of self-interest or by short-term political calculations. Rather, we have decided what made sense according to our own conception of the general social interest, and then tried to persuade politicians, policymakers, and the body politic that the benefits of that course of action would exceed the costs. Our implicit premise was that good economics could also be good politics.

While this is not a role for the economist that the literature acknowledges, it seems to be the way that most economists actively engaged in the policy debate actually function. It is surely also the modus operandi of ''technopols'': those economists/technocrats who have accepted positions of political responsibility.[1] Since technopols are playing an increas-

---

1. The term ''technopol'' was coined by Jorge Dominguez and Richard Feinberg (an early use appears in Feinberg 1992). The term was criticized by John Toye in his discussion of the background paper (in chapter 2) for the conference on which this volume is based, primarily on the ground that the parent term ''technocrat'' originally referred to a proponent of a planned industrial economy rather than to an economist with the pro-competitive attitude

ingly important role in government, at least in middle-income developing countries, it seems worthwhile to ask some questions about their role. Is there enough consensus among economists about what constitute good economic policies to expect that the presence of economists in government will promote better economic policies? Is there any evidence that their presence has actually had positive results? If the answers to the first two questions are positive, can the political influence of technopols be augmented? If so, how?

The conference on which this study is based was intended to focus primarily on the last of these questions, taking for granted that there is a useful measure of agreement among economists on what constitute good economic policies, and that technopols would have a positive influence on economic policymaking and performance were their advice to be followed. In fact, these assumptions attracted critical scrutiny during the conference, and hence they too will be mentioned from time to time in the course of the study. Moreover, we found that to answer our central question required that the inquiry be widened beyond the technopols to the larger political milieu in which they operate. We have sought to examine how economic ideas advanced by reformers have moved through the political system and become policy.

The conference considered the reform histories of 13 countries. Two of them—Brazil and Peru—were countries where efforts at economic reform had been attempted but had failed to take root. For the most part, however, the conference focused on countries that had made some breakthrough in effecting the liberalization of their economies, in a number of cases accompanied by significant macroeconomic stabilization. Not all the countries examined were among those conventionally classified as developing: they also included Australia, New Zealand, Portugal, and Spain, as well as Poland, a country undergoing the transition from socialism.[2]

The success stories on which we concentrated were cases where reforms had not only been initiated but had been "consolidated" as well. We mean by this term that the liberalization of the economy has become irreversible, rather than that the reforms were already yielding clear positive benefits. In general, one would expect consolidation and the appearance of concrete benefits to be associated, since at that point neither the public in general nor the specific interest groups benefiting

---

characteristic of the profession. Since in our view (though not in Toye's) "technocrat" is now widely used to refer to economists and there would seem little prospect of dislodging it, we do not resist the extension to "technopol" or seek to enthrone instead his suggested replacement terms "economist-as-politician" or "econopol." But his further criticism, that "technopol" seems of questionable legitimacy in the context of nondemocratic systems, is accepted below.

2. Several other countries were examined more briefly, either by discussants (Venezuela in chapter 6 and India in chapter 7) or in the panel on the implications for economies in transition (chapter 8, covering Ukraine, Russia, and Bulgaria).

from the reforms will be likely to permit their reversal. However, one argument sometimes advanced for a "big bang" reform strategy is that it makes reversion to the old order infeasible (Przeworski 1991); thus some degree of consolidation might be achieved before gains are apparent. Conversely, it is possible that the public might vote against a reform whose aggregate benefits have become evident if the benefits are spread very unevenly, or if the public is swayed by appeals to some alternative set of values, such as nationalism.

The next section of the study elaborates on the type of economic reform on which we are focusing and outlines briefly the political problems associated with achieving it. The study then provides summary sketches of the case studies presented to the conference, before going on to discuss what generalizations can be established about the political conditions that permit successful policy reform, and the techniques that technopols may deploy to increase their chances of success. The final section examines how the process of policy reform can be promoted by the economics profession and by the international community.

## The Contemporary Meaning of Policy Reform

Perhaps the nearest precedent to the present study—an effort to ask whether a contemporary Machiavelli might have anything to say on how to promote the reforms that mainstream economists tend to favor—is Albert O. Hirschman's (1968) reflections on what he called "reform-mongering." To Hirschman, the archetypal reform was land reform. Land reform was expected to have some beneficial efficiency consequences in the long run, but it was primarily a redistributive reform, with the inevitable losers being the politically powerful class of landowners. Given that direct confrontation with such a class is unlikely to yield results short of a revolutionary situation, Hirschman was led to advocate the "use of ambiguity and obfuscation, less visibly extractive instruments, and timing of initiatives to exploit moments of high popular support" (as his recommendations were summarized by Haggard and Kaufman 1992).

While there are still some of us who would like to see widespread land reform, especially in Latin America, land reform is not typical of what is meant by policy reform, or "structural adjustment," today. Williamson's attempt to summarize the content of the policy reforms being urged by the most influential Washington institutions on Latin American countries in the late 1980s—dubbed, perhaps unwisely, the "Washington consensus"—listed 10 policies, which can be summarized under the headings of stabilization, liberalization, and opening up.[3] The evidence that macroeconomic stability, a market economy, and outward

---

3. The "Washington consensus" was presented in Williamson (1990, chapter 2), and is summarized in the appendix to chapter 2 of this volume. Subsequent criticism focused not

orientation are beneficial to economic growth and (with slight qualifications) a relatively equitable distribution of income is by now reasonably compelling.[4] What is new is the conviction that they are not just policies that are good for the "First World," but that they are also needed to make the transition from the "Second World" and that they are equally desirable for the "Third World" as well. At least in intellectual terms, we today live in one world rather than three.

This is not to proclaim the end of the history of economic thought. The background paper (chapter 2) lists a dozen issues that remain controversial among those who subscribe to the Washington consensus, varying from relatively technical issues such as the need to eliminate indexation in a context of high inflation, or the advisability of using discretionary macroeconomic policies in an attempt to mitigate the business cycle, to ideologically charged issues such as the optimal tax burden, whether there is a role for industrial policy, and the most desirable model of the market economy.[5] One may hope that in due course opinion will coalesce on some of the less emotional of those issues, but one should also be realistic enough to recognize that some of the topics on which near consensus currently prevails may be reopened in the future, just as the near consensus of the 1960s on the feasibility and desirability of demand management or the merits of import substitution subsequently vanished.

Nor should the current consensus be interpreted as a final victory for the political right, as the triumphalist tone of some right-wing scribblers would suggest. It is of course true that the idea of socialism that has long dominated the ideology of the left has suffered a severe blow from both intellectual and political developments in recent years. But that does not mean that the concern for equity and for the poor that has always moti-

---

primarily on the accuracy of that summary of what commanded a wide measure of agreement in Washington, but on the very reasonable claim that widespread agreement—although not complete consensus—extends far beyond Washington, to wherever mainstream economists are in the ascendancy.

In his discussion in chapter 2, however, John Toye questions the scientific status of the consensus: "Is the Washington consensus a statement of what economists actually believe about economic policy (i.e., the outcome of an opinion survey)? Is it instead a statement of what economists ought to believe, at least if they are 'serious' economists (i.e., a synthesis of normative economics)? Or is it a statement of 'wisdom'. . . which liberal economists must believe (i.e., a core vision, a professional creed, or a neoliberal ideology)? Like Superman, the Washington consensus is none of the things that it appears to resemble, and yet is something of all of them." The inventor of the concept affirms that he intended it to be the first of those three things, but finds it difficult to deny that it has taken on a bit of the flavor of the second and perhaps the third as well.

4. This evidence is briefly alluded to in the background paper for the conference (chapter 2), note 7.

5. The alternatives cited are "Anglo-Saxon laissez-faire, the European social market economy, and Japanese-style responsibility of the corporation to multiple stakeholders."

vated the left has suddenly become irrelevant. On the contrary, some take the view that endorsement of the consensus will allow the left to further its traditional concerns more effectively than was possible as long as it was wedded to a doctrine that made impossible demands on computational efficiency, political institutions, and human nature.

Although the current consensus is neither universally accepted, comprehensive in its content, nor beyond question, it would be silly to dismiss it as trivial, if for no other reason than the influence it has exercised over the activities of the international financial institutions. Yet this raises the following puzzle: if the consensus is in fact widely endorsed, why is it not more widely implemented? Unlike land reform, today's policy reforms do not involve primarily the redistribution of assets, robbing a rich and powerful Peter to pay a poor and downtrodden Paul. Rather, they are like an investment that should ultimately benefit the majority by enough to make them happy they made it, but that in the short run will—like all investments—involve sacrifices.

The distribution of these sacrifices over time and across groups is at the heart of the politics of economic reform. It is not just that the costs are short-term while the benefits are long-term, thus running into political constraints from politicians with a short time horizon. It is also that the costs of reform are often concentrated and readily evident while the benefits are diffuse and the beneficiaries are unknown *ex ante* (Nelson 1991). Such a configuration of costs and benefits, complicated by substantial uncertainty concerning the effects of the reforms,[6] raises the crucial question of the conditions under which politicians will risk initiating reform efforts.

Given that belief in the benefits of economic reform is much less widely held among politicians than among economists, and is even less widely endorsed by the general public, let alone by the specific interests that stand to lose, the question of the *strategy* of economic reform becomes central. Economists cannot luxuriate in political agnosticism, telling themselves self-righteously that they have done their duty once they have offered a menu of policies to politicians. Rather, they must be concerned with the conditions under which their advice is followed, and this implies a need to concern themselves with questions of political economy. The purpose of the conference, and therefore of this paper, is to see whether it is possible to illuminate how they can play that role more effectively.

---

6. Rodrik (1993) provides a formal model that demonstrates the possibility of a democratic majority never forming in favor of reforms that are universally expected to benefit the majority. The key assumption of the model is that some electors are uncertain whether they personally will gain or lose. Given that assumption, it is easy to construct cases where a majority of the electorate will perceive itself as likely to lose, and therefore vote against reform, even though those who know they will gain plus those of the expectant losers who actually will gain are in the majority.

# The Case Studies

We chose to seek such illumination by examining 11 cases where countries had made and consolidated fundamental liberalizing reforms, and two others where reform efforts had not taken root. Ideally we sought as the author of each country study an individual who had been in a key policymaking position during the critical period when the economy made the transition from the old model—typically dirigiste, statist, overly protectionist and inward-looking, and often suffering from unsustainable macroeconomic policies—to the new—with greater macroeconomic discipline, market-friendly, and outwardly oriented. Our ideal author had subsequently left the government and found himself a niche in academia, from which he had the time to reflect on his experiences and the independence to speak his mind. He was, of course, someone with an intellectual interest in reflecting on the politics of the transition as well as an economist with total command of the economic issues that had arisen during his period in office.

We believe that we assembled an impressive team of authors, but, needless to say, not all of them satisfied all our rather exacting specifications. The closest to doing so was probably Leszek Balcerowicz, the architect of Poland's shock therapy and minister of finance as well as a deputy prime minister of Poland from September 1989, when the Solidarity government took office, until December 1991.[7]

Rather than treat the various cases in the largely arbitrary order in which they were discussed at the conference, we discuss the countries in alphabetical order below. Note that this includes the two cases—Brazil and Peru—where reform was not successfully consolidated. It is also worth remarking that the most frequent complaint voiced by conference participants was that some other country or countries of interest to them had not been covered: at one time or another we debated including at least twice the number of countries that were ultimately treated, and in almost every case their crowding out was a matter for regret.

## Australia

At the turn of the century Australia may have had the highest per capita income in the world, as the country's small population exploited a rich natural resource base to supply the growing demand for raw materials from the industrial core of the world economy. The country then got the idea, which was frowned on then as now by economic theory (although

---

7. We did have one qualm about inviting Balcerowicz to write on the experience of Poland, since at the time the invitation was extended in mid-1992 there remained considerable doubt as to whether the Polish reforms had been consolidated. Happily, the reforms looked considerably more firm just a few months later than they did when we extended our invitation, following the evidence that the Polish economy had turned the corner.

accepted by Australian economists rather quickly), of using protection to nurture the growth of an industrial base. From 1908 until the 1980s Australia had one of the most protectionist trade regimes in the world: apart from New Zealand, it was the only OECD country that experienced no rise in the export share of production in the postwar period. In other respects Australia moved with the international mainstream. It built a welfare state and, in the postwar years, pursued Keynesian stabilization policies that developed an inflationary bias.

Policy reform started after the election of a Labor government under the leadership of Bob Hawke in 1983. Australia is thus one of three cases out of our 11 where reforms were undertaken by a government that regarded itself as left of center, and this orientation showed up in some components of the program. For example, while the Hawke government had very substantial success in reducing federal government expenditures (from 30 percent of GDP in 1983 to 23 percent in 1989), this was not done at the expense of the disadvantaged. According to the account of Ross Garnaut, who was appointed Hawke's personal economic adviser after he took office in 1983 and contributed the country study on Australia in chapter 3, the government achieved this *inter alia* by curbing middle-class entitlements to social security through a series of income and asset tests, thus safeguarding the position of the poor. It also consulted closely with the trade unions, retained their support on most issues, strengthened their legal position, and secured important productivity-enhancing reforms of the system of industrial relations. One could hardly ask for a clearer demonstration that policy reform does not have to be Thatcherite.

The reforms were undertaken gradually rather than introduced in a single package, but they were in toto nearly comprehensive (with the main exception being the labor market). They covered the restoration of fiscal discipline (from a large deficit in 1983 to a small primary surplus in 1989 and then back into modest deficit under the impact of recession in 1992); a major redirection of public expenditure toward the poor; significant expansion of the tax base combined with a reduction in marginal tax rates, especially on low incomes; far-reaching financial liberalization, encompassing the removal of exchange controls, credit controls, and controls on interest rates; radical trade liberalization, involving the elimination of quantitative restrictions and the unilateral reduction of tariffs to or below typical OECD levels; partial privatization of state-owned business enterprises, accompanied by the introduction of or increase in competition from private business; and systematic attempts to eliminate regulations that served no clear social purpose and to simplify others.

However, Garnaut emphasizes that deregulation in some areas was combined with the promulgation of certain additional regulations motivated by the government's social agenda—to further equal opportunity, to advance the condition of aboriginal Australians, to safeguard the environment, and to reform labor relations. The only major departure from the "Washington consensus" was the decision to float the exchange rate, with no particular care taken to ensure that it remained competitive.

According to Garnaut's account, this ambitious program was primarily the work of two men, Prime Minister Hawke and his treasurer (i.e., finance minister) Paul Keating. Neither was an economist, although Hawke had some exposure to economics while a Rhodes scholar at Oxford and in such positions as member of the board of the Reserve Bank (the central bank). Hawke and Keating did not fight the 1983 election that brought them to power on a program of liberalization, but they were predisposed toward market-oriented and internationally oriented solutions, and they moved determinedly after the election to implement a set of liberalizing policies.

Various devices were used to neutralize the suspicions originating from the conservatism of their own party, including extensive public discussion of the issues and the revival or commissioning of studies that argued the virtues of liberalization (for example, the proposition that financial regulation was an inefficient way of achieving distributional objectives). Hawke encouraged the emergence of economy-wide trade union and business groups that gave greater weight to the general interest in freer trade, as opposed to the old sectoral groups committed to continued or increased protection for their own fiefdoms. Above all, the Hawke government exercised strong leadership, in the context of effective consultation, and in turn enjoyed strong support.

The Hawke government came to power during a recession. Its macroeconomic program embodied firm wage restraint (in cooperation with the trade union movement), which helped secure a respectable rate of growth and the strongest employment growth over a seven-year period that Australia had experienced for more than a century. The structural changes produced the big rise in the export share of production that had eluded Australia earlier in the postwar period. This success presumably helped the Hawke government to win reelection three times (in 1984, 1987, and 1990), making Bob Hawke the longest-serving postwar prime minister before he was displaced by Keating in 1991.

The prosperity of the late 1980s, coupled with financial deregulation, ignited an asset price boom whose collapse helped prolong the recession that set in in 1990. Despite that misfortune, the Labor government won a fifth term under Keating's leadership in the March 1993 election (after the conference was held). The conservative opposition had by then overcome its initial populist antagonism to liberalization; on the contrary, it was now led by an economist (John Hewson) whose commitment to liberalization is unquestionable, and indeed more extreme than that of the Labor party. There thus appears no doubt that reform has been consolidated.

# Brazil

Brazil's vigorous growth performance throughout the 20th century had raised it from its extreme 19th-century poverty to the ranks of the semi-industrial countries when the debt crisis broke in 1982. Brazil was in the Latin American mainstream in pursuing import substitution for most of the postwar period. It had long been a country of high inflation, although this used to mean something rather less than it does today: an annual inflation rate of a mere 100 percent helped provoke the military coup that overthrew democracy in 1964.

The military governments that ran Brazil from 1964 to 1985 pursued a mixed set of policies. The stabilization program initiated by Roberto Campos as planning minister in 1964 was a model of its kind. Other reforms introduced indexation, extensions of social security, and a crawling peg designed to keep the exchange rate competitive in the face of high inflation, which was notably successful in helping to boost exports. But the military governments also nurtured the growth of a large state sector, and they reacted to the oil price increase of 1973 primarily by borrowing from abroad. Add to that the debt crisis of the 1980s and the military's use of populist macroeconomic policies in their later years in an effort to blunt popular opposition to the regime, and the economy inherited by the new democratic government in 1985 suffered from all the ills of the "old model."

The democratic transition started in tragedy as the civilian president elected by the Congress, Tancredo Neves, died shortly before he was due to take the oath of office, leaving his vice president, José Sarney—a political lightweight with no interest in economics, let alone any expertise or convictions—to step unprepared into the presidency. Sarney's first economic team concentrated on redirecting public expenditure away from the megaprojects with which the military had tried to dazzle the world (and succeeded in drowning one of the world's outstanding waterfalls) and on seeking to tackle inflation through the ill-fated Cruzado Plan. This was not nearly as misconceived a program as its subsequent disparagement would lead one to believe, but it nevertheless failed miserably through a combination of initial miscalculation (unrealistically optimistic projections of the budget position and of the real wage that the economy could afford) and political refusal by Sarney to sanction timely adjustments as accumulating evidence showed them to be needed. By the time that crucial congressional elections were over in late 1986 and Sarney was prepared to consider modifying the price freeze that had generated vast excess demand, the trade surplus had vanished and a new inflationary outburst was inevitable. As the Cruzado Plan collapsed, the government reverted to muddling through on macroeconomic policy and proclaimed a moratorium on servicing the foreign debt.

It was in the midst of this crisis that the author of the paper on Brazil, Luiz Carlos Bresser Pereira, was appointed minister of finance. He remained in that position for less than eight months. During that period he concentrated most of his attention on two subjects, macroeconomic policy and renegotiation of the external debt, but his paper also indicates his sympathy to opening up the economy and to domestic liberalization. This is another case where an avowed social democrat took the lead in political advocacy of economic reform, although Bresser Pereira records that he found himself isolated within his own party in challenging traditional populist and ''developmentalist'' attitudes.

Bresser Pereira introduced a price freeze soon after taking office. This was intended as a stopgap measure to ''stop the explosion of the inflationary process'' long enough to allow a more fundamental set of reforms to be designed and introduced. The centerpiece of these reforms was to have been fiscal discipline. In addition to tax increases and the restraint of domestic expenditure, Bresser Pereira sought to improve the fiscal position by renegotiating the external debt so as to curtail expenditure on external debt service. Supplementing—not replacing—this ''orthodox'' stabilization program would be a new freeze, introduced when, as a result of deliberate efforts in the intervening months to correct the exchange rate and public-sector tariffs, relative prices were free of the large distortions that had existed at the time of Bresser Pereira's first stopgap freeze. This was not a program that covered the whole of the ''Washington consensus,'' but one could perhaps forgive a government that had already frittered away its honeymoon and confronted a still-populist public mood for limiting its ambitions.

Bresser Pereira's program was never implemented. He encountered strong opposition to his proposals for renegotiating the external debt, not just from the banks and the US Treasury but also from senior Brazilian diplomats, who argued that Sarney could not risk adding an international crisis to his domestic political and economic woes. In the end Bresser Pereira prevailed on this issue with the president, who agreed that if the negotiations with the banks did not yield an adequate measure of debt relief, Brazil would announce a unilateral curtailment of its debt service. But Sarney subsequently withdrew his support for the domestic component of the planned fiscal adjustment, which involved ''a sizable reduction of expenditures and subsidies, and a tax reform increasing the tax burden.'' Although urged by the president to soldier on, Bresser Pereira insisted on resigning rather than staying on to implement a set of policies that he knew to be inadequate. Subsequent efforts to stabilize under Sarney got nowhere, and by the time he left office, Brazil was experiencing virtual hyperinflation.

In 1990, José Sarney was replaced by the first popularly elected president in 30 years. Hopes were high that Fernando Collor de Mello would follow the example of so many other newly elected Latin American presidents, and his own rhetoric, in adopting modern economic policies. In some respects, notably in liberalizing the trade regime, he did. But his first economic team had no idea how to run a macroeconomic policy, and by the time it was replaced not only had the honeymoon been squandered but the president was under threat of impeachment for reasons having nothing to do with economic reform. His successor, Itamar Franco, seemed in his initial months to display little sympathy for policy reform. Reform in Brazil thus remains not just unconsolidated, but at best still patchy.

## Chile

In the 1960s, Chile was famous (or infamous) for having pushed import substitution to an extreme and for indulging in political business cycles that produced periodically high inflation. Nonetheless, the country enjoyed a modest but fairly steady growth rate of around 4 percent per year. In 1970 Salvador Allende, a Marxist, was elected president, and Chile embarked on a classic populist policy cycle,[8] combined with a massive nationalization program. For the first year output grew, as is usual when demand is expanded and the exchange rate is frozen, but before long shortages and black markets emerged and the economy began to seize up. Severe economic crisis and accelerating inflation provided the backdrop for a military coup that in 1973 brought General Augusto Pinochet to the presidency.

Before long the Pinochet dictatorship appointed a group of economists who came to be known as the "Chicago boys" (since most had been trained at the University of Chicago) to run the economy. They took a series of radical and at that time unfashionable measures aimed at stabilization and liberalization. Combined with the subsequent programs in Argentina and Uruguay, and the earlier reform in Brazil after 1964, the Chilean case gave rise to the claim that "bureaucratic-authoritarian" governments were required to stabilize and/or liberalize Latin American–style economies. This assertion was backed up by the reasoning that the initial effect of such measures was so costly politically, particularly where economic distortions were high, inflation rampant, and politics polarized, that only a military government would be able to push them through. Certainly Chile suffered several years of low growth, low real wages, and rising unemployment before things started to turn around and export-led growth took off (in 1978).

José Piñera, who was one of the technocrats in Pinochet's early team and subsequently minister of labor and then of social security, cancelled his participation in the conference due to his decision to run for the

---

8. See Diaz Alejandro (1981) for the initial diagnosis of this historical regularity, and Dornbusch and Edwards (1991) for subsequent elaboration.

presidency of his country in 1993. We did, however, have the benefit of an article that he had written 18 months before (republished in chapter 5), and which had in fact inspired the Institute's decision to convene the conference. According to Piñera, the policy reforms introduced by the Pinochet government succeeded because of the intellectual coherence of the technocratic team, the comprehensiveness of the package and the speed with which it was enacted, the team's use of the media to build up a constituency for reform, and their total support by a visionary leader.

While the contemporary judgment was that the Chilean reforms were introduced at breakneck speed, the five years required to liberalize trade (for example) no longer looks particularly radical. And while many of us would now think of most of the reforms as Piñera does, as having implemented fundamental economic principles, in retrospect it is also clear that the Chilean team allowed dogma to get the better of them in certain respects. For example, financial deregulation was interpreted to mean forgoing prudential supervision as well as encouraging competition, with the result that many risky loans were made. Of equal importance was the 1979 decision to freeze the exchange rate (which had previously been on a decelerating preannounced crawl), relying on the tenets of international monetarism to stop inflation without a significant loss of competitiveness. Unsurprisingly, given that Chile had backward-looking wage indexation, inflationary inertia proved strong, so that the peso became overvalued and a large current account deficit emerged. The Chilean team (like Chancellor of the Exchequer Nigel Lawson in Britain a decade later) brushed this aside as of no consequence because the counterpart to the current account deficit was a private-sector deficit and the public sector was in surplus. But these two policy errors made Chile extremely vulnerable when the debt crisis broke, particularly given the fact that the capital account had been substantially liberalized.

In 1983 GDP fell by some 15 percent and real wages by something on the order of 35 percent. The Pinochet government started a second round of policy reform following the collapse of 1983, both correcting the faults that had come to light in those years (introducing prudential supervision, abandoning the fixed exchange rate, and modifying wage indexation) and pushing liberalization of the economy further (for example, by privatizing the provision of pensions). The economy began to recover in 1985 and has thereafter shown impressive growth.

Profound political changes followed. Public opinion, which had been hostile to the new policies in the early years, increasingly accepted the reforms, and even political elites on the center-left and left began to adjust their economic views. The democratic opposition recognized that its political credibility depended on resisting the temptation to revert to populist macroeconomic policies, and it came to argue that its social aims could best be achieved within the context of the market-friendly and internationally oriented economic system that had been constructed. It seems fairly clear that its endorsement of the economic achievements of the Pinochet government helped the democratic coalition to win, first, the referendum that removed Pinochet from power, and subsequently the presidential election. Since coming to office in 1990, the new government of Patricio Aylwin has done as it promised by seeking to increase equity while maintaining the economic system that it inherited and operating it as well or better than Pinochet's team had done. Nowhere else in Latin America does policy reform look so securely consolidated.

## Colombia

To an economist, what is most interesting about Colombia is not the narcotics exports that are its curse, but the fact that it has for many years enjoyed a more stable macroeconomic policy than its neighbors. When the price of coffee (its main traditional export) was high, Colombia built up reserves, increased taxes, and tried to prevent its currency from appreciating in a way that would threaten to undermine its legitimate nontraditional exports. Conversely, when coffee prices were low the country engaged in deficit spending, borrowed, and tried to prevent the exchange rate from collapsing.

This rational (dare one say Keynesian?) policy stance was marred in several ways. In the first place, it was associated with tolerance of a rather rapid rate of inflation, between 20 percent and 30 percent per year. Second, the adverse shocks of the early 1980s—low coffee prices and debt crisis—were too great to permit the policy of riding out cyclical downturns to be sustained, and, after initial pursuit of its traditional stabilizing policies, Colombia found in 1984 that, like its neighbors, it had to adjust rapidly if it too was not to be overwhelmed by the debt crisis. The most that one can say is that Colombia was able to make its policy adjustments in a less crisis-driven frenzy than its neighbors (for example, it avoided discrete devaluation and achieved the needed real devaluation by accelerating its long-established crawl), which presumably helped it avoid debt rescheduling and achieve the best growth performance of any Latin American country through the decade of the 1980s. Third, Colombia's admirable record of macroeconomic management was not matched by its microeconomic policies, which remained in the traditional Latin mold of import substitution, regulation, and hostility to foreign investment. In fact, when payments adjustment was recognized to be an urgent necessity in 1984, the immediate reaction was to impose quantitative import controls on almost everything.

Policy reform started in Colombia in 1989, in the closing months of the administration of President Virgilio Barco and was encouraged by his likely (and actual) successor, César Gaviria. The economic crisis of the early 1980s had been successfully overcome by then, so that there was no external pressure for reform, but the government nonetheless began to propose a series of remarkably radical and rapid liberalizing measures. Trade was liberalized through the virtual elimination of quantitative restrictions and drastic reductions in tariffs; the tariff cuts were initially supposed to be spaced over five years but were in fact telescoped into 1991. The result was that Colombia went from being one of the most protected economies in Latin America in 1985 to one of the most open by 1992. The loss of tariff revenue was compensated by a tax reform, involving *inter alia* an extension in the coverage of value-added tax. The government liberalized exchange controls, repealed restrictions on foreign direct investment, promoted flexibility in the labor market, and initiated privatization. The central bank was made independent. There are even proposals to reform the social security system, including thoughts of following the Chilean example in privatizing pensions.

Miguel Urrutia, who wrote the country paper on Colombia, had been Director of the Colombian Planning Department in the 1970s and then had a distinguished career at the United Nations University and the Inter-American Development Bank before returning to Colombia, where he was a member of the board of the central bank at the time of the conference and was subsequently appointed its governor. In seeking to explain his country's remarkable policy changes, he argues that the common feature of all the import liberalization initiatives in Colombia (for there had been other attempts prior to the successful liberalization of 1989–91) was a balance of payments surplus that was producing an embarrassing increase in the money supply that threatened to increase inflation. He points to a number of factors that may help explain why the initiative of the Ministry of Finance and the Planning Department got further in 1989–91 than before. Among interest groups, the increased strength of the exporters was a notable factor, as was the dissatisfaction of industrialists with the slow growth of the domestic market. Urrutia also cites the willingness of the economic team to accompany import liberalization with a real devaluation, and their boldness in abolishing import licenses at a stroke so that they could dismantle the bureaucracy that used to administer them and thus had a vested interest in sabotaging liberalization. The general public was not particularly sympathetic to the changes, but its interest was distracted by constitutional reform and the battles with the drug barons (which had induced an acceptance that deep institutional changes were needed), and there was no strong popular opposition. There was, however, growing intellectual support for the market and free trade among economists in general and those in journalism and government in particular.[9]

---

9. Urrutia notes that the low salaries in government service had caused the old generation of economists to move on to more lucrative pastures, leaving the positions with a significant influence on policy open to a new generation trained in US universities.

Moreover, the president himself is an economist and has been deeply committed to the liberalization of the Colombian economy.

Although the government was united in supporting the liberalization program approved in 1990, it split on the 1991 proposal for telescoping the timetable. The main opponents of acceleration were not the Conservative opposition but the traditional wing of the ruling Liberal party. The acceleration was implemented administratively when the legislature was not in session, so as to sidestep this opposition.

Urrutia argues that the Colombian liberalization is unlikely to be reversed. Consumers are enjoying the fruits of trade liberalization, and most industrialists now support it (the ones who had the most to lose are presumably no longer around, while it is quite normal to find that many of the actual gainers did not recognize their interest *ex ante*, so that support for liberalization is greater *ex post*). The unpopular part of the reform, the tax increases, has been legislated and accepted, so that the budget was even in small surplus for most of 1992. Colombia has apparently implemented and consolidated fundamental reforms without the rest of the world noticing that it was doing anything other than having trouble with the drug barons.

## Indonesia

Despite having achieved an impressive growth rate for the past quarter century, Indonesia is still a low-income country. It has gone through several episodes of reform, notably in the late 1960s and again in the early 1980s, and has been relatively well-governed ever since President Suharto took office in 1966. There have, however, also been periods of backsliding, particularly in the 1970s. It is still unclear whether the cumulative reform efforts have been fully consolidated.

Prior to Suharto's accession to power, Indonesia was in a state of total chaos as a result of the populist, nationalist, and left-wing policies pursued by Sukarno, the previous president. These included massive budget deficits and a fixed nominal exchange rate that had led to acute overvaluation. There had in consequence been half a decade of declining per capita income, while inflation reached almost 600 percent in 1965 (the highest rate recorded in any significant country between the 1940s and the 1980s). In a situation of increasing anarchy, the military moved against the communist party, then reckoned to be the largest communist party outside the communist bloc. Suharto was a general of peasant origin who played a leading role in the brutal suppression of the communists, and subsequently took control and had himself elected president, a position that he has retained to the present day.

Suharto was fortunate in being able to call on a coherent cadre of technocrats to design a program of stabilization and rehabilitation. These technocrats, virtually all of whom were graduates of the economics faculty of the University of Indonesia, and some of whom had also undertaken graduate study at US universities (including a few of the best-known at the University of California–Berkeley, hence the epithet ''Berkeley mafia''), have been a force to be reckoned with in the making of economic policy in Indonesia ever since. The team devalued the currency drastically, balanced the budget (according to the Indonesian definition, which includes aid receipts and bond sales as revenue), tightened monetary policy, and allowed market forces increased scope.

The economy responded rapidly to these policy measures, with falling inflation and recoveries in output and the balance of payments—one of the more impressive examples of expansionary stabilization on record. Presumably this success was aided by the generous debt relief accorded by the country's creditors (in a settlement negotiated on their behalf by Herman Abs, who had negotiated on behalf of West Germany an even more generous restructuring of German debt in 1953). The rapidity of the economic response, coupled doubtless with the ruthlessness with which opposition had been suppressed following the preceding coup attempt, ensured that the economic program faced no opposition.

An unusual feature of Indonesian policy was an early liberalization of the capital account (in 1971). Iwan Azis, author of the country paper on Indonesia and chairman of the economics department at the University of Indonesia from which the technocrats came, suggests that this was a more or less deliberate attempt to tie the government's hands with respect to macroeconomic policy. The technocrats wanted such constraints because they have been in permanent competition for Suharto's ear with a second group, the ''technicians'' or ''engineers.'' While the technocrats generally control the centers of financial power in the government, the engineers typically control the spending ministries. They tend to be devotees of infant-industry protection and import substitution.

A second shock, much milder and with a correspondingly more modest impact on policy, was the so-called Pertamina crisis in 1975. Pertamina, the state oil company, was run by a general and a stronghold of the engineers. President Suharto had given Pertamina authority to undertake development spending outside the petroleum field where it saw a need for policy activism, and it developed an autonomous development agency outside the control of the technocrats. When the latter sought to limit Pertamina's foreign borrowing by getting the International Monetary Fund to write constraints on medium-term foreign borrowing into a conditionality agreement, Pertamina simply borrowed short term instead. The 1973–74 rise in interest rates undermined its ability to service its foreign debt, forcing a default. The central bank had to take over $10.5 billion of Pertamina's debt, almost exhausting its reserves as a result. This fiasco temporarily allowed the technocrats to exert greater discipline over the spenders, although the influx of revenues associated with the oil boom soon gave the spenders leeway again.

After falling back to very low levels in the early 1970s, Indonesian inflation accelerated once more as a result of the oil boom. Since the exchange rate was fixed, the tradeable goods industries began to complain of Dutch disease. In 1978 the government undertook a 50 percent devaluation, despite the fact that the balance of payments was in good shape at the time. The public was taken by surprise and the IMF (but not the World Bank) was disapproving. This devaluation prevented the non-oil tradeable goods industries from suffering the decimation faced by their counterparts in Mexico and Nigeria during the second oil price boom.

The decline in oil prices in the 1980s constituted another shock to the Indonesian economy. Already in 1982–83 the Indonesian government decided that it would not in the future be able to rely on oil exports as its dominant source of foreign earnings. Again, an external shock strengthened the hand of the technocrats, and the government launched a stabilization and structural adjustment program. This involved another large devaluation in 1983, while the commitment to a balanced budget required budget cuts, the postponement of big industrial projects, and a major tax reform designed to tap nonoil revenue. Reform also encompassed financial liberalization, meaning the replacement of credit ceilings and interest rate controls (and subsidized interest rates for favored borrowers) by a market-oriented system employing reserve requirements and open market operations, and domestic deregulation. A second devaluation took place in 1986 after the major oil price decline.

In his paper, Azis discusses the problems that arose in gaining acceptance of those policies. He identifies the need to win the support of the President as the most important factor, which is hardly surprising given that "democratic state" is not among the many labels political scientists have pinned on Indonesia ("praetorian state," "bureaucratic state," "corporatist state," and "authoritarian state" being more typical). But he argues that it is also important to convince members of the government party in the parliament, who do fulfill a representative function; the technocrats devote a fair amount of effort to preparing analyses designed to build parliamentary support for their proposals.

This matters *inter alia* because the technocrats' proposals often have to compete with the dirigiste policies being promoted by the engineers. The continuing influence of the engineers helps explain some of the seemingly contradictory strands in Indonesian policy, such as the fact that the devaluation and domestic liberalization of 1983 were accompanied by an intensification of import controls and the granting of widespread monopoly rights to import.

Indonesia's attempt to promote nonoil exports has been conspicuously successful: these exports almost tripled from $5 billion in 1983 to $14.4 billion in 1990. The rapid growth of recent years thus looks sustainable and is buttressed by the broader trend toward intraregional trade among the members of the Association of South East Asian Nations (ASEAN). Some recent reforms, such as those in the financial sector, are extremely wide-ranging, and other policies, such as the emphasis on agriculture and the encouragement of birth control, are also exemplary. Nonetheless, the persistence of competing policy factions within the government, and newspaper stories after the conference about the dismissal of technocrats from the cabinet and the revived ambitions of the engineers to foster a technological leap, make it difficult to be certain that the reforms have been fully consolidated.

## Korea

The other Asian country covered by the conference was Korea, perhaps the most dramatic case of all of an underdeveloped country turning itself into an industrial powerhouse in a mere third of a century.[10] Korea's drive to catch up with the industrial countries started in the early 1960s under the military government of Park Chung Hee. Following the pioneering example of Taiwan, Park adopted an aggressive strategy of export promotion. This involved an initial devaluation and liberalization of trade in inputs needed to produce exports, and subsequently a switch to a crawling peg in order to keep the exchange rate competitive despite the continuing rather high rate of inflation.

Like Indonesia, Korea hardly fits the picture of a once-for-all change to market-oriented liberalism. The state remained an active player, using moral suasion and access to credit to reinforce the market incentives to export. Trade liberalization was highly selective and cautious: following the initial liberalization of the 1960s, major trade policy reform did not come back onto the agenda until the 1980s. The government also sustained a strong commitment to education, which contributed to a continuous upgrading in the quality of the labor-intensive products Korea was capable of exporting.

The controversy as to whether Korea's success has come about because of or despite the government's extensive intervention in the economy has not yet been resolved. Those who argue "despite" point in particular to the results of the campaign to direct investment into the

---

10. The conference volume contains no paper on Korea, although Il SaKong, who was minister of finance of Korea in 1987–88 and senior secretary to the president for economic affairs in 1983–87, did address the conference on the topic. Unfortunately, his other commitments prevented him from writing a paper, but we nonetheless decided to keep Korea in the sample of countries from which we have tried to extract lessons.

more "advanced" sectors of heavy engineering and chemicals in the 1970s. By the late 1970s, this had led to overexpansion of the favored sectors, strains on the banking system, heavy foreign indebtedness, excess demand, and accelerating inflation.

In 1979, Korean technocrats finally convinced Park to adopt a classic stabilization plan. Implementation was interrupted by the assassination of Park in October of that year, but following the installation of a new military government under Chun Doo Hwan in 1980 the government moved with alacrity not only to stabilize the economy—which it did very effectively—but to initiate a series of liberalizing reforms. The government launched a new round of trade liberalization, privatized the state-owned banking system, and moved cautiously to liberalize the financial system. With high levels of domestic saving and investment and a restored ability to borrow abroad due to strong export performance, the Korean economy recovered quickly, achieving not only a resumption of the high growth that had characterized its performance in the 1960s and 1970s, but also very low levels of inflation.

Following its recovery from the crisis of the early 1980s, Korea came under new foreign pressure to liberalize. Trading partners, particularly the United States, demanded that the government address the growing current account surpluses that appeared in 1986–89. These surpluses emerged primarily as a result of a massive devaluation of the Korean won in effective terms, produced by the policy of continuing to depreciate against the dollar even after inflation had fallen and the dollar had itself begun to depreciate rapidly following the Plaza Agreement. Korea was pressed to accelerate its trade liberalization efforts and to allow its currency to appreciate, as well as to open the financial system and to liberalize the rules governing foreign direct investment.

In 1987–88, the country achieved a relatively peaceful transition to democracy. Like Chile, and unlike some of the other Latin American democracies, the new government continued the basic outward-oriented strategy pioneered by its military predecessors and even accelerated the liberalization of trade. Today Korea is a functioning democracy that is continuing, albeit cautiously, to liberalize its economy.

## Mexico

Mexico enjoyed rapid economic growth for most of the postwar period until 1982, apart from a brief crisis as excessive expansion had to be reined back in 1976. But after that its newfound oil wealth started to come on stream, and aggressive borrowing, using expected future oil earnings as collateral, resulted in several years of very rapid growth around the turn of the decade. When oil prices and the world economy both weakened in 1981–82, and interest rates went through the ceiling, the banks became hesitant about lending more. Mexico found itself unable to continue servicing the debt that it had piled up. Mexico's difficulties in August 1982 are generally considered the starting point of the Latin American debt crisis.

Mexico was at that time a classic example of an inward-oriented economy, with extensive state participation in the economy and increasingly severe macroeconomic imbalances. Oil comprised over 75 percent of visible exports in 1982, as nonoil exports had been squeezed out by the real appreciation induced by expansionist macroeconomic policies and the fixed nominal exchange rate. There were 1,155 state enterprises, there was heavy regulation of the private sector, and import controls were pervasive. The budget deficit was a massive 17 percent of GDP in 1982. The initial reaction of the government of President José Lopez Portillo to the debt crisis did include cutting the budget deficit and devaluing, but these policies were complemented by increased controls. The banks were nationalized, ostensibly to curtail capital flight, and import controls were intensified.

However, a new president, Miguel de la Madrid, took office only four months after the debt crisis broke. Mexico has long been notable for the number of trained economists it places in key policymaking positions, and this was accentuated in the new administration. At first it was not obvious that policy was going to be revolutionized. Macroeconomic policy initially went through stop-go cycles. The abrupt deflation following the moratorium led to a payments surplus in 1984, which combined with the imminence of elections and a terrible earthquake in the capital in 1985 to induce a relaxation. The expansionary policy interacted with the further oil price decline of 1986 to produce a new deficit.

Mexico challenges the conventional wisdom that successful policy reform has to start with macroeconomic stabilization, for even while inflation was accelerating toward its peak of some 230 percent in 1987, the government embarked on a program of trade liberalization, which included joining the General Agreement on Tariffs and Trade (GATT) as well as eliminating quantitative import restrictions and reducing tariffs. The neglect of stabilization was only temporary: the fiscal situation was gradually brought under control, and at the end of 1987 the government negotiated an Economic Solidarity Pact with the government-controlled unions and representatives of private industry. The Pact initially covered a period of $6^{1}/_{2}$ months: it set out the government's macroeconomic policy commitments and matched those with freezes on many prices and wages. The Pact has since been renewed repeatedly, with modifications to increase flexibility and allow prices and wages to reflect economic forces. The objective was to reduce inflationary expectations without having to go through the agony of a further protracted deflation.

A presidential election was held in 1988, which the candidate of the ruling Partido Revolucionario Institucional (PRI), Carlos Salinas de Gortari, narrowly won after a tougher election campaign than had been customary in Mexico. The new president reinforced the commitment to economic liberalization, in the form of deregulation, extensive privatization, an opening to foreign direct investment, and negotiation of a free trade agreement with Canada and the United States (the North American Free Trade Agreement, or NAFTA).

Policy reform, reinforced by the Brady Plan debt restructuring negotiated in 1989, has transformed Mexico's economic prospects. Growth has resumed, albeit not at the high rates prevailing before the debt crisis. Inflation has fallen continuously, and reached single digits in mid-1993. Much flight capital has been repatriated. The government has undertaken a profound reform of the educational system, and since 1989 there has been a major increase in public spending on education. Other dimensions of social policy that had languished during the years of crisis have also received renewed emphasis; notable among these is the Solidarity program, which involves ad hoc village-level expenditures directed to relieving the plight of the underprivileged by providing public goods such as clean water supply, schools, and health facilities. By a stroke of political genius, this program has been financed out of the money raised by privatization. The major remaining doubt concerns the balance of payments, where a large current account deficit has re-emerged, in part because the peso became overvalued again as the crawl allowed by the Pact was not fast enough to keep up with inflation.

It is often true that the economic philosophy of the head of state is a critical factor in determining the direction of economic policy, and nowhere would this seem to have been more true than in Mexico. De la Madrid, and even more his successor Salinas, had a vision of where they wanted the Mexican economy to go. In formulating their plans, both presidents enjoyed the assistance of a talented team of technocrats, and Salinas himself is a trained economist with a Harvard Ph.D.

Their political problems were doubtless less than they would have been in more vigorous democracies, for Mexico remains a country where the PRI not only has enjoyed electoral success, but has exercised corporatist control over key interest groups, including the labor movement. Nevertheless, the conference paper by José Córdoba, President Salinas's chief of staff, emphasizes that gaining political consent for the policy reforms remains a major concern for those in office. Despite the PRI's electoral advantages, electoral contests do provide the opportunity to air policy differences and to criticize the government. The legislature has also become more important, at least as a forum for public debate. Córdoba therefore places particular emphasis on political strategy: the ability of the PRI to orchestrate negotiations among the social partners within the context provided by the Pact; and the conscious targeting of social welfare expenditure to offset the costs associated with the program.

# New Zealand

As recently as World War II, New Zealand was one of the richest countries in the world, but a sluggish growth rate and restrictions on its agricultural exports to Britain (formerly its dominant market) to conform with the European Community's common agricultural policy had by 1984 made it one of the poorer countries in the OECD. The conservative National Party government that ruled prior to this date had tried to counteract the difficulties created by loss of the British market and high oil prices through increasingly interventionist policies and a massive government-directed investment program in energy. By the early 1980s, there were glimmers of concern that this might be making things worse rather than better. There was a large budget deficit, massive protection, and a well-developed welfare state, and many wages and prices were legally frozen.

One of those whose concern glimmered brightest was Roger Douglas, a trained accountant with a Labour Party background who had entered Parliament at a young age and been appointed shadow treasurer (minister of finance). His thoughts had become increasingly laissez-faire, although this was not reflected in the Labour Party's manifesto for the 1984 election. Alan Bollard, director of the New Zealand Institute of Economic Research and author of the country paper on New Zealand, cites evidence indicating that Labour won this election more because of dissatisfaction with the nine-year-old government of Robert Muldoon than because the public wanted anything that it knew the Labour Party was offering. But Labour did win, and it won big.

In New Zealand, even more than in Britain, a winning party gets a remit to implement its program with relatively few checks and balances until the end of the three-year parliamentary term. Roger Douglas, as the new treasurer, found himself in a still more powerful position to determine economic policy than that might usually have implied, since the new prime minister, David Lange, wanted to differentiate his product from that of his meddlesome predecessor and was in any event distracted from economics by a squabble about keeping US nuclear-armed vessels out of New Zealand waters. Douglas was supported in the junior ministerial positions by two able and like-minded colleagues with complementary political abilities, as well as a Treasury staff that had grown increasingly disillusioned with Muldoon's policies and been increasingly snubbed by him because of their inability to conceal the fact.[11] It is difficult to imagine a stronger political base from which to launch a reform program.

---

11. Several members of the Treasury staff took advantage of their period of underemployment under Muldoon to update their economics at US universities. There they absorbed primarily microeconomic developments like public choice, property rights theory, principal-agent theory, contestability, and transactions cost theory. They came back determined to focus on fostering microeconomic efficiency, convinced that it was the neglect of this element that had jeopardized the growth of the New Zealand economy.

A final factor that cleared the ground for radical action was the foreign-exchange crisis that greeted the new government. The pegged New Zealand dollar had been subjected to a speculative attack during the election campaign, and the Treasury and the Reserve Bank had advised Muldoon to devalue. Not only did he refuse, but he persisted in refusing to devalue after the election, even after the prime minister-designate had requested that he do so.[12] The result was that New Zealand suffered a massive loss of reserves, 20 percent of which was a loss of real wealth since the government did eventually devalue by that much. The crisis provided a propitious atmosphere in which to launch a radical program.

Douglas had no qualms whatsoever about implementing policies that he expected to be unpopular, or about defying such conventional wisdom as existed about the desirable sequencing of reforms. On the contrary, he and his associates seem to have believed that they had virtually no chance of getting a second term. They were therefore led to do things as rapidly as they could within the three years available to them, paying little attention to minimizing transitional costs or cushioning the impact on the poor. Doubtless their seemingly cavalier attitude on the latter score arose because they sincerely believed that there was no reason to expect that the reforms would be distributionally biased in favor of one group rather than another.

The program was nothing if not radical. It started with the already mentioned 20 percent devaluation of the currency and the abolition of wage and price controls, and then plunged immediately into financial liberalization, including the abolition of most controls on international capital flows and a start to deregulation. It continued by slashing subsidies to industry and agriculture as well as spending on administration; by broadening the tax base through a new consumption-based tax, compensated by flattening and lowering direct tax rates; floating the exchange rate; and phasing out import licensing and cutting tariffs (although this was not done particularly fast). In its last year before the 1987 election, parliament passed a Commerce Act that created a liberal efficiency-based regime to govern mergers and trade practices, and the government began widespread corporatization and some privatization of state industry.

The Labour government in fact won the 1987 election, albeit with a reduced majority. During the conference Alan Bollard suggested that this victory came about because the public was relieved to see a government that was prepared to take decisive action, even if it was not quite convinced that it liked the actions themselves, and anyway many of the

---

12. By tradition in New Zealand, the outgoing government remains in office for a 10-day transitional period, during which it customarily acts on the advice of the incoming government.

costs of the program—notably in the form of increased unemployment—were still hardly evident at that time. Roger Douglas and his team remained in office for something over a year longer, but the prime minister grew increasingly uncomfortable with their program. During its first term the government had set up a Royal Commission on Social Policy. This reported in 1988, arguing that there was a major trade-off between efficiency and equity that had been wished away by the reformers. This now seems to be beyond doubt, since statistics show a large redistribution of income from the poorest to the richest quintile. When Douglas nevertheless tried to insist on moving to a flat tax, he was dismissed.

It seems, however, that "Rogernomics" was only slowed rather than stopped in its tracks, let alone reversed. In 1989 the government made the central bank independent and gave it a contract requiring it to get inflation below 2 percent per year and keep it there, with no consideration whatsoever for other objectives. Deregulation, commercialization, and privatization have proceeded. Even though the Labour government lost the 1990 election, Muldoon had been ousted from the leadership of the National Party soon after 1984, and the party had by 1990 undergone a fundamental transformation toward a more market-oriented policy stance. Hence there was no major change in policy, and the liberalization effort now appears consolidated.

Positive economic results of this program are only now, after eight years, beginning to become apparent, however. There was no gain in per capita income over that period. Unemployment soared from under 2 percent to over 11 percent of the labor force and has only recently started to edge down. As already noted, income distribution has become noticeably more unequal. The foreign debt exploded to a horrifying 83 percent of GDP. The benefits were a reduction in inflation, from over 15 percent in 1983 to a forecast of less than 1 percent in 1993; improved productivity in what is left of manufacturing; a recent surge in the growth of manufactured exports; a fiscal deficit that is now down to 2 percent of GDP and still trending down; and a growth rate that is up to 3 percent. New Zealand has finally adjusted to Britain's entry to the European Community.

There are two morals. One is that getting the fundamentals right and then being patient does eventually bring its rewards. But the other is surely that enthusiastic implementation of policy reform is not enough: it matters also *how* reforms are introduced. New Zealand's combination of tight money and sloppy fiscal policy, reinforced by the unbalanced specification of the duties of the central bank and the decision to defy the conventional wisdom on sequencing (which advised liberalizing trade and the domestic financial system before the capital account), produced a shockingly overvalued currency. Growth had no chance under such circumstances. Now that real interest rates have at last fallen and the currency has followed them to a more realistic level, growth has revived. But the price that New Zealand paid was high and might well have been prohibitive in other countries.

## Peru

Until the 1980s, Peru's postwar history was not atypical of a number of other Latin American countries: quite healthy growth under democratic governments and import-substitution policies until the late 1960s; a seizure of power by the military, who remained in office for 11 years and bungled the economy; followed by a restoration of democratic rule in 1980.

The country paper on Peru deals with the government of Fernando Belaúnde that took office when the military handed over power. It is written by Richard Webb, who was governor of the central bank throughout Belaúnde's term and for the first months of that of his successor Alan García. We invited Webb to write on his experiences during this period because of a perception that he had been a member of a fairly strong economic team that was seeking the sorts of reforms we have outlined, and yet which clearly did not succeed in reorienting the Peruvian economy in that direction. The issue that we posed to him was why they had failed.

Webb questions his terms of reference. According to Webb, the military regime that preceded Belaúnde cannot be dismissed as misguided ideologues whose ideas needed to be swept away. They had implemented many institutional reforms that were very much in line with the Washington consensus of an earlier (Alliance for Progress) era, such as reform of the educational system, land reform, and the reinforcement of planning mechanisms. They had expanded the state sector in a way that we would now consider imprudent, protection was high, their nationalistic rhetoric (on occasion backed up by expropriation) deterred foreign investment, and they mismanaged macroeconomic policy, but toward the end of their rule they implemented an effective stabilization program and began liberalizing the trade regime. The Belaúnde team aimed to consolidate and advance these gains, supplemented by domestic deregulation and tighter control over public enterprises, rather than to offer a new deal.

The success of the military's stabilization program coincided with a boom in the prices of Peru's primary product exports. This induced doubt about whether the pains of stabilization had really been necessary. It also seduced the military into granting excessive wage increases and subsidies in their final months, leaving their successors with the need to make substantial and unpopular price increases in order to avoid the reemergence of fiscal problems. But prompt and thorough action on this front was ruled out by Belaúnde on the ground that local elections were scheduled four months after his inauguration; as a result, the new government's honeymoon was wasted. His party won the elections, but the economy paid dearly for the delay, since the fiscal adjustments that had been approved five months before were by then too small. The economic team was reduced to monthly haggling with the politicians on the size of public-sector price increases, which were always too small to restore fiscal balance, especially as the president himself was launching new spending programs.

Despite having been granted independence in the constitutional reforms that had accompanied the restoration of civilian rule, the central bank was slow to clamp down on financing the government deficit. But when it finally acted, foreign bankers rushed in to fill the gap. During 1982, even as the debt crisis exploded, there was a fiscal deficit of 7.3 percent of GDP with zero financing from the central bank.

Other reforms sought during the early Belaúnde years do not look particularly radical by present-day standards, although Webb points out that they were branded as such by opponents at the time. Financial reforms encompassed some modest easing of entry restrictions, but the main emphasis was on trying to achieve and maintain positive real interest rates. More radical reforms were ruled out for fear of emulating the unfortunate experiences of neighboring Chile in the early 1980s.[13] Import restrictions were eased in the early months of the government, although the maximum tariff rate remained a hefty 60 percent. Subsidies on nontraditional exports were reduced early in 1982, just as the world economy weakened and the dollar (to which the Peruvian currency was crawlingly pegged) strengthened. The public came to blame the resultant balance of payments problems on trade liberalization.

During the first half of his five-year term, Belaúnde's economic team had been headed by Manuel Ulloa, who although a lawyer by training had developed a good understanding of economics and international finance and had made extensive contacts in Washington during his years in exile. His economic program assumed the continuation of a favorable external environment, which enabled him to give priority to safeguarding the newly restored democracy and limiting his economic actions to moderate reform. By late 1982 the assumption of a favorable external environment had become untenable. Commodity prices were falling and nontraditional exports were stagnant, and then along came the debt crisis and, in 1983, the worst El Niño in many years. The priority became crisis management, in particular of the external sector.

In the second half of his term, Belaúnde dismissed Ulloa and went through three replacement finance ministers, two of whom were tech-

---

13. Recall that in 1982–83 Chile suffered a far more severe recession than Peru, and that it was widely believed that a principal cause had been the rapid liberalization imposed by the Chicago boys, especially financial deregulation.

nocrats (and the third of whom was a civil engineer). A large measure of fiscal discipline was ultimately restored, the main effect of which seems to have been to give President García the leeway to launch his populist experiment. But throughout this period, policy was reactive and dominated by attempts at damage limitation: there was never any effort to exploit the international crisis to launch the country on a new course, or even to confront the crisis head on. Instead, the intellectual climate became increasingly hostile to liberal ideas, which were in fact blamed for Peru's problems; this discrediting of reform ideas led directly to the election of Alan García in 1985.

Richard Webb remarks in his paper on the gulf between the perceptions of the economic team and the ideological views prevalent at the time. There was no elite or public understanding of the desirability of market-oriented reforms or responsible macroeconomic policies; indeed, such policies were discredited under Belaúnde despite the fact that they were not consistently implemented. As a result, Peru suffered from stop-go with a vengeance, particularly under García. Hyperinflation, the utter failure of the García policies, and the spread of the terrorist Sendero Luminoso movement once again changed public perceptions in Peru, to judge from the willingness to accept actions by the current president, Alberto Fujimori, that are many times more drastic than those that were resisted a decade ago. Whether this latest episode will have a happy ending depends both on the technical competence with which the present policies are implemented and on the fragile political climate—topics on which our conference threw no light.

If there is a moral for reformers in Peru's experiences, it surely concerns the risks to new democratic leaders of not tackling difficult economic problems at the outset. The subsequent cycle of policy failure can be traced at least to some extent to the failure of the Belaúnde team to act aggressively and consistently from the outset.

## Poland

Poland was the first of the countries of the communist bloc to establish a noncommunist government, in September 1989. The author of the country paper on Poland, Leszek Balcerowicz, was minister of finance and deputy prime minister in the Solidarity government that took office at that time, and he retained those posts when the government changed in early 1991. He is an economist who was trained at the Central School of Planning and Statistics (as it was then called) in Warsaw, and then in 1972–73 studied at St. John's University in New York, where he had a chance to absorb Western economics.

Balcerowicz provides a pretty clear example of a "kamikaze" technopol—a technocrat who accepts political office with a clear sense of mission, no ambitions for any other position, and a willingness to make whatever personal sacrifices may be called for in order to further the cause of economic reform. In his case the nature of the mission was unusually clear, namely, to tackle the country's near hyperinflation and to replace the centrally planned economy that the Soviet Union had imposed on Poland with a market economy on the Western model. His task was eased by an overwhelming national consensus in favor of making this transition.

Nevertheless, the technical challenge was unusually great. Poland was the very first country to decide that it wanted to try and make a rapid transition from socialism to a market economy, and it had to do that starting from a position of hyperinflation. Intense inflationary pressures had developed in the final years of a weak communist government that had tried to placate the Solidarity opposition by granting wage increases and other benefits that the economy could not afford. The transition to a market economy involved not just the familiar litany of reforms embodied in the Washington consensus, but also the novel challenge of designing the infrastructure of a market economy from scratch.

The Polish program quickly became famous for the "big bang" package of reforms introduced at the beginning of 1990, on the basis of legislation passed by the parliament in the last ten days of 1989. That parliament had resulted from the quasi-free election of June 1989, in which Solidarity had won a crushing victory in the 35 percent of seats that it was allowed to contest. It had managed to assemble a solid parliamentary majority by forming an alliance with two small parties that had formerly been allied with the communists. The program this parliament approved involved expenditure cuts designed to secure fiscal discipline; some financial liberalization and an attempt to establish positive real interest rates; tough tax-enforced wage restraint; widespread price liberalization; the removal of remaining restrictions on private activity and the remnants of central allocation of inputs; elimination of almost all quantitative restrictions on foreign trade; unification of the exchange rate at a devalued and very competitive rate; and the establishment of current account convertibility of the currency, the zloty.

The initial big bang was followed up by a program of radical institutional change, involving privatization (initially of small enterprises), the creation of a social safety net, tax reform designed to eliminate tax preferences and introduce a personal income tax and a value-added tax, the liberalization of inward foreign direct investment, liberalization of the financial sector, and a strengthening of the institutional independence of the central bank. The decision to start off with a big bang reflected a conviction that structural transformation of the economy would be almost hopeless without prior stabilization, although Balcerowicz suggests that political calculations were also involved, namely, the effort to move swiftly when support for radical change was high during a period of "extraordinary politics."[14]

The program resulted in an initial burst of inflation, which was reduced gradually over the following months but never entirely eliminated. It also resulted in a sharp and immediate drop in output. (However, the extent of the actual output decline is a matter of controversy, since statistical coverage of the expanding private sector was minimal.) Unemployment gradually rose. Public dissatisfaction began to be expressed after only about four months. Balcerowicz argues that this was partly due to the unfortunate fact that the program had to hurt the interests of two of Solidarity's principal constituents, namely, the workers and the farmers. The prices of foodstuffs had been liberalized by the communists in 1989, but farm input prices had to be liberalized by the new government as part of the program to bring the budget under control.

The major threat to the program arose in the autumn, however, when Solidarity split into two factions in the presidential election. This made the three non-Solidarity candidates more serious threats than would otherwise have been the case. All three of them attacked the economic program, with the usual claims that the economy could be turned around quickly if only the government would relax its tough macroeconomic policies, increase protection, and introduce an industrial policy. In the event Solidarity's founder Lech Wałęsa won the presidential election, but only after a surprisingly strong showing by a populist outsider.

The new government maintained much the same economic team, and there was no change in economic policy. But major new external shocks hit Poland at the beginning of 1991: the collapse of orders from the Soviet Union, the worsening of the terms of trade as oil prices rose, and the dismemberment of the Council for Mutual Economic Assistance (CMEA, the arrangement that had coordinated trade among the Eastern European economies during the period of Soviet domination). There was a renewed rise in inflation and fall in output, and hence a worsening of the outlook for the budget. The main good news was that Poland finally got a generous debt restructuring from the Paris Club in April 1991.

Parliamentary elections came in October. By now political fragmentation had gone to extremes: the elections were contested by some 60 parties, about half of which won parliamentary seats under the system of proportional representation in effect. Eventually a new government was formed, claiming to make a sharp break with its predecessor's eco-

14. Balcerowicz defines "extraordinary politics" as a period of "clear discontinuity in a country's history. It could be a period of very deep economic crisis, of a breakdown of the country's institutional system, or of a liberation from external domination (or end of war). In Poland, all these three phenomena converged in 1989." He suggests that such a period induces an unusual willingness to suspend the politics of public choice theory and act for the general good, much along the lines sketched by Grindle and Thomas (1991, 105).

nomic policies, and therefore without Balcerowicz. But in practice the realities of power, in particular a refusal by the IMF to give its seal of approval to populist policies (see Sachs, chapter 11), served to prevent any major backsliding. The same was true when that government fell after 6 months and was replaced by a rather stronger government headed by Hanna Suchocka, which made only modest concessions to the special interest groups.

Fortunately Poland began to see an upturn in production by the end of 1991, although the beginning of recovery was recognized only in the second half of 1992. In association with the continuing fall in inflation (to less than 50 percent in 1992), the dramatic shift of employment to the private sector (now 60 percent of the total), the elimination of queues and shortages, and the manageable balance of payments position, one could begin by early 1993 to believe that the reform had been consolidated, even in the context of a highly fragmented and contentious party system. A new election in September 1993, just before this book went to press, produced a plurality for the SLD (the former Communists), who appear likely to head the next government. But since they are taking office with the claim to be the party best able to guarantee the continuation of economic reform, reform would indeed seem to be consolidated.

## Portugal

Portugal fell a long way behind the European mainstream in the 19th and the first half of the 20th century, but growth resumed under the dictatorial rule of António Oliveira Salazar after World War II. The successor to his regime was overthrown by a left-wing military coup in 1974. The new regime undertook widespread nationalization of industry. An intense ideological and political struggle ensued, but the left was routed in late 1975.

Thereafter Portugal established a democratic system. A new constitution was adopted in 1976: despite the defeat of the left, much of the nationalization was enshrined in it. Its adoption was followed by elections in which the Socialists emerged as the largest party. They then attempted to govern alone even though they lacked a parliamentary majority. The preceding chaos had led to the emergence of both extensive unemployment (which went as high as 25 percent) and a balance of payments crisis, so the new government sought to negotiate a standby arrangement with the IMF. The standby was agreed only after a change of government, in which the Socialists formed a short-lived coalition with the right-wing Christian Democrats. Thereafter, following the implementation of an orthodox adjustment program as required by the IMF, the balance of payments recovered rapidly.

A coalition led by the Social Democratic Party (PSD) won the elections of 1979, and won again with an increased majority in 1980, but then lost power after the next election in 1983. A grand coalition that was led by the Socialists but included also the PSD resulted. This government broke up in 1985 after the arch-technopol Aníbal Cavaco Silva, an economist who had served in the Research Department of the Bank of Portugal before entering politics, was elected leader of the PSD and led them out of the coalition. Yet another election followed, in which the PSD emerged as the largest party and formed a minority government.

There was in 1985 no macroeconomic crisis demanding drastic immediate policy changes, just an uncomfortably high rate of inflation (28 percent in 1984) and an unsustainably large budget deficit (12 percent of GDP). The government developed a multiyear program of gradual fiscal correction, which had succeeded in reducing the deficit to just over 5 percent of GDP by 1992.

Despite its name, the Portuguese Social Democratic Party is a party of the center-right rather than the center-left, a member of the Liberal International rather than the Socialist International. It started a program of gradual but determined reform immediately after taking office, but more decisive reforms became possible only after the PSD won an absolute majority in the elections of 1987 on a platform that indicated its intention to liberalize the Portuguese economy. Policies implemented after the election included the liberalization of financial markets and more general deregulation. Privatization became possible only in 1989, after the government succeeded in getting the constitution amended, but it has been pursued vigorously since then.

A major impetus to reform in Portugal has been membership in the European Community, which the country first applied to join in 1977 and finally entered in 1986. Membership is widely popular—unsurprisingly in view of the substantial transfers accruing to poorer member countries such as Portugal, which expects to receive transfers equal to 4.5 percent of GDP in 1993. The Single Market program has required extensive liberalization, which has again been implemented gradually. Portugal has also set its sights on participating in economic and monetary union, and it joined the Exchange Rate Mechanism of the European Monetary System in 1992. Its macroeconomic policy is now focused on satisfying the convergence conditions in the Maastricht Treaty by 1995. These will require further reductions in inflation, in the budget deficit, and in the ratio of debt to GDP. A medium-term adjustment program designed to achieve those objectives, dubbed Q2, has been promulgated. The SDP government has so far succeeded in maintaining electoral support for its program and won reelection in 1987 and 1991.

## Spain

Spain provides perhaps the most convincing evidence for believing that a country can make and consolidate the shift to a liberal economy integrated into the world economy, and simultaneously make the transition to a pluralist democracy. After 1939 Spain was run autocratically by Generalissimo Francisco Franco and suffered all the microeconomic ills of extensive government intervention, although macroeconomic populism was not too much of a problem. The country missed out on European developments in the postwar period because of its anachronistic political system. Yet today it is a respected member of the European Community in the process of catching up with the rich members in Northern Europe. Anyone who denies that the dual transition is possible has to be able to explain away the Spanish experience as a historical aberration. To those of us who want to view Spain as a model rather than an aberration, the issue is to identify potentially replicable features of its experience.

The author of the conference paper on Spain, Guillermo de la Dehesa, was himself Secretary of Commerce from 1982 to 1986 and Secretary of the Economy and Finance from 1986 to 1988. He argues that the process of economic reform actually started, against the general's wishes, under Franco. By 1959 the policies of pervasive controls and import substitution had led to repressed inflation, a chronic external deficit, and the exhaustion of Spain's external reserves. The Spanish authorities had started talking to the IMF and the OEEC (as the OECD then was) about membership. Both institutions—as well as the first indigenous economic technocrats, who had emerged in the Bank of Spain and the Ministry of Commerce, and who were to play a major role in promoting economic reform throughout the transition—had indicated the necessity of a prior stabilization program, involving unification of the exchange rate, a major devaluation of the peseta, monetary and fiscal restraint, and liberalization of price controls and trade restrictions. Franco was eventually persuaded that there was no alternative but to accept their advice, and there followed a gradual opening up of the Spanish economy, which led to an acceleration in its rate of growth. A second boost to trade liberalization was provided by an association agreement with the Community, signed in 1970.

Like Korea a decade later, the Spanish government force-fed steel and other heavy and energy-intensive industries during the late 1960s. The 1974 oil shock therefore created a particularly painful recession, but Franco refused to change course and sanction an adjustment program before he died in late 1975. After Franco's death, King Juan Carlos, whom Franco had designated as his successor, played a crucial role in engineering the political transition to a center-right government under Adolfo Suarez. Memory of the devastating effects of the ideological divisions of the Civil War period acted as a crucial check on both left and right, and led to moderation both in the demands of contending social groups and in the design of the program adopted in late 1977. The Suarez team decided (like the Belaúnde government in Peru) that it could not run the risk of destabilizing the fragile democracy by undertaking any radical liberalization or imposing excessively austere macroeconomic policies. Instead, it sought and obtained a pact with the trade unions, designed to moderate wage inflation (which had exploded following Franco's death) and build a consensus in favor of a social market economy, in return for increased social spending and a more democratic approach to industrial relations. This policy stance, facilitated by a strong fiscal position, was ratified in the 1978 Constitution, which legitimated the market economy.

In late 1982 a socialist government led by Felipe Gonzalez won a decisive majority in the elections and replaced the increasingly enfeebled centrist government of Suarez, which had found itself in a new economic crisis caused in part by the second oil shock and the world recession of 1981–82. Although Gonzalez had campaigned on a traditional socialist platform of increased social expenditure and more nationalization, he revealed himself, once in government, to be a reformist Helmut Schmidt–style social democrat. The government aimed at modernizing the Spanish economy, integrating it fully into the European Community, and catching up with the rest of Western Europe. Five of its fifteen ministers were trained economists, headed by Miguel Boyer at the Ministry of Finance. The government undertook an initial devaluation, tightened fiscal and especially monetary policy, began modest liberalization of the labor market, progressively liberalized the financial and industrial sectors, maintained the pacts defining an incomes policy that had been negotiated by its predecessor, and accelerated the negotiations for entry into the Community, which Spain joined (along with Portugal) in 1986.

The results were gratifying. Foreign investment poured in, especially to manufacturing, where it has constituted as much as 30 percent of total investment; growth was a solid 5 percent a year, inflation slowed, and the budget deficit fell. The black spot was unemployment, which rose to over 20 percent, the highest rate in the Community. The Gonzalez government secured reelection in 1986, 1989, and 1993 and has proceeded to widen its nontraditional socialist agenda to encompass privatization, labor market reform, and independence for the central bank. Despite the reemergence of macroeconomic disequilibrium in the early 1990s, no one today doubts that reform has been consolidated in Spain.

## Turkey

Modern Turkey was founded by Kemal Atatürk on the ruins of the Ottoman Empire following World War I. It developed as an inward-looking, etatist state, although after World War II it took an active part in a number of international organizations. Democracy was overthrown briefly by a coup in 1961 but quickly restored, and the succeeding governments introduced five-year plans and began to place greater emphasis on import substitution. The military intervened briefly once again in 1971. When democracy was again restored, there followed a period of weak and unstable governments. Turkey borrowed heavily from abroad to deepen the import-substitution process, rather than make a lasting adjustment to the 1973 oil price increase. As a result Turkey experienced its debt crisis ahead of its Latin American counterparts. As arrears built up, a center-left government negotiated two standbys with the IMF, in 1978 and 1979, but its half-hearted policies failed to stabilize the economy, and its intensification of trade and payments restrictions failed to achieve balance of payments adjustment.

Electoral defeat in October 1979 replaced the government of Bülent Ecevit with a center-right minority government headed by Süleyman Demirel. He appointed Turgut Özal, a well-trained economist, as planning Undersecretary, where he quickly became the key economic decision maker. His stabilization and liberalization program was announced in January 1980. It aimed to strengthen the fiscal position; combined a large upfront devaluation and with a subsequent crawl of the exchange rate; liberalized trade exchange controls and the financial sector; and abolished most price controls and subsidies. An institutional element emphasized by Yavuz Canevi, governor of the central bank from 1981–86 and author of the paper on Turkey, was the creation of a Money and Credit Board and an Economic Coordination Committee, designed to repair the country's lack of an efficient macroeconomic decision-making mechanism.

By the time the Demirel government had come to power, however, the Turkish political system was becoming increasingly polarized: parties on both the far left and the far right gained in power, labor militancy increased in the face of rapidly rising prices, and social and ethnic violence increased dramatically. Provoked by the failure of the parliament to elect a president, and before there was time to establish whether democracy was capable of sustaining such a bold program, the military once again (in September 1980) staged a coup. They promoted Özal to the post of deputy prime minister in charge of economic affairs and backed the economic reforms that he had instituted, and imposed the social peace that had previously been notably absent. In early 1981 a tax reform, introducing a value-added tax, was added. The regime got substantial aid from the West to help the reform through its early years, reflecting the strategic importance of Turkey as the guardian of NATO's southern flank (the country's geographic location was perceived to be of even greater strategic significance following the Iranian revolution).

The Özal reforms were enormously successful in promoting nontraditional exports. It is of course true that Turkey was lucky in having booming OPEC markets on its doorstep when the program was instituted, but before long Turkish exports were also doing well in Western European and other markets. The share of exports in GDP rose from 7 percent in 1979 to almost 23 percent in 1989. Although the current account remained in deficit until 1988, Turkey returned to voluntary access to capital markets to finance the deficit by July 1983.

Özal resigned after a financial panic in 1982. In 1983 the military restored democracy, having rewritten the Constitution so as to exclude the traditional politicians, limit the number of parties, and severely restrict the freedom of unions. Özal founded the Motherland Party and led it to victory over the military-supported party on a platform that emphasized economic reform. His government pursued a series of microeconomic reforms, including the abolition of exchange controls and further liberalization of the financial sector, and it carried on promoting exports through a rate of currency depreciation in excess of inflation. In addition, a process of privatizing the large state enterprise sector was set in train, although this program encountered a number of problems, remained politically controversial, and has in consequence made limited progress. Özal moved on to become president in 1989, but he continued to guide the economic policies of the government until his Motherland Party was replaced in office in 1991.

The critical weakness of the reform program lay in fiscal policy. The minimum to which the public-sector borrowing requirement (which includes the borrowing of the state enterprises) fell was 4.3 percent of GDP in 1982, and after that it started rising again. Because of its large fiscal deficit, Turkey was unable to dispense with the inflation tax. Having fallen from over 100 percent in 1980 to 27 percent in 1982, inflation rebounded to over 60 percent by 1987 and has stayed that high since. One reason for the weakness of fiscal policy was the easy availability of foreign finance, although there is evidence of election-related cycles as well. The failure to control inflation and the negative distributional consequences of the program led to increasing dissatisfaction with the government, which was voted out of office in 1990 and replaced in 1991 by a coalition that included many of the pre-1980 politicians, who had by this time managed to get lifted the restrictions on their political activity that had been imposed by the military.

Turkish politics in the 1990s seems to be reverting to the pattern of the 1970s, with fragmented parties and a need for coalition governments. Reform is clearly incomplete, given the fiscal situation and the resulting inflation, and privatization remains politically controversial. On the other hand, the current government has negotiated associate membership in the European Free Trade Area (EFTA) as of 1996 and continues to seek a customs union with the European Community, which suggests that the opening of the economy is well consolidated. Indeed, Turkey has been playing an active role in offering a market-oriented model of reform to the Turkic-speaking states of the former Soviet Union in Central Asia and the Caucasus.

## Examining Hypotheses

In the background paper for the conference, John Williamson outlined (as a guide to the authors) a number of hypotheses about the circumstances under which policy reform is possible and the ways in which reform can be promoted. The present section discusses what light the 13 cases discussed at the conference throw on the validity of those hypotheses, plus several others that emerged during the course of the conference. Obviously the sample of cases is not only small but not random: we have favored countries in which there has been some degree of successful adjustment. We do not claim that the hypotheses are being rigorously tested, but the exercise does help illustrate the logic of various propositions that have been advanced concerning the politics of policy reform and suffices to call some of them into question.

In the majority of our cases there was an identifiable date that unambiguously marked the start of reform. In a number of other cases—notably Chile, Indonesia, Korea, and Spain—reform came in several waves: the beginning of the most recent major wave of reform has been taken as the relevant date in what follows unless otherwise specified. There is also some ambiguity in Mexico, where fiscal consolidation and trade liberalization started as early as 1983 but effective stabilization was delayed till 1987 and most liberalization came after that: 1987 was taken as the critical date. For the two countries without consolidated reforms (Brazil and Peru), we took the dates when the authors of the papers on those countries entered office. The dates chosen for each country are shown in the first row of table 1, which is intended to summarize the judgments presented throughout this section.

We group the hypotheses into four clusters: those dealing with economic conditions, political conditions, the position of the team, and the nature of the program itself and how it was sold.

### Economic Conditions

Under this heading we have two hypotheses, regarding the role of crises in motivating and of external help in sustaining reform programs.

#### The Crisis Hypothesis

It has often been suggested that policy reforms emerge in response to crisis. Crises have the effect of shocking countries out of traditional policy patterns, disorganizing the interest groups that typically veto

**Table 1 Assessing the hypotheses in 13 instances of economic reform**

| | Australia | Colombia | New Zealand | Poland | Portugal | Spain | Chile | Indonesia | Korea | Mexico | Turkey | Brazil | Peru |
|---|---|---|---|---|---|---|---|---|---|---|---|---|---|
| Date of reform | 1983 | 1989 | 1984 | 1990 | 1985 | 1982 | 1983 | 1982 | 1979 | 1987 | 1980 | 1987 | 1980 |
| Authoritarian regime | N | N | N | N | N | N | Y | Y | Y | (Y) | N/Y | N | N |
| Rightist government | N(L) | N(C) | N(L) | N(C) | N(C) | N(L) | Y | N(C) | Y | N(C) | Y | N(C) | N(C) |
| Crisis | N | N | (Y) | Y | N | (N) | Y | (N) | Y | Y | Y | Y | N |
| Honeymoon | (N) | N | Y | Y | (Y) | (Y) | N | N | N | N | (Y) | Y | (N) |
| Political base | Y | Y | Y | Y/N | N | Y | Y | Y | Y | Y | N/Y | N | Y |
| Demoralized opposition | Y? | N | Y | Y | Y | Y | N | N | N | N | (Y) | N | Y |
| Social consensus | N/Y | N | N | Y | Y | Y | N | N/Y | Y | N/Y | N/Y | N | N |
| Visionary leader | Y | Y | N | Y/N | Y | Y | Y | Y | Y | Y | N/Y | N | N |
| Coherent team | Y | Y | Y | Y | Y | Y | Y | (Y) | Y | Y | Y | Y | Y |
| Led by technopol | N | (N) | (N) | Y | Y | Y | (N) | (N) | (N) | Y | Y | Y | N |
| Voodoo politics | Y | (N) | (N) | (N) | N | Y | n.a. | n.a. | n.a. | n.a. | ? | n.a. | (N) |
| Comprehensive program | Y | (Y) | Y | Y | Y | Y | Y | N | (Y) | Y | N | N | N |
| External aid | N | N | N | Y | (N) | (N) | Y | N | Y | Y | Y | N | N |

Y = yes, hypothesis satisfied; (Y) = hypothesis satisfied with qualifications; N = no, hypothesis not satisfied; (N) = hypothesis not satisfied, with qualifications; (C),(L) = centrist, left of center, respectively; Y/N = first yes, subsequently no.

563

policy reform, and generating pressure for politicians to change policies that can be seen to have failed.

Despite legitimate concerns about the ambiguity of the concept of a crisis (see Toye, chapter 2), this hypothesis certainly has some relevance to a number of the cases discussed by the conference. It was clearly applicable in Chile, Poland, Turkey, Indonesia in the 1960s, and, in less acute form, Korea; it also applies, with qualification—in that the crisis preceded the response by some five years—in Mexico. Reform efforts in Spain were arguably a belated response to crisis, and were undertaken as soon as a government with sufficient political strength to divert effort from the task of consolidating democracy had come to power. Reform in Indonesia in the 1980s was apparently motivated by an attempt to pre-empt a crisis that was perceived to be likely. In New Zealand a perception of deepening crisis contributed to the electoral victory of the Labour Party, and the foreign-exchange crisis at the time of the government's accession to power helped ease public acceptance of the initial reforms (although it seems likely that Roger Douglas would have rammed through the same reforms anyway). In these last three cases, however, the crises were certainly not of the magnitude experienced by Chile, Poland, Turkey, or Indonesia in the mid-1960s, and this suggests that the threshold at which a country responds to a crisis by initiating reform can vary substantially.

In addition to these cases, one could also note earlier instances from some of the countries examined, including Portugal in 1977, Spain in 1959, Brazil in 1964, and Peru in 1978. One could also cite numerous examples from countries not covered by the conference, including Argentina in 1966 or 1990, Bolivia in 1985, Ghana in 1983, or Uruguay in 1973.

However, there are also three cases where crisis appeared to play no role in stimulating the reform effort: Australia, Colombia, and Portugal. In two of these, Australia and Portugal, reform was initiated by a new government. In the case of Colombia, an outgoing government decided to initiate reform, with the support of an incoming administration of the same party.

To turn to the two cases where reform was not consolidated, Brazil was certainly suffering from a crisis at the time that Bresser Pereira tried to push his reform program, but at the crucial juncture the president backed away despite the existence of a crisis. Peru also had its share of crises, and one of these, in the last years of the military regime, sparked an effective stabilization program and some trade liberalization. But when the debt crisis struck halfway through Belaúnde's term, it prompted muddling through rather than reform. A crisis might have had more positive results if it had broken when Belaúnde first took office, but that was a time when there was no perception of crisis; Webb suggests that this made it more difficult to take necessary action.

An economic crisis is certain to generate policy debate, and one would like to think this in turn will engender efforts to adjust. Sometimes this happens, often by precipitating a change of government (Poland in 1989, Turkey in 1980, Indonesia in 1965, Chile in 1973) but sometimes by making the sitting government realize that it needs to make a policy correction (Korea in 1979, Indonesia in 1982, Chile in 1982, Mexico in the mid-1980s). In the two cases where countries failed to respond to crises, Peru and Brazil, this omission proved to be a costly mistake, not only economically but politically as well. In both cases, the failure to undertake reform ultimately led to new governments coming to power: the one in Peru was inclined to populism, and that in Brazil (where Bresser Pereira had done his best to create an awareness of the crisis of the state) was at least nominally committed to reform. Yet it is also clear that political systems respond differently to crises; there is no situation so bad that it cannot get worse, as Toye observed.

Crisis is clearly neither a necessary nor a sufficient condition to initiate reform. It has nevertheless often played a critical role in stimulating reform. In extreme cases, such as Poland in 1989, the crisis of the ancien regime may be so profound as to create an opening for what Leszek Balcerowicz (chapter 4) calls "extraordinary politics"—a widespread willingness to suspend the usual political rules. These worst of times give rise to the best of opportunities for those who understand the need for fundamental economic reform.

## External Help

A second economic condition for successful reform, the importance of which was asserted by Jeffrey Sachs during an after-dinner speech at the conference (chapter 11), is strong external support, both in the form of intellectual help and in the form of (conditional) foreign aid.

The importance of intellectual influence from abroad can hardly be doubted. The intellectual climate has changed profoundly in the last decade in favor of stability-oriented, market-oriented, and outward-oriented policies. Economists trained in American universities, and therefore presumptively inculcated with those policy attitudes, played at least some role in formulating reforms in Chile, Colombia, Indonesia, Korea, Mexico, and Turkey (although they were also present in Brazil and Peru, where reforms did not take root). Advisers with ties to specific American universities have been associated with several reform efforts: the "Chicago boys" in Chile, the "Berkeley mafia" in Indonesia, MIT economists in Mexico, and those from Harvard in Poland. Intellectual influences from the advanced industrial countries have also been transmitted through the International Monetary Fund and World Bank, which played a key role in reform efforts in the 1980s in virtually all developing countries, often by providing extended training to those who later become technocrats or technopols, as well as through the more obvious mechanism of conditionality.

The influences do not only run from North to South, however; there is increasing cross-fertilization between reformers in different countries. A team of Russians went to Chile to attend lectures on how the Chilean reforms were accomplished, and this visit was followed by their Chilean lecturers going to Russia to give the same course to a broader audience. On the other hand, Alan Bollard commented that, when they started their program, the New Zealand reformers had a hard time finding relevant foreign experience on which they could draw (Reagan, Thatcher, Australia, and Turkey were all seen as only slightly relevant role models). The New Zealand team was apparently more influenced by academic ideas drawn from the property rights and transactions costs literatures than by foreign advisers or precedents.

Important as foreign intellectual influences and examples undoubtedly are, it is also possible for foreign pressures to be ineffective or even, where nationalist sentiments are aroused, counterproductive. The usual reaction to this danger is to affirm that programs need to be "owned" by the country itself. The corollary is, of course, that the international financial institutions need to allow borrowing countries a substantial degree of latitude in program design: this should be preceded by extensive policy dialogue, and the program should not be approved unless it embodies an adequate response to the needs of the situation, but subject to that constraint conditionality should be as unniggardly as possible. A team that does not feel it owns its program is unlikely to pursue it with the enthusiasm and determination that are critical to success, no matter how cleverly or tightly the conditionality terms are defined.

Jeffrey Sachs argues passionately that foreign aid can be critical to the successful launching of a program of economic reform. It was certainly of importance in a number of the cases studied by the conference. Korea was a major recipient of foreign aid in the 1960s, when it first started on its reformed path. Indonesia received very important financial help (including debt relief) in its earlier reform period in the late 1960s, and was a recipient of Japanese assistance during its preemptive adjustment in 1982. Chile received loans averaging $714 million (over 4 percent of GNP) from the IMF and the multilateral development banks during the crucial years 1983–85. Mexico got an emergency bailout of $1 billion from the United States in 1989 and is the US Export-Import Bank's largest client, the World Bank's second largest, and the beneficiary of the first Brady Plan debt restructuring. Poland got a $1 billion stabilization fund to launch the Balcerowicz Plan at the beginning of 1990 and a generous debt restructuring in 1991. Turkey avoided negative transfers (prior to 1983) by virtue of the massive support it received in 1979–81: a total of $5.6 billion from an emergency OECD loan, $1 billion in short-term credits, and a generous debt rescheduling (which can be compared with the less than $2 billion received in the preceding three-year period), followed by a series of structural adjustment loans in the 1980s. In all these instances the aid was generous, and in most cases it was also highly conditional.[15]

Authors of country papers were not asked to consider whether the presence of these conditions was helpful to the reformers in winning arguments with opponents of reform either inside or outside the government. It is certainly plausible, however, that the ability to secure external resources strengthened the hand of the reformers internally, and the papers on both Poland and Turkey confirm the existence of such an effect. Indeed, this is what we regard as the most plausible hypothesis of how conditionality works (rather than the crude view that the international organizations force policies on governments that are united in resisting them).

However, there are also instances among our cases where there was no particular foreign aid to support reform. This was true mostly in the richer countries, notably Australia and New Zealand, whose access to the international capital market provided an alternative mechanism for attenuating the initial costs of reform. Although Portugal received some special help in 1977, both it and Spain were in the 1980s initially limited to importing capital on commercial terms; however, both countries anticipated substantial material benefits from joining the European Community, and both now benefit from EC regional funds that certainly would not have become available without the reform programs that they have implemented.

There were also two developing countries that undertook reforms without special financial support from abroad, namely, Colombia and (in the 1980s) Korea. These are also the countries that liberalized without the pressure of a severe crisis, which helps explain why they neither needed nor received special aid.

A critic of foreign aid could retort by citing a number of countries, such as the Philippines or Zaire, that received aid and squandered it by postponing adjustment. The moral we would draw is not that aid should be avoided, but that it should come with adequate conditionality attached. Admittedly that has its dangers too, particularly the possibility that it might weaken popular support for reform, but this is a risk that seems unavoidable.

## Political Conditions

Under this heading we discuss the claims that reform needs, or at least is easier with, an authoritarian regime; that reform is a monopoly of the

---

15. Dani Rodrik argues (chapter 4) that Turkey missed an opportunity to make an adequate fiscal adjustment in 1980–81 because the conditions on fiscal policy were so loose and the aid so generous as to erode the political perception that it was necessary to take painful fiscal measures.

political right; that reform should be undertaken during a political honeymoon period; that it requires a demoralized opposition; that it needs a social consensus; and that successful reform is possible only with a visionary leader.

## An Authoritarian Regime

One widely held hypothesis is that authoritarian regimes are best at carrying out reform. This hypothesis appears to have been prompted by the record of the military regimes installed in Argentina (1966 and 1976), Brazil (1964), Chile (1973), and Uruguay (1976). Following on macroeconomic crises that democratic governments had been unable to manage, the military governments all launched programs of stabilization and economic liberalization. It was reasoned that, where inflation was high, where protection and government intervention were deeply entrenched, and where leftist and populist political forces wielded a strong voice, the political costs of adjustment were so great that only an authoritarian government of the right would have either the inclination or the capacity to stabilize and liberalize. The experience of the East Asian newly industrializing countries, which pursued successful export-led growth under military (Korea) or one-party (Taiwan and Singapore) auspices, has also been widely cited in support of the hypothesis.

Even brief consideration of the cases in this volume suffices to show that a simple version of the hypothesis cannot be sustained. Of the 11 successful reformers, 4 would generally be classified as authoritarian—Chile, Indonesia, Korea, and Mexico—although they varied substantially in the degree of pluralism permitted. The Chilean military, at one extreme, severely curtailed civil liberties and all avenues of democratic participation during the 1970s; Mexico, in contrast, although dominated by a single party, has permitted other parties to function, maintained a relatively open press, and allowed independent interest groups considerable latitude.

The Turkish case is more complex. The initial plan was formulated by a democratic government, but under strong pressure from the military. The military was instrumental in pressing the reform process further after it seized power, and it undertook some actions, such as banning leftist labor unions, that arguably contributed to the program's economic success. On the other hand, the reforms were continued under the democratic Özal government.

Six cases of successful reform were undertaken by governments that were unambiguously democratic at the time of the reform episode under consideration: Australia, Colombia, New Zealand, Poland, Portugal, and Spain. In three of those cases—Poland, Portugal, and Spain—there had been some reforms before the transition to democratic rule, but a newly democratic government bore the main burden of reform. Nancy

Bermeo (chapter 4) suggests that Portugal provides a particularly good example of reform being accomplished without authoritarianism.

Both Brazil and Peru were newly restored democracies at the time of the reform attempt under study, and arguably the fragility and weakness of their new democratic institutions had something to do with their failure to reform. Brazil had witnessed a period of vastly more effective liberalizing and stabilizing reforms at an earlier date (1964) under an authoritarian military government, and in Peru there had also been some important reform initiatives under military rule.

Thus a first reading of the evidence suggests little association between economic reform and the degree of political liberalism, one way or the other.[16] However, it has sometimes been argued that the most comprehensive and deep reforms all occurred under long-lived authoritarian regimes, with Chile and Korea being the main cases cited. Even this claim seems dubious. If Poland indeed succeeds in consolidating its very profound reform under a democratic system, the hypothesis will be untenable.

Where the level of social conflict over economic policy is high and democratic institutions are weak, it is not surprising that adjustment efforts have often stalled or that an authoritarian regime committed to economic reform sometimes took charge. Brazil in 1964, Chile in 1973, and Turkey in 1980 all fit this pattern. Yet new democratic governments may also be able to exploit the errors of their predecessors if they move swiftly at the outset—that is, if they exploit a honeymoon period effectively (a topic to which we return below). Perhaps particular circumstances may arise where there is a conflict between democracy and economic reform, but the record provides little support for any general claim that a need for economic reform provides a respectable excuse for suppressing or postponing democracy.

## Right-Wing Government

Another common view is that policy reform is inherently right-wing, and therefore only likely to be introduced by right-wing governments. This perception owes much to the fact that right-wing military governments in the Southern Cone and East Asia were among the earliest reformers in the developing world, that President Ronald Reagan and Prime Minister Margaret Thatcher were among the most vociferous propagandists for some of the measures summarized under the Washington consensus, and that domestic and foreign business interests are often—although sometimes selectively and self-interestedly—in the forefront in pressing for policy reform.

---

16. Similar conclusions have been reached by Nelson (1990), Bates and Krueger (1993), and Przeworski and Limongi (1993).

In fact, the governments in our (nonrandom) sample were distributed widely over the political spectrum. Those in Chile, Korea, and Turkey were clearly right of center. Portugal and the Suarez government in Spain were centrist or perhaps center-right. Those in Indonesia and Mexico are difficult to characterize, containing curious mixes of liberalism, nationalism, and populism. Poland combined a labor base with broadly liberal ideas. All these three governments are arguably more centrist than rightist, which could also be said of the Belaúnde government in Peru. Governments in Australia, New Zealand, and Spain (under Gonzalez), by contrast, were clearly center-left. Sarney's government in Brazil might be labeled "populist," although this characterization is more a reflection of its actions than of a principled party platform, which was distinctly lacking.

Despite these problems with categorization, our sample provides little reason to associate economic reform solely with the political right. This is a conclusion that will seem surprising to some: for example, in his discussion of the paper on New Zealand, Max Corden expressed amazement that free marketeers like Roger Douglas should have chosen to join and work through the Labour Party. Just how surprising one finds it to be doubtless depends on whether one characterizes the left-right axis primarily in terms of statism versus free enterprise or in terms of egalitarianism versus privilege.

An associated question is whether, with the benefit of hindsight, left-of-center reformist governments served the best interests of their natural constituency, labor and the underprivileged. The answer varies. In Australia, one can surely give a positive response. In Spain, there would seem to be a sharp distinction between the gains enjoyed by the majority of the working class, who kept their jobs and enjoyed strong growth in real wages, and the costs imposed on the substantial minority of the working class who suffered from a very high and sustained level of unemployment. On the other hand, the Gonzalez government did take particular pains to expand the social safety network so as to mitigate those costs, and some would argue that these costs are in any event more apparent than real because of the size of Spain's informal economy. In New Zealand, however, the statistics on income distribution suggest rather clearly that the benefits were enjoyed by the rich and the losses borne disproportionately by the Labour Party's natural constituency, the poor. This is not to argue that such a result is an inevitable outcome of liberalization, but rather to recognize that it is indeed a potential outcome when no attention is paid to avoiding it.

Not only is it entirely possible that a party that is left-wing (in the sense that it regards the poor as being its natural constituency) may find itself wishing to liberalize the economy, but it may well be that it has a comparative advantage in being able to implement that desire.

This is a result of what Dani Rodrik characterized as the "Nixon-in-China syndrome": center-left governments are more likely to enjoy the trust of labor, in part because they are more likely to be sensitive to ameliorating the costs of adjustment. They may therefore be able to introduce reforms that would never be accepted if imposed by the political right.

## The Honeymoon Hypothesis

The honeymoon hypothesis states that economic reformers are likely to enjoy greater freedom of political maneuver immediately after they take office, when difficult decisions can be blamed as the legacy of the outgoing government. How many of the successful reformers considered by the conference exploited such a honeymoon period to launch their reform programs?

Among the democratic governments, there were several instances that clearly support the hypothesis. Poland provides the outstanding example, with New Zealand providing another case in point. But there are also a surprising number of cases where the reformers did not exploit a honeymoon, either because there was no honeymoon or because the government was otherwise occupied during its honeymoon period. Thus the Hawke government in Australia did not launch itself into economic reforms immediately after taking office, nor did that of Felipe Gonzalez in Spain. The Colombian reforms were started at the tail end of the Barco administration, apparently with little concern about their electoral impact.

We noted above that several new authoritarian regimes (in Chile in 1973, Indonesia in 1966, and Korea in 1961) initiated reforms shortly after taking office, but it seems a questionable use of language to refer to these periods as "honeymoons." Similarly, the military government in Turkey took advantage of its accession to power in 1980 to strengthen the reform program that had been adopted by the preceding civilian government. The timing of the Indonesian reforms of 1982 reflected the emergence of concern about the weakness of the oil price rather than the electoral cycle, and the Korean reforms of 1979 responded to the emergence of economic difficulties rather than electoral concerns. Reforms in another one-party-dominant system, Mexico, likewise appeared to bear little relationship with the electoral cycle. The unimportance of the electoral cycle in countries with a single dominant party is not surprising.

The failure cases are also revealing. Bresser Pereira had no honeymoon to exploit in Brazil, which was arguably precisely his problem; difficult reforms were needed when the advantages of the transition to the new democratic order had already been dissipated. Webb judges that the Belaúnde government in Peru suffered permanent damage from its failure to exploit its honeymoon to push through measures that would have prevented a fiscal deterioration. The experience of these two countries is more suggestive than that of the successful reformers in implying that the existence and effective use of a honeymoon may often be critical in realizing a successful reform, at least in a democracy.

However, Córdoba argues that it would be wrong to interpret the correct principle that a reforming government needs to find a proper opportunity as implying that this must always be a honeymoon period. He notes that, because of the impossibility of blaming a government of which he had been a part and his questionable electoral mandate, Salinas "had to take political measures to create a basic truce between opposing factions and strengthen his personal capacity to govern" before he was able to move ahead on major, controversial reforms—something that was not politically possible until some two years after taking office. The lack of any firm generalizations on this topic was further underlined by events in Pakistan shortly before this book went to press. In July 1993 Moeen Qureshi, a former executive vice president of the World Bank, was called in to head a caretaker government for three months while elections were organized. He adopted a very generous interpretation of the concept of caretaking and proceeded to introduce a wide-ranging set of reforms, including a devaluation, tax increases, and a requirement that candidates for office be current on servicing their loans. Since most of these measures will need to be ratified by the new parliament if they are to stand, one will have to wait to see how much of his unexpected policy revolution will survive. But even at this stage the episode suggests that technopols should exploit whatever opportunities happen to come their way, rather than assume that only honeymoons can present opportunities.

## A Solid Political Base

While a honeymoon period may present an opportunity for a government to initiate new programs, bringing reforms to fruition requires also that they be sustained through time. One would expect that to be difficult unless a government enjoys a solid base of legislative support.

Obviously this factor is less important, or at least less likely to impose a constraint, in a nondemocratic country. The reforming governments in Indonesia, Korea, and Mexico did require legislative support, but elections were not altogether free and parliaments were limited in the scope of their representation and powers. The extra-legislative backing that these governments enjoyed from important groups in society might not have been sufficient to enable them to dominate the political system under terms of open and fair electoral contestation.

The hypothesized importance of legislative support does seem consistent with the majority of the democratic cases studied by the conference. The ruling party had solid parliamentary majorities in Australia,

Colombia, New Zealand, Portugal, and Spain under Gonzalez.[17] In Turkey, the Demirel government, which initiated the reform program, was decidedly a weak one, and this circumscribed its ability to deliver on the program. In contrast, the Özal government initially enjoyed a strong legislative majority, in part due to changed electoral rules, and appeared to weaken in its resolve precisely as the opposition parties grew stronger.

Even with this hypothesis, however, there is one interesting case that serves to qualify the conclusion. In Poland, the Solidarity government first relied on an alliance with two small parties that had previously been allied to the ruling Communist Party in order to get legislation through parliament. Even though it governed in coalition, the parliament was so awed by the landslide won by Solidarity in the one-third of the seats that it had been allowed to contest in the 1989 elections that one can surely call the initial political base a very solid one. The same certainly cannot be said after the elections of 1991, however, yet the fragmented parliament that resulted from those elections permitted the reform program to be maintained largely intact, with only modest backsliding.

It is important also to consider the cases where reform was not successfully consolidated. Sarney in Brazil certainly lacked a solid parliamentary majority, and that was among the problems that impeded Bresser Pereira's efforts to reform. On the other hand, Belaúnde initially dominated the Peruvian political scene but did not exploit that dominance. One other case mentioned at the conference, that of Venezuela, is also interesting in this connection. Miguel Rodríguez (chapter 6) sketches the extensive Venezuelan reforms introduced by President Carlos Andrés Pérez. After a sharp initial decline in output, these reforms delivered impressively rapid growth, yet the reform process has not been consolidated in Venezuela. The primary reason Rodríguez gives is the opposition to the whole process within the president's own party, which effectively precludes reforms that require legislative consent rather than just executive action.

Where the legislature is antireform, as in Russia and Ukraine today (chapter 8) as well as Venezuela (and Brazil), the ability to sustain reforms depends on the development of mechanisms to bypass the legislature. But the examples suggest that it is difficult to do much more than hold the fort under those circumstances. Effective reform does need political support.

---

17. In his paper on Spain, de la Dehesa argued that there is a natural tendency for a large number of fragmented parties to emerge during the transition from dictatorship to democracy, and that it is only after these coalesce into a limited number of larger parties, each representing a wide swath of the political spectrum, that economic reforms become practical.

## A Fragmented and Demoralized Opposition

A government might be able to compensate for the lack of a strong base of support if the opposition is fragmented and unable to challenge it on reforms that are initially likely to be unpopular.

Once again, it is natural to treat the nondemocratic cases separately in examining how widely this hypothesis fits the facts in our sample. In Chile, Indonesia, Korea, and Turkey the opposition was aggressively suppressed immediately following the military coups, although in both Chile and Korea it began to reassert itself over time, and in Turkey an opposition was revived by Turgut Özal when the military redemocratized rather rapidly. In Mexico the opposition was constrained by the limited nature of the democratic system, although during the period under examination opposition on both the right and the left became more, not less, organized.

The hypothesis was clearly satisfied in four of the democratic cases: New Zealand, Poland, Portugal, and Spain. Perhaps Australia qualifies as well. Certainly Russia in 1992 does, as Vladimir Mau notes in chapter 8, where he indeed argues that it was only the extreme weakness of the opposition that provided any reason for believing that reform might succeed. But that still leaves Colombia as a functioning democracy that introduced a reform program with an opposition that, while not particularly strong, was functioning normally. (As it happened, the Conservative opposition was more united in supporting some of the liberalization policies than was the Liberal government.)

The two cases where reform was not successfully executed are again informative. In Brazil, there was certainly a vigorous if somewhat fragmented opposition, and the government lacked a clear majority in the congress. This surely made Bresser Pereira's task more difficult, and it may have been the critical consideration that caused Sarney to back away from his promise to implement a wide-ranging tax reform, and thereby aborted the whole reform effort. In Peru, the opposition had just been decisively defeated, but that still did not give Belaúnde the self-confidence to risk a reversal in the impending local elections and authorize the forceful fiscal adjustment that might have prevented his administration from losing its momentum.

This record suggests that a weak and divided opposition does indeed make the task of a reforming government easier. Of course, this is not to deny that the more vital factor is the existence of a coherent and determined government with adequate political support.

## A Social Consensus

It was suggested during the session on reform programs on the European periphery—Poland, Portugal, Spain, and Turkey (chapter 4)—that a powerful factor impelling reform had been the existence of a social consensus around the objective of "becoming European," including, or perhaps especially, becoming members of the European Community. This objective has a material underpinning in the benefits that it was presumed would accrue upon membership, as well as a social-psychological base. Advocates of social pacts make the more general case that policies reached through consensus are likely to be more durable. Spain is often held up as an example of how such pacts can operate. De la Dehesa indeed argues that economic reform proved easier to implement in Spain once the democratic rules of the political game had been accepted.

How important is it for the success of a program that there be some degree of social consensus around the need for reform? In his speech to the conference, Jeffrey Sachs vigorously attacked the notion that reformers should feel constrained by the need to establish a social consensus or spend their time trying to build one. What they should offer, rather, is leadership, a concept that, he argued, was typically left out of both economic and political economy analysis. If reformers succeed, a social consensus will form in support of their measures; if they fail, no amount of prior social consensus will save them from being cast aside.

This debate was carried further in the concluding session of the conference (chapter 9). Bresser Pereira argued that Sachs was right in cases of acute crisis, where decisive action could produce rapid results, but that long-run reforms required, if not consensus, at least a substantial body of public support. Torres endorsed this view, although he noted that it did not fit the Portuguese experience particularly well, inasmuch as the short-run crisis had been addressed by a coalition government, whereas Cavaco Silva had broken up the coalition to embark on his program of longer-run reform. Stephan Haggard noted that the essence of democracy was that policy formation was a competitive rather than a consensual activity. A society could nonetheless confront problems in adopting reforms where there was a sufficiently basic disagreement over the nature of the model, although one natural consequence of successful reform tended to be ideological convergence. Joan Nelson agreed, and added that it was unusual to find much agreement present at the start.

How do these views compare with the evidence provided by our case studies? Prior social consensus on the desirability of reform does not seem to have been present in many of the cases examined by the conference, notably Chile, Korea, New Zealand (although there *was* widespread agreement that something had to change), or Turkey (in 1980, although Özal won an election in 1983, so that by then there must have been a substantial degree of support). In Colombia the reforms were met by indifference rather than either consensus or opposition. The initial Indonesian reforms in 1966 were imposed from above, but Suharto has gone to considerable lengths to build consensus over the years—an effort that may in fact help to explain the somewhat vacillating character of Indonesian reform. Much the same is true in Korea. Neither Brazil nor Peru had any consensus in favor of reform: in fact, as noted by Barbara Stallings (chapter 9), both are riven by deep divisions about the desirability of moving toward the market. Of course, neither of them have succeeded in reforming.

On the other hand, Australia, Mexico, Poland, Portugal, and Spain are cases where reform was based on an important measure of consensus. In the case of Australia this did not take the form of a prior consensus, but the consensus was something that Hawke nurtured carefully as he developed his gradualistic reform program. Much the same is true in Mexico: Córdoba describes at length the attention that Salinas has paid to building up support for the reforms. In Poland the consensus was on the very general objectives of moving to a market economy and "becoming European," and that consensus began to fray as soon as specific actions were required (in particular, within months of initiating his reforms, Balcerowicz was being assailed from all sides for creating recession). In Portugal and Spain there was also wide agreement on the general objective of joining Europe, but the details of what that involved again proved highly controversial.

The record also shows instances of the Sachs-Haggard phenomenon, where reforms that initially met with intense opposition won widespread endorsement as they came to yield results. Chile is the most dramatic case in point, but Turkey provides another good example. Indeed, all the cases of consolidated reforms must have been characterized by a fair measure of *ex post* public acceptance of the reforms, for otherwise the reforms would not be consolidated.

Does this really mean that we can dismiss public support as an irrelevance and should advocate a strategy of all power (at least temporarily) to the technocrats, so that they can do the right thing unconstrained by democratic niceties? Interestingly, it happens that both of the authors who discussed failed programs are strong critics of the view that the reform should be promoted by allowing technocrats to bypass democratic constraints. Richard Webb describes how in Peru each crisis made the ministers more subservient to the power of the technocrats, but he argues that this is also part of the explanation for Peru's difficulty in sustaining reforms, since "reforms" adopted out of force majeure rather than intellectual persuasion were reversed as soon as the force disappeared. Bresser Pereira[18] argues in his paper that the reform effort in Brazil was doomed to fail given that there was neither public understanding and sympathy nor support from the President. He also argues

18. See also his argument in Bresser Pereira, Maravall, and Przeworski (1993).

that allowing the technocrats to bypass democracy could undermine democracy itself.

This survey makes it obvious that there are no pat answers. In some circumstances it may be politically possible to introduce reforms ahead of public opinion and achieve results sufficiently quickly to sustain them by changing public opinion. In others it may make more sense to build public support as the program is developed. In many cases it may be useful (following Nicolás Ardito-Barletta, chapter 9) to think of a reform program as involving a sequence of reforms, each one of which may initially involve the expenditure of political capital, but which may also help to replenish the government's stock of political capital as its results come on stream. In this conception the political art required by a reformer is to judge just how far he can go ahead of public opinion at any particular time without losing the minimum level of support needed to live to fight the next battle.

One can certainly agree with Sachs that reform initiatives should not be dependent on public opinion polls showing a majority in favor: the function of a leader is to lead, not to quake with fear at the possibility of causing offense. But in a democracy, what the public is willing to accept in the way of good economic policy will at some point constrain what can be introduced, and even in a nondemocracy a prudent leader has to pay attention to avoiding tearing his society apart. Economists who want to see good economic policies implemented have a duty to try and educate the public as well as the policymakers.

## A Visionary Leader

Sachs emphasized the importance of leadership. Piñera had already argued that one of the key conditions for successful economic reform is a visionary leader with a sense of history: an individual prepared to take a long-term view of what is at stake regardless of the short-term political risks.

Of course, there is considerably more latitude in prospect than in retrospect for views to differ about who is "visionary" and who is not. (Many of us would not have classified Pinochet as visionary in 1975, even though he is precisely the political leader to whom Piñera was referring.) Moreover, it is not always correct to assume that great vision is required to initiate reforms. Where economic performance has deteriorated badly (especially under circumstances of hyperinflation), there may be short-term political gains from taking a longer view; good economic policy *can* be good politics even in the short run.

Nonetheless, most of the cases of successful reform in our sample did involve strong leadership from executives with strong commitment, a vision of where they would like their countries to go (even if this was not always combined with any clear sense of how to get there), and a willingness to take risks. Again, the authoritarian cases demand separate consideration. However much distaste one may have for Pinochet's rule, it is clear that he had a vision of a Chile fundamentally transformed and was willing to pursue it regardless of the costs. This was true to a somewhat lesser degree of Suharto in Indonesia, of de la Madrid and Salinas in Mexico, and of Chun Doo Hwan in Korea.

Among the democratic cases it would certainly seem to apply to Hawke in Australia, to Wałęsa in Poland, to Cavaco Silva in Portugal, to Gonzalez in Spain, and to Özal in Turkey. This is not to say that the vision of the leader is enough: in each of those cases it was bolstered by strong social and legislative support, and Özal also benefited both from military backing and from changes in the political system wrought under military rule.

The two cases of unsuccessful reform also appear consistent with the hypothesis, for both Sarney and Belaúnde were very sensitive to short-run political considerations, Sarney making a one-year extension in his term of office the major political issue of the moment and Belaúnde refusing to authorize prompt fiscal adjustment on first taking office because of fears about the impact on local election results. But let justice be done. Both of these leaders also had to worry about preserving their newly restored democratic regimes, and this eminently worthy motive may have deterred them from taking what they perceived to be fool-hardy risks with economic policy.

Yet there is one notable exception to the rule that a visionary leader is essential to the initiation and consolidation of economic reform. This is New Zealand, where reform was apparently possible because the prime minister more or less gave carte blanche to his economic team while he concentrated on realizing his vision, not of a reformed economic system, but of a New Zealand whose territorial waters would be nuclear-free. The economic vision was not that of the leader of the government but of the leader of the economic team, Roger Douglas.

## The Position of the Economic Team

Although the broad political factors we have outlined so far may influence the reform process, so does the internal organization of the economic policymaking apparatus. Two aspects of this involve the presence (or absence) of a coherent economic team, and whether it is led by a technopol.

### A Coherent Economic Team

The hypothesis is that economic reform requires a coherent and united economic team. Reform, it is claimed, simply will not happen unless the team is coherently organized, or if people with conflicting views on economic policy have been appointed in order "to enable the president to get the benefit of competing views" or "to generate creative tension."

This hypothesis was satisfied in every one of our cases of successful reform.[19] The closest to an exception is Indonesia, where the economists ("technocrats") in charge of the financial ministries have to fight a running battle with the "engineers" in charge of the spending ministries, while major decisions involving the choice between them reside with the president. Of course, it could be that it is precisely because the technocrats are not fully in control that it remains unclear whether the reforms have been fully consolidated.

But it must be noted that the condition of a coherent team was also satisfied in both Brazil and Peru, perhaps as well as it was satisfied in several of the cases of successful reform, so clearly a competent and coherent economic team is not a *sufficient* condition for success. The problem in both of those countries was that the team did not receive the support from the rest of the government that was needed to be able to act effectively.

In a number of cases it is clear that institutional reforms were crucial in strengthening the political position of the team vis-à-vis interest groups, competing ministries, the legislature, and even the rest of the executive, to a point where the team was capable of launching and sustaining reforms. For example, Özal moved swiftly upon coming to office in Turkey to increase the independence of the central bank and technocratic ministries and to weaken the hand of the old State Planning Organization, a bastion of dirigisme. He made sure that in the major economic decision-making bodies the technocrats outweighed the elected politicians. Similarly, in Korea Chun Doo Hwan restored the integrity of the Economic Planning Board after a period when Park Chung Hee had circumvented it in order to advance his heavy industry program. In Spain, Gonzalez granted wide powers to his economic czar, Miguel Boyer, to make decisions that cut across the traditional ministerial jurisdictions.

The competence of the economic team cannot compensate for a lack of authority, something that typically requires institutional change within the decision-making structure. It is also conceivable that a team may be excessively cohesive, leaving no one to question plans and to draw attention to downside risks—a danger noted by Córdoba, without admitting that it has actually happened in Mexico. At the same time, the record says pretty plainly that, at least in a reasonably sophisticated economy, a good and united team is a precondition for reform to have a chance.

## The Presence of a Technopol

A question posed in the initial background paper by Williamson was whether it was important to successful reform to have economists in

---

19. However, David Finch has pointed out an earlier instance where it rather clearly was not satisfied, namely, Bolivia in 1956. That program, which stopped a chronic inflation and set the stage for over two decades of respectable growth in a country that had rarely experienced decent performance, was largely designed by visiting experts rather than by a local team.

positions of political responsibility, rather than merely serving as technical advisers. Given that a coherent team is required, is it necessary that the team be led by what we are calling a technopol?

Discussion at the conference suggested that the concept of a technopol was sufficiently blurred to make the answer to this question somewhat ambiguous. Ambiguity arises from whether we are limiting the category to professional economists as opposed to other professionals like accountants (Roger Douglas), whether the economists have to have advanced degrees in the subject to qualify (César Gaviria), and what constitutes a "politically responsible office." But whatever answer one gives to these definitional questions, the answer to the question as to whether technopols were present is: in some cases, but by no means in all.

In the nondemocratic countries it is particularly difficult to distinguish a technocrat responsible to the executive from a technopol with independent political authority. Mexico clearly had economists in key political positions throughout the adjustment period, including the presidency after 1988. Several excellent economists served as ministers in Chile, but the political system did not give them such an active political role as to make it obvious that one would define them as technopols rather than technocrats; the technocrats were completely dependent on Pinochet, lacking an independent base of political power. The economists in the key positions in Indonesia and Korea also seem more naturally classified as technocrats than as technopols, given the closed nature of the political system in both countries.

Turkey provides additional ambiguities. Turgut Özal initially entered government as a technocrat without an independent political base, then remained as a technocrat under the military, but emerged as a remarkably talented politician in 1983, when he won an election against the opposition of the military and became prime minister.

In several of the democracies, economists were elevated to high political positions: Poland had Balcerowicz as finance minister from September 1989 until the end of 1991; Portugal has had Aníbal Cavaco Silva as prime minister since 1985, and now has Jorge Braga de Macedo as finance minister as well; and Spain had Miguel Boyer as finance minister in the early years of the Gonzalez government. Answers are less clear in other countries: neither Bob Hawke nor Paul Keating, the two key figures in Australia, was a professional economist, although both had had some exposure to economic analysis and had thought a lot about economic problems; Colombian President César Gaviria has only an undergraduate degree in economics, although key ministers, including Finance Minister Rudolf Hommes, have doctorates from US universities; and in New Zealand the key minister was an accountant rather than an economist. (Of course, one interpretation might be that this can help explain why the reform program there was technically botched.)

In the two cases where reform was not successful, Bresser Pereira qualifies as a technopol in Brazil. In contrast, Manuel Ulloa in Peru was a lawyer by training rather than an economist, although he had learned a lot of economics and had established a reputation as a wunderkind when he was in office under Belaúnde in the 1960s.

Thus our nonrandom sample does not seem to support any very strong generalizations. And the nonrandomness is in this context a major concern: as Anne Krueger remarked at the end of her discussion, Andreas Papandreou was a member of the economics profession in good standing before he became a Greek politician, yet he pursued distinctly populist policies in office. Economists do not always choose to apply mainstream economics, even if they are good enough politicians to get themselves into elective office.

Although the evidence disproves any claim that the presence of technopols (economist-politicians, if you prefer) is indispensable to successful reform, participants at the conference offered several reasons for thinking that it would be advantageous to have technopols in office. José Córdoba suggested that Salinas has a great advantage through his understanding of economics, which enables him to deal with the routine economic issues that dominate the work of so many presidents in a far more expeditious way than a noneconomist could hope to. Leszek Balcerowicz argued that a technopol's understanding of the subject enables him to offer more effective leadership than is otherwise possible: a strong minister who is completely dependent on the advice of others does indeed seem an impossibility. Balcerowicz also advanced the suggestion that, in contrast to a politician, the self-esteem of an economist holding political office would be more damaged by a failure of his proposals to work than by a failure to get his proposals accepted, even if the latter involved his ejection from office. An economist who had not forfeited his professional reputation by acquiescing in political compromises that yielded bad policy would have somewhere satisfying to go after his ministerial life ended, whereas a politician's career would be over.

A table published in The Economist in August 1993, reproduced here as table 2, suggests that technopols are now more dominant than they were in the period from which our case studies were drawn (although they were still the exception rather than the rule among the G-7 countries). An accompanying lead article recalled that in 1932 "Keynes predicted that over the subsequent 25 years economists would become the most important group of scientists in the world. And once they had worked their magic, he fervently hoped, they would never be important again." The article concluded, "The economists are still waiting for their chance to put the world to rights. They need only one (quarter-century) turn in the sun, then they will go away. Honest." We too endorse the proposition that economists have a central role to play in guiding the

## Table 2   The class of 1993

| | Degree subjects of: | |
| --- | --- | --- |
| | Finance minister | Central bank governor |
| Britain | Law | Economics |
| Canada | None | PPE |
| France | Economics | Law / literature |
| Germany | Law and politics | Economics |
| Italy | Economics | Economics |
| Japan | Law | Law |
| United States | Law | Economics |
| Argentina | Economics | Economics |
| Brazil | Sociology | Economics |
| Chile | Economics | Economics |
| Mexico | Economics | Economics |
| China | None | Mech. engineering |
| Indonesia | Economics | Economics |
| South Korea | Public administration | Economics |
| Taiwan | Economics | Economics |
| Thailand | Economics[a] | Economics |
| Czech Republic | Economics | Economics |
| Poland | Economics | Economics |
| Russia | Economics | Economics |

PPE = philosophy, politics, and economics.

a. MBA in finance.

*Source*: © 1993 *The Economist* Newspaper Ltd. Reprinted with permission. Further reproduction prohibited.

transition with more conviction than the hope that afterward their skills will be unneeded in public life, but that proposition has been only modestly reinforced by the conference.

## The Reform Program

While background economic conditions and political and organizational factors all contribute to the reform effort, so does the design of the program itself. In this section we discuss a number of hypotheses about the nature of the reform program and how it is sold. These concern the need for a program to be comprehensive, "voodoo politics," the use of the media, compensation of losers, and accelerating the gains to winners.

One topic that we do not discuss is the quality of the program itself. Several participants in the conference regretted this, on the ground that good salesmanship will not sell a bad product, but we pleaded division of labor to restrict the terms of reference. The remainder of the volume contains a number of allusions to the topic.

## A Comprehensive Program

The hypothesis claims that reformers need to design a comprehensive program capable of rapid implementation. (Rapid does not necessarily mean instantaneous, which may or may not imply something about a "big bang," depending on how one chooses to interpret that term.) It was suggested in the background paper that "comprehensive" necessarily has to be interpreted relative to the needs of the situation: Poland had to do everything from stopping a hyperinflation to creating the legal infrastructure of a market economy within a matter of months, whereas Colombia's need was confined to liberalizing trade and deregulating the domestic economy.

In that relative sense, the successful programs chosen for study were mostly fairly comprehensive, but this was partly due to the fact that those were the sort of programs we chose to study. The two main exceptions were Indonesia (which has still not fully liberalized trade) and Turkey (which never fixed the fiscal deficit). In addition, several authors noted delays in liberalizing a particular market, although there was disagreement on how damaging this had been. Thus Chile failed to suppress indexation and to introduce prudential supervision during its 1970s reforms, failures that are widely agreed to have been critical causes of the 1982 crisis; Korea took its time in liberalizing imports; and Australia and New Zealand delayed liberalizing the labor market. There were also cases in which many would argue that excessively rapid liberalization proved costly, both economically and politically; the haste of both Chile and New Zealand in liberalizing capital flows provide examples, as does Mexico's rapid trade liberalization under conditions of a growing payments deficit and anemic growth.

Neither of the two cases of unsuccessful reform efforts was based on a comprehensive program. In the case of Brazil, Finance Minister Bresser Pereira felt he had enough on his plate with the attempt to stabilize and to renegotiate the foreign debt, so that liberalization would have to wait. In the Peruvian case, the team was committed to gradual liberalization, but the overarching concern was to do nothing that might threaten the prospects for consolidating democracy.

The programs were not all especially rapid. Australia, Indonesia, Korea, and Portugal all pursued self-consciously gradual programs. Colombia also designed a gradual program but then decided to do all the trade liberalization that was supposed to be spread over five years at one time.

The conference papers are not particularly revealing on the classic issue of whether there are political benefits in designing a comprehensive and rapid program rather than a more gradual one. We did not seek reactions to the proposition of Przeworski (1991) that a big bang serves to burn bridges and thus minimize the possibility of a reversion to the old regime, although Balcerowicz did claim that one of the advantages of early establishment of current account convertibility was that this had served as a constraint on populism. Nor did we invite reactions to the claim that rapid reform serves to preempt vested interests that might otherwise build a coalition to thwart change, although Bollard attests that the New Zealand reformers had such an objective in mind when they chose a rapid reform program. The absence of any strong generalizations suggests that the important element is not simply whether a program is rapid or comprehensive, but whether it is appropriate to the needs of the situation. Unfortunately a judgment on that topic could not reasonably be based on the opinions offered by the authors invited to the conference, who were mostly actors with a major responsibility for having designed the programs and therefore unlikely to be impartial observers. Assessing the appropriateness of programs would have demanded a whole new research program based on assessments by independent observers against a counterfactual. This alternative hypothesis is nonetheless one that future researchers might care to bear in mind.

## Voodoo Politics

This hypothesis suggests that reformers should avoid declaring their intentions to the public prior to gaining power, since policy reform is something that the electorate would never knowingly vote for (a view espoused with great force by Przeworski 1991). Rather, reformers should promise that they can solve economic problems painlessly; following Machiavelli, they should only reveal their true intentions *after* they have won office, taking the public by surprise. Note that if it were also true (as sometimes asserted) that governments can hope to reform successfully only if they gain a mandate from the electorate, then reform would be subject to a Catch-22: it could be effectively implemented only by a government that has no chance of coming to power. (Since reform does sometimes occur under democratic governments, as our cases show, one can immediately infer that at least one of these hypotheses must be wrong.)

Did the parties that introduced major reform programs in our countries declare their intentions in the election that preceded the program? Again, this question does not apply to authoritarian governments, since it was not necessary for them to fool an electorate in order to act. Among the democracies, the results are mixed. There were two cases, Australia and Spain, where the winning party had campaigned on a conventional program of more goodies and then turned around and instituted a program of asking the public to face the facts of life; interestingly, both were center-left governments. Outside our sample of 13 cases, several other reversals of direction by previously populist politicians come readily to mind, such as Carlos Menem in Argentina, Victor Paz Esstensoro in

Bolivia, and Carlos Andrés Pérez in Venezuela. Of those five programs, at least four were successful,[20] refuting the contention that a program cannot hope to succeed unless the government has a prior mandate to introduce reform. In none of those cases, except perhaps Venezuela, does democracy seem to have been weakened by the government doing a U-turn; this supports the contention of Jeffrey Sachs that support will materialize if the program is a success.

The fact that Venezuela provides an exception to public acquiescence in policy reversal is quite suggestive, for in Venezuela, unlike Argentina and Bolivia, there was no public perception that the economy was in crisis when the new government took office. In the two latter cases, large parts of the electorate (admittedly not predominantly supporters of the winning candidate) breathed a sigh of relief when the president abandoned pledges that were recognized to be unrealistic and threatened to make the crisis even deeper, and asked instead for blood, sweat, and tears. In Venezuela, in contrast, the public was taken by surprise when it was asked without warning to abandon the lotus-eaters' life that abundant oil had provided for so long. In both Australia and Spain the policy reversal was carefully explained and gradual rather than a shock.

In two of the other cases in our sample—Colombia and New Zealand—the intention to move in a liberalizing direction seems to have been pretty obvious, even though it was not an explicit campaign theme. In neither, however, was it clear that the government would move as far as it ultimately did, and thus these might count as cases of voodoo politics. There were also at least two cases where the winning party campaigned on an overt promise to liberalize the economy, namely, Poland and Turkey. Admittedly the Polish case presents some ambiguities. Although the Solidarity movement clearly gained political power in large part because of its promise to jettison both the political and economic system of the communists, the short-term costs of the reform program were not made clear to the public in advance. (It is also true that those costs proved larger than had been expected.)

Finally, in neither of the two cases of unfulfilled reform did a party campaign on a promise of reform, although in Peru the general intentions of the winning party were public knowledge.

The more general thesis that advocacy of economic reform involves political suicide can be further tested by asking whether parties that introduced these reforms in our sample countries were punished by the electorate at the next election. In Australia, the Labor government has now won reelection an unprecedented four consecutive times (although admittedly its reforming zeal has tended to wane over time). In Co-

---

20. The arguable exception is Venezuela. This case is discussed briefly by Miguel Rodríguez in chapter 6 as well as by Moises Naim (1993), who argues that the element of surprise was a major cause of public opposition.

lombia there has been only one election since reform started in 1989, and this took place before most of the more radical steps were introduced, but the governing Liberal Party won reelection. In New Zealand the Labour Party won reelection once after introducing the reforms and was then displaced by the opposition at the following election. In Poland Solidarity splintered, in part under the pressures produced by the reforms. In Portugal the PSD won reelection with an absolute majority in 1987 and increased its majority following the next election in 1991. In Spain the socialists have been reelected three times, including a narrow victory in the summer of 1993. In Turkey Özal's Motherland Party won one further election on a reduced majority after its famous victory of 1983, before being displaced as its appetite for reform waned.

That is really a rather successful string of results. It is more consistent with the view that electorates respect decisive and effective government, and that they will reward liberalization efforts, than it is with the "voodoo politics" notion that politicians who believe in liberalization should pretend they do not. The record provides little ground for urging reformers to play voodoo politics, pretending until they take office that their magic touch will dispense with any need for uncomfortable reform. But neither does the evidence of successful reforming governments elected without a mandate suggest that, if a party happens to make silly campaign pledges whose observance would threaten its capacity to govern effectively, it should then compound the folly by actually doing as it had promised. The one thing that a government should not do (to generalize from the Venezuelan experience) is impose without warning or explanation changes that the public cannot see to be necessary.

We thus reject both the view that dishonesty is essential to gain office and that earning an honest mandate is essential in order to be able to implement an effective reform program subsequently. Not only is there no Catch-22, but both horns of the supposed dilemma are invalid.

## Use of the Media

One of the four keys that explain the success of the Chilean reforms was, according to José Piñera, the effective use the reformers made of the media. Even in nondemocratic Chile he perceived it to be important to carry public opinion along. This involved taking the case for reform to the general public, over the heads of the politicians with their vested interests and the professional journalists with their hostility to serious economic argument as something too boring to risk inflicting on their readers.

The conference papers did not reveal much systematic attempt to make the case for reform in the media, apart from the case of Chile, whence the suggestion had originated (although reportedly Korea is another country where the media were consciously used in the same way). The only other support comes from the experience of Venezuela, where Naim (1993) sees the lack of public support as the critical weakness that undermined the program, and argues (as echoed above) that the failure to make the case for reform in the media nurtured the public antipathy. On the other hand, Miguel Urrutia commented that any attempt to use the media systematically to argue one side of the case would be unconstitutional in Colombia. Leszek Balcerowicz also noted the problem of finding time for promoting the reform program with the general public, given the overwhelming demands of managing the economy.

The bottom line is that it would be a mistake to expect too much from an ability to build support for reform through the use of the media. In the sort of pluralistic and market-oriented society that reformers are trying to build, the media will not be the pliant agent that they were in Pinochet's Chile. In any event, as Joan Nelson points out in her contribution to the conference (chapter 9), even if persuasion can help to ease the introduction of specific reforms, "in fairly short order people will judge reforms by their perceived results."

## Compensation

Another hypothesis contends that the chances of successful reform will be enhanced if the losers are provided with compensation, rather than abandoned to become impoverished and embittered opponents. The papers did not reveal any systematic attempts to compensate losers, but this hypothesis was not among those included in the background paper that guided the authors of the country studies, and hence the lack of comment is not definitive. Haggard and Webb (1992) report that in their World Bank project on adjustment in new democracies, compensation broadly conceived was crucial for securing support for programs. But in the more successful cases in their multicountry study—Chile, Mexico, Spain, and Thailand—compensation came in the form of "complementary reforms": measures such as those in the Mexican Solidarity program that provided benefits to a wide segment of the community, but that did so while enhancing welfare and economic opportunity over the longer term and minimizing rent-seeking opportunities. There was little in the way of *direct* compensation schemes for losing groups.

Such direct compensation is a suspect proposition. It comes too close to buying out rent seekers, or at least rent receivers, for the comfort of those of us who regard the essence of economic reform as being an attempt to get away from the rent-seeking society. It would of course be much less alien to those who share the second approach outlined by Robert Bates in his comment on Williamson's background paper (chapter 2), which treats economic reform as an effort to change the group in whose favor the economic system is organized rather than as an effort to get away from favoring specific groups altogether. (Economic reform is in this interpretation typically the result of a political victory of the exporting interests.)

## Acceleration of Gains to Winners

A rather similar hypothesis, which was forcefully argued by Joan Nelson in her contribution to the final panel (chapter 9), is that the prospects of sustaining reform can be enhanced by accelerating the emergence of politically influential groups that can appreciate the benefits they are reaping from the reform program. One action that was employed at one stage in both Korea and Turkey was to provide temporary subsidies to the exporting groups that were expected to benefit from the new regime rather than wait until real devaluation could produce its beneficial effects. Another, advocated by Joan Nelson, is to institute a "high-priority drive for rapid improvement in one or two selected basic services or utilities. . . . The idea of rapid returns does not imply favoritism or subsidies, but rather doing whatever is required . . . to demonstrate concrete progress on some aspect of life that matters to most people."

Once again, the country papers did not report any instances where reforming governments deliberately attempted to accelerate the emergence of winners. Once again, however, this is not definitive inasmuch as the background paper had not specifically requested authors to focus on whether such tactics had been employed. The Colombian paper does note that one factor facilitating the success of import liberalization this time around was the fact that the export lobby had become a politically significant force, in line with the Bates analysis noted in the preceding section.

Despite the absence of corroborating evidence from our case studies, the idea of trying to make sure that some form of "indirect compensation" comes on stream soon enough to sustain support for a reform program seems eminently sensible. It is important that this not be debauched into buying votes, thus yielding the moral high ground that justifies undertaking the reforms in the first place, but it is almost equally important that technopols not adopt a priggish disdain for political realism such as to doom them to political irrelevance.

## A Summary

Summary results as to whether or not each of these hypotheses were satisfied for each of the 13 cases examined in the conference are presented in table 1. The six countries where reform succeeded under indubitably democratic processes are listed in the first six columns, followed by the five cases of success under qualified democracy or authoritarian government, and then by the two cases where reform was not successful. The first row lists for each country the date when the reform episode being examined is deemed to have started. The next 12 rows indicate, in most cases with a simple "yes" or "no," whether the hypothesis was judged to have been satisfied; other entries signify more complex judgments, as amplified in the notes to the table. Three hypotheses are not entered in the table for lack of data, namely, those regarding use of the media, payment of compensation, and acceleration of the gains from reform.

It is obvious at a glance that there are no fully robust empirical generalizations; in every case there is at least one partial counterexample. None of the 15 hypotheses investigated was either necessary or sufficient for successful reform. This is hardly surprising, inasmuch as any problem with a panacea for a solution long ago ceased to be a problem.

But that does not mean that the hypotheses are worthless. A number of the propositions, although not necessarily surprising, receive quite strong support. These include the need for a strong political base, for visionary leadership, and for a coherent economic team. Several others—the possibility of being able to exploit crises or honeymoons and the importance of a comprehensive program—received sufficient corroboration that they should be borne in mind by any reform-minded leader. The finding concerning the importance of conditional external financial support to program success is particularly important for the donor community.

Moreover, some of the negative findings are also important. It is clear that authoritarian regimes are not necessary in order to launch or sustain reforms, and that reform does not have to occur under the auspices of a right-wing government. On the contrary, the evidence suggests that at least in some circumstances center-left governments may have some advantages (notably the ability to make changes that labor perceives as disadvantageous without unleashing disruptive social tensions). The lack of support for both the voodoo politics hypothesis and its converse, that reform can succeed only if it has won a mandate during the preceding election, is also noteworthy; however, these findings need to be qualified by the cautionary note that policy reversals should not be sprung on a public that sees no crisis justifying them.

## The Role of Economists in Promoting Policy Reform

Most policy-oriented economists believe that they have useful advice to give to policymakers, and they tend to say what are intended to be unkind things about failures of leadership and a lack of political will when their advice is disregarded. This fits uncomfortably with the standard professional view that the economist is an expert who informs the policymaker about the range of options, from which the latter selects the one that will maximize the social welfare function[21] that he or she intuits

---

21. Or minimize the loss function, as it is often formulated where the problem is a macroeconomic one.

to be the true expression of society's preferences. But since policymakers are agents who are supposed to be maximizing the welfare of their principal, society at large, an economist who sees that they choose instead to pursue much narrower personal or sectional interests has every right to complain. The question is whether there is a constructive response when their advice is disregarded.

The reaction against the standard formulation was the postulate that politicians are as narrowly motivated by self-interest as is *Homo economicus*. From this comes public choice theory, which has unquestionably produced insights into the behavior of at least some politicians. But unfortunately for those who believe that economics can say some things of interest about how to improve the quality of public policy, public choice theory has no more useful advice to offer about how economists should act in order to promote economic welfare than does traditional normative economics. The advice seems to be to await a summons to write a constitution that will constrain the politicians from exercising their mafia-like proclivity to buy votes, extend their period in office, and grab what they can. Since the politicians postulated by the theory have no interest in such a constitution being written, however, the theory predicts that the wait will be a long one. Public choice theory is a dead end.

Partisan models of political economy provide a more constructive approach. Alesina (1987), for example, hypothesizes that each party represents the interests of a particular social group. He postulates a left-wing party that represents labor and therefore prefers low unemployment even if the cost is higher inflation, and a right-wing party that represents the interests of capital and is therefore prepared to tolerate higher unemployment in order to control inflation. It turns out that the left is electorally disadvantaged in this model because its desire to create a boom after winning an election means that it has to create a recession to get inflation under control again just when the next election is looming, while the right's preferences lead it to a better alignment of the electoral and business cycles.

Such a view of the political process provides a natural place for an economist to offer his or her professional skills to the party that most closely represents the social forces with which he or she empathizes. An economist who empathizes with labor might, for example, be able to educate the left-wing party into understanding that creating an unsustainable boom is not actually in the interests of the party's constituency because it threatens the ability to win a follow-on election.

A party in power confronts a need to command some economic expertise. The economists it employs may be advisers, technocrats, or what we have been terming technopols. Advisers are those with no executive responsibility, whose role is perhaps adequately portrayed by the traditional model in which their duty is to present the policymaker with a menu of options. Technocrats are those who are given some decision-making authority because the politicians find it convenient to delegate power to them.[22] Technopols are those who have some political standing of their own.

One of the key questions posed in the background paper for the conference was whether there is any particular advantage in having economists in the role of technopols rather than technocrats. Both the discussants of the background paper, Robert Bates and John Toye, answered that question in the negative. Politicians who promote economic reform are in Bates's view those whose constituents can be expected to benefit from reform; they rent the expertise of economists in order to help them do the job efficiently but have no need or incentive to share power with them. Toye argues that the skills required by politicians are different from those required by economists, and hence that the normal principle of division of labor suggests that the two groups should be distinct.

The other case is made persuasively, if obliquely, by Arnold Harberger, in a paper entitled "Secrets of Success: A Handful of Heroes" (Harberger 1993). His handful of heroes are the economists who spearheaded the reform programs in Latin American countries over the past 30 years: Roberto Campos in Brazil, Alejandro Vegh Villegas in Uruguay, Sergio De Castro and Hernan Buchi in Chile, Carlos Salinas de Gortari, Pedro Aspe, and Francisco Gil Díaz in Mexico, and Domingo Cavallo in Argentina. Although a number of these served under military regimes in which the concept of a technopol may be questioned, the fact is that all of them (with the exception of Gil Díaz, whose task was a more technocratic one in tax reform and administration) held ministerial offices that would place them in the category of technopols in a democratic system. The question is whether they could have done their jobs equally effectively had they simply been advisers or subordinates rather than themselves being in the key decision-making positions.

Our own view would be that the answer to that question depends very much on the characteristics of the other politicians. If they belong to the political mafia of public choice theory, then the economist will need political authority to prevail. If, on the other hand, they are just as conscientious in striving to maximize the general good as the economist, then a technocratic position can serve just as well.

The objections of Bates and Toye do not seem particularly persuasive. Technocrats, Bates argues, are generally academics; they "lack the normal prerequisites of political influence: wealth and power. Rather, they possess expertise." But power is something that politicians seek through the political process, not something that they are endowed with

---

22. Bates argues in chapter 2 that one possible reason for this willingness to delegate is to curb the collectively self-destructive proclivity of politicians to allocate pork to advance their individual political interests.

at birth; the question at issue is precisely whether it makes sense for those with expertise to seek power, and the answer is surely yes if that will help them bring their expertise to bear more effectively. Toye's suggestion that efficiency demands a division of labor would be compelling if political skills were ones that had been acquired through a long professional training that precluded the study of economics, but in fact most politicians have acquired a professional training in some other field (most often law). If economics gives them expertise that is more relevant than most other fields to providing wise leadership on economic questions, it would seem constructive to encourage some of those who have acquired the skills of the trade to enter politics.

What lessons can we draw about the ways that such economist-politicians, or technopols, should behave in order to advance the cause of economic reform?

One rather clear lesson is that they should not be afraid to proclaim their policy intentions. It is just not true that any hint of a willingness to pursue economic reform will condemn a party to political oblivion, or that parties undertaking such policies face certain electoral defeat in retribution by the public (see the discussion of voodoo politics above). Obviously this does not mean that it is good politics to insist on spelling out the gory details of who can expect to lose (what one might call the Mario Vargas Llosa or John Hewson model). Rather, as Joan Nelson said at the end of her panel discussion (chapter 9), it requires an ability to articulate "a credible image of a reasonably just and attractive society," such as membership in the European Community has offered to those on the European periphery in recent years. Or, as Richard Feinberg (chapter 5) quoted approvingly Alejandro Foxley, the Chilean minister of finance, "Economists must not only know their economic models, but also understand politics, interests, conflicts, passions—the essence of collective life. For a brief period of time you could make changes by decree; but to let them persist, you have to build coalitions and bring people around. You have to be a politician." It is not axiomatic that economists can do this better than politicians with other backgrounds, but on the whole one would think their training gives them an advantage.

A second firm and important finding from the conference is that profound economic reforms have been accomplished by democratic governments, even those in a simultaneous transition from authoritarianism (Spain and, one hopes, Poland). There is no excuse for claiming that democracy needs to be postponed (let alone rolled back) in order to build a market economy or stabilize inflation. In many African countries, where dictatorship has been associated with corruption and economic malaise rather than reform and growth, it seems quite likely that democratization would favor economic modernization.

An economist with democratic principles who finds himself in an authoritarian setting confronts a difficult moral dilemma. He can seek to help the government improve economic policy in the hope that this will contribute not just to the promotion of economic welfare but also to a subsequent political liberalization. But while this is a plausible hypothesis,[23] it is by no means assured; it is also conceivable that good economic performance could help perpetuate authoritarian rule. Hence whether an economist decides to help the government or to join the opposition must depend on his or her personal evaluation of the regime and the probability that economic success will promote political reform.

Similarly, the evidence does not support the claim that economic reform is an inherently right-wing project (unless one defines the left-right axis in statist terms, in which case liberalization is tautologically right-wing). Australia, New Zealand, and Spain all show that left-of-center governments may choose to liberalize: Australia and Spain suggest that this can benefit the left's natural constituency, while New Zealand shows that it need not do so if the reforms are not designed with adequate skill and due concern for their distributional impact.

Many reform programs have been launched in response to the emergence of crises. When a society perceives that the existing order has become untenable, there is likely to be an unusual opportunity to launch fundamental reforms. Balcerowicz exploited the opening for "extraordinary politics" created by the triple crisis that Poland faced in 1989 (breakdown of the economic system, collapse of the political order, liberation from foreign domination) in order to effect a basic transformation of the Polish economy. Bresser Pereira tried to convince Brazil that it faced a fundamental crisis of the state in 1987; he did not succeed sufficiently to get the political space for the "abnormal politics" that would have supported reform, and so Brazil remains in crisis today.

But the experience of Colombia shows that remarkably deep reforms may be possible without any perception of crisis if other conditions are right (in Colombia's case these were an administration that had solid control of the government and legislature, and a public whose attention was focused on drugs and terrorism rather than on economic policy). The lessons would seem to be: exploit the situation if the public perceives the country to be in crisis, seek to raise consciousness of a crisis situation if it exists but the public has not yet woken up to the fact, but do not hold back from seeking reform just because there is no crisis.

However, there are situations in which it may be prudent to postpone ambitions to reform. For example, in retrospect it seems clear that it was a mistake for Brazil to launch the Cruzado Plan in 1985, since its failure began the process of discrediting comprehensive ("heterodox") stabilization plans that has now made it very much harder for Brazil to stabilize. It is surely no coincidence that Brazil at that time lacked two of the features that were suggested above to be close to essential prerequisites

---

23. For which Helliwell (1992) provides some econometric support.

for successful reform, namely, a solid political base and a visionary leader. In the absence of these conditions, economists are better advised to wait for a change of administration or to seek office themselves, as Turgut Özal did in Turkey in 1983.[24]

The only other feature that we have suggested to be a virtual prerequisite for successful reform was a coherent economic team enjoying strong executive support, having effective control over the main levers of policy, and with the bureaucratic authority to design an appropriate program. Institutional arrangements need to be conducive to the coherence and consistency of policy, rather than generate contradictory signals emerging from different policy centers, or cycling among a variety of mutually contradictory efforts. And there need to be some economists available who are sufficiently responsible to accept, and even sufficiently ambitious to seek, high political office, rather than limit their sights to academic debate or lucrative consulting.

Several of the other hypotheses examined also yield useful advice, even though the evidence suggested that none of them identified conditions that are indispensable for successful reform. Some reforming governments exploited a honeymoon while others did not; we cannot say that this factor was consistently important, but it would nonetheless be silly not to take advantage of any opportunity that arises. Similarly, such social consensus as exists should be exploited, and where it is absent efforts should be made to build support, but without forgetting the Sachs dictum that nothing garners support like success: it is not good politics to risk failure by allowing necessary reforms to be held hostage to public opinion polls. Technopols should also explore the possibilities of accelerating the benefits accruing from some reforms that are worth doing in their own right, so as to give a preview of where things can be expected to go if reforms are sustained. But they must not fall into the trap of forfeiting their legitimacy by going back to the old politics of buying support from vested interests.

Several participants in the conference claimed that we had got our priorities wrong in failing to focus on the role that external agents have played in fostering economic reform. Thus John Toye argued that the international financial institutions have been crucial to the reform process. They "did not impose their policies of reform on unwilling countries, as is sometimes alleged. [But] they were . . . vital catalysts in the process of developing countries' deciding to adopt the path of economic reform." David Finch argued much the same case. And Jeffrey Sachs argued strongly that, in a whole series of countries, financial aid had

---

24. The authors will be delighted if Brazilian experience forces them to retract these words, since a number of good friends have now entered the Brazilian government and formed a powerful economic team, but are still working under a president and a legislature that provide neither a visionary leader nor a solid political base.

played a crucial role in supporting the reformers long enough to enable them to start showing results. This contention is consistent with the cases studied by the conference, in at least five of which it is clear that aid was critical to success.

Although the conference was not designed to test the case for the importance of foreign help, either intellectual or material, in nurturing successful reform, we regard it as providing some further support for a case that was already strong. The multilateral agencies have played an important role, both in changing the intellectual climate and providing concrete advice on program design, and in pumping in cash. We are inclined to agree with Barbara Stallings (chapter 5) that the most useful intellectual help came not in the form of hard conditionality ("leverage") but rather by changing the intellectual climate ("linkage"). And, notwithstanding Dani Rodrik's observation that in Turkey the effect of aid was perverse, it has more usually helped sustain precisely the sort of liberalizing reforms that many critics of aid are anxious to see put in place. Of course, it is worthwhile providing financial support only where domestic conditions are right: where the government is committed to reform, has devised a political as well as an economic strategy for pursuing it, and has designed its policymaking structure so as to generate consistent policy.

A lot is at stake in the continuing struggle to transform countries that have long embraced statism, dirigisme, inward orientation, and often populism. The question is whether Brazil will make the same leap that Chile has done, whether China will become a gigantic Hong Kong, whether India will imitate Korea, whether Nigeria will emulate Indonesia, and whether Russia will succeed in following where Poland pioneered. This volume will have been more than worthwhile if it provides some modest help or inspiration to politicians and technopols seeking to lead their countries through the transition.

# References

Alesina, A. 1987. "Macroeconomic Policy in a Two-Party System as a Repeated Game." *Quarterly Journal of Economics* 102, no. 2 (August): 651–78.

Bates, Robert H., and Anne O. Krueger. 1993. *Political and Economic Interactions in Economic Policy Reform*. Oxford: Basil Blackwell.

Bresser Pereira, Luiz Carlos, José Maria Maravall, and Adam Przeworski. 1993. *Economic Reforms in New Democracies: A Social-Democratic Approach*. Cambridge, England: Cambridge University Press.

Diaz-Alejandro, Carlos. 1981. "Southern Cone Stabilization Plans." In W. R. Cline and S. Weintraub, eds., *Economic Stabilization in Developing Countries*. Washington: Brookings Institution.

Dornbusch, Rudiger, and Sebastian Edwards, eds. 1991. *The Macroeconomics of Populism in Latin America*. Chicago: University of Chicago Press.

Feinberg, Richard. 1992. "Latin America: Back on the Screen." *International Economic Insights* 3, no. 4 (July-August): 2-6.

Frank, Robert, Thomas Gilovich, and Dennis Regan. 1993. "Does Studying Economics Inhibit Cooperation?" *Journal of Economic Perspectives* 7, no. 2 (Spring): 159-71.

Grindle, Merilee S., and John W. Thomas. 1991. *Public Choices and Policy Change: The Political Economy of Reform in Developing Countries.* Baltimore: Johns Hopkins University Press.

Haggard, Stephan, and Robert Kaufman, eds. 1992. *The Politics of Economic Adjustment.* Princeton, NJ: Princeton University Press.

Haggard, Stephan, and Steven B. Webb. 1992. "What Do We Know About the Political Economy of Policy Reform?" *World Bank Research Observer* 8, no. 2: 143-68.

Harberger, Arnold C. 1993. "Secrets of Success: A Handful of Heroes." *American Economic Review* 83, no. 2 (May): 343.

Helliwell, John F. 1992. "International Growth Linkages: Evidence from Asia and the OECD." *NBER Working Paper* no. 4245. Cambridge, MA: National Bureau of Economic Research.

Hirschman, Albert O. 1968. *Journeys Toward Progress.* New York: Greenwood Press.

Krueger, Anne O. 1978. *Liberalization Attempts and Consequences.* Cambridge, MA: Ballinger.

Naim, Moises. 1993. *Paper Tigers and Minotaurs.* Washington: Carnegie Endowment for International Peace.

Nelson, Joan, ed. 1990. *Economic Crisis and Policy Choice.* Princeton, NJ: Princeton University Press.

Nelson, Joan, ed. 1991. "The Politics of Stabilization and Structural Change: Is Third World Experience Relevant in Post-Communist Nations?" Paper presented to a workshop on "The Politics of Post-Socialist Economic Reform" held by the Socialist Economic Reform Unit of the World Bank and the Overseas Development Council (12 September).

Przeworski, Adam. 1991. *Democracy and the Market.* Cambridge, England: Cambridge University Press.

Przeworski, Adam, and Fernando Limongi. 1993. "Political Regimes and Economic Growth." *Journal of Economic Perspectives* 7, no. 3 (Summer): 51-69.

Rodrik, Dani. 1993. "The Positive Economics of Policy Reform." *American Economic Review* 83, no. 2 (May): 356-61.

Williamson, John, ed. 1990. *Latin American Adjustment: How Much Has Happened?* Washington: Institute for International Economics.

# APPENDIX

# Conference Participants

Iwan Azis
University of Indonesia

Paul Balaran
The Ford Foundation

Leszek Balcerowicz
Warsaw

Nicolás Ardito-Barletta
International Center for Economic Growth

Robert Bates
Duke University

Thomas Bayard
Institute for International Economics

C. Fred Bergsten
Institute for International Economics

Nancy Bermeo
Princeton University

Alan Bollard
New Zealand Institute of Economic Research

Colin Bradford
OECD Development Centre

Katrina Burgess
Princeton University

Yavuz Canevi
Euroturk Bank

Ed Chow
Chevron

William Cline
Institute for International Economics

A. W. Coats
Duke University

Susan Collins
Brookings Institution

W. Max Corden
School of Advanced International Studies

José Córdoba
Office of Presidency, Mexico City

Jose De Gregorio
International Monetary Fund

Guillermo de la Dehesa
Goldman Sachs, Europe

Jessica Einhorn
World Bank

Kimberly Elliott
Institute for International Economics

Louis Emmerij
Inter-American Development Bank

Richard Feinberg
Inter-American Dialogue

C. David Finch
Washington, DC

Jose Luis Fiori
Inter-American Development Bank

Ross Garnaut
Australian National University

Norio Gomi
Matsushita

Carol Graham
Brookings Institution

Catherine Gwin
Overseas Development Council

Stephan Haggard
University of California at
San Diego

Khristine L. Hall
IBM

Rachel Hall
Institute for International
Economics

Oleh Havrylyshyn
International Monetary Fund

C. Randall Henning
Institute for International
Economics

Gary C. Hufbauer
Institute for International
Economics

Enrique Iglesias
Inter-American Development Bank

Shafiqul Islam
Council on Foreign Relations

Robert F. Kelley
Arthur Andersen

Anne Krueger
Duke University

Carol Lancaster
Georgetown University

Felipe Larrain
Catholic University of Chile

William Lewis
McKinsey & Company

Vladimir Mau
Moscow

Allan Mendelowitz
General Accounting Office

Kalman Mizsei
The Institute for East-West Studies

Joan Nelson
Overseas Development Council

Seamus O'Cleireacain
The Ford Foundation

Chwee Huay Ow-Taylor
Korea Economic Institute

Steve Parker
The Asia Foundation

Luiz Carlos Bresser Pereira
São Paulo

Guy P. Pfeffermann
International Finance Corporation

Ognian Pishev
Embassy of Bulgaria

Jacques J. Polak
Per Jacobsson Foundation

Vasile V. Puscas
Embassy of Romania

Sajjad Rahman
Canadian International
Development Agency

Julio Sergio Ramirez
INCAE

Gus Ranis
Yale University

Borris T. Ratchev
Embassy of Bulgaria

Miguel Rodríguez
World Bank

Dani Rodrik
Columbia University

Subroto Roy
Washington

Willy Van Ryckeghem
Inter-American Development Bank

Jeffrey Sachs
Harvard University

Il SaKong
Institute for Global Economics,
Seoul

Georgeo Sofianos
New York Stock Exchange

Barbara Stallings
University of Wisconsin

Otto Storf
Deutsche Bank

John D. Sullivan
Center for International Private
Enterprise

Francisco Torres
Lisbon

John Toye
Institute for Development Studies

Miguel Urrutia
Banco de la Republica, Bogotá

Rimmer de Vries
Morgan Guaranty Trust

Martin Walker
Czech Embassy

Richard Webb
Brookings Institution

Steven Webb
World Bank

Peter R. Weitz
German Marshall Fund of the
United States

John Williamson
Institute for International
Economics

# Other Publications from the
# Institute for International Economics

## POLICY ANALYSES IN INTERNATIONAL ECONOMICS Series

# BOOKS

U.S. Taxation of International Income: Blueprint for Reform
Gary Clyde Hufbauer, assisted by Joanna M. van Rooij/*October 1992*

ISBN cloth 0-88132-178-8      304 pp.
ISBN paper 0-88132-134-6      304 pp.

Who's Bashing Whom? Trade Conflict in High-Technology Industries
Laura D'Andrea Tyson/*November 1992*

ISBN cloth 0-88132-151-6      352 pp.
ISBN paper 0-88132-106-0      352 pp.

Korea in the World Economy
Il Sakong/*January 1993*

ISBN cloth 0-88132-184-2      328 pp.
ISBN paper 0-88132-106-0      328 pp.

NAFTA: An Assessment
Gary Clyde Hufbauer and Jeffrey J. Schott/*February 1993, rev. ed. October 1993*

ISBN paper 0-88132-199-0      216 pp.

Pacific Dynamism and the International Economic System
C. Fred Bergsten and Marcus Noland, editors/*May 1993*

ISBN paper 0-88132-196-6      424 pp.

Economic Consequences of Soviet Disintegration
John Williamson, editor/*May 1993*

ISBN paper 0-88132-190-7      664 pp.

Reconcilable Differences? United States–Japan Economic Conflict
C. Fred Bergsten and Marcus Noland/*June 1993*

ISBN paper 0-88132-129-X      296 pp.

Does Foreign Exchange Intervention Work?
Kathryn M. Dominguez and Jeffrey A. Frankel/*September 1993*

ISBN 0-88132-104-4      192 pp.

Sizing Up U.S. Export Disincentives
J. David Richardson/*September 1993*

ISBN 0-88132-107-9      192 pp.

Adjusting to Volatile Energy Prices
Philip K. Verleger, Jr./*November 1993*

ISBN 0-88132-069-2      288 pp.

The Political Economy of Policy Reform
John Williamson, editor/*January 1994*

ISBN 0-88132-195-8      624 pp.

## SPECIAL REPORTS

1   Promoting World Recovery: A Statement on Global Economic
Strategy by Twenty-six Economists from Fourteen Countries/
*December 1982*
(out of print)      ISBN paper 0-88132-013-7      45 pp.

2   Prospects for Adjustment in Argentina, Brazil, and Mexico:
Responding to the Debt Crisis
John Williamson, editor/*June 1983*
(out of print)      ISBN paper 0-88132-016-1      71 pp.

# FORTHCOMING

**For orders outside the US and Canada please contact:**

**Longman Group UK Ltd.**
**PO Box 88**
**Harlow, Essex CM 19 5SR**
**UK**

**Telephone Orders: 0279 623925**
**Fax: 0279 453450**
**Telex: 817484**